Criminals and Their Scientists

THE HISTORY OF CRIMINOLOGY IN INTERNATIONAL PERSPECTIVE

This book presents recent research on the history of criminology from the late eighteenth to the mid-twentieth centuries in Western Europe (Austria, Britain, France, Germany, Italy) and in Argentina, Australia, Japan, and the United States. Approaching the history of criminology as a history of science and practice, the chapters examine the discourse on crime and criminals that surfaced as part of different discourses and practices, including the activities of the police and the courts, parliamentary debates, and media reports, as well as the writings of moral statisticians, jurists, and medical doctors. By providing a comparative study of the worldwide reception of Cesare Lombroso's criminal-anthropological ideas, the book seeks to elucidate the relationship between criminological discourse and politics, society, and culture.

Peter Becker is Professor of Central European History at the European University Institute. His previous books include *Verderbnis und Entartung: Eine Geschichte der Kriminologie des 19. Jahrhunderts als Diskurs und Praxis* (2002).

Richard F. Wetzell is a Research Fellow at the German Historical Institute in Washington, D.C. He is the author of *Inventing the Criminal: A History of German Criminology, 1880–1945* (2000).

D1380397

PUBLICATIONS OF THE GERMAN HISTORICAL INSTITUTE

Edited by Christof Mauch
with the assistance of David Lazar

The German Historical Institute is a center for advanced study and research whose purpose is to provide a permanent basis for scholarly cooperation among historians from the Federal Republic of Germany and the United States. The Institute conducts, promotes, and supports research into both American and German political, social, economic, and cultural history; into transatlantic migration, especially in the nineteenth and twentieth centuries; and into the history of international relations, with special emphasis on the roles played by the United States and Germany.

Recent books in the series:

Jürgen Heideking and James A. Henretta, editors, *Republicanism and Liberalism in America and the German States, 1750–1850*

Hubert Zimmermann, *Money and Security: Troops, Monetary Policy, and West Germany's Relations with the United States and Britain, 1950–1971*

Roger Chickering and Stig Förster, editors, *The Shadows of Total War: Europe, East Asia, and the United States, 1919–1939*

Richard J. Bessel and Dirk Schumann, editors, *Life after Death: Approaches to a Cultural and Social History of Europe During the 1940s and 1950s*

Marc Flandreau, Carl-Ludwig Holtfrerich, and Harold James, editors, *International Financial History in the Twentieth Century: System and Anarchy*

Andreas W. Daum, Lloyd C. Gardner, and Wilfried Mausbach, editors, *The Vietnam War and the World: International and Comparative Perspectives*

Detlef Junker, editor, *The United States and Germany in the Era of the Cold War: A Handbook,* 2 volumes

Roger Chickering, Stig Förster, and Bernd Greiner, editors, *A World at Total War: Global Conflict and the Politics of Destruction, 1937–1945*

Kiran Klaus Patel, *Soldiers of Labor: Labor Service in Nazi Germany and New Deal America, 1933–1945*

Criminals and Their Scientists

THE HISTORY OF CRIMINOLOGY IN INTERNATIONAL PERSPECTIVE

Edited by

PETER BECKER
European University Institute, Florence

RICHARD F. WETZELL
German Historical Institute, Washington, D.C.

GERMAN HISTORICAL INSTITUTE
Washington, D.C.
and

CAMBRIDGE
UNIVERSITY PRESS

CAMBRIDGE UNIVERSITY PRESS
Cambridge, New York, Melbourne, Madrid, Cape Town, Singapore, São Paulo, Delhi

Cambridge University Press
32 Avenue of the Americas, New York, NY 10013-2473, USA

www.cambridge.org
Information on this title: www.cambridge.org/9780521120739

GERMAN HISTORICAL INSTITUTE
1607 New Hampshire Avenue, N.W., Washington, DC 20009, USA

First published 2006
This digitally printed version 2009

A catalog record for this publication is available from the British Library

Library of Congress Cataloging in Publication data

Criminals and their scientists : the history of criminology in international perspective /
edited by Peter Becker, Richard F. Wetzell.
p. cm. – (Publications of the German Historical Institute)
"This book grew out of an international conference...in Florence, Italy in
October 1998...sponsored by the German Historical Institute, Washington, DC, and the
European University Institute, Florence" – P. .
Includes bibliographical references and index.
ISBN 0-521-81012-4
1. Criminology – History – 19th century – Congresses. 2. Criminology – History – 20th
century – Congresses. 3. Criminologists – History – Congresses. 4. Criminals – History –
Congresses. I. Becker, Peter, 1962– II. Wetzell, Richard F. III. Series.
HV6021.C75 2004
364–dc21 2003055193

ISBN 978-0-521-81012-8 hardback
ISBN 978-0-521-12073-9 paperback

Contents

Contributors

Philippe Artières is a researcher at the Laboratoire d'anthropologie et d'histoire de l'institution de la culture (LAHIC) of the Centre National de la Recherche Scientifique (CNRS) in Paris.

Peter Becker is a professor of history at the European University Institute in Florence, Italy.

Michael Berkowitz is a professor of Hebrew and Jewish studies at University College London.

Jane Caplan is University Lecturer in Modern History and Fellow of St Anthony's College, Oxford.

Gabriel N. Finder is an adjunct professor of history at the University of Virginia.

Peter Fritzsche is a professor of history at the University of Illinois at Urbana-Champaign.

Mariacarla Gadebusch Bondio is director of the Institute for the History of Medicine, University of Greifswald.

Stephen Garton is a professor of history at the University of Sydney.

Geoffrey J. Giles is a professor of history at the University of Florida.

Mary S. Gibson is a professor of history at the John Jay College of Criminal Justice, New York City.

David G. Horn is a professor of comparative studies at Ohio State University.

Martine Kaluszynski is a researcher at the Centre de Recherche sur le Politique, l'Administration, la Ville et le Territoire (CERAT) at the University of Grenoble, France.

Andrew Lees is a professor of history at Rutgers University at Camden.

Oliver Liang is an official in the International Labour Standards and Human Rights Department of the International Labour Office, Geneva, Switzerland.

Laurent Mucchielli is a researcher at the Centre de Recherches Sociologiques sur le Droit et les Institutions Pénales (CESDIP) in Paris, France.

Yoji Nakatani is a professor of mental hygiene at the Institute of Community Medicine of the University of Tsukuba, Japan.

Nicole Hahn Rafter is a professor in the College of Criminal Justice at Northeastern University.

Marc Renneville teaches history at the University of Paris VIII.

Ricardo D. Salvatore is a professor at the Universidad Torcuato di Tella in Buenos Aires, Argentina.

Richard F. Wetzell is a Research Fellow at the German Historical Institute, Washington, D.C.

Martin J. Wiener is a professor of history at Rice University.

Preface

This book grew out of an international conference on the history of criminology, organized by the two editors, that took place in Florence, Italy, in October 1998. The conference was sponsored by the German Historical Institute, Washington, D.C., and the European University Institute, Florence. The editors wish to thank both institutions for their financial and organizational support, without which the conference and this book would not have been possible. We also want to thank all of the conference's participants, who made the Florence meeting a memorable and productive experience of intellectual exchange across the usual national and disciplinary boundaries. The present volume owes much to comments and suggestions made by conference participants who are not represented as authors in this book. We would also like to thank Daniel Mattern, formerly senior editor at the GHI, who shepherded the manuscript through its initial editorial stages, and Frank Smith, our editor at Cambridge University Press. Keith Alexander and David Lazar at the GHI provided invaluable help in the final stages of preparing the text for publication.

Florence and Washington, D.C.   Peter Becker
                                                   Richard F. Wetzell

Criminals and Their Scientists

THE HISTORY OF CRIMINOLOGY IN INTERNATIONAL PERSPECTIVE

Introduction

PETER BECKER AND RICHARD F. WETZELL

The chapters gathered in this book under the title *Criminals and Their Scientists* seek to contribute to a history of criminology as discourse and practice. They do not follow established models of genealogical reconstructions of criminology as a set of ideas.[1] Although famous representatives of the canon of criminological theories, such as Cesare Lombroso, figure prominently in many of the chapters, such icons of "scientific progress" in the study of crime are discussed not as isolated thinkers, but as participants in a polyphonic discourse with close ties to penal institutions. To avoid the danger of replacing a genealogical with an exclusively social historical perspective, the chapters herein approach criminology as a discursive practice. To be sure, the institutional settings that provided the stage for different criminological actors play an important role in our stories. But professionalization and the institutionalization of criminology as a recognized scientific field and later as an academic discipline cannot fully account for the continuities and ruptures in the history of the study of crime and criminals. Nor can the discursive and institutional strategies of criminologists be explained by a conceptual framework that focuses on divergent class interests.[2]

In an attempt to move beyond ideological and sociological analyses of the development of criminology, we have integrated a genealogical approach with a more comprehensive study of criminology as science and practice. Although a genealogical approach can be useful for understanding

---

1 See Hermann Mannheim, ed., *Pioneers in Criminology*, 2d ed. (Montclair, N.J., 1972); Piers Beirne, ed., *The Origins and Growth of Criminology: Essays on Intellectual History, 1760–1945* (Aldershot, 1994); Paul Rock, ed., *History of Criminology* (Aldershot, 1994).

2 For an excellent discussion of Marxist approaches to the history of criminal justice and criminology, see David Garland, "Punishment as Ideology and Class Control: Variations on Marxist Themes," in *Punishment and Modern Society: A Study in Social Theory* (Chicago, 1990), 111–30; compare also Garland's earlier book *Punishment and Welfare: A History of Penal Strategies* (Aldershot, 1985).

the contributions that eighteenth- and nineteenth-century physicians made to the biological theories of Lombroso and some of his critics, it fails to integrate other varieties of criminological discourse. For the criminological writings of police officials, Victorian judges, or experts in juvenile delinquency, for instance, have a much more complicated relationship to the biological and sociological theories of crime that dominated at the end of the nineteenth century. An alternative conceptual framework was also needed in order to integrate the reconstruction of the discourse into its institutional and political contexts. While the authors of the chapters have used a variety of theoretical and methodological approaches, Michel Foucault's concept of "discursive practice" proved useful for organizing and conceptualizing the volume as a whole.[3] Before providing an overview of the four sections of this book, we shall briefly sketch some general thoughts about a history of criminology as discursive practice.

CRIMINALS AND SCIENTISTS

The title *Criminals and Their Scientists* is meant to provide a framework for discussing a wide variety of discourses and practices in a field that Laurent Mucchielli has aptly called "sciences of crime" (*sciences du crime*) and which would be classified as "criminology" today.[4] The word "criminal" in the title reflects the fact that a considerable part of this discursive field could actually be characterized as "sciences of the criminal" rather than "sciences of crime." For even though nineteenth-century "moral statisticians" and later proponents of "criminal sociology" focused on crime rather than criminals, most nineteenth-century physicians, phrenologists, philanthropists, police experts, and penologists attempted to understand and explain the problem of crime by investigating the mind, lifeworlds, and physical constitution of *criminals*. A focus on the criminal rather than crime thus provides a unifying element of the criminological discourse that makes the binary relationship between criminals and their scientists a plausible starting point for a fresh look at the history of criminology.

The definition of the "criminal" in the criminological discourse was often imprecise. Criminals were frequently represented as "others" whose otherness distinguished them from respectable citizens and made them prone to engage in criminal acts. Many criminological "scientists" categorized as "criminals" not only persons who had committed a crime but anyone who

---

3 Michel Foucault, *The Archaeology of Knowledge*, trans. A. M. Sheridan Smith (New York, 1972), 179ff.
4 Laurent Mucchielli, ed., *Histoire de la criminologie française* (Paris, 1994), 1.

displayed characteristics that were thought to indicate a criminal propensity according to their semiotics of deviance. We are thus forced to use a very broad definition of "criminals," ranging from bourgeois youths who frequented brothels to highwaymen and murderers.

Although, from today's vantage point, the "otherness" of criminals was only elusively defined, contemporary commentators firmly believed in the clarity and visibility of their categories. They were convinced that a subject's failure to comply with the norms for respectable behavior and personality development could be detected through trained observation. Nevertheless, one sometimes also finds an awareness that their project of rendering not only criminal acts but criminal propensities visible and detectable had not been realized. This failure was not only due to the problem of unreported crime, but also to the difficulties of developing a semiotics that would allow for the detection of people who were considered to be in the process of turning to crime.

The diversity of the participants in the criminological discourse and of the sites where knowledge about criminals was produced also calls for some comment about the usage of the term "scientist" in the title of this book. Although religiously inspired philanthropists who visited houses of correction, for instance, do not fit received notions of scientists, the term scientist is, for our present purposes, meant to apply to every active participant in the discourse on crime and criminals. For all participants in this discourse understood themselves as "scientists" insofar as they claimed to have at their disposal a trained and experienced gaze at deviant *others*. The distance they maintained vis-à-vis the subjects of their inquiries endowed them with an institutionally sanctioned authority that characterized both their daily routines and their reflections on the nature of crime.

Criminologists legitimated their authority through the superiority of their skills of observation and analysis over commonsense approaches to the crime problem. In the introduction to his classic *On Criminal Man*, Cesare Lombroso expressed exactly this claim when he emphasized that mass observations were impossible in his field of research. Valid observations could only be made by "competent men."[5] Similarly, Hans Gross, the Austrian author of an influential handbook for judges, advised his fellow magistrates to systematically replace their commonsense understanding of as many different aspects of life as possible with an experienced gaze. From the moment when someone took up judicial office, Gross argued, all his thoughts and activities,

---

5 Cesare Lombroso, *Der Verbrecher (homo delinquens) in anthropologischer, ärztlicher und juristischer Beziehung*, trans. M. Fränkel, 2 vols. (Hamburg, 1887–90), xix.

whether private or official, had to be subjected to the single criterion of their value for his work.[6] Thus the common attribute of the criminological "scientists" was their widely accepted role as expert-observers, which entitled them to speak with authority about criminals in general and individual offenders in particular.

Criminological research was characterized by a close link between discourse and institutional practice. To fully understand the dynamics of the criminological discourse, one therefore has to pay attention to both its theoretical and its practical side and to abandon the traditional differentiation between the production of knowledge in scholarly institutions and its reception in institutions of prevention and repression. Michel Foucault provided a useful conceptual framework for such an analysis in his *Archaeology of Knowledge*. Critical of teleological approaches that anachronistically applied concepts such as "science" or "discipline" to fields of knowledge that did not fulfill the criteria for either, Foucault developed the concept of "discursive formations" (or "positivities") in which common rules, a specific gaze, and a consensus about the phenomena to be studied brought together actors from different backgrounds.[7] This concept of a "discursive formation," rather than a discipline, can be fruitfully applied to an analysis of criminology as discourse and practice. For unlike modern disciplines, "criminological" knowledge from the late eighteenth century onward surfaced on a variety of different sites: in medical treatises, in literary works with psychological interest, in publications from practitioners, in reports from prison and police experts, as well as in laws and decrees.

Although this volume cannot trace all the interdependent manifestations of criminological knowledge, we have tried to cover the most important sites of this discourse. These include the police, the reformatory, and the penitentiary as well as medical and psychiatric institutions. The emphasis we have placed on particular institutions shifts with their changing importance for the production of criminological knowledge. Thus, toward the end of the nineteenth century, the police and its collection of biographical data became less relevant for the reconstruction of the criminological discourse than academic research and criminal-biological documentation centers.

CRIMINOLOGY AS DISCURSIVE PRACTICE

Approaching criminology as a discursive practice rather than a discipline, this volume searches neither for the "birth" of criminology nor for the

---

6 Hans Gross, *Handbuch für Untersuchungsrichter*, 6th ed., pt. 1 (Munich, 1913), 50.
7 Foucault, *Archaeology*, 31–9, 125, 178–81.

genealogy of current criminological thought. Nor is it our intention to evaluate the more or less "scientific" character of the various contributions to criminological discourse. The ethnographic approach of police practitioners and Franz Joseph Gall's phrenological theories receive the same attention as criminal statistics and forensic psychiatry, even though the latter have attracted more scholarly treatment as possible forerunners of modern criminology as a scholarly discipline.[8] Drawing on Foucault's archaeological approach to the history of knowledge, we will present some common features that characterized the criminological discourse from the late eighteenth to the mid-twentieth centuries. These features provided a common framework for a range of different types of criminological arguments, including Gall's phrenological theories, Friedrich Avé-Lallemant's reconstruction of criminal lifeworlds, Cesare Lombroso's theory of atavism, and criminal biology in the Weimar Republic and the Third Reich.

At the core of this highly polyphonic discourse about crime and criminals was a binary relationship in which criminals were confronted by their "scientists" within a system of power and knowledge. The knowledge part of this relationship was determined by the claims of scientists to possess the theoretical and empirical knowledge for analyzing crime in general and individual criminals in particular. The power aspect of the criminal–scientist relationship was structured by institutional practices, in which the scientist, as a practitioner and/or scholar, was engaged in studying, classifying, and disciplining criminals as members of a "class apart." Their official or social authority kept the scientists at a distance from the objects of their intellectual endeavors, and the interaction of criminals and scientists was always hierarchically structured. Nevertheless, because the scientists needed a measure of collaboration of criminals to reconstruct the hidden factors that they believed led men and women astray, criminals retained a measure of independence or *Eigen-Sinn* (Lüdtke).[9]

The criminal–scientist dyad already implies the second common element in the discourse of criminology: the focus on the person of the criminal, rather than the criminal act. This focus on the criminal characterized criminological discourse earlier than is often supposed. Some historical accounts have conflated nineteenth-century criminology with the legal discourse on penal reform and therefore concluded that pre-Lombrosian criminology focused on the crime rather than the criminal.[10] But if the arguments of

8 See, for example, Piers Beirne, *Inventing Criminology: Essays on the Rise of "Homo Criminalis"* (Albany, N.Y., 1993), and Beirne, ed., *Origins and Growth of Criminology*.
9 Alf Lüdtke, *Eigen-Sinn: Fabrikalltag, Arbeitererfahrungen und Politik vom Kaiserreich bis in den Faschismus* (Hamburg, 1993), 9.
10 See, for instance, Monika Frommel, *Präventionsmodelle in der deutschen Strafzweck-Diskussion* (Berlin, 1987).

nineteenth-century penal reformers are properly contextualized and other sites of the criminological discourse are examined, the picture changes dramatically. Such a revised picture emerges from recent studies on the history of criminology that have discovered a rich variety of neglected criminological traditions, such as forensic medicine and phrenology, that clearly focused on the criminal.[11]

Even nineteenth-century criminal jurists did not always focus on the criminal act, but also paid attention to the person of the criminal. To be sure, when they worked with juridical concepts designed to classify different crimes, they focused on criminal acts. But when the same jurists drafted provisions for reducing or aggravating punishment, they discussed both the possibility of insanity as the driving force behind a crime and the best ways to ascertain whether the offender was insane.[12] This interest in the person of the criminal becomes even more striking when one looks at the daily routines of judges and investigating magistrates. For the latter relied on a comprehensive knowledge of what they considered the "signs" of deviance and criminal propensities.

The criminal as the object of criminological curiosity was not the same at all sites of the criminological discourse and did not remain unchanged during the time period covered here. The gaze that criminal anthropologists employed to classify and evaluate men and women certainly differed from that of investigating magistrates. Nevertheless, a shared interest in the criminal's body, psyche, biography, and behavior defined several loosely connected fields of inquiry. Thus the criminal as the object of the criminological discourse surfaced in various forms: as moral being, as biophysical machine, and as the product of a variety of pernicious environmental and hereditary forces. In addition, the discourse about the criminal was characterized by its close links to three further elements: the ideal of a society free from crime and deviance, the notion of prevention, and the resulting suspicion directed at a variety of people who were considered prone to commit crimes. This suspicion stimulated the emergence of various semiotic practices designed to reveal criminal propensities.

Foucault's archaeological method suggests that we ought to go beyond examining the objects of the criminological discourse. Rather, we need to reconstruct the interaction between the authors of the discourse, the constitution of criminological objects of knowledge, and the institutional setting in which criminals and scientists were situated. The analyses of the

---

11 See Mucchielli, ed., *Histoire de la criminologie française,* and Peter Strasser, *Verbrechermenschen: Zur kriminalwissenschaftlichen Erzeugung des Bösen* (Frankfurt am Main, 1984).
12 Patricia Moulin, "Die mildernden Umstände," in Michel Foucault, ed., *Der Fall Rivière* (Frankfurt am Main, 1975), 242–8.

construction of crime and criminals by "scientists" presented in this volume therefore trace the surfacing of criminological objects in several discourses and practices, including practices of social control, the labeling activities of police agents and magistrates, the narratives of moral statisticians, reports in the media, parliamentary debates, as well as the writings of psychiatrists and legal, police, and medical experts. In doing so, they examine the relations between the criminological writing on criminals and the institutional apparatuses of the police, legal system, penal institutions, medical institutions, and welfare offices. They also seek to illuminate the internal dynamics of the criminological discourse, the position of the authors vis-à-vis their objects of study, and the ways in which authority and objectivity are constituted.

This approach does not mean to encourage the reader to ignore the obvious and far-reaching changes in the criminological discourse. The nineteenth and twentieth centuries witnessed major discontinuities in the conceptualization of criminals, in the privileged sites of the criminological discourse, and in the social role of its participants. To account for these transformations, we must consider the changes in the objects of this discourse as well as changes in the social, political, and intellectual environments. For each set of transformations it might be asked whether it occurred because of changes in the nature of crime, the entry of new participants into the discourse, new demands from outside, or the internal dynamics of the discourse.[13]

By approaching the history of criminology from the perspective of a history of discursive practices, this book avoids tracing some sort of steady formation of knowledge. Instead, it pays attention to the rules governing the criminological discourse and to the conditions that shape it, and seeks to reconstruct the polyphonic discourse about crime and criminals to which welfare and police officials, jurists, medical and hygiene experts, psychiatrists, and philanthropists all lent their voices.

SCIENTISTS AND THEIR INSTITUTIONS

The relationship between criminologists and their institutional environment occupies a central place in our explorations of the production, dissemination, and implementation of criminological knowledge. The chapters of this book examine different actors and institutional settings. The power-knowledge fields of medicine, police, law, philanthropy, and penal reform are discussed from various angles.

---

13 On the problem of changes in crime and its relevance for changes in the representation of crime and deviance, see Michel Foucault, *Discipline and Punish: The Birth of the Prison* (New York, 1978), 97ff.

The general relationship between criminological discourse and the normative and institutional arrangements for combating crime and deviance must not be conceptualized as a one-way street but as a relationship of mutual influence. On the one hand, every participant in the criminological discourse, regardless of their own institutional affiliation, was strongly influenced by the institutions of criminal justice and the police and the normative definitions of crime and deviance they applied in their practices. On the other hand, the influence of the criminological discourse reached well beyond the limits of crime and deviance as defined by penal law. For many criminologists did not hesitate to categorize a person as criminal before any crime had been committed. Writing in 1845, long before Cesare Lombroso, the German police expert Gustav Zimmermann presented the benefits of a systematic phrenological survey of the population in the following terms: "Because we should be able to identify on a person's skull the marks of serious villainy, the state should prescribe an examination of the skull for everyone who reaches the age of twenty-five. Everyone found guilty of having a dangerous predisposition should be hanged or confined preventively, depending on his anticipated offense!"[14]

Although Zimmermann was aware that phrenology was far from providing prognoses that were sufficiently reliable to implement such drastic preventive measures, his statement provides evidence of visionary thought experiments that sought to identify criminals before any criminal acts were committed in order to perfect the prevention of deviance. Even though no one was put in jail for bumps on their head, less radical projects for preventive measures found open ears in law enforcement agencies. Populations at risk, to use today's terminology, were more attentively observed and controlled to prevent them from realizing their criminal propensities. Failure to comply with the formal and informal norms that taught people to work, consume, and settle down could easily arouse the suspicion of the authorities.

The role that "common sense" played in criminological evaluations of the dangerousness of socially marginal people from the lower classes introduced a social bias into criminological reasoning. This bias was not the result of a conspiracy of state and capital with the aim of maximizing the potential exploitation of the workforce, but primarily the product of normative expectations regarding the proper life and habits of every citizen that were based on an idealized image of bourgeois respectability. Although the resulting disciplinary measures undoubtedly helped to adapt workers to the new regime of work, the social bias of the criminologists was above all a

---

14 Gustav Zimmermann, *Die deutsche Polizei im neunzehnten Jahrhundert* (Hannover, 1845), 419.

reflection of the colonizing attitude of middle-class observers toward the lives and habits of the lower classes.

From this perspective, one can certainly criticize criminology for never having been a science detached from the normative expectations of the societies of which it has been part. But a critique of this kind does not help us to understand the historical development of criminology any better. Instead, this volume seeks to address the question: Which criminological arguments, topics, and strategies (among a range of possible arguments, topics, and strategies) were activated in a particular criminological discourse and how was this discursive choice related to the intellectual, social, and political context of a particular place and time?

Since these questions describe the research agenda of a lifetime, we cannot claim to provide definitive answers. We do hope that the comparative study of the reception of criminal-anthropological ideas in different countries presented here will contribute to a better understanding of the relationship of the discursive practices of criminology to politics, society, and culture. This should help to elucidate the close interaction between the internal dynamics of a discourse and the demands and pressures coming from the outside. We are not, however, primarily interested in the political-ideological affiliations of scientists or the biased application of criminological knowledge, but in the structuring of the empirical and theoretical field by a certain frame of thought. As Foucault put it:

To tackle the ideological functioning of a science . . . is not to uncover the philosophical presuppositions that may lie within it; nor is it to return to the foundations that . . . legitimated it: it is to question it as a discursive formation; it is to tackle not the formal contradictions of its propositions, but the system of formation of its objects, its types of enunciation, its concepts, its theoretical choices. It is to treat it as one practice among others.[15]

THE BOOK

Part One: Nonacademic Sites of Nineteenth-Century Criminological Discourse

Until the late nineteenth century, criminological reasoning was characterized by a dialectical relationship between legislative and institutional reforms and the empirical proof of their failure by the people who implemented them. The assumptions of the "judicial idealism" underlying these reforms

---

15 Foucault, *Archaeology*, 186.

consisted in the deep-seated belief that the reform of state and society in general and the liberation of reason in particular would finally end any kind of deviance. This belief was closely connected both to the enlightenment faith in reason and to the assumption that only social-integrative acting and living could be considered rational.

Nineteenth-century criminological discourse was diverse and linked to a variety of other discourses, practices, and political objectives. In this period experts in penal law, judges, police practitioners, penitentiary administrators, moral reformers, priests of all Christian denominations, psychiatrists, and writers for a lay audience advanced different theories to explain crime and deviance. Many felt a special need to come to terms with the crime problem in order to reconcile the ideal of equality, which was at the core of all enlightened legal reforms, with the obvious patterns of inequality that continued to persist after the French Revolution.

Addressing this issue, Marc Renneville's chapter looks at the role that the French Revolution and its institutional experiments played in shaping modern criminological thought in France. When the new political and economic order failed to reduce the problem of crime significantly, the enlightened thought experiments designed to abolish crime through a systematic reform of state and society failed as well. This experience of failure, Marc Renneville shows, provided a strong momentum for research into the nature of criminals and for developing new strategies for their confinement and reform.[16]

The book's first section seeks to cover as many of the sites of the criminological discourse as possible and to examine how these sites were embedded into a discursive practice. In addition to penal institutions and legislation, this section also studies the reflections of practitioners and moral reformers on criminals. Martin Wiener's chapter examines the "criminology" of Victorian magistrates. He argues that adapting case law to modern society forced magistrates to introduce implicit anthropological assumptions, which he describes as the standard of the "reasonable man." Under this concept, individual rationality, perfectibility, and self-control were established as the norm for evaluating individual behavior. Wiener also argues that this new standard was an important factor in opening court procedures up to include forensic medical, and especially psychiatric expertise.[17]

---

16 See also Marc Renneville, *La médecine du crime: Essai sur l'emergence d'un regard medical sur la criminalité en France* (Villeneuve d'Ascq, 1997).

17 See also Martin Wiener, *Reconstructing the Criminal: Culture, Law, and Policy in England, 1830–1914* (Cambridge, 1990).

While Wiener's chapter focuses on state institutions and their role in shaping, appropriating, and fostering the discourse on criminals, the three remaining chapters in this section pursue alternative strategies. Andrew Lees reconstructs the efforts of Protestant clergymen to further moral regeneration in Germany. At the core of their activities was a strong moral critique of urban life that provided a noteworthy contribution to the discourse on criminals and deviance by integrating moral-ethical and medical arguments. By putting these reflections in the context of discourses on urbanization and the development of mass culture, this chapter provides important insights into the openness of the criminological discourse.[18]

Michael Berkowitz takes up the important issue of the association of Jewishness with criminality. Until the nineteenth century, both the common man and police experts often considered Jews to be the most dangerous professional criminals. In his chapter, Berkowitz traces the reaction to this theory among the Jews themselves. Although the Jewish response remained marginal within the criminological discourse, it provides an important perspective on one of the voices speaking about criminals.

In the final chapter of this section, Peter Becker looks at the structure of the criminological discourse by focusing on the discontinuities and ruptures taking place toward the end of the nineteenth century. These changes were wide-ranging and affected many aspects of criminology as discursive practice, including the collection of data, the theoretical frameworks for their interpretation, and the position of the author. As Becker shows in his chapter, the evidence produced during the first half of the century by practitioners remained valuable to the criminologists. To shed new light on continuity and change within the criminological discourse, he traces the strategies that turn-of-the-century criminologists developed to integrate information produced by practitioners during the nineteenth century.[19]

*Part Two: Criminology as Scientific and Political Practice in
the Late Nineteenth and Early Twentieth Centuries*

The second section deals with the criminological discourse of the late nineteenth and early twentieth centuries. The single most powerful influence on this discourse emanated from the criminological theories of Cesare Lombroso. Although Lombroso was hardly the first to propose a biological

18 See also Andrew Lees, *Cities, Sin, and Social Reform in Imperial Germany* (Ann Arbor, Mich., 2002).
19 See also Peter Becker, *Verderbnis und Entartung: Eine Geschichte der Kriminologie des 19. Jahrhunderts als Diskurs und Praxis* (Göttingen, 2002).

explanation of crime, his *L'uomo delinquente* (Criminal Man), first published in 1876, was a bold and forceful work that soon attracted sustained attention all over Europe. Medical doctors, in particular, felt compelled to respond to Lombroso's biological explanations of crime. Whether people agreed or disagreed with Lombroso, his work became a reference point for the criminological discourse for several decades.

Following an initial chapter on Lombroso himself, some chapters focus on the reception of Lombroso's criminal-anthropological theories in other countries, some examine the development of the criminological discourse in a particular country, and others discuss its influence on penal policy. The section as a whole shares several themes: first, a shift from the physical characteristics of Lombroso's "born criminal" to a focus on the role of mental abnormalities in criminal behavior; second, the increasing importance of medical doctors in the criminological discourse, in the administration of criminal justice, and in public policy; third, the diversification and specialization of the apparatus of social control, as different problem populations (criminals, the insane, alcoholics, the mentally defective) were separated, and the penal sanction was individualized for different criminal types; fourth, the (potential or actual) expansion of state intervention, as criminology identified new targets (such as persons who had not committed a crime but appeared likely to commit one in the future) and new methods of intervention (such as sterilization), and suggested that the penal apparatus be given more discretion (such as determining the duration of indefinite prison sentences); fifth, the tension between the optimistic and pessimistic implications of the new biological theories of crime, which fostered the hope that it might be possible to develop more effective, therapeutic methods of rehabilitation, but also suggested that, in some cases at least, criminal behavior might be the result of unalterable genetic factors; finally, the ambivalence of the political implications of the new criminological discourse which had both a progressive-humanitarian and a reactionary-repressive potential.

The section begins with Mary Gibson's chapter on Cesare Lombroso's criminological theories. While Lombroso's contribution to criminology is usually summed up as the theory of the "born criminal," Gibson shows that Lombroso's theories were more complex and underwent a significant evolution over the course of his career, as he supplemented his initial atavism theory with degeneration theory and psychiatric categories. Gibson also discusses Lombroso's most influential disciple, Enrico Ferri, who developed a more systematic, multicausal theory of crime that no longer privileged biological over social causes. Finally, Gibson's chapter examines the relationship of criminology to politics. Since Lombroso's and Ferri's criminological work led them to support both liberal-humanitarian and conservative penal policy measures, the policy implications of Italian positivist criminology must be recognized as politically ambivalent.[20]

Next, Nicole Rafter's chapter examines the reception of Lombrosian criminal anthropology in the United States and seeks to explain what made criminal anthropology more appealing than other theories of crime. Her analysis shows that American authors tended to integrate Lombroso's ideas into degeneration theory and shifted the emphasis from criminals' supposed physical characteristics to their intelligence defects. The diverse occupations of these authors, who were physicians, ministers, welfare workers, and educators, serve as a useful reminder of the diversity and fluidity of the professional and disciplinary territory on which criminological discourses unfolded. What made criminal anthropology particularly appealing, Rafter argues, was that visual and graphic illustrations made its foundational texts more accessible and also created a set of visual codes for deviance that were easily understood by those familiar with degeneration theory and Darwinism. Furthermore, in putting forth the concept of the "born criminal," criminal anthropology created a new being endowed with great explanatory power that also "orientalized" the offender, thus creating distance between this "other" and the normal, law-abiding citizen.[21]

The next two chapters examine the reception of Lombroso's criminal anthropology among medical doctors, in Germany and France respectively. Mariacarla Gadebusch Bondio discusses the reception of Lombroso's theories among late-nineteenth-century German psychiatrists. Agreeing with Gibson that Lombroso's theories became considerably more complex over time, Gadebusch Bondio argues that some of Lombroso's German defenders failed to keep up with this growing complexity and thus continued to propagate a rigidly deterministic version of Lombroso's theories that rendered it more vulnerable to critics. She also examines the role that Lombroso's theories played in the criminological writings of Emil Kraepelin, the dean of turn-of-the-century German psychiatry, and Gustav Aschaffenburg, the author of the major German textbook of criminology. Gadebusch Bondio argues that the shift from the "born criminal" to the "degenerate inferior individual" in Kraepelin's and Aschaffenburg's writings reflected a discursive shift from an anthropological discourse to a psychiatric-psychopathological one. Yet the substantive effect of this shift should not be

---

20 See also Mary Gibson, *Cesare Lombroso and the Origins of Biological Criminology* (Westport, Conn., 2002).
21 See also Nicole Hahn Rafter, *Creating Born Criminals* (Urbana, Ill., 1997).

overestimated because even psychiatrists who formally rejected Lombroso's theories adopted elements of his biological explanation of crime. In conclusion, she suggests that the integration of Lombrosian elements into the criminological discourse of German psychiatrists was facilitated by the cultural pessimism, the uncritical confidence in science, and the willingness to sacrifice individuals for the welfare of society that characterized turn-of-the-century German psychiatry.[22]

Laurent Mucchielli's chapter explores the connections between criminology, eugenics, and the social hygiene movement by examining medical debates on the treatment of incorrigible criminals in turn-of-the-century France. Mucchielli demonstrates that the medical profession's support for more repressive penal policies in the 1880s resulted from a "naturalization of crime" in the medical discourse on crime. Arguing against the traditional view that the French countered Lombroso's doctrine of the born criminal by emphasizing the sociological factors of crime, he shows that French physicians were in substantial agreement with Lombroso, both on the importance of heredity and on the role that medicine ought to play in criminal justice. This new medical discourse on crime frequently described criminals as animals. This dehumanizing conception of criminals quickly led to demands for "purging the social body" of such noxious elements, and Mucchielli is thus able to show that turn-of-the-century calls for the death penalty among physicians were based on eugenic reasoning before the term "eugenics" was ever used. In the end, however, calls for sterilization never gained the same momentum in France that they gained in the United States and other parts of Europe. Mucchielli attributes the weakness of eugenics in France not only to the French preoccupation with demographic decline, but to the strong appeal of a public hygiene movement that advocated a preventive approach designed to attack the environmental causes of degeneration, especially alcohol consumption. The chapter thus reminds us that while biological explanations of crime could lead to a pessimistic hereditarian fatalism that looked to eugenics or indefinite detention as the only remedies for an unchangeable criminal disposition, the conviction that criminal behavior resulted from certain biological abnormalities could also fuel a new therapeutic and preventive optimism.[23]

The tension between the optimistic and pessimistic implications of biological theories of crime also plays an important role in the next chapter,

---

22 See also Mariacarla Gadebusch Bondio, *Die Rezeption der kriminalanthropologischen Theorien von Cesare Lombroso in Deutschland von 1880–1914* (Husum, 1995).

23 See also Mucchielli, ed., *Histoire de la criminologie française*; Robert Nye, *Crime, Madness and Politics in Modern France* (Princeton, N.J., 1984); Gordon Wright, *Between the Guillotine and Liberty: Two Centuries of the Crime Problem in France* (New York, 1983).

by Stephen Garton, which examines the impact that the new medical discourse about deviance had on practices of confinement and social regulation
in Australia in the period 1890 to 1930. By the late 1890s, Garton reports,
their reception of the European criminal–anthropological literature had convinced Australian prison officials to think of prisons as "hospitals of moral
disease." The first order of business for turning prisons into "hospitals" for
criminals was to remove other problem populations, especially the insane,
alcoholics, and the newly created category of the "mentally defective" from
prison and place them in separate institutions. Garton thus shows that what
might at first glance appear as "decarceration" was in fact a diversification
of confinement. Once these other types of deviants were removed, prison
reformers proceeded to make further distinctions within the criminal population. The influence of psychiatrists within the penal system also varied
according to the type of criminal. Garton argues that the differentiation
between problem populations and the distinctions drawn among criminals
were largely designed to separate curables from incurables. The optimistic
and the pessimistic implications of the new biological theories of deviance
thus came to coexist by being assigned to two different target groups.

Ricardo Salvatore's chapter examines how positivist criminology's medical conception of the crime problem gave rise to a "medico–legal state" in
Argentina during the period from 1890 to 1940. Argentinean criminologists, like their colleagues in Western Europe and the United States, replaced
Lombroso's notion of a "born criminal" with distinct morphological traits
with that of the mentally abnormal criminal and focused attention on the
concepts of "dangerousness" (the likelihood that someone would commit
a crime or exhibit antisocial behavior) and "social defense" (society's right
to protect itself against dangerous individuals), both of which promised to
extend the state's power to new areas. Salvatore shows that by the 1930s positivist reformers had taken control of a whole range of institutions (including
prisons, courts, police, and insane asylums), where they introduced new
practices of registration and classification. In sum, Salvatore argues that the
positivist reformers gradually colonized the major institutions of social control and provided new "reasons for rule" that transformed the "grammar of
governance." While positivist criminology had a progressive–humanitarian
side that appealed to those committed to serious social reform, Salvatore
shows that its appeal for Argentinean government officials derived from its
promise to confer scientific status, to extend state power, and to provide
"total knowledge" of the lower–class population.[24]

---

24 See also Ricardo D. Salvatore, Carlos Aguirre, and Gilbert Joseph, eds., *Crime and Punishment in
Latin America: Law and Society Since Late Colonial Times* (Durham, N.C., 2001).

The connection between criminology and the politics of order is also a major theme of Yoji Nakatani's chapter on the beginnings of criminological discourse in Japan between about 1910 and 1940. Like their colleagues in most countries, Japanese criminologists abandoned Lombroso's emphasis on morphological characteristics and focused on links between crime and psychological abnormalities. In Japan the concept of "dangerousness" was given a blatantly political twist when it was suggested that involvement with the "dangerous thought" of communism was a sign of psychological abnormality. Nakatani further explores the link between criminology and politics by examining the involvement of leading criminologists in racial research, including studies on the distribution of blood types, which led one researcher to claim that the Taiwanese were genetically "rebellious." Criminologists also played a prominent role in the Japanese eugenics movement, which culminated in the passage of a national eugenics law in 1940.

Part Three: The Making of the Criminologist

This section takes a close look at the micro-practices of criminology: the role played by little tools of knowledge, the discursive space that was defined by conferences and journals, and the hermeneutic practices and semiotic strategies that allowed the criminologist to recognize and analyze the demonic character of seemingly innocent characteristics. The chapters in this section also pay attention to the ways in which the measuring and classifying of people introduced or reinforced norms of different kinds. They thus seek to further our understanding of the relationship between the institutional framework, epistemological issues, and the production of criminological knowledge.

In the first half of the nineteenth century, "criminological" knowledge was produced by various types of practitioners: judges and magistrates, police experts, officials and priests in penal institutions, as well as forensic medical experts. These practitioners used statistical tables and biographical information to distinguish between rational men and delinquents. They produced their knowledge about crime and criminals in close connection with their official task of preventing or punishing delinquency. Their research was one of the side-products of their administrative work and was performed in the police station, at court, or in the prison cells.

To some extent, the same can be said about the "criminologists" of the late nineteenth and twentieth centuries. They also started their research in close connection with other official duties in prison wards, hospitals, or similar institutions. But because of their different role and because of a new master narrative, they looked at criminals in a different way. A main objective of this section is to examine the criminological gaze and the ways in which it was linked to the institutional, social, and "discursive" positions of its bearers. This includes the study of the tools and techniques that criminologists used to access the hidden reality of the criminal's demonic or defective nature. Moreover, this section looks at the relationships between the hegemonic representations of criminals and corresponding semiotic strategies, such as the privileging of the body as a source of evidence, the privileging of the visual, and the reduction of criminals to mere objects of the criminologist's gaze.

This section also seeks to address the institutional framework in which the specialized discourse of criminology could proliferate. At conferences, criminologists not only built networks and exchanged statements and different readings of the evidence, but they also shared new tools and ideas about how to use them best. At the same time that these experts began to meet at specialized conferences, they also started to publish journals devoted to research in the areas that later became known as criminology. This institutional framework shaped the discourse of turn-of-the-century criminology in particular ways.

Martine Kaluszynski's chapter analyzes congresses and journals as two important elements that structured the production and exchange of criminological knowledge. By reconstructing the organization of the international congresses of criminal anthropology in detail, she provides us with a better understanding of the institutions that furnished new and more specialized forms of communication for the mostly academic participants in the criminological discourse. The careful examination of these congresses and their main actors allows us to trace the social, institutional, and political fields in which criminologists were embedded.[25]

David Horn's chapter examines the development and usage of highly specialized tools for criminal anthropological and psychometric research. His analysis focuses on the role that the production and use of these tools played in the discursive practice of criminologists who used them to bolster their claims of scientific authority and objectivity. Horn argues that the emphasis that was placed on the use of scientific tools and methods was a response to two different problems. On the one hand, these tools were instrumental in exploring new fields of evidence in accordance with the

---

25 See also Martine Kaluszynski, *La république à l'épreuve du crime: La construction du crime comme object politique, 1880–1920* (Paris, 2002) and Kaluszynski, "La criminologie en mouvement: Naissance et développement d'une science sociale en France au XIXème siecle" (Ph.D. diss., Université Paris VII, 1988).

criminal anthropological research program. On the other hand, their use also formed part of a defensive strategy to sustain scientific authority at a time when criminal anthropology was coming under increasing pressure from the scientific community and losing its persuasiveness in the courtroom.

It is a peculiar feature of a significant part of the criminological discourse that superficial research techniques went hand in hand with the belief in the direct visibility of evil or moral defectiveness through an experienced gaze. Among the objects exhibited in criminological collections, such as Cesare Lombroso's in Turin,[26] were pieces of tattooed skin from criminals. Although police practitioners had been using tattoos as identifying characteristics for a long time, they became a major focus of the criminological discourse only in the fin de siècle. Thus, tattoos made up one of the pieces of evidence on which the controversy between Lombroso and his French critics turned. This debate is the starting point of Jane Caplan's chapter on the role of tattoos in the discourse on criminality. Her analysis reminds us that one of the pitfalls of positivist criminology of both the Italian and the French variety was its failure to read tattoos as complex signs whose meaning could not be established within a single frame of reference, be it atavism or degeneration. As Caplan shows, most participants in the turn-of-the-century debate ignored the line of continuity between the previous use of tattoos as means of identification and the criminological reading that interpreted them as signs of a deep-seated criminal identity. Most important, however, the privileged role of the tattoo in fin-de-siècle criminological discourse furnished practitioners, such as army doctors, with the opportunity to participate in academic discourse with publications in which observations about tattoos were introduced by reference to the dogma they wanted to follow.[27]

The criminological discourse produced knowledge and disseminated specific readings of the evidence that was considered relevant. Yet criminological narratives and practices were certainly not uniform or uncontested. Outside of criminological circles, these theories were applied, contested, transformed, or challenged – depending on the position of the author. A very specific type of author is discussed in the chapter by Philippe Artières, namely, criminals writing their autobiographies. In this case the strictly hierarchical relationship between criminals and scientists appears to be disrupted. Criminals who took up the pen to reflect about the conditions under which

---

26 See Susanne Regener, *Fotografische Erfassung: Zur Geschichte medialer Konstruktionen des Kriminellen* (Munich, 1999), 171–91.

27 See also Jane Caplan, ed., *Written on the Body: The Tattoo in European and American History* (Princeton, N.J., 2000).

they turned to crime and a life of deviance seemed to take a more active role. But Artières explains that even the criminals' reflections were organized and supervised by the criminologist Alexandre Lacassagne, who was not interested in the authors' evaluation of their lives, but used their writings as evidence for the state of their psychology. Nevertheless, Artières argues, some of the criminals took the liberty of developing a critical stance toward the theories of their criminological master.[28]

The final chapter of this section, Peter Fritzsche's account of media representations of crime and criminals in Imperial Berlin, calls into question academically based criminologists' monopoly on producing criminological knowledge. Fritzsche analyzes the media reports as part of an ethnographic approach to urban life in general and crime in particular that was meant to provide the city dweller with a better idea of his social and physical environment. The motivation of these reports was similar to that of Lombroso's studies. As Fritzsche shows, they responded to an awareness that life within an urban environment was extremely diverse. To appropriate one's city better, one had to know about the diversity, without naturalizing it as the outcome of atavism or degeneration.[29]

Part Four: Criminology in the First Half of the Twentieth Century:
The Case of Weimar and Nazi Germany

This section begins with an overview of the development of criminology in Weimar (1919–33) and Nazi Germany (1933–45) by Richard F. Wetzell. From the late nineteenth century through the end of the Nazi regime, German criminology was characterized by the predominance of research on the biological causes of crime over research on its social causes. This situation was in large part due to the fact that most criminological research was conducted by psychiatrists. Analyzing the development of criminological theories in Germany in terms of two major paradigms, Wetzell argues that the German criminological discourse of the 1920s and 1930s was characterized by a central tension between the hereditarian biases of most psychiatrists and an increasing methodological and conceptual sophistication that promoted a complex view of the interaction of heredity and environment, which made the criminologists' goal of identifying criminogenic genetic factors ever more elusive. Because this tension continued in the Nazi

---

28 See also Philippe Artières, *Le livre des vies coupables: autobiographies de criminels (1896–1909)* (Paris, 2000).

29 See also Peter Fritzsche, *Reading Berlin 1900* (Cambridge, Mass., 1998).

period, the relationship between criminology and Nazism was complex. On the one hand, hereditarian criminal biology clearly contributed to the rise of the eugenics movement, and leading criminologists were eager to connect their field to the "biological politics" and eugenic agenda of the Nazi "racial state." On the other hand, the continuing tension between hereditarianism and more complex approaches in mainstream criminology and the fact that the sterilization of criminals remained controversial even under the Nazi regime demonstrate that the triumph of genetic determinism under the Nazi regime was not as complete as has often been supposed.[30]

Oliver Liang's chapter examines Weimar Germany's most important criminological institution, the Criminal-Biological Service of the Bavarian prison system, which administered "criminal-biological examinations" of prisoners. The reports were designed to help assign the prisoner to the "corrigible," "incorrigible," or "undecided" categories of the "progressive system" of Bavarian prisons, to make available an evaluation of the prisoner for future criminal trials, and to provide a data bank for criminological research. Liang shows that the Criminal-Biological Service enjoyed support from a wide range of bourgeois professionals working within the Bavarian prison system – including medical doctors, jurists, prison administrators, and the clergy – and argues that their support for criminal biology was motivated by a desire to "recast a bourgeois vision of morality" on a biological basis. His analysis of criminal-biological evaluations demonstrates that the biological data the evaluators collected paled in comparison to their extended discussions of sex, gender, class, religion, and politics, which essentially used bourgeois values as a standard for deciding the question of the prisoner's "corrigibility." Thus, Bavarian diagnoses of "incorrigibility" were in fact nothing but moral judgments cloaked in scientific language.[31]

Within Weimar criminology, Bavaria's Criminal-Biological Service was located at the most crudely genetically deterministic and scientifically least sophisticated end of the spectrum. The following chapter, by Gabriel Finder, examines the other end of the spectrum: psychoanalytic criminology. Whereas criminal biology focused on the search for the hereditary factors, psychoanalysts and Adlerian "individual psychologists" sought the causes of crime in unconscious motives deriving from psychological maladjustments originating in childhood. Since psychological disturbances were

---

30 See also Richard Wetzell, *Inventing the Criminal: A History of German Criminology, 1880–1945* (Chapel Hill, N.C., 2000).
31 See also Oliver Liang, "Criminal-biological theory, discourse, and practice in Germany, 1918–1945" (Ph.D. diss., Johns Hopkins University, 1999).

presumably more amenable to treatment than hereditary defects, the psychoanalytic approach had a considerable therapeutic potential that was not lost on some prison reformers. However, the expense of psychoanalytic therapy, the general hostility of mainstream psychiatry toward psychoanalysis, and the judiciary's suspicions about its exculpatory implications prevented psychoanalytic criminology from having any significant practical impact on the criminal justice system. Although the psychoanalytic approach might have been "conducive to the personal freedom of the condemned," Finder argues that its emancipatory potential must not be overestimated because most psychoanalytic criminologists did not challenge the principle of confining offenders and the increased penal flexibility they demanded threatened to expose the individual to increased judicial arbitrariness.

Discussions of alcoholism played an important role in discourses on crime in many countries during the nineteenth and twentieth centuries. Thus Laurent Mucchielli's chapter notes that the French social hygiene movement regarded the fight against alcohol as a key measure for preventing degeneration and thus crime, while Stephen Garton shows that Australian reformers saw the creation of special facilities for alcoholics as an important part of constructing a scientifically based penal system. In the volume's final chapter, Geoffrey Giles examines the German discourse on drinking and crime from Imperial Germany through the Weimar and Nazi periods. Giles shows that whether or not a drunken offender was held criminally responsible often depended on the social class of the offender. His analysis of the discourse on alcoholism and crime argues that the statistical evidence was usually weak and the definition of who exactly was a "drinker" remained unclear. Nor was there any agreement on the appropriate remedy, as some temperance groups demanded total abstinence, while others only called for drinking in moderation. Giles's discussion of treatment facilities for alcoholics draws a depressing portrait of institutions that were often not very different from prisons and usually did little to cure their inmates. When "severe alcoholism" became one of the disorders subject to compulsory sterilization under the Nazi regime, the criteria for what constituted "severe alcoholism" reflected social rather than medical norms in the most blatant fashion. As a result, individuals with criminal convictions who consumed alcohol but displayed no medical symptoms of chronic alcoholism could be sterilized as "severe alcoholics" on the grounds that their criminal behavior was an indication of severe alcoholism. This type of reasoning pushed the logic of linking criminality with biological abnormality to its furthest extreme. If biological abnormality (in this case alcoholism) was a cause of criminal behavior, why not treat criminal behavior itself as a symptom of biological abnormality?

The fact that medical theories were permeated by social values made it easy to rephrase social problems in scientific terms. This opened up new possibilitites not only for the detection of crime, but also for the prevention of crime as a "social disease." Strategies to prevent crime by preventing the existence of criminals can be traced throughout the time period under investigation. These strategies display important elements of continuity and discontinuity because their precise content depended on how the crime problem was conceptualized. Thus the shift from a moral to a medical definition of crime and criminals that took place over the course of the nineteenth century led to a corresponding transformation in the focus of these preventive schemes. Looking at the complex of prevention from the perspective of discourse analysis, this volume seeks to trace the close interrelation between discourse, practice, and the wider political field. In the German case, it was the political transformation reflected in the Nazi seizure of power that allowed some of the most radical "thought experiments" of criminologists to become institutionalized.

ONE

Nonacademic Sites of Nineteenth-Century Criminological Discourse

1

The French Revolution and the Origins of French Criminology

MARC RENNEVILLE

Who will help me read the human heart through its envelopes?
– Louis-Sébastien Mercier[1]

Does the history of French criminology still need to be written? Some recent works assume that it no longer does, but this certainly was not the case a short while ago.[2] Since World War II, criminology has taken a back seat to the issues surrounding criminal law. In fact, at times it has been unclear whether or not criminology had its own history at all. Michel Foucault's famous *Discipline and Punish* dedicated only a few lines to the subject.[3] Although important works on the history of penitentiary systems followed, Foucault's study did not give rise to new research on criminological science.[4] Most likely, this was because criminology was considered a by-product of the penitentiary system.

Without drawing on any particular theory, I seek to locate the origins of French criminology within the history of the state and the individual by focusing on the impact of the revolutionary period, which has been taken into account in histories of the penal system but has been curiously neglected in the history of criminological knowledge. For it is only by resituating the criminological question in this period that one can try to understand the genesis of the contradictory anthropologies of criminal law and the human sciences, involving the competing postulates of free will

---

1 Louis-Sébastien Mercier, *Le tableau de Paris (1782–1788)* (Paris, 1990), 310.
2 Christian Debuyst, Françoise Digneffe, Jean-Michel Labadie, and Alvaro P. Pires, *Histoire des savoirs sur le crime et la peine*, vol. 1: *Des savoirs diffus à la notion de criminel-né* (Brussels, 1995); Laurent Mucchielli, "Naissance de la criminologie," in Laurent Mucchielli, ed., *Histoire de la criminologie française* (Paris, 1995), 7–15.
3 Michel Foucault, *Surveiller et punir (naissance de la prison)* (Paris, 1975; reprint, 1993).
4 Michelle Perrot, ed., *L'impossible prison: recherches sur le système pénitentiaire au XIXe siècle* (Paris, 1980); Jacques-Guy Petit, ed., *La prison, le bagne et l'histoire* (Geneva, 1984).

and determinism. This heterogeneity of knowledge about criminality was frequently underscored by Foucault.[5] Far from reducing that contradiction to a professional conflict, Foucault considered these competing approaches to be strategically aligned and to constitute present-day "governmentality." I suggest here that this functional compatibility was an answer to the way the criminal question was posed in France at the turn from the eighteenth to the nineteenth century. Before turning to the political-scientific context at the end of the eighteenth century, a few historiographical comments are in order.

BETWEEN TWO CESARES: WHAT HISTORY FOR CRIMINOLOGY?

When one tries to define the origins of criminology in general, two questions arise: What should be understood by the term *criminology*? And: When did the birth of this science take place? If one defines criminology as a discourse that aims to undertake the scientific study of crime and criminals, the meaning of criminology is quite broad, because this science produced many schools, each of them claiming orthodoxy and genuine scientific validity.

If French criminology is understood as the study of criminal psychology, it can be said to begin with Bénédict-Augustin Morel (1809–73). If it is a sociology of deviance, its birth can be found in the works of Emile Durkheim (1858–1917). If it is the anthropological knowledge of the criminal, it arises in the works of Cesare Lombroso (1836–1909). If it consists of taking into account the offender's personality in sentencing, then it arises with the research on "psychic abnormalities," as formalized in Joseph Chaumié's circular of 1905.

All these chronologies are legitimate. But one can hardly see what could prevent revisionist schemes: Concerning criminal psychology, why Morel and not Prosper Lucas (1808–85)? If one defends the sociological approach, why not prefer André-Michel Guerry (1802–66) and his "moral statistics" over Emile Durkheim? And as far as anthropology is concerned, did not Franz-Joseph Gall (1758–1828) and Paul Broca (1824–80) anticipate the path later taken by Cesare Lombroso? Any dating based on a specific work lays itself open to a hagiographic reading that is reductive and lacks context.

It is possible to avoid these problems by adopting a strictly institutional approach, combining reception, academic teaching, and professionalization.

5 Michel Foucault, "L'évolution de la notion 'd'individu dangereux' dans la psychiatrie légale," *Déviance et société* 5, no. 4 (1978): 403–22.

The birth date of the national criminologies would then be more recent. In this way, David Garland can claim that English criminology did not exist before 1935.[6] But since the profession of the criminologist still has a precarious status at the end of the twentieth century, it makes more sense to think in terms of "schools" of approaches, trends, or methods, relatively independent from the institutions. Even if one thinks in terms of schools, Alvaro Pires has noted that the birth date of criminology remains an open question,[7] with three possible answers:

1. For some authors, criminology was born in the second half of eighteenth century, with Cesare Beccaria, although he had no clear "scientific" pretensions in his writings;[8]
2. For others, criminology did not originate with Beccaria's juridical treatise, but with the first statistical analyses of criminality by Guerry, Edouard Ducpétiaux, and Adolphe Quételet in the first third of the nineteenth century;[9]
3. For most authors, finally, criminology was born during the last third of the nineteenth century with the "triumvirate" of the Italian "positivist school" (Lombroso, Enrico Ferri, and Raffaele Garofalo), who dictated a shift in the object of study, from the crime to the criminal, and in the method, from juridical reasoning to scientific experiment.

This last possibility is highly questionable. For as soon as Lombroso is elevated to the position of father of scientific criminology, he is usually criticized for methodological carelessness. Nevertheless, of the three choices, the last is the most preferable,[10] even if some difficulties appear, most of all in the definition of "pre-scientific" period, which, according to Pinatel, begins with Plato, Aristotle, Aeschylus, Euripides, and Sophocles.[11] It is certain that several objective factors converged around the middle of the 1880s. In 1885 the first international congress of criminal anthropology took place in Rome, Garofalo (1852–1934) published his *Criminologia*, France passed the law on the transportation of recidivists, and the following year Alexandre Lacassagne launched the *Archives d'anthropologie criminelle*.

---

6 David Garland, "The Criminal and His Science: A Critical Account of the Formation of Criminology at the End of the Nineteenth Century," *British Journal of Criminology* 25 (1985): 131.

7 Alvaro Pires, "La criminologie d'hier et d'aujourd'hui," in Debuyst et al., *Histoire des savoirs*, 1:35.

8 Edwin H. Sutherland, *Principles of Criminology* (Philadelphia, 1934); Henri Ellenberger, *Criminologie du passé et du présent* (Montreal, 1965); David A. Jones, *History of Criminology: A Philosophical Perspective* (London, 1986); George B. Vold and Thomas J. Bernard, *Theoretical Criminology* (New York, 1986).

9 Willem A. Bonger, *An Introduction to Criminology* (London, 1933); Alfred R. Lindesmith and Ya'akov Levin, "The Lombrosian Myth in Criminology," *American Journal of Sociology* 42, no. 5 (1937): 653–71.

10 Robert A. Nye, "Heredity or Milieu: The Foundations of Modern European Criminological Thought," *Isis* 67, no. 238 (1976): 335–55; Georges Picca, *La criminologie* (Paris, 1988); Raymond Gassin, *Criminologie* (Paris, 1990).

11 J. Pinatel, *Le phénomène criminel* (Paris, 1987), 45.

Although the richness and the durability of this journal would appear to be enough to mark the birth of criminology,[12] "criminology" at this time was not limited to "criminal anthropology." To dismiss this as a simple question of vocabulary would miss the fact that there was an animated and complex discussion that juxtaposed many theories, from Lombroso to Durkheim, on to Paul Topinard (1830–1911), Gabriel Tarde, or Lacassagne. Consequently, criminology cannot be considered as a "normal science," which Thomas Kuhn defined as having a minimal consensus on objects and methods.[13] Instead, the field of criminology was structured by several normal sciences coming from different traditions (psychiatry, anthropology, criminal law, hygienics, judicial statistics, and so forth).

When it proved difficult to find the origins of criminology in the last part of the nineteenth century, scholars changed direction and began to look at a genealogy of ideas. Without minimizing the importance of the last quarter of the nineteenth century, Christian Debuyst proposed a new agenda, namely, studying the "peripheral sciences" that were investigating the "delinquency phenomena" long before the term *criminology* became established.[14]

According to Laurent Mucchielli, French criminology began with eighteenth-century physicians. A continuity was established that operated on the level of ideas, witnessing various periods of consensus, open debate, and conflict for the next hundred years. At this level of analysis, it is possible to defend the idea that "the mentalities and penal practices, the big clichés of criminality" were established at the end of the Middle Ages.[15]

But the physicians never had a monopoly on scientific discourses about crime and the criminal. Thus Debuyst found the delinquency problem addressed in the "diffused knowledge" (*savoirs diffus*) and the "problematic positions" (*situations problèmes*) of the eighteenth century.[16] Although such studies pose the problem of continuity, they do allow a collective reconstruction of what Alvaro Pires calls "the field of criminology."[17] My problem here is not to establish when and according to which epistemological or institutional criteria criminology arose as a science, but when and within what context the "criminological question" became, according to Claude Lévi-Straus, a subject that was "good to think about" for both the "natural sciences" and the "human sciences."

---

12 Martine Kaluszynski, "Aux origines de la criminologie: l'anthropologie criminelle," *Frénésie* 2, no. 5 (1988): 17–30.
13 Thomas S. Kuhn, *The Structure of Scientific Revolutions*, 3d ed. (Chicago, 1996).
14 Christian Debuyst, "Pour introduire une histoire de la criminologie: les problématiques de départ," *Déviance et sociéte* 14, no. 4 (1990): 347–76.
15 Mucchielli, ed., *Histoire de la criminologie française*, 461.
16 Debuyst et al., *Histoire des savoirs*, 1:100–101.
17 Pires, "La criminologie d'hier et d'aujourd'hui," 43.

THE END OF THE ANCIEN REGIME AND THE CRIMINAL QUESTION

If human society represses different acts by varying means, it cannot ignore the issue of crime. The "criminal question" was deeply modified in the West when moral theology lost its monopoly. As noted by Debuyst, it was in the eighteenth century that delinquent behavior and moral failing became distinguished.[18] Not that moral culpability disappeared all at once (it never completely disappeared), but it was no longer the dominant explanatory discourse on criminality. However, this break in the representation of the criminal/sinner was neither epistemological nor institutional but political because the foundation of theological representation was shaken in all fields. The same phenomenon was evident regarding the poverty question, which was closely related to the one of criminality: "Convinced of human perfectibility, the Enlightenment writers had the powerful desire to improve the quality of life and felt certain that the condition of the poor was in no way tied to their corruption or to human frailty. They no longer accepted the theory that poverty was a sin and preferred to consider it an effect of 'economic change.'"[19]

Giovanna Procaci noted that the second half of the eighteenth century witnessed a move from a conception of "poverty perceived as an individual destiny to one of poverty understood as a social phenomenon," and emphasized the subversive dimension of these new theories that considered poverty to be a "consequence of despotism."[20] This notion rejected the system of assistance based on charity, and physiocrats such as Anne Robert Jacques Turgot went so far as to theorize that poverty was a by-product of charity. These critics sought to discredit the church's ascendancy and to show that poverty was a social problem that the state had to take care of.

Parallel to the hardening of the repression regarding what Foucault described as the "illegalities of property" (*illégalismes de biens*), this period witnessed a change in the representation of criminality that was very similar to the changes in the conception of poverty.[21] While the philosophical and political agitation undermined the monarchy by openly criticizing its institutions and principles, and dechristianization was slowly progressing, French society vociferously debated the criminal question. The writings of Montesquieu, and even more those of Voltaire, Rousseau, Beccaria, Condorcet, and others, developed a line of thinking that one could call "judicial idealism." Judicial idealism held that criminality was caused not so

18 Debuyst, ed., *Histoire de la criminologie française*, 71.
19 A. Forrest, *La Révolution française et les pauvres* (Paris, 1986), 46.
20 G. Procacci, *Gouverner la misère: La question sociale en France (1789–1848)* (Paris, 1993), 14.
21 Foucault, *Surveiller et punir*, 99–106.

much by corrupted customs or the original sin but by badly organized secular institutions. It is significant that at that time there was no discourse connecting the urban working class and the "dangerous classes," even though in Paris at least, "four-fifths of the violent acts committed between 1765 and 1785 were attributable to journeymen or workers born outside the capital." That is to say, if Paris breathed "order and tranquility" those men who were soon to be labeled "savages" were already in the city.[22] To members of the working classes, poverty and criminality intermingled in reality, but in a remarkable sociopolitical configuration a large part of the elite considered that the danger did not come from the bottom but from the top.

The diagnosis of a natural corruption of the individual was transferred into the institutions. This remarkable moment was studied in detail by Hans-Jürgen Lüsebrink, in his analyses of the literature of the "famous trials," for which Louis-Dominique Cartouche (1693–1721) and Louis Mandrin (1724–55) were the key figures, and his analysis of the memoranda presented at the provincial academies.[23] Of course, literature about crime already existed in the seventeenth century in the *Tragical Stories of Our Times* (Les histoires tragiques de notre temps) by François de Rosset (1614), *The General History of Thieves* (L'histoire générale des larrons) by François de Calvès (1623), *The Spectacles of Horror* (Les spectacles d'horreur) by Jean-Pierre Camus (1630), and in ballads and tales, always useful for biographies of famous criminals. Two important changes took place: the amplification of those discursive circles that were initially confined to a popular public to all levels of society, and their new polemical usage. In the second half of the eighteenth century, the biographies of brigands published in the famous *bibliothèque bleue* often turned against the obsolete monarchy by criticizing its judicial power and by characterizing it as abusive and unfair. The narratives of trials or famous affairs revealed the arbitrary nature of the "lettres de cachet"; of procedural secrecy; and of the use of torture during interrogation.

The controversies in popular and literary representations of criminality can be found in the learned literature as well. Concerns about the criminal question and judicial reform are attested by the numerous examinations of these problems in theses by the learned societies and the academies. In 1777, for example, the Economic Society of Bern solicited proposals for

---

22 Arlette Farge and André Zysberg, "Les théatres de la violence à Paris au XVIIIe siècle," *Annales E.S.C.*, no. 5 (1979): 1012.

23 Hans-Jürgen Lüsebrink, "Les représentations sociales de la criminalité en France au XVIIIe siècle," Ph.D. diss., Ecole des Hautes Etudes en Sciences Sociales, Paris, 1983.

"a complete and detailed project of criminal legislation" that would take into account (1) the principle of proportionality, (2) the nature of the evidence to be retained, and (3) how to reconcile an efficient judicial investigation with "the greatest possible guarantees for liberty and humanity." Voltaire and Jean-Paul Marat sent their own contributions. In 1780 the Academy of Chalons-sur-Marne called for a reflection "about the means to decrease the severity of the penal laws in France, without going against the public severity." Joseph Elzéar Dominique de Bernardi and Jacques-Pierre Brissot de Warville also submitted their reports.

The winds of philanthropy could be felt in most of these memoranda.[24] A reduction in punishment was advocated most often, and the authors considered the harshness of the laws a violation of citizens' rights that partially explained the increase of criminality. Beware those who failed to comply with the recommendations of the academies. At the Chalons-sur-Marne examination of 1780, for example, an author distinguished himself by asserting that excessive lenience by judges was at the origin of criminal behavior. The Academy's judgment was harsh: "He begins by saying that the penal laws are not severe in France. . . . It would be no use to go further in the analysis of this memo, which is very badly written and does not fulfill, in any way, the views of the Academy."

An analysis of fifty memoranda written between 1774 and 1788 by Lüsebrink showed that although half of the memoranda stated that the primary origin of all crimes lay in human nature itself, in the "vices" and "disastrous passions" of the human being, a multitude of social factors was cited to explain the evolution of and the increase in criminality. Human nature was cited as the cause of offenses twenty-seven times, but "social abuses" were cited thirty-eight times, and "juridical abuses," forty-three times.[25]

Of course, the Christian influence remained strong, and when the "human nature" of the offenders was cited as a cause, it was still referred to as sin and fault, and not as illness in the strict sense. The rare presence of medical terms should not be considered here as evidence of a criminological discourse because their use was generally metaphorical. This pathological register was mostly a polemical broadside against the judicial institution. In this way it was, for Brissot de Warville, the excessive frequency of punishment that was "a symptom of illness" for a government because "the man is not born an enemy of society." He did not hesitate to denounce the

---

24 Catherine Duprat, *Le temps des philanthropes: La philanthropie parisienne des Lumières à la monarchie de Juillet*, 2 vols. (Paris, 1993), 1:15–18.
25 Lüsebrink, "Les représentations sociales," 213.

criminality of the upper classes: "Attacks against the security and the liberty of the citizens are one of the greatest crimes, and in this category must be included not only assassination and theft committed by individuals of the people but also those committed by men in high places and the magistrates, whose influence acts on a larger field and with more force, destroying the ideas of justice and task in the mind of the subjects, and replacing them with the right of the strongest, a right that is equally dangerous for those who apply it and those who are subject to it."[26]

Most of these works undermined the bases of the political legitimacy of the state. In his *Plan of Criminal Legislation*, which was subsequently destroyed, Marat wondered whether there was "no government in the world that can be considered legitimate" and whether obeying the laws was not a matter of calculation rather than duty.[27] It was recalled recently that Beccaria's famous *Dei delitti e delle pene* was not only a treatise on rights but also a pamphlet on equality. Hence, the penal question was a pretext to treat "the reform of society and state in a more general manner."[28] Moreover, there is a passage of a work where Beccaria identified himself as a brigand. In these surprising lines, seldom cited, the author devoted himself to what criminologists today would call cost-benefit analysis, but the reasoning of his imaginary offender was miles apart from the one that certain criminologists attribute to Beccaria. Let us recall this passage: "What are [as the offender would say] those laws that we must respect and that make so many differences between the rich and me? He refused me a penny when I asked him and, as an excuse, exhorts me to work, which he could not do himself. And those laws, who made them? Rich and powerful people who never deigned to visit our dark cottages of poverty."[29]

Because the poor benefited little by respecting the laws and the costs for doing so are high, the reformer continued, it was necessary to break "those ties that are disastrous for most men and that benefit only a small number of idle tyrants," to attack "the injustice at its root" and return to "the natural state of independence." Beccaria ended with an imaginary monologue of the

---

26 Jacques-Pierre Brissot de Warville, *Les moyens d'adoucir la rigueur des lois pénales en France, sans nuire à sûreté publique, ou Discours couronnés par l'Académie de Châlons-sur-Marne en 1780* (Châlons-sur-Marne, 1781), 23–4.

27 Pierre Lascoumes, Pierrette Poncela, and P. Lenoël, *Au nom de l'ordre (une histoire politique du code pénal)* (Paris, 1989), 29–30.

28 Mario Sbriccoli, "Beccaria ou l'avènement de l'ordre: Le philosophe, les juristes et l'émergence de la question pénale," in Michel Porret, ed., *Beccaria et la culture juridique des Lumières* (Geneva, 1997), 178.

29 Cesare Beccaria, *Des délits et des peines* (1764; reprint, Paris, 1991), 80.

legitimate offender and by conjuring the ghosts of Mandrin and Cartouche: "At the head of a small troop I will correct the errors of fortune and see the tyrants turn pale and tremble in front of the ones whom their insolent arrogance treated worse than their horses and dogs."[30]

THE PENAL CODES AND PENAL KNOWLEDGE IN REVOLUTION

Hence, what appears in France at the end of the eighteenth century is the emergence of new discourses on a criminality that not only is understood in its religious dimensions but also as a social and political phenomenon. This emergence expressed itself in the popular literature, as well as in penal policies that were proposed to prevent the crimes. Enemies and public servants of the absolutist monarchy attacked the great proliferation of royal laws. In spite of the failure of a last-ditch attempt at reform in 1788, the will to modify the penal law had been supported by the Enlightenment philosophers, who applied themselves mostly to the question of the legitimacy of the right to punish, and the magistrates, who were anxious to rationalize their practice.

These concerns were clearly visible in the penal field through the publication of numerous annotated collections of royal ordinances. The common point made by all the educated men who argued about the criminal question just before the Revolution was the possibility of building a new social order in order to restore the social fabric and to change men.[31] These hopes were often expressed as a "judicial idealism," translated into a shared hope for the capability of the laws — as long as those were just — to reform customs and to regenerate society. Denis Diderot summarized this spirit perfectly in his *Supplément au voyage de Bougainville*: "If the laws are good, the customs are good, if the laws are bad, the customs are bad."[32] Besides, it was not by accident that the figure most frequently called for in a revolution was precisely the legislator, who has the "power to institute, and is capable of carrying out the mutation from savage world to civilized world."[33]

In the minds of some people these laws would even aim at correcting the inequalities of nature: "The social state does not establish an unjust inequality of the rights near the natural inequality of the mean. . . . On the

---

30 Ibid., 131–2.
31 Mona Ozouf, *L'homme régénéré: Essais sur la Révolution française* (Paris, 1989).
32 Denis Diderot, *Supplément au voyage de Bougainville* (1772; reprint, Paris, 1993), 178.
33 Ozouf, *L'homme régénéré*, 462.

contrary, it protects the equality of the rights against the natural but harmful influence of the inequality of means," as Abbé Sieyès wrote in 1793.[34]

Observing the priorities in the complaints coming out of the *cahiers généraux*, the Constituent Assembly was very active on matters concerning the reform of judicial institutions. On June 12 and 13, 1791, Etienne Michel Le Pelletier de Saint-Fargeau (1760–93), in the name of the committees for criminal legislation and the constitution, presented to the Assembly a penal code that, according to Jacques-Guy Petit, was a "synthesis of Enlightenment thought." Le Pelletier based the new system of punishments on the principles of "humane" punishments, "proportionate" to the crime, "fixed and determined," "durable" and "public" and essentially based on a deprivation of freedom at three different levels: jail, detention, and prison.

Le Pelletier placed his hopes in the reform of the criminal through confinement and forced labor, which made the 1791 law a real "code of utopia."[35] His whole proposal was permeated by the juridical idealism that belonged to the reformist philosophy, and it pointed once again to institutions as the source of criminality: "Despotism prevails everywhere. It has been noticed that crime is on the increase; this is not surprising since the individual is degraded; and it could be said that freedom, similar to those strong and vigorous plants, soon purifies any evil in the fortunate ground from which they spring."[36]

Le Pelletier's report was not accepted to the letter. Although Maximilien Robespierre, Jérôme Petion, and Adrien Duport joined him in defending the abolition of capital punishment, this punishment remained in the repressive arsenal. This retention was more than just symbolic, but very revealing in that it sanctioned an exclusive interpretation of the social contract. From this date, in effect, the person of the "delinquent-citizen," as defined by Beccaria, was no longer considered to be inviolable. The positive right of the state was asserted at the expense of the natural rights of the individual. This was based on a new vision of the offender: There are some cases when society applies capital punishment when the offender is not quite a man.

The Legislative Assembly, which met for the first time on October 1, 1791, did not challenge the work of the Constituent Assembly, and adopted the final text of the code on October 6. The great novelty of this first French penal code – which represented a break as much radical as ephemeral

---

34 Emmanuel Joseph Sieyès, "Des intérêts de la liberté dans l'état social et dans le système représentatif," *Journal d'instruction sociale (par les citoyens Condorcet, Sieyes et Duhamel)* 2 (June 8, 1793): 33–48.

35 Jacques-Guy Petit, *Histoire des galères, bagnes et prisons (XIIIe–XXe siècles): Introduction à l'histoire pénale de la France* (Toulouse, 1991), 46–8.

36 Lascoumes, Poncela, and Lenoël, *Au nom de l'ordre*, 353.

because the 1810 code modified its terms – was the fixed nature of the punishments.

The reformers considered the penal code to be the best instrument for fighting the arbitrariness of judges, by putting into practice Beccaria's syllogism: "the major must be the general law, the minor the act in relation with the law, the conclusion will be the acquittal or the sentence."[37] The old system of legal proofs was abolished: The judge would no longer accumulate "complete," "light," "half-complete" evidence, and "distant clues" in order to come to his decision. As a sign of the reformers' Anglophilia, a jury was to render its verdict on the most serious crimes. The power of the judge in these cases was limited to ratifying the decision of the jurors by applying the punishments prescribed by law. The judges did not have any latitude to modify the punishment with what was later called "extenuating circumstances" and what the judges of the ancien régime had called "diminished responsibility."

In spite of the refusal to abolish capital punishment, the French penal code was influenced by the voluntarism of politics and philosophy that guided the party of the most learned reformers. The culpability of offense against religious morality disappeared. The shared belief in the perfectibility of the individual was perceptible, as much in the retention of old, dissuasive punishments (iron collar, public exposition, loss of civil rights) as in the new measures taken to rehabilitate the criminal through work.

If the regeneration of society was effected by enforcing just laws, then it was accompanied by the true education of the citizens. For this purpose Le Pelletier de Saint-Fargeau had written a plan for public education, which he considered a necessary complement to the promulgation of the penal code. Considering that "the human species" had been "degraded by the vice of the old social system," Le Pelletier was "convinced of the necessity to cause an entire regeneration."[38]

Conscious of this necessity and urgency, the doctors also worked at the end of the century on this regeneration through an increased knowledge of man. As far back as 1790, Pierre Jean Georges Cabanis dreamed of prisons that would be "true infirmaries of crime." This was not a simple rhetorical analogy but a true identity link because the doctor-philosopher did mention the county of Oxford, where the prisoners were put in jail and reformed by

---

37 Beccaria, *Des délits et des peines*, 67.
38 Michel Le Pelletier de Saint-Fargeau, "Plan d'éducation nationale présenté aux Jacobins par Félix Le Pelletier, lu à la Convention le 13 juillet 1793 par Robespierre au nom du comité d'instruction publique," in *Oeuvres* (Brussels, 1826), 267–330.

work; thus, "the curative method was discovered, by means of which the crime can be treated as another form of madness."[39]

In 1804 the famous report titled "Relations Between the Physics and the Morals of Man" established the basis for a general science of man, for an "anthropology" that would try to ascertain the factors influencing man's intellect.[40] Yet, this new science could be achieved only by keeping the philosophical work of the Enlightenment at arm's length. Whereas in *De l'esprit* (1758) and *De l'homme* (1772) Claude Adrien Helvétius (1715–71) defended a "psychology" that was based only on physical sensibility and the search for individual physical pleasures, and whereas the perfectibility of man through education seemed unlimited, Cabanis estimated that the way these sensations were received varied depending on the individual's sex, primitive organization, nature, age, health, climate, physical traits, and eating habits. The study of these variations was as useful for the doctor as for the moralist and the legislator because these factors could influence the subject's decision-making capability. Any confusion of the sensations, the impressions, or the instinctive determinations necessarily limited the free will.

While the physiological ideology built a research program that contradicted the certainties of the anthropology that had guided the first codifications, the spirit of the laws evolved in the direction of a rejection of judicial idealism. After Thermidor, it was time for a stabilization of society and its institutions.[41] During the discussion of the civil code in 1804, Portalis openly accepted social inequality as legitimate, justified by the nature and the birth of individuals: "It is not to the right of property that inequality amongst men must be attributed. Men are not born equal in size, force, industry, or talents. Chance and events also create differences between them. Those primary inequalities, which are the very work of nature, necessarily entail those that are observed in society."[42]

The reversal of the debates that took place before the Terror was clear: The priority no longer was to invent a new society but to preserve it. It was necessary to re-establish it and maintain social order. The civil code was followed by the code of civil procedure (1806), the commercial code (1807), the code of criminal procedure (1808), and, finally, the new *code penale* (1810). The preliminary measures and the primary book were presented

39 Pierre-Jean-Georges Cabanis, *Observations sur les hôoutaux* (Paris, 1790), 6.
40 Pierre-Jean-Georges Cabanis, *Des rapports du physique et du moral de l'homme* (Paris, 1980), 554.
41 Bronislaw Baczko, *Comment sortir de la Terreur: Thermidor et la Révolution* (Paris, 1989); Martin S. Staum, *Minerva's Message: Stabilizing the French Revolution* (Montreal, 1996).
42 *Naissance du code civil: La raison du législateur* (Paris, 1989), 274–5.

to the State Council (Conseil d'Etat) on October 4, 1808, discussed, and then adopted on October 3, 1809. On the same day the project was sent to the civil and criminal legislative commission of the legislative corps, which remarked on it. The council adopted this section in January 1810. The same procedure was followed for each section of the code. It was definitively adopted (240 votes to 16) by the legislative corps without public debate and promulgated on February 23, 1810.

With this, the Consulate ended the work of codification with which the Revolution had begun. This is understandable because Portalis thought that penal laws were "less a special sort of law than the sanction of all other laws." However, if penal laws did not have any other aim than supporting the principles that other laws had invoked, one must wonder why the Consulate undertook to draft a new penal code twenty years after Merlin de Douai's first reform. The only survey of the motives for the 1810 code can be found in the presentation of the preliminary explanation and rationale for the reform (*exposé des motifs*) made by Jean-Baptiste Target (1723–1810) in 1801 before the State Council: "Vices are the roots of crimes. Should it be possible to eradicate them, then the law would no longer have to punish. Though for a genius, passionate for the love of good, the improvement of the human race is no chimerical thought, it is a very slow process, to be carried out by wisdom, perseverance, and time. Every day, however, society must be maintained and quick remedies must be found for present calamities: such is the aim of criminal laws and the penal code."[43] A complete change is reaffirmed: Safety becomes more important than the reform of customs. The final code no longer sought to improve individuals or to protect them, but to maintain society.

Indeed, for Target, "real wisdom respects humanity" but should not sacrifice "public safety." The principle of the complete rehabilitation of the offenders was questioned, and on this point Target disagreed with the spirit of the lawmakers in the Constituent Assembly: "An idea of perfectibility, rarely applicable to all men generally, even more rarely to souls that have been altered in crime, and nearly chimerical for those who were soiled by horrible crimes or for whom deep corruption appeared in the repetition of offenses, had embellished in their eyes the principle adopted by our first lawmakers."[44]

---

43 Jean-Baptiste Target, "Observations sur le projet de code criminel," in Jean Guillaume Locré de Roissy, ed., *La législation civile, commerciale et criminelle de la France ou Commentaire et complément des codes français, 1827–1832*, 31 vols. (Paris, 1801), 29:7.
44 Ibid., 16.

The penal code of 1810 marked the final break with the reformist thought of the Enlightenment and the initial move toward the realistic management typical of the nineteenth century. Moreover, the presentation of the code project constantly rode roughshod over the idea of citizenship and the principle of the uniformity of punishment. Indeed, Target remarked that society was made up of classes, some helped by "enlightenment," supported by education, and others degraded by destitution. Although he thought that the distribution of punishments unfortunately could not be carried out according to the "characters" and "tendencies" of individuals, he asserted that the code should take into account the status of the individual as much as the nature of their crime because "the lawmaker's reason" would no longer accept being "fed an abstraction." Thus, customs should be considered.

This development was not so much one of transformation but one of accommodation, control, and pacification. The state would from now on pay full attention to the real society: "The societies to which laws are given should be considered as they are and not as they should be."[45] The nineteenth-century penal code, the code of the criminologists, sealed a durable compromise between monarchical law and revolutionary law. On the one hand, the code of 1810 preserved certain principles of the revolutionary law, including the principles of the legality of punishments (Article 4), equality before the law, and finally that of the division of offenses into three categories: contraventions, offenses, and crimes. On the other hand, the code abandoned the principle of fixed punishments that had been so close to the reformers' hearts by introducing the principle of mitigating circumstances. Even if these were at first limited to contraventions, one of the nineteenth-century trends consisted precisely in extending this modulation to the two other offense categories. The short period of judicial idealism was thus closed, and for a long time.

CONCLUSION: ONE CRIMINAL QUESTION, SEVERAL ANSWERS

At the end of the eighteenth century, France was marked by a period of political and legal transformation that completely changed the problem of how to manage deviancy. The society that evolved after the great Revolution had a new way of perceiving the social bonds and the legal character of the right to punish.

In this new context, the criminal question left to the nineteenth century involved an equation between two unknown quantities, both linked to

45 Ibid., 9.

the relation between individual and society. The first unknown looks like a statement: Crime is persistent. Many reformers thought that economic progress and an increase in the standard of living would make crime increasingly rare – or that it would disappear altogether. A few revolutionaries (Barère, Lanthenas, and so forth) sincerely thought that they would be able to cure society of crime and destitution. These speeches did not deceive the listeners for very long when they were confronted with the daily exercise of power.

Disillusionment came quickly because the problem had to be dealt with, but, in the longer term, these dreams of a government cure were lost because industrialization did not turn out to be the appropriate remedy. Afterward, not only did the persistence of crime have to be explained but also the unexpected relationship between the progress of civilization and the progress of crime. Because it no longer could be said that crime was related to political despotism, other causes were sought. One theory occurred to all specialists, such as doctors, lawyers, moralists, psychologists, theologians, and sociologists: The more a society perfects itself, the more the individual's morality declines. This diagnosis was repeated in the nineteenth century by Morel and Durkheim, among others, but it can still be found in the writings of some criminologists today, with all related commonplaces: Criminality of young people is more severe, a return to "good values" is necessary, and the prison and judicial systems are in crisis.

The second unknown factor in the equation is the individual's right to resist. The formula of the philosophers of the Enlightenment Century was clear from a theoretical point of view: "the consensus of all persons against the arbitrariness of one person." However, if we look at it more closely, judicial idealism found a solution that was incompatible with the exercise of power. The social bond was tied to the fiction of a "social contract," freely consented to by all, which assumed that everybody had good reason to adhere to it. Robert Castel noted that six categories of individuals were going to pose problems for this new idea of sociability throughout the nineteenth century: criminals, vagrants, beggars, children, lunatics, and proletarians. For Castel, however, only the lunatics clearly showed the limit of contractual legalism because only those individuals necessitated neutralization "by other means than the ones of a juridico-policy apparatus."[46] Thus, "the repression of the lunatic will have to lie on a medical ground, whereas the repression of the criminal immediately has a juridical ground."[47]

46 Robert Castel, *L'ordre psychiatrique (l'âge d'or de l'aliénisme)* (Paris, 1976), 56.
47 Ibid., 41.

Was the criminal personality so different from the lunatic's? A priori, it was. A lunatic cannot use his reason. He is insane, cannot take advantage of his freedom and, as a result, cannot understand the social contract: If he breaks it, it is because he does not know it, not because he questions it. Therefore, the offense of a lunatic is not a direct political threat to the power of the establishment. The criminal is the opposite because the imputability of his crime lies in his ability to use his reason and his freedom of will. His actions remain to be understood: Why does the offender choose to transgress the law? Why does a minority refuse the rules of the game? Foucault clearly showed how these questions brought out the contradictions of a repressive machine that theoretically assumed individual freedom of will but whose judicial procedure never ceased looking for the reasons that pushed the individual into committing an offense. On the one hand, the juridical discourse insisted on the freedom of will; on the other, morals claimed a causal relationship. Crime could be understood only in analogy with economic exchange: It would not be "free." In this juridico-moral conflict the offender's freedom quickly became quite chimerical, and justice was entirely unprepared to confront horrible crimes for which no explanation could be found.

If lunacy and criminality were mutually exclusive in the juridical register, they never stopped being systematically combined in the normative register of erudite speeches. Let us consider this question of overlapping in action from another point of view: If we agree with Durkheim that crime is an attempt against the "strong states of collective consciousness" or, to update the expression, to the values of the dominant group, we can see how subversive an offense can be. To commit an offense while being conscious of one's acts is no longer only risking a punishment because you gave in to temptation, as it was according to the system of ancient right; it also is a refusal of the order and the symbolic values of a society that derives its legitimacy from the individuals who compose it. How can a being in possession of intellectual faculties make himself an outlaw and act against his own and everybody else's interest from his own free will?

The reformers of the "century of Enlightenment" answered this question depending on their political situation. Under the ancien régime the social contract was not kept by the government. And if the criminal – this is Beccaria's example – transgressed the law, it was because he has good reason to do so, pushed by hunger and destitution, disheartened by the inequity of laws and corruption of powerful people. But such an argument could not be endorsed by postrevolutionary politicians. If social cohesion was to be preserved, the contractual system demanded that something other than old Christian liberty to do evil be invited, because the moral statistics were showing a spread of evil and criminal offenders were exposing the failure of the carceral system through their recidivism. This second gap was filled with a soft determinism, apolitical and guaranteed by scientific objectivity. The doctors – legists, phrenologists, hygienists – were the first ones to try and cure the new society; soon they were assisted by many specialists in the human sciences, which led to new institutions.[48] Crime paid in those times, and everyone claimed to have discovered the solution to the criminal question. We have not solved it yet.

Far from being a time of confusion, the Revolution has turned out to be a key period for the emergence of French criminology. It was at that time that new judicial and medical representations of the criminal appeared. With the benefit of hindsight, one can see that the opposition between free will and determinism was a polemical artifact that never curbed the repressive machinery. In actual practice, compromise prevailed, both in the theories about criminology and in the judicial system.[49] Research in the French sphere validates recent analyses on the social construction of theories and on the failure of the same when practically applied. In fact, the transformations that occurred in the course of the nineteenth century were already present in Target's report, that is, the decline of the reformers' hopeful expectations and, as early as the middle of the century, the criticism – which was not specific to France – of places of confinement such as prisons and lunatic asylums.

48 Marc Renneville, *La médicine de crime (1785–1885)* (Lille, 1997).
49 See the chapter by Peter Becker in this volume.

2

Murderers and "Reasonable Men"

The "Criminology" of the Victorian Judiciary

MARTIN J. WIENER

Crime is the ineradicable birthmark of fallen humanity.... Crime, then, must be constantly present in the community, and every son of Adam may, under certain conditions, be drawn into it.

Arthur Griffiths, chief prison inspector, 1898[1]

Hitherto noted only very cursorily, as merely the foil against which "scientific" criminologists in Britain developed their discipline at the turn of the twentieth century, the views of the English judiciary about the origins, character, and treatment of crime demand investigation in their own right. At any given moment during the Victorian era a mere fifteen High Court judges tried all serious criminal offenses in England and Wales. These men thereby developed a recognized "expertise" on crime. Their views – pronounced with great authority in crowded courtrooms, reported at length in newspapers, and given force by their sentencing power – were enormously influential. Uniting the knowledge gained by presiding over hundreds of trials with the power to dominate the courtroom and determine the sentence, they were exemplars of Michel Foucault's "power-knowledge" complex. They are forgotten today, yet they form an essential chapter in the history of criminology.

One reason for the neglect of "judicial criminology" has been the formalist legal ideology that maintained (and still maintains) that the work of judges is something quite distinct from their own beliefs and values, whatever they may be. The judicial task, as judges themselves constantly described it, was to set forth "the law" as it had developed through litigation and statute over many years, and not their own views. Such views, in any event, would appear to be very difficult to ascertain because in keeping with this self-image

1 *Mysteries of Crime and Police* (London, 1898), 1.

judges rarely explicitly set forth their personal thinking on crime and criminality in any extended form. The lack of books or articles discussing the subject in general terms (as opposed to reminiscences of particular cases) has helped keep judges out of histories of criminology.

Yet, in nineteenth-century England, as in other times and places, the law was neither fixed nor transparent; rather, it required continual interpretation, particularly because society was undergoing dramatic material and cultural change. Because Parliament (nominally the source of law) was just beginning to involve itself in this task, judges continued to play a large role in the ongoing evolution of law. In adapting old precedents to new circumstances, judges could not help but draw on the ideas and values of their own time and milieu. As they did so they developed an implicit philosophy of human nature and agency; in their criminal work this amounted to an unacknowledged but powerfully influential criminology.[2]

However vague and formally subordinated to the "law," such a criminology can be recovered from judicial decisions and pronouncements, in court and out. In leading cases much of the judges' court remarks are preserved in published law reports. Even cases that had no special interest to lawyers were often recounted in newspaper reports. In addition, in capital cases a guilty verdict led to confidential correspondence between the presiding judge and the home secretary, who, from the 1820s, had the responsibility of deciding whether to allow the prisoner to hang or to commute the sentence to life imprisonment. Much of this correspondence (often revealing of judicial attitudes and values) has survived in the archives of the Home Office. Taken together (as they have never yet been), these two bodies of source material disclose a coherent understanding of "crime" and "the criminal" widely shared among judges and broadly disseminated through the reading and watching Victorian public.

In this chapter I confine my purview in two ways: First, I look at one kind of criminal case, that of murder – one of the rarest but also the most serious; second, I explore one facet of judicial thinking about criminality – the emergence of the standard of the "reasonable man," by whose (imagined) behavior under stress offenders were to be judged.[3] Specifically, reference

---

2 With the rise of "control" theories in criminology, which might be seen as "neo-Victorian," we are perhaps better able to appreciate nineteenth-century conceptions of criminal behavior. For a leading example of such a turn in criminology, see Michael R. Gottfredson and Travis Hirschi, *A General Theory of Crime* (Stanford, Calif., 1990); for another variant, see Jack Katz, *Seductions of Crime: Moral and Sensual Attractions in Doing Evil* (New York, 1988).
3 On the history of the "objective test" of criminal responsibility, see Bernard Brown, "The 'Ordinary Man' in Provocation: Anglo-Saxon Attitudes and 'Unreasonable Non-Englishmen,'" *International and Comparative Law Quarterly* 13 (1964): 203–35; Ronald Collins, "Language, History, and the Legal

to the behavior of the "reasonable man" was supposed to enable the jury to decide whether a murder charge (which carried the death penalty) could properly be reduced to a finding of manslaughter (not punishable capitally).

Criminal cases rarely encouraged the elaborate judicial reasoning sometimes found in civil litigation. Yet occasionally in the criminal courtroom judges did make explicit general arguments, arguments that can be seen to underlie their rulings and instructions in many other trials. In particular, efforts to restrict the defenses of interpersonal violence promoted a general and "objective" standard of self-controlled behavior. Behind repeated statements that particular actions did not constitute provocation was an ever-clearer test by which defendants were to be measured – the expected reaction of the "ordinary, reasonable man" (by the end of the century often colloquially referred to as "the man in the Clapham omnibus").

The notion of the reasonable man was at once "legal" and "empirical"; in it, the self-referential world of law met the more open world of reflection on human nature. Legal scholars have tended to see it only as legal fiction. In a 1975 judgment, for example, Lord Diplock explained the reasonable-man standard (which he argued had ceased to be operative) as a device for facilitating inference about the accused's state of mind. He observed:

Until as late as 1898 persons accused of murder were incompetent to give evidence in their own defense. So the actual intent with which they had done the act which had in fact caused death could only be a matter of inference from the evidence of other witnesses as to what the accused had done or said. In drawing this inference from what he had done it was necessary to assume that the accused was gifted with the foresight and reasoning capacity of a "reasonable man" and, as such, must have foreseen as a possible consequence of his act, anything which, in the ordinary course of events, might result from it.

After the 1898 Evidence of Prisoners Act, he noted, this "objective" test "no longer provided the only means available in a criminal trial of ascertaining the actual intention of the offender" and gradually ceased to be invoked.[4]

Process: A Profile of the 'Reasonable Man,'" *Rutgers Camden Law Journal* 8 (1977): 311–23; Graeme Coss, "'God Is a Righteous Judge, Strong and Patient: and God Is Provoked Every Day': A Brief History of the Doctrine of Provocation in England," *Sydney Law Review* 13 (1991): 570–604; Norman J. Finkel, "Achilles Fuming, Odysseus Stewing, and Hamlet Brooding: On the Story of the Murder-Manslaughter Distinction," *Nebraska Law Review* 74 (1995): 742–803. Since about the time of World War I, "objectivism" has been in retreat in both England and America; in recent decades its retreat has become more like a rout. On the United States, see Kate Stith-Cabranes, "Faults, Fallacies, and the Future of Our Criminal Justice System: The Criminal Jury in Our Time," *Virginia Journal of Social Policy and the Law* 3 (1995): 133–45; on England, see A. Kiralfy, ed., *The Burden of Proof* (Abingdon, 1987). In both nations the 1960s appear to have been the decisive period for the abandonment of this Victorian approach to criminal liability.
4 Quoted in Kiralfy, *Burden of Proof*, 27–8.

However, like modern readings of Jeremy Bentham and his followers as value-neutral "consequentialists," this reading of the notion of the reasonable man assumes the mentality of nineteenth-century jurists to be essentially the same as that of their late twentieth-century successors. In several crucial ways, it was not. Nineteenth-century jurists did not necessarily have a higher estimate of the average man's everyday rationality and self-control than their successors, but they did have a higher estimate of his *potential* rationality and self-mastery, and a much stronger belief in the power of the law to stimulate these potentials and capacities.[5] Bentham shared with most nineteenth-century jurists a belief that there existed in almost all persons the capacity to stand back from impulse and take a longer view of one's own interest. It was a capacity sometimes undeveloped, sometimes damaged, but nonetheless there to be called on and encouraged. As Bentham famously declared, "men calculate, some with less exactness, indeed some with more: but all men calculate."[6] Bentham and his followers expected criminal law to deter socially harmful actions through a clear tariff of efficiently enforced penalties. At the same time criminal law would improve men by rewarding their exercise of self-discipline and punishing their surrender to impulse. As Bentham's disciple, James Mill, argued, the principle of utility "marshalls the duties in their proper order, and will not permit mankind to be deluded, as so long they have been, sottishly to prefer the lower to the higher good, and to hug the greater evil, from fear of the less."[7] In this program the reasonable man was an embodiment both of what men often already were and what they could become, embracing "all of those qualities which we demand of the good citizen."[8]

No longer sharing these deeply grounded beliefs, which had come by the later twentieth century to be viewed pejoratively as both excessively "rationalistic" and "moralistic," Lord Diplock could only see the reasonable-man standard as an intellectual device to get around the restrictions of evidence law. He failed to notice that it also was a statement about human nature – about the shared susceptibilities of ordinary men to criminal behavior and their shared capacities, under the pressure of the law, to resist such a fall

---

5 A pioneering effort to understand the judicial outlook of the time is C. H. S. Fifoot, *Judge and Jurist in the Reign of Victoria* (London, 1959). See also the stimulating essay by Steven Hedley, "'Superior Knowledge or Revelation': An Approach to Modern Legal History," *Anglo-American Law Review* 18 (1989): 177–200. Surprisingly little work has been done along these lines, at least for the criminal law. On the judges and contract law, see the magisterial work by P. S. Atiyah, *The Rise and Fall of Freedom of Contract* (Oxford, 1979).

6 Jeremy Bentham's Economic Writings III, 434.

7 Fragment on Mackintosh, quoted in W. Thomas, *Philosophic Radicals*, 103–4.

8 A. Herbert, *Misleading Cases in the Common Law* (London, 1928), 9.

into criminality. (Women were hardly considered because they rarely stood accused of serious crimes.) Once this mental world is recaptured, however, the reasonable-man standard tells us something not only about the workings of the law but also about how nineteenth-century jurists understood criminality.

In part this standard emerged in the nineteenth century because such beliefs were becoming stronger at that time. The Evangelical revival and the explosive growth of a market economy each in their own way encouraged a belief in free will and in the beneficent effects of the "discipline of circumstances."[9] Yet, the standard also owed much to the emergence of a new need for an explicit standard of behavior in criminal proceedings. Until the early nineteenth century the existence of sufficient provocation to mitigate a killing had been treated as a matter of law, to be decided by the judge alone. Thereafter, as the power of judges retreated before the rise of defense counsel, calling more expert witnesses and enhancing the independence of juries against judges, it became established as a question of fact, for juries to determine.[10] But on what common and consistent basis would juries so determine? If jurors were going to decide whether sufficient provocation existed in a particular case, judges were impelled to provide them a standard by which to do so. In doing this, judges gave explicit expression to a standard that had already implicitly been guiding them.

The expectation of reasonable self-control for all men was first spelled out in the opening year of Victoria's reign. When in 1837 William Kirkham's grown son threw him to the floor, Kirkham fatally stabbed him. Asking the jury to decide whether "there was sufficient time for the passion excited by [being thrown on the floor] to cool before the fatal stabs were given," Mr. Justice Coleridge (later to be Lord Chief Justice) cautioned them, in words that were to be repeated often thereafter, that although the law "will not require more from an imperfect creature than he can perform . . . it considers man to be a rational being, and requires that he should exercise a reasonable control over his passions."[11] Kirkham was convicted of manslaughter only, but the judge gave him the maximum sentence of transportation for life.

---

9 See Boyd Hilton, *The Age of Atonement: The Influence of Evangelicalism on Social and Economic Thought, 1795–1865* (Oxford, 1988); Martin J. Wiener, *Reconstructing the Criminal: Culture, Law, and Policy in England 1830–1914* (Cambridge, 1990).
10 See Brown, "'Ordinary Man' in Provocation"; see Martin J. Wiener, "Judges v. Jurors: Courtroom Tensions in Murder Trials and the Law of Criminal Responsibility in Nineteenth-Century England," *Law and History Review* 17, no. 3 (fall 1999).
11 173 English Reports [hereafter ER] 422.

In 1869 another stabbing between two men led to an unusually direct courtroom confrontation on the law. The defense counsel had urged that the law "ought to be administered with humanity, and with a reasonable allowance for the defects of mankind and for the vast difference between the temper and passions of various men," and described his client, Joseph Welsh, as "a man of hasty temper." Stung perhaps by the defense counsel's description of previous judicial rulings on provocation as "arbitrary," Mr. Justice Keating was moved to speak more abstractly than usual: "The law is that there must exist such an amount of provocation as would be excited by the circumstances in the mind of a reasonable man, and so as to lead the jury to ascribe the act to the influence of that passion" – such as, he explained, "a severe blow – something which might naturally cause an ordinary and reasonable-minded man to lose his self-control and commit such an act."[12] This case was widely cited, and henceforth the "reasonable man" was almost as much a fixture of criminal as of civil trials.

Two aspects of the reasonable-man standard are important for the history of criminology. First, it incorporated a long-existing universalistic conception of human nature. "Ordinary" and "reasonable" were typically used together; "ordinary" men could be generalized about, and an "ordinary" man could be visualized. These ordinary men were both susceptible to falling into criminal behavior and capable of resisting such a fall. Criminal acts could be perpetrated by anyone but also were things that anyone could resist. Criminality was not a settled characteristic of certain persons; the potential for it existed in all. As Arthur Griffiths, the chief inspector of British prisons, observed at the end of the century, "every son of Adam may, under certain conditions, be drawn into it."[13] As Griffiths's language suggests, such a conviction carried into a more secular era a core belief of the religious frame of mind that had long dominated thinking about criminality.[14]

A universalist principle – that human nature was all too prone to fall into criminality but that at the same time all had the capability to resist such a

---

12 *R v Welsh* (1869): *The Times*, Oct. 29, 1869; 11 Cox's Criminal Cases [hereafter Cox CC] 336. At the same time Keating immediately qualified his observation that he "was unable to discover such evidences of provocation in this case" by noting "but of course that would be a question which the jury alone would have to decide." Coss, "God Is a Righteous Judge," and Laurie J. Taylor, "Provoked Reason in Men and Women: Heat-of-Passion Manslaughter and Imperfect Self-Defense," *UCLA Law Review* 33 (1987): 1679–735: Both misleadingly see this case as a turning point in the development of the law of provocation, their exclusive focus on leading cases causing them to miss the gradual judicial adoption of this standard over the previous generation.

13 See note 1 to this chapter.

14 See Cynthia B. Herrup, *The Common Peace: Participation and the Criminal Law in Seventeenth-Century England* (Cambridge, 1987); Daniel A. Cohen, *Pillars of Salt, Monuments of Grace: New England Crime Literature and the Origins of American Popular Culture, 1674–1860* (New York, 1993).

fall – had long underlain the common scaffold injunctions by condemned men to spectators to heed their evil example. For centuries condemned felons had been expected to warn spectators to be mindful of their bad example, and when they failed to oblige, their chroniclers would step in to provide such warning. At his hanging, John Muckett, who in 1811 had kicked his wife to death after she had served him a cold dinner, earnestly exhorted those watching to "bear in mind the dreadful example they had before them of the consequence of suffering a sudden impulse of anger to get the better of their understanding." Three years later William Henry Hollings, who had shot a woman to death, in acknowledging his guilt after conviction, similarly "hoped his fate would furnish a warning to all who heard the case against the indulgence of violent passions. He had loved – he had fervently loved the unhappy girl whose life he had taken away ... he was now prepared to die, in the firm assurance of the forgiveness of the Almighty."[15]

Early nineteenth-century judges sometimes gave fervent expression to this belief, echoing church sermons – one devout Scottish judge declared that an 1830 rape-murder trial he had just presided over showed "the dreadful lengths in wickedness to which the human heart will go when left to itself."[16] The religious overtones later faded, but judges continued to see the law's role as, in the long view, essentially one of moral education. As Baron Bramwell remarked during an 1872 murder trial, "so long as people were subject to violent passions and gave way to them – and he supposed that would be so to the end of the world – the law must repress them by exemplary punishment."[17] This notion of a common human nature, and consequently of criminal justice as a form of disciplinary education, was the fundamental principle that the founding fathers of "scientific criminology" rejected. They placed human variation rather than human similarity at the center of their thinking and, consequently, individualization rather than uniformity at the top of their agenda.

This traditional notion of a common human nature ever-susceptible to sin did not encourage the exploration of specific, personal motives for crime. As Baron Rolfe reminded an 1848 jury, only God could "dive into the

---

15 *The Times*, Sept. 17, 1814.
16 Lord Moncrieff, quoted in *The Times*, July 16, 1830 [reprinted from the *Edinburgh Advertiser*]. As Baron Alderson told the convicted murderer Joseph Connor in 1845, his fate demonstrated "that he who offends against one law of God is guilty of the whole. What was begun in what is called venial sin ended, in your case, in the commission of that crime for which you will suffer. Who in society that offends against God's laws can tell the point where to stop?" [*The Times*, Apr. 10, 1845].
17 *R v Elliot* (1872): *The Times*, Nov. 1, 1872.

human heart";[18] their task was more external. Such judicial observations continued through the century, even as they shed explicit religious forms. Mr. Justice Grantham, summing up in 1887, said "he was afraid it would be a most fruitless task to inquire into the motive for crime because of the impossibility there was of ascertaining what really operated on the minds of human beings. . . . People did have motives which were not patent to the outer world."[19] In this way judges discouraged exploration of the "criminal mind."

Yet – and here is the second aspect of interest to historians of criminology – the reasonable-man standard possessed a Janus face. It simultaneously looked forward and backward. As the standard took hold it did more than simply restate in secularized form older universalistic religious ideas. It also opened doors for "scientific" criminology by shifting attention away from the social situation in which the criminal act occurred to the inner workings of the accused's mind – not (as we have seen) to conscious motives but to the less conscious overall balance of psychic "forces." Before the nineteenth century the nature of the surrounding social context determined the existence and degree of provocation. In this earlier period provocation was conceived, in Jeremy Horder's apt term, as "outrage."[20] Certain actions – not only physical assaults but also grave public insults or sexual violation of one's womenfolk – necessarily "provoked" all men and indeed served as virtual justifications of their violent responses. In a sense such responses were not unreasonable, in that they were expected and almost approved reactions to disgraceful behavior on the part of others. During the later eighteenth century this notion of provocation slowly gave way to another, centered on the psychology of the defendant. Three intertwined social developments stimulated this change in outlook: a diminishing tolerance of interpersonal violence, a waning of the culture of honor, and a waxing of "romantic" interest in the passions and their power.

The late eighteenth and early nineteenth centuries saw increasing criminal prosecution and intensifying punishment of interpersonal violence.[21] As the scope of legitimate violence became narrower, limited essentially to outright self-defense, resorting to violence came to be seen as a weakness – excusable, perhaps, by the frailties of human nature but never justifiable. In the same years the notion of "honor" came under ever more severe censure

18 *R v Stokes* (1848) [quoted in Roger Smith, *Trial by Medicine: Insanity and Responsibility in Victorian Trials* (Edinburgh, 1981), 122].
19 *R v Currell*: *The Times*, March 31, 1887.
20 Jeremy Horder, *Provocation and Responsibility* (Oxford, 1992).
21 See Peter King, "Punishing Assault: The Transformation of Attitudes in the English Courts (1748–1821)," *Journal of Interdisciplinary History* 27 (1996–7): 43–74.

as a relic of feudal barbarism and inimical to "civilization."[22] Its best-known expression, the duel, disappeared after early nineteenth-century courts began to try survivors for manslaughter and even murder. And, finally, even as violent behavior became less tolerated by the law, it became more "interesting" to the broader culture. The era of romanticism around the turn of the century saw much new fascination with extreme states of mind – a fascination not confined to literature. Increasingly employing terms like "storm," "flood," and "transport" to describe violent offenders' states of mind, judges began to acknowledge that strong passions produced a mental condition beyond the reach of reason.[23] Provocation came to be described less as an externally produced outrage than as an external trigger to an internal loss of control over one's passions. Such loss of control was an ever-present possibility for most men. As Baron Graham told the jury in an 1810 case of a French prisoner of war who killed a compatriot, also a war prisoner, "if what he did was the effect of a sudden transport of passion beyond the control of reason, he was guilty of manslaughter [only]."[24]

A generation later jurors were being given a formal standard for determining provocation: The psychic aspect, the loss of control, was now key. The central scene of the criminal drama had moved from the social relations between perpetrator and victim to the dynamics within the psyche of the perpetrator. Jurors were increasingly asked to be psychologists, to look for signs of rationality or their absence in assessing the fact of provocation. As Mr. Justice Tindal told a murder jury in 1833, "the exercise of contrivance and design denoted rather the presence of judgment and reason, than of violence and ungovernable passion."[25] Thus, if a man responded to a grave insult or a blow immediately, without thought, one might find sufficient provocation to reduce the charge. But if he responded by looking for a weapon, one could infer that he remained in control of himself, and the crime would be murder. The external provocation was the same in either case; the accused's mental state in reacting to it determined whether or not it was legal provocation. In a jury's psychological evaluations the "reasonable man" served as a yardstick: Would such a man have lost control in the given circumstances?

22 See Donna Andrew, "The Code of Honour and Its Critics: The Opposition to Duelling in England, 1700–1850," *Social History* 5 (1980): 409–34; G. J. Barker-Benfield, *The Culture of Sensibility, Sex, and Society in Eighteenth-Century Britain* (Chicago, 1992).
23 Horder, *Provocation and Responsibility*, 75.
24 *R v Ayes* (1810): 168 ER 741 (the jury found murder, but the twelve judges [to whom the case was sent by Graham] reduced the verdict to manslaughter). The defendant's being French, ironically, probably bolstered his counsel's argument that he had been overcome by passion.
25 *R v Hayward* (1833): 172 ER 1188.

This increasing interest in the offender's psyche was encouraged by the heightened concern with self-control evident in Victorian efforts at moral reform.[26] Like other social vices, crime was increasingly perceived as the expression of a deep character defect stemming from a refusal or an inability to deny wayward impulses or to make proper calculations of long-term self-interest. If seen as refusal such criminology was continuous with older religious notions. If seen as inability, a note that came to be sounded with increasing frequency, it pointed forward to a "scientific" form of criminology. The question increasingly was whether the line between "unwilling" and "unable" was clear.

In the 1837 case of William Fisher, both older and newer notions of provocation were on display. Told that a man had had sex with his fifteen-year-old son, Fisher stalked the offender for several days, then stabbed him to death.[27] When taken into custody, he appealed to the traditional notion of provocation as "outrage," seeing his action as justified by the situation: He declared that he'd only done what "any father and Englishman would have done under similar circumstances." However, his counsel sought mitigation on the newer ground of understandable loss of control, asking the jurors to "consult your own natures" and weigh what effect such extreme provocation would have on their own self-control. The jury (probably taking into account both arguments) found only manslaughter, and Fisher received a light sentence of one year's imprisonment.

Psychologizing criminal justice led away from a universal, objective standard of provocation. This movement was by two paths. One path led to a "subjective" standard of provocation, one that varied with each individual's nature. As the defense counsel in *Welsh* had urged in 1869, it was necessary to take into account "the vast difference between the temper and passions of various men." Justice depended on what could reasonably be expected of the particular individual in the dock. This argument, rejected in that case, nonetheless kept being put forth. That even "ordinary" men differed in their capacities for self-control, both temporarily (while drunk, for instance) and permanently (if weak-minded, for example), was a point of "common sense," if not common law, frequently appealed to by defense counsels. However, judges almost always opposed such arguments, maintaining an "objective" standard and tending to push for murder convictions in most cases where diminished capacity was argued, while allowing and even encouraging juries to bring in recommendations for mercy. In the judicial

---

26 See Wiener, *Reconstructing the Criminal*.
27 *R v Fisher*. 173 ER 452; also Public Record Office, Home Office [hereafter HO] 26/43.

view neither low intelligence nor intoxication exempted a man from the general legal standard of behavior. Thus, despite defense arguments and petitions after the trial alleging his imbecility, William Williams was hanged in 1861 for murdering his aunt. Home Secretary George Cornwall Lewis privately noted in rejecting the appeals that he was not convinced "of any natural incapacity, but only of entire want of instruction, which I daresay may be taken to be true."[28] As for the intoxication defense, James Fitzjames Stephen stated the usual judicial position when he told the jury in an 1886 wife-murder trial that "if a drunken man, because he was drunk, formed a drunken intent to do grievous bodily harm to another person, and in so doing caused death, he was just as responsible for his actions as if he had not been drunk."[29] This is not to say that judges were always successful in controlling jurors, and not infrequently juries refused to find murder, sometimes obviously swayed by subjectivist arguments. But at least as a matter of law, subjectivism was held at bay in the English courts until after World War II, when it began to make rapid strides toward its present influential position in both English and American law.

A second path away from a single standard of responsibility for all criminal defendants had a more immediate effect – that of an expanding role for the insanity defense. Already in the late nineteenth century the advance of naturalistic ways of thinking about human behavior (especially after Charles Darwin's *Origin of Species* [1859]) made reflective persons less confident about fixing clear responsibility for outrageous acts. One prison chaplain – traditionally a custodian of strong moral discourse – even observed in 1868 before the National Association for the Promotion of Social Science that "the degree of moral responsibility of persons acting under strong natural propensities is very difficult to determine . . . a man may possess a disposition and a temperament which may lead him to commit certain crimes with a certainty which is perhaps only partially recognized."[30] Such attitudes had comparatively little effect (at least for many years) in replacing an objective with a more subjective standard of provocation, for both the legal and medical establishments had much to lose from such subjectivity. These attitudes did, however, foster an expansion of the notion of insanity and paved the way for increasing attention to medical evidence about a defendant's mental state in homicide trials.

---

28 HO 12/130/44840; also see *The Times*, March 27, 1861.
29 *R v Hewett* (1886): *The Times*, May 25, 1886; HO 144/286/B318.
30 Rev. Henry Lettsom Elliot, "What are the principal causes of crime, considered from a social point of view?" NAPSS, Transactions 1868, 335–6.

Ironically, the Victorian judiciary's success in resisting the first path away
from a universalist conception of "the criminal" (that of a "subjective"
interpretation of the reasonable-man standard) encouraged the second path
(that of an increased use of insanity pleas). If "ordinary" men were expected,
regardless of their individual temperaments and situations, to emulate "the
man in the Clapham omnibus" and more tightly rein in their passions,
then the most likely path to avoid a guilty verdict (as defense counsels
came to recognize) became that of showing the prisoner to be *not* ordinary.
If he were a man constitutionally incapable of being reasonable and self-
controlling under stress, then the legal standards of responsibility would not
apply to him. Rather than his *situation*, the defendant's *constitution* became
the key to mitigation of his sentence, but at a heavy price: Rather than
reducing his penal sentence, such a determination would save his life at the
cost of sending him to Broadmoor (an insane asylum), where he was likely
to spend the remainder of his days. In this way, by a more circuitous and
obscure route than on the Continent or in the United States, "scientific
criminology" began to influence English criminal justice.

Whereas early nineteenth-century judges had generally seen little need
for it, medical testimony about the accused's abnormal state of mind became
steadily more common in nineteenth-century trials. Joel Eigen has noted
that "medical participation in [trials in which some form of insanity claim
was made] grew from approximately one trial in ten through the late 1700s
to one in two by the 1840s."[31] By the middle years of the century medical
participation when such claims were made had become almost de rigeur.[32]
Early nineteenth-century judges were rarely impressed by psychiatric arguments. Mr. Justice Best, in the 1823 murder trial of a farmer, John Newton,
listened to the evidence of a surgeon who had worked in asylums and also
to a parade of lay witnesses attesting that they had always considered the
defendant insane. But Best then told the jury that "it was not enough to
excuse the prisoner that he was a wayward or a passionate man, nor even
would it be a defense to show that he had been subject to madness. Such
a fact, if proved, would lead the jury to watch with more anxious care the
evidence which applied to the state of mind in which he was at the time
of the act; but this must be the whole of its influence; for if even a lunatic

---

31 Joel Eigen, *Witnessing Insanity: Madness and Mad-Doctors in the English Court* (New Haven, Conn.,
   1995), 24.
32 See Thomas R. Forbes, *Surgeons at the Bailey: English Forensic Medicine to 1878* (New Haven, Conn.,
   1985), 21; Roger Smith, *Trial by Medicine*; Nigel Walker, *Crime and Insanity in England* (Edinburgh,
   1968–73); Roger Chadwick, *Bureaucratic Mercy: The Home Office and the Treatment of Capital Cases in
   Victorian Britain* (New York, 1992).

had lucid intervals, and in one of these he committed a crime, he would be liable to suffer the penalties of the law."[33] The jury promptly returned a guilty verdict. In 1843 Daniel McNaghten, believing himself the victim of political persecution, shot and killed Prime Minister Peel's private secretary. At his trial he was found insane and committed to an asylum. This notorious case had brought the insanity defense and medical-expert testimony into great prominence. Thereafter, judges did what they could to block the expansion of both, not only pondering the "McNaghten Rules" – that if a defendant knew the difference between right and wrong he would be presumed sane – but repeatedly warning juries of the danger this defense presented to social order and personal security. A year after McNaghten, Baron Alderson kept a jury locked up without food, drink, or heat for twenty-two hours until it rejected an insanity defense and convicted a wife killer of murder. He then urged the home secretary not to stay execution, arguing that "this plea of madness is palliative of unruly passions leading to murder, and is very dangerous."[34] As Baron Bramwell put it in the 1856 trial of the wife poisoner William Dove, "to a man of weak mind and strong animal propensities [as Dove had been portrayed by medical witnesses], the knowledge that the law would not punish him would be to take from him one of the first and most powerful reasons for not repeating his crime."[35]

During the latter half of the century, however, medical evidence came to carry increasing weight. Two official inquiries in the 1870s – a select committee on homicide law in 1874 and a royal commission on indictable offenses in 1879 – heard arguments from defense lawyers and from medical men for revising legal definitions of responsibility. Most strikingly, perhaps, the distinguished lawyer and jurist J. F. Stephen, who in earlier years had argued that the existing law was adequate, now suggested to both inquiries that the McNaghten "knowledge of right and wrong" test be replaced with the more expansive one of "disease of mind."[36] If so diseased, a defendant could not be expected to maintain the self-control of the "ordinary man." Blocked by the opposition of most judges, this suggestion nonetheless gradually advanced in public consciousness and, after 1880, within the Home Office as well.

33 *The Times*, March 24, 1823.
34 *R v Crouch* (1844): *The Times*, May 9, 10, 1844; HO 18/129/16.
35 Quoted in Smith, *Trial by Medicine*, 136. The jury found Dove guilty of murder but recommended him for mercy on the ground of defective intellect. However, the home secretary, on Bramwell's advice, refused to act on their recommendation, and Dove hanged.
36 Special Report from the Select Committee on the Homicide Law Amendment Bill, Parliamentary Papers 1874, IX, Report of the Royal Commission Appointed to Consider the Law Relating to Indictable Offences, Parliamentary Papers 1878–9, XX, 17–18, 67–8.

The attention given it by two official inquiries in the space of a few years suggests that the concept of insanity was becoming more ambiguous and contested. As one might therefore expect, there is evidence that tensions between judges and juries over the insanity defense increased during these same years. After finding Charles O'Donnell guilty of murder in 1876, and making no mercy recommendation, all twelve jurymen nonetheless later submitted a petition to that effect to the home secretary. They explained that when they were about to find insanity, Mr. Justice Hawkins directed them that despite O'Donnell's commitment to an asylum for a fortnight a year earlier, they must presume his responsibility at the time of the killing unless there was specific evidence to refute that. The jurors found such presumption of reasonableness hard to swallow. "Had we been directed," they observed, "that we were at liberty to act upon a probable presumption of insanity to be founded upon the antecedent, contemporaneous and subsequent acts of the prisoner we should at once have acquitted him."[37] O'Donnell nonetheless hanged.

O'Donnell's fate underlines the fact that up until 1880 home secretaries generally seconded the restrictive interpretations of insanity laid down by nearly all judges.[38] But with the accession in that year of the more radical Liberal government and the appointment of Sir William Vernon Harcourt as home secretary, the government proved more receptive to pleas of mental unsoundness, even in cases of very unpopular defendants. When a sixty-five-year-old man, convinced of his wife's infidelity, stabbed her to death in 1881, his neighbors attempted to lynch him. At trial his counsel (unusually well organized for a poor man's) steered clear of traditional character issues (of the defendant and of the victim) and brought in several psychiatrists to testify to the man's proneness to delusion. Despite the resistance of Mr. Justice Cave, Harcourt insisted on an "official" medical examination, which resulted in the judgment that the convict's "nervous system is much impaired" and his committal to Broadmoor Criminal Lunatic Asylum.[39] In such cases sentencing power was in practice beginning to slip from the hands of judges into those of medical men.

An 1882 case of a black seaman, William Brown, illustrates how insanity could come to replace the now less acceptable plea of understandable provocation. Brown, a veteran of twenty years in the Royal Navy, was well respected in the Kent fishing port of Sheerness as a steady workman and a

---

37 HO 45/9422/59678.
38 This included the Liberals H. A. Bruce and Robert Lowe in 1868–74, as well as the even stricter Conservative R. A. Cross in 1874–80.
39 *R v Payne* (1881): *The Times*, Feb. 14, 23, May 10, 1881; HO 144/–/A4796.

kindly mentor of younger men (though his "terrible temper when in drink" was well known). Married to a widely recognized "bad woman" who drank heavily, was unfaithful, and taunted him (despite his devotion to their four children) with racist epithets, he was saved from the gallows after killing her with both a hatchet and a razor by the testimony of sympathetic physicians that he suffered from epileptic fits. On being told of the epileptic episodes in Brown's past his counsel later recalled, "'Thank God,' I said, 'Thank God. . . . When I addressed the jury and drew attention to the character of the man, his love for his children," he felt the case turning in his favor. He reminded them that Brown had tried, almost successfully, to kill himself also. "'Can you doubt that man was mad?' There were heads in the jury box nodding assent." Brown was found insane and sent to Broadmoor.[40]

Findings of insanity or unfitness to plead in homicide trials rose from 99 in the 1860s to 115 in the 1870s, 154 in the 1880s, 160 in the 1890s, and 232 in the 1900s, even while the number of homicide trials fell. Post-trial certifications of insanity also rose, from four in the 1860s to eight in the 1870s and twenty-one in the 1880s, before falling back again to single digits in the face of judicial protests at such circumventing of the normal legal process.[41] By 1883 *The Times* was condemning both the overuse of the insanity plea and the Home Office's increasing susceptibility to such arguments after a murder conviction had been returned.[42] These tendencies did not cease when the Conservatives returned to power. In 1890 Mr. Justice Wills was upset enough to complain to Conservative Home Secretary Henry Matthews of "the extreme and growing frequency of the [insanity] defense in cases of murder" and the Home Office's growing sympathy to this defense. The evidence of an asylum superintendent who examined the prisoner at government expense had just won an insanity verdict for a wife-murderer he was trying, which was unwarranted in Wills's view: "the greater part of the things [the jury] relied upon might as it seemed to me be said of a very substantial part of mankind."[43] Nonetheless, Wills's outburst seems to have

40 *Recollections of Sir Henry Dickens* (London, 1934), 182. See also *The Times*, April 21, 1883.
41 Chadwick, *Bureaucratic Mercy*, 402 (table 6); V. A. C. Gatrell, "The Decline of Theft and Violence in Victorian and Edwardian England," in V. A. C. Gatrell, Bruce Lenman, and Geoffrey Parker, eds., *Crime and the Law: The Social History of Crime in Western Europe Since 1500* (London, 1980), 286–7; information in both from annual Judicial Statistics, England and Wales.
42 *The Times*, Oct. 19, 1883 (leader).
43 *R v Terry* (1890): HO 144/236/A51751; see also *The Times*, July 28, 1890. A similar situation took place the following year when John Miller, who had fatally fractured his wife's skull, was examined before trial by Home Office doctors. Miller's counsel happily made use of their findings that his family "had the hereditary taint of insanity and he himself was of a low mental organisation, weak to resist impulses to violence, and easily thrown off balance by drink." Mr. Justice Lawrance flatly told the jury that this was not enough to meet the insanity test; the jury responded by finding manslaughter. *The Times*, Dec. 11, 1891.

had no effect, and in the course of the 1890s the judges were chagrined to find themselves becoming isolated in their resistance to insanity claims. Indeed, in some ways the Home Office, once the judges' reliable backup, had begun to take the initiative in removing cases from prosecution by administratively finding prisoners unfit to plead or (as that practice was curtailed under judicial pressure) by arranging for jury trials confined to the question of fitness to plead.

As this new position became clear by the end of the century, judges began to retreat – not abandoning the McNaghten rules but frequently interpreting them more flexibly or failing to cite them at all.[44] Judges also gave up efforts to restrict expert testimony to "technical" matters, and it became accepted practice for counsel to ask such witnesses for their general opinion as to the legal responsibility of the defendant.[45] And, even more strikingly, some judges themselves began to use the language of mental disease.[46] Drunkenness, in itself not an acceptable defense, could now become one if reinterpreted as "alcoholic insanity."[47] In the wife-murder trial of John Devlin, a habitual drunkard, the medical officer of Brixton Prison was reluctant to find insanity but admitted under cross-examination that "*delirium tremens* is insanity." Devlin was found to be insane.[48]

When in 1902 William Barnaby stabbed his wife with a sharp Swedish knife, the traditional complaints about her character were made in court. ("Mrs. Barnaby," a policeman stated, "was known as an intemperate, violent woman, while her husband bore the character of a sober, respectable man.") However, the chief thrust of the defense was insanity, or more strictly, epilepsy combined with general low intelligence. The same prison medical officer, though agreeing that the prisoner was an epileptic and of weak mind, refused to agree that he was insane. However, under cross-examination

---

44 One new tactic was to prevent the jury from bringing in an insanity verdict by promising that the prisoner's mental state would be carefully examined after conviction. For example, in the trial of Charles Howell, who murdered his lover in 1903, Mr. Justice Wright conceded that "there might be a kind of insanity which would not excuse him, but which could be inquired into hereafter by those medical gentlemen whose duty it is to advise the Home Secretary" (*The Times*, June 20, 1903). The murder trial of Alfred Nelson, in the same year, saw a similar promise made by Mr. Justice Wright. *The Times*, June 15, 1903.

45 See Tony Ward, "Law, Common Sense, and the Authority of Science: Expert Witnesses and Criminal Insanity in England, c. 1840–1940," *Social and Legal Studies* (1997): 347.

46 In 1899 Wills himself found the fact that a defendant's father and grandfather had both spent periods in asylums convincing evidence of legal irresponsibility. *R v Newland: The Times*, Nov. 24, 1899.

47 See, e.g., *R v Flower 1899* (*The Times*, Dec. 7, 1899), *R v Watts 1900* (*The Times*, Nov. 17, 1900), and *R v Botton 1901* (*The Times*, Sept. 14, 1901).

48 *The Times*, June 26, 1906.

the doctor accepted that "in some cases epileptics were subject to violent impulses, under which they did violent things without malevolence, although a fit was not upon them." Barnaby was not found insane but was convicted of manslaughter only, with the judge concurring, and he received a comparatively short sentence of five years.[49]

In the 1903 case of Samuel Redfern, Mr. Justice Channell told the jury after citing McNaghten, "he himself was accustomed to – and should continue in so doing until a higher authority decided against him – extend the law as there laid down slightly in favor of the prisoner by adding that if from disease of the mind a person is unable to consider what is the difference between right and wrong, then it may very fairly be said that he does not know what is wrong."[50] Such "extension" was formalized in 1915, when in *R v Fryer*, Mr. Justice Bray explicitly abandoned the McNaghten rules in favor of the test of "mental disease."[51]

Thus, by the first years of the twentieth century there was established a broadening recognition of mental unsoundness in the courtroom. Yet it changed less than one might have expected. This recognition constituted much less of a challenge, both practically and theoretically, to the newly developed strict standard of "the ordinary and reasonable man" than did "subjective" interpretations of that standard. Not only did it ensure that defendants in whom insanity was recognized did not, as a rule, return to society, it did not offer a competing vision of "normal" behavior to that of the Victorian judiciary and Home Office. Rather, the shift to mental unsoundness as a defense left that picture and that standard untouched for the great majority of persons and the great bulk of behavior, and simply established that a small number of persons were incapable of attaining it – because they lay, as it were, outside "normal" humanity. Particularly when such persons could be, as was increasingly the case, removed from the criminal justice system before trial by a finding of "unfitness to plead," insanity pleas could be readily reconciled with Victorian expectations of personal self-discipline (the "stiff upper lip" that became the internationally recognized English ideal) for the vast majority of ordinary men and the objective standard of ordinariness and reasonableness by which these expectations were translated into legal thinking. We might say that strict expectations of

---

49 *The Times*, Oct. 23, 1902.   50 *The Times*, Dec. 5, 1903.
51 24 Cox CC 403. Whereas the McNaghten rules were not formally dispensed with until 1957, in the twentieth century they were ever less "hegemonic" in determining the disposition of offenders. See Ward, "Law, Common Sense, and the Authority of Science."

self-discipline for "ordinary men" were made socially and legally tolerable in an ever more "naturalistic" age by progressively easier recourse to defining grave offenders as incapable of reasonable behavior.[52]

Victorian judges, in insisting on universal, objective standards of behavior in homicide trials, thus unintentionally opened a door for the increasing courtroom employment of the language of mental disease and in this way worked together with their "enemy," the emerging discipline of "scientific" criminology. At the same time, and by that same insistence on objective standards, they succeeded in sharply limiting the influence of this new discipline on the practical workings of criminal justice. "Classical" and "scientific" criminology flourished together in a perhaps typically English solution.

---

52 Some tension did continue, and perhaps increased again, as judges often sought to maintain the reasonable-man standard in the face of waning public fear of violent crime and the consequent jury tendency to make allowances for provocation and drunkenness.

3

Unmasking Counterhistory

An Introductory Exploration of Criminality and the Jewish Question

MICHAEL BERKOWITZ

Although the death knell of "the Jewish gangster" and "Jewish crime" has sounded repeatedly, in the beginning of the twenty-first century "Jewish crooks," or more loosely, Jews involved with the underworld or suspected of criminal activity in "legitimate" business, have not vanished. Popular and elite culture has no shortage of Jewish cops and robbers, and occasionally, killers.[1] In academic and media circles, Marlow's "Jew of Malta," Shakespeare's Shylock, and Dickens's Fagin continue to arouse debate.[2] Jewish crooks also inhabit American classics by F. Scott Fitzgerald, Edith Wharton, and Ernest Hemingway; these characters raise few hackles but offer bones of contention to academics. *The Sopranos*, a critically acclaimed television series that premiered in 1999, includes both old and new style Jewish crooks, cooperating and competing with the suburban New Jersey Mafiosi. John Updike's fictional creation, the "moderately famous" Jewish writer Henry Beck, in the twilight of his life, has turned to murdering his critics. Through the exposes of Robert Friedman, and the fiction of humorist Laurence Shames and thriller-writer Reggie Nadelson, the Russian-Jewish mafia has become a fixture of crime reporting and the ever-popular mystery genre. Interestingly, Jews also take the lead, in fact as well as fiction, in subduing the newest Jewish thugs.[3] The musical *Guys and*

---

1 See Albert Fried, *The Rise and Fall of the Jewish Gangster in America* (New York, 1980); Rachel Rubin, *Jewish Gangsters of Modern Literature* (Urbana, Ill., 2000).
2 See James Shapiro, *Shakespeare and the Jews* (New York, 1997). Some critics have incorrectly identified the London fence, Ikey Solomons, with Dickens's Fagin; see J. J. Tobias, *Prince of Fences: The Life and Crimes of Ikey Solomons* (London, 1974). I am indebted to the anonymous reader who supplied this reference.
3 See Laurence Shames, *Mangrove Squeeze* (London, 1999); Robert I. Friedman, *Red Mafiya: How the Russian Mob Has Invaded America* (Boston, 2000).

This chapter is dedicated to the memory of George L. Mosse. I also wish to acknowledge the constructive criticism and bibliographic advice provided by Ralph Austen, Peter Becker, Gabriel Finder, René Levy, Herbert Reinke, and Richard F. Wetzell.

Dolls, recently revived on Broadway and the West End, features the character Nathan Detroit, modeled on Damon Runyon's stories about mobster and super-gambler Arnold Rothstein.[4]

From early modern times to the present, Jews in the West have been aware of their identification with a propensity for criminality. Sigmund Freud wrote that "we hate the criminal and deal severely with him because we view in his deed, as in a distorting mirror, our own criminal instincts."[5] This assertion by the father of the psychoanalytic movement is not simply buried in his voluminous writings. It has been appropriated in the liturgy of progressive Jewry in the last decades of the twentieth century as one of the "Meditations before the Yom Kippur Additional Service." Certainly the inclusion of this quote relates to the celebrity of its author and the central motif of the Day of Atonement. But it may be seen as a historical as well as psychological marker. Although Freud sought universal, scientific truths about human nature, he was also bound to his time and, however tenuously, to his ethnic-national community, the Jews.[6] Just as the jokes in his mental universe were typically "Jewish jokes," most likely the criminals looming large in his weltanschauung were *ganovim*, Jewish crooks.[7]

This chapter examines the question: What has the association of criminality with Jewishness meant to Jews themselves? In addressing this problem, as the initial stage of a larger study including Central Europe, Britain, and the United States, I wish to shed light on little-acknowledged areas of confluence between criminology and anti-Semitism. My remarks here focus primarily on Central Europe and Britain; hence, the contributions of Peter Becker and Martin Wiener, which highlight changes that made the criminological appropriation of anti-Semitic discourse more likely, complement this chapter particularly well. Becker distinguishes between early and later nineteenth-century relationships between religion, ethnography, and criminality, showing the more "modern" variant to be especially susceptible to imbibing racial anti-Semitism.[8] Wiener demonstrates that one of the paths of late Victorian criminology in Britain tended to seize on the imagined

---

4 Leo Kather, *The Big Bankroll: The Life and Times of Arnold Rothstein* (New York, 1994); Eliot Asinof, *Eight Men Out: The Black Sox and the 1919 World Series* (New York, 1977).

5 Sigmund Freud, quoted in *Forms of Prayer for Jewish Worship, III: Prayers for the High Holidays, eighth edition*, ed. Assembly of Rabbis of the Reform Synagogues of Great Britain (London, 1985), 450.

6 See Yosef Haim Yerushalmi, *Freud's Moses: Judaism Terminable and Interminable* (New Haven, Conn., 1991); Dennis B. Klein, *Jewish Origins of the Psychoanalytic Movement* (Chicago, 1985).

7 Sigmund Freud, *The Standard Edition of the Complete Psychological Works of Sigmund Freud*, trans. and ed. James Strachey, in collaboration with Anna Freud, vol. 8: *Jokes and their Relation to the Unconscious* (London, 1960).

8 See Peter Becker's chapter in this book.

"inner workings of the accused's mind," as opposed to social understandings of criminal behavior[9] – which may have overly sensitized the instruments of justice to recognize Jews as perpetrators of crime.

In addition to using criminology to unpack anti-Semitism, I wish to initiate a discussion about the Jewish self-understanding of so-called Jewish criminality, to determine its impact on Jewish self-consciousness. The possibility that there may be an ongoing Jewish discourse on criminality has hardly ever been entertained by scholars. But myths about Jewish criminality were not only a factor in the development of anti-Semitism and in determining the shape of Jewish/gentile relations;[10] realities and fantasies about Jewish robbers were also incorporated into the ways Jews conceived of themselves because they were one of many constituent elements of modern Jewish identity. Nevertheless, of all of the fragments that combined to produce Jewish mentalities, those stemming from the Jewish/criminal nexus are, quite understandably, among the least explicated.

There are a few sophisticated treatments of Jews and crime integrated into broader analyses that do not focus on the evolution of anti-Semitism, such as Florike Egmond's *Underworlds: Organized Crime in the Netherlands* and Mordechai Breuer's selection in *German-Jewish History in Modern Times*.[11] American-Jewish commentators have been most unabashed in including criminals in probing their ethnic experience, notably in the classic by Daniel Bell, *The End of Ideology*, and Irving Howe's *World of Our Fathers*.[12] But the historiography on Jewish criminals tends to look at the "underworld" as a society unto itself and at its dealings with fellow Jews, rather than reflecting on its influence on the Jewish world at large. Where the phenomenon is more broadly considered, it tends to be limited to a specific national-cultural context, rather than being seen comparatively.[13] I propose, then, to take a

9 See Martin J. Wiener's chapter in this book.
10 Otto Ulbricht, "Criminality and Punishment of the Jews in the Early Modern Period," in R. Po-chia Hsia and Hartmut Lehmann, eds., *In and Out of the Ghetto: Jewish-Gentile Relations in Late Medieval and Early Modern Germany* (New York, 1995), 49–71. For the larger context, see Richard J. Evans, *Tales from the German Underworld: Crime and Punishment in the 19th Century* (New Haven, Conn., 1998), and Eric J. Hobsbawm, *Bandits* (London, 1969).
11 Florike Egmond, *Underworlds: Organized Crime in the Netherlands 1650–1800* (London, 1993), 106–51; Mordechai Breuer, "Social Problems Within and at the Periphery of the Communities," in Mordechai Breuer and Michael Graetz, *German-Jewish History in Modern Times*, vol. 1: *Tradition and Enlightenment, 1600–1780*, ed. Michael Meyer, trans. William Templer (New York, 1996), 244–51.
12 Daniel Bell, *The End of Ideology: On the Exhaustion of Political Ideas in the Fifties* (New York, 1965; Cambridge, Mass., 1988), 127–50; Irving Howe, *World of Our Fathers: The Journey of the East European Jews to America and the Life They Found and Made* (New York, 1976), 98–101, 263–4.
13 Two important exceptions are studies of Jewish "white slavery": Marion Kaplan, *The Campaigns of the Jüdischer Frauenbund* (Westport, Conn., 1979) and Edward Bristow, *Prostitution and Prejudice: The Jewish Fight Against White Slavery, 1870–1939* (New York, 1983); see also Todd Endelman, *The Jews*

longer-term and international approach, relative to the existing studies on Jews and criminality.

In the post-Holocaust age, discussion of apparently problematic social roles that Jews have played has been tacitly censored in Jewish historiography. This is a continuation of an earlier "apologetic" tradition of Jewish history that served as a spur to Gershom Scholem, whose pioneering work on Jewish "counterhistory" makes the current project possible.[14] In *From Berlin to Jerusalem* Scholem wrote: "At an early age I developed an aversion to apologetic activities on the part of Jews. The Zionists' attitude in this regard made sense to me, and I am sure it indirectly influenced my later work, which was devoted to the objective investigation and analysis of phenomena which were unaccounted for and conflicted with the apologetic Jewish historiography of the day. At that time, to be sure, I had no way of knowing this."[15] Although Scholem's mania for "objective investigation" found its greatest fulfillment in his studies of Jewish mysticism, particularly the seventeenth-century mystical "false messiah" Sabbatai Sevi, he was also intrigued by another strain in Jewish existence that ran counter to the apologetic trend: the "Jewish underworld" of the "robber bands" in seventeenth-, eighteenth-, and early nineteenth-century Europe, and "das jüdische Element im Gängstertum" (the Jewish element in the world of gangsters), including New York's "Murder, Inc.," into the twentieth century.[16] Are these two areas – kaballah and criminality – totally disparate phenomena that happened to fascinate Scholem? Probably not. Among his central theories, Scholem saw in the latter stages of Sabbateanism and in Frankist libertinism (one of the bizarre offshoots of Sabbateanism) how the criticism born of casting off Sabbatai, as well as the taste of personal freedom experienced in these movements, may have helped pave the way for the Haskalah, the Jewish Enlightenment. The "tragedy" of the false messianism of Sabbatai Sevi, Scholem wrote, also "contained the seeds of a new

of Georgian England, 1714–1830: Tradition and Change in a Liberal Society (Philadelphia, 1979); Bill Williams, *The Making of Manchester Jewry* (Manchester, 1979); Jenna Weisman Joselit, *Our Gang: Jewish Crime and the New York Jewish Community* (Bloomington, Ind., 1983); Lloyd Gartner, "Anglo-Jewry and the Jewish International Traffic in Prostitution, 1885–1914," *Association for Jewish Studies Review* 78 (1982–3): 129–78. The literature on Central Europe is most developed: see Helmut Reinicke, *Gaunerwirtschaft: Die erstaunlichen Abenteuer hebräischer Spitzbuben in Deutschland* (Berlin, 1983).

14 The growing body of literature based on the revision of Gershom Scholem does not diminish his relevance; see Moshe Idel, *Kabbalah: New Perspectives* (New Haven, Conn., 1988); Joseph Dan and Peter Schafer, eds., *Gershom Scholem's Major Trends in Jewish Mysticism 50 Years After: Proceedings of the Sixth International Conference on the History of Jewish Mysticism* (Tübingen, 1993); Ada Rapoport-Albert, ed., *Hasidism Reappraised* (London, 1997).

15 Scholem, *From Berlin to Jerusalem* (New York, 1988), 46.

16 "... *und alles ist Kabbala*": *Gershom Scholem im Gespräch mit Jörg Drews* (Munich, 1980), 8–14.

Jewish consciousness."[17] Perhaps he saw an echo of this, however faint or distorted, in the robber bands – as their freedom, and their equality with gentiles in the underworld, provided some of them with concrete aspirations for the general Jewish/gentile milieu. Other Jews as well heard and read stories about these mixed bands that circulated throughout the Jewish and non-Jewish world. My own teacher, George Mosse, born in Berlin in 1918, shared Scholem's interest in Jewish criminals and routinely began his course in Jewish history with a lecture he called "Jews and Bandits." His main point was that the first instances of democratized acculturation in the West were in integrated groups of thieves, that is, gangs that included both Jews and non-Jews, and did not seem to differentiate or discriminate. Imagine my bemusement when in 1985 I noticed a small item in the *Jerusalem Post* about the apprehension of a gang of Jewish and Arab burglars in Israel that seemed to the police to be "democratic."

Despite these important soundings by Scholem and Mosse, Jewish criminality remains a relatively underworked area, from a historical perspective, partly because the Holocaust has led some to assume that any study of it must necessarily be accessory to an anti-Semitic agenda. Merely to raise the connection of Jews and crime, in a historical manner, may be seen as an invitation to or provocation of anti-Semitism. Surely there always is the danger of having information or arguments taken out of context. Still, I will proceed from the premise that there is much to be gained by engaging this problem from a number of disciplinary perspectives and for the sake of further incorporating Jewry into the common endeavor of humanistic study.

For those whose weltanschauung includes a historical approach to crime, beginning in the nineteenth century or earlier, it may come as little surprise that the subject of Jewish criminals is often taken up in Western popular and academic culture, and within Jewish culture in particular. Up until 1900 Jews were perceived as principal instigators of crimes such as arson, burglary, illegal gambling, fencing of stolen goods, and prostitution. Otto Ulbricht writes that "After 1830, Jewish banditry began to disappear, and after the middle of the century nothing more was heard of it. When full legal emancipation was finally reached in Imperial Germany in 1871, the Jewish crime rate was considerably lower than the Christian one."[18] Unfortunately, the institutionalization of modern criminal statistics in the 1840s coincided with the last decade of significant Jewish criminal activity. But crime was

---

17 Gershom Scholem, *Sabbatai Sevi: The Mystical Messiah*, trans. R. J. Zwi Werblowsky (Princeton, N.J., 1973), 693.
18 Ulbricht, "Criminality and Punishment," 70.

still seen as a problem among the immigrant masses of Jews in the New World, and even in Central Europe – where it almost totally vanished – Jewish criminals would continue to command a disproportionate share of attention. Beginning in the 1870s – and continuing through the 1980s – Jews would be identified with the perpetration of white-collar crimes involving speculative ventures, fraud, and sedition.

Before World War II, and most tragically during the Nazi years, Jews were tainted with the bogus allegation that they had a greater affinity for criminality than non-Jews. The number of Jews involved in crime historically has been minuscule. But given the stigmatization and marginalization of Jews, the perception of Jewish criminality often has been exaggerated in criminological discourses of non-Jewish, majority cultures. Not surprisingly, Jews have responded to the accusation that they bear a special burden for the scourge of crime; typically, their impulse has been to demonstrate the overwhelming truth – that Jews are supremely law-abiding. But because criminality itself is a complicated phenomenon, Jewish attitudes toward criminality are not simple. At times Jews have been fascinated, and even enthralled, by the real and mythical exploits of Jewish crooks – which is not synonymous with an internalization of the anti-Semitic discourse on Jews and crime.[19] Jews' romanticization of "tough Jews" who break the law and flaunt societal conventions is not just a post-Holocaust phenomenon;[20] certainly, an analysis of the extreme popularity of Schiller's *The Robbers* among Jews would reveal a deep resonance.[21] No doubt many Jews of the far left, such as Michael Gold,[22] were moved by Spiegelberg's boast that he was "restoring the fair distribution of wealth, in a word bringing back the golden age."[23] The point that needs to be underscored is that the Jewish view of "Jewish criminals," versus that of schools of criminological thought in the wider world, has, at critical junctures, been starkly at odds.

I wish to emphasize the divergence between what I call the "Jewish" view of Jews and crime as opposed to the non-Jewish criminological discourses in the second half of the nineteenth century, although some of these very theories were originated or propagated by Jews – especially Cesare Lombroso.[24] Through an investigation of how criminality was interlaced with the fate of

19 See Sander L. Gilman, *Jewish Self-Hatred: Anti-Semitism and the Hidden Language of the Jews* (Baltimore, 1986).
20 Rich Cohen, *Tough Jews: Fathers, Songs and Gangster Dreams* (London, 1998).
21 Karl Emile Franzos, in "Chane" and "Esterka Regina" in *The Jews of Barnow*, trans. M. W. MacDowall (Edinburgh, 1882), 103, 201.
22 Michael Gold, *Jews Without Money* (New York, 1935).
23 Friedrich Schiller, *The Robbers and Wallenstein*, trans. F. J. Lamport (London, 1979), 41.
24 On Lombroso's Jewishness, see Nancy Harrowitz, *Anti-Semitism, Misogyny, and the Logic of Cultural Difference: Cesare Lombroso and Matilde Serao* (Lincoln, Neb., 1994), 63–80.

modern Jewry I hope to initiate a more sophisticated appreciation of how criminality, and even allegations of criminality, might influence gender, class, racial, and ethnic-national identity formation.

My main hypothesis is that as criminological thought asserted or suggested ties between biological, anthropological, physiological, and physiognomic bases of criminal behavior that could readily be joined to anti-Semitism, the Jews themselves were markedly ambivalent, even playful, about the identification of Jews with criminality. Within the Jewish world, as early as the eighteenth century, the notion was articulated that crime and criminals existed as something contingent, situational, and transitional – relative to the established order. For Jewish scholars and polemicists, it was easy to demolish the automatic connection between "the Jewish nature" and crime in one fell swoop: Did not crime and profiteering exist with or without Jews? Did it really matter if Jews had been expelled from a given locale? Was there any evidence that these evils were actually eradicated by the removal of Jews? Did not the Jews' contributions to society far outweigh any damage wrought by Jewish crooks?[25] There are even moments when Jewish writers come close to arguing that crime and criminals are "socially constructed," at least a century before such a term would come into intellectual parlance. In a word, their views could not be more different from the view that criminality represents an innate trait. This common latter perspective, as expressed by L. Gordon Rylands in 1889, holds that:

The influence exerted by Heredity, at any rate, is sufficiently obvious in everyday life to attract the attention of observant men; and to such an extent it is tacitly assumed, that we may often hear people discussing the question in what respects a child takes after its father and in what other respects after its mother, and expressing great astonishment if, in any important point, whether physical or mental, the offspring appears to differ markedly from both its parents....[26] Every man inherits certain characteristics by which he is predisposed, more or less strongly, to good or bad actions.[27]

In a cruder form, a pamphlet by Arthur MacDonald proclaimed as its title: "Criminals, paupers, mattoids and other defectives are social bacilli, which require as thorough scientific investigation, as the bacilli of physical diseases."[28]

25 Gerson Wolf, *Die Juden in der Leopoldstadt im 17. Jahrhundert in Wien* (Vienna, 1864), 97–9.
26 L. Gordon Rylands, *Crime: Its Causes and Remedy* (London, 1889), 30.
27 Ibid., 76.
28 "The mattoid (or crank) is an abnormal, characterized by the want of balance; is eccentric and egotistical and may be sane or insane, or simply illusioned, or dangerous, or harmless," Arthur MacDonald, "Need of University Men to Study Men," in *Studies of Modern Civilized Man* (bound pamphlets by the author), 1911–19, located in the Bodleian Library, Oxford.

Concomitantly, such literature avers that there is a universe of morality in which there always is a clear distinction between good and bad, right and wrong, and being for or against the law. Jews, outside of explicitly religious writing, have tended to acknowledge shades of gray.[29] It also appears that there exists a tie between Jewish endeavors to overcome marginality and the identification of such strategies as criminal or deviant. Because definitions of criminality were often tied to perceptions of Jews as engaged or overly engaged in certain "business" activities, the relationship of images of Jewry to shifting boundaries of business ethics and notions of respectability is of particular interest.[30] In other words, commercial activity was more questionable or possibly criminal if Jews were involved. But if, over time, persons other than Jews assumed the same or similar practices, the activity became perceived as a normal, acceptable, and respectable mode of commerce or deportment. Within Jewish communities, notions of criminality seemed to be influenced by the individual's standing and role within his or her own institutional boundaries.[31]

It is clear that distinct currents of criminology were annexed to racist and anti-Semitic stereotypes, resulting in a fatal mix during the Holocaust. Some of these threads, as they were played out in German culture, have been taken up by George Mosse, Sander Gilman, and Henry Friedlander.[32] In contrast to many or most anti-Semitic allegations, which are rooted in anti-Semitic projections having no basis in Jewish life, there was a reality of Jewish prisoners, prostitutes, gangsters, robbers, and robber bands beginning in early modern Europe, that was part of the social landscape that cut across international boundaries – and was observed and commented on by Jews and non-Jews.

It is important to establish some sense of how Jewish crime and criminality was seen in the Jewish world. Of course lawbreaking was ardently condemned because it was antithetical to Jewish and secular law. Interestingly, in Jewish sources there is virtually no resonance of the common anti-Semitic refrain that the Talmud permits lying to gentiles, or taking advantage of them in business.[33] Nevertheless, even a brief perusal of selected

---

29 Bernard S. Jackson, ed., *Jewish Law in Legal History and the Modern World* (Leiden, 1980).
30 "Beilage inbegriffener Ordtnung fuer die Judenschaft zu Worms 28 Nov 1641," in Gerson Wolf, *Zur Geschichte der Juden in Worms* (Breslau, 1862), 78–94.
31 Breuer and Graetz, *German-Jewish History in Modern Times*, 244–51.
32 George L. Mosse, *The Crisis of German Ideology* (New York, 1964); Henry Friedlander, *The Origins of the Nazi Genocide: From Euthanasia to the Final Solution* (Chapel Hill, N.C., 1995); Gilman, *Jewish Self-Hatred*.
33 Among the most infamous tracts are August Rohling, *Talmud-Jude, mit einem Vorworte von Eduard Drumont aus der auch anderweitig vermehrten französischen Ausg. Von A. Pintigny in das deutsche zurückübertragen*

historical and literary sources shows a complicated attitude toward the law. Intellectual positions regarding Jews and crime were notably played out in debates concerning Jewish emancipation and the extension of Jewish rights. Christian Wilhelm von Dohm's "Über die bürgerliche Verbesserung der Juden" (Berlin, 1781) reveals that it was widely accepted that Jews were "guilty of a proportionally greater number of crimes than the Christians; that their character in general inclines more toward usury and fraud in commerce." Still, Dohm contends, "Everything the Jews are blamed for is caused by the political conditions under which they now live, and any other group of men, under such conditions, would be guilty of identical errors."[34] In his attempt to undermine Dohm's plea to enhance the standing of the Jews, Johann David Michaelis responded:

We can see, principally from reports of investigations of thieves, that the Jews are more harmful than at least we Germans are. Almost half of those belonging to gangs of thieves, at least those of whose existence is known to us, are Jews, while the Jews are scarcely 1/25th of the total population of Germany. If this 1/25th part supplies the same number of riff-raff as the whole German people, or even more, then one must conclude that at least in respect to thievery, which I consider to be the lowest of the vices, the Jews are twenty-five times as harmful or more than the other inhabitants of Germany.[35]

Moses Mendelssohn was prompted to address the issue, which he did by ascribing the deeds of Jewish criminals to their abominable social position, and by seeing the Jews' connection with stealing as a transitional rather than permanent aspect of their vocation.

Ritter Michaelis does not seem to know any other vices besides fraud and roguery. I think, however, that where the wickedness of a people is to be evaluated one should not entirely overlook murderers, robbers, traitors, arsonists, adulterers, whores, killers of infants, etc. But even if one were to judge a people's wickedness only by the quantity of thieves and receivers of stolen goods among them, this number should not be viewed in terms of that people's proportion of the entire population. The

von Carl Paasch, 8th ed. (Leipzig, 1890); Johann Jacob Schudt, *Jüdische Merkwürdigkeiten vorstellende was sich Curieuses und Denkwürdiges in den neuen Zeiten bey einigen Jahrhunderten mit denen in alle IV. Theile der Welt sonderlich durch Teutschland zertreuten Juden zugetragen. Sammt einer vollstandigen Franck-furter Juden-Chronik darinnen der zu Franckfurt am Mayn wohnenden Juden vor einigen Jahrhunderten bis auf unsere Zeiten merckwurdigste Begebenheiten enthalten. Benebst einigen zur Erlauterung beigefugten Kupffern und Figuren. Mit historischer Feder in drey Theilen beschrieben von Johann Jacob Schudt* (Frankfurt am Main, 1714–18).

34 Christian Wilhelm von Dohm, "Concerning the Amelioration of the Civil Status of the Jews (1781)," in *The Jew in the Modern World*, 2d ed., ed. Jehuda Reinhart and Paul Mendes-Flohr (New York, 1995), 31.

35 Johann David Michaelis, "Arguments Against Dohm (1782)," in Jehuda Reinharz and Paul Mendes-Flohr, eds., *The Jew in the Modern World*, 2d ed. (New York, 1995), 42.

comparison should rather be made between traders and peddlers among the Jews on the one hand, and among other peoples on the other. I am sure that such a comparison would yield very different proportions. The same statistics, I do not hesitate to maintain, will also show that there are twenty-five times as many thieves and receivers of stolen goods among German peddlers as among Jewish. This is aside from the fact that the Jew is forced to take up such a calling, while the others could have become field marshals or ministers. They freely choose their profession, be it a trader, peddler, seller of mouse traps, performer of shadow plays or vendor of curios.

It is true that quite a number of Jewish peddlers deal in stolen goods; but few of them are outright thieves, and those, mostly, are people without refuge or sanctuary anywhere on earth. As soon as they have made some fortune they acquire a patent of protection from their territorial prince and change their profession. This is public knowledge; when I was younger I personally met a number of men [Jews] who were esteemed in their native country after they had elsewhere made enough dubious money to purchase a patent of protection. This injustice is directly created by that fine policy which denies the poor Jews protection and residence, but receives with open arms those very same Jews as soon as they have "thieved their way to wealth." Although he is inspired by Scripture, Herr Ritter Michaelis seems to have a bias against poverty. Among the Jews, however, I have found comparatively more virtue in the quarters of the poor than in the houses of the wealthy.[36]

Mendelssohn was aware that "a number of Jews existed in Central Europe who supported themselves by both stealing and trading," as Jason Sanders has written. "These thieves benefited from both activities, which mutually reinforced each other. Salesmen on the roads seem to have found ample opportunities to steal, and stealing augmented some traders' meager income. Such Jews frequently were recent immigrants from Eastern Europe, who had not yet secured the right to live in a city. As a result, they attempted to earn a living on the road by trading, begging, and sometimes stealing. Banditry provided an alternative for the poorest of the poor Jews who had difficulties sustaining themselves in low-income, or irregular occupations,"[37] or to enable them to gain a permit to engage in lawful business. To accuse the Jews of immorality, Mendelssohn lamented, was to "confuse cause and effect."[38] It is not surprising, then, that Gotthold Ephraim Lessing chose the stereotype of the Jewish thief as the basis for undermining the myth that the Jews were unvirtuous in his play, *The Jews* (1853). The history of the Jews in Lübeck and Moisling of 1898 includes a twenty-eight-page response, by Gabriel Riesser, to what was termed a spiteful article and lecture by the

36 Moses Mendelssohn, "Remarks Concerning Michaelis' Response to Dohm (1783)," in Reinharz and Mendes-Flohr, eds., *Jew in the Modern World*, 48.
37 Jason Sanders, "From Burglars to Businessmen: Jewish Bandits in Eighteenth- and Nineteenth-Century Germany," unpublished paper, Brandeis University, 1993.
38 Immanuel Wolf and Gotthold Salomon, *Der Charakter des Judentums* (Leipzig, 1817), 141.

jurist Friedrich Christian Benedict Avé-Lallemant, which propounded the "fantasy" of Jewish preponderance in crime.[39] In Britain, as the right of Baron Rothschild to sit in Parliament was debated, it was asserted that Jews "have never, in any age or any country, been prevalent in crime." But the phrase that follows is telling: "Their crimes have mostly been the result of the degraded position to which they have been reduced, the degraded pursuits into which they have been compelled."[40]

Another line of defense against the charge of Jewish criminality was that Jews were distinguished as crime fighters and defenders of the public order. Since 1833, it was argued by a supporter of Rothschild, "Jews have served with honor the offices of sheriffs of counties, and of London, and . . . are holding commissions in our armies, and becoming eminent in our civil government in India."[41] Although Jews were more famous for violating the American Prohibition, they also were touted for combating bootlegging.[42]

It is important to establish, as well, that Jewish criminals were abundant enough to be noticed in various inter-Jewish stock-taking exercises, such as communal histories. The generally turgid chronicles also illuminate Jewish attitudes toward the local and state legal systems by which Jews were supposed to abide. In one of the few humorous asides in a history of the Israelitische Cultusgemeinde of Vienna, Gerson Wolf wrote that it was possible to say something complimentary about the Austrian regime: "Whereas in Prussia and many other German states, where it is still being requested, the Israelite prisoners in Austria are exempt from work on Sabbath and festival days . . . [and] beginning in 1789, sick prisoners were allowed kosher food."[43] The population of Jewish prisoners in many Central European cities was significant enough for communal officials to regularly concern themselves with matters such as kashrut, the provision of high holiday services, and regular exposure to edifying sermons.[44]

There were at least two features of the Jewish relationship with public officials that made it necessary to circumvent certain laws. Wolf notes in his history of Viennese Jewry that gaining permission to live and stay in the city was more a matter of dexterity and craftiness than abiding by the law – which, if upheld, meant that one was forced to be away from one's family,

39 Salomon Carlebach, *Geschichte der Juden in Luebeck und Moisling* (Lübeck, 1898), 137–8, 209ff.
40 Barnard Van Oven, *Ought Baron Rothschild to Sit in Parliament? An Imaginary Conversation between Judaeus and Amicus Nobilis*, 2d ed. (London, 1848), 15.
41 Ibid., 15–16.
42 Herbert Asbury, *The Great Illusion: An Informal History of Prohibition* (Garden City, N.J., 1950), 211–13.
43 Gerson Wolf, *Geschichte der israelitischen Cultusgemeinde in Wien 1820–1860* (Vienna, 1861), 189.
44 Gerson Wolf, *Geschichte der Juden in Wien (1156–1876)* (Vienna, 1876), 228.

and unable to secure a livelihood. Continuous residence, Wolf reported, could only be accomplished through "expedients" – by mildly stretching the truth to obtain the necessary stamps – to get "koshered," as was said. This meant that one would have to go through one line, saying that one was already legally employed – which was necessary in order to receive a residence permit – and another line, saying that one was already living in the district, which was necessary for a work permit – which was, of course, inherently illegal. This was always more difficult for Jews from the East, who were subject to harsher treatment and "night raids" on their hostels. Still, it was so easy (for non-*Ostjuden*) to beat the system that the police took little notice. Wolf tells an anecdote about one family's experience with this process, but is careful to qualify:

We believe that it is not indiscreet to convey the following instance, which the famous mathematician, Professor Simon Spitzer, has spoken of in public. His father lived with his family (a wife and eight children). . . . One day the father did not have the time to get "koshered," so he sent his eight-year old boy, after instructing him as to the procedure, with the necessary money for the purpose. The quick-witted boy did exactly as he was told. He went through the line and then back again. He presented the policeman with his father's pass, and with it, the money. When the policeman asked the boy, "how old are you?" he answered: "Fifty-four." "Married or single?" "Married." "How many children?" "Eight." The boy carried out the necessary make-believe and the matter was over.[45]

Certainly this is not a matter of threatening criminality, but it bespeaks a certain ironic distance from the law, which most likely was not unique to Jews – but which Jews regarded as specific to their own situation. If it was somewhat tricky to keep one's residence, it was infinitely more difficult to run a small business within the confines of the law. The very regulations speak volumes about gentiles' perceptions of and suspicions about Jewish business practices. There seemed to be a great fear that Jews were prone to dealing in stolen goods, so there were a number of stipulations about dealing in products that were "used" as opposed to self-manufactured – with the main concern being that Jews not be allowed to undersell members of the guild. The rules governing clothes-selling and alcohol distribution were amazingly complex and cumbersome, to say the least.[46]

The venue in which Jewish criminality is most explicitly addressed among Jews – albeit in a figurative way – is in literature. There are abundant

---

45 Ibid., 141–2.
46 "Beilage inbegrifferner Oredtnung fuer die Judenschaft zu Wormbs, Wien 28 Nov. 1641," in Wolf, *Zur Geschichte der Juden in Worms*, 78–94.

examples, across time and space, from Carl Spindler's *Der Jude* (1834) to Isaac Babel's *Odessa Stories* (1926), to E. L. Doctorow's *Billy Bathgate* (1989). Here though I deal mostly with the mid–to-late nineteenth century. In a short story titled "Without Authorisation" by Leopold Kompert published in 1882, we are told that "Even to this day, when the State and the ghetto are constantly in relations with one another, there exist so many laws and ordinances that are not proclaimed but dormant, and which hang like invisible swords over the Jews' heads, that the lowest officials can do themselves the pleasure of playing the part of a Haman on a small scale."[47]

In this story, which centers around a Jew who is charged with not having the proper secular certification for his marriage of many years, the key figure is the poor shlemiel's lawyer, Rebb Lippmann Goldberg, "who had a genius for chicanery... the people in the ghetto thought very highly of him... frequently he had gained riches for them by his quibbles and his tricks; and they profited also by his counsel for suits they themselves conducted."[48] In another story Kompert describes how a Jew's success in the *shmate* (clothing) business was based on his ability to engage in what could be seen as dodgy tactics: "Schlome at once set to work with great intelligence and was soon up to all the artifices and tricks that his calling required. In a very short time he could hold and show an old piece of cloth so as to make it pass for new, exhibit admirably a torn silken ribbon so as to conceal its defects, and treat a sample of painted calico of an antiquated pattern in such a way that it would seem to be of the latest fashion."[49]

We are left, then, with a juxtaposition of labyrinthine and contradictory regulations and with the alleged Jewish penchant for navigating their way around them. Moses Mendelssohn possibly located the crux of the problem when he illuminated the mythical distinction, within the emancipation debate, made between so-called producers versus "consumers"; essentially, Jews were cast as being non- or antiproductive, capable only of consuming and reselling. In 1782 Mendelssohn wrote: "Not only making something but doing something also, is called producing. Not he alone who labors with his hands but, generally, whoever does, promotes, occasions, or facilitates anything that may benefit or comfort his fellow creatures deserves to be called a producer; and, at times, he deserves it the more, the less you see him move his hands or feet."[50]

---

47 Leopold Kompert, "Without Authorisation," in *Scenes from the Ghetto: Studies of Jewish Life* (London, 1882), 305.
48 Ibid., 307.
49 Kompert, "Schlemiel," in *Scenes from the Ghetto*, 14.
50 Mendelssohn, "Response to Dohm," 45.

Problems concerning the relationship between Jews and crime also lie at the heart of a short story by Karl Emil Franzos,[51] which concludes a famous compilation of works titled *The Jews of Barnow*. Published in 1873, the story "Nameless Graves" begins by describing a typical Jewish cemetery:

The insignia of the tribe is put first, then the name of the deceased, followed by those of his parents, and after that his occupation in life. Sometimes this last is passed over in silence, for "usurer" or "informer" would not look good upon a tomb, to say nothing of worse things. In such cases friends content themselves with putting, "He was indefatigable in the study of his religion and loved his children" – and, as a rule, this was true. . . . And if any man is so terrible a sinner that no good is to be found in him, they keep silence regarding him. . . . They keep silence. The worst anathema known to this people is, "His name shall be blotted out." And so in such cases they do not inscribe his name on his headstone. There is many a nameless grave in Podolian burial grounds. This is meant as a punishment, as a requital of the evil the man had done while on earth. There are many nameless graves in the "good place" at Barnow, and in some cases the punishment may have been well deserved. It is often the hardest that has reached the criminal. The black deed has been done, and the darkness of the ghetto hid the crime. The Podolian Jews fear the world, and a Christian is supreme in the imperial court of justice. They do not like to deliver their sinful brother into the hands of an alien. They punish him themselves as best they can: He must spend much money on good objects or make a pilgrimage to Jerusalem, or fast every second day for years. His crime is hidden as long as he lives, and it is only after his death that it is discovered. Some very curious things are also looked upon as crimes, and punished in the same way.[52]

Franzos proceeds to tell the story of a Jewish soldier, crippled in war, who was spurned by both Jews and Christians, an occupant of one of these nameless graves; another tale is of a woman whose desire to keep her long beautiful hair, which is forbidden by strict Orthodoxy, leads to her macabre death – and ignominy. The poor souls, in Franzos's eyes, have been victimized not only by Christians but by "ignorant fanatical Eastern Judaism."[53] Therefore, he questions the definitions of crime and criminality imposed from above, in both the Jewish and non-Jewish spheres. It is the task of those who wish to know more about the Jews, and to assist in their enlightenment, to interrogate the nameless graves. This may be difficult, but Franzos writes that their fates are "not impossible to decipher."[54] Both Jewish and gentile society are in dire need of enlightenment.

One might ask: What have these mild cases to do with the more familiar robbers and so-called hardened criminals? Perhaps not a great deal: but

---

51 On Franzos, see Steven Aschheim, *Brothers and Strangers: East European Jews in the German and German-Jewish Consciousness* (Madison, Wis., 1982).
52 Karl Emil Franzos, "Nameless Graves," in *The Jews of Barnow*, 309–11.
53 Ibid., 325. 54 Ibid., 319.

similar sentiments of ambivalence or grudging admiration can be found for more crass, and even sometimes murderous criminals – particularly if they are completely fictional. The leading example is the tremendous popularity of Friedrich Schiller's *The Robbers*, which awaits an extensive study of its reception in English, German, and Yiddish verse and dramatizations.

In Germany a number of books have appeared in the last decades about Jewish gangsters, treated historically. This is not simply a post-Holocaust curiosity or a Nazi, anti-Semitic phenomenon. There seems to be a relatively consistent interest, in the German public at large and among German Jews in particular before 1933, in the Jewish underworld. A review of a book about Jewish gangsters published in the *Jüdische Rundschau*, the Zionist organ in Weimar Germany, seemed more amused than disgusted by the allegation that Jewish crooks had coined the expression "your money or your life." Criminals make for good stories and good history; Jewish criminals promise an exotic variant. Along with Scholem and Mosse, Jason Sanders and Charles Midlo[55] worked on this subject (but both abandoned it before the completion of a book), and this topic has also been seriously treated in Sander Gilman's discussion of "The Language of Thieves" in *Jewish Self-Hatred*, Hans Mayer's *Aussenseiter*, Uwe Danker's *Räuberbanden im Alten Reich um 1700*, Helmut Reinicke's *Gaunerwirtschaft*, and Otto Ulbricht's article in an anthology on Jewish/gentile relations from the late medieval to early modern period.[56]

I now turn to the dissonance between the Jewish and gentile views of Jewish criminals emanating from the so-called scientific realm. This is not to say that German or European criminology constituted a proto-Nazi monolith.[57] Although it is not specifically explicated in the chapters of Becker, Wiener, and Renneville,[58] which illuminate the background, writing about Jews occupied a place in generic criminology from the mid-eighteenth century until the Holocaust. In the third edition of his standard work, *The Criminal*, Havelock Ellis noted:

Another interesting point is the frequency with which these signs refer to the Jews; it seems evident that the Jews, as an outcast class, were at an early period thrown into close connection with the criminal classes; this is also indicated by the frequency of Hebrew words in criminal slang. Like the latter the hieroglyph is a

55 Item no. 743, in Fruma Mohrer and Marek Web, eds., *Guide to the YIVO Archives* (New York, 1998), 190.
56 Gilman, *Jewish Self-Hatred*, 68–86; Hans Mayer, *Aussenseiter* (Frankfurt am Main, 1981); Uwe Danker, *Räuberbanden im Alten Reich um 1700. Ein Beitrag zur Geschichte von Herrschaft und Kriminalität in der Frühen Neuzeit* (Frankfurt am Main, 1988); Reinicke, *Gaunerwirtschaft*; Ulbricht, "Criminality and Punishment."
57 See Richard F. Wetzell's and Gabriel N. Finder's chapters in this book, respectively.
58 See Marc Renneville's chapter in this book.

method of social protection used by outcast classes as a weapon against society; where criminal associations are highly developed the sign language reaches a corresponding development.[59]

In no small measure, it was the "resemblance sometimes found between the criminal ideograms of different countries," significantly among "criminal women and prostitutes"[60] as well, that gave Jewish criminality its international cast.[61] But to a greater extent it was the so-called language of thieves, or thieves' slang, "cant," or Rotwelsch,[62] that appeared to be the central unifying and identifying characteristic of Jewish criminals and the gentiles in their cohort.[63] Friedrich Christian Benedict Avé-Lallemant, who occupies a huge role in establishing the discourse regarding Jews and crime, reported that "Catholics and even Protestants" who were members of Damian Hessel's gang asked that rabbis perform their funeral services because they had been so enmeshed with "Jewish types" and had "lived as Jews";[64] no doubt their language was central to their integration and "Judaization." Martin Luther's *Liber Vagatorum* was the cornerstone of compilations of Rotwelsch that would go through numerous transformations in different national contexts, including the "Beggar Books" in France and editions of the work by Thomas Harman in England.[65] Even Herbert Asbury's history *The Gangs of New York* (1928) has an appendix on "Slang of the Early Gangsters."[66] "Very curious," Havelock Ellis wrote,

are the large number of foreign words, in more or less corrupted form generally, which are to be found in criminal slang. In the German cant Hebrew words are numerous; German and French in Italian; German and English in French; Italian and Romany in English. "Hebrew, or rather Yiddish," Lombroso observes, "supplies the half of Dutch slang, and nearly a fourth of German, in which I counted 156 out of 700, and in which all the terms for various crimes (except band-spieler for cheater at dice) are Jewish."[67]

---

59 Havelock Ellis, *The Criminal*, 3d ed. (London, 1901), 210–11.
60 Ibid.
61 Frank Wadleigh Chandler, *The Literature of Roguery*, 2 vols. (London, 1907), 1:324.
62 *Rotwelsch Grammatik oder Sprachkunst* (Frankfurt am Main, 1755); Friedrich Kluge, *Rotwelsch: Quellen und Wortschatz der Gaunersprache unter der verwandten Geheimsprachen* (Strasbourg, 1901).
63 Juan Hidalgo, *Romances de germania: Volcabulario por la orden del a.b.c.* (Madrid, 1609); Captain Charles Johnson, *A General History of the Lives and Adventures of the Most Famous Highwaymen, Murderers, Street-Robbers, etc. from the Famous Sir John Falstaff to the Reign of K. Henry IV, 1339–1773* (London, 1736), 9, 373, 384.
64 Avé-Lallemant, *Das deutsche Gaunertum*, 16–17.
65 Frank Wagleigh Chandler, *Romances of Roguery: An Episode in the History of the Novel* (London, 1899), 12; Thomas Harman, *The Groundworke of Conny-catching; the manner of their Pedlers-French, and the meanes to understand the same, with the cunning flights of the Counterfeit Crank* (London, 1579).
66 Herbert Asbury, *The Gangs of New York: An Informal History of the Underworld* (London, 1928).
67 Ellis, *The Criminal*, 168.

Gilman has argued that this was crucial to gentile society's assertion that Jews could never learn to speak or appreciate the non-Jewish European languages.

Ironically, the leading figure of the school of criminology that would play a disproportionate role in the development of anti-Semitic racism allied to criminology was Cesare Lombroso, himself a Jew. Although Lombroso maintained that there was no element of anti-Semitism in his work, he clearly felt the need to fend off such charges;[68] his foreword to August Drähm's criminology textbook reveals this as a subtext because he attempted to show that there was no ethnic-national basis to his system.[69]

It seems, however, that the Lombrosian view of criminology was not taken very seriously in the Jewish world; Mendelssohn's situational view would remain typical. In this way, Lombroso is similar to his great devotee Max Nordau, who championed the popularization of the concept of degeneration, related to literature and the arts. That term also would be used as an umbrella for all sorts of scavenger ideologies, many of which were openly or less obviously anti-Semitic.

The recognition that Lombroso was a dominant figure with reservations about applying his notions to Jews, however, did not assure that perceptions of Jewish crime were free of wild exaggerations or were insulated from myths and fantasies concerning Jews. Indeed, one of my arguments here is that the intersection of Jews and crime can be located in purportedly learned discourses as diverse as mesmerism, anarchism, abnormal sexuality, insanity, genetics, and the economics of immigration – which were full of crackpot theories, stereotypes, and self-serving lies. The incursion of Jewish criminality into these domains suggests that the general association of Jews and crime was much broader and more plastic than typically assumed and that such notions could have been nurtured in several different quarters.

There is evidence that Jewish scholars who were themselves interested in criminology fervently denounced and debunked the anti-Semitic applications of Lombroso's methods. One such researcher, who is favorably cited by Krafft-Ebing for offering a corrective to Lombroso, is Moriz Benedikt. Although Benedikt does not identify himself as a Jew, his avoidance of references to Christianity is notable for a work of this type. In *Anatomische Studien an Verbrecher-Gehirnen* Benedikt argued that the scientific study of the brain – which had no relation to the face – was the only way to connect

68 Cesare Lombroso, *Anti-Semitism and the Jews in Light of Modern Science* (1893); see Gilman, *Jewish Self-Hatred*, 290–91.

69 August Drähms, *The Criminal: His Personnel and Environment: A Scientific Study*, introduction by Cesare Lombroso (New York, 1900).

medical anthropology with criminality.[70] He was emphatic that one should guard against trying to make judgments about criminality based on intuition, by gazing at a face or body. Indeed, this would become central to the history of racism. There were deep divisions among criminologists, Benedikt wrote, and a number of tendentious arguments were being propounded. Benedikt himself had suffered from "public, unpleasant agitation" against his person and studies; "criminals," he contended, "are generally not a unitary type but are the products of different physiological makeups, and it is social conditions that make apparent the special form of their appearance" – but again, he speaks of brains, not faces or skulls.[71] Interestingly, Benedikt also took Lombroso to task for asserting that epileptics and others suffering from mental abnormalities had a predisposition to criminality.[72]

Arguably, the greatest disparity between popular, gentile attitudes, toward Jews and crime – versus the views of Jews themselves – lay in the accusation that the Talmud condones and perpetuates Jewish crime. Another association that found almost no reflection in the Jewish world was that of connection between Jewish leftist politics, notably anarchism, and crime. Whereas Jews themselves tended to associate Jewish anarchists with flaunting and undermining the conventions of Judaism,[73] which alienated them from most in the Jewish world, to the outside they were thuggish, violent instruments intent on bringing about a communist order. In Joseph Conrad's *The Secret Agent*, loosely based on the Greenwich Park bombing (1894), crime for the purpose of greed or personal gain is conflated with politically motivated crime. Moreover, there is the notion that Jewish anarchists believe that any and all human life can be sacrificed for their political agenda.[74] "Criminal!" exclaims Conrad's character, the Professor, "What's that? What is crime? What can be the meaning of such an assertion?"[75] Later, the same character says: "I know no pride – no shame – no God – no master."[76] Conrad even puts a conversation about Lombroso, degeneracy, and crime in the mouths of his anarchists. "Lombroso's an ass," one of them asserts.

For him the criminal is the prisoner. Simple, is it not? What about those who put him there? And what is crime? Does he know that – this imbecile who has got on

---

70 Moriz Benedikt, *Anatomische Studien an Verbrecher-Gehirnen für anthropologen, mediciner, juristen und psychologen Bearbeitet* (Vienna, 1879), 135–6.
71 Ibid., 6–7.   72 Ibid., 136.
73 Nathan Goldberg, "Di antireligioze bavegung," in Elias Tcherikower, ed., *Geshikhte fun der yidisher arbeter-bavegung in di Fareynikte Shtatn*, 2 vols. (New York, 1943–5), 2:418–58.
74 Joseph Conrad, *The Secret Agent: Drama in Four Acts* (Canterbury, 1921), 26–7. This version was circulated two years before the published edition.
75 Ibid., 25.   76 Ibid., 68.

in this world of gorged fools by writing about the ears and teeth of a lot of poor, unlucky devils. Teeth and ears mark the criminal! Do they? And what about the law that marks him still better, the branding instrument invented by the overfed to keep down the hungry. Red hot iron on their vile skins – eh? Can't you smell the thick hide of the people burn and sizzle?[77]

Conrad's portrait of the brutal amorality of the anarchists went so far as to paint them as purveyors of pornography[78] and – in shockingly eerie anticipation of the fate of the Jews under the Nazis – advocates of the radical eugenic measures that would result in the extermination of the "weak."[79] Such a view could not have been more different from the way the leading anarchists – such as Saul Janofsky – of both New York and London were perceived in the Jewish world. Hutchins Hapgood wrote that Janofsky was "a little dark-haired man, with beautiful eyes, and a soft, persuasive voice"; he therefore was a fitting leader of the "anarchists of the ghetto" who were "a gentle and idealistic body of men."[80] The bombs they hurled were polemical rather than destructive of life and limb. Essentially, they believed that a more appropriately humane order would emerge with the abolition of government, which by its very nature tends to oligarchy and corruption. Under Janofsky, anarchism was something to think about; it was more a posture of dignified defiance, as opposed to an ideology or plan requiring specific policies. It was frequently referred to as a phase that one passed through, typically as a young person, before deciding on a variety of socialism or Zionism. Figures as diverse as Abraham Cahan, editor of *Forverts*, and Jacob Israel De Haan, a leader of Agudas Yisroel, had tried on anarchism along their journeys.

In the mid-nineteenth century one of the most fascinating figures central to the discourse on Jews and crime was Avé-Lallemant,[81] whose work is rarely consulted by Jewish historians. Given the general aversion to writing about Jews and crime, along with the fact that Avé-Lallemant was appropriated by the Nazis, there is little wonder that his corpus has been treated suspiciously. Although Avé-Lallemant expends a great amount of time and energy detailing the exploits of Jewish crooks and, more impressively, attempting to connect Jewish criminals and crime with various streams of Jewish culture and subcultures, he is not an anti-Semite – at least, not a typical one.[82] He

77 Ibid., 19.   78 Ibid., 9, 35.

79 Ibid., 27.

80 Hutchins Hapgood, *The Spirit of the Ghetto*, ed. Moses Rischin (Cambridge, Mass., 1967), 192–3.

81 Friedrich Christian Benedict Avé-Lallemant, *Das deutsche Gaunertum in seiner sozial-politischen, literarischen und linguistischen Ausbildung zu seinem heutigen Bestande* (Leipzig, 1858).

82 Friedrich Christian Benedict Avé-Lallemant, *Physiologie der deutschen Polizei* (Leipzig, 1882), 4–42, 45.

belonged to a school, also represented by A. F. Thiele, of "judicial idealism" that clearly distinguished between separate Jewish and Christian spheres of morality.[83] Despite Avé-Lallemant's mania for Rotwelsch, which he sees as largely derivative from Yiddish, he specifically praises Yiddish for its linguistic richness.[84] He is not a philo-Semite, either; he is a devout Christian of an authoritarian nature. He tends to ascribe criminality to adverse social conditions, above all – but he also believed that when one is remote from Christianity, and also remote from mainstream, rabbinic Judaism, there is a greater tendency to indulge in criminal mayhem. Avé-Lallemant was particularly fascinated with the practical manifestations of Kabbalah, and some of his findings about late Sabbateanism foreshadow those of Gershom Scholem. Avé-Lallemant was not totally off-base in linking Sabbatai Sevi's followers to both criminality and libertinism.[85] But he goes far afield and creates a direct link to later racist anti-Semitism by crediting Jews with organizing prostitution, including male prostitution, and bordellos, which were responsible for the spread of syphilis; this was seen as part and parcel of satanic practice.[86] My suspicion is that Jews as well as gentiles read Avé-Lallemant – but that they read him differently. Jews could read him simply for the fascinating exploits of the crooks as well as the bizarre connections to esoteric Judaism. After all, Heinrich Heine, too, had written about a seductive rabbi, possibly a follower of Sabbatai, who roamed about the countryside with "a gaggle of prostitutes."

> Aus dem Amsterdamer Spielhuis
> Zog er jüngst etwelche Dirnen
> Und mit diesen Musen zieht er
> Jetzt herum als ein Apollo
>
> Eine Dicke ist darunter
> Die vorzüglich quiekt und grünzelt;
> Ob dem grossen Lorbeerkopfputz
> Nennt man sie die grüne Sau
>
> From the Amsterdam whorehouse
> He's just enticed some wenches,
> And with these Muses he now travels about
> Thinking himself to be Apollo

---

83 See Becker's chapter in this book; A. F. Thiele, *Die jüdischen gauner in Deutschland, ihre taktik, ihre eigenthumlichkeiten und ihre sprache, nebst ausführlichen nachrichten über die in Deutschland und an dessen grenzen sich aufhaltenden berüchtigsten jüdischen gaunder . . .* (Berlin, 1841–3).

84 Avé-Lallemant, *Physiologie der deutschen Polizei*, 46.

85 Friedrich Christian Benedict Avé-Lallemant, *Die Mersener Bockreiter des 18. und 19. Jahrhunderts* (Leipzig, 1880), 13, 17, 22, 54, 76–90.

86 Avé-Lallemant, *Physiologie der deutschen Polizei*, 170–94, 184–202, 258–71.

> Among them is a fatty
> Who really squeals and grunts well;
> Due to the large garland atop her head
> She is generally known as the Green Sow[87]

A successor of Avé-Lallemant, the linguist Friedrich Kluge also saw Jewish crime as an infectious disease. He argued that German university students had come "under the spell of Rotwelsch"; "after Latin and terms from theology," Rotwelsch was the greatest influence on student speech. It exerted, Kluge feared, some kind of mystical power over students.[88] Avé-Lallemant was most explicit about the connection of "magnetism," "animal magnetism," and "mesmerism" to crime. The "animal magnetism" of Mesmer was believed to be "capable of healing diseases of the nerves." It was claimed that Mesmer could "know the state of health of each individual and judge with certainty the origin, the nature, and the progress of the most complicated diseases; he prevents their increase and succeeds in healing them without at any time exposing his patient to dangerous effects or troublesome consequences. . . . In animal magnetism, nature presents a universal method of healing and preserving mankind."[89] Mesmerism also, however, could be seen as the working of an evil force in at least two ways: as an outright sham and as a means of gaining knowledge, which translated into control over potential victims. It was said to work in this way as well: Some criminals were able to use hypnosis, or "animal magnetism," as a means of perpetrating their crimes. Avé-Lallemant believed that it derived from Hebrew mythology, specifically from how humans came to possess the power of God, which was located in the story of the anointing of the High Priest for the tabernacle, and in its exegesis, especially in the mystical literature.[90] Despite the fact that Avé-Lallemant maintained that mesmerism was mostly bogus he thought that there was a relationship between its popularization and crime. He was, in fact, encroaching on territory that is still ill-defined: At what point can one consider a sect that claims to have some kind of inside knowledge or redemptive or therapeutic value a criminal venture?

Jews themselves probably underestimated the extent to which Jewish crooks were perceived as having access to the supernatural. It was thought

---

87 Heinrich Heine, "Der Apollogott," in Klaus Briegleb et al., eds., *Sämtliche Schriften*, 6 vols. (Munich, 1968–76), 6, pt. 1:36.

88 Friedrich Kluge, *Deutsche Studentensprache* (Strasbourg, 1895), 59–63.

89 William B. Carpenter, *Mesmerism and Spiritualism Historically and Scientifically Considered* (London, 1877), 125; translation from Franz A. Mesmer, *Mémoire sur la découverte du magnetisme animal* (Paris, 1779).

90 Friedrich Christian Benedict Avé-Lallemant, *Der Magnetismus mit seinen mystischen Verirrungen: Culturhistorischer Beitrag zur Geschichte des deutschen Gaunerthums* (Leipzig, 1881), 11.

that Jews had special insights into hypnotism, which was part of an "abnormal" psychological makeup. Criminologist August Drähms claimed that it emerged from ancient Near Eastern occult practices because their priests aimed to take "advantage of these means to enhance their particular calling, and thus obtain influence over the masses." This had been continued, however cynically, by Mesmer. At its worst, those who knew the formulations could lull their victims into a trance, like Dr. Caligari, and have them perform deeds – a "semi-conscious automatism" – that were contrary to their own moral sense. Hence, through control of occult sciences, such criminals could create bands of unwitting followers.[91] None of these esoteric explanations, which often found their way into scientific discourse, seems to have resonated within Jewish society.

Avé-Lallemant is also instructive in foreshadowing other tendencies of anti-Semitism. He was clear in linking Jews and Gypsies as the aberrant groups responsible for a disproportionate share of crime. In the end, Avé-Lallemant taught that it was virtually impossible to discuss criminals without referring to Jewish contacts, influences, and sources. And it was in deviant sects of Jewish culture that the ur-sources of criminal subcultures could be discerned.[92] It seems that one of Avé-Lallemant's deepest impulses was to prove that the idea of crime could not have sprung, of itself, from a German Christian society.

In retrospect, it may be said that Jewish criminals were to a large extent accepted as part of the social landscape among preacculturated Central European Jewry. Jews learned about Jewish criminals through the stories they told, but also through non-Jewish inventions, such as Schiller's *The Robbers*, and exaggerations of Jewish involvement in crime, as propounded by Avé-Lallemant. They were reminded of the stereotypes during the many stages of their fight for political rights. Criminals were not seen by Jews as extraordinary individuals but mainly as "unfortunates."[93] This could not have been more different from the view expressed by Drähms that criminals are "the bacilli that infect the collective organism. As such, it is not an accident, nor a misfortune, nor yet an incident that clings to the skirts of advancing civilization, but is the result of distinct causes, whose genesis and amelioration through preventive methods and the application of proper remedial agencies, it is becoming more and more the fashion of contemporary thought to explore. . . . Criminology, therefore, as the patron of pathosociology, reaches the dignity of a science by the same right of necessity that

---

91 Drähms, *The Criminal*, 308–9.   92 Avé-Lallemant, *Die Mersener Bockreiter*, 132–3.
93 Gerson Wolf, *Geschichte der israelitischen Cultusgemeinde in Wien 1820–1860* (Vienna, 1861), 189.

gives the medical profession its place."[94] Perhaps Jews were even less aware of the anti–Semitic potential of criminology, as opposed to race "science" in particular.

Jews have tended to see the very designation "Jewish criminal" or "Jewish crime" with some irony. There was no escaping the view of criminologists, public officials, and the community at large that criminality was related to deviation from the Christian norm, however much it may have been recognized that crime tends to rise out of poverty and privation.[95] Pike's comment in his *History of Crime in England* comes close to the "Jewish" view that "Of a very great number of modern habitual criminals it may be said that they have the misfortune to live in an age when their merits are not appreciated";[96] or the statement of Alexander Smith that "Little villains oft' submit to fate. . . . That Great Ones may enjoy the World in State."[97] No matter what they did, Jews would always be seen as different, unworthy, or beyond the non-Jewish law. This sentiment is encapsulated in Havelock Ellis's contention that

From any scientific point of view the use of the word crime, to express a difference of national feeling or of political opinion, is an abuse of the language. Such a conception may be necessary to ensure the supremacy of a Government, just as the conception of heresy is necessary to ensure the supremacy of the Church. . . . A criminality which is regulated partly by chronology, partly by longitude, does not easily admit of scientific discussion.[98]

Havelock Ellis was credited with saying that crime is "the complex relation which the law creates between itself and the lawbreaker. The law creates the crime." This view was resisted, with great vehemence, by criminologists who argued that crime, in itself, "is an attack upon the social organism," that "every wrongful act in defiance of mandate is both an individual and social menace." There were absolutes that could not be challenged, that were above all manifested "in the state [and] patriotism; and in the highest Christian thought it stands for the universal altruistic sentiment of mankind, the well-being of the race. The essential polarities of the ethical ideal are embodied in the dual concept of right and wrong, the pillar and foundation of the moral constitution."[99] Against the State and Church, according to Avé-Lallemant, were crude sensuality and atheistic materialism, which had

---

94 Drähms, *The Criminal*, vii–viii.
95 Avé-Lallemant, *Das deutsche Gaunertum*, viii, 14.
96 Luke O. Pike, *A History of Crime in England: Illustrating the Changes of the Law in the Progress of Civilisation*, 2 vols. (London, 1896), 509, quoted in Ellis, *The Criminal*, 207.
97 Johnson, *General History of the Lives and Adventures of the Most Famous Highwaymen*.
98 Ellis, *The Criminal*, 7.   99 Drähms, *The Criminal*, 5–6, 2.

to be ardently combated.[100] Nevertheless, Avé-Lallemant was not a direct forerunner to the Nazis. But his obsession with locating the origins of crime outside of Christian society, and as alien to German Christians by their nature and history, was dangerous dogma. In its most extreme form the Nazi state would dedicate itself to the notion that to be Jewish was to be criminal. Jews, even up to the present, tend to cast a suspicious but interested glance toward the strange combination of Jew and criminal; more than occasionally they take subversive delight in the crooks from amongst them who flaunt convention – in myth and reality – and otherwise unsettle the gentile order. As Schiller's Spiegelberg proclaimed: "And Spiegelberg will be the name, in east and west, and into the mud with you, cowards and toads, as Spiegelberg spreads his wings and flies high into the temple of fame."[101]

---

100 Avé-Lallemant, *Das deutsche Gaunertum*, xvi.   101 Schiller, *Robbers and Wallenstein*, 41.

4

Moral Discourse and Reform in Urban Germany, 1880s–1914

ANDREW LEES

I

The intellectual and ideological contexts within which criminological analysis took place were multiform and polyvalent. Men and women who constructed the discursive environment that impinged on the thinking of professional specialists in the area of felonious behavior approached the broader terrain of immorality and wrongdoing from widely varying standpoints. They also had distinctly differing purposes in mind. Reflecting a widespread belief that the rise of the *Grossstädte* (big cities) greatly exacerbated an ongoing moral crisis in their country, many Germans commented critically on contemporary conduct in the late nineteenth and the early twentieth centuries. In so doing they evinced a wide spectrum of thought and feeling. Even if we limit our attention – as I do in this chapter – to members of and spokesmen for the *Bürgertum* (middle class), we discover a great multiplicity of preferences, prejudices, and prescriptions. After first surveying moral criticism of the *Grossstadt* per se, I compare two contrasting strands in the writing of representative individuals who articulated quite different views of the causes that lay behind immorality and the best ways to combat it. I hope thereby to help situate thought about crime within a broader framework in which debates among criminologists can be seen as having echoed and paralleled disputes among other commentators on putative misconduct in an urban and urbanizing Germany and the best ways of responding to it.

II

The rapid rise of the big cities – from Berlin to Essen and from Munich to Hamburg – elicited from many Germans around the turn of the century a complex set of hopes and fears. Cultural responses to urban phenomena displayed a degree of interest that stemmed not only from fascination with the new and exuberant enthusiasms but also from widespread awareness of challenges to be faced and of evils to be overcome.[1]

What I wish to emphasize for now is the current of thinking about cities that was critical both of their perceived failings and more particularly of the moral deficiencies of city dwellers. The *Grossstadt* aroused alarm among many observers not only because of its defects in such areas as housing and public health but also because of what was felt to be its inhabitants' failure to adhere to proper standards of personal and social behavior. Urban centers, it was argued, not only permitted but exacerbated the decline of "morality" in the broadest sense of the term. The big city militated against communal supervision of the individual, fostered selfishness, and produced excessive amounts of crime and other forms of antisocial conduct, such as drunkenness, prostitution, and homosexuality. Having escaped from the social controls that relatives, pastors, and other neighbors had been able to maintain in small towns and villages, inhabitants of big cities increasingly displayed egotistical tendencies that did great harm to the larger collectivity. In a similar vein, it was frequently charged that the immorality of the individual posed a larger threat to established structures of political rule and social stratification. Commentators on city life who sought to defend the status quo against assaults from below frequently charged that uncontrolled and immoral residents of urban centers were all too ready to participate in class conflicts that would ultimately lead to revolution.

Such attitudes can be documented with a wealth of examples, of which only a few will be cited here. In a manner that was reminiscent of similar views expressed earlier by clergymen who belonged to the Church of England, such as James Shergold Boone in the 1840s, and by the well-known Protestant Josiah Strong (among others) in the United States in the mid-1880s, numerous pastors voiced their unease over urban immorality as a supposed threat to German well-being.[2] One of the best known of these men was Adolf Stoecker, who served both as the preacher at the Prussian royal court and as the director of the newly established Berlin City Mission. In a lecture in which he decried "social and religious distress in big cities," he argued vigorously that the *Grossstädte* were sources not only of wealth and

---

1 For a general and comparative treatment of attitudes toward urban development, see Andrew Lees, *Cities Perceived: Urban Society in European and American Thought, 1820–1940* (New York, 1985), esp. 105–255. For a fuller treatment of the themes and the main individuals touched on in this chapter, see Andrew Lees, *Cities, Sin, and Social Reform in Germany, 1880s–1914* (Ann Arbor, Mich., 2002).
2 James Shergold Boone, *The Need of Christianity to Cities* (London, 1844), 10–22; Josiah Strong, *Our Country*, ed. J. Herbst (1891; reprint, Cambridge, Mass., 1963), 176.

pride but also of pain and sorrow. In them, social suffering went hand-in-hand with moral decline and the rise of revolutionary agitation. Crime, prostitution, and begging besmirched an urban environment that was increasingly inhospitable to the Christian faith, and as a result atheistic alternatives flourished. So too, as Stoecker argued elsewhere, did (immoral) exploitation of ordinary Germans by Jews and (immoral) socialism. In a similar vein, Friedrich Schlegelmilch, who worked in the City Mission, penned his own denunciations of city dwellers' moral failings. Having first decried "godlessness" and the decay of family life, he complained that "in the swamp of big-city life . . . the feeling of decency, of moral duty and discipline" had disappeared. "Nowhere except in the big city," he continued, "are there so many failures and so many evil men whose business it is to plunder their neighbors, especially inexperienced ones, to acquaint them with disgraceful vices, and finally to hurl them into the abyss of despair." A few years later, he, like Stoecker before him, connected personal vice and political danger. Socialist majorities in Berlin in elections for the Reichstag, he asserted, showed that it took only a short time for the unspoiled migrant from the countryside to sink to the level of the "big-city proletarian" who threatened the future stability of the whole nation.[3]

Such sentiments were buttressed by many other writers, by no means all of whom were religious conservatives. In his panoramic survey *Grossstadt Dokumente*, the left-leaning Hans Ostwald included many volumes written for general readers that depicted men and women in Berlin and in other cities in their worst light. He also wrote other works about pimps and gamblers,[4] and he commissioned others to help him write about homosexuality, lesbianism, prostitution, white slavery, illegitimacy, young thugs, and usury, as well as about vice in general and crime in particular. As a group, the authors whose works made up this series certainly did not hate the city — which after all provided them with the raw material for their journalistic creativity — but much of what they had to say conveyed a vivid image of it as a place that caused current moral chaos.[5]

---

3 Adolf Stoecker, *Die sozialen und kirchlichen Notstände in grossen Städten* (Stuttgart, 1888), 3, 7, 14–16; Adolf Stoecker, *Reden und Aufsätze*, ed. Reinhold Seeberg (Bielefeld, 1885), 143–274; Friedrich Schlegelmilch, *Grossstadtnot- und hilfe* (Berlin, 1909), 405; *Landflucht und Stadtsucht* (Berlin, 1909), 5–6.

4 Hans Ostwald, *Zuhältertum in Berlin* (*Grossstadt Dokumente* [hereafter GD], vol. 5 [Berlin, 1905]) and *Das Berliner Spielertum* (GD, vol. 35; [Berlin, 1908]). On Ostwald, see Peter Fritzsche, "Vagabond in the Fugitive City: Hans Ostwald, Imperial Berlin, and the *Grossstadt-Dokumente*," *Journal of Contemporary History* 29 (1994): 385–402.

5 Wilhelm Hammer, *Zehn Lebensläufe Berliner Kontrollmädchen* (GD, vol. 20 [Berlin, 1906]); Magnus Hirschfeld, *Die Gurgel Berlins* (GD, vol. 41 [Berlin, 1907]); J. Werthauer, *Berliner Schwindel* (GD, vol. 21 [Berlin, 1906]); Hans Hyan, *Schwere Jungen* (GD, vol. 28 [Berlin, 1906]).

Moral misgivings were also apparent – albeit in a properly subtle and restrained form – at the upper end of the intellectual ladder, in much of the writing by ostensibly dispassionate scholars. In his classic essay on "the metropolis and mental life" the sociologist Georg Simmel included a number of passages in which he made it quite clear that the urban milieu had a deleterious as well as a liberating impact on those who inhabited it. Big-city life, Simmel argued, undermined human solidarity. The modern city dweller felt compelled to defend his independence against the pressures that impinged on him from without. He consequently cultivated a certain isolation that was linked not only to blasé indifference toward other city dwellers but also to "a mutual strangeness and repulsion, which, under the impact of any sort of close contact, would break out immediately into hatred and conflict." Ferdinand Tönnies, whose overall political orientation may best be described as left-liberal, saw the big city as the embodiment of modern *Gesellschaft* (society), which, in contrast to traditional *Gemeinschaft* (community), revealed much selfishness and "many inner hostilities and antagonistic interests." In his view the isolation of the individual described by Simmel manifested itself in the disrepair of family life, and what Simmel referred to as "hatred and conflict" took more specific shape in conflict among classes, which might well "destroy society and the state that it is its purpose to reform."[6]

In many instances critical sentiments with regard to urban morals were closely linked to a fundamentally antiurban orientation that was as backward-looking as it was repressive. Germany was in fact one of the primary breeding grounds of opposition to the urban milieu, which the historian Klaus Bergmann treated some years ago in what is still a classic work on this subject. Writing about "hostility to the big city and agrarian romanticism," he provided us with a masterful account of a current of writing about urban life that helped to prepare the way for, and culminated in the triumph of, the ideology of "blood and soil." National Socialism was indeed in no small measure an outgrowth of anxieties about the moral shortcomings of an urban society.[7]

Two observations that point in a rather different direction must, however, also be emphasized. First of all, as I have already suggested, men such as Ostwald, Simmel, and Tönnies were by no means conservative antiurbanists. Ostwald was fascinated by the city, Simmel saw the city as a place that

---

6 Georg Simmel, "Die Grossstädte und das Geistesleben," in Georg Simmel, *Die Grossstadt: Vorträge und Aufsätze zur Städteausstellung* (*Jahrbuch der Gehe-Stiftung zu Dresden*, vol. 9 [Dresden, 1903]), 187, 189, 195, 199; Ferdinand Tönnies, *Community and Society: Gemeinschaft und Gesellschaft*, trans. and ed. C. P. Loomis (New York, 1963), 77, 227, 229, 231.
7 Klaus Bergmann, *Grossstadtfeindschaft und Agrarromantik* (Meisenheim am Glan, 1970).

stimulated the individual positively as well as negatively, and Tönnies was a progressive liberal.

In the second place – and more generally – criticism of urban morals was frequently linked to ameliorative efforts to civilize city dwellers within the urban environment. Many Germans firmly believed that it would indeed be possible to overcome the cities' moral inadequacies by means of urban institutions and urban practices, and they acted on that belief. The conviction – which had received its classic formulation in the 1840s in England in Robert Vaughan's *The Age of Great Cities* – that urban centers were especially suited to function as focal points for "voluntary combinations of the virtuous in the cause of purity . . . [and] spontaneous efforts in the cause of public morals" continued unabated, and not just among Anglo-Saxons.[8] Many Germans from across the political spectrum shared the belief that the big city had brought human beings together in a manner that need not undermine solidarity; it could instead foster cooperation. The conservative theologian Reinhold Seeberg welcomed not only the urban movement away from small-minded arrogance and groveling servility but also "the educational awareness of being a member of a large community . . . of togetherness and unity." Residents of big cities, he argued, were inclined "to make common cause with others, to establish associations and pursue their goals by pooling their energies."[9] In this spirit, a multitude of reformers responded to what they regarded as the moral crises that were occurring in their cities not by rejecting and attempting to flee these cities but instead by employing them as staging grounds for efforts in the area of urban improvement. In their view, the energies of *bürgerlich* activists were perfectly suited to the task of combating urban ills and working toward the achievement of more civilized and livable cities. As was the case in the area of public administration and the construction of the *Leistungsverwaltung* (efficient administration) for which Germany was internationally and deservedly famous, so too in the area of extragovernmental activity there was a profusion of efforts to overcome the tension between positive and critical attitudes toward urban society. Such efforts took shape in collective endeavors led by individuals who firmly believed that, via the utilization of urban opportunities, middle-class morality could make headway against and perhaps even win out over urban immorality.

It is worth pointing out before proceeding to discuss several of these movements in more detail that the historical literature pertaining to the

---

8 Robert Vaughan, *The Age of Great Cities: Or, Modern Society Viewed in Its Relation to Intelligence, Morals, and Religion* (London, 1843), 296–7.
9 Reinhold Seeberg, "Zur Psychologie der Grossstadt," in Ernst Bunke, ed., *Arbeit für Grossstadt und Land* (Berlin, 1911), 31–2.

topics that concern me is much thinner with regard to Germany than it is
with regard to other countries to Germany's west. There is still relatively little
about Germany that stands comparison with the splendid work by Martin
Wiener on the history of British criminology and by Paul Boyer on perceptions of the urban masses and the pursuit of moral order in the United
States, which constitute the tips of icebergs of writings about these and
related themes in these two countries.[10] German developments have been
treated in important works by Jürgen Reulecke, Detlev J. K. Peukert, Derek
S. Linton, Christoph Sachsse, Rüdiger vom Bruch, Ann Taylor Allen, and
Richard F. Wetzell, which have done a great deal to illuminate our understanding of *bürgerlich* social reform in general and of the narrower topics of
the treatment of young people, social work, and criminology in particular.[11]
There remains nonetheless a scholarly deficit with regard to the German
experience, especially with regard to the relationships among perceptions of
immorality, middle-class reformism, and the urban sphere of activity (what
the Germans would call the urban *Handlungsspielraum*). There is still, moreover, too great a tendency to concentrate either on antimodernism or on
tendencies toward "social control" in a way that militates against a proper
understanding of the variety of views among middle-class Germans who
sought positive as well as negative solutions for what they saw as urban ills.
In the rest of this chapter, I shall attempt to place several pieces of the larger
puzzle in their appropriate places in relation to one another as well as to the
phenomenon of criminology.

III

There was, to be sure, a powerful current of conservatism that manifested
itself clearly and frequently in the pronouncements of men and women

---

10 Martin J. Wiener, *Reconstructing the Criminal: Culture, Law and Social Policy in England, 1830–1914*
    (New York, 1990); Paul Boyer, *Urban Masses and Moral Order in America, 1820–1920* (Cambridge,
    Mass., 1978).

11 Jürgen Reulecke, "Bürgerliche Sozialreformer und Arbeiterjugend im Kaiserreich," *Archiv für
    Sozialgeschichte* 22 (1982): 299–329; Reulecke, "Stadtbürgertum und bürgerliche Sozialreform im
    19. Jahrhundert in Preussen," in Lothar Gall, ed., *Stadt und Bürgertum im 19. Jahrhundert* (Munich,
    1990), 171–97; Christoph Sachsse, *Mütterlichkeit als Beruf: Sozialarbeit, Sozialreform und Frauenbewe-
    gung 1871–1929* (Frankfurt am Main, 1986); Detlev J. K. Peukert, *Grenzen der Sozialdisziplinierung:
    Jugendfürsorge und Jugendsubkulturen 1878–1932* (Essen, 1986); Derek S. Linton, *"Who Has the Youth,
    Has the Future": The Campaign to Save Young Workers in Imperial Germany* (New York, 1991); Rüdiger
    vom Bruch, ed., *Weder Kommunismus noch Kapitalismus: Bürgerliche Sozialreform in Deutschland vom
    Vormärz bis zur Ära Adenauer* (Munich, 1985), esp. the essays on the nineteenth and early twentieth
    centuries by Reulecke and vom Bruch, 21–179; Ann T. Allen, *Feminism and Motherhood in Germany,
    1800–1914* (New Brunswick, N.J., 1991); Richard F. Wetzell, *Inventing the Criminal: A History of
    German Criminology, 1880–1945* (Chapel Hill, N.C., 2000).

whose main concern was to make the case for good order that would be based on control, from without and from within. In their view moral reform was to take place through the denunciation and punishment of wickedness, and it would go hand-in-hand with an authoritarian defense of the political as well as the social status quo. The cultivation and propagation of ideals of personal decency and respectability by members of the middle classes would help enable the *Bürgertum* to define and assert itself not only vis-à-vis the upper but also – and even more – vis-à-vis the lower classes.

Moral criticism and reform as basically conservative discourses appeared most prominently in the writings of Protestant clergymen. Viewing themselves as the chief custodians of their country's moral compass, they constantly sought to draw public attention to private as well as to public vice – all vice, in their eyes, having ultimately public consequences for Germany as a whole. They paid particular attention to evidence of immorality among members of the working classes, although they also reminded their readers that base behavior could be found at all levels of German society. Although many of them were by no means unaware of the harmful impact of material hardship and of other economic and social factors, their main point was to focus on impediments to self-discipline. They wrote from the standpoint that the free will of the individual was ultimately paramount and determinism represented one more excuse for failing to hold the individual accountable for his or her misdeeds. To be sure, individual choices were also seen as being influenced by the contexts within which men and women lived. But the most prominent features of the environment to be borne in mind were not material but cultural: the ideas and the entertainments that served as mental and psychological solvents of individual restraint. Through a whole host of organizations and publications men and women who viewed immorality in this way worked with one another and with others who followed their lead as "moral entrepreneurs" in order to propagate the idea of moral regeneration via moral control. Such regeneration would be at the same time religious in its orientation and national in its ramifications.[12]

More than any other individual, it was Ludwig Weber who worked to spread the "good word." Born the son of a jurist in Westphalia in 1846 and educated at the universities of Bonn and Berlin, Weber was deeply influenced by the example of and his contact with Johann Hinrich Wichern, the founder of the Rauhes Haus, a home for wayward youth in Hamburg,

---

12 I am indebted for this phrase, as well as for a variety of other suggestions, to Fritz Sack, who served as the commentator on this essay at the conference in Florence at which it was presented.

and of the Innere Mission of the Evangelical Church. Wichern's blend of traditionalist Christianity and social concern left an indelible imprint on Weber's outlook throughout his career. During his years as a pastor first in the small cities of Iserlohn and Dellwig between 1871 and 1881 and then in the larger city of Mönchen-Gladbach between 1881 and 1914, Weber sought to bring the power of organized religion to bear in the struggle against moral failings in industrial settings, especially among working-class adolescents.[13]

Weber operated regionally and nationally as well as locally. He involved himself deeply and invested enormous energy in a wide range of socially oriented activities, all of which may be seen as stemming from moral fears. In 1885 he took the lead in forming the Christian Association for the Elevation of Public Morality in Western Germany. Four years later he performed a similar role in the establishment of an umbrella group that was known as the General Conference of German Morality Associations, and he chaired the General Conference as well as the Christian Association for over two decades.[14]

Both organizations served as vehicles for mobilizing their members, a clear majority of whom were Protestant clergymen, enabling them not only to communicate with one another but also to reach larger audiences of outsiders.[15] At regular meetings participants gave and heard lectures, adopted resolutions for transmittal to governing authorities, and developed additional strategies for turning back what they – the self-anointed defenders of virtue – repeatedly portrayed as a rising tide of filth and depravity. The groups also sponsored other activities, including lectures before other groups and the distribution of tens of thousands of pieces of written material. Beginning in 1886 the Christian Association published each month what quickly became known as the *Korrespondenzblatt zur Bekämpfung der öffentlichen Unsittlichkeit* (Journal for Combating Public Immorality). It later became the official organ of the General Conference, which also published several other periodicals as well as numerous fliers and pamphlets (mostly directed at young men,

13 Gert Lewek, *Kirche und soziale Frage um die Jahrhundertwende: Dargestellt am Wirken Ludwig Webers* (Neukirchen-Vluyn, 1963), 18–20, 34–42; Ludwig Weber, *Lebenserinnerungen* (Hamburg, ca. 1906), 2–11.

14 Lewek, *Kirche und Soziale Frage*, 98–101; Weber, *Lebenserinnerungen*, 26–9; Ludwig Weber and [n.a.] Ellger, *25 Jahre der Sittlichkeits-Bewegung: Bilder aus der Geschichte des Westdeutschen Sittlichkeitsvereins und der Allgemeinen deutschen Sittlichkeits-Konferenz, 1885–1910* (Lüttringhausen, ca. 1910), 3–7, 49–51, 171.

15 See the "Liste der Teilnehmer an der Delegierten-Konferenz," in *Verhandlungen der Halle'schen Konferenz der deutschen Sittlichkeits-Vereine vom 8. und 9. Mai 1890* (Berlin, 1890), 6–7. Forty of the fifty-three delegates were clergymen.

who were considered to be especially susceptible to temptation), books, and proceedings of the yearly conventions.[16]

The immoral tide that was to be stemmed and reversed through these efforts consisted for the most part of any form of sexual behavior that was not consecrated by marital vows. In the view of Weber and his fellow moralists, the term *Unsittlichkeit* (immorality) largely referred to the gamut of acts that ranged from simple *Unzucht* (masturbation and pre- or extramarital intercourse) to *gewerbsmässige Unzucht* (prostitution) and, worst of all, *unnatürliche Unzucht* (homosexuality). Any sort of expressive or symbolic activity that might stimulate such behavior also merited condemnation.

The flavor of Weber's thinking and that of his comrades-in-arms about these and related matters can be easily grasped via a lecture he delivered at the convention of the General Conference in 1890 on "The Struggle Against Immorality." "Our era," he proclaimed, "is the era of the big cities, and in these cities sinfulness and misery accumulate, and sinfulness takes on ever more refined forms." He castigated impurity in the first place as a "force of destruction" (*Verderbensmacht*) for bodily health. Assuming a ready familiarity among his listeners with medical arguments pertaining not only to the spread of venereal disease but also to the supposedly harmful consequences of "self-abuse" (*Selbstbefleckung*), Weber quickly moved on to the deleterious implications of immorality for mental and spiritual health. "If a man wallows in the filth of impurity, his heart cannot rise to the ideals that ought to shine as the lodestars of our lives." Sexual immorality thus contributed to crime as well as to irreligion. It also undermined the strength of the nation as a whole. The decline of the ancient Greeks and Romans stemmed from sexual immorality of the sort denounced by Paul in his first letter to the Romans: "these sins of a decadent paganism, which necessarily suffocated from its own vice." In light of this earlier decline, it behooved the Germans to return to the straight and narrow path before it was too late. "Our troops," he observed, "performed superhuman tasks in 1870 because there was still a valiant stock of Germans (*ein deutsches Reckengeschlecht*), so that they could survive a winter campaign." "If," Weber added, "our national energy should languish, then perhaps the possibility of asserting the German Empire and German culture in the heart of Europe will also disappear."[17]

16 John C. Fout, "Sexual Politics in Wilhelmine Germany: The Male Gender Crisis, Moral Purity, and Homophobia," in John C. Fout, ed., *Forbidden History: The State, Society, and the Regulation of Sexuality in Modern Europe* (Chicago, 1992), 275–6. See the back covers of the printed *Verhandlungen* for titles. Many of the briefer items were reprints of lectures given at the conventions.

17 Ludwig Weber, "Der Kampf gegen die Unsittlichkeit," in *Verhandlungen der Halle'schen Konferenz*, 103–4. For other examples of anxiety about national strength, see Rudolf Sohm, *Der deutsche Mann*

Half a decade later, in 1895, Weber developed his ideas at greater length
in collaboration with sixteen other authors who contributed to a volume
he edited on the moral, religious, and social development of Germany
during the preceding thirty-five years.[18] Here, Weber and his fellow authors
(two-thirds of whom were also clergymen) sought to situate rhetorically
the problems of the present within a historical framework that would offer
not only narratives but also explanations.

Almost all the essays implied – and some stated explicitly – that immorality ought not to be viewed simply as a product of circumstances that were
external to the immoral individual. It made just as much if not more sense
to view individual misbehavior as a cause of rather than as a consequence of
social suffering. As Albrecht Romann put it, each human being bore his or
her own responsibility for conduct that did a great deal to bring about the
widespread misery on which, according to "certain statistics," such conduct
was wrongly blamed.[19] To be sure, immoral behavior did not take place in
a vacuum. The point is, however, that it seemed to be linked, in the view
of these men, to other forms of immorality, either behavioral or attitudinal.
Pastor A. Stuhlmann insisted, as Weber did elsewhere, that sexual misconduct stemmed in large part from the consumption of alcohol. "The drunk,"
he wrote, "becomes indifferent toward honor, customs, and decency,
toward the laws and the entire civil and moral order." Alcohol lowered the
barriers against lust and permitted the beast in men to roam freely.[20]

What lay behind both alcoholism and impurity – and other forms of
immorality as well – was, most fundamentally, the declining acceptance of
right doctrines and the rise of wrong ones in their place. As Weber put it
in an introductory essay on the influence of the Church, Christianity was
under assault by a new *Zeitgeist* that reflected the growth of secularism and
materialism among the educated classes. The consequences were inevitable:
"From lack of faith in God, the highest authority and the integrating source
and core of the world, stems insubordination, bellicosity, deceit, theft,

---

und die Sittlichkeit (Berlin, 1901), 2–3, and, with warnings derived from the supposed decadence of
the modern French as well as that of the ancient Romans, Johann Fritsch, *Zerstörende Mächte im
Volksleben* (Berlin, 1903), 34. Both were originally delivered as lectures at meetings of the General
Conference. For a broader discussion of this theme, see George L. Mosse, *Nationalism and Sexuality:
Respectability and Abnormal Sexuality in Modern Europe* (New York, 1985).

18 Ludwig Weber, ed., *Geschichte der sittlich-religiösen und socialen Entwicklung Deutschlands in den letzten
35 Jahren: Zusammenhängende Einzelbilder von verschiedenen Verfassern* (Gütersloh, 1895).

19 Albrecht Romann, "Die Entwicklung des häuslichen Lebens in Deutschland," in Weber, *Geschichte*,
229. For a similar view elsewhere, see August Dieckmann, *Zerstörende Mächte in unserem Volksleben*
(Berlin, 1903), 18.

20 A. Stuhlmann, "Die Schuld des Alkoholmissbrauchs an den socialen Notständen," in Weber,
Geschichte, 184–5. See also Ludwig Weber, *Prostitution und Alcoholismus* (Bielefeld, 1910), 238–40.

suicide, drunkenness, desecration of the sabbath and all the other sins of the people."[21]

Other authors went into considerably greater detail in order to indict specific features of the modern mind. They developed at great length the view that destructive ideas percolated from above into the thinking of ordinary men and women with disastrous consequences for everyday behavior. In the realm of science Darwinism merited the most attention. It not only undermined religion but also seemed to legitimate a spirit of selfishness and ruthlessness in the pursuit of individual advantage.[22] In the area of social and political thought, first liberalism and then socialism pointed the way toward a new, immoral morality. Social democracy was attacked in several essays for its putative effects on the ethical standards of the individual. In Stuhlmann's words, "It overthrows in the hearts and minds of children everything that is conducive to moral conduct." The result was "disgusting undiscipline among young people."[23]

Finally, there was the complaint against modern trends in the area of artistic culture, which had, according to Karl Friedrich Jordan, permeated and polluted popular thinking. Originating in the experimental novels of Émile Zola, literary realism threatened to bring German values down to the low level of the French. Writers who depicted what was ugly and sordid did not encourage their readers to avoid it. Jordan wrote, "On the contrary: It is certain that as a result of being exposed to evil many people become accustomed to it, enter into its spirit, and receive the impulse to engage in it themselves." Dramatic literature was especially suspect. Henryk Ibsen, Hermann Sudermann, and Gerhard Hauptmann all stood accused of having helped pervert public morals. According to Jordan's line of thinking, governmental controls, including tighter censorship, were clearly required in order to stem the tide of cultural pollution.[24]

---

21 Ludwig Weber, "Der Einfluss der Kirche," in Weber, *Geschichte*, 5–9. See also Ludwig Weber, "Aus der Welt der Unzucht und des Verbrechens," in Weber, *Geschichte*, 421–2.

22 E. Dennert, "Der Einfluss der Naturwissenschaft auf die sittlich-religiöse Entwicklung Deutschlands in den letzten 35 Jahren," in Weber, *Geschichte*, 37–44. See also Weber, "Der Einfluss der Kirche," 8–9.

23 H. von Petersdorff, "Der Einfluss der politischen Entwicklung auf die sittlich-religiösen Zustände," in Weber, *Geschichte*, 18–22; Julius Werner, "Der Einfluss der socialen Lehren und Parteibildungen," in Weber, *Geschichte*, 135–41; A. Stuhlmann, "Die neueste Socialdemokratie," in Weber, *Geschichte*, 204. See also Weber, "Die Industriearbeiter," in Weber, *Geschichte*, 365.

24 Karl Friedrich Jordan, "Der Einfluss der Kunst auf die sittlich-religiöse Entwicklung Deutschlands," in Weber, *Geschichte*, 67–83 (quotation on 69). For other indictments of modern literature and art by men associated with the General Conference, see the following, all published in Berlin: Adolf Henning, *Die öffentliche Sittenlosigkeit und die Arbeit der Sittlichkeitsvereine*, 2d ed. (1897), 5–8 (with special attention to Nietzsche); Arnold Waubke, *Eine geistige Krankheit unserer Tage und ihre Heilung* (1899), 6–8; Adolf Bartels, *Geschlechtsleben und Dichtung* (1906); and Friedrich Bohn, *Die Münchener*

It bears noting that despite the generally cultural and censorious orientations displayed by Weber and the men he helped to lead, there were additional explanatory accents. There was among some members of the group a concomitant awareness of social and economic conditions as substantial contributors to the immoral conduct they all bemoaned. Pastor Walter Philipps of Berlin, one of the men who had worked most closely with Weber in the establishment of the General Conference, argued at the first convention that in an urban environment marked by quite bad housing only a level of personal heroism that most individuals simply could not be expected to display would enable them to live unblemished lives.[25] Weber himself clearly admitted and at some points emphasized the force of social circumstances in his attempts to construct an etiology of immoral conduct. In an essay on "The Influence of Material Hardships" he pointed to low wages and long hours of labor in addition to poor housing as factors that led, together with the lack of moral education, to violent criminality, to sexual improprieties, and to "the spirit of revolution."[26] Elsewhere, he drew what seemed to him to be the appropriate conclusions from such remarks. He espoused the view that a "social monarchy" should work with religious leaders in order to devise solutions to social problems that would help to stabilize the social order by combating both personal immorality and social immorality (that is, Social Democracy). Having already begun in the 1880s to support the formation of Evangelical workers' associations, Weber also supported greater rights for members of such groups to form trade unions and to engage in collective bargaining. He took this position both in his writings and through his membership in the Society for Social Reform (*Gesellschaft für soziale Reform*), one of several reformist umbrella groups to which he belonged.[27]

"Jugend" und die neue Moral (1906). Weber warmly welcomed a widely read pamphlet by Otto von Leixner, *Zum Kampfe gegen den Schmutz in Wort und Bild* (Leipzig, 1904), which denounced numerous phenomena within the area of popular culture as incitements to indecent behavior. On efforts to regulate culture that stemmed from moral considerations, see the following: Weber and Ellger, *25 Jahre*, 64–7, 72–4, 95–8, 102–4, 113, 127, 129, 131, 155–8, 171; Robin J. V. Lenman, "Art, Society and the Law in Wilhelmine Germany: The Lex Heinze," *Oxford German Studies* 8 (1973–4): 86–113; Gary D. Stark, "Pornography, Society, and the Law in Imperial Germany," *Central European History* 14 (1981): 200–229; Gary D. Stark, "Cinema, Society, and the State: Policing the Film Industry in Imperial Germany," in Gary D. Stark and Bede Karl Lackner, eds., *Essays on Culture and Society in Modern Germany* (College Station, Tex., 1982), 122–66; and Georg Jäger, "Der Kampf gegen Schmutz und Schund: Die Reaktion der Gebildeten auf die Unterhaltungsindustrie," *Archiv für Geschichte des Buchwesens* 31 (1988): 163–91.

25 Walter Philipps, *Schlechte Wohnungsverhältnisse, eine Quelle der Unsittlichkeit* (Berlin, 1889), 7–11.
26 Ludwig Weber, "Der Einfluss der materiellen Zustände," in Weber, *Geschichte*, 171–8.
27 Ludwig Weber, *Die sozialen Aufgaben und der Anteil der Kirche an ihrer Lösung: Hundert Leit- und Streitsätze* (Gütersloh, 1906), 6–9, 11–12; Lewek, *Kirche und soziale Frage*, 47–78; Weber, *Lebenserinnerungen*, 22–3. See also Ursula Ratz, *Sozialreform und Arbeiterschaft: Die "Gesellschaft für Soziale*

IV

It was, however, in another sector of the German *Bürgertum* that the themes of personal morality and social reform were most closely linked. It was among reform-minded liberals who, while retaining a clear identity as Protestants, operated to a much greater extent than did Weber beyond the confines of confessional campaigns. The classic instance of this approach is to be found in the life and writings of Viktor Böhmert – a man identified by Weber as a potential ally who chose to remain outside Weber's immediate orbit.[28] Böhmert stood at the center of other orbits. Born the son of a Saxon clergyman in 1829 and educated in economics and law at the University of Leipzig, he taught economics in Zurich from 1866 to 1875. He then was named to a professorship at the Technical Institute in Dresden and to the position of chief statistician of Saxony. He held the first position until 1903, the second until 1895. He also pursued a parallel career as a publicist. Between 1873 and 1914 he edited and wrote numerous articles for, among other publications, a quarterly journal known as *Der Arbeiterfreund* (The Worker's Friend), which appeared under the auspices of the Central Association for the Well-being of the Working Classes.[29] He also helped to found and served for many years as the chairman of the Association Against Poverty and Begging in Dresden, the Dresden District Association Against the Abuse of Alcoholic Beverages, and another Dresden group known as the Verein Volkswohl (Association for Popular Well-Being), whose members sought to promote adult education and other wholesome activities during leisure hours. Along the same lines, he participated actively in the affairs of the German Society for Care of the Poor and for Charity and the affairs of the German Society for the Spread of Popular Education.[30]

Like Weber and many other clergymen, Böhmert was appalled by several aspects of the moral landscape in the late nineteenth century. "Two of the worst domestic enemies," he warned, "that haunt the nation as a result of

Reform" und die sozialdemokratische Arbeiterbewegung von der Jahrhundertwende bis zum Ausbruch des Ersten Weltkrieges (Berlin, 1980), 36, 46, 60, 103–4.

28 Weber and Ellger, *25 Jahre*, 43. For comments by Böhmert on Weber, see Viktor Böhmert, *Der Kampf gegen die Unsittlichkeit* (Leipzig, 1888), 11; and "Die Mässigkeits- und Sittlichkeits-Bestrebungen als Grundlage der Sozialreform," *Der Arbeiterfreund* (hereafter *AF*) 28 (1890): 357–8.

29 On the early history of the Central Association, see Jürgen Reulecke, *Sozialer Frieden durch soziale Reform: Der Centralverein für das Wohl der arbeitenden Klassen in der Frühindustrialisierung* (Wuppertal, 1983). The association was established in 1844.

30 For biographical details, see Viktor Böhmert, "Rückblicke und Ausblicke eines Siebzigers," *AF* 37 (1899): 245–67, 376–404; and "Erinnerungen und Lebensauffassungen eines Achtzigers," *AF* 47 (1909): 243–56. See also James S. Roberts, *Drink, Temperance, and the Working Class in Nineteenth-Century Germany* (Boston, 1984), 64–7.

the materialistic tendency nowadays are alcoholism and impurity. Wars and exterior enemies kill only a few hundred thousand in a matter of decades, but alcoholism and impurity claim millions of our countrymen as victims every year." There was no need to fear conquerors from abroad, but there was a need for more godliness and more efforts to combat "the inner enemies of German morality." Manual laborers required especially close attention. The shortening of their workdays afforded them added time in which to drink, which in turn exacerbated sexual misconduct. But noblemen and burghers were also falling from grace, and vigorous efforts were required to set matters right throughout German society – efforts that would have to involve the best energies of individuals and of private associations as well as of governments.[31]

Although echoing Weber's moralizing in many ways, Böhmert's moral message reverberated with a much sharper insistence on the need for what Jürgen Reulecke and Rüdiger vom Bruch have referred to as *bürgerliche Sozialreform* (bourgeois social reform) and what Paul Boyer, writing about American developments, has referred to as "positive environmentalism."[32] Böhmert paid less attention to high culture and to "smut and trash" as supposed causes of bad deeds than he did to the absence of channels through which ordinary people could satisfy their need for pleasure in socially acceptable ways. He sought to construct a social domain in which enlightened members of the middle classes would join forces less for the purpose of suppressing what was deplorable than toward the end of providing rational and ultimately more satisfying alternatives to it.

Attempting to transcend both confessional and political limitations (he repeatedly emphasized the nonpartisan quality of his programs), Böhmert advocated, among other strategies, what he referred to in the title of one of his essays as "the advancement of workers' welfare through a reform of popular sociability (*Volksgeselligkeit*)." The social question, he argued, was by no means simply a matter of the production and distribution of goods but also a matter of the proper consumption of goods, which led directly to the matter of recreation. It was "a question of personal relationships between human beings, a cultural and educational question that must be solved primarily through better customs and habits from above and from below." Looking toward the example set by private associations in Britain and in the United States in the struggle against alcohol, he called for more parks, more coffee houses, more libraries, and more institutions comparable

31 Böhmert, *Der Kampf*, 7, 21; and "Die Mässigkeits- und Sittlichkeits-Bestrebungen," 345, 347, 362–3.
32 See notes 10 and 11 to this chapter.

to Toynbee Hall in East London, the first settlement house. In such settings, he asserted, members of various social classes could come together in the common pursuit of healthy recreation outside their often all too cramped places of residence.[33]

Throughout his later years Böhmert not only advocated such efforts but also reported on them, celebrating what he regarded as a series of vital contributions to the creation of a more humane and potentially more harmonious society. He gave pride of place to the work done by the Dresden Association for Popular Well-Being (Verein Volkswohl), which he headed, describing its recreational facilities for children and adults in great detail. But he was also keenly aware of developments in other cities, which led him to conclude in 1911, toward the end of his long and illustrious career as a social reformer, that the preceding two decades had witnessed a great improvement in the quality of social life. "One no longer speaks," he wrote, "of *workers'* amusements and *workers'* festivals and separate working classes and workers' well-being, but instead of popular entertainments, popular recreations, popular well-being, and popular associations, in which all estates work together not merely as comrades but also as members of executive committees."[34]

In addition to recreational reforms, Böhmert called for – and welcomed – a wide range of other measures designed to improve working-class life in such a way that his overall objective of social harmony between the classes would also be advanced. He called on employers, for instance, to set up profit-sharing schemes for their employees, thus further enhancing a spirit of interclass cooperation. Moreover, although he was reluctant to look to the state for solutions to social questions, he recognized that it too had a role to play in the promotion of social peace, both through the protection of working-class rights to organize and through the provision of social insurance.[35] The main point, however, was to keep pushing for the expansion of a program of urban welfare that would reflect the social engagement of middle-class progressives.

Although the confinements of space do not permit me to adduce here anything like the full range of examples that would be needed in order to

33 Viktor Böhmert, "Die Förderung des Arbeiterwohls durch eine Reform der Volksgeselligkeit," *AF* 27 (1889): 1–18; and "Volksgeselligkeit," *AF* 36 (1898): 1–17.
34 Viktor Böhmert, "Volkswohlfahrt und Volksgeselligkeit im Dresdner Verein Volkswohl von 1888 bis 1910," *AF* 49 (1911): 43–65 (esp. 64). See also Viktor Böhmert, "Die Kulturelle und soziale Tätigkeit des Dresdner Vereins Volkswohl von 1888–1913," *AF* 51 (1913): 392–403.
35 Viktor Böhmert, "Individualismus und Sozialismus – Individualreform und Sozialreform," *AF* 42 (1904): 403–8; and "Was verdanken die Arbeiter und Unternehmer dem wiedererstandenen deutschen Kaiserreich?" *AF* 51 (1913): 124.

make clear the representativeness of Böhmert's responses to urban immorality, I do wish to make some remarks about a second individual who can quite
usefully be set next to him as a proponent and practitioner of *bürgerlich* social
reform. We now turn to Johannes Tews, the leading advocate of *Volksbildung*,
which literally means "popular education" but refers more particularly in
Tews's context to adult education.

Born in 1860 into a farmer's family in Pomerania, Tews compensated
for his lack of initial advantages by utilizing his clearly superior abilities
with great industry. Having spent half a year while he was only fifteen years
old as a substitute teacher in a school in a small town, and having thereafter completed a three-year training program at a teacher-training institute,
Tews soon moved to Berlin. In the nation's capital, about the attractiveness
of which he expressed great enthusiasm, he participated vigorously in the
affairs of the teachers' associations, where he strongly supported democrat-
ically oriented efforts to reform public schools. He also penned numerous
contributions for Theodor Barth's progressive magazine, *Die Nation*, and for
the well-known magazine *Soziale Praxis*. Generally supportive of "social"
liberalism, he placed particular emphasis on the need to provide enhanced
opportunities for continuing education for men and women who had completed their formal schooling. The advancement of *Volksbildung* was his
major objective, and he pursued it for many years as the secretary of the
Society for the Spread of Adult Education (a position he accepted in 1890),
even though he continued to work as a schoolteacher for a decade and a
half after the start of his secretaryship.[36]

What matters here is less Tews's organizational and administrative activity
than his thinking about the relationships between his activities as an educator and the moral condition of his country, a theme about which he wrote
repeatedly. He addressed this subject most pointedly in a lecture he delivered to an association of teachers in Posen, to whom he spoke about "the
meaning of *Volksbildung* for the ethical development of our people." In this
lecture he assessed critically some of the conclusions that had been drawn
from criminal statistics by men whom he described as ignorant or dishonest
reactionaries. Clergymen in particular exaggerated the extent of criminality,
attempting thereby to create an inaccurate impression that modern civilization was degenerating. They sought to uphold a long-standing but not at all

---

36 For biographical background, see Johannes Tews, *Aus Arbeit und Leben: Erinnerungen und Rückblicke*
(Berlin, 1921). For scattered references to him and for the context within which he worked, see
Horst Dräger, *Die Gesellschaft für Verbreitung von Volksbildung* (Stuttgart, 1975) and Paul Röhrig,
"Erwachsenenbildung," in Christa Berg, ed., *Handbuch der deutschen Bildungsgeschichte*, vol. 4: *1870–
1918* (Munich, 1987), 441–71.

convincing tradition among writers according to which there was an inverse relationship between learning and morals. Hostility to *Bildung*, which could be traced as far back as the period when Jean-Jacques Rousseau was writing his diatribes against the arts and sciences and detected more recently in the writings of Cesare Lombroso, served as an attitudinal weapon in the hands of men who were waging a defensive war against modern progress.[37]

By contrast, Tews strove to explain the causes of what he believed was not an increasing but instead a decreasing rate of criminality by means of a quite different strategy of interpretation. In his view, criminal behavior – which admittedly was still too high, even though it was declining – stemmed in large measure from causes that were quite different from the growth of educational opportunity. The increasing density of a growing population led to various sorts of friction, the refinement of legal thought resulted in the ascription of criminal characteristics to more and more actions, and sentences of imprisonment following convictions tended to stimulate rather than discourage criminal behavior. Fortunately, however, such tendencies were more than outweighed by progressive developments in the area of education, the beneficial impact of which was clearly evident from the fact that in Prussia the educationally retrograde East was more prone to criminality than the more advanced West.[38]

Tews thus stood out more as a defender than as a critic of the big-city milieu, whose remaining defects were to be remedied by means of urban actions and institutions. "The cultivation of the intellect, which has freed humanity from the yoke of barbarism and from economic need," he wrote, "will also contribute to its liberation from the dross and the filth of immorality." In this way it would help to reinforce the leading role of the metropolises in the formation of a social conscience, which Tews was later to celebrate with unmistakable admiration in a book on big-city education. "Social sensitivity," he wrote, "becomes livelier when human beings move closer to one another." The big cities, he asserted, were the places in which "the sense of community" could develop most vigorously, and continuing education for adults, fostered by the initiatives of independent associations, were to play an extremely important role in this connection.[39]

Here was an unmistakable counterpart to the beliefs and efforts of Viktor Böhmert: a view of "immorality" that was based on the fundamentally optimistic conviction that deviant behavior was susceptible to ameliorative

---

37 Johannes Tews, *Die Bedeutung der Volksbildung für die sittliche Entwickelung unseres Volkes* (Berlin, 1901), 7, 10–12.
38 Ibid., 20–23, 27.
39 Johannes Tews, *Grossstadtpädagogik* (Leipzig, 1911), 13.

action by means of the rational management of leisure time in pedagogical settings, in which members of the *Bürgertum* would work to improve morals by spreading improved culture and sociability. Like Böhmert, Tews developed projects for ethical elevation in ways that involved not simply using the city as a staging ground for morality leagues but also capitalizing on the cities' advantages in a whole host of other ways. Moral improvement, urbanism, and positive environmentalism were all parts of the same overall strategy for utilizing the resources of civil society in ways that did not directly involve the state in order to make an urban society more civilized and more moral.

V

Analyses of and strategies for combating "immoral" conduct constituted central components of discursive efforts by German burghers to develop and maintain a sense of social identity that set them apart in their own minds in the social hierarchy.[40] "Victorian" moralizing in Imperial Germany may be regarded not only as a formative element in a project of cultural self-definition but also as an important aspect of an attempt to achieve a certain degree of social mastery: mastery over the increasingly problematic world of the *Grossstadt*, which seemed to seethe with moral disorder; and mastery over the urban masses, whose putative misconduct as individuals seemed to go hand-in-hand with the larger threat posed by Social Democracy. Indeed, self-mastery was often preached as an essential ingredient of the strategy for legitimating an ongoing role for men of the middle classes as moral guarantors of social stability. Much of this discourse had unquestionably defensive implications, and much of what I have written in this chapter pertains to men whose social and political conservatism was unmistakable. In line, however, with Thomas Nipperdey's insistence on transcending the view of the late Kaiserreich as an *Untertanen-Gesellschaft* (society of subjects),[41] I would emphasize that the language of moral concern also lent itself to progressive projects of social reform. Moral defensiveness stimulated not only calls for repression but also a wide range of proposals for and

40 On efforts at definition via distinction, see Jürgen Kocka, "Bürgertum und bürgerliche Gesellschaft im 19. Jahrhundert: Europäische Entwicklungen und deutsche Eigenarten," in Jürgen Kocka, ed., *Bürgertum im 19. Jahrhundert: Deutschland im europäischen Vergleich*, 1 (Munich, 1988), 26–7; and David Blackbourn, "The German Bourgeoisie: An Introduction," in David Blackbourn, ed., *The German Bourgeoisie: Essays on the Social History of the German Middle Class from the Late Eighteenth to the Early Twentieth Century* (London, 1991), 9–10.

41 Thomas Nipperdey, "War die Wilhelminische Gesellschaft eine Untertanen-Gesellschaft?" in Thomas Nipperdey, *Nachdenken über die deutsche Geschichte: Essays* (Munich, 1986), 172–85.

movements toward a society marked by interclass cooperation and social harmony.

Discourse on morality among spokesmen for the German *Bürgertum* reflected diverse concerns and pointed in various directions, including not only repression but also reform. Pervasive fears of alcohol and sexuality in an increasingly urban society that was marked by the rise of Social Democracy stemmed from a great deal more than a conservative longing for a return to a *heile Welt* (harmonious world), they frequently pointed toward amelioration of rather than flight from the big city, and they had not only defensive but also progressive implications. Varying treatments of the theme of moral reform reflected divergent tendencies within the middle class. Although some critics of immoral behavior emphasized the need for control from above, many others were much more sensitive to the need for positive inducements to behave well. Although religious conservatives painted a picture of present conditions that was fundamentally gloomy, men who were closer to the ideological center regarded with satisfaction what they saw as encouraging trends that held out a real prospect of both social and moral improvement – trends that embodied the continuation of *bürgerlich* activism in independent associations as well as the growth of state intervention.

The interpretive tensions among the contemporary commentators on immorality and moral reform who have been treated in this chapter were analogous to the tensions that pervaded much of the writing during this period that was produced by men who were more specifically concerned with the phenomenon of crime. Among "moral entrepreneurs" as well as among "criminologists" there was an ongoing debate between advocates of control and repression and advocates of efforts to bridge the gap between moral discourse and social science. An important part of the context for criminology was a vigorous debate about the relationships between control and reform in general, beneath which large elements of the debates among the criminologists can also be subsumed.

What I wish to emphasize in conclusion is the way in which the social environmentalism that was represented by men such as Böhmert and Tews was echoed in much of the writing about unlawfulness per se. In his chapter on "The Criminologists' Gaze at the Underworld" Peter Becker clearly shows that among men who sought to combat the "criminalists'" view of criminals as "fallen angels," there was considerable attention devoted to social as well as to hereditary conditioning. Peter Fritzsche, in his chapter on the journalistic reporting of the murder of Lucie Berlin, points still more clearly to the ways in which violent crime served for many observers as an indicator of social ills. To be sure, there is a great deal of evidence that the views of those who emphasized individual responsibility were contested not only by social environmentalists but also by followers of Cesare Lombroso and his view of criminality as an outgrowth of the criminal's inheritance. It bears emphasis, however, that even in Germany hereditarianism – though certainly ascendant – was by no means triumphant, at least before World War I. To mention only a few of the men who placed primary emphasis on social factors, Abraham Baer, Franz von Liszt, and Gustav Aschaffenburg were unquestionably among the leading students of crime during the Imperial period.[42] Indeed, as Richard F. Wetzell shows in his chapter, the intellectual sway of criminal biology was vigorously contested by social environmentalists during the Weimar and the Nazi years as well as in the period on which I have focused in this chapter.

---

42 Abraham Baer, *Der Verbrecher in anthropologischer Beziehung* (Leipzig, 1893); Franz von Liszt, *Strafrechtliche Aufsätze und Vorträge*, 2 vols. (Berlin, 1905); Gustav Aschaffenburg, *Crime and Its Repression*, trans. Adalbert Albrecht (Boston, 1913).

5

The Criminologists' Gaze at the Underworld

Toward an Archaeology of Criminological Writing

PETER BECKER

When criminologists scrutinized the bodies and minds of criminals at the end of the nineteenth century, they explored new fields of criminological evidence but lost sight of the social practices and everyday lives of their subjects. They met criminals in hospital wards and penitentiaries where the subjects of their intellectual curiosity were removed from their proper social, cultural, and familial matrix. Within this institutional setting criminologists had only restricted access to criminals' identities. This restriction was not seen as a real constraint because it was fully compatible with the criminologists' conceptual framework. Only on some occasions did criminologists feel the need to include additional evidence in their narratives that lay beyond the reach of clinical experiments and anthropological examinations. When they felt compelled to introduce information about the criminals' lifeworld, reproduction, habits, and social institutions, criminologists usually turned to literary accounts and the knowledge of practitioners in the field, such as the German police expert Friedrich Christian Benedikt Avé-Lallemant, who was writing several decades earlier than his criminological counterparts.

Criminological discourse underwent a systematic transformation during the last decades of the nineteenth century. Practitioners working in the field of crime detection and prevention, and arguing from the perspective of a moral-ethical paradigm, lost ground. Their role in the production of criminological knowledge was taken over by doctors, anthropologists, psychiatrists, and criminal law experts who looked at the problem of crime and deviance from the perspective of social and/or biological determinism. These authors had difficulty integrating the knowledge of practitioners and medical experts of the first two-thirds of the nineteenth century into their narratives, as they were based on a different master narrative. In the first three sections of this chapter I discuss some strategies that criminologists used to exploit the evidence presented by earlier writers. I will, however, begin with a brief introduction to the two types of criminological discourse. In the conclusion, a comparison between the discursive strategies of criminologists and practitioners will look at the transformation from the earlier to the later discursive formation from another perspective.[1]

A large portion of this chapter uses the criminologists' look at the reflections of practitioners on criminal identity. The criminologists' sporadic reading and quoting of the works of earlier practitioners was part of a more general pattern. The criminologists' open and explorative approach required and enabled them to integrate a wide variety of evidence: Friedrich Schiller, Franz Joseph Gall, Fyodor Dostojevsky, and medical as well as legal experts of the nineteenth century stood next to criminalistic practitioners within the intellectual horizon of criminologists; all these sources contributed to the emergence of new theories about crime and the criminal. An analysis of the integration of the criminological insights of practitioners into the arguments of criminologists should provide evidence for a discussion of the limits and possibilities of a transfer of evidence across the divide of two different discursive formations.

The concepts and the methodology of this chapter are inspired by Michel Foucault's archaeology of knowledge, especially by his reflections on the transformation and change of discursive formations. The archaeological method directs our interest to the rules that structured criminological discourses as well as to the role assigned to these discourses within a field of nondiscursive practices. From Foucault's perspective, these rules define many different aspects of discursive practice, such as the position of the writing and speaking subject, the privileged sites of empirical investigation and theoretical reasoning, the admission of certain objects as evidence, and the ways in which individual pieces of evidence are linked to each other in order to produce a coherent narrative. Foucault's archaeology demands consideration of further elements, tracing several different levels, from the primary relations between the objects, their representation in the discourse, and the formation of discursive strategies.

A comprehensive archaeology of the two discursive formations of criminological writing cannot be accomplished in the space of this chapter. Most of the aspects mentioned must remain in the background of the argument,

---

1 In this chapter I continue the argument that I developed in a book on the representation of criminals in nineteenth-century criminalistic and criminological discourse. See Peter Becker, *Verderbnis und Entartung: Eine Geschichte der Kriminologie des 19. Jahrhunderts als Diskurs und Praxis* (Göttingen, 2002). Comprehensive references to document the reconstruction of the two differing narratives can be found in this volume. For the purpose of this chapter, I restrict the references mostly to the reconstruction of links and interfaces between the two narratives. For helpful comments and thoughtful critique I am strongly indebted to Glenda Sluga and to all participants of the 1998 conference on the history of criminology in Florence.

such as the links between each discursive formation and nondiscursive practice on the one hand and the position of the researchers/authors to their
objects on the other hand. I focus, instead, on one particular aspect of an
archaeology of criminological writing, namely on the transformation of one
discursive formation into another. Using Foucault's archaeological method,
we will be able to avoid the pitfalls of constructing a history of criminological thinking in which the names of great thinkers are assembled like pearls
on a rosary. The archaeological method will therefore provide a suitable
conceptual framework to understand the continuities and changes among
the writings of criminalistic practitioners and their academically based
counterparts.

TWO APPROACHES TO CRIMINAL IDENTITY

Starting in the late nineteenth century, criminologists began to develop a
theoretical and empirical stance toward the bodies and minds of individual
criminals, while neglecting to research the *criminal underworld*. The social,
psychological, and physiological constitutions of criminals were carefully
cataloged and studied. The results were used to support contested theories
about the origins of criminal activities. Even though there was no agreement
on one single theory, the theories shared basic elements.[2] They offered an
explanation for the inception of criminal activities that held genetic and/or
detrimental environmental factors responsible. From this perspective, criminals, tramps, and prostitutes were the victims of forces beyond their control
because they faced the world without the necessary mental and physiological resources to cope with the demands of a modern, highly competitive
world. At the heart of the criminologists' shared belief in the incomplete
mental and physical evolution of degenerates and atavistic beings is a master
narrative, the sense of which is best captured by the phrase "impaired men."

Criminological discourse and practice aimed at an "objectivizing of
the subject" in what Michel Foucault calls "dividing practices." Foucault
describes this concept as follows: "The subject is either divided inside himself
or divided from others. This process objectivizes him. Examples are . . . the
criminals and the 'good boys.'"[3] Foucault's notion can easily be applied
to our analysis of the criminologists' gaze as directed at criminals. Using

---

2 For a more detailed account of criminological thought at the turn of the centuries, see the chapters by
Mary Gibson, Martine Kaluszynski, and Laurent Mucchielli in this book. See also Laurent Mucchielli,
"Hérédité et milieu social: le faux-antagonisme franco-italien," in Laurent Mucchielli, ed., *Histoire de
la criminologie française* (Paris, 1994), 189–214.
3 Michel Foucault, "Afterword. The Subject and Power," in Hubert L. Dreyfus and Paul Rabinow,
eds., *Michel Foucault: Beyond Structuralism and Hermeneutics*, 2d ed. (Chicago, 1983), 208.

his trained eye the anthropologist or medical expert acting as criminological observer "divided" criminals into physical, emotional, and psychological beings. The experts applied their specialized physiological, anatomical, anthropological, and psychiatric knowledge to divide the bodies of their subjects into meaningful entities.[4] Highly specialized methods of examination were supposed to support the criminological argument that deviations from the norm could be explained as the result of an individual's impaired evolution. Moreover, there was a further realm where dividing practices were of crucial importance: the organization of the criminologists' empirical field of evidence. They studied the "alien beast" in isolation, that is, in hospital wards and prisons.

Theories of degeneration and atavism directed attention to the physical, mental, and emotional characteristics of criminals, all of which could be quantified, graphically represented, and communicated in a seemingly "objective" manner. Crime and deviance were therefore considered a form of behavior that could best be tackled by a clinical approach. Criminals as objects of the clinical gaze were abstracted from their social environment and subjected to a specialized gaze on their bodies and their responses to psycho-physiological experiments, which were so important to criminological researchers.[5] The application of a clinical method had further impact on criminological reasoning. The rules for the anamnesis (the procedure of establishing a past medical history) of crime as a form of disease directed the attention of the investigating criminologist to the realm of heredity.

The conceptual and physical isolation of the criminal from his social environment was a distinctive feature of the criminological approach. This becomes all the more obvious if we compare the criminologists' to the criminalists' style of studying criminals. The authors, whom I refer to as criminalists, were practitioners in law enforcement agencies, and some used their spare time to reflect on crime and criminals in a rather systematic way. Their thoughts were published as monographs and in specialized police journals, or were communicated in memoranda to the policy-making authorities. These authors dominated the discourse on crime and criminals in the pre-1848 period (*Vormärz*) and the subsequent era of reaction in the 1850s and 1860s.

When they tried to make sense of the stunning insight that the modernization of state and society did not lead to a reduction, let alone the

---

4 This dividing gaze materialized not the least in the numerous criminological museums, where skulls, pieces of skin, and other significant parts of the criminals' bodies were displayed for research and teaching.
5 See David Horn's chapter in this book. An in-depth discussion about the usage of tattoos as criminological evidence can be found in Jane Caplan's chapter in this book.

disappearance of crime and deviance, these practitioners used a moral-philosophical perspective instead of an anthropological one. Attentive observers saw themselves confronted with threatening evidence: Criminal activity was increasing and seemed to corrupt more and more people. Following Immanuel Kant, criminalists firmly believed in every single person's free will to choose between a moral and an immoral life.[6] In this approach to criminal identity they incorporated legal and empirical knowledge in much the same way their English counterparts did. They all shared a high estimation of the potential rationality and self-mastery of "reasonable men," as Martin Wiener argues in this book.[7]

The German criminalists differed from their English counterparts in one important respect: They found a theoretical solution to account for the obvious conflict between every individual's potential for self-determination and the many occasions when people lost full control over their behavior. Based on their own observations and on readings of forensic cases, criminalists especially blamed the disastrous consequences of alcoholism, gambling, and the like for trapping people in a vicious lifestyle.[8] They readily acknowledged that a life consumed by corruption could have ensnarled someone in situations where it was no longer possible to make an autonomous choice. This kind of reasoning was already of crucial importance during the French Revolution as a means of transforming legal idealism into the bureaucratic management of crime, as Marc Renneville points out in his chapter. French authors of that time were moved by the same disillusionment as their German counterparts. Even though French authors readily acknowledged the importance of a person's background for the explanation of criminal careers, their research was not as strongly biographical as the studies of German criminalists.[9]

The biographical method enabled criminalists to hold liable even those criminals who acted under restricted freedom of choice. Forensic

---

6 Kant used the concept of *Gesinnung*, meaning one's maxim for the way of acting, as the crucial dividing line between good and evil: This argument can be traced especially in Kant's writings on religion. See Immanuel Kant, *Die Religion innerhalb der Grenzen der blossen Vernunft (1793)* (Werkausgabe, vol. 8) (Frankfurt am Main, 1977), 669, and was closely linked to his conception of the "radical evil." See Christoph Schulte, "Böses und Psyche: Immoralität in psychologischen Diskursen," in Carsten Colpe and Wilhelm Schmidt-Biggemann, eds., *Das Böse: Eine historische Phänomenologie des Unerklärlichen* (Frankfurt am Main, 1993), 302ff; Christoph Schulte, *Radikal böse: Die Karriere des Bösen von Kant bis Nietzsche* (Munich, 1988), 106.
7 See Martin J. Wiener's chapter in this book.
8 A telling example of this awareness is the book of the Berlin-based criminal police expert Merker on the reasons for the increasing number of property offenses: Johann Friedrich Karl Merker, *Hauptquellen der Verbrechen gegen die Eigenthums-Sicherheit in Berlin, mit Hindeutung auf die Möglichkeit der Verminderung derselben* (Berlin, 1839).
9 See Marc Renneville's chapter in this book.

psychiatrists and criminalists believed that everyone should be held responsible for their choice of a vicious life. This conceptual framework permitted legal and medical experts to blame criminals for punishable acts that were committed in a state of mental derangement.[10] Friedrich Nietzsche criticized this legal and philosophical approach in a highly sarcastic manner by pointing to the surprising separation of the concept of freedom from the realm of acting: "Freiheit also, so oder so zu sein, nicht so oder so zu handeln." (Freedom therefore to be one way or another, and not to act in one way or another.)[11]

Criminalists were therefore interested not only in the criminal and his/her personality at the time of committing a crime but also in his/her biography. From the biographies they could learn about the decisive turning points when someone voluntarily turned away from being a reasonable man and chose an immoral course. A turning point was not necessarily linked to crime but rather to a perpetrator's first manifestation of a detached view of bourgeois morality, which revealed itself through contempt for productive work, an excessive consumption of liquor, gambling, and premature contacts with prostitutes. The criminalists were deeply convinced that these first steps on the "downward slope" usually led to destitution, crime, or insanity. Only one possible remedy was identified: the prolonged reeducation of the "fallen" in family-like institutions, such as the Rauhes Haus in Hamburg, funded by the state and charitable organizations.[12] From this perspective, reform measures were feasible especially for juvenile delinquents, who had to be taken out of their corrupting environments and "regenerated" by strict discipline, moral improvement, and the habituation of a new lifestyle.

---

10 See Johannes Baptista Friedreich, *System der gerichtlichen Psychologie*, 2d ed. (Regensburg, 1842), 106; Johann Christian August Heinroth, *Grundzüge der Criminal-Psychologie; oder, Die Theorie des Bösen in ihrer Anwendung auf die Criminal-Rechtspflege* (Berlin, 1833), 85–6. A brief introduction to Heinroth's theories can be found in Klaus Dörner, *Bürger und Irre. Zur Sozialgeschichte und Wissenschaftsgeschichte der Psychiatrie*, 2d rev. ed. (Frankfurt am Main, 1984), 257ff.

11 Friedrich Nietzsche, *Menschliches, Allzumenschliches: Ein Buch für freie Geister (1878)* (KSA 2) (Munich, 1988), 63.

12 On this institution, see Johann Hinrich Wichern, *Zur Erziehungs- und Rettungshausarbeit: Aufsätze, Berichte und Tagebuchblätter*, pt. 1: *Das Rauhe Haus*, Gesammelte Schriften Johann Hinrich Wicherns, vol. 5 (Hamburg, 1902), esp. 187ff. On reeducation in Germany, see also Christoph Sachsse and Florian Tennstedt, *Geschichte der Armenfürsorge: Vom Spätmittelalter bis zum 1. Weltkrieg* (Stuttgart, 1980), 229ff; the Hanover police expert Carl Georg Ludwig Wermuth emphasized the need for sufficient spatial distance from a corrupted family background as a precondition of a successful reeducation of children ("Zusammenstellung der wesentlichen Verhältnisse der Königlichen Polizei-Verwaltung zu Hannover von 1846–1862," Hauptstaatsarchiv Hannover, Dep. 103, IX, Nr. 76, 60f). On the theory and practice of these institutions outside Germany, see Jeroen Dekker, "Rituals and Re-education in the Nineteenth Century: Ritual and Moral Education in a Dutch Children's Home," *Continuity and Change* 9 (1994): 132ff.

The "criminology" of the practitioners was based on fundamental philosophical and anthropological conceptions of the late eighteenth and early nineteenth centuries. One of the main premises was the fundamental equality of respectable citizens and professional criminals with respect to their potential to strive for moral and ethical perfection, or at least to resist numerous temptations. In practice, only a limited number of people were considered able to achieve the high standards of bourgeois respectability. An ever-increasing number of people were seen as constantly threatened by moral corruption. These people, mostly men, defined a middle group whose members had to be protected by the law and the police against temptations of many kinds. One of the most serious temptations was identified as being exerted by a third group of people, professional criminals (*Gauner*). Their sportive and easygoing lifestyle, their elegance and affluence, their attempts to corrupt innkeepers and other respectable citizens, and their efforts to bribe policemen, were identified as a central threat to the security of state and society.[13] In the writings of practitioners, *Gauner* were characterized as members of the criminal underworld and conceptualized as negative instances of the bourgeois ideal type.[14] In short, they were conceptualized as *fallen men*, an image which acted as a master narrative in this discourse.[15]

This short outline of the discursive formations and the two corresponding master narratives about crime and criminals should reveal their distinctiveness but also the connections between them. There was, however, a major difference regarding the links between these master narratives and nondiscursive practices. Criminalists wrote as practitioners with an immediate interest in turning their insights into new or refined strategies to combat and prevent crime. Criminologists, who dominated the production of insights about criminals from the late nineteenth century onward, looked at criminals mostly from their academic vantage points in anthropology, medicine,

13 See, for example, Franz Andreas Wennmohs, *Über Gauner und über das zweckmässigste, vielmehr einzige Mittel zur Vertilgung dieses Übels,* vol. 1: *Schilderung des Gauners nach seiner Menge und Schädlichkeit, in seinem Betriebe, nach seinem Äussern und als Inquisiten* (Güstrow, 1823), 86f; see also Carl Falkenberg, *Versuch einer Darstellung der verschiedenen Classen von Räubern, Dieben und Diebeshehlern, mit besonderer Hinsicht auf die vorzüglichsten Mittel sich ihrer zu bemächtigen, ihre Verbrechen zu entdecken und zu verhüten: Ein Handbuch für Polizeibeamte, Criminalisten und Gensd'armen,* 2 vols. (Berlin, 1816), 1:157ff.

14 In contemporary writings, the world of *Gauner* was rather closely linked to Jews. The most dangerous criminals were believed to come from Jewish origins. A more detailed analysis of this part of the criminalists' argument can be found in Peter Becker, "Randgruppen im Blickfeld der Polizei: Ein Versuch über die Perspektivität des 'praktischen Blicks,'" *Archiv für Sozialgeschichte* 32 (1992): 283–304, here 294; see also Michael Berkowitz's chapter in this book.

15 See Peter Becker, "'Gefallene Engel' und 'verhinderte Menschen': Über 'Erzählmuster,' Prostituierte und die Kriminalistik des vorigen Jahrhunderts," in Detlev Frehsee, Gabi Löschper, and Gerlinda Smaus, eds., *Konstruktion der Wirklichkeit durch Kriminalität und Strafe* (Baden-Baden, 1997), 333ff.

and psychiatry. Their aim was not so much focused on a refinement of police procedures but rather on the design of a new set of preventive strategies.

Despite these unbridgeable differences, there were correspondences between the two approaches. Both criminologists and practitioners were not merely interested in the criminal as someone who had committed a specific crime but rather in the criminal as an anthropological, sociological, or moral-ethical *type*. Both of them were not only intellectually concerned with crime and deviance. Their work was intended to contribute to the development of administrative techniques to rid society of criminals and deviants.[16]

The common basis of shared interests and strategies of criminologists and practitioners did not preclude the emergence of a variety of different constructions of the criminal type. Criminalists used evidence different from criminologists; their focus was on biographies, social networks, and the social as well as physical reproduction of the criminal world. Some of their books and articles follow an almost ethnographic style, even though their "thick description" was very specific and aimed at the final destruction of the social realities under scrutiny.[17] The "ethnographic" accounts of the criminal underworld were based on the same binary code that informed the construction of criminal identities. The underworld was represented as a negative mirror image of bourgeois society. It was structured along the same lines as the world of respectability: Families, crafts, associations, and cooperative forms of "work" seemed to dominate the criminal as well as the bourgeois world. In the criminal world, all institutions were tainted, however, by a lack of loyalty, a lack of interest in the common good, and a lack of reason.[18] Drawing on analogies on the social reproduction in bourgeois society, families and wider social networks in the criminal world were considered to be of crucial importance. Genealogies that were carefully assembled by the practitioners were among the evidence used to prove this point.

Criminologists, by contrast, had a stronger interest in the body than in the lifeworld of criminals. A highly specialized, categorizing approach to the observation of the skull, skin, organs, and reflexes of criminals was said

---

16 This approach was based on shared beliefs about the importance of prevention. It was therefore linked but not restricted to theoretical discussions within the legal profession about prevention which Monika Frommel discussed in *Präventionsmodelle in der deutschen Strafzweck-Diskussion. Beziehungen zwischen Rechtsphilosophie, Dogmatik, Rechtspolitik und Erfahrungswissenschaften* (Berlin, 1987).
17 See Becker, *Randgruppen*, 300ff.
18 Peter Becker, "Kriminelle Identitäten im 19. Jahrhundert. Neue Entwicklungen in der historischen Kriminalitätsforschung," *Historische Anthropologie* 2 (1994): 150ff.

to reveal an inborn "inferiority." Criminological writers were nevertheless interested in some characteristics of the criminal underworld, those that fit their own argumentational needs. They looked – among other things – at techniques that practitioners had reconstructed as the main elements of the various criminal crafts, at the language of thieves, and quoted from the criminal cases as such. To integrate these bits and pieces into their own narratives they employed three main strategies: The first, *replacement*, was employed by Hans Gross. He used the criminalists' description of the *Gauner* but did not apply it to contemporary professional thieves. Rather, he projected the characteristics of the *Gauner* onto Gypsies as an anthropologically – and ethnically – defined group. This enabled him to "naturalize" an ethical-moral stigma. The second, *parallelization*, was very dear to Cesare Lombroso and can be found both in his references to the criminal underworld and in his reflections on the arguments of his critics. In part because of the explorative character of his writing and research, he paralleled evidence and theoretical concepts even when they were openly contradictory. The third, *serialization*, was perfected by the Austrian psychiatrist Richard von Krafft-Ebing. He arranged selectively quoted criminal cases one after another, thereby achieving a synergetic effect because these cases provided an interpretative context for each other.

HANS GROSS AND THE STRATEGY OF REPLACEMENT

In Gross's most influential book, the *Handbuch für Untersuchungsrichter* (Manual for Investigating Magistrates), we find a revealing contradiction on two levels between the traditional wisdom of earlier practitioners and the modern, scientific knowledge of criminologists. On a first level, Gross juxtaposed traditional demands for authenticity and objectivity with modern reflections on the necessary subjectivity of individual perception, memory, and representation. On a second level, he reconstructed the main criminal figures both from the perspective of modern criminology and from the viewpoint of the practitioners of the pre-1848 and reactionary eras.

In this section I analyze the salient contradictions between traditional legal notions of objectivity and modern psychology. Gross tried to solve this problem, as I will argue, by transforming the claims of truth and objectivity by the investigating magistrate into mechanical reproductions of material evidence. In the second part of the argument, I outline Gross's strategy of replacement with regard to the description of criminal types, which allowed him to transfer the moral-ethical characteristics of the *Gauner* to the ethnically defined group of Gypsies.

Replacement I: Mechanical Representation Instead of Reasonable Evaluation

Until the introduction of public and oral criminal procedures in the mid-nineteenth century, inquisitorial investigation dominated the criminal trials in most German states. This type of procedure was characterized by a strong emphasis on written depositions. Ludwig Hugo Franz von Jagemann, a famous legal expert from Baden, aptly summarized this peculiarity with the Latin phrase: "Quod non est in actis, non est in mundo." (What you don't find in the files does not exist in the external world.)[19] Under these conditions, the investigative magistrate had to bear significant responsibility when he summarized depositions of witnesses and suspects or when he described the scene, means, and victims of a crime with the help of his clerk. Contemporary legal experts repeatedly reminded the magistrate of his obligation to represent objectively all information about the crime. However, objectivity was not understood as the mechanical reproduction of depositions but rather as the skillful, reasonable recreation and evaluation of events.[20]

From this perspective, the reconstruction of an absolute truth about criminal events was threatened by misperceptions, by the lack of talent, ambition, and discipline of the magistrate, and, finally, by the skillful deceptions of *Gauner* who appeared in court or at police offices. In his handbook of advice for his fellow magistrates, Jagemann focused on the proper questioning of witnesses and suspects and on the writing of minutes of the court proceedings. This guidance was meant to encourage his fellow magistrates to pursue their duties with eagerness, discipline, and reason. The Lübeck police expert Avé-Lallemant approached the same objective, that is, the improvement of the magistrates' and policemen's accounts, from a different angle. He directed the attention of police officials and magistrates to the habitual deceptions practiced by *Gauner*, described their most common deceptive schemes, and provided some recommendations for counterstrategies.[21]

Magistrates and police officials saw themselves confronted with *Gauner* whose long practice had already turned them into professionals. As Richard Evans has argued, *Gauner* used deceptions mainly as a means to elude police

---

19 Ludwig Hugo Franz von Jagemann, *Handbuch der gerichtlichen Untersuchungskunde*, 2 vols. (Frankfurt am Main, 1838), 1:657.
20 See my article on strategies which were used to guarantee objective representations: Peter Becker, "Objective Distance and Intimate Knowledge: Concerning the Structure of Criminalistic Observation and Description," in Peter Becker and William Clark, eds., *Little Tools of Knowledge* (Ann Arbor, Mich., 2000).
21 Friedrich Christian Benedikt Avé-Lallemant, *Das deutsche Gaunerthum in seiner social-politischen, literarischen und linguistischen Ausbildung zu seinem heutigen Bestande*, 4 vols. (Leipzig, 1858), 2:375ff.

examinations.[22] Pretended noble descent, important protectors, and the like were employed to impress the authorities. Even after they were taken to court they usually insisted on their false identity. This strategy was often quite successful, as we learn from an analysis of wanted posters in police weeklies.[23]

Gauner also ran their deceptive schemes as part of their criminal trade, when they acted as swindlers or as spies for burglars. When we look at the practitioners' accounts of fraud and deception, the clear distinction between perpetrators and victims suddenly begins to blur, however. The victims do not appear as innocent prey. On the contrary, the most successful swindling schemes lured victims into criminal activities such as forgery, fraud, and embezzlement. Instead of making criminal or at least unethical profits, the would-be swindlers found themselves duped. The clear distinction between perpetrators and victims disappeared in other schemes as well. *Gauner* exploited the superstitious beliefs of the population while at the same time being superstitious themselves.[24] These borderline cases were usually not at the center of the practitioners' reflections on *Gauner*. They entertained a view of bourgeois society in which a firm and lasting distinction existed between respectable citizens and *fallen men*.

It is revealing of the practitioners' ambivalent attitude toward *Gauner* that their respectable appearance was always interpreted as a disguise, even though the *Gauner* were considered to be recruited from all classes and professions. In order to reinvent the *Gauner* from respectable origins as impersonators of their previous respectability, criminalists had to assume a radical change of identity during his or her fall. From this perspective, criminals joined – independent of their social descent – the ever-growing criminal underworld after their fall and posed a real threat to the trust that was the foundation of modern economic activities.[25]

The dichotomy of deviant and respectable people structured the strategies of criminalists in every respect. Therefore, it was also influential in the evaluation of a person's credibility. Respectable citizens were expected to show honesty and authenticity, among other qualities. For that reason,

---

22 See case number 3 in Richard J. Evans, *Szenen aus der deutschen Unterwelt: Verbrechen und Strafe 1800–1914* (Reinbek bei Hamburg, 1997), 199ff.

23 The *Hannoversche Polizeiblatt* had a column on *Gemeinschädliche Umhertreiber* (dangerous vagrants) in which the editors tried to make their audience aware of this problem. On this police journal, see Leo Lucassen, *Zigeuner: Die Geschichte eines polizeilichen Ordnungsbegriffes in Deutschland 1700–1945* (Cologne, 1996), 139ff, and Dirk Riesener, *Polizei und Politische Kultur im 19. Jahrhundert: Die Polizeidirektion Hannover und die politische Öffentlichkeit im Königreich Hannover* (Hannover, 1996), 70ff.

24 See, for exemple, Albert Hellwig, *Verbrechen und Aberglaube. Skizzen aus der volkskundlichen Kriminalistik* (Leipzig, 1908).

25 Avé-Lallemant, *Deutsches Gaunertum*, 2, 33ff.

their representations of social and physical realities seemed trustworthy and reliable. Only pathological conditions of mind or senses, or predominant self-interest could preclude the revelation of the one and only truth to the judge, as Jagemann argued.[26]

Gauner and other people guided by strong self-interest were therefore the main threats to an objective representation of criminal acts. They duped the criminalists' practical gaze in order to prevent a truthful reconstruction of the crime. Because practitioners could always explain misrepresentations of reality with an intention to conceal or falsify the facts, they could forego critical attitudes toward language and sense perceptions.[27] They held fast to the conviction that the one and only truth could be established, which could be identified as one of the main pillars of legal proceedings. This pillar was shaken only by psychological and physiological experiments toward the end of the nineteenth century. At this time, criminologists and legal experts were still far from following Friedrich Nietzsche in his claims that a substantial difference between true and false did not exist.[28] But they began to consider such a wide array of distorting influences on the individual's perception, memory, and representation of reality that the chance to reconstruct this reality through the existing legal proceedings seemed to recede into the distance.

Gross tried to maintain the distinction between truthful and deceptive witnesses. Because he did not ignore the results of contemporary psychological research, his argument shows an interesting twist in his reliance on the intentions of the observer rather than on the results of his observations for defining the distinction between truth and falsehood. Gross had to concede that even sincere witnesses could have misrepresented events due to their education, physical constitution, gender, age, and the pathological malformations of their senses.[29] Gross was obviously caught between the implications of his reception of modern psychological and physiological findings on the one hand and the quest for absolute truth on the other. Modern psychological research showed that perception, memory, and testimony were influenced by many factors through which the perceived situation and/or action could have been unconsciously altered. The language spoken in foreign dialects, the illumination of the "stage," the excitement of the onlooker, the rapidity of movement, the interpretative approach to

---

26 Jagemann, *Handbuch*, 1, 562ff.   27 Jagemann, *Handbuch*, 1, 565.
28 Friedrich Nietzsche, *Jenseits von Gut und Böse: Vorspiel einer Philosophie der Zukunft (1886)* (Munich, 1988), 53.
29 Hans Gross, *Handbuch für Untersuchungsrichter*, 6th ed. (Munich, 1913), 75ff.

reality, previous head injuries, and insinuations by the judge were among the many influences that Gross mentioned.[30]

This was certainly not sufficient reason for Gross to support a relativistic approach that was incompatible with the legacy of the European legal system. Rather, he clung to the arguments of practitioners in which bad intentions, that is, partisanship and interestedness, were identified as the main sources of evil. Therefore, he considered children to be ideal witnesses due to their naiveté. Love and hatred, ambition and disloyalty, religion and social status were unknown to them. He described the good-natured heart of children as the mirror that reflected the outer world. Nevertheless, children were not perfect witnesses for other reasons, as Gross had to concede. They lacked the ability to make reasoned interpretations of their perceptions, which made them too receptive to the insinuations of authorities from within or outside their family.[31]

The ideal witness therefore was a mature person whose personality and position favored a disinterested while reasonable interpretative approach. These qualities were usually associated with officials and expert witnesses. Practitioners of the pre-1848 period and the Reaction had already emphasized the exceptional position of officials with regard to the credibility of their depositions. These superior qualities were the key to providing the official investigation and the resulting protocols with their aura of authenticity and objectivity. Officials were, however, usually not present at the crime scene, when the criminal act unfolded. In order to document and reproduce the events in question, exceptionally reliable witnesses had to be found. Because detectives and magistrates could not trust everyone's perception and representation, they looked for other sources of information and turned to the material evidence of crimes.

The physical remnants could be collected by officials and "questioned" by technical means. The graphs, charts, numbers, and microscopic images that resulted from this "questioning" had to be read by expert witnesses whose standing and official position guaranteed objectivity. Modern research therefore put an end to the reliance on language as a privileged approach to the truth about criminal acts. At the same time, new technology promised police and legal experts an "objective," depersonalized reconstruction of crime scenes.[32] In following this promising path, they did not engage in

---

30 Gross, *Handbuch*, 77ff.   31 Gross, *Handbuch*, 118ff.

32 Lorraine Daston argues that the replacement of narratives with technical, mechanical devices for documenting evidence was one of the main scientific strategies to further objectivity in the modern sense. See "Scientific Objectivity With and Without Words," in Becker and Clark, eds., *Little Tools of Knowledge*.

reflections about a more discursive style of ascertaining truth or about the ways in which language and concepts shaped their own perception of reality. They simply replaced the testimony of witnesses as objects of their quest for truthful representations with a highly technical analysis of material evidence.

Replacement II: Gauner and Gypsies, or the Naturalization of Moral Stigmas

Gauner were described in the extensive, specialized literature of the practitioners as professionals. They were different both from "ordinary" criminals, who turned to illicit means in hard times, and from people who committed violent crimes under conditions of exceptional emotional distress. *Gauner* did not suffer from a bad conscience but rather pursued their trade systematically and skillfully. The practitioners pointed especially to the *Gauner*'s ability to disguise their criminal intent both from respectable citizens and from the authorities.

During the pre-1848 and reactionary eras, numerous authors described the *Gauner*, his habits, and his recruitment with disgust and fascination. Their accounts provided readers with a comprehensive view of the criminal underworld that was conceptualized as the negative counterpart of an idealized bourgeois world. The respectable citizen's constant striving for moral improvement found its equivalent in the *Gauner*'s persistence in evil-doing that could not be corrected by the intervention of secular or religious authorities. In the criminal underworld, the social harmony of bourgeois society turned into a selfish struggle for power and dominance. The modesty of respectable citizens was transformed into sexual, alcoholic, and materialistic excesses. The reasonable citizen was upright, virtuous, and self-disciplined within a well-structured society. The *Gauner* was portrayed as timid and sly, but without the will to accept the constraints of law and order.[33]

Modern criminological research at the turn of the century was more or less incompatible with the practitioners' *ethnographic* description. Criminological writings did not, however, systematically drop negative moral qualities of criminals; rather, they searched for new ways to account for them. They abandoned the idea of free choice in a career of wrongdoing and replaced it with anthropological, physiological, and evolutionist ideas. Proof of their theories was sought in a wide range of sources. The writings of practitioners were among them, but these were only of secondary importance.

Hans Gross's handbook is an interesting case in point for this incoherent reception of earlier wisdom. He divided the traditional knowledge about

---

33 See Becker, *Kriminelle Identitäten*, 155ff.

Gauner into two categories. The habitual and skillful deception of *Gauner* was discussed in Section 7 on *Gaunerpraktiken* (tricks), whereas the moral qualities and social habits of *Gauner* were used for a description of Gypsies as an ethnic and criminological type.

The presentation of *Gaunerpraktiken* followed the line of argument that I previously described. The idea of the willful and skillful impostor was somewhat at odds with the contemporary psychological and criminological research to which he wanted to introduce his readers. Gross did not relate the problem of impostors to the threat posed by inferior and degenerate people, even though his analysis of degeneration as a security problem alluded to the existence of possible links. One of them, pathological forms of lying and deception by degenerates, could have been used to understand the success of some swindlers. He could have followed the lines of reasoning pursued by Nietzsche, who pointed to the swindler's belief in his own deceptions as the main precondition of his or her success.[34]

But Gross did not follow the conceptual trail blazed by Nietzsche. He kept pathology and deception separate and gave himself and his readers much more flexibility in dealing with lawbreakers who sooner or later came in contact with policemen and magistrates. To label the "poetic" representation of a suspect's biography as pathological would have filled insane asylums with criminals, vagrants, and prostitutes. In the writings of Gross and in the practical work of the police and the courts, the swindlers' lack of authenticity was therefore located between pathology and willful deception.

From the viewpoint of Gross and his fellow criminologists, *Gauner* and other degenerates had at least one characteristic in common: They could not be easily identified as such. Only legal and medical experts, "competent men" in Lombroso's terminology,[35] could decipher the hidden references to the habits of *Gauner* as well as the body and the mind of degenerates. Their task was complicated by the absence of any single, telling sign: Only the trained eye of the specialist analyzing the whole could reveal the truth about a person. Every person was therefore suspect. Gross's paragraph about the difficulties in dealing with degenerates throws an interesting light on the ubiquity of degeneration in the mind of contemporary experts:

Degenerates, psychological inferiors, neurasthenics, psychotics, and endogenous nervous people do not comprise a specific class of mentally unhealthy people: Even epileptics, hysterics, tramps, exhibitionists, and countless others of this kind are degenerated and, due to their degeneration, one of the aforementioned disorders

34 Nietzsche, *Menschliches, Allzumenschliches*, 1, 72.
35 Cesare Lombroso, *Der Verbrecher in anthropologischer, ärztlicher und juristischer Beziehung*, 3 vols. (Hamburg, 1887), xix.

appeared. In addition to these, there is an immense group of people who are degenerated but whose epilepsy, hysteria, etc., did not fully develop. They remain *tantum
degenerati* throughout their lives, without turning out to be ill. Nevertheless, they
cannot be considered normal . . . and degenerates therefore cause an exceptional
number of problems for the criminalist that are – without exception – difficult to
solve.[36]

Gross and his contemporaries reacted with paranoia and heavy-handedness
to the threat posed by the ubiquity of degeneration. In the end, their paranoia
motivated them to stress the importance of an authoritarian approach in
which contested meanings were not resolved discursively but rather through
reference to the authority of experts.

Even though there were many structural similarities in the arguments
of criminologists and criminalists, there was one main difference regarding
the treatment of the social fabric of the criminal underworld. Criminologists looked at inferior and degenerate people, impostors, and swindlers as
individuals and not as part of a carefully protected criminal underworld. In
the writings of practitioners, the social network and interaction of *Gauner*
were important subjects. This aspect of the practitioners' writings was quite
difficult to include in modern criminological narratives. Gross overcame
this problem by replacing the members of the criminal underworld with
the ethnically defined group of Gypsies.

The moral qualities of Gypsies that Gross introduced with a quotation from a contemporary authority in the field are almost identical to
the descriptions of *Gauner* in earlier texts: Gypsies are described as having "a strange blend of vanity and meanness, affectation, sincerity, and real
carelessness; almost a complete lack of manly judgment and reason, which is
complemented by harmless cunning and slyness; moreover, they show a disgraceful toadyism in their behavior and their very existence, which is aimed
at cheating others; they do not show any consideration for truth and lie with
an unblushing boldness because of their complete lack of shame." From his
own experience, Gross added the cowardly nature of Gypsies to this list in
order to accomplish a comprehensive account of the Gypsies' psychology.[37]

When the practitioners described the *criminal underworld*, they stressed
the unfavorable consequences of children's early exposure to an immoral
lifestyle. In Gross's reflections on Gypsies we find a similar concern. Conforming to the replacement of moral with ethnic qualities, Gross presented
the young generation of Gypsies as born and not socialized into their
immoral life. Their inborn tendencies resulted, he argued, from the Gypsies'

36 Gross, *Handbuch*, 236.   37 Gross, *Handbuch*, 504.

thousand-year-long habit of living on the earnings of others. He prized the idea of a radical dissociation in the cultural evolution of "respectable" Europeans and Gypsies. At a certain moment in time, they seemed to have diverged and taken different paths. Whereas the first group invested its energies in cultural, social, and metaphysical advances, Gypsies perfected their parasitic habits. This specific evolution gave them a significant advantage over the "normal" criminal.[38]

Gross's train of thought, especially the idea that moral characteristics could be bred and transmitted genetically, seems irrational from today's point of view. His contemporaries were, however, much more used to this flexible combination of anthropological, evolutionist, and moral arguments. Erich Wulffen, a high-ranking official in the Saxon Ministry of the Interior, used a similar line of argument to identify the inherent tendency toward prostitution in all women when he argued, "In every woman the nature of a whore is physiologically and psychologically dormant. This is the result of her anthropological evolution. Using women's biological tendencies, men have bred her for this whorish nature."[39]

Replacing *Gauner* with Gypsies signaled a shift toward a wider focus in criminological arguments. This shift aimed at the naturalization of moral stigmas that were presented as the result of a thousand years of cultural evolution. The consequences of this style of thought are obvious and openly addressed by Gross: Gypsies were comparable to migrant birds who contracted all sorts of diseases during their travels. This made Gypsies dangerous to respectable people. Moreover, their innate tendency to steal was not the result of education. Therefore, they could not be taught better habits. Gross hesitated to draw the obvious conclusion from his findings and left this task to others: The logic of his argument pointed already to the need to isolate Gypsies from society – in whatever ways possible.[40]

CESARE LOMBROSO AND THE STRATEGY OF PARALLELIZATION

Lombroso studied crime and criminals in an explorative way, for which Mary Gibson's chapter provides further proof.[41] Lombroso's starting point consisted of medical, psychological, and anthropological observations, but

---

38 Gross, *Handbuch*, 507.
39 Erich Wulffen, *Der Sexualverbrecher: Ein Handbuch für Juristen, Verwaltungsbeamte und Ärzte, mit zahlreichen kriminalistischen Originalaufnahmen* (Berlin, 1921), 678.
40 See Michael Zimmermann, *Rassenutopie und Genozid: Die nationalsozialistische "Lösung der Zigeunerfrage"* (Hamburg, 1996), 125ff.
41 I refer to the third edition of *L'uomo delinquente* (1884) on which the translation into German was based.

he also extended his interests to ethnographic, historical, literary, and public knowledge. Based on his extensive body of references, he wanted to locate criminals within an evolutionist framework.[42] Signs of an *atavistic* quality were first identified on the criminal's body.[43] In order to prove the parallel nature of mental and physical atavism, he aimed at the reconstruction of the psychology of primitive man. For this purpose, he referred extensively to ethnographic reports on savages, which he placed on a par with the ancient predecessors of Europeans.[44]

Lombroso was unable to find matching evidence on the psychology, habits, and lifestyles of criminals in his own clinical observations. He thus had to turn to writings by his Italian friends and especially to "ethnographic" accounts of the criminal underworld that were written by practitioners in the decades before Lombroso appeared on the scene. In this section, I trace Lombroso's main references to the practitioners of the pre-1848 period and the Reaction. My main focus is on his strategies to integrate information about *fallen men* into his narrative, which was guided by the idea of criminals as *impaired men*.

In his masterpiece, *L'uomo delinquente* (Criminal man), Lombroso referred to the writings of the German practitioner Friedrich Christian Benedikt Avé-Lallemant on three occasions. The first reference occurred during his discussion of the thieves' language; the second provided evidence for the peculiar handwriting style of criminals; and the third appeared as part of his study of criminal gangs. In the writings of practitioners such as Avé-Lallemant these references played an important role. Their ethnographic approach to the criminal underworld was based on the expectation of finding a negative mirror image of bourgeois society. Communication and associations were considered important to respectable citizens; therefore, the gaze of practitioners was predisposed toward finding corresponding evidence within the criminal world. Moreover, the practitioners presented their narratives as the outcomes of risky expeditions to an unexplored world. The familiarity with and the use of the language spoken by the alien "tribe" of *Gauner* proved their expertise in these matters. Avé-Lallemant used so much of the underworld language in his narrative that much of it was incomprehensible to the uninitiated.[45]

---

42 See Daniel Pick, *Faces of Degeneration: A European Disorder. c. 1848–c. 1918* (Cambridge, 1989), 120ff.

43 See the chapters by Jane Caplan and David Horn in this book.

44 See Gilles Boetsch and Michèle Fonton, "L'Ethnographie criminelle: les applications de la doctrine lombrosienne aux peuples colonisés au XIXème siècle," in Mucchielli, ed., *Histoire de la Criminologie*, 139–56.

45 See Avé-Lallemant, *Gaunerthum*, 2, 140ff.

Lombroso referred to these writings in a very characteristic way: These references stood next to quotes from other sources, taken from a variety of different publications. Together, they provided a differentiated representation of criminality and criminals. By quoting rather extensively from his sources Lombroso integrated information into his narratives, which were not held together by his theoretical concept. His criminological narrative was therefore pointillist. Comparable to neo-impressionistic paintings, the totality of references placed next to each other should have crystallized in the mind of readers in support of Lombroso's concept of *atavism*.

Lombroso's analysis of the language of thieves can be used to illustrate the pointillist style of his narrative. The chapter on thieves' cant follows a standard format in this book. It is divided into fourteen sections, which are numbered consecutively and in which Lombroso reflected on origin, linguistic geography, word formation, and usage. From this we can learn that a variety of different factors contributed to the existence of the language of thieves and shaped their character: the common experience of a certain lifestyle and "profession" (Sections 6, 8, and 9), the fantasy and creativity of idle and cynical people (Sections 2, 3, and 10), the integration of terms from foreign languages (Sections 4 and 11), and the adherence to an antiquated terminology (Section 5 and 12). On several occasions, Lombroso tried to use the evidence to emphasize the atavistic character of this language. He even dedicated one of the smallest sections (less than half a page) to a summary of the atavistic character of the thieves' cant: Like savages, criminals tended to reproduce natural sounds – such as the trickling of water and the noise of people walking – or to personify abstract and material objects. On these grounds, he claimed that the language of thieves resembled the language of savages and that its atavistic character bred similar versions of this language all over the world.[46]

Lombroso's argument is not conclusive. The atavistic character of the language of thieves does not follow from his presentation. Without providing a theoretical framework, which could have explained the relevance of lifestyle, profession, and tradition in shaping this language in terms of an atavistic recurrence of primitive origins, his reference to social and cultural influences on the emergence of thieves also supports contradictory interpretations. This chapter is certainly not outstanding with regard to its incoherence. The same inconsistency can be found in most of Lombroso's other chapters and lends his narrative a rather eclectic character. It even

---

46 Lombroso, *Verbrecher*, 398.

dominates his treatment of theoretical models. When his theory was criticized, he looked for new explanations in which atavism and pathology
supposedly had a common basis.[47] The integration of these two elements
was achieved not through a synthesis but rather through a parallelization of
theoretical models. Parallelization was at the heart of his pointillist presentation of evidence and was a guiding principle in his use of photographs; it
also greatly influenced his theoretical arguments.

From this finding, we can draw some conclusions about Lombroso's
narrative: the strategy of parallelization was well suited to his explorative
approach to different types of evidence and theoretical arguments. At the
same time, it prevented him from developing theoretically coherent arguments. The strategy of parallelization introduced a characteristic friction
particularly between the theoretical and empirical parts of his narrative.
Lombroso did not only collect and publish evidence to support his theories;
the empirical and theoretical portions of his arguments represent two different, yet connected, strands of investigation.

KRAFFT-EBING AND THE STRATEGY OF SERIALIZATION

Numerous references to published criminal cases can be found in Richard
von Krafft-Ebing's classic *Psychopathia sexualis*. His style of presentation differed from the ones that Lombroso and Gross used, in that its approach
was less explorative. He identified degeneration as the main problem and
deviant sexuality as the appropriate site to study it. Selective quotes from the
forensic literature and therapeutic practice[48] provided the empirical basis for
his well-developed tableau of deviant sexuality. Krafft-Ebing quoted from
his sources frequently, but less extensively than Lombroso. He reduced the
complex narratives of criminal cases to a skeleton of information that was
meaningful within his own theoretical framework: sexual motives, personality profiles, and hereditary taints.

Krafft-Ebing used this argumentative strategy extensively. In *Psychopathia
sexualis* he referred to 250 short case studies within six chapters. Brief quotes

---

47 A good summary of the differences between the Italian and French "schools" can be found in Robert
Nye, *Crime, Madness, and Politics. The Medical Concept of National Decline* (Princeton, N.J., 1984), 97ff;
Marc Renneville, "La réception de Lombroso en France (1880–1900)," in Mucchielli, ed., *Histoire
de la criminologie*, 107–35; Peter Strasser, *Verbrechermenschen. Zur kriminalwissenschaftlichen Erzeugung
des Bösen* (Frankfurt am Main, 1984), 79ff.
48 On the selectivity of Krafft-Ebing's style of references, see Gisela Steinlechner, *Fallgeschichten: Krafft-
Ebing, Panizza, Freud, Tausk* (Vienna, 1995), 21ff.

dominate. They are arranged serially, taken out of their previous narrative context and placed in a standardized way according to Krafft-Ebing's theoretical argument.[49] This produced a synergetic effect because every single case provided an additional context for all the other cases.

Krafft-Ebing's narrative gives the reader less flexibility in terms of the interpretation of evidence. The role played by hereditary diseases, corrupting influences on the nervous system, and a variety of temptations within and outside bourgeois households are obvious factors that, to him, explained the development of a degenerated constitution and resulted in one of many sexual pathologies. Here as elsewhere, criminological narratives focused on violent crimes and not so much on offenses against property. *Psychopathia sexualis* is quite representative in this respect because it aimed at an analysis of degeneration and its harmful consequences. Violence – in Krafft-Ebing's book mostly sexually related and motivated offenses – was not directly explained by willful, evil acts but rather as the unfortunate outcome of a degenerate constitution. The emphasis on destiny complicated the integration of case studies of violent crimes that were published in the first half of the nineteenth century. When authors of the first half of the nineteenth century tackled the problem of violent crime, they strove to present violent criminals as *fallen men* and to identify rational motives and/or the influence of mistaken reason. One case, reported by the famous German legal expert Anselm von Feuerbach, is typical in this regard. It provides a good starting point for this section because it also was quoted in Krafft-Ebing's masterpiece.

Feuerbach considered Andreas Bichel, a Bavarian serial murderer who targeted young women, an unusual criminal, describing him in the first edition of his publication on unusual forensic cases.[50] Bichel is characterized as a weak and timid man who killed young girls to steal their clothes and other belongings. The murderer is represented as perfidious and not openly malicious, pretending to subject himself to the demands of the social and moral order because of his "effeminate," anxious character. Bichel's avarice was strong enough to override his orderliness. The influence of avarice was so strong that he finally committed several murders. Feuerbach summarized Bichel's character as follows: "If these characteristics of cruelty, harshness,

---

49 Richard von Krafft-Ebing, *Psychopathia sexualis. Mit besonderer Berücksichtigung der konträren Sexualempfindung (1912)* (reprint, Munich, 1984). The number of 250 case histories is taken from the 1912 edition, which was completed by A. Fuchs. The first edition presented forty-five case studies, a number which increasingly grew from edition to edition.
50 Paul Johann Anselm Feuerbach, "Andreas Bichel, der Mädchenschlächter," in Paul Johann Anselm Feuerbach, *Merkwürdige Criminal-Rechtsfälle*, 2 vols. (Giessen, 1811), 2:3–30.

avarice, and timidity joined by the rudeness of the mind, the lack of education and formation, even a limited intelligence, which tends to stare stupidly
at one point, then the character has achieved a state in which crimes such as
the ones committed by Bichel are possible."[51] During the criminal investigation Bichel revealed himself as a determined villain who openly confessed
to only those parts of the crime that were already confirmed by independent
sources. His stubborn lying encouraged Feuerbach to describe Bichel as a
fallen man. All in all, the murderer was held responsible both for his deeds
and for allowing himself to develop such destructive forms of avarice. With
this reading of Bichel's personality Feuerbach was in line with well-known
contemporary psychiatrists.

Johann Christian August Heinroth, a famous forensic psychologist during
the first half of the nineteenth century, was an adamant advocate of criminal
responsibility in cases where criminals showed clear signs of insanity. From
his viewpoint, everyone had to take responsibility for exposing himself to a
situation in which one's ability to act reasonably and responsibly was diminished. This basic principle of the master narrative of the *fallen man* is well
expressed in a passage in Heinroth's book, in which he reflects upon the case
of a man who had abused and murdered a child: "No man is born a beast.
If a man becomes a beast, it is his own fault. . . . No man is evil by nature;
he might degenerate gradually if he gives in to evil temptations against the
voice of his conscience."[52]

Heinroth's and Feuerbach's arguments were fully compatible with the
discursive practice of criminalists, which was based on the master narrative
of the *fallen man*. Toward the end of the century the moral–ethical look at
the biography of criminals was replaced by the criminologists' interest in
the constitutional weaknesses of criminals and in the influences that finally
caused these weaknesses to erupt in gruesome murders. Criminological
narratives focused on genealogies and physiognomies instead of social habits
and biographies of criminals in order to decipher and explain the degeneration of their subjects.[53] This shift in argumentative strategy is illuminated
in Krafft-Ebing's presentation of the Bichel case. He used Feuerbach's case
study as one of the references in the chapter on sexually motivated murder.
To avoid the problem of Lombroso, that is, the inclusion of information
that had the potential to contradict his theoretical argument, he quoted
very selectively and only from the penultimate paragraph. In the paragraph,
Feuerbach briefly mentioned the possibility of Bichel's sexual interest in his

51 Feuerbach, "Andreas Bichel," 20–21.   52 Heinroth, *System*, 328.
53 See also Christian Phéline, *L'image accusatrice* (Laplume, 1985), 57ff.

victims but regarded this factor as only a secondary influence on his modus operandi and his motivation to commit the murders.

By comparison, Krafft-Ebing focused his analysis of the Bavarian *Mädchenschlächter* (girl slaughterer) on the reconstruction of a pathological personality. This directed his attention toward the "sexual" and allowed him to integrate even those elements of Bichel's psychological profile that Feuerbach mentioned but disregarded in his interpretation. One of those elements was Bichel's limited intelligence, which Feuerbach described as "the limited intelligence that tends to stare stupidly at one point."

Krafft-Ebing considered the Bichel case one of the most dreadful but also one of the most telling cases for the close link between sexual lust and the desire to murder.[54] In his slightly modified quotation from Bichel's testimony, Krafft-Ebing presented only the reference to dismemberment of the victims' bodies and Bichel's bizarre cannibalistic desires. Sexual lust and pathological drives appear, in his quotation, to be the hidden motives for the killings. This impression is supported by the inclusion of Bichel's case in a series of sexual murder cases. Placed next to Vacher, the ripper, and other sexually motivated murderers of women and close relatives, the interpretation of Bichel's killings is understandable only in the context of sexual lust and desire to murder. The rational, economic motive for Bichel's murder, which Feuerbach identified with the desire for the women's belongings, was not even mentioned in Krafft-Ebing's reading of the case.[55]

With abridged, serial quotations from different sources, authors such as Krafft-Ebing tried to overcome the problem of a complexity of motives that led to killings. The monotonous repetition of descriptions of murder, lust, and hereditary taints was one of the solutions to this problem. This style of narrative gave the impression that these cases revealed a common driving force that was hidden only from the untrained gaze and exerted its influence at all times and at all places.

CONCLUSION: THE TRADITION OF CRIMINOLOGICAL KNOWLEDGE

The criminological and criminalistic discourse on crime and deviance was open to contributors from many areas. Practitioners and theoreticians, scholars and literary writers, theologians and followers of a materialistic doctrine

---

54 Krafft-Ebing, *Psychopathia sexualis*, 75.
55 Parallel to changes on the level of the criminological discourse there were changes in the way of acting and in the motives of murderers, as social historical studies on violent crimes show. See A. Parella, "Industrialization and Murder: Northern France, 1815–1904," *Journal of Interdisciplinary History* 22 (1991): 631ff.

contributed in different ways to the reconstruction of criminal identities.[56] Their arguments were guided by one of the two master narratives described in this chapter. These master narratives structured two discursive practices in rather specific ways: the first was dominated by criminalists, the second one by criminologists. The dividing line between the two practices can be drawn in the last two decades of the nineteenth century. The first discursive practice had its main site in the offices of practitioners, the second one in the academy, in examination rooms of penitentiaries, and in laboratories. The authority of statements resulted, in the case of criminalists, from their experience and reason in the use of data on biographies and lifestyles of criminals; criminologists, however, legitimated their findings with reference to clinical and psychological experiments. Finally, criminalists perceived criminals as members of a criminal underworld or "counter world," whereas the criminologists were more interested in the criminal as an individual subject to hereditary and environmental influences.

Looking at criminology as a discursive practice structured among other things by a specific master narrative about the origins of criminal careers, we are able to reach beyond the confines of disciplinary history. Furthermore, this enables us to pay tribute to the intellectual scope of the authors of criminological publications. Focusing on discursive practices instead of concentrating on schools of thought gives us access to the common ground between authors of different criminological beliefs. If we look at just one aspect, the role played by the master narrative of *impaired men*, we can easily observe that Lombroso and his French critics concurred with each other on several important points: They both held an impaired biological and sociopsychological evolution responsible for criminal careers and agreed on its main legal and administrative implications.

The two master narratives were less deterministic in structuring criminological research than scientific paradigms. Directed by one of the two master narratives, criminologists and practitioners were able to blend theoretical and empirical knowledge into reasonable, widely acceptable arguments on the origins of crime and the best ways of combating and preventing it. The two master narratives also provided a frame of thought that directed the attention of researchers to certain evidence and suggested a specific reading.

Neither a discursive practice in general nor a specific master narrative in particular determined certain representations of crime and criminals. On the

---

56 On the moral discourse and the urban reform movement as an important context for criminological writing, see Andrew Lees's chapter in this book; representations of crime as part of a new representation and apprehension of urban spaces at the turn of the centuries are analyzed in Peter Fritzsche's chapter in this book.

contrary, there always was a potential for change in the logic of criminalistic and criminological discourse, in the dynamics of institutionalized information gathering, and in the socioeconomic changes that were effected by these discursive practices and affected them at the same time. The discursive practice of criminalists came under pressure by the emergence of new scholarly disciplines, such as hygiene and physiology, by their own "thought experiments," by the implications and persuasion of the ethnographic approach, and by reliance on a patchwork of empirical and theoretical positions that were open to a variety of different receptions by later authors.

The two master narratives differed above all in the meaning they bestowed on social problems. Prostitution and alcohol abuse, premature encounters of juveniles with vice, and the negative influence of waywardness and of lacking education are important issues in both master narratives.[57] The relevance of productive *labor* as a crucial signifier of social and psychological normalcy was another common element. The same is true for the fear of professional criminals as the main threat to state and society. Practitioners used to read these problems as signs of an imminent moral collapse, whereas criminologists understood them as signifiers of the degeneration of individuals and of the social body. Despite these different readings, the common concerns can be seen as interfaces through which empirical evidence could be exchanged.

The protagonists of the two master narratives did not live and write independently of their social context. Criminalists, as the main representatives of the master narrative of the *fallen man*, were practitioners and were therefore confronted with social problems on a daily basis. Criminologists entered the discussion on social problems as physicians, legal experts, and anthropologists, and were motivated by their claim to be able to develop interdisciplinary, scientific solutions to pressing social problems. Representing deviants, outcasts, and criminals as *fallen men* allowed criminalists to hold the paupers of the first half of the nineteenth century responsible for their miserable existence and explain the lack of success in the criminalists' efforts to prevent, or at least to combat crime and deviance successfully.

Understanding criminals as one of the many embodiments of degeneration allowed the individualization of deviance as a social problem. Degenerate men and women were too weak to build a strong counter-society. They posed a threat because of their inability to live up to the standards of state and society. This was at least the basic premise on which the criminologists built their arguments. This approach resulted from the mobilization of medical-scientific theories for the explanation of crime and

57 See the chapters by Peter Fritzsche and Andrew Lees in this book.

deviancy. Supported by the stunning success of the new medical-scientific knowledge to explain and solve a wide variety of medical and hygienic problems, medical experts successfully claimed their priority in dealing with social problems. They still acknowledged the genuine social and moral quality of deviance and crime but looked for new social, anatomical, and psychological factors to account for them scientifically. Criminologists were driven by the same illusion of a society free of deviance and conflicts already dear to the practitioners. In contrast to the practitioners, criminologists tried to achieve this – nightmarish – dream by focusing on the conditions under which a man's fall was made possible by his constitution and/or his social environment. They identified the existence of *impaired men* as the main problem and accordingly represented criminals and outcasts as people without the physical, social, and intellectual abilities needed for their successful integration into society. A close cooperation between medical and legal experts seemed to be necessary against this threat.

The reflections on *fallen men* and *impaired men* both dealt implicitly with the conditions under which an individual could be successfully integrated into civil society. Within the master narrative of the *fallen man*, the criminalists identified the *Gauner's* excessive selfishness, egoism, and boundless pursuit of profit as an abuse of civil liberties and as an obstacle to their integration. The very existence of *Gauner* indicated the ambivalent character of these liberties, which could be granted only to people with sufficient self-discipline, orientation toward the common good, and patriotism.[58] This argument was based on a binary model, which distinguished sharply between respectable and deviant people. When the practitioners reflected on the appropriate strategies to prevent the fall of an individual, they used a slightly different model in which the dichotomy between good and evil was overcome by the inclusion of a third group of people. These people were considered to lack the strong moral resolve of the first group, without having already turned their back on the bourgeois moral order. Their lack of moral resolve made them vulnerable to temptations of different kinds. It was for them that the police and the law had to provide constraints that could prevent their fall.

Within the master narrative of *impaired men*, there also was a binary model in place that distinguished sharply between degenerated and "healthy" individuals. The very existence of degenerate people was linked to hereditary

---

58 On the role of patriotism for the socialization of egoistic men, see Rudolf Vierhaus, "'Wir nennen's Gemeinsinn' (We call it public spirit): Republic and Republicanism in the German Political Discussion of the Nineteenth Century," in Jürgen Heideking and James A. Henretta, eds., *Republicanism and Liberalism in America and the German States, 1750–1850* (Cambridge, 2001).

taints and to the destructive influences of an unhealthy social environment. Eugenic and hygienic measures were thought to prevent the spread of degeneration.[59] The structure of the criminological argument was similar to the criminalistic one, however, because it took a third group of people into consideration: People whose constitution was fragile but stable enough to allow them to live respectably so long as they were kept away from wrongful temptation. For them, the police and the law still had to provide the necessary protection.

The two master narratives directed the attention of researchers to certain fields of empirical evidence. Criminalists understood crime as a willful abuse of reason. Their attention was directed at the biography and lifeworld of suspects in order to locate the traces of a wrong attitude toward life. This evidence revealed the existence of *Gauner* and their socialization into a criminal underworld. The criminalists' binary mode of thinking secularized firmly established Christian ideas of good and evil, and bestowed new meanings on them.[60] They replaced the devil's insinuations and the evil influence of natural drives with the concept of a willful decision to pursue a wrongful life. From this perspective, a person could be held legally and morally responsible for the consequences of their fall, such as pauperization, insanity, and criminality.

It is characteristic of the criminalists' approach that they were not really interested in those cases of violent crime that could not be explained with rational, economic motives. Their focus was directed at professional thieves and swindlers, the lifeworld of the *Gauner*, and the collaboration among professional criminals. They were less interested in murderers motivated by jealousy or other passions. If they took up this issue, they emphasized that these murderers also were victims of a self-inflicted moral-ethical waywardness. It is also telling for the criminalists' approach that they did not pay much attention to the fate of children who were born into the criminal underworld, for these children did not have a chance to make a decision between a righteous or wrongful life. They were the strongest evidence against the theoretical basis on which the master narrative of the *fallen men* was built.

---

59 For discussions of these measures, see Richard J. Evans, *Rituals of Retribution: Capital Punishment in Germany, 1600–1987* (London, 1996), 437; Mariacarla Gadebusch-Bondio, *Die Rezeption der kriminalanthropologischen Theorien von Cesare Lombroso in Deutschland von 1880–1914* (Husum, 1995), 164ff; Richard F. Wetzell, "Criminal Law Reform in Imperial Germany" (Ph.D. diss., Stanford University, 1991), 306. On the request to prevent epileptics, alcoholics, criminals, and lunatics from marrying, see Gustav Aschaffenburg, *Das Verbrechen und seine Bekämpfung. Kriminalpsychologie für Mediziner, Juristen und Soziologen, ein Beitrag zur Reform der Strafgesetzgebung* (Heidelberg, 1903), 186.
60 On this redefinition, see Strasser, *Verbrechermenschen*, 82–3.

Even though passion as a motive for murder and the fates of the children of *Gauner* had the potential to shake the theoretical foundation on which the master narrative of the *fallen men* was built, practitioners did not suppress evidence related to these themes. This information was part of the surplus of observations that were the outcome of the practical and intellectual curiosity of police experts. In systematic accounts of the origin of crime and its remedies, criminalists tended to ignore this kind of evidence and focused instead on information that corroborated the idea of criminals as *fallen men*. Literary accounts, materialist scientific treatises, and phrenological theories preserved the evidence for later use by criminological authors.[61]

Criminologists focused on violent crime, irrational motives, and the determining influence of early socialization into the criminal underworld. They took issue with problems that criminalists could not deal with successfully. Degeneration theory provided a more promising framework for the explanation of random violence than the belief in an abuse of reason. Criminologists were, however, less successful in dealing with professional criminals. Faced with this challenge, criminologists either pathologized the personality of these criminals or "naturalized" it by transferring it to members of ethnically defined groups, such as Gypsies.

The shift from the master narrative of *fallen men* to the one of *impaired men* redefined the position of practitioners within the criminological discourse; they lost their role as active contributors. From the late nineteenth century onward, they were restricted to popularizing new criminological knowledge and to translating its implications into suggestions for administrative reform. In their reform proposals they blended traditional concepts about official authority with new ideas about technical competence in order to restrict even further the rights of suspects in criminal procedures. They considered their superior reason, enriched by a scientific, objective analysis of material evidence, as the only way to solve a crime successfully. Whereas their demands for far-reaching penological reforms were endorsed by criminologists and found widespread support,[62] their requests for a systematic reform of the code of penal procedure and of the organization of the police force had to wait until the Third Reich abolished the rule of law.[63]

---

61 Klaus Eder, "Die Zivilisierung staatlicher Gewalt: Eine Theorie der modernen Strafrechtsentwicklung," in Friedhelm Neidhardt, Rainer Lepsius, and Johannes Weiss, eds., *Kultur und Gesellschaft: René König, dem Begründer der Sonderhefte, zum 80. Geburtstag gewidmet* (Opladen, 1986), 238, argues that in penal law, too, procedures were needed to preserve options for later developments.

62 On the proposals of criminal police officers in the early twentieth century, see Patrick Wagner, *Volksgemeinschaft ohne Verbrecher: Konzeptionen und Praxis der Kriminalpolizei in der Zeit der Weimarer Republik und des Nationalsozialismus* (Hamburg, 1996), 137ff.

63 See Wagner, *Volksgemeinschaft*, 193ff.

The lack of concurrence between the history of institutions and the history of discourses can be traced in the relationship between the organization of the police and the two discursive criminological practices. The master narrative of the *fallen man* motivated a systematic reorganization of the police archives and the creation of personal files. Police departments such as that in Hannover began to rearrange their archives as early as mid-century. This reorganization was intended to provide the police with the proper infrastructure for meeting the challenge posed by the *Gauner* and his skillful deceptions. The shift to the master narrative of *impaired men* was part of the transition from one discursive practice to another. As a result, the privileged sites of the discourse moved from the offices of practitioners to the laboratories and examination rooms, where anthropological and psychophysiological measurements could be taken. These sites were not incorporated into criminal procedures until the 1920s.

This transition to a new discursive practice therefore had the potential to severely influence legal procedures; this potential was, however, for a rather long time not realized, even though the personnel working in these institutions was strongly influenced by the master narrative of *impaired men*. There were good reasons for the delay in redefining legal procedures along these lines, though. *Fallen men* were defined by social and biographical characteristics that could be firmly established and used as evidence to increase or decrease the penalty. *Impaired men* were defined anthropologically; there was, however, no consensus on the signs by which to recognize their degeneration unambiguously. An individual's degeneration therefore could not easily be introduced as a criterion for the legal evaluation of a subject so long as the rule of law protected the personal rights of the defendant. Only when the rule of law was abolished could these vague anthropological concepts finally become the basis of criminal procedure.

TWO

Criminology as Scientific and Political Practice in the Late Nineteenth and Early Twentieth Centuries

6

Cesare Lombroso and Italian Criminology

Theory and Politics

MARY S. GIBSON

Cesare Lombroso is well known to historians and current criminologists alike, but he is often recognized for little more than contributing the notion of the "born criminal" to criminological theory. Yet his ideas were complex and changed significantly over his lifetime. A reductionist view of Lombroso's criminal anthropology is not the fault of the readers because many of his works have never been translated or were drastically shortened for foreign publication. Even for those scholars who read Italian it is difficult to locate copies of the various editions of his books. Those writings that are available tend to be discussed in a vacuum, without any understanding of their particular Italian context.

In this chapter I attempt to eliminate some of the imprecision that curiously envelops such a major figure in the history of criminology. First, I trace the evolution of parts of Lombroso's theory through an examination of the five editions of his seminal work, *Criminal Man*. Second, I examine the work of his disciple and colleague, Enrico Ferri, for the purpose of placing Lombroso within the wider circle of Italian intellectuals who formed the "Positivist School" of criminology. Although a collective portrait of the many adherents of this school is beyond the scope of this chapter, the analysis of Ferri will provide an example of the prominence of criminal anthropology within Italian academic circles.

Finally, I explore the relationship of politics to positivist criminology. Both Lombroso and Ferri belonged to the Italian Socialist Party (Partito Socialista Italiano, or PSI) at a time when theories of biological and racial determinism were more often associated in other nations with the Right. A leader of the PSI, Ferri published a book arguing that criminal anthropology and socialism were both "scientific" and therefore compatible. Although not all Italian socialists subscribed to positivist criminology, it did attract allies from across the political spectrum. This political malleability of positivist criminology derived from its complex and sometimes contradictory theory, which counseled harsh punishment for born criminals but progressive "penal substitutes" for "occasional criminals," those individuals supposedly free of a biological propensity for deviance. In Italy, then, positivist criminologists became champions of both "conservative" measures, like life imprisonment and the death penalty, and "liberal" alternatives to prison, like parole and suspended sentences. The Italian experience thus seems to throw into question any automatic link between specific criminological theories and political allegiances.

CESARE LOMBROSO

Recognized as the master of positivist criminology, Lombroso was a generation older than Ferri and first enunciated most of the theories that were later tested, and sometimes revised, by his colleagues. Lombroso's radically new approach to the issue of crime came primarily from his training in medicine rather than law. Born in 1835 into a Jewish family in northern Italy, Lombroso pursued his medical studies at the Universities of Padua, Vienna, and Pavia, graduating from the latter in 1858.[1] At the outbreak of the wars of Italian unification in 1859, he volunteered as a doctor in the revolutionary forces and was stationed in Calabria until 1863. Like many young doctors of that period, Lombroso identified science with the Risorgimento, believing that empirical research was crucial to destroying the obscurantism of the old regimes on the peninsula and building a foundation of knowledge for a new, united, and liberal Italy. In an early positivist enterprise he measured and studied three thousand soldiers in Calabria in addition to his routine duties as a physician.[2] From 1863 to 1872, as the director of a succession of insane asylums in Pavia, Pesaro, and Reggio Emilia, Lombroso continued to focus on human subjects as the source of knowledge, in this case conducting research on the insane. Once appointed to the Chair of Legal Medicine and Public Hygiene at the University of Turin in 1876, he turned his attention to a third group, inmates of the Turin penitentiary. Although he changed professorships several times – to a chair in psychiatry

---

1 The best biography of Lombroso is the one written by Renzo Villa, *Il deviante e i suoi segni: Lombroso e la nascita dell'antropologia criminale* (Milan, 1985). Other biographies include Pier Luigi Baima Bollone, *Cesare Lombroso ovvero il principio dell'irresponsabilità* (Turin, 1992). Baima Bollone, as a professor of legal medicine, stresses the medical context of Lombroso's research. A more dated work is Luigi Bulferetti, *Cesare Lombroso* (Turin, 1975). In English, the best biographical overview remains Marvin Wolfgang, "Cesare Lombroso," in Hermann Mannheim, ed., *Pioneers of Criminology* (1955; reprint, Montclair, N.J., 1972).
2 Wolfgang, "Lombroso," 170.

and clinical psychology in 1896 and one in criminal anthropology in 1906 – Lombroso continued to serve as a prison physician in Turin, examining two hundred prisoners each year.[3]

According to Lombroso, the central idea for his life's work in criminology came to him in 1871 in a flash of insight while doing an autopsy on the body of Giuseppe Villella, a notorious brigand. Contemplating the skull of Villella, as Lombroso often reminisced, "I seemed to see all at once, standing out clearly illumined as in a vast plain under a flaming sky, the problem of the nature of the criminal, who reproduces in civilised times characteristics, not only of primitive savages, but of still lower types as far back as the carnivores."[4] The discoveries that prompted this epiphany were a small hollow at the base of the skull and, underneath it, an enlarged segment of the spinal cord. The latter reminded Lombroso of an anatomical feature typical of some "inferior races" in Bolivia and Peru as well as "the lower types of apes, rodents, and birds."[5] Even late in life Lombroso referred to the skull of Villella – which he preserved until his death – as the "totem, the fetish of criminal anthropology," because the crucial notion of atavism – or the reversion of criminals to a lower state of physical and psychological evolution – had sprung from it.[6] Yet Renzo Villa, in his excellent intellectual biography of Lombroso, has shown that Lombroso's earliest reports of this autopsy were contradictory in terms of dates, the specific features of the skull, and even the crimes committed by Villella.[7] It thus appears that Lombroso fabricated, or at least embellished, the story of Villella's skull in order to fashion a dramatic founding event for his new discipline of criminal anthropology. This episode also showed him bending his data to fit preconceived theories, a practice that would become all too common in the writings of positivist criminologists.

Despite Lombroso's perpetuation of the myth that criminal anthropology sprang fully formed from the skull of Villella, he owed debts to both earlier and contemporary thinkers. As an indefatigable reader in several languages and a doctor trained in part in Vienna, Lombroso drew on a large and international body of literature not only in medicine and penology but also in history and linguistics in formulating his theory of crime.[8]

---

3 Wolfgang, "Lombroso," 171.
4 Cesare Lombroso, *Criminal Man, summarized by G. Lombroso Ferrero* (New York, 1911), 6–7.
5 Lombroso, *Criminal Man*, 6.   6 Cited in Villa, *Il deviante*, 176.
7 Ibid., 148–9.
8 For an early review of writers who inspired Lombroso, see Giuseppe Antonini, *I precursori di C. Lombroso* (Turin, 1900); Villa also carefully traces Lombroso's precursors in *Il deviante*. In English, see the polemic against the "myth" that Lombroso founded scientific criminology by Alfred Lindesmith and Yale Levin, "The Lombrosian Myth in Criminology," *American Journal of Sociology* 42 (1937): 653–71.

He was influenced by the positivism of Auguste Comte, the recapitulation theory of Ernst Haeckel, the phrenology of Franz Joseph Gall, and
the degeneration theory of Bénédict-Augustin Morel. Villa has minimized
the influence of Darwin on Lombroso, arguing that the latter – although
familiar with the *Origin of the Species* before its translation into Italian –
was more deeply affected by other sources. Most importantly, Villa identifies comparative linguistics, and especially the work of Paolo Marzolo, as
decisive in Lombroso's early conception of evolution and the possibility of
reversion to earlier stages of civilization. Himself a doctor, Marzolo tried
to reconstruct the linguistic evolution of humanity through the empirical
collection of phrases and modes of communication thought to be typical
of earlier stages of civilization.[9] And indeed Lombroso's lifelong interest in
the jargon and art of criminals attests to his youthful linguistic studies. Like
physical deformities, "primitive" cultural artifacts constituted signs of evolutionary failure. Yet, even if Lombroso's earliest research was not directly
informed by Darwinism, he was eclectic enough to draw on Darwin's
name by the 1880s, if only to enhance the prestige of his school. And
the influence of Darwinism on his younger colleagues, such as Ferri, is
undeniable.

A prolific writer, Lombroso produced over thirty books and one thousand articles during his lifetime. His most famous work, *Criminal Man*, went
through five editions between 1876 and 1897.[10] With Guglielmo Ferrero
he issued a companion book, *The Female Offender*, in 1893, with a second edition ten years later.[11] Topics of other monographs included insanity,
genius, race, legal medicine, and political crime.[12] Many of Lombroso's articles, as well as innumerable book reviews and short commentaries, appeared
in the *Archives of Psychiatry, Criminal Anthropology, and Penal Sciences* (hereafter *Archives*), a journal founded by Lombroso and his burgeoning group

---

9 Villa, *Il deviante*, 92–102; in honor of Paolo Marzolo, Lombroso named his firstborn child Paola
   Marzola Lombroso.
10 The five editions of *L'uomo delinquente* (Criminal Man) appeared in 1876 (256 pages); 1878
   (746 pages); 1884 (610 pages); 1889 (1,241 pages in two volumes); and 1897 (1,903 pages in three
   volumes, plus a volume of tables and illustrations). None of these editions was ever translated into
   English; the version of *L'uomo delinquente* available in English was compiled by Lombroso's daughter,
   Gina, and published in 1911 after his death. *Crime, Its Causes, and Remedies* was a compendium of his
   ideas written late in life for foreign readers (published first in French in 1899 and in English in 1911).
   It therefore is not possible for English-language readers to follow the development of Lombroso's
   ideas through the various editions of his major work, *L'uomo delinquente*.
11 *The Female Offender* was translated into English as early as 1895, but in an abridgement of the Italian
   original.
12 A good bibliography of books by Lombroso can be found in Villa, *Il deviante*, 283–8. Excerpts from
   some of his lesser known writings are now available in Cesare Lombroso, *Delitto, genio, follia: Scritti
   scelti*, ed. Delia Frigessi, Ferruccio Giacanelli, and Luisa Mangoni (Turin, 1995).

of disciples in 1880.[13] As one of the most prominent intellectuals in late-nineteenth-century Italy, Lombroso was also invited to write for more general publications like *Nuova antologia*, geared toward middle-class readers. His opinion was sought not only on issues of criminal justice but on quite separate topics, such as foreign policy.

As a scientist, Lombroso rejected the armchair theorizing of the classical school for empirical research. As he repeated throughout his life, the focus of study should not be the crime but the criminal.[14] Unlike classical criminologists, who drew up scales of crime and punishment based on moral principles, Lombroso espoused observation of the bodies of criminals to find the facts. Experimental science therefore became the model for positivists, replacing the deductive mathematical analogies of the great eighteenth-century penologist Cesare Beccaria. To his credit, Lombroso spent vast amounts of time collecting data by examining inmates in Italian prisons. For him, the prison was a laboratory where he took a variety of odd machines to measure and experiment on the physical body. He also performed autopsies on dead criminals and examined bones of ancient peoples preserved in archeological museums. Lombroso's books are filled with the results of his observations and experiments: Lengthy tables illustrate the data, and pages of photographs train readers in the detection of abnormality.

That Lombroso's theory changed throughout his professional career is clear from a comparison of the five editions of *Criminal Man*. Issued as a short volume of about 250 pages when it first appeared in 1876, it grew to three volumes of text totaling 2,000 pages by the fifth edition. This final edition also included a fourth volume or *Atlante*, which constituted a curious appendix filled with a variety of illustrative evidence, including maps of criminal geography, graphs of the distribution of crimes, photographs of offenders, and representations of the tattoos, handwriting, and art of prison inmates. Lombroso's daughter, Gina, issued a short synopsis of her father's work in 1911, two years after his death, also under the title *Criminal Man*. Because this posthumous volume is the only one to have been translated into English, many readers do not have access to the original formulation of Lombroso's theory or to the evolution of his ideas during the height of his popularity in the last three decades of the nineteenth century. Gina's synopsis, as well as a compendium produced by Lombroso for foreign audiences,

---

13 Founded as the *Archive of Psychiatry, Criminal Anthropology, and Penal Sciences*, the journal revised its name several times, most importantly replacing "penal sciences" with "legal medicine" after 1904.
14 For example, see Cesare Lombroso, "Criminal Anthropology: Its Origin and Application," *Forum* 20 (1895–6): 34. This article is one of only a few writings directed by Lombroso to an American audience.

Crime: Its Causes and Remedies, lack the wealth of detail and broad scope of the last editions of *Criminal Man*. They also synthesize a rambling and often contradictory set of observations into a falsely compact and coherent theory.

As a comparison of the five editions of *Criminal Man* reveals, Lombroso revised, or at least expanded, his theory in three main areas: the classification of criminals, the identity of the born criminal, and punishment. Whereas positivist criminology later became known for its careful system of classification, the first edition of *Criminal Man* lumped all lawbreakers together in a single group that was then compared to the insane and, sporadically, control groups of "normal" men. The phrase "born criminal" did not yet appear because it was coined four years later by Ferri.[15] In 1876 Lombroso simply referred to "criminals in general," and systematically listed their physical characteristics: compared to "healthy" individuals, they exhibited small and deformed skulls; greater height and weight; light beards; crooked noses; sloped foreheads; dark skin, eyes, and hair; large ears; protruding jaws; less muscular strength; and little sensitivity to pain. This last, according to Lombroso, constituted the exterior sign of inward moral obtuseness because criminals rarely exhibited remorse for their crimes. Unable to control their passions, they indulged in wine and gambling. Lacking intelligence, they were good at crime because they needed only to repeat the same behavior. Lombroso also included chapters on tattoos among prisoners, as well as their slang, their writing, and their art, although these characteristics would seem social rather than biological in derivation. But from Lombroso's eclectic point of view, the scientist had to be alert to any and all external clues to a fundamental internal atavistic nature. The criminal was an ill person, and the criminologist had to be creative in locating and reading the symptoms.

In the second edition of *Criminal Man* Lombroso used the term "habitual criminal" to name the carrier of the physical, moral, and intellectual anomalies already defined for "criminals in general." He also began to build a system of classification, establishing two new categories: the "insane criminal" and the "criminal by passion." The first edition had already argued that criminals and the insane shared many abnormal anatomical and biological traits. By the second edition Lombroso argued that some criminals were themselves insane and deserved specific treatment different from either the sane criminal or the noncriminal insane. Completely new was the chapter on criminals by passion, included in response to critics. Criminals by passion

15 Villa identifies its first use in an article by Ferri in the *Archive*, 1 (1880): 369.

were unlike habitual criminals in many ways: They tended to have high reputations before committing their crimes; they repented immediately; and their motives were "generally generous and often sublime."[16] These might include anger against an adulterous spouse or commitment to a banned political ideal. In both cases, the jealous husband or political rebel would uncharacteristically lose control of his emotions momentarily, but did not exhibit the physical or moral anomalies of a common murderer.

In the final three editions of *Criminal Man* Lombroso continued to elaborate new categories of deviants. Some were borrowed from Ferri, who had urged his teacher to extend his analysis beyond atavism. While never as clear and systematic as Ferri in his classification, Lombroso nevertheless introduced a series of criminal types that became stock figures in the popular imagination. Most obviously, he adopted Ferri's label of the "born criminal," a tag that quickly gained international recognition, but also drew instant criticism, as opponents ridiculed Lombroso's inability to identify any single anomaly that disfigured all born criminals. In response, Lombroso proposed that any individual exhibiting a cluster of anomalies be labeled atavistic, although he was always vague in setting a minimal number of malformations necessary for being so categorized. He also maintained that even "isolated" anomalies marked a criminal as constitutionally flawed and therefore potentially dangerous. Such fuzziness in definition became alarming in light of his theory of punishment, which depended on the precise categorization of offenders.

Lombroso also expanded the category of the insane criminal to distinguish three further variations: the "alcoholic criminal," the "hysteric criminal," and the "mattoide." In the first case, drunkenness could turn even an individual possessing few anomalies onto a path of crime because "by itself, it gives courage, incites the passions, dims the mind and conscience, and disarms any reserve so that one commits crimes as an automaton, almost a somnambulist."[17] Thus, although not necessarily atavistic, alcoholics exhibited the same character traits as born criminals: impulsiveness, cruelty, lack of remorse, and laziness. Often inheriting a weak constitution from alcoholic parents, they were predisposed to violent acts like homicide and rape.

The category of the hysteric criminal was also elastic, as some of its members had few signs of mental illness, such as convulsions or low intelligence. But all possessed "an egoism, a preoccupation with themselves that makes them eager for scandal and public attention as well as an excessive

16 Cesare Lombroso, *L'uomo delinquente*, 2d ed., 133.
17 Cesare Lombroso, *L'uomo delinquente*, 5th ed., 2:415.

impressionability so that any little thing makes them bilious, cruel . . . and irrational."[18] Whereas most hysterics were female, mattoides were invariably male and represented one of Lombroso's most innovative classifications. Meaning "half crazy" in lay terms, mattoide entered positivist terminology to designate unstable but heroic individuals who combined the vulgar with the sublime. Self-fashioned prophets and revolutionaries, they rose from humble origins to harangue the masses with utopian ideas. Combining "unusual and well-expressed ideas" with those that were "mediocre and base," their voluminous writings marked them as truly mad.[19] In adding three categories that relied little on physical anomalies, Lombroso began to "psychologize deviance," a trend that was amplified by his successors.[20] He also widened the net of criminality to include persons labeled dangerous not because of past crimes but because they possessed neurotic traits reminiscent of born criminals.

Finally, the last editions of *Criminal Man* included an entirely new category, that of Ferri's "occasional criminal." Lombroso was always uncomfortable with the category of the occasional criminal, complaining that it "does not offer a homogeneous type like the born criminal and the criminal by passion, but is constituted of many disparate groups."[21] In his schema, these groups included the pseudocriminal, marked by few if any anomalies; the criminaloid, who exhibited enough anomalies to be predisposed to crime; and the habitual criminal, now a label for recidivists who began their careers as pseudocriminals but had reached the depravity of born criminals. In all cases these individuals broke the law because environmental pressures or temptations overcame their natural goodness.

By the final edition of *Criminal Man*, then, Lombroso had recognized a spectrum of deviant types outside of the born criminal. Some were comprised of individuals with few anomalies, like the three subcategories of the occasional criminal, whereas others were intermediaries between the occasional and born criminal. The latter included some subcategories of the insane criminal and the criminal by passion. This proliferation of categories increased the weight of sociological factors in Lombroso's explanation of the causes of crime. Because of the notoriety of the concept of the born criminal, Lombroso is rarely credited with including environmental factors in his discussion of the etiology of deviance. Yet, as early as the first edition of *Criminal Man*, he argued that "there is no crime that is not rooted in multiple causes," including education, hunger, and urbanization.[22] In the

18 Ibid., 2:445.
19 Ibid., 2:470.
20 The phrase is Villa's; see *Il deviante*, 200.
21 Lombroso, *L'uomo delinquente*, 5th ed., 2:491.
22 Lombroso, *L'uomo delinquente*, 1st ed., 120.

later editions he devoted increasing space to the sociological causes of crime and lowered the percentage of criminals in the category of the biologically perverse from over 50 percent to 33 percent.[23] Even with this drastic reduction of his original category, Lombroso could retain a general theory that denied free will because he conceptualized environmental and biological forces as equally deterministic.

Despite his increasing willingness to acknowledge the role of external forces on the individual, Lombroso remained throughout his life most enthusiastic about analyzing the identity of the born criminal. Although he relied on the research of others to paint a portrait of the occasional criminal, he continued indefatigably to collect primary data on the innate factors that pushed certain individuals into a life of crime. The identity of the born criminal, however, did not remain static throughout the revisions of *Criminal Man*. In the first edition, he identified all born criminals as atavistic. After describing the anomalies in the size and shape of a series of skulls, he remarked on "the singular coincidence between the abnormalities found in criminal men and those observed in the normal skulls of the colored or inferior races."[24] Not surprisingly, according to the positivist maxim that exterior physical defects signaled interior moral depravity, such similarities extended to the emotions. The ferocity of criminals, for example, was "common to ancient and savage peoples but rare and monstrous today."[25] Atavism even explained the popularity of tattoos among lawbreakers because "tattoos are one of the special characteristics of primitive man and of those in the wild."[26] In short, criminals were "savages living in the middle of a flourishing European civilization," identifiable by their physical and moral anomalies.[27] They represented throwbacks on the evolutionary scale, a freakish reappearance in modern European civilization of its brutish past.

By the third edition of *Criminal Man* Lombroso admitted that the concept of atavism was inadequate to explain the presence of multiple anomalies in all born criminals. Such a radical reconsideration resulted partially from the widespread criticism of his key concept, including that from his follower Ferri. Rather than abandoning his beloved notion of atavism, Lombroso simply added the concept of degeneration to explain physical and psychological malformations that had resulted from fetal disease rather than constitutional weakness. Such a disease might prevent a normal fetus

---

23 In the fifth edition of *L'uomo delinquente*, Lombroso holds that 40 percent of all criminals are "born criminals" (1:vi); two years later, *Crime: Its Causes and Remedies* includes the lower figure of 33 percent.
24 Lombroso, *L'uomo delinquente*, 1st ed., 13.   25 Ibid., 67.
26 Ibid., 54.   27 Ibid., 108.

from, in Haeckelian terms, recapitulating all the stages of human evolution. Their development blocked in the womb, babies could thus be born with a "predisposition" to crime, legible in anomalies left by the disease. The theory of degeneration allowed the interplay of biology and environment because social factors contributed to alcoholism, venereal disease, or malnutrition, which in turn could cripple the health of a mother and her fetus. But even if caused by external forces, degeneracy became a hereditary condition that progressively weakened future generations.

Although the adoption of degeneration theory, of French origin, might be seen to signal a defeat for criminal anthropology, it actually broadened its scope and applicability. Lombroso could now count any malformation, even if not attributable to atavism, as one of a cluster of anomalies needed to identify a born criminal. Furthermore, it widened the psychological dimension of his theory because he held that many symptoms of degeneracy were mental rather than physical. As part of this tendency to psychologize deviance, he developed two new categories of the born criminal: the morally insane and the epileptic. Introduced in the third edition of *Criminal Man*, moral insanity designated individuals who appeared normal in physique and intelligence but were unable to distinguish between good and evil behavior. Generally classified as borderline cases between normality and madness, the morally insane were pronounced by Lombroso as identical to atavistic criminals in their compulsion to harm others and their lack of remorse. Once tested for physical sensitivity, they exhibited, as Lombroso expected, a dullness of touch compatible with their moral vacuity. To support his thesis of "the analogy and complete identity between the morally insane and the born criminal" he enumerated studies that had found widespread moral insanity among the prison population.[28]

In the fourth edition of *Criminal Man* Lombroso finally enunciated his last subcategory of the born criminal, the epileptic. Although subscribing to the common notion of the time that epileptics might commit crimes during convulsions, he also proposed the category of "hidden epilepsy," which could promote deviant acts even in the absence of physical trauma. Thus epilepsy became a universal substructure of all criminal behavior, encompassing both moral insanity and atavism. In the final edition of *Criminal Man* Lombroso declared the difference between the three categories to be primarily that of scale: "as the morally insane criminal merges with the congenital criminal, only differing in an exaggeration of its characteristics,

28 Lombroso, *L'uomo delinquente*, 5th ed., 2:55.

so the epileptic delinquent... offers an exaggeration of the morally insane criminal... and as when two things resemble a third, then all three are equal, so it is certain that born criminality and criminal insanity are nothing but special, if variant, forms of epilepsy."[29] From this perspective Lombroso began to find a combination of atavism, moral insanity, and epilepsy in many of his subjects of research. He thus gained flexibility in classifying them as born criminals because even "isolated" physical atavisms became significant when combined with the innate moral depravity of moral insanity or epilepsy. As the definition of the born criminal became increasingly elastic, criminal anthropologists gained ever-widening discretion to label a variety of deviants as born criminals.

A third theme undergoing significant modification over the five editions of *Criminal Man* was that of punishment. In the first edition Lombroso made only scattered references to the penal implications of his theory of atavistic criminals, suggesting, for example, that they were not likely to be deterred by the death penalty because of their extreme insensitivity to pain.[30] By the second edition, however, he had inserted a special section on "therapy for crime" in order to make his new science useful to lawyers and magistrates. Again, his decision to devote increasingly large sections of each edition to punishment came largely at the behest of Ferri, who – being a lawyer himself – realized that his colleagues had little interest in theory unless it had explicit prescriptions for sentencing. Thus, by the final edition of *Criminal Man* Lombroso devoted three hundred pages to a detailed discussion of the appropriate punishments for various categories of lawbreakers.

Although his practical advice became increasingly specialized over the years, Lombroso's basic philosophy of punishment never changed. In opposition to the Enlightenment principles of Beccaria, he counseled that punishment be tailored to individual criminals rather than to their crimes. He explicitly rejected the principle of moral responsibility, arguing that criminals acted out of compulsion, whether from their innate physical and psychological degeneracy or from the social environment. Yet, even if criminals did not freely choose to break the law, society still had the right to punish them in its own defense. This principle of social defense was itself not so different from Beccaria's belief that the major purpose of punishment was to prevent those guilty of crime from further threatening society. Lombroso directly broke with Beccaria, however, over the mode of determining appropriate punishments. To Lombroso, a mathematical scale of crimes and punishments

29 Ibid., 2:189. 30 Lombroso, *L'uomo delinquente*, 1st ed., 60.

was too abstract because both born and occasional criminals might steal or even murder. Therefore, the law should allow judges wide discretion to assess the degree of "dangerousness" in each defendant as a basis for issuing the appropriate sentence. In short, the positivists rejected the classical penchant for determinate sentences in favor of flexible, unconditional penalties.

In place of the classical scale of crimes and their punishments Lombroso argued for the correlation of types of criminals with punishments. Thus, mistakes in the classification of offenders could bring undeserved consequences. Despite his early rejection of the death penalty, Lombroso gradually came to advocate it for born criminals convicted of a series of bloody crimes or for members of organized gangs, like mafiosi and brigands, who threatened the security of the state. In so doing he betrayed the liberal principles of his youth and defied a public consensus that had led to the abolition of capital punishment in the Zanardelli Criminal Code of 1889. To his adversaries he responded that, "to say that this punishment goes against the laws of nature is to pretend not to know that it is written in very clear letters in [nature's] book and that the entire progress of the animal world, and thus our own, is based on the struggle for existence, involving immense slaughter."[31] Society need have no pity for such born criminals because they were "constituted for evil" and "do not resemble us, but instead ferocious beasts."[32] Capital punishment would simply accelerate natural selection, ridding society of the unfit.

For born criminals who had committed less heinous crimes and for habitual criminals Lombroso recommended perpetual incarceration, preferably on islands or in the remote countryside. Work would be mandatory because "we must worry less about their well-being than about putting them to use."[33] In this way they would defray the costs of their incarceration while being prevented from further menacing society or corrupting occasional criminals. Like capital punishment, life imprisonment emulated "the process of natural selection, to which we owe not only the existence of the race but possibly also of justice, which depends on the elimination of those who are most violent."[34] Insane criminals also would be separated from society for life but be kept in special criminal insane asylums, where they would receive treatment. A crusader for these special institutions as a humane alternative to incarceration, Lombroso even envisioned the establishment of specialized mental institutions for groups like alcoholic or epileptic criminals.

---

31 Lombroso, *L'uomo delinquente*, 5th ed., 3:587.   32 Ibid.
33 Lombroso, *L'uomo delinquente*, 5th ed., 3:582–3.
34 Ibid., 3:583.

For criminals by passion and occasional criminals, Lombroso sought alternatives to penitentiaries. Unlike the classical school, which had vaunted prisons as a humane and enlightened alternative to corporal punishment, positivists derided them as "schools of vice." They would only ruin reformable criminals by mixing them with congenital deviants. When unavoidable, prisons should be modeled on the "Pennsylvania," or cellular system, where inmates lived and worked in separate cells to prevent communication and moral contamination. Preferable to prison were fines or, if the defendant was poor, community service. For nondangerous criminals Lombroso counseled the courts to impose house arrest, police surveillance, or simply judicial reprimands. He was also enthusiastic about suspended sentences and parole, two modern alternatives to incarceration pioneered in France and the United States that he pushed to have introduced into the Italian criminal code.

The variety of punishments proposed by Lombroso raises the question of his political allegiance. Today, support for the death penalty or incarcerating criminals for life based on biological traits characterizes a conservative criminology concerned above all with retribution and the maintenance of order. However, liberals prefer indeterminate sentences supplemented by parole as humane tools to encourage the reform of lawbreakers. That positivism was the font of both conservative and liberal approaches to criminality shows that it was more multifaceted than usually conceded. It also illustrates the difficulty of automatically identifying certain intellectual theories with a specific political position. Positivist criminology was not innately of the Right or the Left but could be compatible with both positions, depending on historical circumstances and which part of its doctrine was being emphasized.

A fervent supporter of the liberal Risorgimento in his youth, Lombroso gradually came to embrace a humanitarian socialism by the end of his life. Although he never theorized about the compatibility of socialism and positivism as clearly as Ferri would, he joined the Italian Socialist Party in 1893, wrote for its newspapers and periodicals, and served as a socialist representative on the city council of Turin from 1899 to 1905. His socialism has been described by one biographer, Luigi Bulferetti, as "sentimental" because Lombroso was not particularly orthodox and did not believe, for example, in economic determinism.[35] He was, however, extremely sympathetic to the poor and worked, while on the city council, for better hospitals, schools, and day care for the working class.[36] Delfina Dolza, the author of a recent biography of Lombroso's two daughters, evaluates

35 Bulferetti, *Cesare Lombroso*, 361, 385.   36 Ibid., 426.

his political position more positively. She sees Lombroso as emblematic of "positivist" intellectuals who, wishing to educate the public, felt "a moral duty to put their own research at the service of the collectivity."[37] This conviction that scientific research could discover truth and improve society was similar to the Progressive spirit in the United States at the turn of the century. Thus, Lombroso's life shows a continuity between his championing of science as necessary to the new, secular society being born in the Risorgimento and his later adhesion to socialism. In 1909, the year of his death, he still described himself as a "convinced follower of socialist thought."[38]

Lombroso's personal and intellectual contacts were not, however, limited to socialists. Because he was perhaps the best-known professor in Turin during the 1880s, his house became the center of cultural interchange for both locals and visitors.[39] His guests included a wide spectrum of intellectuals, including Ellen Key, Achille Loria, Robert Michels, Gaetano Mosca, Max Nordau, and Max Weber. According to Michels, "all of these people, although differing in age, temperament, language, and mentality, felt themselves drawn together into one bundle by the boundless esteem and sincere affection that each of them, taken separately, felt in his or her own heart for Lombroso."[40] Such statements testify to Lombroso's many attractive qualities: his restless energy, curiosity about all subjects, imaginative if not always careful opinions, and enthusiasm for popularizing his doctrine beyond academic circles.

Of Lombroso's many legacies, the one that best captures both the fascinating and repugnant aspects of his thought was the Museum of Criminal Anthropology, still located in Turin. Housed in the Museum was a macabre collection of hundreds of objects amassed by Lombroso over a lifetime, beginning in his student days in 1859. Considered by Lombroso as "data" relevant to criminal identification, these objects included skulls, skeletons, pickled brains, photographs, wax effigies of "deviant" faces, patches of dried skin bearing tattoos, weapons of crime, and art created by inmates.[41] In building his collection Lombroso accepted gifts from anthropologists, wheedled artifacts left behind in Italian prisons, and – with the help of his

---

37 Delfina Dolza, *Essere figlie di Lombroso: Due donne intellettuali tra '800 e '900* (Milan, 1990), 52.
38 Quoted in Dolza, *Essere figlie*, 65.   39 Villa, *Il deviante*, 206.
40 Quoted in Dolza, *Essere figlie*, 53–4.
41 Baima Bollone devotes a chapter to the Museum in Cesare Lombroso, 143–63. For photographs of selected objects in the Museum, see Giorgio Colombo, *La scienza infelice: Il museo di antropologia criminale di Cesare Lombroso* (Turin, 1975) and the final section of Umberto Levra, ed., *La scienza e la colpa: Crimini, criminali, criminologi: Un volto dell'Ottocento* (Milan, 1985).

students – robbed graves. He proudly organized public expositions of this material in connection with the National Exposition of 1884 in Turin, the first Congress of Criminal Anthropology of 1885 in Rome, and the Universal Exposition of 1889 in Paris. Put under the direction of his son-in-law, Mario Carrara, in 1904, the Museum remained after Lombroso's death as a school in the positivist science of reading the body for signs of immorality, insanity, and criminality.

ENRICO FERRI

Born in 1856, twenty-one years after Lombroso, Enrico Ferri was to become his most visible and indefatigable disciple. Even before meeting Lombroso he wrote a law thesis, defended in 1877, critiquing the notion of free will and arguing that individuals were not morally responsible for their behavior.[42] Ferri believed that the free choice of all members of society, whether mentally competent or not, was constrained to some degree and that it was useless for judges to try to measure such an abstract concept. But if criminals did not bear moral responsibility for their criminal acts, they did have a legal responsibility to repay society for damage to persons or property. Thus, he did not throw out the notion of punishment but rather shifted its foundations from moral retribution to social defense.

Such an interpretation clashed radically with that of the classical school and thus with most of Ferri's professors at the universities of Bologna and Pisa, where he did postdoctoral work under the guidance of Pietro Ellero and Francesco Carrara, respectively. Despite his unorthodoxy, he was offered the chairs of both Ellero and Carrara after their retirements. While writing his thesis Ferri was not yet convinced that lawyers should become involved in the empirical work of criminal anthropology; but by 1879 he was visiting Lombroso in Turin and learning to examine prisoners. In 1880 he helped Lombroso launch the *Archives* and contributed to the first volume.

Perhaps because of his legal training, Ferri's writings were more systematic than Lombroso's. It was Ferri who kept pushing Lombroso to develop a definitive classification of criminals, a task that was never completed in

---

42 The thesis titled "L'imputabilità e la negazione del libero arbitrio" was published in 1881 by Zanichelli of Bologna. For Ferri's biography, see entries in the *Encyclopedia italiana di scienze, lettere ed arti*, 36 vols. (Treccani, 1936), 15:64; Florian et al., *Dizionario di criminologia*, 2 vols. (Milan, 1943), 1:361–5; and Franco Andreucci and Tommaso Detti, eds., *Il movimento operaio italiano: Dizionario biografico, 1853–1943*, 6 vols. (Rome, 1978), 2:342–8. In English, see Thorsten Sellin's chapter on Ferri in Mannheim, *Pioneers of Criminology*. A bibliography of his principle writings can be found in the appendix of *Enrico Ferri: Maestro della scienza criminologica* (Milan, 1941), 261–70.

the latter's writings because he kept inventing new categories or revising old ones. Perhaps in exasperation Ferri created his own system of classification, one that changed little over his lifetime and seems to have inspired Lombroso's multiple attempts. Ferri arranged his categories along a scale of dangerousness, beginning with the occasional criminal, who had few abnormal physical and psychological traits and was therefore fairly innocuous; more of a threat to society, in increasing order, were criminals by passion, who were normal except for rare outbreaks of emotional violence; habitual criminals, who were occasional criminals pushed to recidivism by life in an evil environment; insane criminals with maladies familiar to psychiatrists; and, finally, born criminals. Although responsible for coining the term *born criminal*, Ferri's determinism was somewhat softer than Lombroso's; for example, in response to French critics of criminal anthropology, he allowed that born criminals were merely predisposed to crime and could lead normal lives if raised in the proper environment.[43] He was even more optimistic about the reformability of the other four categories, thus becoming a proponent of innovative measures to prevent crime and rehabilitate offenders. This strain of social reform has often been ignored in analyses of positivist criminology.

Ferri's classification of offenders formed part of what he came to call "criminal sociology," which he differentiated from both classical jurisprudence and, to a lesser extent, criminal anthropology. As a lawyer, he criticized the classical school, which considered crime only a "juridical problem" to be properly named and defined.[44] Whereas the majority of humanity immediately asks why a heinous crime has been committed, the classical jurist limits himself to questions such as: "What is the name of the crime committed by that man under such circumstances? Must it be classed as murder or patricide, attempted or incompleted manslaughter, and, if directed against property, is it theft, or illegal appropriation, or fraud?"[45] From Ferri's point of view, "rivers of ink have been spilled" over defining the difference between legal notions, such as incompleted and attempted crime, while classical legal education ignored the social dimension of crime.[46] Criminal sociology would repair this imbalance by directing its attention to the social phenomenon – the criminal – rather than the juridical fact of the crime.

To answer the question of the causes of crime Ferri developed a model of multiple causation. Showing great respect throughout his life for the

---

43 Enrico Ferri, *The Positivist School of Criminology: Three Lectures* (Chicago, 1913), 91–2.
44 Ibid., 71.   45 Ibid.
46 Ibid., 75.

"genius" of Lombroso and even labeling himself at times a criminal anthropologist, Ferri softened his master's emphasis on inherited stigmata and pathological epilepsy.[47] Although these physical and psychological defects were significant, they constituted only one of three categories of criminal causation. The second category was telluric, referring to forces in the physical environment, such as climate, the fertility of the soil, or the time of day. Social factors – including poverty, illiteracy, and bad families – constituted the final category. Although an ardent and active socialist, Ferri denied that poverty alone led to crime, because most of the poor led honest lives. The etiology of every crime lay in a combination of the three categories – anthropological, telluric, and social – so that even the occasional criminal acted under some type of mental imbalance brought out under certain environmental conditions.

That all crime was determined – either by instinct or the environment – was to Ferri a source of optimism rather than pessimism. At least it offered a way to measure criminality and understand its causes. The principle of free will, subscribed to by the classical school, could not be measured and thus contradicted "the law of causality, which is at the very foundation of modern scientific thought." Just as Galileo had destroyed the misperception that the earth, and therefore humanity, was the center of the universe and Darwin had destroyed the "anthropocentric illusion" that man is essentially different from plant and animal life, now positivists were using the same scientific reasoning to overthrow the myth of free will.[48] Instead, criminal sociology offered the prospect of a bright future in which positivists could isolate all the material causes of crime and identify which combination of factors had motivated each delinquent.

Positivist criminology also promised more justice because punishment would no longer be based on moral retribution, which was dear to nineteenth-century classicists. Ferri went back to Beccaria's original emphasis on prevention, although giving it a new interpretative twist. For Ferri, "penalties have the same relation to crime that medicine has to disease," and therefore criminology had to follow the recent evolution of medicine toward isolating the microbes that cause illness.[49] Once the etiology of crime had been analyzed, legislators needed to "apply the rules of social hygiene" in order to provide a telluric and social environment that discouraged deviance.[50] Social hygiene would rely essentially on what Ferri labeled "penal substitutes" like protection for orphans, improved education,

---

47 Ibid., 77.
49 Ibid., 98.

48 Ibid., 64.
50 Ibid., 99.

good housing, and the elimination of poverty. Those who still defied the law, especially if classified as occasional criminals, would be given suspended sentences, fined, or at most sent to humane reformatories to be educated and trained to work. The most incorrigible – insane and born criminals – would be sentenced to mental asylums and penitentiaries respectively, but always under an indeterminate sentence so that even the most vicious would have hope of release. Each institution, whether orphanage, reformatory, mental hospital, or prison, would be run by experts trained in positivist criminology who would scientifically customize the treatment of inmates and accurately recognize the signs of recovery necessary for release or parole.

Of all the positivist criminologists, Ferri was the most active in the PSI. Yet his conversion to socialism came late, after a much publicized sparring with Filippo Turati in the early 1880s over the role of biological determinism in crime.[51] During that period Ferri, like Lombroso, was still drawn to republicanism and resented the attacks of some socialists on the pioneering work of positivist criminologists. But Ferri became radicalized in the next ten years and joined the PSI in 1893, a year after its founding. The next year he published an impassioned defense of the compatibility of Darwinism – seen as the essence of criminal anthropology – and Marxism. Titled *Socialism and Modern Science*, this book helped to establish positivism as an important philosophical strain in Italian socialism.

According to Ferri, the compatibility between Darwinism and Marxism rested, first, on their agreement that society is not static but evolves and progresses. Because Darwinism had established change as fundamental to society, he argued that the capitalist system was not the economic embodiment of the struggle for existence, as many bourgeois writers claimed, but was bound to be superseded. According to Ferri, it would be "ridiculous" for a Darwinist to believe in the immutability of property relations because the economy – like the political structure, the family, and culture – was subject to continual evolution.[52]

Second, both Darwinism and Marxism were compatible in their materialism, with the former privileging biological facts and the latter economic conditions. As opposed to religion or idealist philosophies that appealed to God or some type of universal spirit to explain the world, positivist criminology and socialism were both scientific and empirical. Ferri saw no contradiction between biology and economics, arguing that economic

---

51 Ferri, *Socialismo e criminalità: Appunti* (Turin, 1883).
52 Ferri, *Socialism and Modern Science (Darwin-Spencer-Marx)* (New York, 1900), 96–7. This was a translation of *Socialismo e scienza positiva (Darwin, Spencer, Marx)*, published six years earlier.

conditions "are the resultant of the *ethnical* energies and aptitudes acting in a given *physical* environment," phrases that echoed his anthropological and telluric categories.[53] Criminal sociology needed to meld with socialism and its emphasis on the dynamic development of the proletariat in order to avoid "sterility," whereas socialism could assure its maturation from utopianism to science by becoming positivist. Based on such an understanding, "the two currents of evolutionist naturalism and scientific socialism will increasingly come to resemble each other and finally become identical by drawing their energies from the eternal ocean of life and of empirical truth."[54]

Finally, Ferri denied that the Darwinist principle of the struggle for existence was antithetical to a peaceful socialist society free from class conflict. He predicted that competition would become more benign and increasingly intellectual rather than economic as society progressed to a higher stage. Thus, each individual who worked for the collective could be guaranteed economic support without contradicting Darwinian principles. Yet he insisted that some individuals would always fail in the struggle for existence and continue to commit crimes even in a socialist society. Although the social determinants of crime could be eliminated, human anthropology and the physical environment would always remain in some ways outside human control. As a natural fact, inborn criminality, like physical disease, would always exist because "crime . . . is a department of human pathology."[55]

Ferri found a public platform for his political ideas as a left-wing member of the Chamber of Deputies after 1886, first as a republican and then as a socialist. He used his position to oppose the increasingly repressive policies of the liberal governments of the 1890s toward the peasants and the urban working class. When the Pelloux government in 1899 tried to push through parliament a series of decrees undercutting civil rights, Ferri – a brilliant orator – participated in the successful filibuster, talking "for hours and hours without ever saying . . . things that were not useful or pertinent to the discussion."[56] By 1903 he had risen high enough in the PSI to be given the editorship of *Avanti!*, the party newspaper. One biographer has labeled him "the most powerful man in the party" during this period.[57] His name also appeared frequently in *Critica sociale*, the highly respected intellectual weekly of the PSI. Despite his differences with the editors, Turati and Anna Kuliscioff, he was honored with a salute in 1891 to the first issue of his journal, *The Positivist School*, received respectful and sometimes

53 Ferri, *Socialism*, 164.   54 Ferri, *Positivismo*, 327.
55 Ferri, *Socialism*, 43.
56 Andreucci and Detti, *Dizionario biografico*, 2:346, quoting a contemporary of Ferri, A. Angiolini.
57 Ibid.

enthusiastic reviews of his books, and had the opportunity to air his views on the compatibility of positivism and socialism.[58] Ferri's views represented only one current of Italian socialism, however, and his analysis of criminality was labeled "conservative" by some colleagues in the party because he insisted that an equal distribution of wealth could not rid society of the born criminal.

In addition to politics, Ferri turned to several other arenas to spread his positivist faith. His best known book, *Criminal Sociology*, went through five editions between 1881 and 1929, the year of his death.[59] After helping Lombroso found the *Archives* in 1880 he established his own journal, *The Positivist School*, which was slanted more toward law than toward medicine. This magazine gave positivists a voice in a field that was still dominated by organs of the classical school, such as the *Rivista penale* of Luigi Lucchini. More than any other criminologist, Ferri was known as a great and stirring orator, and he lectured on positivist criminology throughout Europe and Latin America.[60] He also was a brilliant criminal lawyer, gaining a national reputation as early as 1885 for his successful defense of a group of peasants from his native province of Mantua who had been arrested for insurrection. Ferri published several collections of his speeches as a defense lawyer, with the explicit aim of illustrating to the public how positivism worked in practice in the courtroom.[61]

Equally concerned to convey positivist principles to his students, Ferri founded in 1912 a special institute within the law school at the University of Rome called the School of Applied Law and Criminal Justice. Ferri had received a professorship at the University of Rome in 1906, thirteen years after being fired from the University of Pisa for his membership in the PSI. The institute had two purposes, the first of which was to integrate criminal anthropology, psychology, and legal medicine into the traditional law curriculum.[62] Ferri recruited noted positivist criminologists like Sergio

---

58 See *Critica sociale* for the "Saluto" to The Positivist School in 1 (1891): 138; reviews of *Sociologia Criminale* in *Critica sociale* 2 (1892): 206–7, and *L'omicidio nell antropologia criminale* 4 (1894): 191–2; and Ferri's article titled "La scienza e la vita nel secolo XIX," 7 (1897).

59 The first two editions were titled *I nuovi orizzonti del diritto e della procedura penale* and appeared in 1881 and 1884; the third edition, titled *Sociologia criminale*, appeared in 1892 followed by the fourth in 1900 and the fifth in 1929–30. It was translated into Spanish in 1887, Russian in 1889, French in 1893, German in 1896, English in 1917, and Japanese in 1923. See "Dati bio-bibliografici" in *Enrico Ferri: Maestro*, 261–70.

60 On Ferri as an orator, see Scipio Sighele, "Ferri Oratore," in *Enrico Ferri: Maestro*, 161–71. Ferri was invited twice to give a tour of lectures in Latin America, in 1908 and 1910; he also gave courses at the University of Brussels (1885–1903) and the École des hautes études in Paris (1889–1901).

61 *Difese penali, studi di giurisprudenza, arringhe civili*, 2d ed. (Turin, 1923), 1:1–2.

62 On Ferri's school, see Giulio Andrea Belloni, "La Scuola d'applicazione," in *Enrico Ferri: Maestro*, 207–19.

Sergi (son of the famous Giuseppe Sergi), Benigno di Tullio, Sante De Sanctis, Alfredo Niceforo, and Salvatore Ottolenghi as his teaching staff for such subjects. Second, he sought to turn the school into a laboratory where students would learn to examine criminals, dissect the corpses of victims of criminal homicide, and use instruments of criminal identification. Replicating procedures learned many decades earlier from Lombroso, Ferri took students to prisons, criminal insane asylums, and juvenile reformatories to make them familiar with the human "data" processed by the courts. He delighted his students and gained fame for his ability to walk into a prison and identify murderers based solely on their physical features.[63] Ferri's specialty was a course called "The Theoretical and Practical Examination of Real Trials," in which he replaced the abstract discussion of legal principles with a close reading of famous criminal cases, including those he had won. Although its name has been changed, the Institute of Criminal Law in Rome still proudly displays Ferri's bust in its library.

CONCLUSION

Lombroso and Ferri were major protagonists in the debates that raged at the International Congresses of Criminal Anthropology, initiated by the Italians in Rome in 1885. At this first meeting Lombroso's theory of atavism reigned virtually uncontested as the European consensus on the etiology of crime. By the second congress of 1889 in Paris, however, the French counter-attacked with an alternate theory that stressed the environmental roots of degeneracy. Yet, as Laurent Mucchielli argues, the French position rested heavily on heredity, so that their opposition now appears more nationalistic than substantive. The chapters by Mariacarla Gadebusch Bondio, Nicole Rafter, and Ricardo Salvatore attest to the fame of Lombroso in countries as diverse as Germany, the United States, and Argentina, although his foreign followers sometimes modified his theories to fit local intellectual traditions and political exigencies.[64] Lombroso boasted that other nations had incorporated many of his ideas into their criminal justice systems and continually berated the Italian state for being slow to adopt policies like parole, criminal insane asylums, and reform schools for juvenile delinquents.

Although criminal anthropology suffered setbacks in the international arena, positivist criminology developed steadily as a well-respected and

63 An example is cited in the "Rievocazione" in *Enrico Ferri: Maestro*, 11. He boasted about this ability as early as 1889 in a letter to Napoleone Colajanni; see Salvatore Massimo Ganci, ed., *Democrazia e socialismo in Italia: Carteggi di Napoleone Colajanni* (Milan, 1959), 278–81.
64 See the chapters by Mariacarla Gadebusch Bondio, Laurent Mucchielli, Nicole Rafter, and Ricardo Salvatore in this book.

popular discipline in Italy through the 1880s and 1890s. One mark of its health was the growing number of disciples who collaborated with Lombroso. With the exception of the anthropologist Giuseppe Sergi, who was born in 1841, these disciples were decidedly younger than Lombroso, attesting to the continuing attraction of his personality and ideas on students in a variety of fields. The second generation of positivist criminologists, born between 1852 and 1869, included not only Ferri and Garofalo but also Salvatore Ottolenghi and Mario Carrara, both of whom trained in legal medicine; Eugenio Florian, Scipio Sighele, and Adolfo Zerboglio, who all trained in law; and Sante De Sanctis, who trained in psychiatry. The fascination of criminal anthropology stretched even into a third generation of men like the sociologists Alfredo Niceforo and Guglielmo Ferrero and professors of clinical medicine, Giacinto Viola and Nicola Pende. Along with Lombroso, this large group of disciples not only trained other students but also carried their positivist convictions into their careers in the courts, prisons, insane asylums, reformatories, and other public institutions. Criminal anthropology was not confined to the ivory tower and would continue to influence public debates about Italy's system of criminal justice through the fascist period.

7

Criminal Anthropology

Its Reception in the United States and the Nature of Its Appeal

NICOLE HAHN RAFTER

Why do some ideas immediately grab people's attention and elicit assent whereas others, equally worthy, fail to attract notice? This is in part an issue of receptivity; I raise it here in the course of mapping the routes through which, starting circa 1890, criminal anthropology entered American thinking. I identify four situational factors that predisposed Americans to criminal anthropology: the socioeconomic context, the intellectual context, the criminal justice context, and the unsettled state of the professions and disciplines related to criminal anthropology. After assessing receptivity, I identify the authors who introduced U.S. audiences to criminal anthropology and compare their work to that of Cesare Lombroso, the Italian founder of the field, noting areas in which the Americans simply parroted the born-criminal doctrine and others in which they modified it. In the final section of this chapter I discuss sources of the doctrine's appeal, arguing that the visual codes of criminal anthropology conveyed criminological information more efficiently, powerfully, and pleasurably than other modes of explaining crime.

AUDIENCE RECEPTIVITY

Like some people, some theories are lucky, appearing at the right place at the right time. This was certainly true of criminal anthropology, which was introduced to the United States in the 1890s, a time when Americans concerned with social control were primed for exactly this sort of doctrine.

My thanks to Mary Gibson of the John Jay College of Criminal Justice in New York City for providing me with a copy of Lombroso's *Atlante*, the illustrated appendix to the 5th edition of *L'uomo Delinquente* (Turin, 1897), and to Dario Melossi and Richard Wetzell for their helpful comments on an earlier version of this chapter.

The Socioeconomic Context

During the second half of the nineteenth century, urbanization and industrialization transformed the United States from an agricultural into an industrial economy and its living centers from isolated small towns to interconnected urban centers. New social classes emerged, including those composed of wealthy industrialists, middle-class professionals, and an underclass with few economic or political resources. Financial instability throughout the late nineteenth century exacerbated such problems as poverty, the integration of immigrant populations, and public health. The professional middle classes grew concerned about the steadily growing underclass, whose members seemed strange and dangerous. It was difficult to understand where they originated, how they came to be so poor, and why they lived in such degrading conditions.

Social-control workers, a subgroup of middle-class professionals, began to conduct scientific studies of those they called "the dependent, defective, and delinquent classes" (meaning the poor, the chronically ill, and the criminal), but they studied these populations with little sympathy or comprehension.[1] Problems such as poverty seemed to be the result of free will, not social forces. In fact, late-nineteenth-century social-control workers found it difficult even to distinguish among dependents, defectives, and delinquents. They believed that poverty, chronic illness, and criminality were interrelated and indeed interchangeable problems, merely different manifestations of an underlying degeneracy.[2]

The socioeconomic situation, then, encouraged acceptance of a doctrine such as criminal anthropology that cast a socially problematic group as foreign and threatening. The considerable distance between, and tensions among, social classes made the underclass appear alien and criminalistic.[3]

The Intellectual Context

"In the nineteenth century," Charles Rosenberg has remarked, "science for the first time assumed a significant place in the hierarchy of American

1 I use the term *social-control workers* to refer to men and women of the late nineteenth and early twentieth centuries who engaged, as volunteers or paid professionals, in "charity" or "social welfare" work. They included alienists (psychiatrists), commissioners on the state boards of charity, early intelligence testers and other psychologists, full-time eugenics crusaders, public health officials, social workers, sociologists, statisticians, and superintendents of institutions for the feeble-minded (mentally retarded), insane, delinquent, and criminal. For a discussion of the location and significance of this group in the shifting social-class structure of the late nineteenth century, see Nicole Hahn Rafter, "Eugenics, Class, and the Professionalization of Social Control," in George Bridges and Martha Myers, eds., *Inequality, Crime, and Social Control* (Boulder, Colo., 1994), 215–26.
2 See, e.g., Richard L. Dugdale, *"The Jukes": A Study in Crime, Pauperism, Disease and Heredity; also Further Studies of Criminals* (New York, 1877).
3 See C. Wright Mills, *The Power Elite* (London, 1956).

values."[4] Although science did not displace God, it did generate its own set of beliefs about the origins and meaning of human life. Charles Darwin's stunning theory of evolution, in particular, led to reinterpretations of life as a scientifically determined struggle for survival.

By the mid-nineteenth century science had profoundly affected thinking about crime, in part through the doctrine of phrenology, according to which human behavior is determined by the development of various "faculties" of the brain, expressed by the shape of the skull. Although phrenology was a way of explaining all human behavior, not simply criminal behavior, it encouraged Americans to think about crime in terms of biological abnormality.[5] Phrenologists' promotion of the medical interpretation of deviance as a sickness was another way in which they anticipated criminal anthropology. Thus, the intellectual context in which criminal anthropology took root was one in which Americans were already familiar with some of its key assumptions, including the ideas that criminality is a form of sickness, that there is something significant about the criminal's brain, that biology mirrors morality, and that crime can be addressed through science.

Phrenology's heyday had passed by 1860; more current in the 1890s was another biological explanation of crime – degeneration theory, which held that socially problematic people are devolving from normality. Degeneration, proponents of this theory taught, can manifest itself in various forms – pauperism in one member of a family, chronic illness or idiocy in another, criminality in a third; the specific manifestation is less significant than the underlying malady of degeneration. Richard L. Dugdale, Josephine Shaw Lowell, Charles Richmond Henderson, and other writers described degeneration as a heritable tendency to decay, one that afflicts most dependents, defectives, and delinquents.[6] But their doctrine, though hereditarian, was neither fully deterministic nor wholly pessimistic. Based on the Lamarckian concept of the inheritance of acquired characteristics, degeneration theory held that devolution can be reversed by clean living and self-discipline, so that eventually a degenerate family can evolve back to middle-class normality. Popular throughout the Western world in the late nineteenth century, degeneration theory prepared audiences for criminal anthropology by

---

4 Charles E. Rosenberg, *No Other Gods: On Science and American Social Thought* (Baltimore, 1976), 2.
5 See, e.g., Eric T. Carlson, "The Influence of Phrenology on Early American Psychiatric Thought," *Arch. Psych.* 115 (1958): 535–8; John Davies, *Phrenology: Fad and Science – A 19th Century American Crusade* (New Haven, Conn., 1955); and Roger Cooter, *The Cultural Meaning of Popular Science: Phrenology and the Organization of Consent in Nineteenth-Century Britain* (Cambridge, 1984), a study that applies to the United States as well as Great Britain.
6 Dugdale, *"The Jukes"*; Josephine Shaw Lowell, "One Means of Preventing Pauperism," National Conference of Charities and Correction, *Proceedings 1879*: 189–200; Charles R. Henderson, *An Introduction to the Study of the Dependent, Defective, and Delinquent Classes* (Boston, 1893).

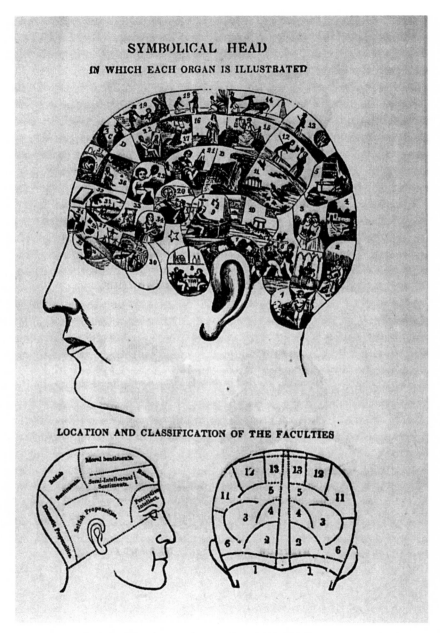

Figure 1. According to phrenologists, the atrophy, underdevelopment, or overdevelopment of specific faculties could lead to criminal behavior. From J. G. Spurzheim, *Education: Its Elementary Principles Founded on the Nature of Man* (New York, 1883), p. 322. Photo: Ann Arouson.

tracing criminality to bad inheritance and presenting criminals as devolved creatures, reversions to a lower form of life.[7]

Another influential factor in the intellectual context was the advent of eugenical thinking. By 1880 American social-control specialists openly advocated policies that would prevent degenerates from reproducing, and by the turn of the century, when Americans had become familiar with Sir Francis Galton's term *eugenics*, the goal of controlling reproduction by the unfit had become the basis for a vigorous social movement.[8] Although Cesare Lombroso himself did not advocate eugenic solutions, his doctrine was entirely compatible with eugenics.[9] Americans already crusading for eugenic measures found in criminal anthropology seemingly scientific support for their own program.

The Criminal Justice Context

From time to time crime becomes a compelling social issue. In the United States the late nineteenth century was one of those times. Americans debated the causes of crime, developed the idea of degrees of criminality, and mobilized for scientific reforms of the criminal justice system – all steps that increased receptivity to criminal anthropology. Some Americans were disturbed by the inability of the police to identify "revolvers," those who were arrested for repeated offenses. Others lamented the inability of prisons to reform offenders. At an 1870 meeting in Cincinnati, reformers resolved to totally revamp penal philosophy and practice. Formulating the new philosophy of penal reform, they pictured the criminal as sick and in need of rehabilitation, and they described rehabilitation as a process requiring "scientific" penology.[10] Delegates to this 1870 prison congress advocated indefinite

---

7 J. Edward Chamberlin and Sander L. Gilman, eds., *Degeneration: The Dark Side of Progress* (New York, 1985); Daniel Pick, *Faces of Degeneration: A European Disorder, c. 1848 – c. 1918* (Cambridge, 1989); Nicole Hahn Rafter, *Creating Born Criminals* (Urbana, Ill., 1997).

8 Mark H. Haller, *Eugenics: Hereditarian Attitudes in American Thought* (New Brunswick, N.J., 1963); Nicole Hahn Rafter, "Claims-Making and Socio-Cultural Context in the First U.S. Eugenics Campaign," *Social Problems* 39 (1992): 17–34.

9 Apparently, Lombroso spoke eugenically only in a posthumously published article written shortly before his death in 1909, and this in a casual remark about how life confinement of insane criminals would protect society, "making at the same time their propagation impossible." Cesare Lombroso, "Crime and Insanity in the Twenty-First Century," *Journal of Criminal Law, Criminology, and Police Science* 3 (1912): 60. However, although this is the only eugenic remark by Lombroso that I have found, one might get a different impression from material not yet translated into English.

10 The proceedings of the 1870 congress were published as E. C. Wines, ed., *Transactions of the National Congress on Penitentiary and Reformatory Discipline, 1870* (Albany, N.Y., 1871). The concept of scientific penology is outlined in the paper that Zebulon Brockway, the most influential American penologist of the nineteenth century, delivered at the congress; see Zebulon R. Brockway, "The Ideal of a True

sentencing, with release dates to be determined by scientific experts. The reformers further advocated prisoner classification by degree of reformability and an analogous classification of prisons, so that one institution in each state could be designated for incurables, those whom Lombroso later called "born criminals."

In France a police official named Alphonse Bertillon met the concerns over recidivism with a method of precisely recording the physical features of each person arrested. Through an intricate method of filing and retrieval, Bertillon's documents could lead the police to the prior records of someone they had arrested.[11] This method was widely adopted in the United States. At the turn of the century, before the invention of fingerprinting, *bertillonage* marked an outstanding advance in the scientization of criminalistics and penology. Although the system was not based on a theory of crime, it did give the impression that criminality could be read from the body, an idea not only compatible but entirely congruent with criminal anthropology.[12]

The late nineteenth century, in short, was a period in which both policing and penology were professionalizing, becoming more scientific, and making stronger claims to expertise. In addition, criminal justice officials began to create better records and make greater use of statistics. These concerns and developments meshed well with criminal anthropology. In fact, Lombroso, who kept a close watch on developments in the United States, thought that one of the major penological experiments in late-nineteenth-century America, the introduction of indeterminate sentencing at the Elmira, New York, Reformatory, was designed to test his own theories.[13] He was mistaken, but it is true that there was little criminological distance between Elmira's experiments and Lombroso's teachings.

The Professional Context

The late nineteenth century saw the emergence of new specialties in social-control work: penology, psychology, public-health medicine, psychiatry, social work, sociology, and statistics. The state boards of charity – the

---

Prison System for a State," in E. C. Wines, ed., *Transactions of the National Congress on Penitentiary and Reformatory Discipline, 1870* (Albany, N.Y., 1871), 38–65. The concept was popularized by books such as Henry M. Boies, *The Science of Penology* (New York, 1901).

11 Alphonse Bertillon, "The Bertillon System of Identification," *The Forum* 11 (1891): 330–41; Alphonse Bertillon, *Signaletic Instruction* (Chicago, 1896).

12 "For Bertillon, the criminal body expressed nothing," Allan Sekula observes in "The Body and the Archive," *October* 39 (1986): 30.

13 Gina Lombroso-Ferrero, *Criminal Man According to the Classification of Cesare Lombroso* (1911; reprint, Montclair, N.J., 1972): xxix–xxx.

ABSTRACT OF
THE ANTHROPOMETRICAL SIGNALMENT

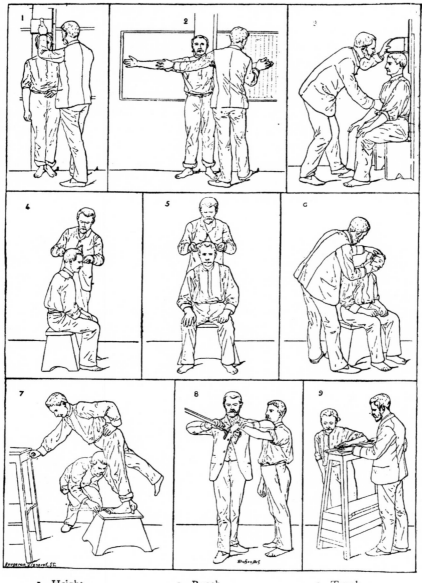

1. Height.	2. Reach.	3. Trunk.
4. Length of head.	5. Width of head.	6. Right ear.
7. Left foot.	8. Left middle finger.	9. Left forearm.

(ii)

Figure 2. Although Bertillon measured criminals for purposes of identification, he found no meanings in the criminal body. From Alphonse Bertillon, *Signaletic Instruction* (Chicago, 1896), Frontispiece.

philanthropic groups that managed institutions for the so-called dependent, defective, and delinquent classes – evolved into more specialized welfare bureaucracies with positions that required training. But at the time criminal anthropology arrived in the United States the social-control specialties were still in the process of formation. The various professions and disciplines related to criminal anthropology lacked clear jurisdictional boundaries, and in many cases their representatives vied for professional territory and the right to claim expertise.[14] To some members of these new social-control specialties, criminal anthropology offered an authoritative basis for dealing with criminals – and thus for claiming professional status. It provided scientific information and had clear policy implications. For penologists in particular, criminal anthropology offered a way to distinguish themselves from the older and more custodial prison keepers or wardens and to establish themselves as professionals.

In the United States, then, criminal anthropology fell on fertile ground. The people most concerned with crime control were receptive to the idea of the criminal as a biologically distinct and inferior being. But although it is important to identify receptivity factors, this type of analysis can overemphasize criminal anthropology as an import and obscure the fact that Americans had identified the criminalistic degenerate, a first cousin of Lombroso's born criminal, before they ever heard of Lombroso. In other words, both Lombroso and his American followers were part of an international culture in which, as at no other time in Western history, criminal anthropology was likely to seem plausible.

THE DIFFUSION OF CRIMINAL ANTHROPOLOGY IN THE UNITED STATES

Criminal anthropology made its way into the United States by means of five main routes: first, Moriz Benedikt's book *Anatomical Studies upon Brains of Criminals*, translated and published in the United States in 1881;[15] second, articles by Americans who knew of Lombroso's work indirectly or directly;[16] third, Havelock Ellis's *The Criminal* (1890), a popular book based

14 See Rafter, *Creating Born Criminals* and Leila Zenderland, "The Debate over Diagnosis: Henry Herbert Goddard and the Medical Acceptance of Intelligence Testing," in Michael M. Sokal, ed., *Psychological Testing and American Society, 1890–1930* (New Brunswick, N.J., 1987), 46–74. See also Stanley Cohen, *Visions of Social Control* (Cambridge, 1984).

15 Moriz Benedikt, *Anatomical Studies upon Brains of Criminals* (New York, 1881).

16 Joseph Jastrow, "A Theory of Criminality," *Science* 8 (1886): 20–22; Henry Charles Lea, "The Increase of Crime and Positivist Criminology," *The Forum* 17 (1894): 666–75; William Noyes, "The Criminal Type," *American Journal of Social Science* 24 (1888): 31–42; Hamilton D. Wey, "A Plea for

Table 1. *Major Books on Criminal Anthropology Published in the United States (1893–1911)*

Author	Title	First Pub.	Other Pub.
Arthur MacDonald	*Criminology*	1893	–
Henry Boies	*Prisoners and Paupers*	1893	–
Charles R. Henderson	*An Introduction to the Study of the Dependent, Defective, and Delinquent Classes*	1893	1901, 1908, 1909
Eugene Talbot	*Degeneracy*	1898	1904
August Drähms	*The Criminal: His Personnel and Environment*	1900	–
W. Duncan McKim	*Heredity and Human Progress*	1900	1901
Henry Boies	*The Science of Penology*	1901	–
G. Frank Lydston	*The Diseases of Society*	1904	1905, 1906, 1908
Philip Parsons	*Responsibility for Crime*	1909	–

Source: Library of Congress, National Union Catalog, for all except Drähms.

Full citations for books listed are: Arthur MacDonald, *Criminology*, 2d ed., with an introduction by Cesare Lombroso (New York, 1893); Henry M. Boies, *Prisoners and Paupers* (New York, 1893); Charles R. Henderson, *An Introduction to the Study of the Dependent, Defective, and Delinquent Classes* (Boston, 1893); Eugene S. Talbot, *Degeneracy: Its Causes, Signs, and Results* (London, 1898); August Drähms, *The Criminal: His Personnel and Environment – A Scientific Study* (1900; reprint, Montclair, N.J., 1971); W. Duncan McKim, *Heredity and Human Progress* (New York, 1900); Henry M. Boies, *The Science of Penology* (New York, 1901); G. Frank Lydston, *The Diseases of Society* (Philadelphia, 1904); Philip A. Parsons, *Responsibility for Crime* (New York, 1909).

heavily on Lombroso's *Criminal Man*;[17] fourth, translations of Lombroso's work,[18] although for the most part these were not available until after 1910; and fifth, American books that popularized Lombroso's theory. It is on this fifth group that I concentrate here.[19] There were nine of these books, written by eight different authors (see table 1).

The authors of these books on criminal anthropology were all well-educated, male professionals, but they were occupationally diverse. Some were involved in social-control work. (Henry M. Boies was a member

Physical Training of Youthful Criminals," National Prison Association, *Proceedings 1888*: 181–93, and "Criminal Anthropology," National Prison Association, *Proceedings 1890*: 274–90.

17 Havelock Ellis, *The Criminal* (London, 1890).

18 Cesare Lombroso, "Introduction" to Arthur MacDonald, *Criminology* (New York, 1893), vii–x; "Criminal Anthropology: Its Origin and Application," *Forum* 20 (1895), 33–49; introduction to August Drähms, *The Criminal* (1900; reprint, Montclair, N.J., 1971), xxvii–xxviii; *Crime: Its Causes and Remedies* (1911; reprint, Boston, 1918); "Crime and Insanity in the Twenty-First Century"; Cesare Lombroso and William Ferrero, *The Female Offender* (1895; reprint, New York, 1915); Lombroso-Ferrero, *Criminal Man*.

19 For more detail on the other four routes, see Nicole Hahn Rafter, "Criminal Anthropology in the United States," *Criminology* 30 (1992): 525–45. This article also outlines how I define American books on criminal anthropology and how I went about identifying them.

of Pennsylvania's Board of Public Charities; Drähms had been a resident chaplain at San Quentin; and Charles R. Henderson had been a welfare worker.) Others were educators (Henderson, G. Frank Lydston, Arthur MacDonald, Philip Parsons, and Eugene Talbot), physicians (Lydston, W. Duncan McKim, and Talbot), or ministers (Drähms and Henderson). Professional heterogeneity characterized most of these men. McKim held both Ph.D. and M.D. degrees; Lydston, a physician, was also a university professor and successful author; Henderson, a minister heavily involved in welfare work, taught sociology at the University of Chicago; MacDonald, a psychologist and educator, claimed to have studied theology, medicine, psychiatry, and criminology; and Talbot, a professor of dental and oral surgery, held both M.D. and D.D.S. degrees.

Thus, like Lombroso, who moved into criminology from medicine, the Americans came to criminology from the outside, as amateur specialists. This situation was inevitable, given that the social sciences were not yet clearly defined disciplines. At that point the field of criminology had no "inside," no training program or core of knowledge and goals. The eight U.S. authors who popularized criminal anthropology had few qualifications other than an ability to digest source materials and speak authoritatively. But this was an advantage for criminal anthropology: If social-control work and related disciplines had been more mature, amateur specialists in criminal anthropology would not have been able to write as authorities about the causes of crime.

The books addressed somewhat different audiences but were generally directed toward educated laypersons, especially the growing body of social-control workers. Again, the immaturity of these professions was favorable for criminal anthropology because there was no body of contradictory information. The only way to criticize criminal anthropology, at first, was through religion, an approach that Lombroso's supporters dismissed as unscientific.[20] Thus, the "professional readers" at whom Lydston and the others aimed their books had little access to alternative theories.[21]

What did these major U.S. works on criminal anthropology say? How closely did they adhere to Lombroso's own work? Most of the American authors repeated – indeed, lovingly repeated – Lombroso's litanies of the physical and behavioral anomalies of the born criminal: his pointed head, heavy jaw, and long arms; his laziness, frivolity, and moral insensibility; his fondness for tattoos. However, even while devoting entire chapters to the born criminal's stigmata, five of the eight American authors expressed

---

20 See, e.g., G. Frank Lydston, *The Diseases of Society* (Philadelphia, 1905), 17–18.
21 Ibid., 9.

doubts about his very existence.[22] Drähms, for example, felt that the criminal anthropologists had not conclusively verified their theory, while MacDonald was aware of other, more sociological theories of crime for which there also seemed to be scientific evidence.[23] Although these five were unable to resist reporting Lombroso's galvanizing findings, they qualified their reports, usually without resolving the tension between their enthusiasm for criminal anthropology and their doubts about it.

Insofar as they deviated from Lombroso's teachings, the Americans did so not by rejecting his theory but by supplementing it, particularly by placing greater emphasis on the criminal's weak intelligence.[24] In *Criminal Man*, Lombroso paid little attention to the criminal's mentality aside from stating that "*Intelligence* is feeble in some and exaggerated in others."[25] Four of the eight U.S. criminal anthropologists, in contrast, carried Lombroso's implications to their logical conclusion by finding that criminals were intellectually as well as ethically weak, mentally as well as morally imbecilic.[26]

The U.S. authors further supplemented Lombroso's work by more thoroughly integrating criminal anthropology with degeneration theory. Lombroso did not immediately realize that degeneration could explain the criminal's bad heredity; at first he relied on the notion of atavism.[27] His American followers, writing after degeneration theory had been around for a while, made it the basis for their hereditarianism. Moreover, their deeper immersion in degeneration theory led them to place more emphasis on the interconnections among degenerate types. Henderson's book was titled *An Introduction to the Study of the Dependent, Defective, and Delinquent Classes*, and McKim wrote that "vice, crime, and insanity may be regarded as merely different phases of degeneracy which so resemble one another that we are often at a loss when we would distinguish between them."[28]

---

22 MacDonald, Henderson, Lydston, Drähms, and Parsons.

23 Drähms, *Criminal*, 7, 27; MacDonald, *Criminology*, 272a, 272b.

24 Here I make inferences only on the basis of those of Lombroso's works that have been translated into English. A fuller view might lead to different conclusions.

25 Lombroso-Ferrero, *Criminal Man*, 41 (emphasis in original); see also Lombroso and Ferrero, *Female Offender*, 170–71.

26 Talbot, Lydston, MacDonald, and Drähms.

27 See Mary Gibson's chapter in this book; Maurice Parmelee, "Introduction to the English Version" of Cesare Lombroso, *Crime: Its Causes and Remedies* (1911; Boston, 1918), xxix; Marvin Wolfgang, "Cesare Lombroso," in Hermann Mannheim, ed., *Pioneers in Criminology*, 2d ed. (Montclair, N.J., 1972), 247, 249. For another view, see Peter Becker, "Controversy over Meanings: The Debate Between Cesare Lombroso and his Critics about the Signs and the Habit of Criminals," paper delivered at the 1994 annual meeting of the American Society of Criminology, in Miami, in which he argues that Lombroso derived his theory of the criminal as atavism not from Darwin but from other evolutionists who stressed recapitulation, the idea that every human starts at step one in the evolutionary process. In this view, criminals differ from the lawful in that they do not evolve as far.

28 McKim, *Heredity and Human Progress*, 64.

Like Lombroso, half of the major U.S. criminal anthropologists showed little or no interest in eugenics. The other four, however, championed eugenic solutions. Two supported life sentences on the grounds that these would prevent criminals from breeding.[29] Boies and several others recommended marriage restrictions: "The marriages of all criminals should be prohibited, but the utmost vigilance should be exercised to prevent the marriage of the instinctive."[30] Some even advised sterilization.[31] McKim, the most extreme, recommended death by carbonic acid gas as the "surest, the simplest, the kindest, and most humane means for preventing reproduction among those whom we deem unworthy of this high privilege."[32] He endorsed criminal anthropology *because* it fit well with eugenics, and two of the other authors (Boies and Lydston) also may have been drawn to Lombroso's theory for eugenic motives. Thus, even though there was no necessary connection between the two doctrines, links were easily made, a compatibility that led to greater eugenic content in the work of American criminal anthropologists than in Lombroso's.

In the United States, then, criminal anthropology was promoted by neophyte criminologists, amateurs who became overnight specialists in the field. They directed their books at other well-educated citizens, men and women who were equally likely to be concerned about social control and equally unprepared to examine criminal anthropology critically. The promoters repeated Lombroso's contentions about the born criminal as a savage atavism whom nature had thoughtfully stigmatized so he could be easily recognized. However, the eight authors also Americanized the born criminal, adding such characteristics as low intelligence and degenerate relatives. Some also Americanized the solutions to innate criminality by advocating eugenics.

THE PLEASURES OF CRIMINAL ANTHROPOLOGY

What made criminal anthropology attractive, not just to Americans but to others as well? What were the sources of its persuasiveness and appeal? How did its visual rhetoric work?

One way to approach these issues is to compare the work of Lombroso and his closest English-speaking follower, Ellis, with that of their criminological predecessors, the phrenologists, and of three contemporaries known for their

---

29 Boies, *Prisoners and Paupers*; Parsons, *Responsibility for Crime*.
30 Boies, *Science of Penology*, 239; see also Boies, *Prisoners and Paupers*, 280; Lydston, *Diseases of Society*, 557–62; and Parsons, *Responsibility for Crime*, 198–9.
31 Boies, *Prisoners and Paupers, Science of Penology*; Lydston, *Diseases of Society*.
32 McKim, *Heredity and Human Progress*, 188.

criminological work: the Scottish prison physician J. Bruce Thomson, the English psychiatrist Henry Maudsley, and the Hungarian physician Moriz Benedikt.

Phrenology constituted an important forerunner of criminal anthropology, not only in its substantive claims about the relationship of criminality to the body, but also in its use of visual imagery. Phrenologists made images of the head in several media, including line drawings and porcelain busts. (Novelty items such as walking sticks topped with phrenological heads were also popular.) Moreover, because phrenologists often illustrated the functions of the various mental faculties with tiny pictures, their visual language was highly accessible.

By contrast, J. Bruce Thomson, the Scottish prison physician who in about 1870 wrote an influential article on criminal anthropology, and Henry Maudsley, the great English psychiatric criminologist, apparently used no illustrations at all in their major works on crime.[33] This put their work at a disadvantage in terms of popular appeal. Similarly, although Benedikt's *Anatomical Studies on Brains of Criminals* included numerous line drawings of animal and criminal brains, there was little variety in these illustrations, and their explanatory codes are almost impossible to decipher. In addition, it is difficult to grasp the illustrations' point through visual inspection alone.[34]

Lombroso and Ellis, like the phrenologists and Benedikt, illustrated their texts with line drawings, but their drawings depicted a far greater variety of objects – not only brains and skulls but also maps, prison cell hieroglyphics, measuring tools, bodies, and body parts. Moreover, while the illustrations of the phrenologists and Benedikt were somewhat abstract (e.g., representations of standardized human faculties or, in Benedikt's case, of a typical bear's brain), Lombroso's and Ellis's tended to be more specific and immediate: drawings of actual people, often people in action, or of specific tattoos and prison cell markings.

In addition, Lombroso and Ellis used a greater range of media to convey their criminological points. Both made liberal use of photographs, with Ellis including several of the haunting composite photographs pioneered by Galton. Lombroso used photographs of statues as well as actual people, and he had a museum that displayed actual criminological artifacts including bits of tattooed skin.

---

33 J. Bruce Thomson, "The Psychology of Criminals," *Journal of Mental Science* 17 (1870): 321–50; Henry Maudsley, *Responsibility in Mental Disease* (1874; New York, 1876).

34 Indeed, it is difficult to understand Benedikt's thesis even after reading the book carefully and studying the pictures at length.

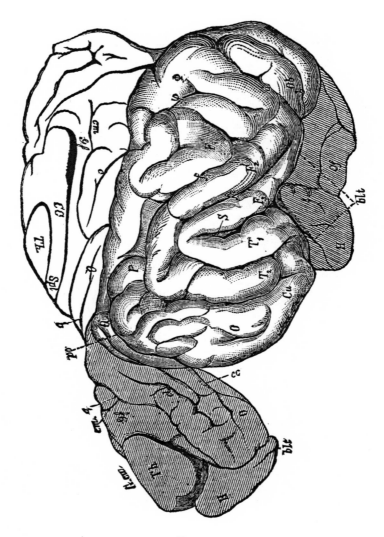

BEAR.

(With the medial and basilar surfaces turned and brought to view.)
F. 1, F. 2, F. 3.=1st, 2d, and 3d frontal gyri.
O. O.=Occipital lobe.
P.=Parietal lobe.

Figure 3. It is difficult to grasp the point of Benedikt's illustrations, including this diagram of a bear's brain, although his book claims that criminals have anomalous brains. From Moriz Benedikt, *Anatomical Studies upon Brains of Criminals* (1881; reprint, New York, 1981), p. 164.

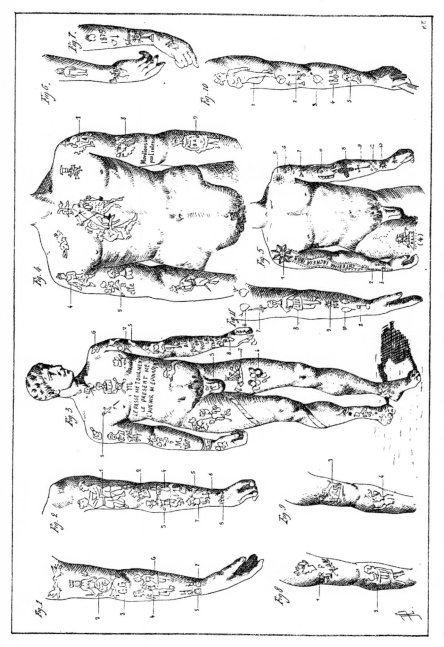

Figure 4. Lombroso interpreted criminals' tattoos as evidence of the criminal's primitive nature. From Cesare Lombroso, *Atlante*, Appendix to the 5th edition of *L'uomo Delinquente* (Torino, 1897), Tav. LXV.

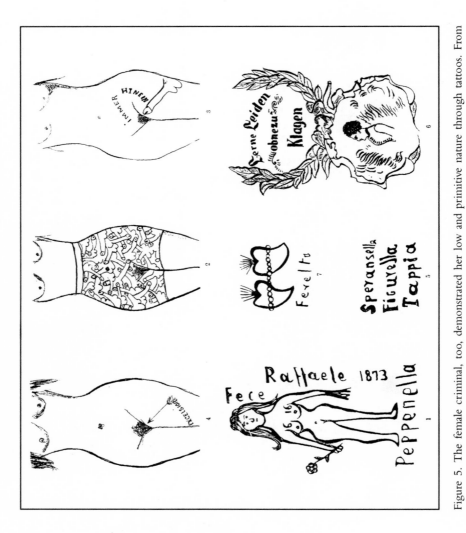

Figure 5. The female criminal, too, demonstrated her low and primitive nature through tattoos. From Cesare Lombroso, *Atlante*, Appendix to the 5th edition of *L'uomo Delinquente* (Torino, 1897), Tav. LXVI.

Figure 6. Photographs of Russian female offenders illustrating their coarse nature and facial anomalies. From Cesare Lombroso and William Ferrero, *The Female Offender* (New York, 1915), Plate I.

Thus, in answer to the question of what made criminal anthropology appealing I would point out, first, that criminal anthropology was much more visual and graphic than other theories of crime. Its foundational texts were lively and accessible. Moreover, its photographs, maps, and drawings of

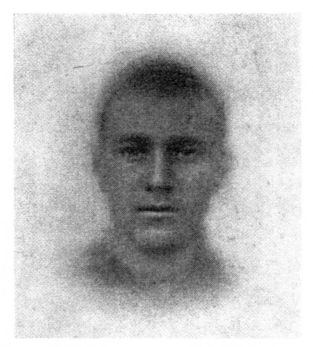

Figure 7. One of the most remarkable illustrations in Havelock Ellis's *The Criminal* is a composite photograph of 38 criminals at the Elmira Reformatory. Galton invented this technology in a search for the average or typical criminal face. From Havelock Ellis, *The Criminal* (London, 1890), Plate XV.

measuring tools carried an assertion of scientific status, bolstering criminal anthropologists' claims to objectivity.[35]

But although Lombrosian images appealed as science, they also were excellent fictions. They stimulate strong emotions, and although they do not actually tell stories, they inspire us to think narratively as other criminological images available at the time do not. In this regard we might note that the verbal discourses of criminal anthropology also often contained anecdotes (see the texts of Benedikt, Maudsley, and Thomson). In this regard, criminal anthropology harks back to the phrenological writing of Eliza Farnham, who provided narratives of particular cases.[36] Narratives have more popular appeal than dry, academic texts.

---

35 See David Green, "Veins of Resemblance: Photography and Eugenics," *Oxford Art Review* 7, no. 2 (1985): 3–16; Sekula, "Body and the Archive."

36 Eliza B. Farnham, "Introductory Preface" and "Appendix" to M. B. Sampson, *Rationale of Crime* (New York, 1846).

A second source of criminal anthropology's appeal lies in the area of ontology. Through their discursive and visual texts, criminal anthropologists created a new being: the born criminal. This figure has enormous explanatory power. Once we have grasped who he is – the essence of his being – we understand completely why he is subhuman, lacking in free will, prone to tattoo himself, savage, and so on. Similarly, once we comprehend the nature of Lombroso's female offender, we can find signs of her crude sexuality and violent propensities in photographed faces of this type. What criminal anthropologists did, to borrow words from Judith Butler, was to "endow ontology" and "materialize" bodies.[37] This ontological dimension of criminal anthropology explains the force of its images. Bursting with energy, occasionally shocking, sometimes horrific, these images sparkle with ontological vitality. The images of criminal anthropology are much more riveting and stimulating than those of phrenology and degenerationism.

A third source of criminal anthropology's appeal lies in the realm of epistemology. Lombroso and Ellis created a new set of visual codes for criminality, illegality, and illegitimacy. These codes were easily intelligible to those familiar with Darwin's work and degeneration theory, and they pointed toward policy conclusions that fit well with then-current social philosophies such as Social Darwinism and eugenics. The codes were easily intelligible because they meshed with broader cultural themes and assumptions. In a period when the concepts of "good inheritance" and "bad inheritance" were really surrogates for "middle class" and "lower class," for example, the images of criminal anthropology made it clear that criminality and bad heredity were lower-class attributes. The images literally incorporated Lombroso's key insight, that Darwin's theory applies to criminal behavior as well as to the evolution of species, and that criminals are throwbacks to primitive forms of life. Lombrosian imagery also incorporated folk notions, such as the ideas that crooked is less good than straight, dark is inferior to white, and non–Anglo-Saxon facial features signify brutality. The images fit perfectly with then-current hierarchies of gender, race, sexuality, social class, and physical ability. In short, the images of criminal anthropology conferred on criminals' bodies scientific and moral meaning.

Fourth and finally, criminal anthropology appealed because its imagery "orientalized" offenders. It created an Other – the exotic, dangerous, sexy born criminal. This point relates to but is a bit different from my earlier point

---

37 Irene Costera Meijer and Baukje Prins, "How Bodies Come to Matter: An Interview with Judith Butler," *Signs* 23, no. 2 (1998): 280; Judith Butler, *Bodies that Matter* (New York, 1993).

about ontology. The images of criminal anthropology are attractive (at least to me) because they are ontological fun. They bring a new being, the born criminal, into existence, and there is pleasure merely in watching them bring this off. But at the same time, these images also appeal because the new being they create is so strange – lurid, horrifying, titillating, forbidden. Moreover, although these images depict only criminals and their artifacts, like many orientalizing discourses they actually establish a set of binary terms, in this case law-abiding versus criminal. Law-abidingness, although invoked only through implication, is socially central and normative.[38] Once we look at these pictures, we know how *not* to appear.

In her study of *Bodies that Matter* Judith Butler discusses the characteristics of "abject" bodies, by which she means bodies that are excluded from discourse and *"not* constructed."[39] One of their characteristics is that the personal histories of abject bodies do not matter to audiences; indeed, we do not even think about their background and life courses. The criminal bodies of the Lombrosians do not entirely fit into Butler's category because they have, after all, been constructed and materialized, but Butler's insight about personal history does apply here: We would not think of identifying with most of the people depicted by Lombroso and Ellis. These figures are so different, so "oriental," that in reading these books we tour an exotic world in which it is impossible even to imagine the history of the people represented. They are like African Pygmies or harem women: so distant and strange that we can be astonished, scornful, condescending, or amused, but never sympathetic. (In Farnham's somewhat earlier phrenological images of criminals, in contrast, the offenders, though odd, still belong to our own species.)[40] Instead of trying to understand criminal anthropological bodies in Butler's terms, as "abject bodies," perhaps we should borrow Jennifer Terry and Jacqueline Urla's term and call them "subordinated bodies" or "subordinated Others."[41]

A few of the Americans adopted Lombroso's visual strategies. Of the nine books that popularized criminal anthropology in the United States, six had few or no illustrations, and a seventh, Talbot's *Degeneracy* (1898), included images that focused more on anatomical deformities than criminality per se. However, Lydston's *Diseases of Society* (1904) included several photographs

---

38 "The ideal human body has been cast implicitly in the image of the robust, European, heterosexual gentleman," wrote Jennifer Terry and Jacqueline Urla, "an ideal defined by its contradistinction to a potpourri of 'deviant' types" (Jennifer Terry and Jacqueline Urla, "Introduction: Mapping Embodied Deviance," in Terry and Urla, eds., *Deviant Bodies* [Bloomington, Ind., 1995], 4).
39 Butler, *Bodies that Matter*, 16. Original emphasis.
40 Farnham, "Appendix."   41 Terry and Urla, "Introduction."

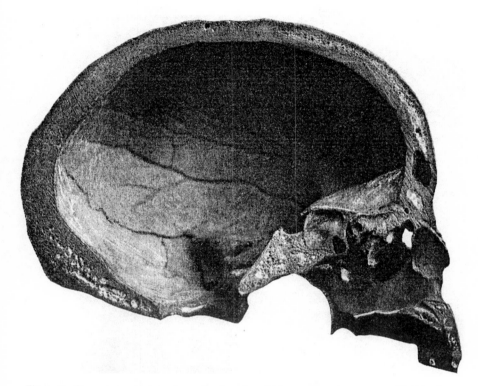

Figure 8. One must speculate about the meanings Lydston meant to convey with this photograph of a Skull of a Negro Murderer; the author himself does not explain but merely presents the illustration as though its significance is self-evident. From G. Frank Lydston, *The Diseases of Society* (Philadelphia, 1905), Frontispiece.

and line drawings of criminals, most spectacularly a frontispiece titled "Skull of a Negro Murderer." Boies's *Prisoners and Paupers* (1893) was even closer to Lombroso's work in its combination of representational innocence and guile. Its photographs included a statue of Sophocles, illustrating the body of the ideal man; numerous photos of immigrants disembarking at Ellis Island, illustrating physical inferiority; and a group portrait of misshapen Elmira inmates, illustrating the degeneracy of criminals.

I have separated different effects – the visual clout of criminal anthropology, its ontological intensity, its epistemological power and inventiveness, and its orientalizing quality – here, but perceptually these impressions work together. Moreover, they fuse not only with one another but also with the discourse they illustrate. In criminal anthropology verbal and visual texts work closely in tandem to clarify, repel, and delight.

Figure 9. Boies used this statue of Sophocles to illustrate the body of the ideal man and provide a telling contrast to the deformed criminals pictured later in his book. From Henry Boies, *Prisoners and Paupers* (New York, 1893), Frontispiece.

CONCLUSION

In this chapter I have analyzed American receptivity to criminal anthropology, the diffusion of the theory in the United States, and the sources of its appeal. Although I have not addressed the issue of its impact, it is worthwhile noting that Lombroso prided himself on Americans' "almost fanatical adherence" to his teachings. Much criticized in Europe, he comforted himself with the belief that "One nation . . . – America – gave a warm and sympathetic reception to the ideas of the Modern School."[42] Lombroso's assessment of his influence in the United States, inflated though it is, reminds us that for a while, from about 1890 to 1910, his version of criminal anthropology generated so much interest in the United States that nine books discussed the theory in depth. Possibly only two other theories of crime in U.S. history have generated more attention.[43] In late-nineteenth-century America, criminal anthropology was indeed the right doctrine at the right time.

42 Lombroso-Ferrero, *Criminal Man*, xxix.
43 One was defective delinquency theory, according to which "feeble-mindedness" or mental retardation is the cause of criminal behavior; this theory was widely accepted in the early twentieth century. More recently, Travis Hirschi's control theory has been widely discussed and tested; see Travis Hirschi, *Causes of Delinquency* (Berkeley, Calif., 1969).

8

From the "Atavistic" to the "Inferior" Criminal Type

The Impact of the Lombrosian Theory of the Born Criminal on German Psychiatry

MARIACARLA GADEBUSCH BONDIO

HERMOGENES: For my part, Socrates, I have often talked with Cratylus and many others, and cannot come to the conclusion that there is any correctness of names other than convention and agreement. For it seems to me that whatever name you give to a thing is its right name; and if you give up that name and change it for another, the later name is no less correct than the earlier, just as we change the names of our servants; for I think no name belongs to any particular thing by nature, but only by the habit and custom of those who employ it and who established the usage. But if this is not the case, I am ready to hear and to learn from Cratylus or anyone else.

SOCRATES: It may be that you are right, Hermogenes; but let us see.

– Plato, *Cratylus*[1]

DEFINING THE OFFENDER

Different meanings and interpretations of "reality" are implied in scientific definitions. Definitions are limiting through their labeling role, especially when the reality in question is not an inanimate object but a deviant individual. They function as useful conventions only if we are conscious of how dangerously static they are. Theoretical systems that scientifically explain forms of criminality are therefore connected with hermeneutic, terminological, and definitional problems.[2] Concepts such as those of the "born criminal" or "atavism," which were introduced by Cesare Lombroso and his followers and became common in the criminological debates at the end

---

1 Plato, *Cratylus*, vol. 4, trans. H. N. Fowler (Cambridge, 1977), 384d–385a.
2 See David Garland, "Criminological Knowledge and Its Relation to Power: Foucault's Genealogy and Criminology Today," *British Journal of Criminology* 32 (1992): 403–22.
I would like to call attention to the following books that appeared too late for me to take into account here: Richard F. Wetzell, *Inventing the Criminal: A History of German Criminology, 1880–1945* (Chapel Hill, N.C., 2000); Mary Gibson, *Born to Crime: Cesare Lombroso and the Origins of Biological Criminology* (Westport, Conn., 2003); Valeria P. Babini, *Il Caso Murri. Una storia italiana* (Bologna, 2004).

of the nineteenth century, became more popular and seemed to acquire increasing autonomy from the theories that gave rise to them.

Around 1880, after the Italian publication of *Criminal Man*, Lombrosian theories gained popularity in Germany.[3] They caused vehement discussions and became the objects of severe criticism and the basis for new, daring scientific positions. Not only criminologists and criminal lawyers took part in this debate; so too did psychiatrists, prison doctors, and intellectuals.

This chapter examines the special role some psychiatrists played in the diffusion of criminal anthropology in Germany. The German response to the new ideas of Lombroso on the criminal man can be seen as a complex process of reaction and assimilation or, better yet, as a formal rejection combined with an essential assimilation and revision of fundamental components of the theory of the criminal man (born criminal and atavism). Today, Germany's reception of Lombrosian theories is a recognized fact in the history of criminology. But as late as 1985, Renzo Villa, in his otherwise excellent book on Lombroso, gave very little space to the German reception.[4] New research in the last fifteen years has shown how deeply Lombroso's teaching influenced German criminology.[5] Positivistic science in the second half of the nineteenth century was characterized by a strong belief in quantitative research methods common to the exact sciences. The application of this empirical means of collecting data to disciplines such as criminal anthropology and psychiatry led to interesting, sometimes dubious results, such as the well-known attention to the bodies of delinquent men and women, which scientists began to measure with instruments in an almost obsessive manner.[6] This work translated into measurable quantities, morphological characteristics and anomalies, such as sensitivity to pain. The illusion of defining or quantifying the degree of abnormality, establishing a boundary between normality and illness, is perhaps one of the most

---

3 Cesare Lombroso, *L'uomo delinquente studiato in rapporto alla Antropologia, alla Medicina Legale e alle discipline carcerarie*, 1st ed. (Milan, 1876), 1. German ed.: *Der Verbrecher in anthropologischer, ärztlicher und juristischer Beziehung*, trans. Moritz O. Fränkel (vol. 1: Hamburg, 1887; vol. 2: Hamburg, 1890), atlas (Hamburg, 1898).

4 "Rare is the presence of Lombroso in Germany: except for isolated exponents, as the most devoted prison doctor Hans Kurella, it is impossible to speak of a school" (Renzo Villa, *Il deviante e i suoi segni: Lombroso e la nascita dell'antropologia criminale* [Milan, 1985], 253).

5 See Richard F. Wetzell, "Criminal Law Reform in Imperial Germany," Ph.D. diss., Stanford University, 1991; Richard F. Wetzell, "The Medicalization of Criminal Law Reform in Imperial Germany," in Norbert Finzsch and Robert Jütte, eds., *The Institutions of Confinement: Hospitals, Asylums, and Prisons in Western Europe and North America, 1500–1950* (New York, 1997), 275–83. I dealt with the problem in greater depth in Mariacarla Gadebusch Bondio, *Die Rezeption der kriminalanthropologischen Theorien von Cesare Lombroso in Deutschland von 1880–1914* (Husum, 1995).

6 See Mariacarla Gadebusch Bondio, "Das Bild vom Bösen: Photographie als Instrument zur Stigmatisierung der Devianz," in Volker Hess, ed., *Normierung der Gesundheit*, Abhandlungen zur Geschichte der Medizin und der Naturwissenschaften, no. 82 (Husum 1997), 93–118.

typical aspects of positivistic medicine. Statistics, classifications, and typological schemes (photographs) adorned the treatises of physicians and alienists as well as the books of criminologists and criminal jurists; they seemed to lend objectivity and credibility to various theories and hypotheses.[7]

The absorption of Lombrosian theories played an undeniable role in the processes of "medicalization" and "pathologization" of the criminal individual.[8] Here, my analysis focuses on a group of psychiatrists who played a leading role in setting new trends in nineteenth-century psychiatry. Foremost among the protagonists of the German debate on the essence of criminal man were Gustav Aschaffenburg, Emil Kraepelin, Hans Kurella, Paul Näcke, and Robert Sommer. All of these scientists shared a common social purpose: protecting society from degeneration and delinquency. Deeply "imbued with a sense of social responsibility," as Paul J. Weindling has noted, German doctors contributed to developing a system of social control and believed that an effective system of crime prevention could be realized.[9] In this context, it is interesting to see in which ways medical authority assumed increasing importance in defining and explaining criminal phenomena that seemed to pose a growing danger to bourgeois society. It is not my purpose here to show how Lombrosian theories contributed to the development of new social perceptions of existing problems such as deviance. Instead, I focus my attention on the ways in which German psychiatrists were able to integrate the Lombrosian discourse into their theories.

POSITIVIST SCIENCE AND THE IMPERIAL STATE ALLIED AGAINST CRIME

The perceived need for the scientific study of criminality in the second half of the nineteenth century characterized Imperial Germany and other industrialized European countries where acute social problems (proletarianization of the lower classes, increased unemployment, prostitution, and vagrancy) upset the "normal" citizen, the bourgeois. Increased attention to crime, more than an objective rise in actual delinquency, constituted an ideal basis for accepting new explanations and interpretative models of

---

7 See Stefania Nicasi, "Il germe della follia. Modelli di malattia mentale nella psichiatria italiana dell'Ottocento," in Paolo Rossi, ed., *L'età del positivismo* (Bologna, 1986), 327–32; Giulio Barsanti, Simonetta Gori-Savellini, Patrizia Guarnieri, and Claudio Pogliano, eds., *Misura d'uomo. Strumenti, teorie e pratiche dell'antropometria e della psicologia sperimentale tra '800 e '900*, Istituto e Museo di Storia della Scienza di Firenze (Florence, 1986); Laura Lanzoni, "Il tempo della mente: Gabriele Buccola e le ricerche psicometriche nell'Istituto psichiatrico di Reggio Emilia," *Physis* 34 (1997): 511–43.

8 On the psychiatrization of criminal danger, see Michel Foucault, "About the Concept of the 'Dangerous Individual' in 19th-Century Legal Psychiatry," *International Journal of Law and Psychiatry* 1 (1978): 1–18.

9 Paul J. Weindling, *Health, Race, and German Politics Between National Unification and Nazism, 1870–1945* (Cambridge, 1993), 2.

deviance.[10] Because criminal anthropology offered a new "scientific" interpretation of criminals and a "rational" answer to questions about the dangerous elements in civilized society, I concentrate on this particular sector
of the German scientific world.

In the second half of the nineteenth century, psychiatry was establishing
itself as a medical discipline at universities and in society.[11] Through the creation of organized and state-sanctioned forms of delimitation, illicit behavior
became more strictly regulated. In exemplary fashion, Michel Foucault has
outlined the process of the establishment of lunatic asylums, correctional
institutions for delinquent youth, and so forth, as spaces that symbolized
the isolation of abnormal individuals.[12] In this process physicians, particularly psychiatrists, played a central role in observing, defining, judging, and
treating the deviant.

The interest of the German imperial state in scientifically based control
of its population and labor force can be recognized in statistical research.
Criminal statistics were introduced in Germany in 1830, but the results
of this early census were characterized by regional differences in defining
criminals and crimes. In 1882 the first national criminal statistics marked a
new bureaucratic intensity in the study of criminality.[13] Karl Mittermaier
emphasized the role of criminal statistics as a science that, with its exact
methods, could provide information about the degree of the morality of the
general population (*Moralität des Volkes*).[14] In 1871 a census of the insane
was taken in Prussia: The *Preussische Irrenzählung* created census cards for
the mentally ill, just like the criminal record cards that had been adopted
by the police. These criminal record cards were standardized by Alphonse

10 On the development of criminal statistics and their role in the general perception of delinquency as a growing social danger, see Hans Jürgen Collmann, *Internationale Kriminalstatistik:
Geschichtliche Entwicklung und gegenwärtiger Stand* (Stuttgart, 1973), 5–19; Helmut Graff, *Die deutsche
Kriminalstatistik: Geschichte und Gegenwart* (Stuttgart, 1975), 51–6; Dirk Blasius, *Kriminalität und Alltag*
(Göttingen, 1979), 26; Albert Funk, *Polizei und Rechtsstaat: Die Entwicklung des staatlichen Gewalt-
monopols in Preussen 1848–1986* (Frankfurt am Main, 1986), 207–11.
11 On the development of psychiatry as a discipline, see Klaus Dörner, *Bürger und Irre: Zur Sozialgeschichte
und Wissenschaftssoziologie der Psychiatrie* (Frankfurt am Main, 1984); Heinz-Peter Schmiedebach,
*Psychiatrie und Psychologie im Widerstreit: Die Auseinandersetzung in der Berliner medizinisch-psychologischen
Gesellschaft (1867–1899)* (Husum, 1986), 55–60.
12 Michel Foucault, *Überwachen und Strafen: Die Geburt des Gefängnisses*, 8th ed. (Frankfurt am Main,
1989), 351–61.
13 See Hans Jürgen Collmann, *Internationale Kriminalstatistik. Geschichtliche Entwicklung und gegenwärtiger
Stand* (Stuttgart, 1973), 5–19; Helmut Graff, *Die deutsche Kriminalstatistik. Geschichte und
Gegenwart* (Stuttgart, 1975), 51–6; Herbert Reinke, "Kriminalität als 'zweite' Wirklichkeit von
Tätigkeitsnachweisen der Justizverwaltung: Bemerkungen zu Kriminalstatistiken im 19. Jahrhundert
als Materialien einer historisch orientierten Kriminologie," *Kriminologisches Journal* 2 (1987): 177.
14 Karl Joseph Anton Mittermaier, "Praktische Ergebnisse der Criminalstatistik zur Ausstellung
wichtiger Fragen des Strafrechts und Strafverfahrens," *Der Gerichtssal* 13 (1861): 23.

Bertillon and constituted an effort to coordinate an internationally applicable system of identification.[15] In this process of increasing control of social life, behavioral models also became more differentiated and were administered by the state.[16] In the middle of the nineteenth century – despite improvements in public hygiene – economic crises, the marginalization of the lower classes, the spread of tuberculosis, alcoholism, and malnutrition, weakened the confidence of industrialized society in continuing progress.[17] The naturalistic and realistic novels of Émile Zola, Honoré de Balzac, and Charles Dickens, as well as the dramas of Gerhart Hauptmann, give detailed fictional representations of the dark atmosphere of industrialized cities.[18]

The establishment of a *Grossstadt Medizin* (big-city medicine) contributed to the specialization and professionalization of physicians and represents an important aspect of Bismarck's health policy, to which the 1883 health insurance reform belonged.[19] The relationship of the individual to health and illness, life and death, normality and abnormality, became more and more complex and mediated by the medical monopoly. Because it increasingly became the task of physicians to determine the military fitness, ability to work, and legal responsibility of citizens, they were gradually transformed into agents of the state.[20] Interested in normative regulation and precise definitions of health and illness, the state contributed to the rise in power of the medical community.[21] The alliance between imperial state and science increased the self-confidence of the liberal *Bildungsbürgertum* (educated middle class), with its secularized and rational ideals.[22] A deep belief in exact and objective methods dominated psychiatry and found eminent supporters in Italy, with authorities such as Andrea Verga and Cesare Lombroso,

15 See Alfons Bertillon, *Identification Anthropometrique: Instructions signalétiques* (Melun, 1893).
16 For statistical sources, see Werner Conze, "Sozialgeschichte 1850–1918," in Hermann Aubin and Wolfgang Zorn, eds., *Handbuch der deutschen Wirtschafts- und Sozialgeschichte*, 2 vols. (Stuttgart, 1976), 2:611; Jacques Donzelot, *La police des familles* (Paris, 1977).
17 See, e.g., Thomas Mckeown, *Die Bedeutung der Medizin. Traum, Trugbild oder Nemesis?* (Frankfurt am Main, 1982), 215–19.
18 See Marie-Christine Leps, *Apprehending the Criminal: The Production of Deviance in Nineteenth-Century Discourse* (Durham, N.C., 1992), 135–50, 166–205.
19 Reinhard Spree called this a process of *Zwangssozialisation* (compulsory socialization). See Reinhard Spree, *Soziale Ungleichheit vor Krankheit und Tod* (Göttingen, 1981), 157.
20 See Paul Weindling, "Hygienepolitik als sozialintegrative Strategie im späten Deutschen Kaiserreich," in Alfons Labisch and Reinhard Spree, eds., *Medizinische Deutungsmacht im sozialen Wandel des 19. und frühen 20. Jahrhunderts* (Bonn, 1989), 37–55.
21 See Theodor Schieder, "Kultur, Wissenschaft und Wissenschaftspolitik im Deutschen Kaiserreich," in Günter Mann and Rolf Winau, eds., *Medizin, Naturwissenschaft, Technik und das zweite Kaiserreich* (Göttingen, 1977), 10.
22 See Gerd Göckenjahn, *Kurieren und Staat machen: Gesundheit und Medizin in der bürgerlichen Welt* (Frankfurt am Main, 1985), 315–26.

as well as Wilhelm Griesinger, Kraepelin, and Richard von Krafft-Ebing in Germany. These scientists nourished the illusion of finding scientific explanations and solutions for problems like mental illness.[23] In this mechanistic, materialistic view of natural and social phenomena, personalities such as Rudolf Virchow, Emil Du Bois-Reymond, Hermann Helmholtz, Oskar Vogt, Ludwig Büchner, and Jacob Moleschott gave new impulses to the establishment of new biological and evolutionary theories in medicine. After the diffusion of Bénédict-Augustin Morel's degeneration theory in the 1860s (the *Traité des dégénérescences* appeared in 1857), parallel to Charles Darwin's theory, pathological deviation from normality, such as physical and psychological degenerations, were explained through a nosological frame of reference and understood as being regulated by laws of heredity and environment.[24] With his atavism hypothesis, Lombroso provided a decisive boost to the harmonization of Darwinism and degeneration theory, which was enormously successful in the psychiatric world thanks to its formulation by Valentin Magnan.[25] The born criminal was interpreted by Lombroso as a throwback to a primitive state of savagery and was placed in a new etiological paradigm.[26]

In addition, the debate on the question of legal responsibility (Article 40 of the Prussian penal code)[27] also emerged in the 1860s and found a solution in 1871 with the new definition of legal responsibility (Article 51 of the penal code).[28] The function of psychiatrists as expert witnesses in matters of the insanity defense was firmly established. In the 1880s and 1890s, the years following the introduction of Article 51, vehement discussions about psychiatric evaluations and the concept of diminished legal responsibility

---

23 On the introduction of methods of experimental psychology in Italy and the conflicts between medico-organic and psychological approaches to insanity studies, see Lorena Lanzoni, "Il tempo della mente. Gabriele Buccola e le ricerche psicometriche nell'Istituto psichiatrico di Reggio Emilia," *Physis* 34 (1997): 511–43.

24 See Axel Liégeois, "Hidden Philosophy and Theology in Morel's Theory of Degeneration and Nosology," *History of Psychiatry* 2 (1991): 419–27; Rafael Huertas, "Madness and Degeneration: From 'Fallen Angel' to Mentally Ill," *History of Psychiatry* 3 (1992): 391–411, and "Madness and Degeneration, III. Degeneration and Criminality," *History of Psychiatry* 4 (1993): 141–58.

25 On the development of the Lombrosian theory of atavism, see Mary S. Gibson, "Cesare Lombroso and Italian Criminology: Theory and Politics," in this volume.

26 See ibid.

27 "Ein Verbrechen oder Vergehen ist nicht vorhanden, wenn der Thäter zur Zeit des Thates wahnsinnig oder blödsinnig oder die freie Willensbestimmung desselben durch Gewalt oder durch Drohung ausgeschlossen war" (§40, quoted in Heinz-Peter Schmiedebach, *Psychiatrie* [Husum, 1986], 63).

28 "Eine strafbare Handlung ist nicht vorhanden, wenn der Täter zur Zeit der Begehung der Handlung sich in einem Zustande von Bewusstlosigkeit oder krankhafter Störung der Geistestätigkeit befand, durch welchen seine freie Willensbestimmung ausgeschlossen war" (quoted in Hans Georg Güse and Norbert Schmacke, *Psychiatrie zwischen bürgerlicher Revolution und Faschismus* [Regensburg, 1976], 210).

developed. Many psychiatrists took part in the "Versammlungen des Vereins der deutschen Irrenärtzte," and discussed such questions as the existence of the born criminal (Robert Sommer, Hans Kurella, K. Wilhelm Pelman, Arthur Leppmann, Emanuel Mendel, Adolf Knecht, Auguste Forel, Abraham Baer, Aschaffenburg, and Kraepelin).[29] The boundary between the born criminal and the mentally ill and the presence of stigmata of degeneration in such individuals were among the most intensively debated issues. Two psychiatrists were especially active in these debates: Kraepelin, who defended psychiatry at the German Lawyers' Annual Meeting (Deutscher Juristentag) in Innsbruck and fought for the introduction of the concept of diminished responsibility in the criminal justice system,[30] and Aschaffenburg, who supported an aggressive approach to criminality according to a biological–social model.

HANS KURELLA AND MAX NORDAU: CULTURAL PESSIMISM

To understand Lombroso's reception in the German psychiatric community, it is necessary to deconstruct a myth in the traditional criminological historiography, namely that of Kurella and Nordau as the primary disciples, defenders, and diffusers of Lombroso's theories in Germany. Some works by Lombroso as well as the biography by his daughter offer hints that Kurella and Nordau were loyal proponents of Lombroso's teachings.[31] Lombroso's biographers have mostly accepted these characterizations – which were confirmed by Kurella and Nordau – as true without verifying them. But a detailed comparison of the positions of these two German advocates of Lombroso with the thought of their "maestro" is completely lacking. Marvin E. Wolfgang,[32] Renzo Villa,[33] and Luigi Baima Bollone[34] have characterized Kurella as Lombroso's best friend in Germany and as a defender of his theses. Karl-Heinz Hering pointed out that at first Kurella was Lombroso's faithful companion and adds that he was "more Catholic than the pope."[35] Luigi

29 See Thomas Peter Schindler, "Psychiatrie im wilhelminischen Deutschland im Spiegel der Verhandlungen des 'Vereins der deutschen Irrenärzte' von 1891–1914," diss. med., Berlin, 1990, 157–67.

30 See Emil Kraepelin, "Zur Frage der geminderten Zurechnungsfähigkeit (Vortrag auf dem 27. Deutschen Juristentag 1904 in Innsbruck)," *Monatsschrift für Kriminalpsychologie* 1 (1904–5): 477–93.

31 Cesare Lombroso, *L'uomo delinquente* (Milano, 1876), xxix; the reprint edition is Cesare Lombroso, *Crime: Its Causes and Remedies* (Montclair, N.J., 1968), xxxiii–xxxvi; Gina Lombroso, *Cesare Lombroso: Storia della vita e delle opere narrata dalla figlia* (Turin, 1915), 1, 210, 287.

32 Marwin E. Wolfgang, "Cesare Lombroso," *Quaderni di criminologia clinica* 3 (1961): 27–97.

33 Renzo Villa, *Il deviante e i suoi segni* (Milan, 1985), 79, 253.

34 P. Luigi Baima Bollone, *Cesare Lombroso ovvero il principio dell'irresponsabilità* (Turin, 1992), 223.

35 Karl-Heinz Hering, *Der Weg der Kriminologie zur selbstständigen Wissenschaft* (Hamburg, 1966), 82.

Bulferetti recognized a sort of deformation of Lombroso's ideas on genius by Nordau.[36] But almost all the biographies stress the parallels between the degeneration theory of Lombroso and that of Nordau and between the concept of determinism in Kurella and in Lombroso.

At the beginning of the twentieth century Reinhard Frank, a professor of criminal justice, wrote an article on the diffusion of Lombroso's theories in Germany and recognized some misunderstandings: "One often sees that the popular version of scientific theories cannot appropriately reflect their true contents. Even the Lombrosian theories undergo a strange misunderstanding. When his theories on the criminal nature were heard abroad for the first time a quarter of a century ago, there was an indignant outcry throughout Europe."[37]

Frank argued that the widespread notions that Lombroso equated the criminal with the mentally ill and therefore proclaimed punishment superfluous and without merit were false for three reasons: (1) From the beginning Lombroso had not only underlined the difference between criminals and the mentally ill but had also researched this industriously; (2) Lombroso had not tried to eliminate punishment but rather pleaded for the introduction of punishments that were based on the principle of rehabilitation rather than retribution; (3) the degree of punishment would be decided according to the danger that the individual posed to society and not according to the degree of guilt. Therefore, Frank saw Kurella, Moriz Benedikt, and Sommer as the only three followers of Lombroso in Germany. What Frank pointed out was neglected or simply ignored by his contemporaries.

KURELLA: DETERMINISM AS A SCIENTIFIC GUARANTEE

Lombroso's most famous book, *Criminal Man*, first appeared in Germany in 1887, more than ten years after the first Italian edition.[38] The German translation was based on the third edition – in which Lombroso had already introduced his typology of criminals and had also transformed the anthropological atavism theory into a pathological one. In this new etiology of delinquence the concepts of moral insanity and epilepsy were more important than the atavistic cause. Lombrosian theories were already known in

---

36 Luigi Bulferetti, *Cesare Lombroso* (Turin, 1975), 239, 395.
37 Reinhard Frank, "Le teorie di Cesare Lombroso in Germania," *Archivio di Antropologia Criminale, Psichiatria, Medicina Legale e Scienze Affini* 30 (1909): 585.
38 Cesare Lombroso, *Der Verbrecher in anthropologischer, ärztlicher und juristischer Beziehung*, trans. Moritz O. Fränkel, 2 vols. (Hamburg, 1887; reprint, Hamburg, 1890). An atlas was published in Hamburg in 1898.

the German scientific world prior to the appearance of *Criminal Man*. In 1869 Lombroso published a book on clinical contributions to psychiatry in German,[39] and articles on the results of Lombroso's psychiatric research can be found in the well-known *Archiv für Psychiatrie* at the end of the 1860s.[40] His anatomical discoveries also were regularly reported in Virchow's *Archiv*. But it was only after the first International Congress of Criminal Anthropology in 1885 that Lombroso's theories became increasingly popular among a vast and heterogeneous group of interested people.

What role did the psychiatrist and *Nervenarzt* Kurella play in the diffusion of Lombrosian theories? Kurella translated many of Lombroso's works into German. A deep and genuine admiration for the Italian "maestro" left traces in Kurella's letters, some of which are preserved in Turin.[41] Almost all of his publications between 1892 and 1913 deal directly or indirectly with criminal anthropology.[42] Three main foci can be recognized in his elaboration of Lombrosian theories: (1) The conflict between individual psychology and the elaboration of a general criminal typology; (2) the question of determinism in science, particularly in criminal anthropology; (3) the interpretation of the stigmata of degeneration.

First, recognizing the impossibility of defining general types of criminals on the basis of their psychological characteristics, which are per se subjective, Kurella unintentionally pointed out a problematic aspect of Lombrosian typology.[43] Kurella also saw the difficulties of clearly distinguishing between the criminal and the mentally ill, an effort in which Lombroso was increasingly engaged. Over the years Lombroso departed from the original intention of the Italian positivist school to examine criminal man (and woman) as

---

39 Cesare Lombroso, *Klinische Beiträge zur Psychiatrie, physikalische, statistische Studien und Krankengeschichten* (Leipzig, 1869).
40 See Wilhelm Griesinger, "Neue italienische Literatur über Psychiatrie. Irren-Anstalten," *Archiv für Psychiatrie und Nervenkrankheiten* 1 (1868–9): 454–5, 461–77; Moritz O. Fränkel, "Eine mittlere Hinterhauptsgrube am Schädel eines Verbrechers," *Archiv für pathologische Anatomie und Physiologie und für klinische Medizin* 22 (1871): 560–2; Moritz O. Fränkel, "Verbrecherschädel," *Allgemeine Zeitschrift für Psychiatrie* 34 (1878): 403–4.
41 See Mariacarla Gadebusch Bondio, *Die Rezeption . . .* (Husum, 1995), appendix, 244–5, 250.
42 Hans Kurella, "Cesare Lombroso und die Naturgeschichte des Verbrechers," in Rudolf Virchow and Wilhelm Wattenbach, eds., *Sammlung gemeinverständlicher wissenschaftlicher Vorträge* (Hamburg, 1892); Hans Kurella, *Naturgeschichte des Verbrechens* (Stuttgart, 1893); Hans Kurella, *Die Grenzen der Zurechnungsfähigkeit und die Kriminalanthropologie* (Halle, 1903); Hans Kurella, "L'importanza di Cesare Lombroso nella sociologia," in Luigi Bianchi, ed., *L'opera di Cesare Lombroso* (Turin, 1906), 307–18; Hans Kurella, *Anthropologie und Strafrecht* (Würzburg, 1912); Hans Kurella, *Die Intellektuellen und die Gesellschaft* (Wiesbaden, 1913); Hans Kurella, "Probleme und Fortschritte der Kriminalanthropologie," *Centralblatt für Nervenheilkunde und Psychiatrie* 11 (1900): 257–72.
43 Hans Kurella, "Cesare Lombroso und die Naturgeschichte des Verbrechers," in Rudolf Virchow and Wilhelm Wattenbach, eds., *Sammlung gemeinverständlicher wissenschaftlicher Vorträge* (Hamburg, 1892), 1, 5.

a psycho-physical unity. His first goal was to systematize his theory and give policemen and lawyers a useful instrument for exact identification through a typology. As demonstrated by his *Palimsesti del carcere*,[44] the publication that combined the most detailed psychological information, Lombroso's interest in the psychology of the criminal was only casual, whereas his efforts to define the criminal in well-recognized categories, based mostly on anthropological data, were a constant in his later work. The shortcoming in Lombrosian criminal anthropology most criticized by contemporaries, namely, that it paid too little attention to the individual psychological aspects of criminals,[45] was not recognized by Kurella as a fault but only as contrasting with his typological attempts. For Kurella, Lombroso remained the first person who examined the criminal individual, showing the abnormal aspects of body and mind.

Second, according to Kurella, the foundation of a science rested on establishing connections between the individual and nature and society: "Like every science, and most of all like psychology, criminal psychology has to be deterministic, it has to assume the law of causality in the sphere of will [*Willensleben*]."[46] Kurella considered Lombroso's teaching a perfect example of "biological determinism." Precisely this definition was later accepted by most historians of science. Luigi Bulferetti, one of Lombroso's later biographers, preferred to talk about a "naturalistic determinism" that would gradually detach itself from its anatomical physiological basis and develop in a sociological direction.[47] Kurella undoubtedly contributed to the simplification of the born-criminal theory. Deeply convinced of its truthfulness, he emphasized in *Naturgeschichte des Verbrechens* (1893) that the born criminal must be regarded more as a kind of primate than as an "atavus."[48] Like the prison doctor Abraham Baer, who in the same year published his work *Der Verbrecher in anthropologischer Beziehung*,[49] or Paul Näcke in his aggressive criticism of the existence of degeneration stigmata,[50] Kurella drew on the

44 Cesare Lombroso, *Palimsesti del carcere* (Turin, 1888).
45 Within the positive school Patrizi criticized Lombroso's use of psychology: Mariano L. Patrizi, *Addizioni al "dopo Lombroso": Ancora sulla monogenesi psicologica del delitto* (Milan, 1930); A. Bertolani, "Mariano Luigi Patrizi," *Archivio di freniatria* 59 (1935): 671–8.
46 Hans Kurella, *Naturgeschichte des Verbrechens* (Stuttgart, 1893), 3.
47 Luigi Bulferetti, *Cesare Lombroso* (Turin, 1975), 385.
48 Hans Kurella, *Naturgeschichte des Verbrechens* (Stuttgart, 1893), 52.
49 See Adolf Abraham Baer, *Der Verbrecher in anthropologischer Beziehung* (Leipzig, 1893).
50 The conflict between Näcke and Lombroso became evident in 1896 at the Fourth Congress of Criminal Anthropology in Geneva, where Näcke discussed the use of the concept of moral insanity. After a nebulous argument on terminological questions, he concluded that the "moral deficient" has to be considered a "genuine born criminal." See Paul Näcke, "Considerations générales sur la psychiatrie criminelle," in *Compte rendu des travaux de la quadrième session du Congrès International d'Anthropologie Criminelle* (Geneva, 1897), 1–11. Näcke developed his critical position toward Lombrosianism in many articles that were published in the *Archiv für Kriminalanthropologie und Kriminalistik*.

initial formulation of Lombroso's theory without considering its development. Thanks to pupils like Enrico Ferri, however, Lombroso was led to consider the interaction of endogenous and exogenous elements in criminal behavior. Lombroso recognized that the question of whether the born criminal is determined by his nature to commit crime cannot be easily decided: A complex synergy of different factors can but does not necessarily have to lead someone to do something illegal. Lombroso's position on these implications of his own theory remained unclear until almost 1881. During the 1890s critics split into two factions: those who, according to Kurella's interpretation, saw the born criminal as predestined to crime and those who, basing themselves on Lombroso's later works, gave more importance to exogenous factors as catalysts for an existing disposition to crime. Psychiatrists and jurists like Robert Sommer, E. Bleuler, and Reinhard Frank realized the importance of this change in the thought of Lombroso and his school and thus were able to reach a differentiated critical conclusion. Sommer, for example, confirmed the existence of a born criminal but, basing his ideas on Baer's research, refused to accept that this "morally abnormal individual" was characterized by morphological stigmata. Sommer therefore distinguished between endogenous criminal natures (*endogenen Verbrechernaturen*) and the mentally ill: the first were generally in full possession of their faculties (*zurechnungsfähig*).[51] Sommer, who declared himself a follower of Lombroso, had sensed the dangers of the Lombrosian theories, the immeasurable potential of their deterministic content if taken to their logical conclusion.[52] Bleuler looked at the influence of external factors on delinquency: If the congenital impulse for crime was not accompanied by factors that lead to its realization, then this instinct remained merely a predisposition.[53] Frank noted that a born criminal could die "without having committed a crime," and underlined the fact that such individuals should be defined as "latent" criminals.[54] These examples show how an accurate reading and revision of the born-criminal theory could weaken its biologically deterministic foundations.

See, e.g., Paul Näcke, "Degeneration, Degenerationszeichen und Atavismus," *Archiv für Kriminalanthropologie und Kriminalistik* 1 (1899): 200–21; "Die Kastration bei gewissen Klassen von Degenerierten als ein wirksamer sozialer Schutz," ibid., 3 (1900): 58–84; "Sind wir dem anatomischen Sitze der 'Verbrecherneigung' wirklich näher gekommen, wie Lombroso glaubt?" ibid., 12 (1903): 218–28; "Die Überbleibsel der Lombrososchen kriminalanthropologischen Theorien," ibid., 49 (1912): 326–39.

51 Robert Sommer, "Die Criminalpsychologie," *Allgemeine Zeitschrift für Psychiatrie* 51 (1895): 782–98, esp. 792–8.

52 Ibid., 788.

53 Eugen Bleuler, *Der geborene Verbrecher. Eine kritische Studie* (Munich, 1896), 34–5.

54 Reinhard Frank, *Vergeltungsstrafe und Schutzstrafe. Die Lehre Lombrosos* (Tübingen, 1908), 32.

Third, an interesting and specific explanation for the German rejection of Lombrosian criminal anthropology was given by Kurella at the Seventh International Congress of Criminal Anthropology in Turin, in 1906. This contribution was published six years later as *Anthropologie und Strafrecht* (1912). After an initial acceptance of the new discipline from Italy, Kurella argued that Rudolf Virchow played a key role in its rejection. The core idea on which the discussion turned was purely anthropological: Lombroso was said to have discovered in the skull of a murderer atavistic stigmata that confirmed his hypothesis (the most striking was the *fossula occipitalis mediana*, which he observed in the skull of the famous criminal Giuseppe Villela). The born criminal exhibiting these attributes could be compared to "diluvian human races," especially Neanderthals, and, at the same time, to natural people. Lombroso correctly interpreted Neanderthals, discovered in 1856, as a well-diffused prehistoric race, whereas Virchow identified them as a "pathological specimen." Following Lombroso and the anthropologist Hermann Klaatsch, Kurella demonstrated the similarities between the child, primitive man, and orangutan, which were found among "Negroes," the Neanderthal race, and criminals.[55] Kurt Strauch also was involved in this debate on anthropological questions, which grew up around very different interpretations of morphological and anatomical abnormalities. A forensic doctor and pathologist in Berlin, Strauch tried to find a consensus among the theories of Lombroso and Virchow, with whom he worked as an assistant. The characteristics of inferior human races were explained by Strauch as "signs of developmental disruption" or, in agreement with Lombroso, as stigmata of degeneration. Some anomalies, for example hairy hands and hairy feet, could be seen from a phylogenetic point of view as regressive forms, "remaining at a lower stage of evolution."[56] If one observes such evolutionary defects in a criminal, "these signs do not prove an illness, a nosos, but only a significant deviation from the norm, an anomaly, a pathological state in Virchow's sense."[57] Here it is evident how the use of terms is confused by Strauch. By distinguishing between "illness" as a "nosos" and a "pathological state" as a deviation from the norm, Strauch argues *ad absurdum*. Such individuals would not be genuinely ill but neither would they be entirely healthy: They would be inferior and, in bad social conditions, would develop into antisocials or criminals.

---

55 Hans Kurella, *Anthropologie und Strafrecht* (Würzburg, 1912).
56 Curt Strauch, "L'importance des anomalies physiques des criminels dans la théorie et dans la pratique médico-legale," *Bericht über den Internationalen Kongress für Kriminalanthropologie* (Cologne, 1911), 152.
57 Ibid., 153.

It must be pointed out that during this congress, at which anthropological themes attracted considerable attention, Kurella – talking about the hostility aimed at criminal anthropology – had also underlined that three cultural components had to be assimilated into the new discipline: positivism, sociology, and *Rassenhygiene* (eugenics). Only the lawyer Ernst-Heinrich Rosenfeld protested against this proposed integration of eugenics into criminal anthropology and recognized a danger in the negation of the rehabilitative capacity of criminals.[58] Kurella's reference to eugenics can be better understood in light of his fundamentally pessimistic nature combined with his strong belief in the application of biological laws to cultural and social phenomena. In his book *Intellectuals and Society*, Kurella saw a society in decay and hoped for a new selection of talented individuals through heredity.[59] He found that the best individuals were filling the mental hospitals or becoming morphine addicts or sexual perverts.[60] A catastrophe seemed to him to be threatening society, and in contrast to Lombroso, he had no hope for a socialist society, which he saw as a "platonic idea" and a "senile fantasy." An "anthropology of talents" was what Kurella wanted to develop from Lombroso's criminal anthropology.[61] He saw the only possible solution to social decadence in the selection of gifted families and the "eliminat[ion] of nervous degenerates and those who have inherited instincts for sexual perversions, gambling, and drinking."[62] Kurella reviewed the often unclear Lombrosian theory with blind trust in determinism and a hopeless application of Darwinistic laws to society, so that his reformulation was condemned to become more static and vulnerable to critics.

NORDAU AND THE DANGER OF GENIUS

Another example of the ambiguous role of Lombroso's defenders in Germany is Max Nordau.[63] Nordau dedicated his masterpiece *Entartung* to Lombroso, who criticized the book immediately after publication.[64] Lombroso could not accept Nordau's extreme revisions of his genius theory,

---

58 See Ernst-Heinrich Rosenfeld, "Über den Zusammenhang zwischen Rasse und Verbrechen," in ibid., 88.
59 "In the meantime I had the possibility to know also the teaching of Lombroso on the neuropathic nature of the genius and as in 1895 I had the chance of a long stay in Lombroso's house I could see more deeply into his ideas and materials and I developed the strong intention of starting from a different point from Lombroso's, not with the rare high levels of geniality but with the middle levels of average talents, or better the sphere of dilettantes" (Hans Kurella, *Die Intellektuellen und die Gesellschaft* [Wiesbaden, 1913], 4).
60 Ibid., 54.   61 Ibid., 108.
62 Ibid., 57.   63 See Michael Berkowitz's chapter in this book.
64 Max Nordau, *Entartung* (Berlin, 1893), vii.

especially because Nordau often referred to Lombroso's own concept of *genius*. Paul Näcke polemically identified the congruence of the theories of the two scientists: "Nordau defines Zola – without proving it – as a degenerate in a very superficial way as Lombroso would do, whom Nordau follows mostly in a shameful but also stubborn way."[65]

How can one distinguish the two conceptions of genius from each other, and how could Nordau ignore these differences? Both authors based their theories on the concept of *degeneration*. Lombroso had already used this concept in the 1850s to explain the personality of Girolamo Cardano, long before the theory of Bénédict-Augustin Morel was known in Italy.[66] An autonomous theory of genius took shape in Lombroso's research on points of overlap among genius, mental illness, criminality, and degeneration. The pathological aspects of genius were the point of overlap with Nordau's concept of genius. Analyzing the psycho-physiological components of art, Nordau found that sometimes painters and writers were degenerate and therefore dangerous to society. In the second Italian edition of *Entartung* (1896) Lombroso distanced himself from Nordau's evaluation of symbolism. Nordau considered the symbolists to be mentally ill and refused to consider them as artists, whereas Lombroso did not find a contradiction between madness and genius.

Richard Wagner was, for Lombroso, the best example of someone who was not only mentally ill but also extremely creative.[67] Exceptional individuals could be superior human beings. Wagner could be seen as a maniac, maybe as an epileptic and sexual psychopath with a persecution complex (he felt persecuted by the Jews), but he remained a genius. In most cases neurosis and genius would accompany each other.[68] Using an anatomical explanation, Lombroso tried to present a convincing medical legitimation of his theory: A particular organic predisposition had been observed in exceptionally gifted individuals; that was, a larger quantity of nerve cells, mostly in the anterior brain lobes. These nerve cells were stimulated by a large quantity of sensations. Madness influenced genius, according to Lombroso, by increasing cerebral stimulation, but it was not the direct cause of genius.[69]

65 Paul Näcke, "Emile Zola: In Memoriam: Seine Beziehungen zur Kriminalanthropologie und Sociologie," *Archiv für Kriminalanthropologie und Kriminalistik* 11 (1903): 80, note 97.
66 See Cesare Lombroso, "Su la pazzia di Cardano," *Gazzetta Medica Italiana. Lombardia* 40 (1855): 341–5.
67 Cesare Lombroso, "La degenerazione del genio e l'opera di Max Nordau," introduction to Max Nordau, *Degenerazione* (Turin, 1896), xxx–xxxii.
68 Ibid., xxiii.   69 See ibid., xxviii.

Nordau reversed this theory by differentiating between evolutionary and degenerative atavistic anomalies and found that the former group characterized the real genius, the latter the degenerate pseudo-genius.[70] The works of artists might be divided into healthy and pathological ones. Degenerate art was, according to Nordau's view, a form of literature in which sexual psychopathies, such as homosexuality, were represented. By supporting these "perverted ideals," such works could lead society to sterility; this was the reason why Nordau regarded it as necessary to censor these forms of art. Lombroso criticized the censorship of so-called amoral art as nonsense, a fear of new ideas, or *misoneismo*. He pointed out that art could only be understood in its own cultural context. Nordau was dominated by a strong cultural pessimism that Lombroso could not share. In spite of their differences, in 1906 Lombroso dedicated the English edition of *Crime: Its Causes and Remedies* to Nordau with these words: "To Max Nordau. To you, as the ablest and best beloved of my brothers . . . to answer those who, not having read my *Criminal Man* (of which it is the necessary complement), nor the works of Pelmann (sic), Kurella, Van Hamel, Salillas, Ellis, Bleuler, and others, accuse my school of having neglected the economic and social causes of crime, and of having confined itself to the study of the born criminal, thus teaching that the criminal is riveted irrevocably to his destiny, and that humanity has no escape from his atavistic ferocity."[71]

In Nordau's as in Kurella's writings we can see how some aspects of Lombroso's theories were distorted.[72] At the same time, the continuous exchange of dedications, acknowledgments, and other references is evidence of a deep friendship that bound Lombroso to the two German scientists, even at the cost of threatening the clarity of their scientific positions. Lombroso probably felt a certain isolation and hostility from German colleagues and appreciated these signs of almost devotional solidarity. Surely another important reason for Nordau to refer so frequently to Lombroso's authority was the need to legitimize his ideas. Actually, Nordau's theory of genius became well known in fin-de-siècle society, and remained almost inseparably tied to that of Lombroso. Similarly, Kurella's role as a spokesman for Lombroso in Germany was accepted as an obvious fact, and many historians of

---

70 Max Nordau, *Degenerazione*, trans. O. Oberosler, 2d ed. (Turin, 1896), xviii.

71 Cesare Lombroso, *Crime: Its Causes and Remedies* (Montclair, N.J., 1911), xxxiii.

72 Surprisingly, Huertas defines Nordau as "true to the strictest Lombrosianism" and sees his text on degeneration as "clearly Lombrosian." He also considers the two theories concerning genius as completely compatible. See Rafael Huertas, "Madness and Degeneration, IV. The Man of Genius," *History of Psychiatry* 4 (1993): 309, 312.

criminology still uncritically use his texts as sources that report and explain the theories of the Italian criminal anthropologist.

PSYCHIATRISTS STUDY THE "BORN CRIMINAL"

At the inauguration of the Forensic-Psychological Association in Heidelberg on June 23, 1905, the law professor Eugen von Jagemann gave a speech on the relations between physicians and lawyers concerning questions of forensic psychology.[73] He naturally referred to the Lombrosian theories and their diffusion in Germany, theories that he defined as "extravagant," thereby rejecting the role that was given to somatic stigmata by the definition of the born criminal.[74] Jagemann agreed with the characterization of most criminals as degenerate but was convinced that these individuals could also produce active and healthy children. Australia provided an example to support this idea. In defense of the cooperation between jurists and physicians, Jagemann mentioned two representatives of German psychiatry: Emil Kraepelin and Gustav Aschaffenburg, whose significance was fundamental for the development of German forensic psychiatry. Jagemann underlined the paradigmatic significance of Kraepelin's forensic-psychiatric courses and Aschaffenburg's integration of statistical methods with individual analysis. A look at the relationship between these two psychiatrists and their approaches to the scientific explanation of criminality will give a more complete picture of the German reaction to Lombroso's criminal anthropology.

BETWEEN DEGENERATION AND SOCIAL ILLNESS: KRAEPELIN'S CONCEPT OF THE CRIMINAL

Kraepelin's first publication, *Die Abschaffung des Strafmasses* (1880),[75] already bore witness to his deep interest in criminological problems. As a young psychiatrist Kraepelin supported the elimination of the system of retributive justice and was convinced that society could only be protected by the indefinite detention of criminals. For Kraepelin, the rehabilitation of criminals had to be seen as the goal of indefinite punishment, which could be compared, in his conception, with the treatment of lunatics. He applied a sort of medical model to criminals and rejected the notion of "morality" as a criterion

---

73 Eugen van Jagemann, "Mediziner und Juristen gegenüber den Fragen aus der forensischen Psychologie," Vortrag zur Eröffnung der forensisch-psychologischen Vereinigung in Heidelberg, am 23. Juni 1905 gehalten, *Monatsschrift für Kriminalpsychologie und Strafrechtsreform* 2 (1905–6): 337–57.

74 Ibid., 342.

75 See Emil Kraepelin, *Die Abschaffung des Strafmasses* (Stuttgart, 1880).

of judgment in the classical justice system.[76] Already in his first writings Kraepelin acknowledged the role of criminal psychology in establishing the fine line between crime and madness. To define which kind of punishment a delinquent should receive, an individual analysis of the specific causes was necessary: "The individuality of the criminal person, his natural disposition, the conditions in which he grew up, as well as the factors that influenced him, leading him in the end to the criminal act, all these contribute to the definition of punishment at best as extenuating circumstances."[77]

When examining the category of habitual criminals Kraepelin stressed their lack of a sense of morality. In 1883 – in his *Compendium der Psychiatrie* – Kraepelin defined the concept of *sittlicher Schwachsinn* (congenital idiocy) more precisely and related it to that of the born criminal.[78] To follow the development of the medical-biological interpretation of criminality, we must analyze Kraepelin's masterpiece, the *Compendium*. He did not wish to address this theme originally.[79] But the thin compendium became a thick textbook, the eighth edition of which appeared in four volumes between 1909 and 1915. (The ninth edition was published in 1927, after his death.) His psychiatric nosology was based on meticulous clinical research using diagnostic cards (*Zählkarten*), of the type introduced by Bertillon at that time for use by the police.[80] The theme of moral insanity represented a leitmotif in Kraepelin's psychiatric book because it was connected with the question of the born criminal. In the first six editions the morally ill person was defined as one who possessed intelligence but – in contrast to normal "socialized" individuals – had no inhibitions in satisfying egoistic impulses.[81] These individuals were characterized, according to Kraepelin, by pathological instincts. He attributed to the Italian school the merit of having recognized this pathological emotional disposition in born criminals.[82]

In the sixth edition of his book Kraepelin analyzed moral insanity more thoroughly: Accurate research on habitual criminals showed that most of them were morally deficient. The development of a moral sense could be stunted by bad education and alcoholic parents, among other things, and by "angeborene sittliche Unfähigkeit" (innate moral incapacity).[83] In this context Kraepelin referred to the Lombrosian school and spoke about the

---

76 On Kraepelin and his relationship to criminal anthropology, see Wetzell, "Criminal Law Reform."
77 Kraepelin, *Die Abschaffung*, 18.
78 Kraepelin, *Compendium der Psychiatrie*, 1st ed. (Leipzig, 1883).
79 Kraepelin, *Lebenserinnerungen* (Berlin, 1983), 28.
80 Matthias Weber and Eric J. Engstrom, "Kraepelin's Diagnostic Cards: The Confluence of Clinical Research and Preconceived Categories," *History of Psychiatry* 8 (1997): 375–85.
81 See Kraepelin, *Compendium* (1883), 352.   82 Ibid., 353.
83 See Kraepelin, *Psychiatrie*, 6th ed. (Leipzig, 1899).

born criminal as an individual who was not fully developed. Anthropological data could show the physical defects of these persons, whom he tried to place into specific clinical groups.[84] The anatomical and functional characteristics of born criminals were defined by Kraepelin as "expressions of a general degeneration."[85] Analyzing categories of individuals, such as vagabonds, prostitutes, and habitual delinquents, he observed that they were "mentally and often physically inferior." In the seventh edition of the *Compendium* he defined them as "born criminals."[86] For Kraepelin two significant problems in defining moral insanity were the lack of physical stigmata and the question of legal responsibility or its absence in these individuals (with well-developed intelligence), who would not be considered as suffering from full-fledged mental illness. Showing the relationships between moral insanity, criminal instincts, and degeneration, he adopted the concept of the born criminal as degenerate for some categories of criminals. Kraepelin remained skeptical with regard to the physical and morphological characteristics of criminal types and thought that more data had to be collected.

To complete this short synthesis of Kraepelin's conception of criminality we must consider his article in 1906 on "Crime as a Social Illness,"[87] which offered a social Darwinist reformulation of his original ideas. Kraepelin's "engagement" in social issues can only be understood in the context of the political climate of aggressive nationalism and imperialistic policy in which he, as a politically engaged scientist, assumed a defensive role in order to save society from degeneration.[88] According to Kraepelin, crime was the result of personal and general causes, not the product of free will: "If we define illness as processes in our body that hamper or make life goals unreachable, we can understand crime as an illness of the social body that prevents the realization of a prosperous social life."[89]

This parallel between the individual and the social body allowed an analogous attitude toward the causes, explanations, and treatment of illnesses and social problems of delinquency. Kraepelin observed that certain presuppositions were essential to crime: An inferior predisposition (*minderwertige Veranlagung*) was the basis of moral inferiority (*sittliche Minderwertigkeit*). He added that the children of alcoholic or mentally ill parents were normally degenerate and grew up without sufficient moral education. Kraepelin tried to divide

---

84 Ibid., 584.   85 Ibid.

86 Emil Kraepelin, *Psychiatrie: Ein Lehrbuch für Studierende und Ärzte*, 2 vols., 7th ed. (Leipzig, 1904), 815–41.

87 Emil Kraepelin, "Das Verbrechen als soziale Krankheit," in Franz von Liszt, ed., *Vergeltungsstrafe, Rechtsstrafe, Schutzstrafe: Vier Vorträge* (Heidelberg, 1906), 22–44.

88 Eric Engstrom, "Emil Kraepelin: Psychiatry and Public Affairs in Wilhelmine Germany," *History of Psychiatry* 2 (1991): 114.

89 Kraepelin, "Das Verbrechen als soziale Krankheit," in Liszt, ed., *Vergeltungsstrafe*, 23.

criminals into types and to define the borderline between criminals and the mentally ill. His scheme covered three main groups: The first consisted of those influenced by external causes (such as occasional criminals); the second group was composed of individuals who could be defined as "inferior personalities" and represented the real enemies of society (as recidivists); the third group presented the category of those who can barely be distinguished from the mentally ill (mentally ill criminals / criminally insane);[90] it therefore was very difficult to consider them responsible for their actions. Kraepelin represented the criminologist as a knight in the struggle against degeneration, a supporter of general education (*Volkserziehung*), and a "social politician."[91] Prevention of crime constituted an important part of this plan, which could be realized only through active cooperation between forensic and penal-law sciences. But what exactly did Kraepelin mean by the term *crime prevention*? Although Kraepelin defined crime as a social illness, the social causes of it were mostly localized in the individual, and attempts at prevention were concentrated on those individuals who represented a danger to society. Convinced that life in big cities implied a negative estrangement from nature, provoking forms of degeneration that could be directly connected with "civilization," Kraepelin had a very dark conception of modern life in industrialized cities: "Domestication" seemed to him to make individuals weak and sterile, subject to the negative effects of drugs (alcohol and cocaine, but also coffee and tea) and unfit for life's struggles. He characterized these individuals as *entwurzelt* (rootless) and expanded this concept to the national level.[92] He spoke against internationalism as a dangerous cause of rootlessness and saw the only hope for an improvement in this dramatic situation in "mass psychiatry" (*Massenpsychiatrie*).[93] Crime was explained by him as biologically based and better defined through a new nomenclature. The integration of delinquency into a social Darwinist view of social phenomena also entailed a fundamental "prognostical and therapeutical pessimism" for Kraepelin. The idea of a state in which security and order are genuine dominated Kraepelin's scientific and social program. The idea of a general and diffused degeneration became obsessive in his representation of society as biologically determined. He used the concept of the born criminal to stigmatize those who, as recidivists and incurable moral defectives,

---

90 See ibid., 30.   91 Ibid., 35.

92 See Emil Kraepelin, "Über Entwürzelung," *Zeitschrift für die gesamte Neurologie und Psychiatrie* 63 (1921): 5; on the question of *Staatsfeindlichkeit* in the nineteenth century, see Johanna Blecker, "Die Stadt als Krankheitsfaktor: Eine Analyse ärztlicher Auffassungen im 19. Jahrhundert," *Medizinhistorisches Journal* 18 (1983): 118–36.

93 See Emil Kraepelin, "Ziele und Wege der psychiatrischen Forschung," *Zeitschrift für die gesamten Neurologie und Psychiatrie* 42 (1918): 195.

represented the greatest danger to the state not only because of their illegal behavior, but as individuals who perpetuated the degeneration of the human race through heredity.[94]

"SOCIAL DEFENSE": ASCHAFFENBURG'S MODEL OF CRIME PREVENTION

Kraepelin introduced the main concepts of the positivist school in his program for the defense of society and emphasized some aspects, such as the endogenous biological disposition to crime. The "born criminal" was preserved as a concept in spite of oscillations and shifts of meanings. Like Kraepelin, Aschaffenburg believed in the individualization of punishment and in the importance of incapacitating criminals (*Unschädlichmachung*). In defining the role of social influences in human behavior Aschaffenburg distanced himself from the theory of Franz von Liszt, who saw "normal" behavior as a result of a complex of different motivations (of individual and social origin) and criminal behavior as a product of negative socialization.[95] Aschaffenburg was closer to Kraepelin's explanation of crime: Human behavior had to be seen as the result of external and internal motives that operated on a certain character and personality.[96] Character was, for Aschaffenburg, a product of disposition, development, intelligence, and affective experience, among other things, so that the question of responsibility could hardly be answered. It's worth noting that, according to Enrico Ferri, Aschaffenburg spoke of a "social responsibility" and rejected the concept of "moral responsibility." Thus he maintained the concept of responsibility but rejected the concept of freedom of the will. Aschaffenburg's magnum opus *Das Verbrechen und seine Bekämpfung* (1903, 1906, and 1923), dedicated to Kraepelin, is structured similarly to Lombroso's *Causes and Remedies of Crime* (German ed., 1902): (1) social causes; (2) individual causes; and (3) remedies. Aschaffenburg based his observations on statistical data, individual research, and serial statistics. The "organic" paradigm led him to structure his representation of criminal phenomena according to the explanatory scheme of the natural sciences. He attached great significance to the methodology of research and expressed skepticism toward individual psychology. For an

---

94 See Emil Kraepelin, "Psychiatrische Randbemerkungen zur Zeitgeschichte," *Süddeutsche Monatshefte* 17 (1919): 130–45.

95 See H.-G. Güse and N. Schmacke, *Psychiatrie*, 195; on Franz von Liszt, see Hans Heinrich Jescheck et al., eds., *Franz von Liszt zum Gedächtnis* (Berlin, 1969); Karl-Heinz Hering, *Der Weg der Kriminologie zur selbstständigen Wissenschaft* (Hamburg, 1966), 168–81; Richard Wetzell, "Criminal Law," 165–73.

96 See Gustav Aschaffenburg, "Der Einfluss Kraepelins auf die Kriminalpsychologie und Kriminalpolitik," *Archiv für Psychiatrie und Nervenkrankheiten* 87 (1929): 87–95.

effective criminal policy, Aschaffenburg considered it useful to define general causes of crime.[97] However, he stressed the importance of psychiatric studies of criminals, which could help to assess the personalities of these individuals.[98] The common goal of psychiatrists and jurists had to be the universal interest, for which the interests of the individual had to be sacrificed. Aschaffenburg described his concept of psychology: The goal of his attempts was to trace a generally valid profile of criminal types. Typical characteristics could be ordered into useful typologies. It is interesting to see how Aschaffenburg tried to define the role of psychology in understanding crime: He criticized psychoanalysis as unscientific and ignored the fact that at this time Freud, together with his follower Wilhelm Stekel, elaborated an interpretation of crime that was not incompatible with the Lombrosian theory of atavism.[99] In defining criminals Aschaffenburg adopted the concepts of passivity and weakness. Like Liszt, who spoke about "Neurasthenie" (neurasthenia), he saw criminals as people who were too weak to resist external stimuli for crime. Exogenous causes (climate, race, religion, city/country, occupation, alcohol) assumed an important role in his first works but became less important in his later writings.[100]

Prostitution was also discussed in this part of his book and was defined as a dangerous form of crime, typical of psychopathic characters that were found among mentally inferior women.[101] The predisposition of these persons to moral deficiency was common to other categories, such as fanatically querulous individuals, pathological liars, and so forth. But with these individuals Aschaffenburg also addressed the endogenous causes of crime, which were very hard to separate from the exogenous causes. The Lombrosian theory seemed to Aschaffenburg to have been opposed in Germany with more impetus than objectivity.[102] He recognized a positive development of the

97 See Gustav Aschaffenburg, *Das Verbrechen und seine Bekämpfung*, 3d ed. (Heidelberg, 1903; reprint, 1923), 6.
98 See Gustav Aschaffenburg, "Kriminalpsychologie und Strafrechtsreform," *Monatsschrift für Kriminalpsychologie und Strafrechtsreform* 1 (1905): 1–7.
99 On Freud's and Stekel's interest in the atavism theory, see Sigmund Freud, *Drei Abhandlungen zur Sexualtheorie*, 5th ed. (1905; reprint, Leipzig, 1922); Wilhelm Stekel, *Störungen des Trieb- und Affektlebens*, 10 vols. (Berlin/Vienna, 1912–28), 1:174–5; Rüdiger Herren, *Freud und die Kriminologie* (Stuttgart, 1973), 105–34.
100 See Gustav Aschaffenburg, *Das Verbrechen* (1923), 531–5; Gustav Aschaffenburg, "Psychoanalyse und Strafrecht," *Süddeutsche Monatshefte* 28 (1931): 793–7.
101 See Mariacarla Gadebusch Bondio, "La tipologizzazione della donna deviante come prostituta, delinquente e degenerata nella medicina ottocentesca," in Marco Beretta, Felice Mondella, and Maria Teresa Monti, eds., *Per una storia critica della scienza* (Milan, 1996), 283–314.
102 See Gustav Aschaffenburg, *Psychiatrie und Strafrecht: Rede zur Gründungsfeier der Universität Köln vom 5.5. 1928* (Cologne, 1928), 30; Gustav Aschaffenburg, "Kriminalpsychologie und Strafrechtsreform," *Monatsschrift* (1905): 2.

theory over the years: "I find the born criminal theory in its original form erroneous, and I cannot share the ideas of Lombroso in many cases. But I feel obliged, as an opponent of Lombroso, to declare that without him, criminal psychology would never have flourished as it has, and that today we can enjoy its fruits only thanks to his work."[103]

According to Aschaffenburg the born criminal did not exist. He did, however, point out that the scientific research of Ernst Kretschmer on the connection between *Körperbau* (physique) and character showed that Lombroso was headed in the right direction.[104] Thus, he accepted the use of the phrase "stigmata of degeneration" and recognized their existence, not considering them proof of inferiority or of a criminal predisposition but rather a signal of eventual inferiority. Like Kraepelin, Aschaffenburg placed the criminal between the healthy and the mentally ill individual. The born criminal was redefined by Aschaffenburg as a social enemy, as someone who, owing to his "insufficient constitution" or "inferior disposition," could not satisfy the demands of life and society. Here the predisposition to crime obtained an essential significance and could be understood only through the complex relationships between individual and society. In Aschaffenburg's conception of society the prevention of crime became a central function: Castration and sterilization were seen as extreme but acceptable instruments of an effective criminal policy.[105]

It is worth noting that in his last article before he emigrated to the United States in 1935, Aschaffenburg mentioned Lombroso and his significance for criminology. He stressed a certain gratitude toward the Italian psychiatrist who had shared a similar, ambiguous position toward difficult questions like sterilization, castration, and the death penalty. Aschaffenburg's work had achieved a synthesis of Kraepelin's and Liszt's theories and was to exercise a major influence on a generation of lawyers and psychiatrists in Germany. In spite of his agnosticism in regard to the eugenics question, his criminological works are imbued with a biological conception of crime, but in a more sophisticated elaboration when compared with the Lombrosian anthropological model of delinquence. Aschaffenburg shared the replacement of the principle of individual ethics by community ethics (*Gemeinschaftsethik*), which was fundamental to Kraepelin's *Massenpsychiatrie*. It cannot be emphasized enough that this was the key point of eugenic demands in criminology.

---

103 Gustav Aschaffenburg, *Das Verbrechen und seine Bekämpfung* (Heidelberg, 1923), 191.
104 Ibid., 193.
105 Aschaffenburg spoke on this theme at the Seventh International Congress of Criminal Anthropology. Gustav Aschaffenbug, "Begrüssung des Kongresses," *Bericht über den internationalen Kongress für Kriminalanthropologie* (Cologne, 1911), 17–23.

Hans von Hentig's radical eugenic theories regarding the selection of individuals in criminal justice (*strafrechtliche Selection*), through the sterilization of specific groups of criminals, for example, represented a further drastic step in the direction of applied eugenics.[106]

Thus, the diffusion of social Darwinist thinking connected with the birth of eugenics must be seen in correlation with three other important factors that contributed to their success in Germany: The presence of a fundamental cultural pessimism, a blind confidence in scientific explanations of deviance, and the belief in the need to sacrifice individuals for the benefit of society. All these were the common elements of the psychiatric theories on the criminal that were analyzed here. In addition to an easily applicable typology, Lombroso's research stimulated further investigations of the criminal as the object of precise "scientific" analysis; but, in order to be effective, his discourse had to be revised on a pathological rather than anthropological basis. The shift from the concept of the born criminal to that of the degenerated, biologically inferior individual not only represented an enlargement of the category of antisocial individuals but also implied a moral judgment with serious implications, as demonstrated by the dangerously ambivalent use of the principle of social defense.

---

106 See Hans von Hentig, *Strafrecht und Auslese: Eine Anwendung des Kausalgesetzes auf den rechtbrechenden Menschen* (Berlin, 1914).

9

Criminology, Hygienism, and Eugenics in France, 1870–1914

The Medical Debates on the Elimination of "Incorrigible" Criminals

LAURENT MUCCHIELLI

A EUROPEAN MOVEMENT, 1850–1900

The growing radicalism with which deviant behavior came to be naturalized starting in the mid-nineteenth century, and especially once the notions of degeneration and criminal heredity began to spread, is common knowledge.[1] Prosper Lucas's *Traité philosophique et physiologique de l'hérédité naturelle* (1847), and even more, Bénédict-Augustin Morel's *Traité des dégénérescences physiques, intellectuelles et morales* (1857) and Jacques Moreau de Tours's *La psychologie morbide dans ses rapports avec la philosophie de l'histoire* (1857) are major landmarks in this respect. All of these authors postulate the existence of "hereditary morbid predispositions," indicated by external physical "stigmata." The notions of "moral folly" and "epilepsy," later adopted by Cesare Lombroso,[2] were already found in the writings of Morel, who took some of his inspiration from James Cowles Prichard, an English physician.[3] It is not surprising, then, that the publication of *L'Uomo delinquente* (1876) was preceded by writings elsewhere in Europe, whose biological determinism was equally adamant.

---

1 See Ian Dowbiggin, *La folie héréditaire (ou comment la psychiatrie française s'est constituée en un corps de savoir et de pouvoir dans la seconde moitié du XIXè siècle* (Paris, 1993); Daniel Pick, *Faces of Degeneration: A European Disorder, c.1848–c.1918* (Cambridge, 1989), 44ff; Marc Renneville, "Entre nature et culture: le regard médical sur le crime dans la première moitié du XIXème siècle," in Laurent Mucchielli, ed., *Histoire de la criminologie française* (Paris, 1994), 29–53; Marc Renneville, *La médecine du crime: Essai sur l'émergence d'un regard médical sur la criminalité en France (1785–1885)* (Lille, 1997), 542ff.
2 Lombroso studied medicine between 1852 and 1858, precisely at the time when these first great treatises on criminal heredity were widely circulated. Generally speaking, he was a great reader of Morel, Haeckel, and Broca, and later of Darwin and Spencer (Pick, *Faces of Degeneration*, 112–13). The theory of atavism was formulated by several French authors some years before its use by Lombroso (Claude Blanckaert, "Des sauvages en pays civilisés. L'anthropologie des criminels [1850–1900]," in Mucchielli, ed., *Histoire de la criminologie française*, 61–3).
3 See Jean-Claude Coffin, "La 'folie morale,' figure pathologique et entité miracle des hypothèses psychiatriques au XIXème siècle," in Mucchielli, ed., *Histoire de la criminologie française*, 89–106.

Like Lombroso, Henri Maudsley (1835–1918) studied medicine in the mid-1850s and specialized in neurophysiology, psychiatry, and forensic medicine.[4] Thanks to *The Physiology and Pathology of Mind* (1867), followed by *Body and Mind* (1870) he soon became renowned throughout Europe. His writings contained all of the elements of the naturalization of crime, along with the claim that medicine is capable of ridding society of its deviants. His reasoning rested on a belief in the absolute natural determinism of behavior: "The fixed and unchanging laws by virtue of which events occur are as powerful in the domain of the mind as in any other part of nature's domain."[5] Even the traditional boundary between the "normal" and the "pathological" disappeared, to be replaced by completely mechanical biological functioning. The willpower of the mentally ill was considered of no consequence, even if the exact way in which these neurophysiological mechanisms functioned was still unknown.[6] Fortunately, this "distinct class of creatures doomed to evil," this "degenerate or morbid variety of the human species" was easily identified. "Marked by special characteristics of physical and mental inferiority," it was identifiable by the naked eye: "a family resemblance betrays them." These creatures were "scrofulous, often misshapen, with an angular, poorly shaped head, . . . stupid, shiftless, balking, deprived of vital energy, and often epileptic."[7] According to Maudsley, no remission was possible for these unfortunate monsters. For the good of the species and of human society, they had to be maintained in isolation and barred from marrying to prevent them from reproducing.[8]

Thus physicians reasoned in very much the same way in Italy and in England, then. It is hard to imagine why the situation should have been different in France. Indeed, the alleged French exception – especially Alexandre Lacassagne's alleged "sociological conception" advanced by some French historians[9] – has already been challenged.[10] As critical a physician as Paul Dubuisson, who was close to Lacassagne, unambiguously stated that "we agree with the new school [of criminal anthropology] on the hereditary

---

4 Pick, *Faces of Degeneration*, 202–3.
5 Henry Maudsley, *Le crime et la folie*, 4th ed. (Paris, 1885), 285.
6 Ibid., 26.   7 Ibid., 27–8.
8 Ibid., 268.
9 Martine Kaluszynski, "La criminologie en mouvement: Naissance et développement d'une science sociale en France à la fin du XIXème siècle. Autour des *Archives d'anthropologie criminelle* d'Alexandre Lacassagne," Ph.D. diss., University of Paris VII, 1988; Pierre Darmon, *Médecins et assassins à la Belle époque. La médicalisation du crime* (Paris, 1989).
10 Laurent Mucchielli, "Hérédité et 'Milieu social': Le faux antagonisme franco-italien, la place de l'École de Lacassagne dans l'histoire de la criminologie," in Mucchielli, ed., *Histoire de la criminologie française*, 189–214; Marc Renneville, *Alexandre Lacassagne (1823–1924): Un médecin-anthropologue face à la criminalité* (Gradhiva, 1995), 17, 127–40.

nature of intellectual and moral faculties, and it may be said that scholars now unanimously agree on this point."[11] The same consensus was also
discernible in discussions in medical circles on responsibility and the foundations of punishment.

THE NATURALIZATION OF CRIMINALS AND EARLY THEORIES
ON THE DEFENSE OF SOCIETY

Consensus Among Republican-Minded French Physicians: Defending Society Against the Incorrigible

For an entire year – between July 1863 and July 1864 – the French Medical
and Psychological Association debated the moral responsibility of criminals.
Although the issue was not a new one among psychiatrists, the determinist
position took a new, more radical turn that gradually became the norm in
French medical circles. This was mainly due to a young doctor, Eugène
Dally, who unhesitatingly proclaimed his materialist convictions in opposition to the traditionalist positions voiced by the likes of Jean-Pierre Falret.
In his contribution, Dally gave a clear, synthetic presentation, paving the
way for a new medical theory of dangerousness and the defense of society.
This theory was predicated on the idea that human nature could not be
modified. "It is recidivism that is socially dangerous, and recidivism shows
that the criminal cannot be cured. But lawmakers make the mistake (a mistake grounded in their faith in an absolutely free substance) of believing
that reform is possible, indefinitely possible."[12] Or further: "The rule is that
criminals, as a result of their physiological and psychological dispositions,
do not tend to recover; they belong to the category of individuals affected
with hereditary, constitutional ailments."[13]

To believe that these recidivists, who committed serious, violent offenses,
were morally responsible was misleading, and there was no sense in debating
endlessly on the extent of their folly in an attempt to preserve the principle
of responsibility (his opponents spoke of "attenuated responsibility" or of
"partial responsibility"). Fundamentally, Dally proposed that moral responsibility be dissociated from legal responsibility. Irrespective of whether the
criminal was responsible for his acts or not, the fact was that he was a

---

11 Paul Dubuisson, "Théorie de la responsabilité," *Archives d'anthropologie criminelle* (1888): 3, 35.
12 Eugène Dally, "Considérations sur les criminels et sur les aliénés au point de vue de leur responsabilité," *Annales médico-psychologiques* 2 (1863): 292–3.
13 Dally in "Discussion sur la responsabilité partielle des aliénés," *Annales médico-psychologiques* 3 (1864):
270.

threat to society, which in itself justified that he be punished. Punishment, then, was not grounded in vengeance or in expiation, but simply in "social utility."[14] In practice Dally suggested that these socially dangerous individuals be dealt with by creating asylums for the incurably ill and by preventing the worst murderers from doing any further harm by condemning them to "life imprisonment," or even – in some "exceptional" cases – to death.[15]

At the time, one of Dally's opponents was probably right in claiming that "No one of us is ready to accept Dr. Dally's doctrine of moral irresponsibility."[16] Many still agreed with Alfred Maury's statement that "society, in order to defend itself, needs to accept the principle of responsibility, which tends to improve humanity at the same time as it safeguards it."[17] Many also were concerned with avoiding the accentuation of what already looked like "a sort of antagonism" between physicians and jurists on the question of responsibility. Dally's argument does not seem to have convinced people at the time: "The doctrine I am supporting does not by any means disarm society; to the contrary, it fortifies social defense by placing it on its true terrain."[18] But a look at the situation fifteen years later shows that the idea had progressed.

In 1879 Dr. Hubert Boëns wrote on crime in *La philosophie positive*. At the time this periodical, headed by Emile Littré, was the organ of the non-religious disciples of Auguste Comte, all free-thinkers, fervent republicans, and, frequently, freemasons. A great many physicians were found in this intellectual milieu, along with some of the most outstanding theoreticians and founders of the Third Republic, including Jules-François-Camille Ferry and Léon Gambetta. Boëns wrote that his objective was "to demonstrate the necessity, following from recent progress in physiology and biology, of modifying the sociological principles on which judges base their decisions as to the responsibility of criminals, and determine those cases that fall within the jurisdiction of present criminal law."[19] He then suggested that individual rights and the principle of responsibility be replaced by the rights of society and the principle of dangerousness:

In our opinion, in the presence of a criminal act that has threatened the existence of one or several members of the community, there are only three questions to be examined and answered: What damage did the criminal cause? What are the possible

---

14 Dally, "Considérations sur les criminels et sur les aliénés au point de vue de leur responsabilité," 291–2.
15 Ibid., 293.
16 Fournet in "Discussion sur la responsabilité partielle des aliénés," 272.
17 Ibid., 269.   18 Ibid., 270.
19 Hubert Boëns, "La criminalité au point de vue sociologique," *La philosophie positive* 2 (1879): 77.

consequences of this crime . . . for society? What is the probability that the offender, if placed in similar circumstances, would again commit an act of the same kind? The objective is to protect the regular, sensible, useful members of the community against the malfeasant aggressions of some poorly structured, perverted, malevolent individuals, almost always useless to the general well-being, who are to society what pests are to our countryside: dangerous.[20]

In the face of such danger, according to Boëns, society had the right to defend itself, and in 1879 he undertook to clarify both the theory and the practical measures required; that is, death or the impossibility of reproduction:

In Switzerland and Belgium the so-called Liberal Party, which counts more doctrinaires than progressives in its ranks, has made the abolition of the death penalty an article of its political credo. It will change its mind. The death penalty is a social right. Simply, respect for the rights of man demands that this [sanction] only be applied to profoundly vicious individuals, in those cases where no doubt is possible, and behind closed doors . . . this sanction is just, and necessary to purge the social body and maintain its particular organization. Moreover, people who commit murder must be prevented from having offspring, in the name of sexual selection and by virtue of the principle *Similia ex similibus nascuntur*. The murderer by system, by vicious organization, must be cut off forever and absolutely from the life of the community. We cannot put him in a position to perpetuate his race or to recover his freedom, however momentarily.[21]

Boëns, well aware that the free-thinking republicans were demanding the abolition of capital punishment in reference to the 1789 Declaration of Human Rights, proposed an argument that "seems, at first glance, somewhat paradoxical," namely that the republican conception of individual rights should be reserved for "good citizens," as opposed to those "ferocious beasts" who, as proved by the "pathological anatomical sciences," were afflicted with "incurable lesions."[22] Basically, then, what he proposed was not a reversal of the concept of human rights but rather a break with the idea of a unified category, by placing incurable criminals outside of "humankind."

Are They Still Human? Widespread Agreement with Lombroso

In many respects this position met with eager assent within the French medical community. Those French physicians who agreed with the neo-Lamarckian version of degeneration did of course criticize this atavistic

20 Ibid., 91–2.
22 Ibid., 79, 80–82, 96.

21 Ibid., 94–5.

theory of the born criminal.[23] But even if the exact mechanisms behind the physiological determination of crime continued to be debated, no one – with the exception of the Parisian anthropologist Léonce Manouvrier – really challenged its reality, its etiological predominance, and its fatal hereditary repetition.[24] Similarly, although the atavistic theory in itself came to be challenged, the comparison of criminals with animals was already commonplace, as shown, for instance, by the expert testimony in the Troppmann affair, a criminal justice case widely publicized in 1869.[25] In 1881, Dr. Gustave Le Bon curtly wrote that legal and philosophical considerations on the responsibility of criminals were totally "childish," and that the lawmaker's problem should be put in infinitely simpler terms:

> If I am bitten by a viper or a rabid dog, I do not care to know whether the animal is responsible for its misdeed or not. I try to protect myself by preventing it from doing any further harm or harming others: This is my only concern. . . . We may pity those individuals whose structure condemns them to act wrongly, pity those whose lot it is to be stupid, ugly, or in poor health, just as we pity the insect that we crush in passing or the animal we send to the slaughterhouse; but this compassion is vain and can in no way change their fate.[26]

Similarly, although Maurice de Fleury (future member of the Academy of Medicine, a republican, but one who never concealed his attraction to spiritualism) denounced Lombroso's theory as "oversimplified" in *L'âme du criminel*, it was only to excite the imagination with a description of the absolute evil of the criminal soul, the product of a tainted mind. In effect, the sacrifice of the weakest and most abnormal was written in Nature's "great plan" and death was, in point of fact, a deliverance for these poor creatures, nature's errors:

> And yet we care for them; we raise them in cages, we preserve them from death. For what purpose, God almighty! Is it really human to allow these monsters, these creatures of darkness, these nightmarish larvae to breathe? Do you not think, to the contrary, that it would be more pious to kill them, to do away with that ugliness and that unconsciousness that cannot be made noble, even by suffering? I glimpse the possibility of the legal, authorized elimination of all these incurable beings. Death without suffering, almost a consolation, a release: A gentle death, hardly sad, annihilating useless ugliness and narrowing the intolerable field of vain horror, of evil for no reason.[27]

---

23 Marc Renneville, "La réception de Lombroso en France (1880–1900)," in Mucchielli, ed., *Histoire de la criminologie française*, 107–35.
24 For example, Charles Féré, *Dégénérescence et criminalité* (Paris, 1888), 57ff.
25 Michelle Perrot, "L'affaire Troppmann (1869)," *L'Histoire* (1981): 30, 32.
26 Gustave Le Bon, "La question des criminels," *Revue philosophique* 1 (1881): 538–9.
27 Maurice de Fleury, *L'âme du criminel* (Paris, 1898), 138.

There is an endless store of quotations illustrating how French physicians of the time vied in eloquence in their stigmatization of the inhumanity of criminals. All viewed this inhumanity as inscribed on the body, where it was more or less directly visible.

Criminals were not human, then, it was thought, and for that reason human laws – however radically coercive – need not apply to them. Debased to the ontological status of a disease, a germ – in short, a thing – the criminal was nothing but a noxious element to be eradicated just as one would eradicate cholera or the plague. It is precisely this radical but logical conclusion that was denounced by some jurists whose belief in free will and responsibility led them to defend the idea that criminals may be reformed. Louis Proal, councilor at the Court of Aix, was one of the best known of these critics: "Crime alters human nature but does not suppress it. The criminal does not cease to be a member of the human race. . . . A metaphor does not suffice to change a man into a malfeasant beast. No doubt, man may lower himself to bestiality. . . . But by nature, a criminal is neither a tiger nor a monkey, nor a wolf, nor a fox nor a mole; a criminal is a man."[28] This position was in fact systematically denounced as "metaphysical" by the vast majority of physicians who participated in the controversy discussed here, and by Lacassagne in particular.

The Specific Case of Lacassagne's Hygienist Doctrine

Alexandre Lacassagne (1843–1924) was an expert in forensic medicine and an important institutional figure. His fascination with Lombroso, who was his scientific model at the start of his career, led Lacassagne to establish himself as the leading figure in French criminal anthropology, although he lived at a distance from Paris. He owed this position to the strategy of distinguishing himself from Lombroso, in which he succeeded from the start, at the first conference on criminal anthropology held in Rome in 1885. At the time he countered the "fatalism" of the Italian psychiatrist with the role of the "social environment" and asserted that "societies have the criminals they deserve." The phrase became popular. Basically, however – that is, in his thinking on the importance of heredity, the uselessness of the current methods of punishment, and the role of medicine in reforming all of society – Lacassagne was in full agreement with the biopolitical ambitions of such theorists as Lombroso and Maudsley. To understand his thinking properly, one must simply place it in the hygienist's perspective and in the

---

28 Lucien Proal, "Le déterminisme et la pénalité," *Archives d'anthropologie criminelle* 5 (1890): 373–4.

framework of a belated reference to phrenology. For instance, in his first major scientific paper he wrote that the "social environment" is "a collection of individuals whose mental evolution varies," and added that this distinction "is indispensable if we are to estimate the true value of the influence of sanctions and chastisements on a social environment." A distinction that proves, in effect, that for a specific category of individuals ("the occipital strata"), "one must have the courage to state that the criminal code is merely a social illusion."[29] His hygienist doctrine never varied:

Physical and mental degeneration factors are, we repeat, caused by diseases and addictions such as alcoholism, syphilis, and tuberculosis. Their effects on the parents have repercussions on the children, in the form of physical stigmata of degeneration, described and studied in detail by Lombroso and his school of thought. [This is why] we remain true to our aphorism: Societies have the criminals they deserve.[30]

This hygienist tradition may be defined as an all-encompassing project for sanitary and social control, conceived by physicians at the end of the eighteenth century and implemented with increasing efficiency from the period between 1820 and 1830 onward but which really peaked in the late nineteenth and early twentieth centuries, owing in particular to the impact of what is known as the "Pasteur revolution." The policing of morals involved fighting crime as well as prostitution, drinking, vagabondage, and extramarital sex, and also involved reform schools for children.

Nearly a century after the foundation of the *Annales d'hygiène publique et de médecine légale* (1829), Etienne Martin, student and successor of Lacassagne, was still determined to exert this medical control, but in a spirit that no longer had anything philanthropic about it; it probably was, in his case as well as for Lacassagne, closer to the utopia of eugenics as it has been defined elsewhere.[31] His praise of medical science and his protest against "the desperate slowness" of penal reforms led him to conclude his preface

29 Alexandre Lacassagne, "Marche de la criminalité en France de 1825 à 1880: Du criminel devant la science contemporaine," *Revue scientifique* 1 (1881): 674–5.

30 Etienne Martin and Alexandre Lacassagne, "Des résultats positifs et indiscutables que l'anthropologie peut fournir à l'élaboration ou l'application des lois," *Archives d'anthropologie criminelle* 16 (1901): 541.

31 See Laurent Mucchielli, *Utopie élitiste et mythe biologique: l'eugénisme d'Alexis Carrel* (Esprit, 1997), 238, 81. Lacassagne often pointed out that medicine should be the basis for rethinking the foundations of society. In 1902, for instance, he claimed that "One may predict the time at which true statesmen – not those improvised versions that arise during transitional periods, but those who, later on, in an organised society, will educate themselves for those high and noble functions – will understand that it is no longer possible to govern or to lead men without positive knowledge about human nature" (Lacassagne, "La médecine d'autrefois et le médecin au XXème siècle," *Archives d'anthropologie criminelle* [1902]: 17, 80–81). He even went on to state that "the future of humankind, human happiness after all, is produced in physics and chemistry laboratories" (ibid., 79).

to the twenty-fifth volume of Lacassagne's *Archives d'anthropologie criminelle* with these words:

> If social therapeutics does not march in step with the findings brought to our attention by observers of the fight against crime, it is because society, which is subjected to that wrongdoing for which it is responsible, is still caught up in ideas and prejudices as to responsibility and punishment, and in budgetary constraints where alcoholism is concerned. These concerns annihilate all good will and every attempt to make progress. It is therefore still up to us [physicians] to combat this spirit of routine, by accumulating convincing proof of the need to fight the scourge of criminality, and making it self-evident to all, not out of such violent reactions as those expressed by the crowd, moved by the desire to avenge a wrong, but out of scientifically established, reasoned social prophylaxis. This will lead us to deliberately rid policed society of those poorly formed, tainted elements who disturb its functioning.[32]

In its foundations (that is, lineage), then, there is no difference between the hygienist positions of Lacassagne and his most important students and those of most medical criminologists of the time. Often, in fact, hygienism was even more drastic in its suggestions as to how to combat criminality.

HOW CRIMINAL JUSTICE TREATED "THE INCORRIGIBLE": PHYSICIANS AND CRIMINAL LAW

Recidivism was a recurrent theme in the writings of nineteenth-century criminal law specialists, a veritable "creative obsession," in the words of B. Schnapper,[33] that incessantly disturbed the work of controlling and normalizing the "bad poor" through imprisonment and forced work.[34] In the 1791 Criminal Code recidivism was already considered an aggravating circumstance that could lead to deportation to the colonies. The philanthropic period from 1830 to 1840 represented a short lull in the gradual trend toward stricter control that continued under the Second Empire, when some major statistical tools were developed, including the retrospective serialization of data collected in the criminal justice administration and the establishment of the criminal record. Henceforth, recidivism could be measured, year after year, and the fact that it increased almost continuously prompted more severe repression. It was in this connection that the idea of transportation gradually returned to the forefront of penal controversy as an easy way to

---

32 Martin, "Préface à la 25ᵉ année," *Archives d'anthropologie criminelle* 25 (1910): 7.
33 Bernard Schnapper, "La récidive, une obsession créatrice au XIXè siècle," in *Le récidivisme: XXIè congrès de l'Association française de criminologie* (Paris, 1983), 25–64.
34 Jacques-Guy Petit, *Ces peines obscurs: La prison pénale en France (1780–1875)* (Paris, 1990).

rid society of the most hardened criminals. It first fueled the law of May 30, 1854, "obliging sentenced offenders to remain in the colony after the end of their sentence for a time equal to its duration, or, for those sentenced to more than eight years of hard labor, for the remainder of their life." But many liberal republicans and socialists viewed this law as too symbolic of the coercive methods of the empire. Nonetheless, a great many of their successors denounced the counterproductive effects of imprisonment and demanded more severe punishment. It was in fact the republicans who, in the 1870s, revived the issue of the elimination of recidivists and who laid the groundwork for the first major eliminatory measure adopted in 1885: transportation. Physicians did more than simply encourage this movement. Starting at the turn of the 1880s, they were so sure of their theory and of the accuracy of their anthropometric measurements (later known as *bertillonage*) that they soon raised the question of the widespread use of the death penalty, and some of them then went on to demand the sterilization of degenerates.

Prison – The "School of Crime"

The denunciation of prison as a "school of crime" is probably as old as prisons themselves. However, throughout the first half of the nineteenth century this fact was not viewed as a reason for definitively giving up the hope of reforming people through imprisonment (and, in particular, through solitary confinement). At the very start of the Third Republic, champions of solitary confinement were still in the forefront. But a shift occurred in the 1880s and physicians then became, logically, the most vehement opponents of the development of prisons, including solitary confinement. As Gustave Le Bon, who was an invaluable caricaturist of the clichés of his time, said:

If society decides to avenge the offense committed by a criminal by imprisoning him, it has the right to use that infantile procedure; but at the same time, it should remember that it will pay a high price for that vengeance. The criminal, from whom it often had little to fear before he entered the prison, will have become extremely dangerous by the time he leaves it. . . . The idea that prisons may improve criminals can no longer be defended by any competent person nowadays. . . . [It is] a definite fact, acknowledged by the judges themselves, proved by the statistics, that far from protecting society, our correctional system simply produces an army of enemies of society. This is a rapidly growing army, and we may already predict that the day will come when modern civilizations will be unable to rid themselves of it without paying the price of one of those gigantic hecatombs that makes history shudder.[35]

---

35 Le Bon, *La question des criminels*, 535–7.

At that point the political events of the time caught up with the sanguinary imaginings of Dr. Le Bon. Indeed, it seemed possible to act immediately and "without offending our humanitarian feelings" by implementing transportation. In conclusion to a line of reasoning that Lombroso would have endorsed, he stated that this was a scientifically and economically ideal solution, in all respects.[36]

"The Politics of Riddance" (Charles Lucas): Toward Transportation

After the Paris Commune (1871) the men on the political scene – republicans and legitimists – were frightened. The theme of "the army of crime," of the crowds of vagabonds, drunk with violence (and alcohol) on the verge of submerging the social order, was present everywhere. Combating not only recidivism but recidivists – an all-important change in language – was on the agenda. For the first time, in the survey of judges launched by parliamentary representatives in 1872, the question was raised: "Should transportation be applied to individuals sentenced to hard labor only, or to recidivists as well?"[37] Once the storm passed, however, the supporters of solitary confinement were able to win the battle to prepare what was to become the June 5, 1875, law on cellular imprisonment.[38] But the dream of confinement quickly came up against the eternal obstacle of its prohibitive cost. No sooner had the General Prison Association (Société générale des prisons) been founded, in 1877, than it put the problem on the agenda and in turn raised the question of the "deportation" or "transportation" of recidivists.[39] At last, supporters of the latter triumphed in broad daylight, thanks to the political determination of the new republicans. Moral and social order were the key elements of the governmental program of the republicans led by Léon Gambetta. The new plan for combating recidivists, based both on the conviction that some criminals were incorrigible and on the electoral dividends to be derived from this "safety" measure, was defended from the outset by two of Gambetta's close associates: Joseph Reinach and René Waldeck-Rousseau.[40] They received considerable support from medical circles at the time.

---

36 Ibid., 537–8.   37 Schnapper, "La récidive, une obsession," 44.
38 Robert Badinter, *La prison républicaine (1871–1914)* (Paris, 1992), 41ff.
39 Martine Kaluszynski, *Production de la loi et genèse des politiques pénales. La Société générale des prisons 1877–1900* (Grenoble: Centre de Recherche sur la Politique, l'Administration et le Territoire [CERAT/GIP], Rapport terminal, 1996), 80.
40 Gordon Wright, *Between the Guillotine and Liberty: Two Centuries of Crime Problems in France* (New York, 1983), 143ff.; Badinter, *La prison républicaine*, 111ff.

In 1881, at his inaugural lecture as holder of the chair in forensic medicine at the Lyons Faculty of Medicine, Lacassagne gave advance support to a project with which he was quite familiar. A childhood friend of Gambetta's, a member of the Positivist Society[41] and as opportunistic in science as Gambetta was in politics, he explained the cerebral causes of criminality. He ended his lecture by singing the praises of physicians and their responsibility to society, which he immediately shouldered personally when he wrote: "At the present time, it will be the physicians, once again, who will show judges that some criminals are incorrigible, some are organically bad, defective individuals, and they will obtain not only their imprisonment... but their deportation to an isolated place, far from contemporary society, which is too advanced for them."[42] As a good hygienist, he even warned skeptics that "As long as this selection is not done, we will continue to hatch and to raise crime in hothouses, so to speak, and we will witness an increase in the two great modern plagues that are derivatives of crime: suicide and prostitution."

Gambetta's project also received support from Emile Yvernès (1830–99), a renowned jurist and statistician, and director of judiciary statistics at the Ministry of Justice. In the 1882 *Compte général de l'administration de la justice criminelle*, he published a major retrospective study of 1826–80. Following a denunciation of the "excessive indulgence" of judges, he discussed the need for transportation in the case of "incorrigible vagabonds and thieves, estranged from any work, living on charity and by plunder, for whom we should relinquish attempts at reformation," "those wrongdoers, whose criminal life proves that they are and will remain enemies of any social order."[43]

Statistics had settled the question and corroborated both the diagnosis and the remedies recommended by medical science. It was up to parliament to draw the proper conclusion. The law on the transportation of recidivists – voted definitively on May 12, 1885, by 385 votes to 52 – established the "presumption of incorrigibility," so to speak.[44]

This law was widely enforced. Less than twelve years after it had come into effect, Bérard, former state prosecutor and the new parliamentary representative of the Ain *département*, reported that thanks to this law some 4,000 dangerous individuals had been removed from metropolitan France,

41 Kaluszynski, *La criminologie en mouvement*, 165–7.
42 Lacassagne, *Marche de la criminalité en France de 1825 à 1880*, 684.
43 Emile Yvernès, *Compte général de l'administration de la justice criminelle en France pendant l'année 1880 et rapport relatif aux années 1826 à 1880* (Paris, 1882), xciii, cxxxi.
44 Schnapper, "La récidive, une obsession," 55.

a quite insufficient figure, in his opinion, but indicative, nonetheless, of a "salubrious" reaction against the "deplorable indulgence" of the courts.[45] Relegation did not satisfy everyone, however, even when it was more systematic. The director of the Lyons prison for minors, for instance, a supporter of solitary confinement under all circumstances, felt that "it is perfectly proved by repeated observations that the threat of transportation has hardly any effect on the vast majority of those who are sentenced to hard labor."[46] Hardened criminals allegedly viewed it as a lesser evil. But this argument could be even more easily used to demand more widespread recourse to capital punishment.

The Principle of the Death Penalty

For some time historically minded criminologists maintained the view that Italian medical criminologists alone, as opposed to practically all the rest of European criminologists, favored the death penalty. Here again this picture does not reflect historic reality.

It is a well-known fact that Lombroso was always in favor of the physical elimination of the hard core of incorrigible, born criminals, although he did call for the broad use of alternatives to imprisonment for petty offenders, on the one hand, and for the creation of real asylums for the criminally insane on the other. In his work on *The Causes and Remedies of Crime* he distinguished two types of individuals and treatments within the "incorrigible" category. For the first, more docile group, "deportation" (of the French type) seemed sufficient, and even worthwhile for the community because it might furnish free manpower for the most arduous tasks.[47] But that would not be sufficient "when, despite prison, deportation, and hard labor, these criminals repeat their sanguinary crimes and threaten the life of honest people for the third or fourth time – then there remains nothing but *extreme selection*, painful but definitely effective, the death penalty."[48] It should be emphasized that what was involved here was not the establishment of a sanction. Like most of his colleagues, Lombroso believed neither that capital punishment was viewed by public opinion as achieving atonement nor that it had a deterrent effect

---

45 Alexandre Bérard, "La relégation. Résultats de la loi du 27 mai 1885," *Archives d'anthropologie criminelle* 12 (1897): 245–64.

46 M. Raux, "Note relative à l'exécution de le peine de travaux forcés, la transportation et la relégation, l'application du régime d'emprisonnement individuel, la substitution de certaines peines de réclusion aggravée à la peine de mort ou aux travaux forcés à perpétuité," *Archives d'anthropologie criminelle* 11 (1896): 605.

47 Cesare Lombroso, *Le crime: Causes et remèdes*, 2d ed. (Paris, 1907), 516–17.

48 Ibid., 518 (emphasis added).

on other criminals. Putting incorrigible criminals to death was nothing, in his view, but a way of defending society by applying the law of natural selection to creatures who were no different from animals:

Alas, the death penalty is only all too plainly written in the book of nature, as it is in the book of history; . . . the progress of the organic world is entirely grounded in the struggle for existence, with the ensuing ferocious hecatombs. Far from making us more compassionate, we are hardened against any pity by the fact that there are such creatures as those born criminals, organized to do evil, who are atavistic reproductions not only of the wildest of men but also of the most ferocious animals; for with the exception of the Indian fakirs, we humans have not reached the point of zoophilia at which we are ready to sacrifice our lives for their benefit.[49]

It was definitely eugenics, then, that underlay Lombroso's recommendation that society "purge prisons of those criminals who, through their glorification of vice, make any attempt at reformation vain; by doing so we would apply, once again, to society that selection process to which we owe the existence of our race, and probably also justice itself, which gradually came to prevail as the most violent individuals were eliminated."[50]

This line of reasoning was consistently, actively protested by a large minority of jurists of spiritualist leanings.[51] Within the French medical community, however, Lombroso's position was tempered more than it was challenged, and many people endorsed it fully. A periodization is no doubt required here. Indeed, immediately after the 1885 relegation law was passed, the punitive expectations or anxieties of many French scholars were more than fulfilled. The latter could then agree with Gabriel Tarde that, even though it was legitimated in law by the principle of defending society and in fact by the acknowledgment of the incorrigibility of major criminals, "capital punishment, *at least in the way it is or has been practised*, [was] repulsive, insurmountably repulsive."[52] It was with relief that many people, such as his friend Dr. Armand Corre,[53] were won over by this argument, which, he admitted, was more "sentimental," "aesthetic," or even "religious" than rational. But how fragile an argument it was! When the social and political climates change, a virtue is once again made of necessity. Suffice it to

---

49 Ibid., 518, 520.   50 Ibid., 517.

51 This does not mean that the spiritualist position necessarily led to such opposition. To the contrary, spiritualism also led Henri Joly, one of the best-known criminologists of the time, to support the principle of capital punishment for "a small number of villains, dehumanized by their own fault." Not only that, he believed in its exemplary, redemptive nature: "I would not be loath, I must admit, to having hundreds of prisoners present, on their knees" (Henri Joly, *Le combat contre le crime* [Paris, 1891], 334–5).

52 Gabriel Tarde, *La philosophie pénale* (Lyon, 1890), 559 (emphasis added).

53 Armand Corre, review of Tarde, *Archives d'anthropologie criminelle* 6 (1891): 103.

change the method of execution – cleaning it up for spectators, and making it painless for the sentenced – and sensitive souls cease to be offended.

Some fifteen years after his support of Tarde's "sentimental" reservations, Corre was again called on to take a stance on the death penalty in 1906 when the minister of justice, Guyot-Dessaigne, proposed a new bill abolishing that form of punishment. Passions were unleashed, and this time Corre took the diametrically opposite position.[54] He took a strong stance in favor of capital punishment, violently denouncing "a current of inane, repugnant sentimentality, intellectual ramblings, so-called philosophic and scientific theories shaped in solitary studies, spurred by vanity and calculating ambitions. . . . It brims over with compassion, but mostly for people who least deserve compassion."[55] Lacassagne, opportunistic as usual, adopted a more sober but nonetheless resolute attitude. Setting himself apart from a discussion among "statesmen, sociologists, and lawmakers," he intended to elucidate the viewpoint of physicians and other "medical criminologists, who base their knowledge and assertions on scientific studies."[56] They did not have "beautiful pages of philosophy, with moving oratory" to offer but "definite proof that holds and arrests the mind desirous of pure logic and intent on never indulging in idle talk." Unaware of how "striking" his expression was, to say the least, Lacassagne indignantly wrote: "There is little concern with knowing whether science views beheading as a necessary evil and the executioner as an indispensable surgeon for the ulcers of our civilization and the gangrene of our vices."[57] His personal position was clear: Because beheading was too violent and produced visible reflexes in the head several seconds after its fall, he recommended "English-style" hanging, behind walls, within prisons.[58]

Techniques for Capital Punishment: Cleaner Solutions

In the chapter of his *Philosophie pénale* quoted above, Tarde gave notice of what the development of gentler techniques – he actually had electrocution in mind – for the elimination of the incorrigible might lead him to conclude: "Were the day to come when that progress, apparently slight, was achieved, the greatest objection to the death penalty, which is to say the repugnance

---

54 Julie Le Quang Sang, "L'abrogation de la peine de mort en France: une étude de sociologie législative (1791–1985)," Ph.D. diss., University of Paris X, 1998, 255ff.
55 Corre, "A propos de la peine de mort," *Archives d'anthropologie criminelle* 23 (1908): 231.
56 Lacassagne, "Peine de mort et criminalité," *Archives d'anthropologie criminelle* 23 (1908): 57.
57 Ibid., 59.
58 Lacassagne, *Peine de mort et criminalité* (Paris, 1908), 179.

it elicits, would vanish."[59] The controversy over the efficiency of these techniques had in fact already been going on for several years.

In 1886 the General Prison Society launched a survey of capital punishment techniques in the Western world. The inventory of the solutions applied at the time showed a split between hanging (used in Austria, Belgium, and England before its abolition, in Russia, in Spain by strangulation, and in the United States), beheading by guillotine (used in France, Greece, most of Italy, and those Swiss cantons that enforced the death penalty), or by axe (in Denmark, Finland, Germany, Norway, and Sweden). Discussions on the comparative merits of the various methods continued for many years.

In France the guillotine continued to have many fervent supporters, but there was no lack of opponents, who advanced the possibility that sensation, and perhaps even consciousness, might be prolonged for a short time after decapitation. The controversy was very much alive, especially at the Académie des Sciences and the Société de Biologie in the mid-1880s. In 1888 an important protagonist in the debate, Paul Loye, published the results of his studies on the immediate effects of beheading. He had experimented at length on dogs, observed many beheadings, and performed experiments on severed heads. According to Loye, his findings unambiguously showed that sensitivity ceased instantaneously and that this technique was therefore preferable to hanging or strangling. He proudly concluded: "Moralists and philanthropists should be reassured: death by beheading cannot be a torture."[60]

The question remained a moot one, however, for a new technique had emerged: electrocution. In France a bill had been brought before the Senate as early as 1884 for the legalization of this method, which was believed to be less barbarous. Four years later electrocution was introduced in the State of New York, and by 1890 it had become very popular, according to Garde. Lacassagne, for one, was fascinated by the research done in the United States (J. Mount Bleyer). He noted, for instance, that some people recommended "the strangest techniques; Professor Packard (of Philadelphia), for instance, recommends having the condemned breathe in carbon dioxide in a special chamber, to cause death without suffering, and Dr. Ward Richardson (of London) had the idea of a cell in which the condemned would breathe vapors of an anaesthetic until death ensued."[61] But Lacassagne definitely

---

59 Tarde, *La philosophie pénale*, 569.
60 Loye, *La mort par la décapitation* (Paris, 1888), 277.
61 Lacassagne, "Les exécutions électriques aux États-Unis," *Archives d'anthropologie criminelle* 7 (1892): 433.

viewed electrocution as the most credible alternative to the guillotine. It was first administered to a condemned man on August 6, 1890, following testing on animals. Lacassagne wrote a detailed description of the convulsive reactions of the body during the two shocks – the first did not suffice – on the basis of the reports of American specialists in forensic medicine, then gave a meticulous description of the autopsy of the cadaver. The press and public opinion, he noted, were shocked by the convulsions, which might indicate that the man had suffered. For this reason, "a second experiment was required; it was complete because not just a single condemned man, but four, were executed."[62] Although he felt that the method was still insufficiently reliable, he was very satisfied with these "experiments" on human beings, which had "the merit of having placed the study of the physiological mechanism involved in death by electricity on our agenda."[63]

As for Lombroso, he declared himself opposed to electrocution on the basis of principles that Lacassagne did not consider. In effect, Lombroso emphasized the fact that "the anxiety" of "awaiting death" during the "long preparations required by the application of an electrical current" represented "great pain." He also judged beheading too bloody and was one of the very first to recommend an unheard-of solution, summarized as follows by a commentator: "The use of a gas such as chloroform or ether, producing asphyxiation in the course of pleasant hallucinations. No preparation is needed, and the person departs unawares for the beyond."[64] Several years later this idea was endorsed by many people, including the most fervent French champions of eugenics (Binet-Sanglé, Carrel, Richer).

The New Eugenic Function of Capital Punishment

The reasoning behind the claims of the physicians of the time may be viewed as eugenic before the term was coined. If criminal behavior was simply the outcome of a tainted heredity (irrespective of whether atavism or degeneration was seen as the culprit), then it was clear that the only way to prevent such behavior was to banish such criminals from society once and for all and to prevent them from reproducing; this would then result in a selection process through which the "social body" would gradually be "made healthier." From a strictly intellectual point of view (although

---

62 Ibid., 437.   63 Ibid., 440.
64 Anonymous, "L'avis de Lombroso sur l'électrocution," *Archives d'anthropologie criminelle* 17 (1902): 64.

it was not necessarily the only one), this was an obvious fact for most medical criminologists. It was quite logical, then, that Georges Genil-Perrin, a specialist in forensic medicine and a psychiatrist, could write in 1913: "Morel wished to crown his work by the publication of a *treatise of physical and moral hygiene*; his shadow must be thrilled with pleasure in the Olympia of psychiatrists, as it witnesses the awakening of the fight against degeneration, whence was born the new science of *Eugenics*."[65] Similarly, following the turn of the century it is not surprising to find calls for banishing criminals and the insane,[66] and more generally, barring alcoholics from marrying.[67] Such remarks were still marginal in the 1880s and 1890s, however, at a time when deportation, followed by capital punishment, were in the forefront of discussions on punishment. It was not until the turn of the century that the issue of eugenic solutions as such, and of sterilization and castration in particular, arose.

In 1901 the debate on the castration of criminals was launched by Servier, a retired professor of medicine, in the *Archives d'anthropologie criminelle*. He based his argument on the postulate that decapitation was "a barbarous procedure, a small shame on civilisation."[68] Capital punishment was an absolute necessity, however, and Servier pointed out that it served not only one or two, but three essential functions: "First, it annihilates the dangerous criminal . . . and then it inspires healthy fear in people who may be tempted to follow suit. This is what just about everyone thinks. However, the death penalty has still another effect, one that is not always noticed, although it is very important: It eliminates a degenerated procreator, and thus becomes a powerful factor for the improvement of the race . . . by nipping tainted conceptions in the bud."[69]

He added: "I believe that the latter argument, the least considered until now, is precisely the one that carries the greatest weight." Indeed, Servier, rightfully using Lombroso as a reference, pointed out that heredity was "*the keystone of human action*" and for that reason "the copulation of assassins represents a constant threat for the future because of the probable poor quality of the resulting offspring. There is a serious risk that the sons of a murderer

---

65 Georges Genil-Perrin, "L'évolution de l'idée de dégénérescence mentale," *Archives d'anthropologie criminelle* 28 (1913): 379.

66 See, e.g., Lavergne, "Mariage et psychopathes," *Archives d'anthropologie criminelle* 27 (1912): 616–29.

67 See, e.g., Paul Garnier, "La criminalité juvénile: Étiologie du meurtre," *Archives d'anthropologie criminelle* 16 (1901): 576–86; Lacassagne, "Du rôle des médecins dans la réforme du code civil," *Archives d'anthropologie criminelle* 21 (1906): 75.

68 Servier, "La peine de mort remplacée par la castration," *Archives d'anthropologie criminelle* 16 (1901): 130.

69 Ibid., 130–31.

will enter this world with the sanguinary penchants of their father deep down in their hearts."[70] For this reason, "instead of beheading murderers, we should turn them into eunuchs," as was first suggested some years previously in the United States.[71] This was the only way to eliminate these "degenerate reproducers," to "annihilate their race," and in doing so contribute in a major way to the "improvement" of the human race as a whole.[72] Technically speaking, Servier viewed this solution as extremely simple and hygienic.[73] In comparison with capital punishment, he believed he had unquestionably established "the humanitarian superiority of castrating."[74]

Where Should the Eugenics Program Stop?

As if appalled by the breadth of the potential extent of this simple new procedure, Servier did devote the last paragraph of his paper to one reservation as to how widely this "selection of males" should be applied. This undertaking was to have a scientific foundation: "No doubt, by pursuing the destruction of the tainted seed in the loins of thieves, we would arrive at the extinction of a great many of those families cited as examples by criminologists, in which theft is a practice handed down from father to son." In doing so, however, "society would commit an abominable abuse of power and a crime of lèse-humanity."[75]

This ultimate moral reservation is no doubt extremely important for any understanding of the rest of the history of eugenics in France. Starting at the turn of the century, many physicians in other countries extended the "natural" field of preventive castration much farther. In 1910, for instance, Lacassagne published the inventory established by Dr. Robert Renthoul of Liverpool. The list and number of degenerates cited by the latter were impressive. For his own country in 1909 he counted "no less than 128,787 persons officially certified as being affected with mental derangement," plus, naturally, the innumerable unidentified insane. He went on to specify that "this statistic does not include the great many children whose intelligence is deficient. . . . Their number probably reaches 150,000, and all are prospective fathers and mothers of an even greater number of deranged children."[76] Furthermore, in addition to the deranged, in the strict sense, there were 34,015 epileptics, plus the countless mass "of criminals,

70 Ibid., 131–2.
71 Ibid., 135.
72 Ibid., 132.
73 Ibid., 138.
74 Ibid., 141.
75 Ibid., 141.
76 Robert Renthoul, "Stérilisation proposée de certaines personnes atteintes de dégénérescence intel-lectuelle," *Archives d'anthropologie criminelle* 25 (1910): 516–17.

vagabonds, alcoholics, and prostitutes, all of whom are truly afflicted with mental derangement."[77] But that was not all: "There is also the category of individuals who are on the edge of the precipice, so to speak: there are the choreic, the neurotic, the feeble-minded, the extravagant, the erratic, those individuals whose mental faculty is so weak that one or two glasses of beer are enough to deprive them of any ability to distinguish between good and evil. The total, then, makes one shudder." The number of degenerates to be sterilized would have been in the millions, no doubt. Renthoul did not hesitate for a second, however: "Is it not time for us to pay serious attention to this important natural question, to this senseless, useless production of a growing number of degenerates? For it touches us all, closely; our present criminal inaction is based on hypocrisy and false moral scruples, and has no true relation with the useless suffering of so great a number of poor degenerates."[78]

Conclusion: Why Was the French Situation Relatively Atypical?

The long history of theories on criminal justice and crime in France is characterized by constant ideological swings. We find oscillations between an optimistic pole based on a dynamic, egalitarian conception of human nature that translates into confidence in reform and social reintegration through work, and a pessimistic pole grounded in a static, hierarchical conception of human nature that translates into the search for adequate forms of exclusion from society. These two human and social conceptions were never really mutually exclusive, however. There was ongoing debate between them, with one or the other prevailing more or less distinctly at different periods. The former conception had the upper hand between 1791 and 1848, for instance, whereas there was greater wavering during the ensuing decades. A definite reversal occurred in the 1880s with the growing prevalence of the latter conception. Biomedical theories, and more broadly the gradual institutionalization of what may be termed the "human medical sciences" (physical anthropology and psychiatry, and their participation in the founding of the new discipline, "criminology"[79]), played a central role in this process. These sciences legitimated segregation as a way of dealing with the social question in the name of science – the supreme source of truth for republicans in this fundamentally anticlerical century. They even succeeded

---

77 Ibid., 517.   78 Ibid., 518.

79 There was also the new field of "psychophysiology," institutionalized in France toward the mid-1880s under the impetus of Ribot. See Mucchielli, "Aux origines de la psychologie universitaire en France (1870–1900): enjeux intellectuels, contexte politique, réseaux et stratégies d'alliance autour de la *Revue philosophique* de Théodule Ribot," *Annals of Science* 55 (1998): 263–89.

in challenging the very notion of punishment, to be replaced by a conception that may be termed "sociomedical utilitarianism,"[80] that is, the principle of the defense and progress of society viewed not as an organized body of autonomous individuals possessing inalienable rights, but as a living organism with limbs, or cells to be eliminated in order to keep the organism healthy.[81]

Nonetheless, calls for the massive sterilization of deviants, such as those voiced in the United States, were never prevalent in France during that period. To be sure, Lacassagne – who was to become a member of the French organizing committee for the first International Congress on Eugenics, held in London in July 1912[82] – gladly published Renthoul's paper. True, too, over fifteen French physicians expressed similar opinions during the 1905–14 period.[83] It may even be claimed that physicians already had a functional technical arsenal ready to work. In addition to the continuous improvement of bertillonage, pursued by students of Lacassagne in particular as part of the fight against recidivism, physicians were soon able to propose screening for abnormality in schools as well as in the army.[84] As shown by the work of William Schneider,[85] however, the fact is that eugenics was never as well accepted in France as in the Anglo-American and Scandinavian countries. The fact that France was particularly obsessed with demographic decline – depopulation, as it was called at the time, especially in Bertillon's important last book[86] – is the main reason advanced by Schneider. But the long-standing presence and political predominance of the hygienist program for

---

80 See Robert Nye, *Crime, Madness, and Politics in Modern France: The Medical Concept of National Decline* (Princeton, N.J., 1984), 68–70. Nye was the first scholar to formulate a synthetic analysis of the questions dealt with here, and one to whom historians working on this period are greatly indebted. Using an approach similar to our own, he writes of a "republican [and medical] theory of punishment." We prefer "sociomedical utilitarianism" inasmuch as the very notion of punishment is emptied of its foundations here.

81 We have restricted our discussion to the issue of reputedly "incorrigible" criminals, but other criminological and criminal justice issues were also debated during that punitive "Belle époque." Often, for instance, the same physicians also supported the reinstatement of corporal punishment in prison, using pain to tame the young people, known as "Apaches" at the time, who had committed violent offenses. See, e.g., Lacassagne, "Les châtiments corporels en Angleterre," *Archives d'anthropologie criminelle* 26 (1911): 35–46; H. Laurent, *Les châtiments corporels: la peine capitale, le fouet aux apaches* (Paris, 1911).

82 J. Léonard, "Les origines et les conséquences de l'eugénisme en France," *Annales de démographie historique* (1985): 203–14.

83 See the many examples cited by Anne Carol, *Histoire de l'eugénisme en France: Les médecins et la procréation. XIXe-XXe siècle* (Paris, 1995), 163–84.

84 See, e.g., Haury, "Une tentative de défense sociale dans l'armée. Le dépistage des anormaux psychiques," *Archives d'anthropologie criminelle* 25 (1910): 519–38.

85 William Schneider, *Quality and Quantity: The Quest for Biological Regeneration in Twentieth-Century France* (Cambridge, 1990).

86 Alphonse Bertillon, *La dépopulation de la France* (Paris, 1911).

the prevention of the three scourges that obsessed physicians at the time –
tuberculosis, syphilis, and above all, alcoholism – also should be stressed,
probably even more than Schneider does. In effect alcoholism was viewed
as the cause of degeneration and its ensuing social problems.[87] Although the
nosological validity of the doctrine of degeneration was often challenged
at the time, most hygienists consider that its "overall etiological validity
remains unshaken, because it is unshakeable."[88] Like the insane and prostitutes, criminals were mostly viewed as degenerates, and the preventive fight
against the causes of degeneration was given precedence over the treatment
of its consequences: The organization of the preventive fight against alcoholism took precedence over the issue of treating criminals.[89] Many people really viewed alcoholics as public enemy number one. Paul Brouardel
furnished a memorable example with the apocalyptic portrait he drew in
1889 at the opening session of the Congrès international d'hygiène et de
démographie, over which he presided: "The alcoholic is a mentally weak
creature, capable of the worst intentions. He is dangerous for himself and
for his fellow citizens. These people represent more than half the inmates
of prisons; they fill the hospitals and insane asylums. The alcoholic ruins
his family and the community, which must first assist him and his wife in
their destitution, and are then obliged to provide assistance for his scrofulous, idiotic, epileptic children, unfit to work and to provide for their own
pittance."[90]

One last reason should be mentioned: the fact that a majority of jurists –
and probably a large minority of physicians[91] – expressed strong, principled

---

87 See Alain Corbin, *Les filles de noce: Misère sexuelle et prostitution au 19ème siècle* (Paris, 1982); Pierre
    Guillaume, *Du désespoir au salut: les tuberculeux* (Paris, 1986); Dominique Nourrisson, "Tuberculose
    et alcoolisme ou du bon usage d'un aphorisme," in J.-P. Bardet et al., *Peurs et terreurs face à la contagion*
    (Paris, 1988), 199–217; and, more generally, on public hygiene policies, see Robert Cauvais, "La
    maladie, la loi et les moeurs," in Claire Salomon-Bayet, ed., *Pasteur et la révolution pastorienne* (Paris,
    1986), 281–330; Jack Ellis, *The Physician-Legislators of France: Medicine and Politics in the Early Third
    Republic, 1870–1914* (Cambridge, 1990); Lion Murard and Patrick Zylberman, *L'hygiène dans la
    République (1870–1918)* (Paris, 1996).
88 Genil-Perrin, *L'évolution de l'idée de dégénérescence mentale*, 379.
89 "Alcoholism is synonymous with crime," according to Dr. Legrain (*Un fléau social: l'alcoolisme* [Paris,
    1896], 13), former collaborator of Magnan and one of the leaders of the fight against alcoholism.
    Sixty-four percent of prisoners were alcoholics, according to his estimation. The link between crime
    and alcohol was so obvious that the Ministry of Justice issued an official instruction on Decem-
    ber 22, 1906, demanding that the headings for criminal statistics be modified to facilitate the
    evaluation of the role alcohol played (Maurice Yvernès, "L'alcoolisme et la criminalité," *Archives
    d'anthropologie criminelle* 27 [1912]: 17). Lacassagne, a good hygienist himself, had always emphasized
    this problem, contending that "statistics on alcoholism are superposable with those for criminality,
    whence an obvious [sic] causal relationship" (Lacassagne and Martin, "Les données de la statistique
    criminelle," *Archives d'anthropologie criminelle* 21 [1906]: 845–6).
90 Paul Brouardel, "Discours de M. le professeur Brouardel," in *Actes du Congrès international d'hygiène
    et de démographie à Paris en 1889* (Paris, 1889), 11.
91 Jacques Léonard, *La médecine entre les pouvoirs et les savoirs* (Paris, 1981), 270–72.

opposition to the biological theories that explained everything by heredity, and to their logical conclusion in eugenic solutions. Indeed, those physicians who supported eugenics constantly complained about the persistence of an excessively broad, philanthropic conception of human rights and about the belief in the beneficial effects of education, all of which they stigmatized as "sentimentality." Now, it is worth our while to give some thought to this complaint. We may hypothesize that for reasons tied to French cultural history these principles, which reflect a political philosophy, played a peculiar role in France's exceptionalism with regard to the eugenic programs adopted at the time in several English-speaking countries. The extent of their role remains to be determined, however, through investigation of sources other than scientific writings.

10

Crime, Prisons, and Psychiatry

Reconsidering Problem Populations in Australia, 1890–1930

STEPHEN GARTON

In the 1890s nearly 1.5 percent of the population of New South Wales (Australia's most populous colony/state) were in prison. By the 1920s this rate had fallen dramatically to only 0.4 percent. This was not merely the effect of a severe economic recession and a subsequent period of growth. Prison admissions in Australia throughout the nineteenth century had been very high, and they declined quickly throughout the first half of the twentieth century. Like so much else in the field of crime, policing, and imprisonment, this trend was hardly unique to Australia. Similar patterns occurred in Britain, Canada, and America, a phenomenon described by Andrew Scull as the first great wave of "decarceration."[1] This is a misleading concept. When we examine the history of other institutions of "penality" very different patterns emerge. In New South Wales, during the same years of decline in prison admissions, mental hospital residents rose from 0.7 percent to 1.5 percent of the population. In addition, there were no government-run inebriate asylums in 1890 but by 1930 there were two such institutions and many more private institutions. Similarly, in 1890 there was only one asylum for the "mentally defective" but by 1930 there were at least six, and although the numbers admitted to juvenile reformatories had not changed, the number of neglected and delinquent children under some form of state supervision had increased dramatically through the operation of the children's court. What we can see is not so much "decarceration" as diversification, proliferation, and specification, all steps toward an unrealizable but nonetheless powerful ideal of "individualization."[2]

1 Andrew Scull, *Decarceration: Community Treatment and the Deviant: A Radical View* (Englewood Cliffs, N.J., 1977).
2 All figures from New South Wales (hereafter NSW) comptroller-general of prisons, annual reports (1890–1930); NSW inspector-general of the insane, annual reports (1890–1930); and NSW inspector of charities, annual reports (1890–1930).

The appeal of "individualization" and the myriad reforms it legitimated are familiar to historians of criminality, penality, and welfare in Britain, Europe, and America. The groundbreaking works of such scholars as David Garland, David Rothman, and Martin J. Wiener (and numerous others) have charted many dimensions of both the discursive representations of problem populations and the policies introduced to deal with such populations.[3] Australia, as a British colony (and after 1901 a dominion), although thousands of kilometers from the metropolitan centers of Europe and America, had important and influential reformers who were receptive to the international developments in penality and criminology. Whereas the foundation of European colonization in Australia as a site of convict transportation created its own tensions and peculiarities, this did not isolate Australia from more general currents of change. In the late nineteenth and early twentieth centuries, a sustained and diverse series of reform measures were pursued by governments and administrators seeking to reconfigure the means by which the state dealt with "undesirables," the mentally afflicted, and the "immoral." Underpinning these reforms was a new language of "disease," "heredity," "fitness," and "degeneracy" that gave shape to novel ways of understanding the meaning of crime, insanity, responsibility, and delinquency. These new discourses operated in diverse ways. On the one hand, they constructed more specific and precise problems (the inebriate, the moral imbecile, the feebleminded, the psychopath and so on). On the other hand, they also blurred the old distinctions between problem populations, creating more categories from which one could generalize, such as the "unfit," the "incurable," or the "degenerate."

This was also an international language of reform that Australian reformers found appealing. If the Australian example demonstrates anything, it is the global impact of the new discourses of criminology, degeneracy, and unfitness. At one of the points on the globe furthermost from the metropolitan sites where these discourses originated, they had a demonstrable effect in providing a new lens to view problem populations, a new rationale for particular reforms and, as the statistics on the changing rates of incarceration noted above indicate, they had a marked effect on actual practices of confinement and social regulation. One of the most obvious conclusions that can be drawn from such evidence is that these discourses were international and global in their impact. And although we need to map the peculiarities

---

3 See Martin J. Wiener, *Reconstructing the Criminal: Culture, Law and Policy in England, 1830–1914* (Cambridge, 1990); David Garland, *Punishment and Welfare: A History of Penal Strategies* (Aldershot, 1985); and David Rothman, *Conscience and Convenience: The Asylum and its Alternatives in Progressive America* (Boston, 1980).

of local political culture and social formation that shifted the emphasis of particular discourses, slowed or speeded reform, stalled or prevented some reforms while allowing others, all of which created national and regional differences, this should not blind us to the more general character of these developments, ones which we might, for the want of any clearer specification of their significance or meaning at this point, see as a series of complex responses to modernity (although what this concept means in relation to penality requires much more discussion and analysis). Nor were these transformations confined to the mere quantity or diversity of incarceration. As other work suggests, it also had effects on the gendered and ethnic character of confinement.[4] But these dimensions of the question are beyond the scope of this chapter. Here I seek to chart the impact of new ideas on Australian penality and the responses to them from a number of influential Australian penal reformers and doctors.

I

In 1904 Frederick William Neitenstein, the head of the Prisons Department in New South Wales, set off on a round-the-world tour, visiting numerous prisons in Britain, Europe, and America; it was a chance to cement his relationship with various administrators and reformers. For many years Neitenstein had been a vigorous correspondent with major figures in the field of criminology, notably Havelock Ellis and Cesare Lombroso, as well as a host of lesser figures, such as the Matron of the Massachusetts Reformatory for Women. The report of his journey provides fascinating insight into the state of prison administration in the Western world in the early twentieth century.[5] Like many Australian administrators before and after him, Neitenstein was assiduous in cultivating international contacts (and many, like him, also traveled extensively overseas, creating a major archive of comparative data on prisons and asylums throughout the world from the 1860s to just before World War I).[6] He was a bower bird of penal knowledge,

---

4 I have sought to explore some of the gender dimensions of incarceration in mental hospitals in this period in *Medicine and Madness: A Social History of Insanity in New South Wales, 1880–1940* (Kensington, 1988).

5 Frederick W. Neitenstein, *Report of the Comptroller-General of Prisons on Prisons, Reformatories, Asylums and Other Institutions Recently Visited by Him in Europe and America* (Sydney, 1904).

6 Some of the major books and reports include Frederick Norton Manning, *Report on Lunatic Asylums* (Sydney, 1868); George Tucker, *Lunacy in Many Lands* (Sydney, 1887); "Report of the Chairman, Indeterminate Sentences Board, on Reformatory Prisons and Institutions in Europe and America," *Victoria Parliamentary Papers* 3 (1910): 405–36; and Sir Charles Mackellar, "Report on the Treatment of Neglected and Delinquent Children in Great Britain, Europe and America," *NSW Parliamentary Papers* 4 (1914): 1207–1475.

soliciting advice and collecting information on the latest developments with a view to assessing what was most appropriate for the Australian situation.

His tour also allowed him to reassert his contribution to penal adminis-tration in Australia for a domestic readership. Neitenstein had a long and distinguished career, first as superintendent of the Nautical Training Ship for Juveniles (1878–95) and then as comptroller-general of prisons (1896–1909). During that time he gained a reputation as a vigorous and effective reformer that was subsequently perpetuated by historians who viewed his period as comptroller-general as the "golden years" of Australian prison reform.[7] Of greater interest is the exact nature of these reforms. Neitenstein assumed responsibility for prisons in New South Wales at a time of consider-able upheaval. The economic recession of the 1890s had placed considerable strains on government assistance and social regulation. Large demonstrations of unemployed, extensive food queues, pleas from charities for increased assistance to cope with the worsening problem of destitution, and rising labor movement activism unsettled Australian governments that were ham-pered by an entrenched fiscal crisis and unable to respond to many of these calls. In this climate, other indicators of social unrest assumed greater signif-icance in the minds of political, social, and business leaders. Larrikin gangs (an Australian term for hooligans), which had been active for a number of years, appeared more menacing, and when crime and imprisonment rates began to rise in the early 1890s there were widespread fears of a crisis in the social order. There were calls for increased policing and harsher sentences, and in-prison flogging and "the gag" were reintroduced (almost twenty years after they had been abandoned) as deterrents, particularly for the youthful offender.[8]

By the mid-1890s the worst of the economic crisis had abated, but more significantly deterrence and harsh physical punishment were seen as failures. Neitenstein's appointment as head of the Prisons Department was a sign of a new reformist attitude, inspired as it was by widespread debate in Britain, Europe, and America on the need to assert the importance of rehabilitation more than retribution in the treatment of criminals. Of course, Neitenstein was not alone in this desire for reform. Previous prison administrators, such

---

7 For a contemporary appreciation of his work, see Bernhard Ringrose Wise to Neitenstein, Aug. 7, 1901, in Frederick W. Neitenstein papers, Mitchell Library, Sydney, mss 1833/1. For later views, see John Ramsland, *With Just But Relentless Discipline: A Social History of Corrective Services in New South Wales* (Kenthurst, 1996), 140–75; Mark Finnane, *Punishment in Australian Society* (Melbourne, 1997), 68–75; and Merrilyn Sernack-Cruise, "Penal Reform in NSW: Frederick William Neitenstein, 1896–1909," Ph.D. diss., University of Sydney, 1980.

8 See Attorney-General and Justice Department Special Bundle, "Reintroduction of the Gag in NSW Gaols," Archives Office of NSW, 5/7731.

as Harold MacLean, had sought to bring Australian developments into line with "modern" thinking, but his efforts had been hampered by a cautious legislature. Neitenstein's appointment was an indication of a new political will to tackle the problem of prison reform in a more sustained and "progressive" way. Other Australian colonies also had active prison reformers, such as Thomas Walker in Western Australia, and John Evans and Charles Strong in Victoria, but Neitenstein was acknowledged by his peers and later historians as the leading penal reformer of the period.[9]

Neitenstein's debt to broader criminological discourses is very evident in his reference to prisons as "hospitals for moral disease," drawing very directly on Havelock Ellis.[10] Here we have a familiar and very important shift, from a legal and utilitarian discourse of "moral calculus," deterrence, and punishment graduated to fit the severity of the crime, to a newer language of disease. The connecting threads across this shift are the ideas of moral weakness and reform. But as Martin Wiener has shown, the meaning of these terms changed significantly across the century. In the early nineteenth century, there was a faith in the capacity of individuals, in the right circumstances, to morally improve themselves. Training and the right environment became mechanisms for restoring moral will and the capacity to control immoral impulses. By the end of the century, moral states were "naturalized," immorality was more ingrained, more inherent in the nature of the individual and hence less amenable to easy reform. But the responses to this naturalization were complex and in some ways contradictory. They could lead equally to an optimistic faith in new ways of "curing" social problems and to a fatalistic acceptance that these problems would always exist. Australian developments were in part attempts to grapple with the desire to individualize treatment and the fear that some were beyond treatment.

Although Neitenstein was a careful and assiduous student of international criminology, he was selective in his reading of this literature. One key concept in Lombroso's early work – atavism – is clearly absent from Neitenstein's thinking and almost all other Australian discussions of crime. We can only speculate on this absence because neither Neitenstein nor anyone else of significance provided a critical rationale for this neglect. But it does seem likely that in colonies largely founded as convict settlements (except for South Australia) the idea of atavism threatened the comfortable assertion that Australia had thrown off its disreputable past. In

---

9 For some discussion of this broader context, see Finnane, *Punishment in Australian Society*, 65–84.
10 NSW Prisons Department, *Annual Report* (Sydney, 1896), 44. For the parallels with Ellis, see his discussion of prisons as "moral hospitals" in Havelock Ellis, *The Criminal*, 4th ed. (London, 1910), 336.

turn-of-the-century Australia there were many claims that the new nation
had become a "social laboratory" where the most advanced social thinking
and practice was in evidence. By 1912 Australia had introduced comprehensive pension schemes, factory and shop acts, a minimum wage, concili-
ation and arbitration systems, female suffrage, workers' compensation, and
a maternity allowance, all of which were proclaimed as progressive reforms.
(Even Lenin was moved to warn European workers of the "bourgeois"
nature of the Australian experiments lest they believe that capitalism could
work.) Australian political culture was rife with self-confident assertions of
the virtues of environmentalist social reform. It was certainly not a culture
that wished to contemplate ideas of a darker potential in its population, a
potential all the greater in Australia because of its past. Instead, Australian
penal reformers like Neitenstein sought out environmentalist answers and
strategies wherever possible. But they were aware of the problems of recidivism and the evidence for a criminal class. Here, however, they opted for
ideas of degeneracy and defectiveness rather than atavism in an effort to
situate the problem in a present amenable to change rather than a past that
was beyond amelioration.[11]

For Neitenstein the ideal of prison as a "hospital" environment involved
two processes. The first was to make the prison itself an agent of reform. To
this end he worked to transform conditions within prisons through more
rigorous regimes of classification and observation, incentives for obedience
and greater opportunities for suitable employment, and religious and moral
instruction. Neitenstein, however, was convinced that these innovations
would fail unless other urgent problems were addressed. The most serious
was the size and composition of the prison population. For Neitenstein, if the
prison was to become a "moral hospital," it had to treat the disease of crime
and that "disease" alone. If that was the case, then it was imperative to keep
out other problem populations. In his view it was essential to remove from
prison "feeble old vagrants, diseased and friendless incapables, dipsomaniacs,
lunatics," whereas others, such as "habitual criminals, the sexually insane,
imbeciles, juveniles, and women," had to be placed in different institutions
or separate prisons.[12]

Australian prisons, however, traditionally were large repositories for
"undesirables," which in part explains the high rates of imprisonment. This
reflected a deeper structure of social regulation, where police and magistrates

11 For more general discussions of Australia's reputation as a "social laboratory," see Brian Dickey, *No
   Charity There: A Short History of Welfare in Australia* (Melbourne, 1987), 72–108, and Stephen Garton,
   Out of Luck: Poor Australians and Social Welfare (Sydney, 1990), 62–83.
12 Prisons Department, *Annual Report* (1896), 46–7.

were the most significant authorities in many local areas. Australia, as a series mainly of former convict colonies, carried the twin burden of a pervasive fear of a "convict taint" in the population and the absence of social institutions other than the police to deal with the consequences of the expansion of settlement. The convict taint was a trope of nineteenth-century social policy.[13] Authorities believed that this justified higher levels of policing, and this conviction remained long after the end of transportation. By the 1890s Australia had 193 police per 100,000 people, when the comparable rate in Britain was only 137. More police produced higher rates of arrest, which in turn were taken to confirm the reality of the convict taint. It was not just the quantity of police that counted. Australian forces took their style of policing as much from the militia model of the Irish Constabulary as they did from the paternalism of the London Metropolitan Force. The combination of the two, however, leaned more toward the heavy-handedness of the Irish model, especially in rural areas, again producing higher arrest rates and a greater inclination by magistrates to imprison.[14]

The other factor that made police and magistrates central to social regulation was the absence of other structures. Australia was a sparsely populated country fueled by high levels of immigration (forced and unforced) pushing out an ever expanding frontier. This frontier was a dangerous one. A series of protracted conflicts between settlers and indigenous populations ensued for nearly 150 years. Police and magistrates were everywhere to ensure order and protection for settlers. But the danger of the frontier and the character of settlement (pastoral rather than agricultural) also prevented large-scale habitation, and hence there was insufficient population to form parish organizations, charities, mutual provident societies, or a host of other systems and institutions for dealing with such social problems as destitution, disability, illness, insanity, poverty, and unemployment. Police and magistrates often were the only authorities in many areas to deal with such problems. As a consequence they had many duties in addition to that of policing. They conducted censuses; acted as notaries for births, deaths, and marriages; provided information to colonial governments on a variety of matters pertaining to agriculture, fisheries, and so on; distributed food relief to the poor; and incarcerated the insane, in the first instance in police lock-ups. The effects of this are very evident in the construction of a lunatic asylum population

---

13 For a useful account of the use and effect of this discourse, see Henry Reynolds, "That Hated Stain: The Aftermath of Transportation in Tasmania," *Historical Studies* 14, no. 53 (1969): 19–31.

14 The figures on policing and the general character of policing are discussed more fully in Mark Finnane and Stephen Garton, "The Work of Policing: Social Relations and the Criminal Justice System in Queensland, 1880–1914 (Part I)," *Labour History* 62 (1992): 52–70.

in Australia. In practice, police were responsible for the admission of three-quarters of all inmates of insane asylums, and because their concerns were public order and dangerousness, most of the people they detained (who were subsequently certified by doctors) were men. Unlike England, where the bulk of the asylum population was female, in Australia (and other frontier societies like California and Ireland) lunatic asylum inmates were mainly men.[15]

Neitenstein's first task, then, was to work toward persuading police and governments that prison was not the place for a number of populations, such as the insane, the aged and infirm, the inebriate, and the imbecilic. He was far from alone in this aim. There were many doctors, philanthropists, politicians, and reformers whose assessment of the treatment of different problem populations was similar – prison was not the place for such groups. Two groups were particularly significant – the inebriate and the insane. At the 1887 New South Wales Intoxicating Drink Inquiry, almost all witnesses agreed that the system of treating inebriates as criminals was profoundly flawed. Frequent short sentences in prison did nothing to get to the root of the problem. Here all were agreed that inebriety was a disease, not a crime, requiring prolonged treatment in an asylum.[16] There inebriates could be subjected to a sustained regimen of treatment until their problem was rectified. Subsequent inquiries concurred. In 1906 a South Australian Royal Commission Report argued that "the disease of inebriety . . . should be treated pathologically, just as people with an ordinary disease."[17]

Similarly, Australian psychiatrists were particularly concerned about the incarceration of lunatics in police lock-ups and prisons. By the early twentieth century they mounted a vigorous campaign to change the requirement for certification before treatment. The insistence that two doctors certify insanity before incarceration was an effort to provide a safeguard against "wrongful confinement." But for psychiatrists, this inhibited their proper role as providers of medical therapy. They claimed that certification meant that people were being left untreated until their condition deteriorated to such an extent that they required compulsory confinement. It was then that

15 For a broader discussion of this problem, see Stephen Garton, "Policing the Dangerous Lunatic: Lunacy Incarceration in NSW, 1870–1914," in Mark Finnane, ed., *Policing in Australia: Historical Perspectives* (Kensington, 1987), 74–87.

16 "Report of the Intoxicating Drink Inquiry Commission," *NSW Legislative Assembly Votes and Proceedings* 7 (1887–8): 45–9.

17 "Report of the Royal Commission on the Treatment of Inebriates," *South Australian Parliamentary Papers* 2, no. 22 (1906): iii. For a more general discussion of this shift, see Stephen Garton, "'Once a Drunkard Always a Drunkard': Social Reform and the Problem of Habitual Drunkenness in Australia, 1880–1914," *Labour History* 53 (1987): 38–54.

many became dangerous and fell into the hands of police. By then they were beyond medical help. What was required was early treatment – in clinics, public hospitals, and private practices – before certification, when symptoms were not entrenched and when people were curable. In 1901 the inspector-general of the insane, Eric Sinclair, argued that the continuing distinction between mental disease and bodily sickness, cemented in language, legislation, and practice, was blinding society to the fact that "the insane ... should be treated as cases of ordinary illness not as prisoners and outcasts."[18] In this sphere, the aims of prison reformers like Neitenstein and psychiatrists like Sinclair were as one. All agreed that prison was no place for inebriates or the insane. They required separate institutional treatment, and, in the view of psychiatrists, many of the insane should not have been incarcerated at all but rather admitted to clinics and hospitals as patients, not inmates.

Neitenstein and prominent psychiatrists also agreed on the need to treat another population in a different way. By the end of the nineteenth century the discourse of mental defectiveness achieved considerable prominence. Australian psychiatrists, influenced by the work of Henry Maudsley, Francis Galton, Havelock Ellis, and others, were active promoters of eugenic conceptions of the socially and hereditarily unfit. For them mental defectiveness lay at the heart of many social problems. In this, they opted for a largely intellectual definition of defectiveness. They embraced such techniques as IQ tests (developed and refined by such scientists as Alfred Binet, Theodore Simon, Henry Goddard, and Lewis Terman) as the best means of both conceptualizing and diagnosing mental defectiveness. Despite the importance of intellectual deficiencies as the framework for understanding hereditary defectiveness, they also made allowance for other explanatory frameworks, notably degeneracy and moral defectiveness, for those who were criminal but able to pass all the usual intellectual tests. In the Australian context the idea of degeneracy was taken to indicate those who had weakened their own constitution through drink and moral dissipation, a group that some doctors believed could be cured. But the increasing influence of intellectual definitions of deficiency led to a greater interest in "moral imbecility," which suggested that such problems were inherent and thus largely untreatable. Thus, intellectual or mental defectives and moral defectives needed to be diagnosed and differentiated from those who were amenable to medical treatment. A special committee established to investigate the problem at the 1911 Australasian Medical Congress declared in its report that "few

18 Inspector-General of the Insane, *Annual Report* (1901), 5.

people outside the medical profession realize the gravity of the problem of the mentally deficient, its relation to crime and to the multiplication of the unfit in the community."[19]

Doctors, particularly psychiatrists, were very prominent in eugenic circles in Australia. They, like prison administrators, had a very direct interest in solving the "problem" of mental defectiveness. But even here Australian reformers tended to err on the side of optimism. There was a strong environmentalist strand in Australian eugenic thought. Leading doctors and psychiatrists felt that many social evils had environmental origins and, more importantly, that most of these evils were a complex combination of hereditary deficiencies and environmental stimuli. Thus, there was scope for reformers and doctors to combat environmental causes and prevent hereditarian deficiencies from being realized. This confidence may, in part, explain the relative unimportance of sterilization as a eugenic strategy in Australia. There were a few small groups that advocated sterilization (notably the Racial Hygiene Association, which after World War II became, as it remains today, the Family Planning Association, although radically different in name and policy from its first incarnation). But the majority of reformers and the medical profession believed that sterilization of defectives was both legally risky (it muddied the waters on the issue of informed consent) and largely unnecessary when preventive medicine could alleviate environmental problems, and permanent segregation in asylums, farm colonies, and institutions for defectives could ensure that those beyond medical intervention would lose the opportunity to transmit their hereditary deficiencies.[20]

This belief in the potential for environmentalist intervention underscores the importance of the distinction between curable and incurable populations in fin-de-siècle penality. Prison reformers like Neitenstein and psychiatrists like Eric Sinclair were convinced that there were some in their charge who were beyond help. The discourse of mental defectiveness provided one means of explaining this. What followed from this was the conviction that mental defectiveness was at the heart of problems like recidivism and chronic mental illness. If this was the case, then mental defectiveness was a problem separate from that of criminality or mental illness, and one that

---

19 "Report of the Committee of Inquiry into the Feeble-Minded," *Australasian Medical Congress Transactions* 1 (1914): 703.
20 For a detailed discussion of this environmentalist strand in Australian eugenic thought, see Stephen Garton, "Sir Charles Mackellar: Psychiatry, Eugenics, and Child Welfare in New South Wales, 1900–1914," *Historical Studies* 22, no. 86 (1986): 21–34, and "Sound Minds and Healthy Bodies: Reconsidering Eugenics in Australia, 1914–1940," *Australian Historical Studies* 26, no. 103 (1994): 163–81.

should be dealt with separately. Sinclair supported the widespread eugenic belief that defectives should be placed in separate residential facilities "under continuous supervision ... preventing their further multiplication by marriage."[21] In the first three decades of the twentieth century, governments responded to these ideas by establishing a number of institutions specifically for the purpose of permanently incarcerating those diagnosed as mentally defective. But Sinclair's support for this policy arose not only from his belief in eugenic ideas of defectiveness but also from what he saw as the potential benefits for mental hospitals. Like Neitenstein, he believed that if mental hospitals could be cleansed of inappropriate and incurable populations, such as the defective, reformers and doctors could devote their efforts to treating curable populations. These ideas were very influential. They carried the day in parliamentary debates on reform, and, as a consequence, there was a significant transformation in the institutionalization of problem populations in Australia before World War I. The significant increase in the number of inebriate asylums, mental-defective facilities, and mental hospitals, and the emergence of new strategies such as the children's court had a marked impact both on the number of admissions to prisons and the character of those admissions. Diversification was a very active reform ideal in Australia. Mental defectiveness, then, became a means for reformers and doctors to rationalize and explain such issues as recidivism or mental-hospital recovery rates, and why some patients and inmates seemed intractable. But underpinning the support for mental-defective facilities was also a faith in the capacity of doctors and prison reformers to treat specific social problems. As Sinclair declared in 1913: "The progress of medical science ... tends to deal more largely with ... the curable cases as compared with the incurable."[22]

II

A central part of Neitenstein's reform program was to rid the prison of populations who were best handled in other institutions. For him these were not problems of crime prevention and treatment. The other part of his program, however, was a new system for dealing with criminals, with a view to "curing" this problem. Neitenstein was, however, working within a vacuum in Australia. There was no established criminology school there and those charged with crime policy were largely dominated by the judiciary. Legal

21 Inspector-General of the Insane, *Annual Report* (1911), 1.
22 "Evidence of Eric Sinclair, Royal Commission on the Administration of the Mental Hospital and Reception House for the Insane at Darlinghurst," *NSW Parliamentary Papers* 1 (1913): 640.

ideas of crime and punishment focused on the act of crime rather than the perpetrator, and judicial authorities in Australia were reluctant to cede their authority in these matters to new experts, largely medical, who claimed to know "the criminal."[23] Part of the importance and influence of Neitenstein and other penal administrators such as Harold MacLean and John Woods was that they operated at the interface between medical and legal conceptions of crime and worked hard to integrate both perspectives into the operation of the Australian penal system. Here Neitenstein drew directly on ideas from Cesare Lombroso, Enrico Ferri, Havelock Ellis, and other prominent international criminologists. He adopted the common notion that there were different types of criminal offenders. Although he did not recognize the five or six different types defined by Ellis, he did draw a sharp distinction between the occasional, the juvenile, and the professional criminal. The first two classes had to be treated with "paternal mildness," the latter with sustained and disciplinary certainty.

The key to successfully differentiating these classes was a thorough reform of sentencing policies. For Neitenstein and other reformers, notably Harold MacLean, William Crick, and John Neild, sentencing practices that focused on the criminal act rather than the criminal were the source of the endemic problem of recidivism in prisons. Sentences, he argued, needed to be deterrent and reformative, not merely punitive. The first step, in his view, was to ensure that first-time offenders and juveniles did not go to prison, where they might be infected with the contagion of crime or be so demoralized by the experience that they turned to crime as a way of life. Much of the impetus for sentencing reform came from Britain, where similar issues were being debated. These ideas found fertile ground in New South Wales. In 1895 the First Offenders Act came into operation, allowing suspended sentences for first-time offenders convicted of summary offenses. The 1899 Justices Fines Act allowed summary offenders to pay off their fines in installments instead of being forced to serve out their fine in jail. More significant, the 1905 Neglected Children and Juvenile Offenders Act established a children's court, whose express purpose was to support children where possible and to keep them at home with their parents rather than in institutions through a system of probation. Persistent juvenile offenders and those found to be mentally defective were diverted, respectively, to reformatories for moral training and education or to special farm colonies for

---

23 For discussion of this tension between medical and legal ideas on crime, see Stephen Garton, "The Rise of the Therapeutic State: Psychiatry and the System of Criminal Jurisdiction in New South Wales, 1890–1940," *Australian Journal of Politics and History* 32, no. 3 (1986): 378–88.

permanent segregation.[24] For first-time offenders and juveniles, fines and probation were considered far more satisfactory judgments than imprisonment. It gave them a sharp shock and a warning that any further slip into crime would be more severely punished in the future. For juveniles it was even more important to "intercept the budding criminal" and encourage the parents to provide a more positive home environment or divert the more intractable into a comprehensive juvenile reformatory system, where they could be subjected to a sustained regime of physical drill, education, useful work, and moral reform. Those who failed to respond to these strategies, or whose intellectual deficiency was considered too serious to respond to a positive environment, were sent to institutions for permanent segregation.[25] This was a further refinement of the notion that prisons should treat only "genuine" criminals.

Safeguards were needed to ensure that professional criminals did not slip into the first-offender class and thus escape just punishment. Classification techniques therefore became a vital and integral part of criminal and prison administration. The common use of pseudonyms and simple disguises by criminals, plus the vast distances between police stations in Australia (not to mention the significant migratory habits of Australian men in search of work) made it very difficult to check whether someone who was arrested had previous convictions. For Neitenstein adequate identification and classification of criminals was a crucial plank in his reform program. He was greatly interested in Lombroso's notion of criminal types and Alphonse Bertillon's system for identifying criminals through precise anatomical measurements. His first initiative was to introduce Bertillon's new techniques to supplement the traditional photographs of all prisoners (which had been used since the 1870s). But as Neitenstein recognized, this was an imperfect system. By 1902 he had instituted a new system utilizing Francis Galton's new fingerprint technique for the identification of repeat offenders.[26]

If prisons could be purged of those populations best treated elsewhere, and authorities could be confident of their capacity to identify genuine criminals, then, Neitenstein believed, the prison could play an important role in "treating" crime. Again, sentencing policy, according to Neitenstein, was the stumbling block to success. If prisons were to be "hospitals for

---

24 For general discussions of these developments, see Robert van Krieken, *Children and the State: Social Control and the Formation of Australian Child Welfare* (Sydney, 1992), and Stephen Garton, "Bad or Mad? Developments in Incarceration in NSW, 1880–1920," in Sydney Labour History Group, ed., *What Rough Beast? The State and Social Order in Australian History* (Sydney, 1982), 89–110.

25 See Comptroller-General of Prisons, *Annual Report* (1896), 44–65.

26 "Report by Comptroller-General on Prisons, Reformatories, and Asylums," 103.

moral disease," then it was essential to place "these offenders in a position long enough for scientific treatment" to work. At present, he argued,
this was impossible because (continuing his hospital metaphor) "patients
can be released before cure and remain long after their cure." The system
of repeated short sentences for minor offenses was counterproductive for
those who might benefit from prison discipline and a positive evil in relation to the professional criminal. If sentences addressed the crime and not
the criminal, then dangerous criminals were being released time and time
again to continue their attacks on society. If the aim was to "treat" crime,
Neitenstein argued, then criminals had to be placed in prison for as long
as it took to effect a cure. To this end, he was a vociferous advocate of the
indeterminate sentencing system, first developed in America.[27] There were
limitations to the indeterminate sentence. Criminals could only be kept up
to the maximum sentence handed down by the court. This could mean that
some were released even though they had not "recovered." Neitenstein was
also realistic enough about the prospects for reform to recognize that some
offenders were beyond help. The indeterminate sentence, in his view, had
to address two principles, that of treatment and that of protection. Treatment was clearly a priority. But indeterminate sentences were also there
to "protect society from the outlaws whose only business in life is to prey
upon society."[28] Neitenstein became a firm advocate of permanent detention for "habitual criminals"; "one of the deadliest and costliest products
of civilisation."[29] Neitenstein's views on "habituals" found a very sympathetic audience in Australia. In 1905 the New South Wales attorney-general,
Charles Wade, presented a bill to parliament for the permanent detention
of habitual criminals. It passed in Parliament to general acclaim from all
sides and was enacted that year. It provided for the permanent detention of
any offender convicted of three serious felonies. Such a prisoner could be
released if it was determined that the person had "recovered," but otherwise
it was primarily a measure to protect society from the worst offenders. By
1913 fifty-seven persons were detained under this act.[30]

Neitenstein may have been skeptical about the prospects of reform for
habituals, but he was full of hope for others in the prison system, at least
at first. In the late 1890s he attempted to marry the disciplinary rigor of
Walter Crofton's and Edmund DuCane's systems in Ireland and England
with a new sensitivity to the individuality of prisoners. DuCane's regime

27 See Comptroller-General of Prisons, *Annual Report* (1896), 44–6, and "Report by Comptroller-
   General on Prisons, Reformatories, and Asylums," 7–9.
28 "Report by Comptroller-General on Prisons, Reformatories, and Asylums," 8.
29 Ibid.
30 Comptroller-General of Prisons, *Annual Report* (1913).

was intensely criticized in England for its uniformity, its severity, and its failure to address the problems of recidivism. A growing aversion to the severity of penal discipline and a loss of faith in its positive effects made English prisons the object of renewed criticism.[31] But this pessimism did not infect Neitenstein. He remained convinced that education, work, religious instruction, and physical drill were the means of inculcating the will, character, and self-control necessary for effective citizenship.

To facilitate the effects of these physical and educative regimes it was also essential to provide prisoners with incentives to reform. Following Crofton, and before him Alexander Maconochie, Neitenstein introduced a mark and grade system into the prisons. Prisoners were divided into seven classes, with a graduated scale of privileges and conditions associated with each. Good behavior and demonstrable reform were rewarded with marks (recalcitrant behavior, resistance, or rebellion with the loss of marks) and the accumulation of marks could earn promotion to a higher division. Neitenstein also believed that such a system of reform was most effective if the prisoners were separated from each other. Thus, no prisoner could infect another with bad habits, and disciplinary regimes would work to greatest effect free from outside or extraneous influences. This, however, was impractical given the costs involved. In this context he favored "restricted association," where prisoners would congregate for periods of work and share cells but would otherwise be separated. He undertook a major campaign to build as many single cells as possible and had meals served in cells. Electric lights were introduced to encourage reading, and prison libraries were stocked with books. Prisons themselves had long been differentiated by the type of prisoner they held, with Grafton and Bathurst for serious, long-stay offenders, Berrima for the sick and aged, a special section at Parramatta for the criminally insane, and Darlinghurst and Long Bay Gaol for less serious offenders. Neitenstein maintained and refined these categories, closing down prisons such as the labor camp at Trial Bay, which he considered inappropriate to the new regime of "moral reform." He also succeeded in having the first women's prison built in the state.[32]

Neitenstein's successors continued their work in the "scientific, humane, rational, reformative, deterrent and economical" framework that he had set.[33] There were modifications and refinements, mainly directed toward keeping even more "noncriminal" cases, especially inebriates, out of the

---

31 For a useful discussion of this change of temper, see Wiener, *Reconstructing the Criminal*, 321–36.
32 Comptroller-General of Prisons, *Annual Reports* (1896–1909).
33 This was clearly announced by Neitenstein's successor, Samuel McCauley. Most of the subsequent holders of this position for the next twenty years had been men trained by Neitenstein. See Comptroller-General of Prisons, *Annual Report* (1909), 1.

system. There also were further efforts to refine the classification system within prisons. Intelligence testing was first tried in prisons before World War I and became the norm after the war to better assess to which classification level prisoners should be assigned, based on their presumed capacity to reform. Few held out hopes for the "defectives," and they were usually sent to the lower grades. Psychological testing also gained a foothold in the 1920s. In 1929 a psychological laboratory was opened at Long Bay Gaol with the aim of more expertly diagnosing sexual perverts, inverts, and other psychological "misfits" who might benefit from psychiatric treatment.[34]

Here, in a small way, was an important collaboration between psychiatrists and prison officials in their effort to more expertly differentiate between the curable and the incurable population. Psychiatrists also gained a foothold in other areas of the criminal justice system. In the absence of an established institutional location for criminologists within universities or government departments, doctors, particularly psychiatrists, came to dominate the discourse on crime in Australia. They had been an important influence on Neitenstein, and his adoption of a discourse of "disease" had, in large measure, been a response to the close and productive relationships he enjoyed with prominent psychiatrists in Australia. Neitenstein and prominent psychiatrists forged an alliance to convince the legal profession (which also supplied a significant proportion of politicians in Australia) that crime was best seen as a problem of "the criminal" rather than "crime." They had only limited success, however. The legal profession maintained its control of judicial processes and continued to treat most offenders on the basis of their acts rather than their "natures." But ideas of degeneracy and deficiency began to make inroads into legal discourse and practice, and for some offenders medical intervention became a crucial part of the regime that governed their fate.

III

By the late nineteenth century many psychiatrists believed that they had an important role not only in the management of their specific problem population, the insane, but other problem populations, notably the inebriate and the criminal. They did so on the assumption that these other populations were in fact wrongfully classified as willful transgressors of laws and codes of moral self-control. Instead, psychiatrists argued that these populations were the victims of mental diseases and deficiencies and thus not responsible for

---

34 Comptroller-General of Prisons, *Annual Report* (1927–9), 7–8.

their actions. If this was the case, inebriates and criminals should not be subject to legal regulation but medical treatment. The growing number of inebriate asylums at the end of the century was one response to this discursive shift. Serious inebriates were increasingly sent to asylums for extended periods of treatment rather than prison. Or, if repeat offenders, they were confined in special wards within mental hospitals. The efforts of psychiatrists to have a greater say in the handling of criminals, however, met some opposition from entrenched legal institutions and values that clung faithfully to ideas of laws, rights, and just punishment.[35]

Ideas of "disease" seemed more plausible in relation to serious offenders, mainly murderers and sexual offenders. Here, doctors made headway in convincing the legal profession to accommodate medical ideas. The psychiatric critique focused on the McNaghten Rules, which established the test by which competence to suffer the full weight of the law was determined. Under this test a successful insanity plea depended on a determination that at the time of the criminal act the offender was unable to distinguish between right and wrong. In other words, the offender had no understanding of the moral meaning of his or her acts and, if so, could not be held responsible for the crime. This was a very restrictive criterion and one that many doctors in Britain, most notably Henry Maudsley, found wanting. Australian psychiatrists took up these arguments. In 1892 Frederick Norton Manning, inspector-general of the insane in New South Wales, argued that the McNaghten Rules were "false in theory and unsatisfactory in practice." The legal definition of insanity, he claimed, took no cognizance of delusions and compulsions, which meant that offenders may have been able to discern right from wrong but had no control over their behavior.[36] Over the next few decades Manning's arguments received enthusiastic support from Australian psychiatrists, who continued to assert that "criminology was a branch of medicine."[37]

These are familiar arguments and claims, and they parallel those of doctors in Britain, Europe, and America, who sought to make their expertise

---

35 For more general accounts of these developments in Britain and America, see Nicholas N. Kittrie, *The Right to be Different: Deviance and Enforced Therapy* (Baltimore, 1971); Nigel Walker, *Crime and Insanity in England*, vol. 1: *The Historical Perspective* (Edinburgh, 1968); and Wiener, *Reconstructing the Criminal*, 269–75.

36 F. N. Manning, "Proposed New Test for Insanity," *Intercolonial Medical Congress Transactions* 1 (1892): 59–60, and "Insanity in its Relation to the Law," *Intercolonial Medical Congress Transactions* 1 (1892): 631–8.

37 See W. A. T. Lind, "Criminology as a Branch of Medicine," *Medical Journal of Australia* 2 (1916): 20; J. W. Springthorpe and W. L. Mullen, "On the Plea of Insanity in Criminal Trials," *Intercolonial Medical Congress Transactions* 1 (1892): 647–64; and J. V. McCreery, "The Psychology of Crime," *Australasian Medical Congress Transactions* 3 (1908): 26.

more central to the work of the courts. This struggle has been analyzed by a number of historians, and most have noted a general relaxation in the application of the McNaghten Rules in Britain by the end of the nineteenth century. The arguments of alienists convinced legal authorities that greater flexibility was required to ensure justice, even though they refused to formally abandon the rules for fear, as Martin Wiener argues, of opening up the floodgates to vexatious insanity pleas.[38] But a glance at the statistics on those detained in hospitals for the criminally insane suggests that such a relaxation did not go very far before World War II. There were small increases in such committals, although, as Nigel Walker argues, admissions were increasingly occurring at the pretrial rather than the trial stage. But by the 1930s only half of all English murder trials resulted in a successful insanity plea or a decision of unfit to plead.[39] Australian statistics confirm this resistance to change. Between 1880 and 1940 there was no significant increase in the number of inmates in institutions for the criminally insane. (Admission rates did rise, but as a proportion of the general population they fell quite significantly.)[40]

These patterns, however, are misleading. The focus on trials, murder cases, and insanity pleas misses a significant dimension of the increasing influence of psychiatry on the criminal justice system in Australia. For a small but difficult group of prisoners, psychiatry provided an alternative form of regulation. This group largely consisted of "sexual perverts," child molesters, and parents charged with infanticide. Murder cases were still seen as the domain of the courts, advised by psychiatrists. But for these other cases the McNaghten Rules were considered too crude an instrument – most passed this test and were thus liable to imprisonment. For prison administrators and doctors this was an unsuitable group in prison; they usually were the objects of considerable harassment from other prisoners and were deemed by most administrators to be suffering from a different and more entrenched disease than that of innate criminal tendency. Increasingly the decision was made to certify such cases as insane at the pretrial stage. In the 1880s 11 percent of inmates in criminal mental hospitals were certified at the pretrial stage; by the 1930s this figure had risen to 56 percent. But this, too, is only part of the picture. In a considerable number of such cases psychiatrists who were called in to advise on the diagnosis and appropriate

38 See Wiener, *Reconstructing the Criminal*, 269–75. See also Walker, *Crime and Insanity in England*; Roger Moran, *Knowing Right from Wrong: The Insanity Defence of Daniel McNaughten* (London, 1981); and Roger Smith, *Trial by Medicine: Insanity and Responsibility in Victorian Trials* (Edinburgh, 1981).
39 See Walker, *Crime and Insanity in England*, 122–3.
40 NSW Inspector-General of Mental Hospitals, *Annual Reports* (1880–1939).

course of action persuaded police to drop the charges altogether, allowing the accused to then be certified as insane and transferred to an ordinary mental hospital. Thus, they did not appear in any crime or prison statistic at all. The crucial judgment here became "dangerousness." If an offender was thought to be a continuing danger to others, psychiatrists generally advised that the charges be upheld, and the offender was then either certified at the pretrial or trial stage and sent to the criminal mental hospital. But if there was no apparent danger, it was easier, more efficient, and quicker to have the charges dropped and the offender certified and sent to an ordinary mental hospital.

The extent of this process of keeping offenders outside of the criminal justice system altogether is impossible to quantify. Such cases do not appear in ordinary statistical series or in any public reports on the operation of the police, courts, and hospitals. Confidential archives sometimes reveal particular cases where such decisions operated. On balance, however, it is reasonable to assume that the number of such cases was small, perhaps fifty or so a year, and a further twenty or so were sent to criminal mental hospitals. Certainly, the vast bulk of serious offenders remained the province of police, magistrates, the courts, and prisons. Nonetheless, it was an important intervention, one that incorporated medical decision making further into the operations of the criminal justice system – well beyond that circumscribed by the McNaghten Rules.[41]

IV

Australian prison reformers, politicians, and psychiatrists actively embraced the new discourses of penality circulating in Britain, Europe, and America in the late nineteenth and early twentieth centuries. They were perhaps influenced by history and an inclination to see that crime, delinquency, inebriety, and madness had deep roots in Australian life and that hereditary dispositions nourished these roots. The Australian colonies had traditionally responded to the threat of their "convict taint" with a widespread and intense system of police surveillance, thereby peopling its prisons, mental hospitals, and industrial schools with large populations (of mainly men and boys). By the end of the nineteenth century the new discourses on "criminal types," "hereditary deficiency," and "degeneracy" served to confirm old prejudices in Australia, but these pessimistic prescriptions were also

---

41 For a general discussion of these developments and closer analysis of the evidence, see Garton, "Rise of the Therapeutic State," 378–88.

countered by a newer, optimistic sense of the potential for environmental intervention. There was a sense of hope that by differentiating the curable from the incurable new strategies might be effective in alleviating many social ills. These ideas suggested that the established method of incarceration, mainly prisons, was not the appropriate or most effective policy for combating many social problems. Reformers came to argue that what they faced was not a generalized "dangerous" population, but a series of distinct and special "problem populations," each with its own origin, habits, forms, and, hopefully, remedies.

The result of these new discourses was a significant reconfiguration of incarceration practices in Australia. Groups such as juveniles, inebriates, and "sexual perverts" were culled from the prisons and moved to other institutions – inebriate asylums, mental hospitals, farm colonies, and industrial schools. Others who were deemed to be occasional criminals, those without an entrenched criminal taint, notably juveniles, fine defaulters, and first offenders, were given greater opportunities through probation, suspended sentences, and mechanisms for fine payment to avoid prison altogether. This was a considerable liberalization of the criminal justice system. However, those deemed to be genuine professional criminals were given harsher sentences and, if found to be repeat offenders, even indeterminate sentences. To ensure that these decisions could be made on "sound" principles, an array of new techniques were employed to help identify specific populations by their shared characteristics – fingerprints, Bertillon measurements, intelligence tests, and, later, psychological examinations. Although the police and the courts maintained their tenacious hold over the operations of the criminal justice system, they were persuaded that doctors, particularly psychiatrists, had a limited but important role to play in diagnosing problem populations and advising on the best course of treatment.

Here we can see the operation of two specific policy trajectories – individualization and typification – both, in part, a legacy of Lombroso's efforts to define "criminal types" but both also moving well beyond his focus on crime to encompass a wide range of problem populations. On the one hand, the ideal was to tailor treatment and punishment to the specific needs of each individual case. Thus, each person was assessed for his or her specific characteristics. On the other hand, such assessments operated around practices of classification. Individuals were defined as particular types and, once classified, sent to the corresponding institution or streamed into a noninstitutional solution as was deemed appropriate. But this was not just a matter of redefining existing populations, dividing them up in new ways, and specifying particular punishments and treatments. It also was a process of producing new populations and changing the characteristics of others. Certainly, the number of juveniles subjected to some form of state regulation greatly increased in early twentieth-century Australia. We also can see, at a time of falling prison admissions, a significant rise in mental hospital admissions. These hospital admissions were of a very different type than those of the nineteenth century. By the interwar years, most were women rather than men, a consequence of a shift from the police to families and doctors as the key determiners of who was insane. Thus the map of early twentieth-century penality in Australia underwent significant transformations under the influence of new discourses of criminology, eugenics, degeneracy, and deficiency, creating institutions and practices of continuing power and significance.

11

Positivist Criminology and State Formation in Modern Argentina, 1890–1940

RICARDO D. SALVATORE

With Pinero, Ramos Mejia [and] Cabred, Argentina was the first country that understood and applied my father's ideas, and it was for me and for him a great joy to come here in 1906 and see for ourselves all that had been done in this field; but I see that from that year until today, Argentina has continued to lead the nations that understood my father's directives in the fight against crime entirely and organically and applied them in a much better way.

– Gina Lombroso, July 29, 1936[1]

The period from 1880 to 1930 was a crucial epoch for the formation of the nation-state in Argentina.[2] Those who have examined this process have alternatively emphasized the fiscal and administrative resources that made possible the existence of a national state, the mechanisms that engendered a system of oligarchic political hegemony, the juridical basis of sovereignty and governance, and the construction of a national project.[3] Few, however, have focused on the cultural and disciplinary aspects of state-making.[4] Until quite

---

1 Quoted by Osvaldo Loudet, *Figuras próximas y lejanas al margen de la historia* (Buenos Aires, 1970), 201.
2 Scholars have duly noted the importance of the Conquest of the Desert (1879), the federalization of Buenos Aires (1880), the system of nonconfessional elementary education (1884), the foundation of a solid monetary system (1898), the law of obligatory military conscription (1902), and the electoral reform act (1912) as key moments in the process of consolidation of the nation-state, concordant with the process of modernization.
3 Oscar Oszlak, *La formación del estado argentino* (Buenos Aires, 1982); Natalio Botana, *El orden conservador* (Buenos Aires, 1979); Torcuato Di Tella and T. Halperin Donghi, eds., *Los fragmentos del poder* (Buenos Aires, 1969); Victor Tau Anzoátegui, *Formación del Estado Federal Argentino* (Buenos Aires, 1965); Fernando Sabsay and Antonio José Pérez Amuchástegui, *La sociedad argentina: Génesis del estado argentino* (Buenos Aires, 1973); Tulio Halperin Donghi, *Proyecto y construcción de una nación* (Bogotá, 1985) and Tulio Halperin Donghi et al., eds., *Sarmiento, Author of a Nation* (Berkeley, Calif., 1994); and Nicholas Shumway, *La invención de la Argentina* (Buenos Aires, 1993).
4 Corrigan and Sayer speak of a "cultural revolution" at the roots of the process of state-making. See Philip Corrigan and Derek Sayer, *The Great Arch: English State Formation as Cultural Revolution* (Oxford, 1985). On social control in its relation to the state, see Dario Melossi, *El estado del control social* (Buenos Aires, 1992).

recently key areas of state intervention such as health, education, welfare, and penal policy – areas in which state structures, practices, and rhetoric were crucial for the constitution of political and social subjects – have remained marginal to the historian's research agenda.[5]

As a result, the expansion of the Argentine state as a cultural and institutional complex – its structures of governance, its reasons for rule, its practices – have remained relatively unexplored. This oversight is remarkable for a country and period that is taken as paradigmatic of rapid economic, social, and cultural modernization. A similarly pessimistic assessment applies to the analysis of positivism, a powerful current influencing Argentine politics, society, and culture during this period.[6] With a few salient exceptions, positivism has been treated as an intellectual current with little if any influence on the institutional formation and everyday practices of the state. As a consequence, scholars have failed to acknowledge the crucial role of positivist social reformers in the expansion and renovation of the oligarchic state (1890–1916) and in its regime of governance.[7]

Positivism and state-making were inextricably connected. Positivism contributed to redefining the scope of sovereignty, the instruments of power, and the hegemonic pretensions of the oligarchic state. More than a mere intellectual trend, positivism provided the ruling elite with the institutional spaces, the technologies of power, and the rhetoric needed to exercise power more effectively in the period of transition toward a more democratic republic. Obtaining positions within the institutional apparatuses of the state (in the areas of education, health, justice, and welfare), positivists were able to redirect the oligarchic state's agenda toward the so-called "social question" and to establish a new regime of governance that was less dependent on open repression and political exclusion. Because it was based on a medical conception of social problems and because it used the criminal justice system to experiment with categories, policies, and institutions, I shall call this new regime of governance the *medico-legal state*.

Positivist criminology – a new discipline formed in Argentina between about 1890 and 1910 at the conjuncture of European and North American

---

5 Héctor Recalde, *La salud de los trabajadores en Buenos Aires (1870–1910)* (Buenos Aires, 1997); Mirta Z. Lobato, ed., *Política, médicos y enfermedades* (Buenos Aires, 1996); and Adriana Puiggrós, *Sujetos, disciplina y curriculum en los orígenes del sistema educativo argentino* (Buenos Aires, 1990).

6 See Oscar Terán, *José Ingenieros: Pensar la Nación* (Buenos Aires, 1986) and *Positivismo y nación en la Argentina* (Buenos Aires, 1987); Hugo Biagini, *Como fue la generación del 80* (Buenos Aires, 1980), and *Educación y progreso* (Buenos Aires, 1983); and Ricaurte Soler, *El positivismo argentino: Pensamiento filosófico y sociológico* (Buenos Aires, 1968).

7 Among the exceptions, see Hugo Vezzetti, *La locura en la Argentina* (Buenos Aires, 1983); and Eduardo Zimmerman, *Los liberales reformistas: La cuestión social en la Argentina, 1890–1916* (Buenos Aires, 1995).

intellectual currents – was crucial to the formation of this "state within the state." Its key categories (dangerousness, social defense, semialienation) and policies (indeterminate sentences, individualized treatment, classification of deviants) helped to refashion institutions, practices, and mentalities that significantly altered the nature of the state. A central hypothesis running through this chapter is that the emergence and diffusion of positivist criminology had a profound and lasting influence on the "disciplinary grid" of the Argentine state. In particular, I propose that: (a) disciplinary institutions adopted ideas, concepts, and policies for the control, rehabilitation, and resocialization of "deviant" populations suggested by positivist criminologists; and (b) the state's everyday practices came to reflect (in relation to the general population) concepts, categories, and procedures pioneered by criminologists. All these transformations in the leadership, practices, and programs of state institutions affected the very nature of the regime of governance.

The focus of this chapter is not positivist criminology per se (as a discipline or intellectual current), but the process of the dissemination of positivist criminologists' ideas, research methods, techniques of behavioral control, and social policies. This, I believe, was the ultimate legacy of Cesare Lombroso's ideas in the Argentine context. Elsewhere, I have dealt with the transformation that José Ingenieros and his disciples effected in Lombroso's concepts and research agenda.[8] There I emphasized the important role of positivist criminology as an "interpretive grid" for the social problems created by economic modernization, noted the "medicalization" of criminological interpretations and interventions, and sketched the interconnections between prisons, representations of crime, and public policy. Here I am interested in gauging the impact of positivist criminology on the reshaping of the Argentine state during the period 1890–1940. With this objective in mind, I shall try to map out this process of dissemination in a vast but limited territory of power: the legal and medical professions, the judicial system, and the institutions of confinement and treatment of "populations at risk." I shall focus my inquiry on the 1930s – a period generally characterized as a moment of conservative restoration and exclusionary and fraudulent politics – when a second generation of criminologists seemed to have taken control of major nodes of decision making and institutionalized treatment.

---

8 In previous works I have examined the emergence of positivist criminology in Argentina in the context of an export economy based on casual labor and a society with growing social tensions. See Ricardo D. Salvatore, "Criminology, Prison Reform, and the Buenos Aires Working Class," *Journal of Interdisciplinary History*, 23:2 (Autumn 1992), 279–99; and "Penitentiaries, Visions of Class, and Export Economies: Brazil and Argentina Compared," in Ricardo D. Salvatore and Carlos Aguirre, eds., *The Birth of the Penitentiary in Latin America* (Austin, 1996), 194–223.

POSITIVIST CRIMINOLOGY BETWEEN 1900 AND 1940

Although the founders of the Sociedad de Antropología Jurídica (1888) must be credited as the pioneers of positivist criminology in Argentina, it was José Ingenieros who, in the first decade of the twentieth century, disseminated the new doctrine and made it a legitimate intellectual and policy-oriented endeavor.[9] His research at the Instituto de Criminología (within the National Penitentiary), his medical practice in public hospitals, his editorial work for the journal *Archivos de Psiquiatría y Criminología*, and his lectureships at the University of Buenos Aires gave renewed impetus to the discipline. These activities encouraged physicians, lawyers, professors, and bureaucrats to join the crusade for indeterminate sentences, the segregation of inmates according to dangerousness, labor therapy, and individualized treatment inside prisons.

The reception of Ingenieros's theories, clinical methods, and programs reflected the novelty with which his work was associated. Although accepting the main tenets of the Italian *Scuola Positiva*,[10] Ingenieros sought to redefine the science of criminology on the basis of psychopathologies, presenting his work as a creative synthesis of the "anthropological" and "sociological" schools. The delinquent personality, he argued, presented in different degrees the various influences of biological (physio-psychological) and environmental (social) factors. Building on his own clinical research as well as on a growing volume of international and local publications, Ingenieros tried to integrate recent developments in medical science into criminology. Findings in psychiatry and psychology, he thought, held the keys to interpreting criminal behavior and, hence, to the more effective reformation of criminals. In this regard, his criminology can be said to have taken a "psychological bent."[11]

Ingenieros countered Lombroso's morphological, genetic, and atavistic notions of delinquency with a notion of crime as a combination of moral,

---

9 To be fair, the names of José María Ramos Mejía, Francisco de Veyga, Carlos Moyano Gacitúa, Eusebio Gómez, and others should be added to the list of disseminators of the new doctrine, but the intellectual prestige of Ingenieros overshadowed all competition.

10 In his influential *Criminología* (Madrid, 1913), Ingenieros upheld the experimental method in the study of crime and punishment, conceived of crime as both a biological and a social phenomenon, presented social defense as the single most important criterion for penal sanctions, and advocated prisons that combined different therapies conducive to behavioral modification.

11 Ingenieros's interest in the question of mental illness was strong. He wrote a thesis on the simulation of madness in 1900. A few years later he completed *La simulación en la lucha por la vida* (Buenos Aires, 1903), a book about simulation as part of the economic struggle of modern societies. In 1904 he published *Histeria y Sugestión* (Buenos Aires, 1904), a study in clinical psychology focused on hysteria. Many of his articles in *Archivos de Psiquiatría y Criminología* dealt with questions of abnormality and mental illness. Finally, he wrote *La locura en Argentina* (Buenos Aires, 1920), an intellectual and institutional history of madness.

intellectual, and volitional "anomalies." His classification of delinquents, presented at the International Congress of Psychology in 1905, was based on combinations of these basic "anomalies." Assimilating the delinquent personality into a "psychological syndrome," he was able to divide the wide spectrum of abnormal behavior exhibited by delinquents into distinct psychopathologies.[12] A variety of conditions previously attributed to heredity or environment contributed to shaping the delinquent personality, one that varied according to the type of psychopathology. The delinquent personality, argued Ingenieros, was perfectly identifiable using a combination of clinical exams (anthropometric measurements, family and clinical histories, and psychological tests).

Besides spreading the doctrine of the Scuola Positiva, Ingenieros can be credited with the development of a model of research and intervention that had tremendous potential. Institutions of social control (such as prisons, police stations, and public hospitals) served as the sources of evidence for criminological research; they were the "laboratories" producing and validating hypotheses about crime and punishment, abnormality, and mental illness. The knowledge obtained from these sequestered populations served to augment criminologists' professional prestige and could later be used to influence public policy. Clinical cases were important not only because they reinforced the validity of positivist principles but also because the "life stories" contained in them helped outsiders (the elite, the public) decipher the mind, culture, and attitudes of the new immigrant working classes.

Ingenieros's "plan of social defense" was ambitious, encompassing strategies for the prevention (prophylaxis), explanation (etiology), and treatment (therapy) of delinquency. The prevention of crime included questions of child and maternal welfare, the regulation of work, education, public health, and immigrant selection. A research program combining clinical studies with statistical analysis was to test the validity of existing theories of crime, producing useful classifications for policymakers. The plan contemplated separate institutions of confinement according to the subjects' anomalies, sex, and age. Within these institutions, medical doctors were to control the method and extension of the penal sanctions. The treatment of inmates had to be adequate to each individual's psychopathology. A combination of incentives and penalties, among which labor was central, was supposed to produce reformation among delinquents who were not "habitual" or "congenital."

---

12 See Rafael Huertas García-Alejo, *El delincuente y su patología. Medicina, crimen y sociedad en el positivismo argentino* (Madrid, 1991), 69–103.

The evolution of criminology and penal policy between 1910 and 1940 can be measured by the success of the new Sociedad Argentina de Criminología (SAC, an association founded along positivist principles in 1936) in recruiting new members and disseminating the acquired doctrine. Under the direction of Osvaldo Loudet, one of Ingenieros's disciples, the society rapidly acquired professional prestige and was able to translate this prestige into political influence. The first Latin American International Congress of Criminology, convened in Buenos Aires in 1938 and organized jointly by the government and the SAC, was a good expression of that prestige and influence. The society's *Anales* and the papers and proceedings of the congress make evident the remarkable success with which a new generation of criminologists took over Ingenieros's ambitious program and carried it into effect.

In 1936 Loudet summarized the project of positivist criminology in a five-point policy and research agenda. First, researchers had to study the delinquent's personality, trying to assess the interconnections between biological and sociological determinants of his or her "antisocial behavior." They would be assisted in this endeavor by new developments in psychopathology and clinical psychiatry. Second, Loudet recommended concentrating research efforts on the economic and social conditions of crime. The relationship between economic activities and types of crime needed further investigation, as did the connection between immigration and the increase in physical and mental anomalies among the Argentine population. Third, Loudet challenged criminologists to improve the methods of confinement and institutional therapy so as to realize the vision of the pioneers. In particular, criminologists had to persuade judges of the suitability of indeterminate sentences as a means of rehabilitation. Fixed penalties limited the possibility of reform according to medical principles and, for this reason, were to be rejected. Fourth, criminologists had to engage in a series of preventive interventions intended to remove potential delinquents from their social context; children and the mentally ill represented the most likely targets of state tutelage. The fifth area of intervention was policing. It was the responsibility of criminologists to see that the federal and provincial police forces incorporated modern, "scientific" methods of investigation, identification, and registration.

Loudet's agenda did not represent a radical break with the past, but an extension of Ingenieros's objectives and program that was adapted to the realities of the time. Some of the definitions advanced by Ingenieros two decades before had become widely accepted among the new generation of practitioners of criminology. These included the classification of crime according to the three types of "anomalies" (volitional, intellectual, and moral), and the program of "social defense," with its preventive, etiological, and therapeutic components. If Loudet's agenda sounded much less revolutionary than Ingenieros's *Criminología*, it was because the school had achieved a certain degree of consensus about their science, the causes of crime, and basic penal policies. On topics such as the psychological dimension of crime, the need for indeterminate sentences, and the medical supervision of the process of rehabilitation, Loudet was preaching to the converted.

At the center of the new consensus about social control were the interlocking doctrines of "social defense" and "dangerousness" (*estado peligroso*). By social defense, positivists understood society's right to defend itself against individual or collective aggressors (not only delinquents but also those who challenged the established norms of social interaction). An individual was said to be in a state of dangerousness when, by his or her psychic condition or acquired habits, he or she was likely to commit a crime, or, more generally, to exhibit some degree of "antisocial" behavior. Combined, these concepts legitimized a new power to supervise, control, and punish behavior that, in classical penology, would not have qualified as "crime." Alcoholism, mental illness, prostitution, and venereal disease, for example, could now be treated as homologous to crime. The very ambiguity and open-ended nature of the concept of "dangerousness" gave criminologists reasons to apply it to a growing number of anomalies and subjects. Criminologists were convinced that, in order to have a truly preventive policy, it was necessary to extend this concept of "dangerousness" to the pre- and post-delictive phase. This implied nothing less than a fundamental revision of the juridical definition of crime.[13]

How did criminologists' discourse change between 1910 and 1938? More than was the case with the earlier generation, "dangerousness" became the accepted foundation of penal policy. This doctrine radically altered the received notion of penal responsibility. On the slippery ground of "disease" and "anomalies," there could now be violations of penal statutes whose perpetrators were devoid of all penal responsibility. Or, conversely, those considered not legally responsible (*incapaces de derecho*) in classical theory might now be held responsible for the simple condition of posing a "danger" to society.[14] The displacement of responsibility from the individual to society

---

13 As crime came to be viewed as a social disease associated with individuals' misadaptation to the struggle for life, criminologists attacked the notion of crime as a violation of a penal statute.

14 Alfredo J. Molinario, "La peligrosidad como fundamento y medida de la responsabilidad," *Primer Congreso Latino-Americano de Criminología* [hereafter *Primer Congreso*] (Buenos Aires, 1939), vol. 1, 221–45.

also entailed a change in the role of the penal sanction, from retribution to social defense. Adapting penal sanctions to the physical and psychological condition of the accused required the violation of a key juridical norm – the notion that the same crime must always carry the same penalty.[15]

The growing importance of pathology and psychiatry in the reshaping of criminology resulted in an increased belief in the efficacy of the "scientific method." With clearer taxonomies, better tests, and an unambiguous symptomatology, criminology seemed to have acquired a more solid (scientific) foundation. No longer trapped by the sterile dichotomy of criminal anthropology versus sociological criminology, researchers were free to engage in a thorough search for the true causes of delinquency, a search bounded only by the possibilities of experimental research and the availability of clinical evidence. The "psychological bent" refocused the researcher's gaze on the terrain of weaknesses, abnormalities, and psychopathologies. "Today there is no doubt," wrote Alejandro Raitzin, "that the anthropological signs of criminality, so tenaciously pursued by Lombroso and his disciples, fall under the framework of the more general concept of *semialienation*."[16] A general condition of mental/social misadaptation, more inclusive than madness and devoid of any traces of atavism, was the new territory of the criminologist.

Criminality, previously imagined as a cultural complex or environmental niche (the so-called *mala vida*), could now be assimilated into a disease of the body, mind, and spirit, and, as such, was detectable by clinical examination. Yesterday's born delinquent had been replaced by the abnormal, dangerous individual, ill-adapted to the social competition for economic resources. This brought closer to reality the possibility of medical knowledge controlling the wheels of justice.[17] Comparing the thematic interests of positivist criminologists in the 1910s and 1930s, one can identify other important displacements. Vagrancy and the maladaptation of immigrant workers to the demands of local labor markets, so important for Ingenieros's contemporaries, were no longer decisive issues in the late 1930s.[18] In the context of the Great Depression, labor shortages ceased to be an overwhelming concern. Unlike earlier penologists, positivists of the 1930s found inexhaustible

15 Jorge Eduardo Coll, "Sobre la Responabilidad Social. La técnica jurídica de la peligrosidad en el Proyecto del Código Penal Argentino," *Anales de la Sociedad Argentina de Criminología*, vol. 3 (1937), 89–104.
16 Alejandro Raitzin, "Semi-alienación, doble peligrosidad," *Primer Congreso*, vol. 2, 226.
17 Freudian profound psychology and experimental psychology now held the standards for determining what was and was not an abnormal personality. On the reception of Freud in Argentina during this period, see Hugo Vezzetti, *Freud en Buenos Aires* (Bernal, 1996).
18 See Salvatore,"Criminology, Prison Reform, and the Buenos Aires Working Class," 288.

sources of reflection about theory, society, and state policy in the family and in childhood.[19] The abrupt decline of immigration created a new interest in reproduction (natalism, family welfare). The exacerbated problems of urban poverty and child abandonment reactivated earlier concerns about the inability of poor parents to take care of their children. Questions of mental health now attracted greater attention as criminologists tried to extend state control over these areas.[20]

DISSEMINATION

By the 1930s positivist reformers could show important achievements in relation to the objectives set by Ingenieros two decades before. They had taken control of a whole network of institutions concerned with the treatment of delinquents, minors, and the mentally ill. They had conquered important spaces in the centers of higher education, from which they could disseminate their ideas and programs to the educated classes. They had helped to establish key institutional practices by which the state related, in a "modern" fashion, to the lower classes. And they had made the notions of "social defense" and "dangerousness" more acceptable among the managers of institutions of social control and among the cultural and political elite.

Institutional Control

To carry their ideas into practice positivists managed to build an impressive network of institutions. By 1910 various offices were performing tasks directly related to the positivist project: the Anthropometric Office (1889) and the Service of Observation of the Mentally Ill (1899), both within the Metropolitan Police, the morgue attached to the Institute of Legal Medicine (1896), the Medico-Legal Office within the House of Correction for Minors (1905), and the Institute of Criminology within the National Penitentiary (1907). Other centers, such as the Minors' Colony at Marcos Paz, the Hospice of Mercedes, and the National Colony of Alienated, were also part of the positivist "disciplinary archipelago." Within these institutions positivists conducted research, experimented with methods of classification and treatment, and designed preventive policies.

19 Juan J. O'Connor, "Apreciación por el Tribunal Infantil de los factores biológicos y sociológicos en las reacciones antisociales de los menores," *Primer Congreso*, vol. 2, 50–53. For an attempt to create a full taxonomy of children's psychological states, see Rogelio de Lena, "Necesidad de una clasificación y nomenclatura precisas en delincuencia infantil," ibid., 84–8.
20 For a criticism of the concept of "moral madness," see Nerio Rojas, "Límites entre el delincuente 'nato' y el 'loco,'" ibid., 89–93.

By the 1930s the institutional network had expanded significantly. Positivists were in command of the General Direction of Penal Institutes, the organ that set policies for all federal prisons and reformatories. Its director, José Paz de Anchorena, was a devout positivist who had collaborated in Ingenieros's journal. At the head of the Patronato de Menores, the umbrella organization coordinating policies dealing with abandoned and delinquent children, was Carlos de Arenaza, another positivist reformer and longtime director of the Minors Division of the Metropolitan Police. Gonzalo Bosch, also a member of the school, directed the Hospicio de Mercedes, a center for the treatment of mental disease with a special pavilion for mentally ill delinquents. Other positivists held positions of key strategic importance in the Prison for Indicted Felons, the National Register of Recidivists, the National Patronate of Ex-Convicts, and several new provincial reformatories for minors and women.

Academic and professional entrenchment provided positivists with an appropriate forum for conducting their pedagogical work promoting individualized treatment, social defense, and "dangerousness." Professorships at major universities, in both medicine and law, gave the positivist school public visibility.[21] Although often thought of as academic enclaves, these professorships actually provided connections into the world of policing and criminal justice. From their professorhips (*cátedras*), the positivists were able to integrate various nonacademic spaces (morgue, laboratory, museum, police station) into a common project.[22] Membership in professional associations (whose number was growing) complemented the prestige of the *cátedra*, offering opportunities for acquiring social capital.[23] Many of the directors of institutions of social control belonged to the SAC, directed by Loudet.

The judicial apparatus was not immune to positivist advances either. Although judges continued to be divided between those who subscribed to medico-scientific explanations of crime and penal responsibility and those who preferred more traditional, "juridical" conceptions, progress was evident in this terrain, too. Cornelio Moyano Gacitúa, one of the leading

---

21 In La Plata, Buenos Aires, Santa Fé, and Córdoba positivists held professorships in legal medicine, penal law, criminology, psychology, and other related courses. In addition, they offered special seminars on forensic medicine, juridical anthropology, psychopathology, etc., to those members of the legal or medical profession willing to enter these novel fields.

22 Jorge Salessi, *Médicos, maleantes y maricas. Higiene, Criminología y Homosexualidad en la construcción de la nación argentina* (Rosario, 1995), 165–77.

23 Professional associations whose members favored positivist ideas and remedies included the Argentine Society of Criminology, the Argentine Medical Association, the Society of Psychiatry and Legal Medicine, the Argentine Anthropological Association, the Argentine Psychological Association, and others.

figures of the movement, was appointed to the Supreme Court. Antonio Sagarna, another positivist who contributed to projects about "dangerousness" and the organization of the federal penal system, was made minister of justice and later was appointed to the Supreme Court. Lower courts, too, were influenced by the positivists, particularly in the new jurisdictions. The establishment of Courts for Minors, with their small army of social-service workers (called *inspectores delegados*) and their "preventive" interventions — the sequestration of "abandoned" children and their allocation among foster families and reformatories — came closest to the notion of "dangerousness."

Thus, by the late 1930s positivist criminologists were found throughout the state apparatus: from prisons to courts, and from police stations to mental hospitals. Professional prestige, a faith in rehabilitation, and the social services demanded by a rapidly growing population accounted in part for this success. Political support also was important. Just as Ingenieros and his group were backed by Minister Joaquín V. González, the different initiatives promoted by Loudet and his colleagues found encouragement from Minister of Justice Dr. Jorge E. Coll. A devout positivist who had reached his position after a long career in the administration of reformatories and other institutions of welfare, Minister Coll actively and openly promoted the notion of "dangerousness." He had drafted, in collaboration with Eusebio Gómez, the 1928 bill establishing "dangerousness" as the basis of penal policy.[24]

So entrenched were positivists in the institutions of social control that, toward the late 1930s, they began to consider "dangerousness" a reality. In the opinion of Juan P. Ramos, a distinguished constitutional lawyer, Argentina already had well-developed institutions that could carry into effect the positivist program of social defense — these institutions, he added, were all headed by "our professors."[25] Although Ramos referred in particular to prisons, reformatories, and institutions for monitoring ex-convicts, his assertion could have extended to the police, to the courts, and to other institutions not directly involved in the treatment of delinquents.

Practices and Programs

The increasing influence of criminological positivism was also noticeable in the everyday practices and procedures of state institutions. Through direct

24 The Buenos Aires congress was for him the culmination of a protracted international struggle for the affirmation of positivist criminology. In his inaugural speech, minister Coll presented positivist criminology as a scientific movement destined to revolutionize penal justice. "Discurso del Ministro Jorge Eduardo Coll," in *Primer Congreso*, vol. 1, 47–51.

25 "Discurso del dr. Juan P Ramos," *Primer Congreso*, vol. 1, 446–50.

intervention or through persuasion, positivists influenced the ways in which the state dealt with subject populations. Between 1900 and the late 1930s, various state institutions established practices of identification, registration, classification, research, diagnosis, and treatment that corresponded closely to positivist objectives and programs. These practices, explained below, ushered in new disciplinary relationships between the state and the segments of the population considered "at risk," relationships that prefigured new forms of governability.

Responding to the imperatives established by positivists, various institutions incorporated practices of classification, clinical inspection, and physical measurements as part of their everyday routine. Physical exams in schools, prisons, reformatories, and police stations became more routine in the 1920s and 1930s, a measure of the enhanced influence of doctors in the formation of social policy. The Cuerpo Médico Escolar, a corps of physicians monitoring health conditions in schools, taught teachers how to measure the stature, weight, and thorax circumference of elementary school students.[26] In the 1920s, under the leadership of Loudet, the Penitentiary of Buenos Aires introduced "medico-psychological indices" to rate the dangerousness of inmates, a practice soon followed by other penal institutions.[27] During this time hospices for the mentally ill and reformatories for children started measuring intelligence quotients (IQs) as a means to determine the inmates' "mental weakness."[28] To classify their inmates according to personality traits, diseases contracted, and family background, reformatories for minors implemented periodic medical exams, extensive recordkeeping, and systematic questionnaires.[29]

After an extensive search for an accurate method of identification (which included experimenting with Bertillon's "talking portrait") the police embraced dactyloscopy (the Vucetich system) as the most reliable system.[30] The method, pioneered among prison inmates and police arrestees in the

---

26 The first attempt to take anthropometric measurements of school children was undertaken by the Comisión Escolar in 1881. Later in 1888 the Cuerpo Médico Escolar took over this task, extending it to all the schools under the jurisdiction of the Consejo Nacional de Educación. See Emilio R. Coni, *Memorias de un medico higienista* (Buenos Aires, 1918), 231–5.

27 Apparently, the practice of classifying inmates according to their dangerousness was already established in the prisons of Buenos Aires province by 1938, according to the report by the director of Penal Establishments. Santiago Hernández, "Plan de racionalización carcelaria del gobierno de la Provincia de Buenos Aires," *Primer Congreso*, vol. 3, 385–9.

28 José Belbey, "La delincuencia de los debiles mentales," *Anales de la SAC*, vol. 3 (1937), 189–200.

29 For an argument in favor of extending these classificatory practices, see Lena, "Necesidad de una clasificación," 84–8.

30 Luis Reyna Almandós, "La identificación dactiloscópica civil y la prevención del delito," *Anales de la SAC*, vol. 2 (1936), 53–64.

1890s, gradually became the standard of identity for the whole of the Argentine population. Beginning in 1906, the Buenos Aires police started to distribute identity cards (*cédulas de identidad*) with fingerprints to all citizens who requested them. The popularity of these identity cards impressed even police authorities. By 1920 the central registry included almost one million records, reaching half of the total population by the end of the 1930s.[31] The period 1900–1930 also saw the formation of an impressive apparatus for the production of crime statistics, a result of the expansion of state surveillance.[32] The number of arrest records (*prontuarios*) of the Federal Police's investigative division rose from 3,500 in 1902 to 292,500 in 1909.[33] The creation of a National Register of Recidivists in 1919 facilitated the collaboration among various data-producing agencies and made available to the justice system a key indicator of "dangerousness."[34]

But perhaps the most durable mark that positivist criminologists left on the Argentine institutional landscape had to do with their research. Positivists built a research apparatus that was novel in two respects: It linked "social problems" with institutional techniques of behavioral control and rehabilitation, and it engaged state bureaucracies in the production of "scientific" knowledge. Research programs of a positivist nature thrived because of the availability of sites of intervention that produced new "evidence" about subject populations. The data gathered with the help of surveys, censuses, interviews, and clinical studies helped to produce statistical or clinical "truths" that validated the claims of positivists in the terrain of theory and policy.

Accustomed to classifying populations according to environment, biology, and personal history, institutions started to view their inmates or patrons in a medical way. Resorting to expert medical advice became indispensable and "diagnosis" and "therapy" controlled the individual fate of inmates. What distinguished this moment of state expansion was the simultaneous emergence of an impetus to measure, register, diagnose, and treat the bodies, minds, and spirits of subject populations in a "scientific," medical way. If this impetus spread across state institutions it was because the positivist agenda for the production of knowledge depended on state practices of subjectification and control.

---

31 Miguel A. Viancarlos, "Los servicios técnicos de la Policia de la Capital. Su Organizacion y evolución hasta el presente," *Anales de la SAC*, vol. 3 (1937), 141–87.
32 The General Register of Criminal Statistics in the province of Buenos Aires dates from 1910.
33 Salessi, *Médicos, maleantes y maricas*, 155.
34 The Register was moving over 72,000 files by 1936. Victor Paulucci Cornejo, "Registro Nacional de Reincidencia – Su funcionamiento," *Anales de la SAC*, vol. 3 (1937), 39–54.

Persuasion

University *cátedras* (professorships) disseminated the theories and principles of positivist criminology in multiple directions. In these controlled environments, professors could train the new cadres of practitioners and believers who would later carry the principles of the Scuola Positiva into institutions of research and policy. Positivists' clinical research engaged bureaucrats and administrators in practices that made them participants in the enterprise of reform and modernization. The *cátedra* was a privileged site for the critique of penal policy, a locus of enunciation for the crusade for medico-scientific approaches to social policy. The conviction with which professors challenged traditional studies of law and, particularly, classical penology facilitated diffusion of the doctrine.

Within the universities the influence of positivist criminologists was noticeable but not hegemonic. In the late 1930s courses on legal medicine were already an integral part of the medical-school curricula, and any professional who so desired was able to take seminars in various specialties related to medico-legal studies. But in the law schools, positivists failed to make legal medicine (much less legal psychology) an integral part of the regular curriculum.[35] Outside the university the resonance of the professors' discourse was ample. Endowed with an impressive apparatus of publication, the positivists' message reached multiple audiences within the bureaucracy, professionals, and the lay public.[36] In the courts, in the police stations, and in the prisons and reformatories, we can find echoes of this persuasive discourse. The personal influence of the representatives of science left enduring impressions among bureaucrats and administrators. In addition, reasons of institutional proficiency, self-perception, and modernity facilitated the acceptance of positivism. To those engaged in the everyday management of masses of subjects (inmates, patients, and students), the promise of rehabilitation was a powerful reason for accepting the new doctrine. Prison wardens, policemen, asylum administrators, and reformatory workers preferred to conceive of their work as part of the medical treatment of society's ills. The scientific and progressive nature of the methods used was another essential component of the doctrine's appeal.

---

35 At the Criminology Congress of 1938 various speakers argued in favor of introducing legal medicine into the lawyers' undergraduate curricula, a position the congress approved as a recommendation to Latin American governments.
36 Publications produced at no cost, using the labor of the inmates of the penitentiary, disseminated the ideas and findings of the positivists into a community of experts and lay readers. Salessi, *Médicos, maleantes y maricas*, 172–3.

Police authorities, for example, were dazzled by the new technologies of identification and investigation. Thus, it is not surprising to find police functionaries who recall the massive registration and identification of citizens of the 1920s and 1930s as a period of rapid modernization in the force.[37] This, combined with new uses of forensic evidence in court (photography, bone studies, autopsies, ballistics, etc.), persuaded many within the force that the much-awaited era of "scientific policing" had finally arrived. The police force was now in touch with the principles of physics, chemistry, optics, and biology that could enhance its capacity to solve crimes. Biological metaphors could help legitimize the expanded powers of the police over civil society. Ramón Falcón, the chief of the Federal Police (1906–9), spoke of social problems in medical terms: Workers' strikes were "social diseases" propagated by foreign "germs" (anarchist agitators) and subject to "social prophylaxis."[38]

The positivist paradigm also found supporters within the prisons. The memoirs of Osvaldo Solari Bosch, a teacher at the National Penitentiary during the 1930s, give us an inside perspective on the reception of positivist principles.[39] A believer in rehabilitation, Solari Bosch took as his mission the conversion of his prisoner-pupils into honest, hard-working individuals. He followed the method recommended by the criminologists: separating the subjects into categories associated with certain propensities and behaviors. More importantly, he sought individual knowledge of each prisoner-pupil: Each inmate had certain personality traits and a history ready to be discovered. Knowing the particular "weakness" of each inmate, a teacher could target his moral tales (reading exercises in class) in a specific direction. Monitoring the changing psychological states of prisoners was Solari Bosch's leading preoccupation. The prison school was his "laboratory," a font of knowledge providing powerful insights about criminals.[40] The "psychologism" of his analysis, his belief in individual treatment and classification,

---

37 Laura Kalmanowiecki represents the "radical years" (1916–30) as a period of professionalization of the Buenos Aires police, predicated on distancing from militarism and enhanced involvement with the public. In the early 1930s, she argues, the police expanded its surveillance apparatus to control the activities of communists and "radicals." Laura Kalmanowiecki, "Military Power and Policing in Argentina, 1900–1955," Ph.D. diss., New School for Social Research, 1995. For a different perspective, see Beatriz Ruibal, *Ideología del control social a principios del siglo XX* (Buenos Aires, 1991).
38 Salessi, *Médicos, maleantes y maricas*, 117.
39 Osvaldo Solari Bosch, *Escuela de Penados (Crónica de la Penitenciaría Nacional)* (Buenos Aires, 1971).
40 The inferences he obtained from this observation, though, differed from those drawn by criminologists. Solari Bosch found no pathological situation and tended to attribute the changing moods of prisoners to the alienating conditions of the penitentiary (45).

and his aim to investigate the personal history and social environment of each inmate demonstrate the impact of positivist criminology inside the prisons.

Convergence

Elementary education, public health, and the treatment of mental illness adopted methods of vigilance, discipline, and prevention that seemed akin to those promoted by criminologists. In elementary education, according to Adriana Puiggrós, the medical model proved persuasive chiefly because sanitary and health issues opened the way into questions of morality, family, and sexuality.[41] The discourse of public hygiene served as a counterpoint to the preaching of the Catholic church and, in addition, permitted people to build (on the "dangers" of contagious diseases) a whole range of disciplinary interventions targeting schoolchildren and their families. In ways resembling those of criminology, pedagogues insisted on the separation of bodies, the classification of students according to propensities and deficiencies, and the policing of families. While the Cuerpo Médico Escolar disseminated norms about hygiene and family morality, home visits by school officials (*visitadores escolares*) projected the inquisitive gaze of the state into children's families.[42] The new pedagogy regarded a lack of discipline in school as a disease and treated "infected" pupils as delinquents or dangerous children.

In the area of public health we encounter a similar convergence. Progressive "social physicians" and proponents of public hygiene (*higienistas*) such as Guillermo Rawson, Eduardo Wilde, José Penna, Emilio Coni, or Samuel Gaché contributed to defining an area of state intervention (health risks for workers, prostitutes, and the poor) that prepared the way for the preventive policies of criminologists.[43] The fear of contagion triggered by mass inmigration nurtured a regime of observation, information gathering, and control of population movements that took multiple institutional forms: the National Department of Hygiene, the Office of Public Assistance (Asistencia Pública), the *lazareto* at Martín García island (to quarantine immigrants),

---

41 See Puiggrós, *Sujetos, Disciplina y Curriculum*, chapters 4 and 7.

42 For the project of "patriotic education," see Carlos Escudé, *El fracaso del proyecto argentino* (Buenos Aires, 1990); and Lilia Ana Bertoni, "Soldados, gimnastas y escolares: La escuela y la formación de la nacionalidad a fines del siglo XIX," *Boletín del Instituto de Historia Argentina y Americana "Dr. Emilio Ravignani"* 13:1 (1996), 35–57.

43 Similar preoccupations about social threats produced collaborations between hygienists and criminologists. Overlapping and exchanges in positions were common. Emilio Coni, a leading hygienist, wrote about forensic practice (*Código de Higiene y Medicina Legal*). José Maria Ramos Mejía, one of the founding members of the new criminology, was appointed director of the Departamento de Higiene.

and the various public hospitals that were recently modernized. The public health apparatus produced important disciplinary measures (among them, the compulsory denunciation of these diseases, and the forced hospitalization and isolation of patients) and a valuable experience in mass education (the public campaigns of the Argentine League Against Tuberculosis, the conferences and pamphlets of the Sociedad Luz).[44]

Meanwhile, a psychiatric apparatus replaced the traditional philanthropic associations in the treatment of insanity. *Alienismo*, the specialized knowledge dealing with mental illness, and its technology of "moral treatment" entered the territory of insane asylums (*manicomios*), opening new spaces for the treatment and study of the insane. Leading the way were the Hospicio de las Mercedes and the Colonia Nacional de Alienados. It was within these sites of observation that the doctrine of "moral insanity" appeared, which referred to a wide spectrum of transgressions against social norms.[45] The confluence between positivist criminology and mental health policy engendered the figure of the insane delinquent (*loco-delincuente*) whose coercive internment preceded the diffusion of the concept of "dangerousness" by almost two decades.[46] In addition, criminal cases involving insanity affirmed the pivotal importance of the *pericia médica* (judicial medical report) in judicial decisions.[47]

Thus, criminologists found their work facilitated by the activities of mental health experts, social physicians, and pedagogues who had created the approach, institutions, and categories upon which the "dangerousness" was to rest. Affinities resulted from the convergence of these projects. The normalization of school children and the inclusion of the insane within the orbit of public health officials found common ground in the medical approach to social problems, a perspective that was shared by criminologists. These reform movements expanded the social dimension of the state and established the "necessity" of intervention and research in nontraditional areas. The association of poverty with disease, which was crucial to the progressive slant of criminology, originated in the texts of social physicians and hygienists. Normalizing pedagogues and psychiatrists (*alienistas*), in turn,

---

44 See Héctor Recalde, *La salud de los trabajadores*, chapter 5. For socialist campaigns against alcoholism, see Dora Barrancos, *La escena iluminada* (Buenos Aires, 1997).

45 Vezzetti, *La locura en la Argentina*, 127–32.

46 See Máximo Sozzo, "Control social e intersección institucional psiquiatría-justicia penal," in Encarna Bodelón and Teresa Picontó Novales, eds., *Las transformaciones del estado y del derecho contemporáneos* (Madrid, 1998), 47–76.

47 The judicial "medical report" (*pericia médica*) emerged in practice from the Vivado case, an 1877 criminal case that confronted *alienistas* and physicians over the fate (prison sentence or hospitalization) of a *loco-delincuente*. Vezzetti, *La locura en Argentina*, 140–42.

had established the centrality of notions of "normality" and "abnormality" in public policy. Protective gestures toward abandoned children, working mothers, and the insane, that is, the notion of "state responsibility," were already ingrained in the public discourse of pedagogy, mental health, and hygienism.[48]

"DANGEROUSNESS" IN LAW AND JUSTICE

Although the positivist reformers were highly successful in disseminating the notions of "social defense," "dangerousness," and the scientific study of delinquency, they were unable to secure the passage of a revised penal code that embodied their theoretical principles and institutional practices.[49] The penal codes drafted by reform commissions headed by positivists were either shelved or modified beyond recognition before they came under consideration by the legislature. The lack of significant legal reform has been regarded as evidence of the limitations of the reforms as well as a sign of the continued control of congress by the oligarchy. While this criticism is valid for the period prior to 1910, it is not accurate for the 1930s. In fact, the reformers who participated in the Criminological Congress of 1938 seemed enthusiastic about their achievements on the crucial terrain of legislation and judicial practice.

To be sure, the "Dangerousness" bill drafted by Indalecio Gómez and Jorge Coll in 1928 and approved by the senate in 1933 never became law. Nevertheless, some crucial provisions in existing law, which were the products of minor reforms in penal and procedural laws, allowed judges to put into practice key positivist principles. In Alfredo Molinario's view, "dangerousness" had already been "legislatively consecrated" in Argentina through the institutions of judicial pardon, suspended sentencing (probation), and conditional release (parole).[50] With these legal instruments, judges were able to hand down sentences that deviated from the proportional schedule of punishments prescribed in the penal code and thus move toward indeterminate sentences. At the very least, these provisions enabled judges to consider the offender's psycho-physical condition before sentencing. Artemio Moreno went further, arguing that some articles of the penal code forced judges to base their sentences on considerations typical of "dangerousness."

---

48 Susana Belmartino, "Las obras sociales: Continuidad o ruptura en la Argentina de los años 40," in *Política, médicos y enfermedades*, 210–46.
49 Beatriz Ruibal, "Medicina legal y derecho penal a fines del siglo XIX," in *Política, médicos y enfermedades*, 193–207.
50 Alfredo J Molinario, "La peligrosidad como fundamento y medida de la responsabilidad," *Primer Congreso*, vol. 1, 244.

Before sentencing (articles 40 and 41), judges had to evaluate the relative "dangerousness" of the accused.[51] To grant penalties of "conditional application" (art. 26) – suspended sentences – judges had to consider the "moral personality" of the accused. Similarly, two aggravating circumstances of homicide, "impulse of brutal perversity" and "violent emotion" (art. 44), referred to psychological states that demanded an expert opinion. In Moreno's view, Argentine legislation already contained "the truest and most fecund basis for the individualization [of punishments]."

The concept of "dangerousness" was already permeating the institutional practice of the justice system. As early as 1905 the Argentine police had come to accept the concept of "dangerousness" as the basic criterion for monitoring people, a principle that was ratified at the second International Police Conference of 1920.[52] According to the 1921 penal code, criminal cases involving mental illness entered a special track (leading to a "measure of curative safety") in which the role of the medical expert was crucial.[53] Dangerousness was the only reason that validated indeterminate hospitalization. Centers of medico-psychological research created by the positivists were already providing valuable services to criminal judges. The indeterminate sentence, a key ingredient in the positivists' arsenal, was already a common practice. Judges had gradually incorporated consideration of the mental and physical "normality" of the accused into decisions about sentencing and probation and were using medical reports to establish dangerousness.[54] For the prisoners in the National Penitentiary, medical power was a hard reality. Their petitions for parole or a reduction of their sentence were systematically rejected or accepted on the basis of medico-psychological reports. Any reference to the persistence of "anomalies" in the inmate's individual file significantly reduced his chances of release. Conversely, any reduction in his dangerousness index served as a green light for parole.

These developments were a result of the greater importance attributed to medical reports and of the conviction of judges about the solidity of psycho-pathological knowledge. Judge Domingo Abate, while suspicious of Lombrosian categories and procedures, had come to accept the necessity

51 Artemio Moreno, "La formación científica del Juez del Crimen," *Primer Congreso*, vol. 1, 136.
52 *Conferencia Internacional Sudamericana de Policía*, Buenos Aires, 20/29 de febrero de 1920. Convenio y Actas (Buenos Aires, 1920).
53 Sozzo, "Control social e intersección institucional."
54 "We can assert without exaggeration that in the Argentine Republic there already exist institutions that perform an integral study of the condemned, which formulate a true judgment of dangerousness in advising the administrative authorities and the tribunals the granting or rejection of the referred benefit [probation]." Angel E. González Millán, "La importancia del informador social en el estudio de la delincuencia adulta," *Primer Congreso*, vol. 3, 392.

of medico-psychological reports. After long experience as a sentencing judge (*juez de sentencia*), he was persuaded that organic weakness and psychological abnormality were important factors in criminal behavior. He was therefore ready to trust positivist criminologists' diagnoses of crime and to use their clinical reports in evaluating criminal cases.[55]

The resolution of criminal cases still hinged on the notion of culpability, which could not be easily dissociated from the notion of intentionality. Even so, medical terminology and biological conceptions of responsibility started to infiltrate the arguments of plaintiff and defense. In cases of homicide or injury during the 1880s and 1890s, passion, now translated into a medical condition rooted in the nervous system that could develop into perversion, served as a basis for diminished culpability.[56]

Still, the positivists wanted more, namely, to extend the notion of dangerousness to the predelictual phase. They still had to persuade judges that dangerous individuals who had committed no crime should be subject to the same penal sanctions as criminals. In particular, positivists called for the power to confine *alienados en libertad* (mentally "abnormal" persons in the general population) before they committed any crime.[57] They pointed to research that claimed to demonstrate the dangerousness of some types of mentally abnormal persons (*alienados*) and were ready to exert pressure on the judicial and legislative apparatus to have their preventive policies approved.[58] In the case of abandoned children, the criterion of dangerousness had been in operation for some time. Street children who were considered dangerous were jailed and then placed in reformatories until they were judicially "rescued" and distributed to private families or employers.[59] By the 1930s minors were being detained and institutionalized if they exhibited signs of abnormalities, without regard to whether or not they had committed any crimes.[60]

---

55 Consistent with his view he recommended that the Congress of Criminology make mandatory the medical examination of all those processed by the criminal justice system. Domingo Abate, "El exámen médico integral de los procesados peligrosos," *Primer Congreso*, vol. 2, 263–7.

56 Kristin Ruggiero, "Passion, Perversity, and the Pace of Justice in Turn-of-the-Century Argentina," in Ricardo D. Salvatore, Carlos Aguirre, and Gilbert Joseph., eds., *Crime and Punishment in Latin America* (Durham, N.C., 2001).

57 Jose Belbey y Felipe Cia, "El peligro de los alienados en libertad," *Primer Congreso*, vol. 2, 252–62.

58 The preventive institutionalization of *alienados* and *semi-alienados* was a move of significant implication for social control. José Ingenieros had estimated in 1919 that there were approximately 15,000 *alienados* and 10,400 *retardados* in Argentina; of the former 8,800 were institutionalized. José Ingenieros, "La Locura en la Argentina," in *Obras Completas* (Buenos Aires, 1962), vol. II, 254–7.

59 Donna Guy, "Girls in Prison: The Role of the Buenos Aires Casa Correcional de Mujeres as an Institution for Child Rescue, 1890–1940," in *Crime and Punishment in Latin America*.

60 Juan Carlos Lando, "Protección a la minoridad en la Provincia de Buenos Aires," *Primer Congreso*, vol. 2, 73.

Given the major expansion of disciplinary power in relation to delinquents, minors, and the mentally ill, positivists could proudly claim that
they had established dangerousness on a solid foundation. And, they had
done so with only piecemeal changes in legislation. Much of this achievement was due to the dissemination of medical power in the interstices of
the state, particularly in areas responsible for health, justice, and security.
The pressure that judges and lawyers felt to modify their visions of crime
and criminal justice according to the dictates of the new medical disciplines
cannot be accounted for solely by the influence exerted by a generation of
criminologists. The emergence and consolidation of the medical profession
(c. 1870–1900) as a new configuration of power and knowledge influencing
public policy is crucial for understanding the success of positivist criminologists,[61] not only because physicians pioneered the modernization of the
disciplines that later formed the medico-legal complex but also because of
the active presence of physicians in the politics of the conservative state. The
most influential politicians raising social issues were medical doctors. They
campaigned against overcrowded tenements, polluted water, lack of sewage
disposal, infectious disease, and alcoholism. Their campaigns, a dimension of
the "civilizing process," enriched traditional politics and added complexity
to the Argentine state. The professionalization of medicine and the emergence of the *médico-funcionario* (the physician at the service of the state in
safeguarding public health) preceded the rise of criminological positivism
by at least two decades.[62] Beginning in the 1870s, the hygienists established
the fear of contamination as part of the public agenda and built a powerful
apparatus of surveillance on this basis.

A STATE WITHIN A STATE

There are at least two ways of conceptualizing the presence of a "medico-
legal state" in early twentieth-century Argentina. One is to resort to a spatial
metaphor of inclusion, the image of "a state within a state." According to
this perspective, the dissemination of positivist criminology appears as an
enterprise of colonization. A group of reformers takes control of marginal
areas of the state apparatus and starts from there to build the social networks,
programs, and prestige they need to influence state policies and, in the long
run, transform state practices. An alternative approach consists in imagining

---

61 For a history of the main medical association, see Carlos Reussi y otros, *Historia de la Asociación
Médica Argentina y de sus secciones* (Buenos Aires, 1992).
62 The creation of the first professional association (the Circulo Medico Argentino) and the first professional journal (*Revista Medico Quirúrgica*) are both products of the 1870s.

the state as a terrain of hegemonic power constructed (and supported) by an array of arguments or "reasons for rule." From this perspective, a group of reformers manages to transform not so much the institutions of the state as the prevailing interpretations of society and politics. Reformers make their new paradigms and programmatics acceptable to the rulers by providing appealing reasons for the convenience of the new policies in terms of gains in governability and legitimacy. In this second scenario, the hegemony of positivist discourse stems from a vast exercise in persuasion.

Let us examine the implications of these interpretations. Working within the framework of the conservative regime, in the interstices of power opened by the very process of modernization, positivists managed to build an impressive apparatus of social control. In institutional sites liberated from conservative, oligarchic control they established a new micro-physics of power, based on a scientific understanding of the populations under treatment. Reformers presented their preventive interventions and their therapeutic practices as humane, scientific, and efficacious counterpoints to the repressive and exclusionary policies that characterized the oligarchic regime.

Similarities in the treatment of subject populations in hospitals, prisons, schools, insane asylums, and orphanages marked the success of positivist reformism in these particular niches of disciplinary power. Or, seen from the other perspective, this homology measures the permissiveness of the regime with regard to reforms that, because of its institutional boundaries, appeared as unthreatening to the existing sociopolitical order. Perhaps these reformers were a group of critical guests invited to participate in the regime's adventure of order and progress. Underscoring this metaphoric inclusion was a basic agreement about the limits of the reforms. To the extent that reformers did not challenge the underlying (conservative) principles of property, order, family, and government, they were allowed to conduct their experiments of social engineering in secluded and bounded spaces.

The division of labor implicit in this tacit agreement between positivist reformers and the conservative ruling elite – one that precluded areas such as monetary and credit policy, international relations, or agriculture from the reach of reformers – can be explained in terms of convenience, tolerance, or weakness on the part of the conservative leadership. Or, on the other side of the coin, one could ponder the effectiveness of positivist reformers in building the alliances that allowed them an institutional space for the deployment of their policies and principles. But, at a certain point, the spatial metaphor exhausts its energy as we realize that the collaboration between these two elites was built on communicative interactions and was solidified by language.

Under the alternative perspective, positivists appear as contributing a new "interpretive grid" to questions of social integration and governance. The ideas advanced by positivist reformers – the notion of dangerousness, the premise of social defense, the medicalization of crime, and the individualization of treatment – provided new foundations for the order envisioned by the architects of the "feasible republic" (*república posible*).[63] The collaboration between positivists and conservatives depended on the former's ability to comprehend social reality and, consequently, to advance social policies that anticipated a new regime of governance. In a variety of communicative interactions, positivist speakers (professionals) tried to convince judges, lawyers, and state functionaries (rulers) of the necessity to study and treat social problems in a scientific, medical way. This was the crucial contribution of criminologists to state formation. Faced with the intractable social question (and the failure of traditional, coercive solutions) the ruling elite invited new actors, already settled within state clusters, to offer alternative solutions, novel interpretations, and new "reasons of rule."

What elements made the positivist discourse persuasive? The apparent modernity and scientific flavor of the positivist project were important aspects of its appeal. Even jurists distrustful of the intrusion of medicine into the terrain of justice could agree that legal proceedings had to keep up with technological progress. A modern judicial process could no longer depend solely on testimony, now that the new technologies made available new areas of evidence (autopsies, ballistics, graphology, photography, dactyloscopy, and medico-psychological reports). The possibility of extending state jurisdiction to areas and people that the liberal state had not imagined also was appealing to the governing elite. In some of its strong versions, the concept of "social defense" included the preventive confinement of all people with physical, emotional, or mental "anomalies": from "sexual perverts" to overeaters (*glotones*), from alcoholics to "eccentrics," from epileptics to prostitutes.[64] If this was so, the potential for social disruption would be minimized.

Also appealing to the ruling elite was the promise of a comprehensive knowledge of the working classes. Like the medico-psychological indices designed by Loudet, positivist research strategies tried to encompass the totality of the lives of subject populations. A potential delinquent had to be studied at home, in the street, in school, and at work if he was to be

---

63 Natalio Botana and Ezequiel Gallo, *De la República posible a la República verdadera (1890–1910)* (Buenos Aires, 1997).

64 Alejandro Raitzin, "Semi-alienación, doble peligrosidad," *Primer Congreso*, vol. 2, 223.

adequately classified and treated.[65] This strategy could yield an abundant harvest of new information about relatively unknown social subjects. A profound and thorough investigation of individuals in confinement was the basis for a new political utopia: the possibility of a "total knowledge" of the subaltern classes as a new precondition for rule.[66] In addition, the institutionalization of deviants according to the rules of dangerousness entailed the depoliticization and individualization of social groups that until then had remained threatening to the state. Acquiescence to the rule of experts anticipated the possibility of more modern (and authoritarian) forms of state control.

The widespread acceptance of positivist interventions and principles by socialists, anarchists, and other liberal reformers shows that, in addition to its conservative side, positivist discourse had a progressive, critical side.[67] The concern of positivist reformers for the welfare of children, women, and the elderly, expressed as a relentless criticism of the policies of the conservative state, must have attracted many young spirits who were willing to extend their protection and care to the victims of the "struggle for life."[68] The adaptability of positivist social-control recipes to different political agendas also proved crucial for the diffusion and endurance of this type of discourse. In Italy the construction of dangerousness was associated with authoritarian forms of power;[69] in Argentina positivism added legitimacy to quite distinct political projects: the conservative order of 1890–1916; the middle-class politics of the period 1916–30; and the conservative, fraudulent regimes of the 1930s.[70] Its resilience in the face of changing political climates and its increasing diffusion bear witness to the important role of positivism in providing governments with a series of arguments, policies, and institutional solutions regarding the problem of social disorder.

The dialectical synthesis between progressive and repressive interventions advanced by positivist reformism served as a way to avoid the polarization between left and right, the mark of international politics since the end of World War I. Indeed, the positivists managed to maintain an intermediate

---

65 Osvaldo Loudet, "La historia clínica criminológica," *Primer Congreso*, vol. 3, 11–49.
66 As a prison administrator observed in 1938, this was only feasible in relation to populations in confinement. Santiago Hernández, "Plan de racionalización carcelaria del gobierno de la Provincia de Buenos Aires," *Primer Congreso*, vol. 3, 388.
67 See Patricio Geli, "Los anarquistas en el gabinete antropométrico," *Entrepasados* 2 (1992): 7–24.
68 The critical stance is present in many positivist reformers' writings. Consider, for example, José Belbey, "La delincuencia de los debiles mentales," *Anales de la SAC*, vol. 3 (1937), 198.
69 See Mary Gibson, *Prostitution and the State in Italy* (New Brunswick, N.J., 1986).
70 David Rock, "Radical Populism and the Conservative Elite, 1912–1930," in David Rock, ed., *Argentina in the Twentieth Century* (Pittsburgh, 1975), 66–87.

course in this ideologically divergent world. This was explicitly recognized by Justice Minister Coll in his speech to the delegates to the Criminological Congress of 1938: Thanks to the efficient interventions of a state committed to social defense, the country could keep its liberal, constitutional traditions in the face of a growing polarization between nationalist and radical tendencies.[71] The preventive and totalizing features of state policy as imagined by positivist criminologists – and their kindred spirits in pedagogy and welfare institutions – promised to keep social conflicts circumscribed and exceptional. By institutionalizing and medicalizing social problems, the state could better cope with attacks from left and right.

CONCLUDING REMARKS

Between the two visits mentioned by Gina Lombroso (1906 and 1936), positivist criminology had gained terrain in Argentina, reaffirming and expanding Ingenieros's program of social defense. In spite of contending schools and principles, positivists had developed a consensus about public policy and had spread the doctrines of "social defense" and "dangerousness" outside of the professional field. Consolidation, extension, and intensification are the appropriate words to describe this process. From Ingenieros to Loudet, Argentine criminology had consolidated its psychological bent, asserted the centrality of dangerousness, reaffirmed the prestige of psychological lab research, become more concerned with social issues, and openly and actively promoted the enhancement of medical power within the justice system.

Gina Lombroso's assessment that Argentina had understood and applied her father's ideas prior to and better than any other country was only partially true. For the administrators, scientists, and professionals who gathered in 1938 in Buenos Aires to assess the state of the positivist project had already radically redefined Lombroso's project in the direction of psychopathology and mental health. Only in a general sense – that of promoting a science of the delinquent – can it be said that Ingenieros and Loudet continued or deepened Lombroso's program.[72] But, on a different level, Gina Lombroso's assessment was accurate. For positivists had managed to establish, within the interstices of the Argentine state, a vast apparatus of social control and research affecting the procedures of the police, the courts, and the prisons.

---

71 Speech by Minister of Justice J. E. Coll, *Primer Congreso*, vol. 1, 49.
72 Osvaldo Loudet was persuaded that instead of searching for a species with specific morphological characters, criminologists should engage in a comprehensive search for the physiological and psychological determinants of antisocial behavior. "Programa de la Sociedad Argentina de Criminología," *Anales de la SAC*, vol. 1 (1936), 15.

Just as importantly, the positivists' programs had provided the state with new facts, theories, and policies to reinterpret Argentine politics and society.

Positivist criminologists had been successful in a wide range of activities and objectives. The conception of social problems as diseases, the individual monitoring of patients, the classification and separation of inmates according to degrees of dangerousness, and the enhanced power of physicians in determining the duration of confinement became common practices in many institutions of social control. Masses of populations (immigrant workers, children, women, the poor, the mentally ill) were placed under the gaze and scrutiny of the medical establishment and their problems treated in institutional environments as diseases. Positivist principles influenced the decisions of courts, the methods of policing, and the administration of prisons. Moreover, positivist assumptions and methods were persuasive to the very administrators of these institutions of social control.

I have suggested two ways of conceptualizing the relationship between positivist reformers and the oligarchic state: as a new paradigm of research that transformed into a grammar for governance and as a process of gradual annexation of sites of institutional power. In actuality, both interpretative strategies are complementary. As we saw, by the 1930s positivist criminologists had "colonized" important institutions of social control and had established a firm basis for a vast research project (encompassing child abandonment, delinquency, and madness). At the same time they had disseminated novel procedures for the handling of masses of population throughout the landscape of the state, and thus established the foundations of a new regime of governance that was at once progressive and disciplinarian. They did so in part because of their ability to reinterpret the project of progress at a crucial inflection of a crisis of legitimacy.

The persistent preaching of positivist criminologists was successful in the long run. Ingenieros's early critique of the existence of insane people in prisons and his call for secluding them in specialized asylums (*manicomios*) later became a firm policy of the state. This apparently minor reform was, in fact, an important factor in the expansion of the powers of the state vis-à-vis dangerous individuals, regardless of their delinquent activities. We have noted the inroads made by positivists in the administration of justice. Although unable to radically alter the penal code, positivists managed to influence the ways the justice system worked, from its investigative procedures to the sentencing process, from the management of institutions of confinement to the organization of social welfare.

The Argentine state of the 1930s was different from that of the 1890s not only because of the democratic political reform of 1912, but chiefly because of the incorporation of practices of observation, identification, classification, research, and treatment pioneered by the positivists. As a result of the reformers' success in influencing public policy on issues of public health, mental illness, crime, and education, this state was highly interventionist and deeply penetrative of the private realm. It was prepared to discipline masses of people in institutional settings, because a new kind of machine was functioning at its core: one that was more efficient and silent, monitoring and disciplining the bodies, souls, and minds of vast segments of the population according to a medical rationale. Progressive and repressive at the same time, this state could more easily make the transition toward populist policies when this became a necessity.

What then was the legacy of the Italian School in Argentina? Looking at the 1930s, Ingenieros's criticism of Lombroso seems distant and quite irrelevant for the questions of the decade. Criminologists had already accepted – and hence, took as natural – notions of a criminal personality, psychopathologies, criminological examinations, environmental conditions, and the like, as if Ingenieros (or Enrico Ferri plus Gabriel Tarde) had won the battle of words.[73] The consolidation of a psychological perspective on criminality and the realization of the social defense program designed by Ingenieros signified the decline of theoretical debates and the emergence of a basic consensus about the terms of the problem and the tasks ahead. The Criminological Congress of 1938 presided over by Loudet showed the degree of this consensus and the expansion of positivist criminologists' power of persuasion and intervention. The Argentine state, at different levels and institutions, was carrying out the program of measuring, classifying, confining, and treating the different "dangerous populations" in terms that reflected positivist conceptions and policies. A new mode of governance, the *medico-legal state*, had replaced the practices and theory of the old oligarchic state. This was the true legacy of the Italian School. For, once the original impulse (positivist criminology) lost its novelty as an intellectual current, the procedures, methods of discipline, and categories characteristic of dangerousness survived as everyday state practices and reasons for rule.

---

73 Ingenieros had criticized Lombroso for his inability to see that the morphological traits of degeneration served as indicators only of degeneration and that this trait was not exclusive to delinquents. He also criticized Lombroso's exclusive reliance on anthropological evidence and his ambivalent and changing definitions (born delinquent, moral insane, moral atavism).

12

The Birth of Criminology in Modern Japan

YOJI NAKATANI

THE BEGINNINGS OF CRIMINOLOGY

After the Meiji Restoration of 1868, when feudalism was abolished, Japanese society underwent drastic changes during the Meiji period, which lasted from 1868 to 1912. The government reformed the legal system based on European models, paying particular attention to the French system. Various laws were enacted, including the Penal Code of 1880 and the Civil Code of 1896–98.[1] Along with these legal reforms dealing with crime, a body of scientific thought appeared, first in the fields of criminal statistics and penology. At about the same time that the government began issuing official statistics on the incidence of criminal activities, legal scholars were being exposed to the statistical analysis of criminal behavior, mainly by Lambert A. J. Quetelet. Concurrently, penologists and physicians were engaged in efforts to reform the penitentiary system and to improve unsanitary prison conditions.

Because Japan had been established as a modern state by political and administrative reforms, particularly by the promulgation of the Meiji Constitution of 1889, jurists became aware of the importance of measures for defending the social order. During the last decade of the nineteenth century this included exposure to the theories of contemporary Italian and German criminologists.

The enactment of the New Penal Code of 1907 emphasized criminal policy, namely the prevention of crime, which strongly encouraged studies on crime and offenders. In the same year, some jurists founded the

---

1 On the history of the legal system for the insane in Japan, see Yoji Nakatani, "Relationship of Mental Health Legislation to the Perception of Insanity at the Turn of the Twentieth Century in Japan," in Yasuo Otsuka and Shizu Sakai, eds., *Medicine and the Law: Proceedings of the 19th International Symposium on the Comparative History of Medicine – East and West* (Tokyo, 1994), 227–50.

Association of Penal Science. An important change that occurred during this period was the involvement of psychologists and medical doctors, who were more interested in an empirical approach to criminal behavior and the characteristics of offenders.[2]

GROWTH OF INTEREST IN CRIME

Beginning around 1910 and continuing throughout the decade, both scholars and the general public evinced a growing interest in the problem of crime. This was evidenced by the appearance of a wide range of publications dealing with crime and related matters (scientific journals, textbooks, popular magazines, and novels), and during this period specialists began forming societies and professional organizations. One such organization was the Japanese Association of Criminology, founded in 1913. The prospectus of the Association states: "The prevention and suppression of crime, indispensable for the social order, is the main objective of legislation. In order to meet these needs, we must establish the causal relationship that exists between the characteristics of offenders and the influence of the social environment. These findings will enable us to take appropriate social and legal measures."[3] The association was composed of specialists from various fields: psychology, psychiatry, legal medicine, law, and sociology. The emphasis, however, was placed on the psychological and psychiatric approach. The secretary of the association was Seiichi Terada, a pioneer in the psychology of crime who translated Cesare Lombroso's famous work *L'uomo delinquente* into Japanese.[4]

Although many publications appeared during this period, I will concentrate on two journals, the *Journal of Abnormal Psychology* and the *Archives of Criminology*, because they both included many articles written by criminologists and clearly represented the concerns people had about the problem of crime and offenders.

The *Journal of Abnormal Psychology* was started as the bulletin of the Japanese Association of Psychiatry, founded in 1917. The name of the association might suggest that it was a medical society, but in fact it was a group composed mostly of nonprofessionals. Kokyo Nakamura, the founder of the association and editor-in-chief of the *Journal*, was a novelist with a unique

---

2 On the early involvement of German doctors in criminology, especially prison psychiatrists, see Richard F. Wetzell's chapter in this volume.
3 "Prospectus for the Inauguration of the Japanese Association of Criminology," *Annals of the Japanese Association of Criminology* 1 (1914): 1 (in Japanese).
4 Cesare Lombroso, *L'Uomo Delinquente*, 5th ed. (Turin, 1897), translated into Japanese by Seiichi Terada (Tokyo, 1914).

career.[5] In his youth he had suffered from persistent neurasthenia and had visited many physicians. In addition to the incurability of his own condition, his brother's psychosis and eventual suicide further aggravated his distress. These painful experiences engendered in him the belief that "materialistic medicine" was incapable of curing illness unless coupled with "medicine of the mind." Referring to the notion of the inseparability of mind and body, he searched for a sort of holistic approach to medicine, which he attempted to augment through his self-taught experience of hypnosis and psychotherapy. As expressly stated in the preface to the first issue, the purpose of the journal was to study the broad range of abnormal psychological phenomena, which were not always pathological in the narrowest sense.[6] The members of the association and contributors to the *Journal* included, aside from psychologists and medical doctors, many literary scholars, religious thinkers, journalists, and businessmen. A total of 103 issues were published before the *Journal* was discontinued in 1926.

The various themes and styles of articles in the *Journal* reflect the diversity of motives and interests of the contributors. There are reviews of contemporary Western scientific trends: Freudian psychoanalysis, Bergsonian psychology, and the theory of sexual perversion by Richard von Krafft-Ebing. Considerable attention was paid to hypnosis and related psychological phenomena such as automatism, somnambulism, and multiple personalities. A surprisingly large number of articles dealt with supernatural phenomena such as telekinesis, mind reading, spiritualism, mystic experiences, possession, prophetic dreams, ghosts, and life after death. There are even reports of "experiments" conducted with people purported to possess supernatural powers.[7] In a public session organized by the association, a well-known performer supposedly copied letters and images on dry plates using only the power of his mind, which produced a heated debate on the credibility of his act. Also, readers of the *Journal* were encouraged to submit reports of their own mysterious experiences, which were then commented on by specialists.[8]

Crime and suicide were preferred subjects of the *Journal*, being referred to as typical examples of behavior caused by abnormal psychology. In addition to research reported by specialists, there were many documents concerning

---

5 He described his own career in "Prospectus for the Foundation of the Japanese Association of Psychiatry," *Journal of Abnormal Psychology* 1 (1917): 79–80 (in Japanese).

6 "Preface to the First Issue," *Journal of Abnormal Psychology* 1 (1917): 1–2 (in Japanese).

7 Kakutaro Nakagiri, "Experiment of Telekinesis," *Journal of Abnormal Psychology* 2 (1918): 43–54 (in Japanese).

8 The journal specified four items as subjects for the readers' column: spiritual phenomena, bizarre behavior of the lunatic, life of the criminal, and biography of eccentric persons. This amalgam of categories shows how "abnormal psychology" was conceived at that time.

actual criminal cases: Each issue included a "Diary of Abnormal Psychology," a column written in diary style that cited recent newspaper articles. Although the criteria for inclusion in this column remain unclear, the main topics seem to be major crimes such as mass murder, atrocious crimes committed by perverted and insane persons, unsolved criminal cases, and suicides committed by unhappy couples.

The *Archives of Criminology* were started in 1926 as the bulletin of a local academic circle, the Association of Criminology in Kanazawa. The editor-in-chief and chairman of the association was Tanemoto Furuhata, a professor of legal medicine at the Kanazawa Medical College. Contributions to the early issues were limited to persons residing in the Kanazawa area: researchers at the medical college, magistrates and prosecutors of the district court, high-ranking officers of the prefectural police, and lawyers. But the *Archives* soon became a nationwide journal and continued to publish until 1943.

The motivation of the circle is evident in the opening remarks made at the first meeting and also in the preface of the *Archives*: "The unfavorable influence of the World War, together with the spread of materialism, has resulted in a rapid increase in the crime rate and in increasingly more sophisticated methods used by offenders, both of which urgently require the extensive cooperation of legal medicine, criminal justice, and other related professions."[9] The *Archives*, therefore, were expected to provide improved knowledge and a means for dealing with the increasing menace of crime. Accordingly, the majority of the articles were devoted to research reports related to investigational methods: examination of blood types, fingerprints, and handwriting; autopsy of the victim's body; the mechanics of poisoning; and the psychology of suspects. Compared to the *Journal of Abnormal Psychology*, the *Archives* appear to be significantly more academic. Nevertheless, the *Archives* also contained less-than-scientific articles, including essays and letters in which judges, prosecutors, police officials, prison administrators, instructors of reformatories, and others freely stated their opinions about the causes of crime and offered suggestions for preventing crime and for reforming offenders.

Thus, an interesting feature that the *Journal of Abnormal Psychology* and the *Archives of Criminology* share is the coexistence of two completely different types of discourse: one a scientific report and the other a popular, nonacademic statement. This implies that the early development of criminology in Japan was enriched by the popularization of knowledge on crime.

---

9 Yoshio Shigemi, "Prospectus for the Inauguration of the Association of Criminology in Kanazawa," *Archives of Criminology* 1 (1928): 1–3 (in Japanese).

RECEPTION AND APPLICATION OF WESTERN TRENDS

With regard to the reception of contemporary Western trends, it is important to note that Cesare Lombroso's criminal anthropology became well known in Japan at a time when his doctrine was losing influence. After the International Congress of Anthropology in 1889 in Paris, Lombroso encountered severe criticism particularly from advocates of sociological theories on crime. Although some of Lombroso's works were introduced to Japan as early as the 1870s, his main ideas remained unfamiliar to scholars until the 1910s. Consequently, Lombroso was always referred to as one of the founders of positivistic criminology, representing the Italian school with Raffaele Garofalo and Enrico Ferri. Most Japanese scholars simplified Lombroso's theories into a "born-criminal doctrine," to the extremes of which they kept a certain distance. Among the public, Lombroso became famous as an erudite critic rather than a criminologist when his book *L'uomo di genio* was translated into Japanese by a decadent poet in 1916.[10]

There was another reason for Lombroso's limited impact in Japan. At the time when Japanese psychiatrists became aware of studies on offenders, they were strongly influenced by German medicine, in which Lombroso's concepts were unanimously rejected.[11] As a result, most Japanese textbooks described the concept of the "born criminal" as one of the prototypes upon which German authors elaborated their concepts of "abnormal character" or "psychopathy."

As far as the causes of crime were concerned, Japanese criminologists paid considerable attention to the biological theories of the German criminologists Gustav Aschaffenburg, Johannes Lange, and Karl Birnbaum. However, they were also concerned with environmental factors, most likely because they were facing a rapid increase in the crime rate after World War I. This tendency seems to parallel the renewal of interest in social causes in the United States while crime saw a tremendous increase during the war.[12]

An attempt to integrate environmental and biological approaches was made by Shufu Yoshimasu. As a psychiatrist and penal reformer, he conducted a large-scale survey of prisoners during the late 1920s. Referring to German studies, especially to Edmund Mezger's dynamic explanation of crime and Franz Exner's research on recidivism, Yoshimasu worked out a "dynamic scheme of criminal behavior." According to this scheme, a

---

10 Cesare Lombroso, *L'uomo di genio* (Turin, 1894), translated into Japanese by Jun Tsuji (Tokyo, 1894).
11 See Richard Wetzell's chapter in this volume.
12 See Nicole Rafter's chapter in this volume.

person's future risk of offending against the law could be assessed in accordance with both environmental and biological attributes of the individual, including psychopathy, early onset of the criminal career, history of recidivism, broken family, lax school attendance, occupational instability, and hereditary disposition.[13]

Criminal investigation, forensic medicine, and penal policy were enriched with new knowledge about offenders. In these fields, Germany's "modern school" of criminal law and the contemporary trends of penal policy in the United States were influential. The leader in this area was Ryo Masaki, a legal scholar who, along with Tanemoto Furuhata, was editor-in-chief of the *Archives of Criminology*. He expressed doubts about the efficacy of general deterrence by harsh punishment, and enthusiastically promoted reforms of the penitentiary system. Rejecting the idea of retribution, he took the educationalist approach intended to afford more opportunity for resocialization, focusing on the particularity of offenders. He even stated that "crime is a sort of illness that can be cured only by scientific methods of improving the offender's personality." From this standpoint, an offender with diminished responsibility would deserve a longer term of imprisonment that would provide more opportunity for treatment.[14]

The efforts to realize more socialized and scientific treatment of prisoners resulted in a series of reforms of the penal system. The enactment of the Juvenile Law of 1922 introduced probationary supervision, which was followed by the establishment of the Parole Examination System in 1931 and the decree introducing the Progressive Stage System for Prisoners in 1933.

Thus, scientific criminology clearly had not just a theoretical, but a practical impact, emphasizing the prevention of crime. This impact may be attributed to the fact that the early development of criminology occurred at a time when social problems were becoming serious due to rapid modernization of society.

DIFFERENT ASPECTS OF THE CONCERN ABOUT CRIME

Referring to the writings appearing during the thirty-year period from 1910 to the late 1930s, I will discuss various aspects of concern about crime from a larger viewpoint.

---

13 Shufu Yoshimasu, "Psychiatric Study on the Social Prognosis of Offenders," *Psychiatrica et Neurologia Japonica* 40 (1936): 728–31 (in Japanese).
14 Ryo Masaki, "Objective of Imprisonment and the Scientization of Penal Policy," *Archives of Criminology* 5 (1931): 1–9 (in Japanese).

Rise in the Crime Rate

Many people expressed a fear of increasing crime. Although in most cases this was a vague impression, the criminal statistics partially confirmed their fears.[15] The number of people convicted of crimes shows a gradual increase beginning in the mid-1920s: 137,804 in 1920; 163,192 in 1930; and 188,203 in 1936, the highest number in the prewar period. This trend paralleled the increase in the number of reported thefts: 13,121 in 1920; 16,508 in 1930; and 20,574 in 1936. The number of offenders convicted per 100,000 people was also on the rise: 245.8 in 1920; 252.1 in 1930; and 265.7 in 1934. Moreover, the number of penal code offenses brought to the Public Prosecutor's Office showed an even more dramatic rise: 227,255 in 1910; 298,525 in 1920; and 427,092 in 1930. A sharp rise occurred in 1929, and the trend peaked in 1934 at 545,360.[16] This rapid increase was partially due to the fact that the police became more inclined to arrest persons committing petty crimes and public order offenses, against which charges were easily dropped.

The cause of this trend seems complicated, but experts of criminal statistics have provided some explanations.[17] The relatively low crime rate at the beginning of the twentieth century may be due to the general improvement in the standard of living. However, beginning in 1910, inflation and the soaring price of rice led to an increase in the number of property crimes. Even though this increase leveled out between 1918 to 1923 as a result of the prosperity following World War I, the trend reaccelerated in 1924 due to economic recession, which was aggravated by the great Kanto earthquake that struck Tokyo and Yokohama in September 1923. The steady increase in the crime rate during this period can be attributed mainly to poverty in the farming districts and to the increase of unemployment in the cities.

Concern about the menace of crime, however, was influenced more by the particular aspects of the trend rather than by the aggregate figures. This can be understood by looking at some of the important traits, which I discuss in the following sections.

Juvenile Crime and Urbanization

Although no precise statistics are available for juvenile crime during this period, it is interesting to note that some administrators of prisons and

---

15 Annual Report of Criminal Statistics, Ministry of Justice.
16 On the details of the criminal trends in Japan, see Minoru Shikita and Shinichi Tsuchiya, *Crime and Criminal Policy in Japan: An Analysis and Evaluation of the Showa Era, 1926–1988* (New York, 1992).
17 Ibid.

reformatories perceived a worsening of the situation in the 1920s. In the *Archives of Criminology*, the director of a provincial prison reported that the number of youths incarcerated in his prison increased by 40 percent from 1923 to 1927.[18] According to another report by the director of a reformatory, a rapid increase was seen in the 1920s in the number of minors referred to the family court in the Kyoto, Osaka, and Kobe regions.[19] Because these worrisome trends were more noticeable in the cities than in the countryside, specialists often related this change to the bad influences of urban culture on the younger generation.

Beginning in the first decade of the twentieth century, when Japan was transformed into an industrial state, a population migration took place on a large scale from farming districts to industrial centers, producing a sharp rise in the urban population. In 1913, 72 percent of the population lived in townships with a population of less than 10,000. By 1930, this had fallen to 59 percent. However, 14 percent of the population lived in cities of 50,000 or more in 1913, and this number had swelled to 25 percent by 1930. Driven by "city fever," a large number of young people flocked to the industrial centers, where they were forced to work in shops or factories under very poor conditions. The situation was not greatly improved by the passage of the Factory Act of 1916, which limited the working day for women and children to eleven hours and prescribed a minimum working age of twelve.[20]

Specialists in juvenile crime worried that not only the discontent produced by the low standard of living but also the temptations of the urban environment would induce young workers to commit immoral acts. In fact, there emerged many venues for recreation, such as restaurants, cafes, dance halls, theaters, movie houses, department stores, and brothels. Among these forms of entertainment, moviegoing was considered to be the most harmful. Introduced from the United States in 1896, movies rapidly became a popular form of amusement, particularly after 1929 when the first "talking pictures" were released. The audience was mostly young workers. According to a survey on recreation among city residents, which was conducted by the Ministry of Education in 1921, movies were the most popular form of entertainment for about one out of every three respondents. The movies were considered harmful not only because movie theaters offered places for delinquents to gather but because the stories in the films were sometimes

18 Yumatsu Usui, "On the Causes of Juvenile Crime," *Archives of Criminology* 3 (1930): 13–19 (in Japanese).
19 Junzo Ogawa, "Juvenile Criminals in the Kyoto, Osaka, and Kobe Region," *Archives of Criminology* 4 (1931): 382–3 (in Japanese).
20 Yoshiteru Iwamoto, "Hometown, Emigration, and Foreign Land," in Naohiro Asao et al., eds., *Synoptic History of Japan*, 18 vols. (Tokyo, 1994), 97–132 (in Japanese).

easily mimicked. After the release of a French movie entitled *Gigolo*, there was a rash of juvenile crimes imitating the story, and the Tokyo Prefectural Police consequently created a regulation prohibiting children under fifteen from viewing such movies.[21]

Riots and the Left-Wing Movement

Concern about the rising crime rate was also linked to the fear of political unrest, especially after the war, when social discord was intensified by a series of events: strikes in factories, rioting in cities, the appearance of left-wing organizations, and terrorism by fanatics of both the left and right wing.

Serious inflation in 1918 and the growth of the urban proletariat contributed to the spread of strikes in the factories. The Federation of Labor, which was founded in 1919 and had thirty thousand members, continued to grow over the next few years. The development of the labor movement as well as the Russian and German revolutions encouraged the formation of left-wing parties. With the support of the Comintern, the Communist Party was established in Japan in 1921 and immediately declared an illegal organization.

Another important event was the "rice riots" of 1918, which started in a rural town as a housewives' protest meeting against the rising cost of rice and rapidly spread to the big cities where mobs attacked and sometimes burned the buildings of rice dealers and moneylenders.

In what context were these political upheavals perceived by criminologists? The *Archives of Criminology* contained many articles discussing this matter. Psychologists repeatedly expressed concern about the epidemic of strikes and riots. The mentality of the working class, they argued, was characterized by a lack of scientific knowledge and understanding, superstition, a tendency toward imitation, and excitability. As a result, these people were highly prone to reckless action, presenting a typical example of "mass psychology."[22] From the viewpoint of the defense of the social order, public prosecutors regarded the riots as intentional, suggesting that they were more ideologically inspired and organized than their precedents, which seemed simply induced by mass psychology.[23] The police officials in charge of

---

21 Taketoshi Yamamoto, "Essay on Mass Media," in Naohiro Asao et al., eds., *Synoptic History of Japan*, 289–303 (in Japanese).
22 Mizuyo Shimozawa, "Psychology of Strikes," *Journal of Abnormal Psychology* 5 (1920): 389–96 (in Japanese).
23 Tokisaburo Sugimoto, "Memoirs on the Arson in Hibiya," *Archives of Criminology* 4 (1931): 375–8 (in Japanese).

regulating left-wing parties were particularly concerned about the profiles of arrested rioters and members of the Communist Party. These persons, it was said, usually had familial, educational, and medical problems, and this fact would be a clue for reforming them and for preventing "the collapse of the embankment," that is, preventing the unlimited expansion of communism.[24]

The view of Hideo Egami, an instructor of psychology at a high school, was more pedagogical. He analyzed the ongoing "deterioration of thought" among youth and found that psychological problems played an important role in this process. He then attributed receptivity to "dangerous thought," or "the seductive appeal of Marxism" among students to the psychological peculiarity of youth: curiosity for novelty, compassion, eagerness to learn, a tendency toward imitation, and ambitiousness. For Egami, it was therefore crucial that teachers and parents be able to detect such tendencies and intervene as soon as possible to correct the "errors" of potential left-wingers.[25]

Thus, involvement in communist activity became a psychological problem and, accordingly, a subject for criminologists. This kind of behavior was usually interpreted as resulting from a "fault" or "illusion" on the part of vulnerable individuals. In the *Archives of Criminology*, a prison physician proposed to "bring these individuals to their senses" by persuasion (much as parents should do with their children).[26] This paternalistic attitude was clearly stated in the opinion of a chief justice of the court of appeals: "Despite the decline of the Communist Party due to strict police regulation, there remain students, teachers, and even scholars who are devoted to Marxism. It is a pity that they are exploited as a tool of the Comintern and are dishonored by being arrested." It was essential, he stressed, that those "stray sheep" be awakened from their dream by making them recognize the Comintern's plot to conquer the world.[27]

These opinions of specialists can be related to a particular tendency of Marxism, which thrived in Japan in the 1920s. The Marxist movement was supported mainly by youth in their twenties. The majority were unmarried, well-educated men from middle-class families. Thus Marxism attracted those people who felt compassion for the poor as well as strong indignation

24 Kiichiro Sakata, "Recent Trends of Socialist Movement," *Archives of Criminology* 2 (1927): 131–9 (in Japanese).
25 Hideo Egami, "Psychology of Youth and Their Thought," *Archives of Criminology* 4 (1931): 328–37 (in Japanese).
26 Keiji Kuroda, "Essay of a Criminologist," *Archives of Criminology* 5 (1931): 154–63 (in Japanese).
27 Hosui Tateishi, "Love of Family, Marxism, and Patriotism," *Archives of Criminology* 8 (1934): 285–9 (in Japanese).

about the corruption of the privileged class. Accordingly, the movements tended to be idealistic and dogmatic.

Terrorism

The rise in terrorism also gave rise to fear among criminologists. Assaults on party politicians by right-wing fanatics occurred repeatedly. First, Takashi Hara, the first commoner ever to become prime minister, was assassinated in 1921. Then, Prime Minister Osachi Hamaguchi was shot and wounded in 1930, which was followed by the assassination of Prime Minister Tsuyoshi Inukai by young army officers in 1932. After the assault on Hamaguchi, a psychiatrist commented in the *Archives of Criminology* that a scientific method of criminology should be applied to terrorists, because many of them were either insane, degenerate, mentally retarded, or adolescents with high levels of suggestibility.[28]

The most shocking incident, though, was the assault on the Emperor Showa, then prince, in 1923. The perpetrator, Daisuke Nanba, a twenty-four-year-old anarchist, fired into the car that was carrying the prince to Parliament, but the prince was not harmed. During the trial he did not hesitate to profess his homicidal intent and accordingly was hanged a year later. The documents from the investigation and the trial reveal an interesting profile of the assassin.[29] He was born to a reputable family in one of the outlying prefectures, and his father was a member of the House of Representatives. Although all his brothers were bright, his performance in school was mediocre, and he even failed the entrance examination for a prestigious high school. He then left his hometown to attend high school in Tokyo, where he was exposed to radical thinking. He began to have compassion for the poor in the slum neighborhoods in Tokyo and to feel indignation over the authorities' harsh oppression of the socialists. His hatred then turned to the privileged class to which, he thought, his father also belonged. According to his testimony during the trial, he did not have any resentment toward the prince himself, but he reasoned that the imperial family helped the ruling class to oppress the people and that terrorism was the last resort to awaken the proletariat, who were still operating under an illusion about the imperial system.

It is interesting to read the memoirs written by jurists who had close contact with Daisuke Nanba. Rikisaburo Imamura, the lawyer who defended

---

28 Junji Kaneko, "Essay on the Assault of the Prime Minister," *Archives of Criminology* 4 (1931): 55–6 (in Japanese).
29 A psychiatric report on Daisuke Nanba argued that he was completely sane.

Nanba, analyzed his life history in order to clarify the cause of the "unprecedented disgraceful affair." Imamura compared Nanba's profile to that of
other left-wing terrorists. The common characteristics he found were
"despair due to poor health, and strong self-respect." Imamura's explanation of Nanba's behavior is as follows: He suffered from renal disease and
was convinced that he had only a few years to live. The desire to end his
life as a hero drove him to commit this reckless act. Books and pamphlets
on socialism and anarchism also helped Nanba give voice to his immature
thoughts. He further cites an episode that showed the extent of Nanba's
belief: Despite Imamura's efforts to make his client repent for his foolish act,
Nanba shouted "banzai (long life) for the Japanese proletariat!" in front of
the judge at the time of sentencing. Imamura later confessed that he took
great pains to understand Nanba's thinking but was only disappointed by
his tenaciousness.[30]

Hideo Yokota, the presiding judge for Nanba's trial, also stated that it was
hard for him to understand Nanba's act. For Yokota, the core of the problem
was that Nanba was a "dropout." Born to a good family, he ended up "falling
into communism" due to the influence of several unfortunate circumstances:
his mother's premature death, his father's harshness, and the destructive
effects of the urban environment. Yokota suspected that the confluence of
these factors brought about Nanba's "moral corruption," and he strongly
emphasized the role family and education should play in preventing the
indulgences that would allow youth to slip into communism.[31]

Mass Media and Crime

Another important trend that contributed to the development of criminology was the popularization of knowledge about crime. As mentioned above,
both the *Journal of Abnormal Psychology* and the *Archives of Criminology* carried
many nonacademic contributions, including essays on sensational criminal
incidents, excerpts of newspaper articles, experiences of police officers, and
reviews of foreign and domestic detective novels. According to an essay in
the *Archives of Criminology* of 1931, interest in crime was growing rapidly
among the general public, as evidenced by the large number of books and
popular magazines featuring stories about crime.[32]

---

30 Rikisaburo Imamura, "Memoirs," in *Documents of Modern History*, 3 vols. (Tokyo, 1988), 53–64 (in Japanese).
31 Hideo Yokota, "On the Affaire of Toranomon," in *Documents of Modern History*, 163–82 (in Japanese).
32 Keiji Kuroda, "Essay of a Criminologist," *Archives of Criminology* 5 (1931): 154–63 (in Japanese). He
   complained that even though knowledge about crime became popular, criminology as a discipline
   was rather underdeveloped.

This interest in crime was probably fed by the mass media, which saw unprecedented growth in the 1910s and 1920s. Two major newspapers had begun publication at the beginning of the century and soon had achieved a large circulation. One had a circulation of 160,000 in 1910, 440,000 in 1921, and 1,050,000 in 1932. This rapid increase in subscribers was due mainly to an increase in the number of people who were educated enough to read newspapers, particularly members of the growing urban middle class. By 1923 the illiteracy rate in Tokyo had dropped to 8 percent. Added to the already established daily newspapers was a steady stream of new weekly and monthly magazines. In the 1930s each of the two major monthly magazines aimed at housewives had a circulation of one million or more.[33]

POLITICS AND CRIMINOLOGISTS

Finally, it is important to examine the links between criminology and the resurgence of nationalism that occurred in the 1930s, when Japan invaded Manchuria in 1931 and withdrew from the League of Nations in 1933. I will concentrate on two conservative movements: racism and eugenics. These movements developed parallel to the development of criminology, and some leading criminologists were involved with one or both.

Racism

Japan had made astonishing political and economic progress in the late nineteenth and early twentieth centuries, which was highlighted by the victory over Russia in 1905. These successes encouraged Japanese leaders to compete with European powers. As a result of the subsequent rise in Japan's international status and its acquisition of colonies in East Asia, the Japanese people became more aware of the physical and cultural diversity among different peoples.

This concern can be seen in the works of Tanemoto Furuhata. In the *Archives of Criminology*, he reported numerous studies on blood types and fingerprints.[34] At that time, these two topics attracted the attention of specialists

---

33 Yamamoto, "Essay on Mass Media."
34 Tanemoto Furuhata's main works on blood types and fingerprints in the *Archives of Criminology* include "Identification of Individuals," 1 (1928): 18–30; "Heredity of Fingerprints and its Application for Anthropology" 2 (1929): 20–28; "Trends of Study on Fingerprints" 2 (1929): 110–15; "Paternity Test through Blood" 2 (1929): 140–46; and "Particularity of the Japanese Nation through Distribution of Blood Types" 2 (1929): 311–29. In these articles he cited methods of criminal identification developed by European scientists such as Alphonse Bertillon and Francis Galton. But he insisted that identification through fingerprints originated in Japan, where a thumbprint had been customarily used in place of a signature.

not only as tools of criminal investigation but also as means for identifying the specific characteristics of race. In his reports Furuhata detailed large-scale surveys and concluded that he had identified the racial uniqueness of Yamato-minzoku (the archaic term for "the Japanese nation") based on the distribution of blood types and fingerprints. He argued that, rising from multiple origins, Yamato-minzoku was a sort of big family (the culmination of a longstanding process of fusion and integration). What is most interesting about Furuhata's argument is the contrast between the very sophisticated scientific analysis used to prove his hypothesis and the old-fashioned rhetoric he employed to state his findings. Using many clichés suggestive of ultranationalism, he asserted that Yamato-minzoku, ruled by the emperor (a descendant of God), was characterized by an incomparable racial uniqueness and was therefore superior to other racially mixed nations.

Takeji Furukawa, a pedagogue, carried out another blood-type study with a similar hypothesis and conclusion. He compared the distribution of blood types among two different peoples, the Formosans, found on Taiwan, and the Ainu, a people spread throughout Northeast Asia, including Northern Japan, particularly on the island of Hokkaido. Furukawa's motivation for the study may have derived from a political incident. After the occupation of Taiwan following Japan's victory over China in 1895, the inhabitants continued to tenaciously resist their occupiers. Insurgencies in 1930 and 1931 killed hundreds of Japanese settlers. The purpose of Furukawa's study was to "penetrate to the essence of the racial traits of the Taiwanese, who recently revolted and behaved so cruelly." Based on the finding that 41.2 percent of a Taiwanese sample had type O blood, he assumed that their rebelliousness was genetically determined. This reasoning was supported by the fact that among the Ainu, whose temperament was characterized as subordinate, only 23.8 percent had type O blood. Furukawa contrasted the passiveness of the Ainu with the intransigence of the Taiwanese, who refused to be "moralized." In conclusion, Furukawa suggested that the Taiwanese should intermarry more with the Japanese in order to reduce the number of individuals with type O blood.[35] His proposal was consistent with the policy of integration adopted by the Japanese governors.

The Taiwanese mentality was analyzed from yet another perspective. Hideo Egami, a psychologist and one of the main contributors to the *Archives of Criminology* in 1929 conducted research sponsored by the Ministry of Education. He carried out fieldwork for the purpose of determining the

---

35 Takeji Furukawa, "Racial Traits of the Taiwanese and the Ainu Through Blood Types," *Archives of Criminology* 4 (1931): 130–34 (in Japanese).

characteristics of the Taiwanese: their moral and religious sensibility, native intelligence, and customs. He then compared the data with those obtained from Japanese counterparts. The results were satisfactory, for the Taiwanese subjects showed the desired effects of the integration policy, which supported the possibility that the Taiwanese would one day become a part of the Japanese nation. Understanding the psychology of "savages" was meaningful for him because of a perceived urgency to "make them enjoy, as soon as possible, the benefits of Koka (becoming subordinate to the Japanese emperor)."[36]

The core of Japan's ethnic policy was to assimilate the inhabitants of colonies and occupied areas in order to establish the "Greater East Asia Co-Prosperity Sphere," a policy that contrasted sharply with the exclusionist policy adopted by the Nazis.[37]

Eugenics

At the beginning of the twentieth century, the enactment of sterilization laws in the United States aroused the curiosity of several Japanese scholars. Hisomu Nagai, a professor of physiology at the Imperial University of Tokyo, was concerned about the future of the Japanese nation and began to spread the principles of eugenics, proposing sterilization as an effective means of reducing the element in the population having "malignant heredity." However, health professionals as a whole did not subscribe to these ideas, nor were they even interested in this problem because at that time they were too busy dealing with chronic diseases, tuberculosis, and malnutrition.

From the late 1920s to the early 1930s, eugenics was widely discussed as a means of solving the problem of overpopulation. In 1930 Hisomu Nagai organized the first meeting of the Japanese Society of National Hygiene, which brought together about eight hundred attendees. It should be noted that Tanemoto Furuhata was a member of the board of directors. The stated purpose of the society was to study heredity and its relation to the Japanese people's physical constitution. Meanwhile, the enactment of the Sterilisierungsgesetz (sterilization law) in Germany aroused debate about eugenics in Japan. Opponents criticized the excesses of Germany's

---

36 Hideo Egami, "Moral Sensibility of the Japanese and the Taiwanese," *Archives of Criminology* 3 (1930): 261–83 (in Japanese). The works of Furukawa and Egami were examples of anthropological studies to which Japan's territorial expansion to East and South Asia gave an impetus.

37 Under the Nazi regime, Jews and gypsies were often regarded as predisposed to commit crime. (See Richard Wetzell's chapter in this volume.) On this point, the German racist discourse differed from the Japanese counterpart, in which criminal disposition was not emphasized as a racial trait.

legislation and demanded more careful consideration, suggesting that the current knowledge of heredity was not sufficient to justify taking such radical steps.[38] The proponents of sterilization, headed by Nagai, rejected these critics, arguing that it would be reasonable to sacrifice a minority for the sake of the "eternal life of a nation." They stressed that Japan's prosperity had been brought about by the superiority inherent in Yamato-minzoku and that it therefore was of the utmost importance to prevent "racial degeneration."[39] The Japanese Society of National Hygiene actively promoted eugenics research, including a study on the Ainu, who were regarded as an example of an "inferior race."[40]

Furthermore, the society was engaged in the formulation of a bill for sterilization. The Ministry of Health also began to prepare drafts of legislation, conducting a survey in 1939 of families of mentally ill people on the basis of which the Ministry of Health contended that some forms of mental illness were strongly heritable. In order to popularize such eugenic ideas the Ministry of Health organized an "Exhibition of National Eugenics" that proved to be a great success, drawing over one thousand visitors a day. The exhibits were composed of two distinctly different elements: scientific knowledge and religious concepts. The display appealed to the audience based on the findings of ethnology and then preached to them the value of a eugenics policy that would help Japan, a divine nation, to overcome its present difficulties. This idea was symbolized by an exhibit showing a tree buffeted by a storm yet standing strong, upon which were painted the words "Kodo-Seishin" (Spirit of the Empire).[41]

In 1940 the bill for the National Eugenics Law was passed and enacted by the Diet. The purpose of this law was to foster an increase in the healthy population by improving the people's physical constitution. It aimed to do so by promoting an increase in the number of individuals with healthy predispositions and a decrease in the number with unhealthy predispositions.

---

38 Jinichi Kikuchi, a forensic psychiatrist, raised strong objections to the eugenics movement promoted by the Japanese Society of National Hygiene. His criticism addressed not only the eugenicists' lack of psychiatric knowledge but also the risk of the abuse of eugenic measures by the ruling class. He warned that sterilization would be exclusively applied to "abnormal proletarians."

39 Proponents often argued that sterilization had already been practiced in many Western countries and that current genetics, especially Ernst Rüdin's research, had provided sufficient evidence supporting the effectiveness of the measure.

40 In 1933 the Japanese Society of National Hygiene formed a committee under the chairmanship of Hisomu Nagai. Aiming to explain the decrease in population of the Ainu, the committee performed a series of surveys on physical conditions, especially tuberculosis, syphilis, and eye disease. The fact that this project was expected to offer preventive measures against racial degeneration suggests the close relationship of eugenics to racism.

41 Yutaka Fujino, *Japanese Fascism and Eugenic Ideas* (Kyoto, 1998) (in Japanese).

The law further stipulated that sterilization could be performed on patients with specific disorders: hereditary mental illness and deficiency, as well as serious types of hereditary morbid character and malformations.[42] A person with such a patient as a blood relative also could be sterilized. However, only the person affected could apply for an operation; in the case of a minor or an incompetent person, a father or spouse could apply. Even an administrator of a mental hospital or prison could apply for it, if the person's disorder was determined to be extremely serious.[43]

How many people were actually sterilized under this law? According to statistics from the Ministry of Health, the number of sterilizations totaled 538, which included 217 men and 321 women, from 1941 to 1947, when the law was abolished. For the most part, these were persons with severe mental illness or mental deficiency. This figure seems rather small when compared to that of Germany, where over 56,000 people were sterilized in 1934 alone.[44] The reason for this limited practice of sterilization in Japan is not clear. I suspect, however, that two major factors hindered the practice. First, because there were relatively few mental hospitals at that time, it was difficult to systematically deal with patients who met the sterilization criteria.[45] Second, even though some psychiatrists, especially leaders in academic circles, argued for the value of the project, most doctors were reluctant to become involved in the practice.[46]

CONCLUSION

Tracing the early history of criminology in Japan, I have argued that the "science of crime" developed through the contributions of specialists in three

---

42 The inclusion of criminals in the sterilization law was a matter of debate during the Nazi era. (See Richard Wetzell's chapter in this volume.) In Japan, criminal behavior was not included among the criteria of sterilization, unless it was regarded as a sign of a "hereditary morbid character." Furthermore, the number of sterilized persons with hereditary morbid character was low.

43 The German law provided a powerful judicial organization (Erbgesundheitsgerichte), which made decisions about sterilization. The Japanese law stipulated that a local governor, assisted by a board of specialists, was responsible for the decisions.

44 Ernst Klee, *"Euthanasie" im NS-Staat: Die "Vernichtung lebensunwerten Lebens"* (Frankfurt am Main, 1983).

45 According to the statistics of 1941, the total number of psychiatric beds was about 20,000, which was disproportionately small for the patient population. A large number of psychiatric patients were sequestered in their own homes.

46 There were several reasons for psychiatric practitioners' reluctance regarding sterilization. First, most of them showed little interest in the ideology of the eugenics movement, even though they recognized possible benefits of sterilization for patients with hereditary diseases. Second, they contended that interruption of reproduction would conflict with the Japanese values based on the family unit. Finally, they thought of sterilization as an unnatural act that was in conflict with their medical ethics.

disciplines: forensic medicine, psychiatry, and psychology. On the one hand, an increase in the crime rate led scientists to establish methods for criminal investigation. The technical progress in forensic medicine subsequently aroused an interest in the biological differences among races. However, this new field could not have been explored if people had not faced the problem of Japan's international status and racial identity. This is the reason why the rhetoric of racism easily mixed with anthropological discourse. Psychiatrists and psychologists involved in the study of crime also became concerned about social problems that seemed to endanger the soundness and stability of the Japanese nation. It is therefore understandable that some leaders of criminology were ready to accept the ideas of racism and eugenics.

At the root of these scientific trends was the fear of the growing menace of crime, which was widespread and was intensified by the perception of particular aspects of criminality: the decadence of youth, moral corruption caused by urbanization, the mass psychology of the lower class, and the infiltration of anarchism and Marxism. All these changes were reflections of the economic and political upheavals Japan experienced in the first half of the twentieth century. Criminologists played a role in helping the nation to face this crisis, mainly by making the phenomenon of crime a subject of scientific research. A similar process can be found in the United States. It has been argued that when criminal anthropology reached U.S. shores in the late nineteenth century, crime was becoming a compelling issue due to the transformation of society, and people concerned with social control were primed for exactly this sort of doctrine.[47]

To conclude, although Japanese criminology showed peculiarities related to Japanese politics and society, it also illustrates how the science of crime developed in connection with the modernization of society.

---

47 See Nicole Rafter's chapter in this volume.

THREE

The Making of the Criminologist

13

The International Congresses of Criminal Anthropology

Shaping the French and International Criminological Movement, 1886–1914

MARTINE KALUSZYNSKI

International congresses took on particular importance at the end of the nineteenth century. Numerous, diverse, and varied, these forums for communication, legitimacy, and power became essential for ideas, movements, and individuals as places to exchange views and, especially, to make their existence known. What were these congresses about? Were they primarily about curiosity, necessity, legitimacy, gaining political advantage – or about research?[1]

The advantages of international congresses are so numerous and varied that each involves its own set of motivations. Through this case study of the international congresses of criminal anthropology – an analysis requisite to an understanding of the internal and external life and evolution of an intellectual movement – I will identify the various facets of these congresses and the stakes involved in their content, form, and attendance. I will also demonstrate the structuring role that these forums played, both nationally and internationally, in the development of the discipline and even more so in the development of a certain notion of a juridical "Europe" and the foundations of a juridical "international."

Before discussing these international congresses, a few words are in order on the science of criminology, its origins, doctrines, and debates. It was in the last quarter of the nineteenth century that a particular body of knowledge formed out of a hodgepodge of numerous other disciplines. Criminology, or rather criminal anthropology, attempted to analyze the phenomenon of crime scientifically in order to understand and reduce it. The first appearance

---

This chapter was translated from French by Julie Johnson, San Francisco, California.

1 This chapter is based on Martine Kaluszynski, "Les congrès internationaux d'anthropologie criminelle (1883–1914)," *Mi neuf cent: Revue d'Histoire intellectuelle* 7 (1989): 59–70. See also Robert Nye, *Crime, Madness, and Politics in Modern France* (Princeton, N.J., 1984) and David G. Horn's chapter in this book.

of French judicial statistics in 1825 proved important in that they formed the basis of many criminological studies. The way also was paved by scholars such as Adolphe d'Angeville and Lambert Adolphe Quételet. The latter observed that criminal acts occur with a consistency and regularity that reflects certain laws, and maintained that there exists a "penchant toward crime." The fundamental contribution of these works was the idea that man can be studied scientifically, quantifiably, with calculation and precision. Statistics and anthropology were combined to develop a scientific discourse.

Cesare Lombroso was the first to formalize the orientation of this new approach, contributing the idea that the root cause of crime was to be found in physical or mental abnormalities. His book, *L'uomo delinquente*, published in 1876, met with great success. According to Lombroso, all hardened criminals were atavistic reincarnations of a primitive stage in the evolution of man. Their behavior was not due to the pressure of circumstances and the outside world but arose from a natural disposition. Such individuals were biologically stunted and thus deficient in the very mechanisms of adaptation to human society. In Lombroso's words they were "human animals of a particular sort, born criminals who are destined to remain so." Darwin's influence is very clear, and Lombroso drew from it the linear idea of evolution that led him to affirm that criminals were evolutionarily backward individuals who had failed to reach the final evolutionary stage, that of man, of humankind. This view met with a flurry of criticisms attacking its method, theses, principles, and the immense role attributed to biology in theories whose cornerstone was the assertion of a veritable structural determinism of criminal behavior, which was viewed as a fatal consequence of specific stigmata of criminality.

One of the main legacies of Lombroso's theories was the belief that criminals constitute a separate race bearing the stigmata of a particular biological or psychological structure that forms a distinctive and indelible mark. Despite the ambiguity of these works, Lombroso remained a dominant figure. The ensuing debate gave new impetus to the young discipline. In fact, one very positive result of Lombroso's writings was that they promoted the study of the criminal, which had been previously neglected. Whereas before only the crime had been considered, now scholars shifted their attention to the criminal and his or her personality. This represented a radical change in the object of study, a shift in focus from the crime to the criminal, and a dramatic upheaval in the notions of crime and criminal justice. It was in this specific context and in this atmosphere of passionate debate that the "French school" of criminology became established and developed.[2]

---

2 See Martine Kaluszynski, "La criminologie en mouvement: Naissance et développement d'une science sociale en France au XIXème siècle. Les Archives de l'anthropologie criminelle d'Alexandre

The young Third Republic extolled the values of order, stability, and work, and was determined to use every means to ensure that these values be upheld. The technological and industrial revolution was accompanied by a rare flourishing of disciplines that was due not only to the quality of scientific, literary, and artistic production but also to its variety, contrasts, and contradictions. During this century of working-class misery and major upheavals, passion, and burgeoning ideas, violence was perceived as negative; crime and criminality were subjects that reflected the worries and fears of a society in transition. Anxieties beyond the scope of crime itself – a feeling of economic and social "insecurity" – were displaced and gravitated to the visible pole of unrest and disorder.

In the French school we find a group of men united around a set of ideas about the phenomenon of crime who were initially drawn to each other by their shared opposition to Lombroso's theories.[3] Grouped in Lyon around a journal, *Les Archives de l'anthropologie criminelle*, and a leader, Alexandre Lacassagne, these men wrote for this journal and joined ranks at meetings from 1886 to 1914. The term *criminal anthropology*, while contested, came to cover all scientific aspects of the phenomenon of crime, even though such aspects sometimes departed significantly from Lombroso's original theories, such as his notions of the born criminal, the genetic transmission of individual defects, and a humanity doomed to a gradually rising tide of criminality.

The French movement focused on the influence of the "social milieu,"[4] which was regarded as a veritable hotbed of criminality. Its doctrines were eclectic. The criminal was seen as subject to many different influences, particularly sociological influences. Crime was viewed as a social phenomenon that was intimately correlated with the social milieu in which the criminal lived. The criminal was an individual who appeared normal but was predisposed to crime as a result of an unstable brain equilibrium that put him at the mercy of external triggers (pathological processes, atmospheric conditions), especially social ones (poverty, idleness, laziness, imitation). The French school countered the inevitable fatalism of the anthropological theory

---

Lacassagne," Ph.D. diss., Université Paris VII, 1988, or Kaluszynski, *La Republique à l'épreuve du crime: La construction du crime comme object politique, 1880–1920* (Paris, 2002).

3 Léonce Manouvrier is one example: He criticized Lombroso in the name of anthropology and, considering Lombroso a "manipulator" of the discipline, argued his point of view in terms of three themes: definition of the object of study, the condition of scientific observation, and the relativity of the distinction between law and ethics. See Philippe Robert, Pierre Lascoumes, and Martine Kaluszynski, "Une leçon de méthode: le mémoire de Manouvrier de 1892," *Déviance et Société* 2, no. 3 (1986): 223–46.

4 That explains why the French school was given the name "social environment school" (école du milieu social). Over the course of the nineteenth century, the concept of environment was applied in two new areas: in biology under the impetus of Geoffroy Saint Hilaire, and in the moral sciences by Auguste Comte and Hippolyte Taine, both of whom had a significant impact on Lacassagne.

with social initiatives. Nevertheless, biological theories were not absent from their writings. While less dominant than among the Italians, they still occupied a respectable place in the corpus of the *Archives*, as did anthropometric articles. The French movement – that is, the group of people whose articles appeared in the *Archives* – included many foreigners and provincials, but consisted mainly of medical doctors, especially experts in forensic medicine, psychiatrists, and military doctors. Only very few of the authors were jurists (such as René Garraud and Gabriel Tarde), mostly academics rather than practioners of law; a few were government bureaucrats.

The criminological discourse was also very medically oriented: the criminal was approached in clinical terms, and the facts were presented in the form of a diagnosis. Society was often treated as a biological organism that must be protected from disease: mental defects, lunacy, criminality. These writings also promoted the very important notion of hygiene. Both moral and physical hygiene constituted a key element of the discourse and seemed to coincide with the desire for a wide-ranging cleansing of society.[5] The criminological discourse particularly revolved around the criminal and criminality and everything having to do with the body. The *Archives* were full of reflections on criminals, who were often broken down into categories and subcategories (the female criminal, the child, the lunatic). They also included articles on tattoos, hypnotism, and "exoticism," which showed a fascination with strange or exotic phenomena, among which crime was simply an exceptional element. On the whole, the *Archives* neglected criminal law as such and focused instead on "penality," that is, criminals and their treatment.

Lacassagne thus led a movement that developed in parallel to that of Lombroso. From 1886 to 1914 he met with no real opposition in France and served as the movement's official spokesperson at international meetings. With his large following, he embodies the birth of French criminology.

KNOWLEDGE-BUILDING INSTITUTIONS: JOURNALS AND CONGRESSES

The terms *school* and *movement* are used without any tangible evidence of their existence; but these references are not artificial. A team, a spirit, a

---

5 See, for example, Alexandre Lacassagne, *Base et organization d'une société de médecine publique* (Paris, 1877); Lacassagne and Paul Dubuisson, "Cremation," *Dictionnaire encyclopédique des sciences médicales*, vol. 23 (Paris, 1879); Lacassagne, *Les Etablissements insalubres de l'arrondissement de Lyon: Compte rendu des travaux du Conseil d'hygiène publique et de salubrité du Département du Rhône* (Lyon, 1891). Moreover, Lacassagne was a member of the Society of Public Medicine and Professional Hygiene as well as a member of the Consultative Committee for Public Hygiene in France.

group crystallized around an academic department, a university: the medical school of the University of Lyon. Although initially unorganized, the group formed around a leader (Lacassagne) and around a journal (*Les Archives de l'anthropologie criminelle*), which served as a driving force for organizing, exchanging ideas, and developing a movement.[6] At the International Congresses of Criminal Anthropology, the group stood united in their ideas and theories about crime. These two elements – the journal and the congresses – played a key role in shaping, establishing, and anchoring an emerging body of knowledge. In order to further a comparative perspective, I will focus on the International Congresses of Criminal Anthropology, highlighting the French perspective but taking into account other countries.

THE IMPORTANCE OF INTERNATIONAL CONGRESSES IN THE FIELD OF CRIMINAL JUSTICE

The study of crime took the form of publications, reports, and doctrine, and gradually became "disciplined" through "institutions for the discussion, evaluation and dissemination of the results of research."[7] Similarly, the twelve international prison congresses,[8] supported in France by the Société générale des prisons, played an important role in developing and legitimizing the French movement. Through these meetings a European juridical space beyond national borders began to take shape that was characterized by shared ways of thinking. This formation of a scientific community (both national and international) also contributed to the formation of a body of knowledge.[9] All of these elements contributed to the recognition of that body of knowledge, its definition, and a certain know-how. The result was a specialized body of knowledge, induced, constructed, and debated among specialists motivated by public debates aimed at a specific goal and practical outcomes.

It was through the congresses that the discipline originated and became firmly established. The regularity of these meetings stabilized the movement,

---

6 Published from 1886 on as *Archives d'anthropologie criminelle et des sciences pénales* (*Médecine légale, judiciaire, statistiques criminelles, legislatives et droit*), the title was altered in 1903 and 1907, but the words *Archives d'anthropologie criminelle* (hereafter *AAC*) remained unchanged. Publication was suspended in 1920. Lacassagne died in 1924 without having been able to resume publication of the journal that was commonly called the "Lacassagne Archives."

7 Pierre Favre, *Naissance de la science politique en France* (Paris, 1989), 8–10. Favre even writes that "science doesn't truly appear until these institutions exist."

8 London (1872), Stockholm (1878), Rome (1885), Saint Petersburg (1890), Paris (1895), Brussels (1900), Budapest (1905), Washington, D.C. (1910), London (1925), Prague (1930), Berlin (1935), and The Hague (1950).

9 Favre, *Naissance de la science politique*, 10.

giving it a history, a tradition, and "rites" that became institutionalized. The international dimension of these meetings also lent an air of "consensus" to the discussions, which took place under the banner of "science," thereby transcending spiritual, political, and national divisions: "Nebulous times are yet one more reason to gravitate toward the serene domain of science. . . . For people of every stripe, it provides a neutral ground where they can meet and work together to solve the major problems that are so compelling for everyone."[10]

THE INTERNATIONAL CONGRESSES OF CRIMINAL ANTHROPOLOGY

These international congresses[11] where quarrels between schools and ideas were played out allow us to trace the political development of French and European criminology. Eight congresses were planned from 1885 to 1914: Rome (1885), Paris (1889), Brussels (1892), Geneva (1896), Amsterdam (1901), Turin (1906), Cologne (1911), and Budapest (1914). The last one never took place. The lifespan of these congresses paralleled that of the criminological movements, especially the French movement, which came to an end with World War I but had in fact lost its steam before then.

These international congresses became possible because, along with Italy and France, other countries such as Spain,[12] Holland (with G. A. van Hamel) and Belgium (Adolphe Prins, Paul Héger, E. Heuze, Raymond de Ryckere, Henri Jaspar) were developing similar criminological approaches. The *Archives* column written by Alexandre Likhatcheff shows a burgeoning movement in Russia, whereas no major works were being produced in England or the United States[13] other than articles on forensic medicine (*Journal of Mental Science* and *The Medico-Legal Journal*). In 1893, Paul Ladame, who wrote the German column in the *Archives*, noted that "the Germans have long been indifferent, if not hostile to such research,"[14] yet it was in Germany that Lombroso had published his first piece on criminal anthropology.[15] At first, only one German journal regularly included articles

---

10 Charles Lucas in *Revue Pénitentiaire* (1877): 14.

11 There were no national criminal anthropology congresses.

12 In 1888, the journal *La Revista de anthropologia criminal y ciencas médica legales* began publication under the leadership of Dr. Angel Alvarez Talandriz and Raphaël Salillas.

13 See the news columns of Henri Coutagne, who was responsible for reporting on English and Anglo-American news in the *AAC* and who did not hide the awkwardness of the task; see *AAC* 3 (1886): 666.

14 Paul Ladame, "Chronique allemande," *AAC* 8 (1893): 526.

15 The first mention of the famous *occipital fossa* appeared in an article in Rudolf Virchow's *Archiv* in 1871. (See Paul Ladame, *AAC* 8 [1893], 526.) But German science took no immediate notice of the publication in 1876 of Lombroso's *L'uomo delinquente*.

on criminal anthropology, namely the *Centralblatt für Nervenheilkunde und Psychiatrie, mit besonderer Berücksichtigung der Degenerationsanthropologie*, edited by Dr. Kueller until 1892, then by Dr. Sommer (from Würzburg). Then, in 1898, a specialized journal was created, the *Archiv für Kriminalanthropologie und Kriminalistik*, edited by Professor Hans Gross, a professor of criminal law at the German-speaking university of Prague. Thus, in several countries, a movement of ideas was forming that the international congresses would structure.

The congresses were places of exchange and dissemination, but also places of conflict and power, where adversaries who had either clashed or allied themselves in their writings confronted each other face to face. The programs and duration (often several days) of these congresses as well as the personalities present and the topics discussed made them rich events. They provided a concentrated overview of the range of criminological notions of the era and of various countries around the world. They therefore merit systematic study.[16] Here, we will examine only certain aspects of these congresses, with an emphasis on their "spirit" more than their content.

STRUCTURE AND ORGANIZATION OF THE CONGRESSES

Several elements characterize the form, structure, and "corpus" of these congresses. First, they were held at regular intervals (three, four, or at most five years apart). Each country with a vested interest in criminology served as host and organizing country, the Italians twice, which is understandable given the dynamic, founding role that this country played. The venue for the next meeting was always decided during the closing session of each congress. At times this involved some discussion,[17] but usually the choice seems to have been made by majority vote according to a tacit agreement.

The organizing countries invested a lot of energy into preparing each congress. It was a point of honor to ensure that everything went smoothly

16 By analyzing the contents and scope of all reports from each country, one would be able to identify the emergence of certain themes and their exact development at the congresses and in each country concerned. Biographical research on the major scholars present would also be useful and relevant. It would also be informative to examine the congresses against the sociopolitical context and development of the host countries. Lastly, it would be useful to systematically track, country by country, whether or not the resolutions adopted were implemented, when, how, and so on.

17 In 1892, three proposals were made: Amsterdam for 1894 (proposed by Sarraute), Geneva for 1896 (proposed by Dimitri Drill, Soeren Hansen, Etienne Magitot, Léonce Manouvrier, and Alphonse Struelens), and Chicago for 1896 (World's Fair). The first two proposals were adopted, the second by unanimous consensus. In 1896, a large majority of congress attendees decided that the 1901 congress would be held in Amsterdam. Two petitions with signatures were circulated, one for Paris, one for Amsterdam. Upon discussion, Paris was rejected as being too wild, a "hub of iniquity for workers and conferences" (*AAC* 11 [1896]: 546).

so that one would emerge from the "test" with an enhanced reputation. The organizing committee was generally composed of well-known scholars in the field from the host country, except in 1901 in Holland, where the organizing committee consisted mostly of Dutch politicians. The honorary presidents elected by each organizing committee were well-known people from other countries. Here France, Italy, and Belgium were very well represented.

No information is available on how these events were financed. Were there national or international subsidies, or special grants? The only concrete information we have is the cost of the registration fees for the congresses (twenty French francs in 1889 and 1896), which included a free copy of the published conference proceedings.

The form of the congresses appears to have been relatively traditional, each with an official sponsor, and the opening sessions were attended by a minister (usually the minister of justice)[18] and other government officials. Ritual opening and closing speeches framed the meeting. The opening speech was always moderate, "neutral," and welcoming in tone. It set the stage for events and players, but without excessive passion or controversy. By contrast, the closing speech was usually more significant: it took stock of and memorialized the congress. In the manner of a brilliant synthesis, it reaffirmed a victory, a knockout, the triumph of an idea, or brought closure to a lingering controversy. Always oriented toward science and progress – the stock beneficiaries of the genre – the closing speeches were often lyrical and glowing, and emphasized optimism and reconciliation after the heat of contentious congresses.

The sessions were organized into half-days that included reports, comments, discussions, and sometimes visits to exhibitions organized in association with the congresses.[19] Over all these years, the program remained quite traditional, generally divided between criminal biology and criminal sociology. The social aspect of the meeting was also important: the visits, the banquets, the intermissions, and all the extras that were part of the congresses. Each meeting offered a prime opportunity for the organizing country to showcase its talents, innovations, and model institutions.[20] Each

18 The French minister of justice was present in 1889 at the Palais du Trocadéro in Paris, and the Belgian minister Jules Lejeune was present in 1892 at the Palais des Académies in Brussels.

19 In 1885 there was a criminal anthropology exhibit that showed craniums and tattoos. See Dr. A. Motet, "Rapport sur l'exposition d'anthropologie criminelle," *AAC* 1 (1886): 88–96. In 1899 there was a general anthropological exhibit, with a section on legal and criminal anthropology.

20 The 1889 congress included a presentation on anthropometry by A. Bertillon and a visit to the police prefecture. The 1892 congress offered a visit to the Saint-Gille prison; the 1896 congress offered visits to the museum of archaeology, the anthropometric service, and the psychiatric hospital. The

meeting was also enhanced by evening receptions and banquets, which were important because they were more conducive to meeting people, sharing ideas, and deepening connections than the academic sessions themselves.[21]

Attendance at the congresses appears to have been truly international: France, Italy, Belgium, Germany, Switzerland, Holland, Hungary, Brazil, Mexico, Peru (1889), and China were represented. Medical and legal organizations sent representatives, but such affiliations were not noted until 1892. Such was the composition and organization of these major meetings. This general overview has primarily outlined their overarching structure and tenor, and in so doing, shown that the International Congresses of Criminal Anthropology were fairly traditional in form and conception. A comparison with other congresses would probably reveal similarities in this regard.

THE FUNCTIONS OF THE CONGRESSES

A second observation regarding these congresses relates to the role(s) they played and the various functions they served. As a place where a discipline was established and emerging scientific ideas legitimized, a place of intellectual exchange and dissemination, each international congress could either fulfill or dash expectations. The congresses also involved implicit agendas, such as strengthening networks, providing opportunities for showcasing one's achievements, and by symbolically boosting one nation or another.

Establishing a Discipline

The first congress took place in Rome in 1885 at the instigation of Cesare Lombroso. Organized by the Italian school at the Palace of Fine Arts, this congress was initially national in scope, which explains the predominance of Italians at most levels (organizing committee, speakers, program).[22] It was here that Lacassagne, confronting the all-powerful Lombroso, politely attacked the determinist theories and advanced his hypothesis of the

---

1901 congress proposed outings to the Verers de Meerenberg model asylum, and the 1911 congress, visits to prisons and asylums.

21 In 1889 Paul Brouardel invited people to the lounge of the dean of the faculty and Emile Magitot threw a gala reception at the mansion of Prince Roland Bonaparte in the country outside Villeres. In 1892, there was a royal reception at the palace in Brussels and a reception by the minister of justice. In 1896 there were receptions, dinners, a gala evening at the Amsterdam opera; and in 1906 festivities in honor of Lombroso's jubilee.

22 Gabriel Tarde noted: "Compared to the program dealing with biological issues, the program of the four sessions of the sociological section seems quite meager to me" (Tarde, "Actes du Congrès de Rome," *AAC* 3 [1888]: 74).

importance of the social environment, and proposed the following formula: "The criminal is a microbe that proliferates only in a certain environment. It is probably the environment that produces the criminal, but like a medium that has no microbes, it cannot make crime germinate on its own. Microbe and medium, the biological and the social, are hence the two fundamental aspects of criminality and constitute the essential data of criminal anthropology." This first challenge started the Franco-Italian polemic, and, following this congress, in 1886, Lacassagne launched the *Archives de l'anthropologie criminelle*.

Constructing a Discipline

Criminology has been a discipline that consists of different schools and approaches. These congresses brought together protagonists who opposed each other in their writings between meetings. Thus the Italians secured supremacy in 1885, despite Lacassagne's discreet challenges. The 1889 congress in Paris, on the other hand, brought victorious advances by the French and marked the beginning of the duel between Lombroso and Léonce Manouvrier, an epistemological and methodological debate that turned on the question of the existence of anatomical traits unique to criminals and on the term "criminal anthropology," which Manouvrier, an anthropologist by training, could not accept in its Lombrosian usage. The anti-Lombrosian offensive continued at the 1892 congress and it seemed that the notion of the born criminal had been definitively laid to rest. But at the Geneva congress in 1896 the Italians rallied their forces and fought back. Lombroso refused an honorary presidency so he would be free to speak. He vigorously argued his view, and a resolution proposed by Manouvrier against Lombroso was rejected to applause. The Italian school regained ground and momentum. In Amsterdam in 1901, the Italians had wind in their sails. Rebellion seemed to have been nipped in the bud; the opposition was silent. And Lombroso, author of the inaugural report, was rejoicing. In 1906 his jubilee was celebrated in Turin. Lombroso's victory was beyond question, confirmed, ratified, enshrined. They had not been able to "kill" the founding father. Everyone celebrated both his person and his work, controversial as it was. Everyone bowed down, gave homage, caught in the trap of consecration. In a sense, the congress of 1906 put a definitive end to the passionate quarrels. The scientific jubilee in honor of Lombroso closed the circle. The 1911 conference in Cologne was lifeless and unenthusiastic, marking both the death and culmination of a discipline. While they lasted, the conferences had organized and structured a milieu.

Exchange and Dissemination

The congresses were also places of exchange and dissemination, where new technologies were introduced, such as Alphonse Bertillon's anthropometric method of identification, which was gradually adopted by police forces throughout the world and became one of the standard elements of forensic science.[23] The congresses' headline themes were telling: child protection, crime prevention, and social defense. The three main figures of the International Union of Criminal Law founded in 1890 – Franz von Liszt, G. A. van Hamel, and Adolphe Prins – were all avid participants in the criminal anthropology congresses before founding their more juridically oriented association.

A Place Rich in Initiatives

If one looks closely at the resolutions adopted from 1885 to 1911, it appears that most of them were implemented by the individual countries. France provides a compelling example when it comes to the teaching of forensic medicine and criminal anthropology, the need to have delinquents undergo a psychological and moral examination, the establishment of forensic police work, and so on. But were the conferences launching such initiatives or merely giving their stamp of approval to developments that were already under way?

A "Media Spotlight"

While French jurists were skeptical and scarce at national meetings, they flocked to the international meetings because they understood their attraction as a media spotlight. By their presence or absence, people could impact the atmosphere and direction of a congress. For example, in 1889, the presence of two women, Pauline Pigeon, director of the school of the Saint-Louis Hospital, and Clémence Royer, a prominent scientist and philosopher who had translated Darwin's works into French, caused quite a stir. Of course, very few women attended these meetings of mainly male scientists.[24] In 1901, Judge Jean-Marie Bernard Paul Magnaud – who had

---

23 France reluctantly adopted this system, and it was not until 1893 that a criminal identification department was established, but it was well received in the United States. A private company put the method into practice and provided public authorities with the personnel and equipment required to organize a department.

24 This did not prevent Ferri from believing that women would gravitate to criminal anthropology, since they were excluded from criminal law conferences, and because, he said, "despite or because of

become known as the "good judge" for acquitting persons who had stolen out of poverty and hunger – was the star of the congress. But absence made the biggest impression on a congress, especially when it was boycotted by a whole group. In 1889, the Italian socialist school, then represented by Napoleone Colajanni, did not attend, but the incident was quickly forgotten. In 1892, however, the entire Italian school boycotted the congress: Lombroso, Enrico Ferri, Rafaele Garofalo, and others. A joint letter bearing forty-nine signatures (including those of Lombroso and Ferri) explained that this nonattendance was due to the fact that the international commission charged with the preparation of the congress had failed to produce the data it was supposed to collect. This cordial but intransigent letter certainly appears to have been a pretext relieving Lombroso – unsettled or angered by attacks against him – from having to appear before his opponents. The absence of the Italians had quite an effect and put a damper on the Brussels congress. In 1896, France sent no official delegates,[25] but no known motive explains this gesture. In 1901, the absence of Paul Brouardel, Léonce Manouvrier, Gabriel Tarde (due to a death), Paul Garnier, and Jacques-Joseph Valentin Magnan was noted. That same year, Belgium did not attend. The participation or absence of a group thus significantly shaped the congresses.

A Place of Power: Doctors and Jurists

The international congress enabled a discipline to develop, individuals to make their voices heard, and nations to engage one another on a scientific and intellectual plane. But these congresses were also animated by less obvious agendas, and thus played a more powerful role than the simplest stated objectives might indicate. They highlighted the existence and importance of networks, be they spiritual, intellectual, or professional.

While the first criminal anthropology congresses were attended mainly by medical doctors and anthropologists, jurists started participating in 1896 and had a substantial presence in 1901. The French jurists who attended (mainly members of the Société Générale des Prisons – Albert Riviere, Théophile Roussel, Jules Voisin, Camille Ferdinand-Dreyfus) were not very representative of the French criminological movement, which consisted

---

its determinist beginnings, women see and sense that in this moral, individual, and social discipline practically aimed at abating the scourge of criminality, their involvement, reflections, and sentiments can be useful" (*AAC* [1901]: 519–20).

25 E. Martin wrote, "Many remarks were made about all the nonparticipation, and particularly that of our government. It is inexplicable, in fact, that our ministers did not even respond to the official invitation sent to them by the Swiss government. Negligence or forgetfulness? I don't know. But in any case our kind neighbors were vexed" (*AAC*, [1896], 481–2).

primarily of doctors and forensic medical experts. But their participation was emblematic of the weight and power lawyers held on the national level. With their growing influence, legal issues were being raised at these meetings where matters of criminal law previously had been all but absent. This impact is characteristic of what Yves-Henri Gaudemet has rightly called the "Lawyers' Republic" because through their training, ethics, language, and objectives jurists exercised an enormous influence on their environment and on the society as a whole. It is hardly surprising to see lawyers involved in issues of crime; but criminal anthropology was a different matter. Most jurists had developed a hostile attitude toward this discipline because of the unsettling impact its theories were having on the right to punish and the fact that lawyers now had to contend with medical experts in court. Faced with such vocal skepticism, medical doctors remained on the defensive.[26] The two professions thus maintained a tacit separation between their respective territories. This latent socio-professional conflict was actually a power conflict and a struggle over political power.[27] Thus the penetration of jurists into the criminal anthropology congresses is an example of a victorious advance into a symbolic space. It has to be understood in the context of professional jealousy and rivalry, curiosity, and the desire to have a presence. The significant involvement of jurists in 1901 may also have been a sign that they were relaxing and softening their skepticism – at a time when the quarrels among doctors, biologists, and anthropologists were also dying down.

Doctors and lawyers may have been mutually jealous, but they also had a lot in common. They met with each other, and frequently collaborated. Doctors called on the judicial system to protect them against charlatanism and those who practiced medicine illegally. Out of a rivalry the two professions began to define a common body of ideas. Both lawyers and doctors saw themselves as bearers of order and progress, motivated by their respective sciences. Doctors focused on hygiene and maternal protection. Working toward similar goals of protection and effectiveness, lawyers advanced their own projects and perspectives through law and legislation.

Tactically, it appears that on a broader level, "legal" interests infiltrated these congresses and oriented them toward legal issues: treatments, crime prevention, and so forth. This occurred as a slow transition of the congresses into areas of "technical" expertise (the only ground for consensus) in which

26 See Désiré Méreaux (alias Paul Dubuisson), "Histoire d'un duel entre deux mentalités," *AAC* (1906).
27 See Martine Kaluszynski, "Identités professionnelles, identités politiques: médecins et juristes face au crime en France à la fin du XIXème siècle," in Laurent Mucchielli, ed., *Histoire de la criminologie française* (Paris, 1995), 215–35.

lawyers were the experts. Remember that the International Union of Criminal Law (Union Internationale de Droit Pénal) was formed by early stalwarts of the criminal anthropology congresses: Adolphe Prins, Franz von Liszt, G. A. van Hamel. Perhaps, at a certain point, law became the necessary instrument and jurists the driving force for action and reform?

These jurists were not isolated scholars. Some members of the Société Générale des Prisons constructed a corpus of thought on punishment. In this sense, they contributed to the foundation of "criminology," broaching the same issues but from a different angle. In fact, so great was their contribution that "criminology" became categorized as a legal science and became institutionalized.

A Place of Diplomacy

Lastly, no one can deny the diplomatic role these congresses played. The attending scholars were standard bearers for their respective countries. Through the talents and notoriety of these representatives, nations won points on the playing field of international relations. One example of cultural supremacy bestowed on a country through these congresses was the choice of the official language. For every congress up until 1906 that language was French. That year speeches were also delivered in German, English, and Italian. But the real blow to France came at the 1911 congress in Cologne, when German was selected as the official language. The report by Etienne Martin in *Les Archives de l'Anthropologie Criminelle* was very cool and to the point: "What future can the international congresses and their influence on the advancement of ideas have?"

A Place of "Politics"?

We have arrived at the end of the international congresses. Among the countless things the First World War destroyed, it dealt a fatal blow to this movement already in decline. The congresses offered a wealth of intellectual stimulation and encounters to those who participated in the convivial atmosphere of these multiple-day meetings, which combined work with pleasure. For us distant observers today, they are a gold mine of information.

I would like to emphasize one term: *reform*. It is difficult to qualify the movement connected to the congresses, just as it is difficult to assign a political orientation to these meetings. The individuals who attended them, however, are a good indicator. Since they were of different nationalities, it would be a delicate matter to define their spiritual or political affiliations in a general way. But there definitely was one common characteristic that connected most of these individuals and that characterized the congresses: the desire for reform, for advancement, for progress. More broadly, it was the faith in science – the new religion of rationalism thought capable of structuring and explaining any phenomenon, including criminality.

"International congresses," noted van Hamel in the opening speech of 1901, "are overnight camps, where hikers on an extended trip gather for the evening to exchange opinions, to share the results of their research, to offer each other encouragement and valuable information."[28]

These congresses also provided a stage for a wide variety of performances: scientific, intellectual, dramatic, and comical. They were important venues because of their prestige, great presence, composition, and effects. More a time for taking stock than moving forward, they summarized exchanges that had occurred in articles and reviews since the last conference, galvanized authors, and promoted emerging work and ideas. They were a place of ideas and ideology, not practical achievements. Even though each conference closed with many resolutions, those resolutions were only rarely or partially implemented, and disillusionment was not uncommon.

Nevertheless, these congresses were essential to the development of a "movement," regardless of its origin, nature, form, or objectives. Participants had to make a good showing, for appearances, words, a speaker's standing, the force of his convictions, his talent, made more of an impact than the most rigorously constructed scientific presentation.

The invention of criminology is indicative of transformations in the way people conceptualized the world and the social order in the early years of the Third Republic. The realization of policies in this area was characterized by two elements: First, efforts went into amassing a body of knowledge and applying rigorous methodologies in order to then, second, develop the instruments, techniques, projects, and laws needed to implement policy. Knowledge and power do not constitute two distinct realms that occasionally interact; they are organically connected. As Michel Foucault has observed: "No relationship of power exists except in correlation with the development of a field of knowledge; nor does any knowledge exist that does not suppose and simultaneously constitute relationships of power." These practices and bodies of knowledge made crime into an object of scholarly discourse. They opened up a field of study, with its rivalries and competition. They formed

---

28 Van Hamel, "Discours d'ouverture, Actes du Congres d'Amsterdam, 1901," *AAC* (1901): 510.

and shaped interests in which scientific, professional, and political ways of thinking were inextricably linked.

In order to implement its policies, the Republican regime fostered the development of networks, laboratories for ideas, and associations where the conceptual tools for public action were hammered out. It also legitimized the role of experience, experimentation, knowledge, and expertise – for which the international congresses were a perfect medium.

14

Making Criminologists

Tools, Techniques, and the Production of Scientific Authority

DAVID G. HORN

INTRODUCTION

A number of studies over the past twenty years have focused on the production of "the criminal" in the late nineteenth century – on the discursive construction, that is, of a new object of both scientific knowledge and sociotechnical intervention.[1] This chapter focuses, in a complementary fashion, on the production of the criminologist – on the fashioning of a new kind of scientific expert qualified to read the criminal body and diagnose social dangers.[2] In fact, it might be more apt, as the title of this volume suggests, to speak of the co-production of criminals and scientists. Criminal anthropology's claims to the status of science were, on one hand, dependent on the presence of bodies that lent themselves to a discriminating quantification: In the laboratory, the prison, the university lecture hall, and the courtroom the anthropologist would be required to point with some measure of confidence to bodies that were marked off from the normal, or that announced their dangerousness. At the same time, the facticity of "the criminal body" was dependent on the authority of figures like Cesare Lombroso, who in publications and in testimony before juries had to struggle to contain the variability of real bodies' surfaces, to overcome criminals' multiple forms of resistance to scrutiny, and to disqualify competing claims

---

1 See, for a range of examples, Michel Foucault, "About the Concept of the 'Dangerous Individual' in 19th-Century Legal Psychiatry," *International Journal of Law and Psychiatry* 1 (1978):1–18; Marie-Christine Leps, *Apprehending the Criminal: The Production of Deviance in Nineteenth-Century Discourse* (Durham, N.C., 1992); Laurent Mucchielli, ed., *Histoire de la criminologie française* (Paris, 1994); Pasquale Pasquino, "Criminology: The Birth of a Special *Savoir*," *Ideology and Consciousness* 7 (1980):17–32; Allan Sekula, "The Body and the Archive," *October* 39 (1986):3–64; Renzo Villa, *Il deviante e I suoi segni: Lombroso e la nascita dell'antropologia criminale* (Milan, 1985).
2 This chapter is part of a larger project of mine to trace, following a variety of genealogical threads, the history of our turning to the body as a locus and kind of evidence, and to make visible the cultural specificity of the very idea that bodies can testify (or be made to testify) to legal and scientific truths.

of knowledge. And this scientific authority, I suggest, had much to do with the *practical* abilities of physicians and others to regularize tools and measurements, to stabilize interpretations, and to deploy the rhetoric of the "expert."

If we ask what it could have meant to be a criminal scientist toward the end of the nineteenth century, we are obliged first to recognize the relative absence of institutional markers of such a status. The "Italian school" was, for a time, little more than an informal network of physicians, biological scientists, and jurists dispersed throughout Italy, committed to carving out a new epistemological space. Although many of its members taught at universities (in departments of pathology, physiology, law, and the like) there was no chair in criminal anthropology until 1905 (and this only an *ad personam* appointment to honor Lombroso at Turin).[3] Much of the making of the new science of criminals went on elsewhere: in laboratories, museums, journals, prisons, asylums, and, later, at international conferences.[4] Indeed, rather than speak of the *production* of criminologists in the nineteenth century, we might instead speak of a self-fashioning or, as Patrizia Guarnieri has suggested, of the cultivation of an "image."[5]

The identity of the new criminology was, at any moment, tied to the relative fluidity or fixity of disciplinary boundaries, to changes in the structure of the university, and to the evolving role of the physician in Italian culture.[6] Here I wish to explore the roles played by tools, techniques, manuals, and other elements of *practice* in the elaboration and consolidation of a criminological science.[7] In so doing, I call attention to the performative qualities of the new anthropology – to the acts of manipulating instruments, tabulating measurements, and testifying about numbers that aimed at elevating the work of criminologists above the level of popular wisdom and at the same time sought to create a new kind of scientific "common sense."

---

3 Sandra Puccini and Massimo Squillacciotti, "Principali tappe dello sviluppo statutario delle discipline etno-antropologiche italiane (Appendice B.)," in *Studi antropologici italiani e rapporti di classe, dal positivismo al dibattito attuale* (Milan, 1980), 202–12.

4 On criminological museums as sites of knowledge production, see Giorgio Colombo, *La scienza infelice: Il museo di antropologia criminale di Cesare Lombroso* (Turin, 1975). For a discussion of the importance of conferences, see the chapter by Martine Kaluszynski in this volume.

5 Patrizia Guarnieri, "Misurare le diversità," in Giulio Barsanti et al., eds., *Misura d'uomo: Strumenti, teorie e pratiche dell'antropometria e della psicologia sperimentale tra '800 e '900* (Florence, 1986), 126.

6 For a discussion of the growing authority of medicine and physicians in nineteenth-century Italian culture, see Guido Panseri, "Il medico: Note su un intellettuale scientifico italiano nell'Ottocento," in Ruggero Romano and Corrado Vivanti, eds., *Storia d'Italia: Annali*, 9 vols. (Turin, 1978–86), 4:1133–55.

7 For insightful discussions of the history of anthropometrical instruments and techniques, see Barsanti et al., eds., *Misura d'uomo*, and especially the essays by Pogliano and Guarnieri.

What I have in mind is to attend to the varied and messy kinds of work (manual, theoretical, interpretive, rhetorical) that were required to go from the manufacture, say, of a Zwaardesmaker double olfactometer in Geneva to its manipulation in a cramped prison cell in Turin, to the transcription of olfactory thresholds in a preprinted form, to testimony on the witness stand about the sensory atavism of a criminal defendant – testimony meant both to speak to the particular circumstances of the defendant and to affirm the competence of the scientific criminologist, and him alone, to recognize social dangers.

In these pages I do not, however, undertake such a detailed project. Rather, this chapter isolates, without any pretense that they are decisive, two moments in the development of Lombroso's criminological science: the publication in 1867 of a report on experiments in electrical algometry and the publication in 1905 of *La perizia psichiatrico-legale*, a manual intended to guide and prepare the expert witness for the courtroom.[8] Much, of course, happens in the intervening period (to Lombroso, to the Italian school, and to criminology internationally), and the contrasts between the two publications are many (not least, their styles and rhetorical devices). I focus on the differences between a criminological science that, in 1867, was being fitfully elaborated in relation to creative deployments of novel instruments and a science that, in 1905, was in search of consolidation – here, instruments and their manipulations were made (or at least expected) to recede into the background. And finally I suggest that the continuities and fractures (temporal and cultural) in the *discourses* of criminology might productively be examined in relation to the fate of tools, techniques, and practices.

SCIENCE AND COMMON WISDOM

As many have noted, the founding of an "Italian" or "positive" school of criminology was marked, at least in its creation mythology, by its disavowal of the "classical school" and by the displacement of a discourse of "reason-ableness" by a discourse of dangerousness.[9] However, the emergent scientific discourse was at the same time engaged in an effort to define its relationship to other existing understandings of the body.[10] If attention to criminals and

---

8 Cesare Lombroso, *La perizia psichiatrico-legale coi metodi per eseguirla e la casuistica penale classificata antropologicamente* (Turin, 1905).

9 For a sense of these displacements and their limits, compare the essays in Parts 1 and 2 of this volume. Also see Pasquino, "Criminology."

10 Compare Guarnieri's discussion of asylum doctors' efforts to distance themselves from popular and previous medical understandings of madness. "Misurare le diversità," 136.

their bodies was the response to a "classical" or "metaphysical" focus on criminal acts and the problem of will, criminal anthropology also felt the need to mark its distance, particularly through practices of quantification, from alternative knowledges of embodied dangerousness. Ironically, criminologists (and especially Lombroso) often relied precisely on these knowledges to buttress and make intelligible their own claims. Thus, Lombroso at times drew on the discourses of physiognomy and phrenology, which had purported to find signs of interior intellectual and moral states on the body's surfaces, particularly at the level of the head and face.[11] And although he insisted on the modernity of criminal anthropology, Lombroso also was not above calling on "the ancients," particularly Homer and Avicenna, to say there was nothing new about his criminological claims.[12]

More broadly, knowledge of deviant bodies was not presumed to be exclusive to anthropologists. Artists, writers, the "lower classes," and even children, according to Lombroso, were aware of and could reproduce in paintings and poems the contours of criminal physiognomy,[13] and the various editions of *L'uomo delinquente* are filled with examples of folk wisdom. Folk taxonomies were, in Lombroso's view, rooted in "natural instincts": Honest men and (especially) women were innately repulsed by the ugliness of the criminal type, and the conclusions of "instinctive observers" found expression in proverbs, folk songs, and jokes. Lay observational practices could, in fact, be put to the test: Lombroso's daughter recounts that her father "once placed before forty children twenty portraits of thieves and twenty representing great men, and 80 percent recognized in the first the portraits of bad and deceitful people."[14] Even Lombroso's mother, we are told, knew a potential murderer when she saw one.[15]

But if these folk and nonscientific typologies (which were themselves made objects of anthropological analysis) served to reinforce the findings of the criminologists, they might also have risked calling into question the privileged position of the anthropological observers, or (as some critics

---

11 See Sekula, "The Body and the Archive," 11–12; Barbara Maria Stafford, *Body Criticism: Imaging the Unseen in Enlightenment Art and Medicine* (Cambridge, 1991), 84–129. Whereas the focus on the head was in some ways "commonsensical" and continuous with popular practices of reading faces, Sekula suggests it also worked to "legitimate on organic grounds the dominion of intellectual over manual labor" (12). The anthropology of criminal women also privileged the genitals as loci of deviance.

12 Cesare Lombroso et al., *Polemica in difesa della scuola criminale positiva* (Bologna, 1886), 42.

13 Lombroso et al., *Polemica in difesa*, 11; Gina Lombroso-Ferrero, *Criminal Man, According to the Classification of Cesare Lombroso* (Montclair, N.J., 1972 [1911]), 48–51.

14 Lombroso-Ferrero, *Criminal Man*, 50.

15 Cesare Lombroso, *L'uomo delinquente, in rapporto all'antropologia, alla giurisprudenza ed alle discipline carcerarie*, 5th ed., 3 vols. (Turin, 1896), 1:310.

charged) the *scientific* status of their theories.[16] However, for Lombroso and his colleagues the anthropologist was distinguished from the artist, from the observant folk, and from the child by his specialized techniques for measuring and reading the body: by a corporeal literacy that made possible both an exegesis and a diagnosis.[17] Similarly, Lombroso rejected what he termed the "qualitative and deterministic" readings of the phrenologists[18] in favor of physiological experiment and *anthropometry*: the precise measurement of the dimensions and relations of parts of the body, a practice that had been joined to social statistics by Adolphe Quetelet.[19]

It is not enough, however, to say that it was quantifying *readings* that distinguished criminal anthropology from alternative and popular knowledges. (Of course, some criminological readings remained avowedly qualitative – even aesthetic.) In a sense, what differentiated the scientist from the popular reader of faces was the ability to enter prisons, asylums, schools, and orphanages to perform tests; the authority to enlist "volunteers" from the populations of "normal" women and men; the access to instruments that were expensive and often difficult to manipulate; and the means to disseminate results (journals, conferences, university lecture halls, and, of course, the witness stand). On the one hand, we need to keep in view the power relations that enabled physicians and biological scientists to move freely in nonpublic spaces, to compel subjects to remove their clothes, to probe and manipulate the body, and even to inflict pain. On the other hand, I argue, we need to explore further the importance of tools and technical practice in the formation of a scientific identity for criminal anthropology.

Anthropometry and physiological experiments were, in obvious ways, dependent on the availability of both docile subjects and an appropriate selection of reliable instruments. Lombroso, in *La perizia*, suggests that a well-appointed laboratory would include an Anfosso tachianthropometer (for measuring anatomical proportions), Broca's auricular goniometer (facial angles), Sieweking's esthesiometer (sensitivity to touch), an Eulenberg baristesiometer (pressure discrimination), a Nothnagel thermesthesiometer (thermal sensitivity), a Zwaardesmaker olfactometer (olfactory sensitivity), a Regnier-Mathieu dynamometer (muscular force), a Mosso ergograph (fatigue), and a modified campimeter (visual field), as well as a more

16 Lombroso et al., *Polemica in difesa*, 11.
17 On the exegetical practices of anthropologists, see the chapter by Jane Caplan, this volume.
18 Lombroso et al., *Polemica in difesa*, 5.
19 On the links between anthropometry and photography, see Sekula, "The Body and the Archive," 19–23; on anthropometry's relation to racist evolutionary thought, see Steven Jay Gould, *The Mismeasure of Man* (New York, 1981), 73–122.

mundane selection of compasses, measuring tapes, eye charts, magnets, and odoriferous substances.[20] We might well ask how this bewildering array of instruments came to be found in medical laboratories, a question that might lead us to the conditions of the instruments' design, manufacture, and international circulation. But the selection of instruments (why these and not others?) also tells us something about which measurements could and could not count as significant at particular moments in the history of criminology and about how the body was imagined and mapped *through* tools. In a sense, each instrument produced the body anew, giving rise to an index, a threshold, or a capacity that could not have mattered previously.[21] The coherence and authority of criminology would come to depend on scientists' ability to contain a potentially limitless proliferation of measurements and to deploy those instruments that promised to demonstrate systematic and significant differences between pathological and normal bodies.

TOOLS AND THE PRODUCTION OF DIFFERENCE: ALGOMETRY

In 1867 Lombroso invited four male colleagues, whom he judged to be "free of cutaneous and nervous disease,"[22] to his laboratory in Pavia to conduct an unusual experiment. Lombroso proposed that the men apply the electrodes of a Ruhmkorff induction coil, connected to a medium Bunsen battery, to various parts of each others' bodies, gradually increasing the current until each man indicated that he felt pain. The men held the electrodes, which had been fitted with sponges dipped in a saline solution, to their gums, nipples, tongues, lips, eyelids, the soles of the feet, and the glans of the penis – thirty-nine separate locations in all. Lombroso reports that the pains he and his associates sustained were of varied qualities. On the index finger, the pain was experienced as a "series of hot pricks"; on the palm of the hand as a "cramping and tearing"; on the back as a "scalding pain"; on the tip of the elbow as a "knife blade that passes through the joint"; on the forehead as "a kind of burning that pierces superficially and branches out, vinelike, to the roots of the hair"; on the glans of the penis as "though a red-hot

---

20 Lombroso, *La perizia*, 490–544. Also see Francis Galton, "On the Anthropometric Laboratory at the Late International Health Exhibition," *The Journal of the Anthropological Institute of Great Britain and Ireland* 14 (1885):205–21.

21 On the relations between the refinement of instrumentation, the construction of models, and the evolution of conceptual frameworks, see Timothy Lenoir, "Models and Instruments in the Development of Electrophysiology, 1845–1912," *Historical Studies in the Physical and Biological Sciences* 17 (1986):1–54.

22 Lombroso identifies Camillo Golgi and two young friends named Bettoni and Pisa. "Algometria elettrica nell'uomo sano ed alienato," *Annali universali di medicina* (1867):104.

wire were passed through it."[23] But although these qualitative differences evidently made an impression, it was *quantitative* differences that would hold the researchers' attention.

The presence of the induction coil in Lombroso's medical office points us toward both a nineteenth-century fascination with electricity and its potential medical uses (Gina Lombroso-Ferrero reported that her father had been using the device to provide electrotherapy to his patients),[24] and toward a competitive international traffic in scientific instruments. Heinrich Daniel Ruhmkorff, an instrument maker in France, had begun producing his more efficient version of the induction coil (a modification of earlier coils developed by Masson and Breguet, Neef, Wagner, and others)[25] in 1851; his coils were of such a level of refinement and manufactured on such a large scale that Ruhmkorff's name was for a time applied to induction coils generally.[26] In later research, however, Lombroso (and many of his contemporaries) would rely on an inductorium developed by the German physiologist Emil DuBois-Reymond, which added a separate current interrupter to the circuit.[27] And although earlier studies of sensitivity to electricity had been performed by the German physiologist Ernest Von Leyden, Lombroso would later give his own name to the algometrical apparatus he had assembled in Pavia.[28]

What all of these instruments had in common, and what enabled the move from therapeutic (and other) uses to quantitative physiological research, was the ability to administer electrical shocks that were *graduated*: By moving the inducing and induced coils toward or away from each other, operators could regulate with some consistency the shock delivered, even though no instrument was yet available to measure its voltage. Thus, in his experiments on pain Lombroso could propose to measure "thresholds of sensitivity" as a function of the distance between the inducing and induced coils when pain

---

23 Ibid., 102.
24 Gina Lombroso-Ferrero, *Cesare Lombroso: Storia della vita e delle opere, narrata dalla figlia* (Turin, 1915), 102. On the history of electrotherapeutics, see Leslie A. Geddes, "A Short History of the Electrical Stimulation of Excitable Tissue Including Electrotherapeutic Applications," Supplement to *The Physiologist* 27(1)(1984): S1–S47; George Beard and Alphonso Rockwell, *On the Medical and Surgical Uses of Electricity*, 8th ed. (New York, 1891).
25 Frederick Collins, *The Design and Construction of Induction Coils* (New York, 1909), 1–12.
26 Herbert W. Meyer, *A History of Electricity and Magnetism* (Norwalk, Conn., 1972), 180.
27 Geddes, "A Short History," S18.
28 See Cesare Lombroso, "Algometria ed estesiometria elettrica: rettificazione di priorità," *Annali universali di medicina* (May–June 1867):654–6. For a discussion of the further development of the electric algometer, see Luigi Roncoroni and Giovanni Albertotti, "Le sensibilità elettrica generale e dolorifica esaminate col Faradireometro in pazzi e normali," *Archivio di psichiatria, scienze penali ed antropologia criminale* (hereafter: *Archivio*) 14 (1893):23–9.

was first reported. He and his colleagues recorded the threshold distance for each application and collected the results in a table.

Lombroso observed that parts of the body varied consistently in their sensitivity to pain. In all the men the gums, glans, tip of the tongue, lips, and nipples proved the most sensitive to pain; the soles of the feet and the big toe the least sensitive. In general, the top and front of the body proved more sensitive than the bottom and back. Lombroso explained these differences largely in terms of variations in the thickness of the epidermis (which accounted, in his view, for the sensitivity of the penis and the tongue) and the quantity and "nobility" of the nerves (which accounted for the sensitivity of the face).[29] Second, and perhaps more important, the individuals varied consistently in their *overall* sensitivity and in relation to their intellect – the most intelligent member of the group, we are told, also proved the most sensitive to pain.

But the significance of the correlation between intellect and sensitivity only became apparent when Lombroso repeated his experiments on a different set of subjects: 23 volunteers (11 women and 12 men) whom he identified as mentally and physically "healthy" and 63 institutionalized persons (40 women and 23 men) whom he identified as "mentally ill" [*alienati*].[30] Here, it was not only individuals who revealed a patterned variability, but groups. Men, it appeared, were systematically less sensitive than women – a result, Lombroso speculated, of men's thicker skin. But after skin thickness, the most important cause of differences appeared to Lombroso to be the "level [*grado*] of intelligence," or rather the state of mental health: The mentally ill were systematically and markedly less sensitive than healthy subjects. Lombroso found that the mad "seemed almost not to feel currents that were very painful for healthy men."[31] What is more, they could not properly identify the *site* of pain: One subject, for example, moaned that his tooth hurt while in fact his hand was being shocked. In the case of the

29 Lombroso, "Algometria elettrica," 106.
30 Neither the "recruitment" of subjects nor the experimental protocol is discussed in Lombroso's article. Another study reports experiments on forty girls from a Bologna orphanage, sixty prostitutes examined in a "dermo-syphilitic" clinic, and fifteen women "of good standing" who consented to be examined "after much difficulty." Measurements of sensitivity among the orphan girls were limited to the hands, forehead, tongue, and cheek, whereas prostitutes were tested in eleven places. "Naturally," we are told, "all of the exams performed on prostitutes could not be extended to all the normal women." Still, twelve of fourteen normal women apparently agreed to have shocks applied to their clitorises. See Raffaele Gurrieri and Ettore Fornasari, *I sensi e le anomalie somatiche nella donna normale e nella prostituta* (Turin, 1893), 5–6. In addition, prostitutes were subjected to a thorough physical exam and asked about their medical and sexual history, whereas normal women had only their age and visible "degenerate characteristics" recorded (18–24).
31 Lombroso, "Algometria elettrica," 103.

mad, insensitivity (or "obtuseness," as Lombroso called it) was taken to be a sign of an underlying organic defect. This suggested not only the possibility of mapping, through precise measurements of electrical currents, madness in relation to sanity, but also of distinguishing experimentally among different kinds of mental illness (maniacs, monomaniacs, apathetic melancholiacs, erethismic melancholiacs, the demented, and pellagroids).[32]

What Lombroso's experiments seemed to promise, at least to his contemporaries, was not only a refined understanding of the nature and manifestations of organic anomalies but also a means of a more general *diagnosis*: of making visible a wide variety of conditions that threatened to remain hidden but that might pose social dangers. Scientists in Europe and the United States would soon test the sensitivity of epileptics, deaf-mutes, underachieving schoolchildren, and a whole range of suspected and convicted criminals.[33] In the case of criminals, algometry, as it came to be called, would be made a routine part of the examinations performed by penologists and criminologists retained as expert witnesses in courts of law.[34] Pain was not enlisted to extract the truth about illegal *acts*, as had been the case with torture, but rather to produce evidence of the biological nature of individuals and groups, and about the dangers that accompanied a "failure to evolve."

Of course, measurements of pain sensitivity constituted simply one among many metrical practices at the disposal of criminal anthropologists. To the extent that pain thresholds were stable, quantifiable, and served to differentiate, they could function interchangeably with the cephalic index, the angle of a jaw, or the bizygomatic diameter of the face. More often than not, claims anthropologists made about the dangerousness of particular individuals involved *multiple* signs of the body's degeneration or atavism. But it is worth noting the boldness of the claim that *pain*, which many nineteenth-century scholars had identified as private, subjective, and highly variable – in sum, beyond the reach of quantification – could be made both

---

32 The demented, pellagroids, and apathetic melancholiacs presented diminished sensitivity, whereas erethismic melancholiacs presented increased sensitivity. Inexplicably, many mentally ill persons seemed to be more sensitive on the forehead than were normal persons. Ibid., 120.

33 See, for example, Edward James Swift, "Sensibility to Pain," *The American Journal of Psychology* 11(1899–1900):312–17; Gurrieri and Fornasari, *I sensi e le anomalie somatiche*; Salvatore Ottolenghi, *La sensibilità dei sordomuti* (Rome, 1895); Roncoroni and Albertotti, "Le sensibilità elettrica."

34 See, for example, Lombroso, *La perizia psichiatrico-legale*; Cesare Lombroso, *Lezioni di medicina legale*, 2d ed. (Turin, 1900); Salvatore Ottolenghi, *Polizia scientifica: Identificazione fisica e psichica; investigazioni giudiziarie* (Rome, 1907). On the rise of legal medicine in Europe and the United States, see Michael Clark and Catherine Crawford, eds., *Legal Medicine in History* (Cambridge, 1994). For Italy in particular, see Patrizia Guarnieri, *A Case of Child Murder: Law and Science in Nineteenth-Century Tuscany*, trans. Claudia Miéville (London, 1993) and Angelo Zuccarelli, "L'evoluzione odierna della medicina legale e l'antropologia criminale," *Psichiatria: Gazzetta Trimestrale* 5(1887):149–64.

objective and public. Indeed, it was the link that pain established *between* the body's surface and interior states (including the ability to feel "moral" anguish) that made algometers and algometry of particular interest to criminologists.

The relations of pain sensitivity to pain perception and to endurance, which so preoccupied many late-nineteenth-century physiologists, were never posed by Lombroso in a systematic way. Rather, he took for granted that painful sensations were unambiguously felt and would be faithfully reported. In this respect, pain experiments seemed to him to avoid precisely the problem of "subjectivity" that had plagued tests of "general sensitivity." Lombroso criticized Leyden's work in electrical esthesiometry and Weber's work on tactile sensitivity[35] because subjects might not always be "attentive" to their sensations; the problem of paying attention was greatest, he observed, in "common people."[36] By contrast, in experiments involving painful shocks, Lombroso assured his readers, there was no question of subjects' failing to pay attention. The only problem he acknowledged was with the mentally ill, who could not always be relied upon to describe the intensity or the *site* of their pain. But in this case, argued Lombroso, the experimenter could rely on grimaces and involuntary muscle contractions.[37]

Other experimenters offered more nuanced accounts. Salvatore Ottolenghi observed that the difficulties involved in measuring pain grew out of variations in the subject's attitude toward the experiment, his or her readiness to acknowledge pain when felt, the "sincerity of subjective phenomena," the difference between sensitivity and excitability, variations in resistance, and the possibility of suggestion or autosuggestion.[38] Two other researchers, surprised to find that "cultured" men seemed in one experiment to be less sensitive to pain than male hospital orderlies, reasoned that the first group better understood the importance of the examination and knew to wait until the pain reached levels that were truly unbearable.[39]

Some of Lombroso's contemporaries raised more troubling questions about the stability of pain thresholds, about the physiological effects of pain of short duration, and about the suitability of electrical algometers for

---

35 See Ernst Heinrich Weber, *De Tactu* (1834), reprinted in *The Sense of Touch*, trans. Helen E. Ross (New York, 1978).

36 Lombroso, "Algometria ed estesiometria elettrica," 655.

37 Lombroso, "Algometria elettrica," 104.   38 Ottolenghi, *La sensibilità dei sordomuti*, 16.

39 Roncoroni and Albertotti, "Le sensibilità elettriche," 428. Richard Behan found susceptibility to pain depended chiefly on the build of individuals ("those of a thin and neurotic build suffer much more severely than do the heavier and more robust") and on the "degree of mentality": "the higher the development and the more vivid the imagination, the greater is the susceptibility." *Pain: Its Origin, Conduction, Perception, and Diagnostic Significance* (New York, 1916), 115.

administering pain.[40] Lombroso argued that nothing was better suited to the measurement of sensitivity than electricity because nothing was less harmful.[41] Paolo Mantegazza, however, found that electrical currents produced "disagreeable sensations" that were different from the majority of pains and were differently tolerated by different individuals. Some, Mantegazza observed, even found these sensations to be pleasurable.[42] In the end, the most serious charge Mantegazza leveled was that Lombroso had measured nothing and had merely observed the stimulant action of electricity on the muscles. (Mantegazza, for his part, preferred to administer traumatic pain by crushing the paws of animals, using sharp probes, or applying boiling water and ice cubes to the skin. None of these methods allowed for gradations, but Mantegazza's interests were in the physiological effects of traumatic experiences.)

Lombroso responded that although admittedly there was no evident correlation between sensitivity to electrical shocks and sensitivity to touch, there *were* more constant relations between sensitivity to electrical pain and sensitivity to pain generally, a correlation he confirmed by pricking and pinching his subjects and by applying cylinders of ice to their bodies. Moreover, he noted, the loci identified as most sensitive to electrical shock were precisely those known to the ancients and to more recent practitioners of torture, and included the sites where pain is most strongly felt during illness (for example, toothaches and migraines).[43]

PAIN AND CIVILIZATION

For all its purported utility in making distinctions, pain sensitivity was, unlike for instance "facial diameter," much more than indexical. In making sense of pain thresholds Lombroso and his contemporaries drew on (and purported to confirm) the widespread notion that sensitivity – not just to pain but also

40 These questions were among those raised in a public feud between Lombroso and Paolo Mantegazza, by 1867 professor of pathological physiology at Pavia and author of *Fisiologia del dolore* (Florence, 1880). The debate, which by all accounts destroyed a professional and personal relationship, was ostensibly centered around the question of whether pain increased the pulse (as Lombroso had argued) or decreased it (as Mantegazza had earlier claimed on the basis of experiments with animals and humans). But also at issue were disciplinary boundaries (criminology and physiology), techniques for administering and measuring pain, and the credit for coining the term "algometry." For a discussion of the feud, see Luigi Bulferetti, *Cesare Lombroso* (Turin, 1975), 160; Lombroso-Ferrero, *Cesare Lombroso*, 101–3; Villa, *Il deviante e i suoi segni*, 124–5.

41 For a survey of algometrical methods, see Franz Geotzl, Daniel Burrill, and Andrew Ivy, "A Critical Analysis of Algesimetric Methods with Suggestions for a Useful Procedure," *Quarterly Bulletin of Northwestern University Medical School* 17(4)(1943):280–91.

42 Mantegazza, *Fisiologia del dolore*, new edition (Florence, 1930), 323–4.

43 Lombroso, "Algometria elettrica," 113–14.

to pleasure of varied kinds – was linked to levels of evolutionary progress, to race, and to "civilization." The outlines of this hierarchy of suffering, what Martin Pernick has labeled a "great chain of feeling,"[44] were fairly consistent across disciplinary and national boundaries. The story told by Fülöp-Miller in his volume *Triumph over Pain* is typical: Plants and lower animals are less sensitive than higher animals, children less sensitive than adults, "savages" less sensitive than "the civilized," Eastern Europeans less sensitive than Western Europeans.[45] Travelers' accounts that had affirmed the extraordinary sensory abilities of non-European peoples (and particularly the sense of smell) now came under attack.[46]

The link between civilization and sensitivity could be construed in a number of ways: that civilization made humans soft, vulnerable, and weak, or that it better allowed them to make aesthetic judgments. But underlying these different readings was the assumption that savages felt no pain (and, for that matter, little pleasure). This notion had become so much a part of common scientific wisdom by the time Lombroso conducted his experiments in 1867 that he could invoke it to dismiss the charges of his principal critics:

[Mantegazza] must be well aware that the Dakota [and] the Otomac exhibit a pain sensitivity so obtuse as to sing war hymns while their limbs roast in a slow fire, that the Tahitian and the Negro feel pain so little as to invent for ornaments cuts made in the most sensitive regions of the body. The savage woman of Australia has gone so far as to contradict the most sacred laws of the Bible when it comes to the pains of childbirth, insomuch as in some tribes it is the husband who is confined while the wife who has given birth is obliged to work. And do we not see, we doctors, among our masses the peasant who tolerates for several days in a row, without even noticing, pains due to pleurisy and wounds that for men of more refined intelligence would be intolerable?[47]

In fact, Mantegazza would make similar claims in his own work on pain.[48]

---

44 Martin Pernick, *A Calculus of Suffering: Pain, Professionalism and Anaesthesia in Nineteenth-Century America* (New York, 1985), 157.

45 René Fülöp-Miller, *Triumph Over Pain*, trans. Eden and Cedar Paul (New York, 1938), 397.

46 Francis Galton, *Inquiries into Human Faculty and Its Development* (London, 1883), 32.

47 Lombroso, "Sull'algometria elettrica," *Rendiconti (Reale istituto lombardo di scienze e lettere)* 1:8 (1868):395.

48 "Sensitivity is certainly less among the inferior races, both because their organization is simpler and because sensation is propagated in a more restricted field of sympathies." Mantegazza, *Fisiologia del dolore*, 313. For him, "ethnic differences in sensitivity" were due not only to biology but also to "the habit of suffering," to the use of narcotics, and to the presence or absence of stimulants (caffeine). He cites as evidence his own experiences as a surgeon in the Americas, and ethnographic and anecdotal accounts of childhood games, rites of passage, and expressions of grief.

Not content to rely on folk wisdom or on a loosely organized ethnographic record, anthropologists would also proceed to measure variations in pain sensitivity among males and females of different age groups and social classes; the results – that children are less sensitive than mature men and the poor less sensitive than the rich – appeared to give new scientific support to received wisdom.[49] Lombroso also was able to perform tests of the sensitivity of a group of Dinka visiting Europe from central Africa. (Virchow had also made them subjects of physiological experiments.) Algometrical experiments, Lombroso reported, revealed the Dinkas' "great obtuseness," a finding that appeared confirmed by the tribe's habits of scarification and breaking off of teeth.[50] And lest we assume these experiments were undertaken only at the margins of the human sciences, it is worth noting that studies of sensitivity (as well as other sensory capacities) would later be made parts of two important scientific expeditions: the Cambridge Anthropological Expedition to Torres Straits, headed by Alfred C. Haddon,[51] and the expedition to Cape Horn undertaken by the French Academy of Sciences.[52]

By the end of the century the insensitivity of criminals had also become part of common wisdom. For example, American criminologist Arthur MacDonald wrote in 1893 that "It is generally admitted that sensibility is less among criminals."[53] In Britain, Havelock Ellis noted that "the physical insensibility of the criminal has indeed been observed by everyone who is

49 Salvatore Ottolenghi, "La sensibilità e l'età," *Archivio* 16 (1895):540–51 and "La sensibilità e la condizione sociale," *Archivio* 19 (1898):101–4. Ottolenghi found that some 25 percent of the lower classes possessed an upper-class sensitivity, whereas 28 percent of the upper classes had the diminished sensitivity of the poor, suggesting anthropological and physiological inequalities were less "fatalistic" than had been supposed (103).

50 Cesare Lombroso and Mario Carrara, "Contributo all'antropologia dei Dinka," *Archivio* 17 (1896):349–63.

51 See William McDougall, "Cutaneous Sensitivity," *Reports of the Cambridge Expedition to the Torres Straits, vol. II: Physiology and Psychology* (Cambridge, 1901), 189–95. "In view of the oft-repeated statement that savages are less sensitive to pain than white men," wrote McDougall, "it seemed a matter of some interest to obtain a measure of the threshold of sensibility to pain" (194). McDougall's experiments, under the supervision of William H. R. Rivers, found Murray Islander men had a sense of touch "twice as delicate" as English men (chiefly "inmates" of the Cheadle Convalescent Hospital) and a sensitivity to pain "hardly half as great" (195). The Cambridge expedition also addressed visual acuity, color vision, hearing, smell, taste, "muscular sense," variations in blood pressure, and "reaction times." For a contemporary critique, see Edward B. Titchener, "On Ethnological Tests of Sensation and Perception with Special Reference to Tests of Color Vision and Tactile Discrimination Described in the Reports of the Cambridge Expedition to Torres Straits," *Proceedings of the American Philosophical Society* 55 (1916):204–36.

52 Paul Hyades and Joseph Deniker, eds., *Mission scientifique du Cap Horn, 1882–1883, vol. VII: Anthropologie, ethnographie* (Paris, 1891).

53 Arthur MacDonald, *Criminology* (New York, 1893), 70. For MacDonald, analgesia helped to explain the remarkable "hardiness" of criminals.

familiar with prisons. In this respect the instinctive criminal resembles the idiot to whom, as Galton remarks, pain is a 'welcome surprise.'"[54] For the Italian sociologist Raffaele Garofalo, the mere fact of widespread tattooing among prison populations offered itself as compelling evidence.[55] But Lombroso found anecdotal evidence from prisons unsatisfactory, not least because many who were confined in prisons were also mentally ill. Moreover, he wrote, "the subject of the pain sensitivity of criminals is too important and delicate for [him] to be content with only approximate data, not verified through direct experiment."[56] Only such experiments, he argued, could offer the further precision that sensibility is highest in the case of con artists and lowest for those who committed assaults and robberies, or that sensitivity was greater on the left side of the body than on the right. (The prevalence of left-handedness [*mancinismo*] was taken to be a further sign of the atavistic nature of criminality.)[57] Other experimenters found that criminals not only were less sensitive to pain but also had diminished "general" and tactile sensibility, and obtuse senses of hearing, taste, and smell.[58] Criminals were, however, more sensitive than normal people to the weather ("meteoric sensibility"), to pressure, and to the effects of magnets, and possessed generally acute eyesight. ("In this [respect], too," it was argued, "the criminal resembles the savage.")[59]

Most consequential, however, was the link criminologists worked to establish between physical sensitivity and moral sensitivity. As Ellis put it, criminals suffered from "psychical analgesia."[60] Psychologist G. B. Verga argued that moral sensitivity was nothing but a "perfection of peripheral

---

54 Havelock Ellis, *The Criminal*, 5th ed. (Montclair, N.J., 1973 [1914]), 123.

55 Raffaele Garofalo, *Criminology*, trans. Robert Millar (Montclair, N.J., 1968 [1914]), 92. Ellis noted that tattooing did not spare "parts so sensitive as the sexual organs, which are rarely touched even in extensive tattooing among barbarous races." *The Criminal*, 123.

56 Cesare Lombroso, *L'uomo delinquente*, 4th ed., 3 vols. (Turin, 1889), 1:323.

57 Cesare Lombroso, "Il mancinismo sensorio ed il tatto nei delinquenti e nei pazzi," *Archivio* 4 (1883):441–7. (The experiments cited had been performed by Antonio Marro.) Cf. Giuseppe Amadei and Silvio Tonnini, "La sensibilità laterale nei pazzi," *Archivio* 4 (1883):511–12; Cesare Lombroso, "Sul mancinismo e destrismo tattile nei sani, nei pazzi, nei ciechi e nei sordomuti," *Archivio* 5 (1884):187–97.

58 See, for some examples, Salvatore Ottolenghi, "L'olfatto nei criminali," *Archivio* 9 (1888):495–9; "L'occhio del delinquente," *Archivio* 7 (1886); "Il gusto nei criminali in rapporto coi normali," *Archivio* 10 (1889):332–8; Giuseppe Gradenigo, "L'udito nei delinquenti," *Archivio* 10 (1889):325–31.

59 Lombroso-Ferrero, *Criminal Man*, 25–6, 245–51. Although some evaluations relied on devices specifically developed for the task (Lombroso's algometer, Weber's esthesiometer, Nothnagel's thermesthesiometer, Landolt's campimeter, and Ottolenghi's graduated osmometer), others were decidedly low-tech. To evaluate hearing, Lombroso recommended "speaking in a low voice at a certain distance from the patient, or . . . holding an ordinary watch a little way from his ear" (251).

60 Ellis, *The Criminal*, 140.

sensitivity, which conducts external impressions to the interior of the brain."[61] The incapacity to feel pain therefore not only was a sign of an underlying social danger, but was itself a social danger. As Garofalo commented, "This physical insensibility, moreover, prevents any vivid representation in their minds of the suffering which they cause to others, since they themselves either would not feel such suffering or would feel it but little."[62] More troubling still, the Hungarian-born criminologist Moriz Benedikt cited examples of criminals who regarded themselves as privileged persons: They "hold the delicate and sensitive in contempt" and "take pleasure in tormenting others whom they regard as inferior creatures."[63]

If moral insensitivity could be linked to an organic defect, it was only logical that it, too, could be investigated in the laboratory. Thus, for example, studies of the blushing reflex purported to show the criminal body's inability to react appropriately to "moral stimuli" (a severe reprimand, an awkward question about a bodily function, the fixed and reproachful stare of the anthropologist). This confirmed what had been known "by the people and for centuries": An absence of blushing was a "sign of a dishonest and savage life."[64] Another set of experiments deployed newly invented pletismographs and sphigmographs to measure the changes in blood flow and pressure produced by both physical and psychic pains and pleasures: A diminished "vascular reaction" was a sign of insensitivity.[65]

REWRITING WOMEN'S SENSITIVITY

If Lombroso's studies relied upon and worked to reinforce common wisdom about pain and civilization, they would also come to challenge popular beliefs, particularly in the case of women.[66] Recall that in Lombroso's 1867

---

61 Cited in Lombroso, *L'uomo delinquente*, 4th ed., 1:591–2.
62 Garofalo, *Criminology*, 115. "It must be admitted," Garofalo reassured his readers, "that this lack of vulnerability, very frequent in other races, as, for example, the Chinese, is seldom found among Europeans, and is especially rare in the city population, where even the lower social strata have acquired a certain degree of refinement."
63 Ibid.
64 Lombroso, *L'uomo delinquente*, 4th ed., 1:348. Cf. Bartolomeo Bergesio, "Sull'arrossimento nelle pazze," *Archivio* 5 (1884):112–13; Giuseppe Amadei and S. Tonnini, "Dell'arrossimento nei pazzi," *Archivio* 5 (1884):113–14.
65 Cesare Lombroso and Alberto Cougnet, "Sfigmografia di delinquenti ed alienati," *Archivio* 2 (1881):234–5. See also Angelo Mosso, *La paura* (Milan, 1884), which discusses the development of the pletismograph. For Mosso, the extreme "*irrequietezza*" of the blood vessels of the hand meant that "every most minor emotion, during waking or sleeping, changed in surprising fashion [the hand's] volume" (p. 117).
66 For a detailed discussion of experiments designed to test the sensibility of women, see Mary Gibson, "On the Insensitivity of Women: Science and the Woman Question in Liberal Italy, 1890–1910,"

study he had found women to be more sensitive to pain than men, a result that was subsequently confirmed by a number of other studies. But this conclusion proved to be at odds with an evolutionary model that linked women with savages, criminals, and children as not fully developed, not yet civilized. Lombroso characterized woman as a "big child"[67] and as a "man arrested in his intellectual and physical development."[68] The signs of woman's failure to evolve or mature were varied, ranging from an underdeveloped moral sense to a predisposition to cruelty, to a "physiological incapacity" for truthfulness. That women habitually lied was confirmed by proverbs and rooted both in atavistic biology ("savages always lie") and in the social need to hide menstruation from men and sex from children.[69] Women's bodies were said, moreover, to be marked by traces of youth and the past: prehensile feet, left-handedness, dullness of the senses, and an inability to experience pleasure.[70]

By the 1890s Lombroso's algometrical experiments seemed to confirm that women also possessed a limited ability to sense pain. Lombroso and his collaborator Guglielmo Ferrero now dismissed the popular notion that women were more sensitive to pain: Their earlier experiments, it seemed, had not taken into account that women react more loudly to pain, a sign of their "greater irritability."[71] Similarly, when the researchers Luigi Roncoroni and Giovanni Albertotti found normal women to be generally less sensitive to touch than normal men but more sensitive to pain, they pointed to a possible source of error in measurements of pain sensitivity: "Woman, having a more developed sense of fear, complains of pain when it is not yet unbearable, whereas men can better be persuaded to resist until the pain becomes truly vivid."[72]

In addition to telling a story about the evolutionary status of women and men generally, and in the context of debates over the political rights and duties of the sexes,[73] algometrical studies were also used to differentiate

Journal of Women's History 2(2)(1990):11–41. See also David Horn, "This Norm Which Is Not One: Reading the Female Body in Lombroso's Anthropology," in Jennifer Terry and Jacqueline Urla, eds., *Deviant Bodies: Critical Perspectives on Difference in Science and Popular Culture* (Bloomington, Ind., 1995), 109–28.

67 Cesare Lombroso and Guglielmo Ferrero, *La donna delinquente, la prostituta e la donna normale*, 3rd ed. (Turin, 1915), 98.

68 Ibid., 4.   69 Ibid., 95–8.

70 Lombroso assembled a series of scientific and anecdotal sources that agreed on the "reduced sexual sensitivity" and passivity of women. Ibid., 43–8.

71 Ibid., 52.

72 Roncoroni and Albertotti, "Le sensibilità elettrica," 428.

73 Gibson, "On the Insensitivity of Women."

among women to make claims for the atavistic nature of female criminals, especially prostitutes, and to argue for the naturalness of maternity. Raffaele Gurrieri and Ettore Fornasari's study is typical: The researchers found that prostitutes were generally more obtuse than normal women[74] and that prostitutes who had never borne children showed particular insensitivity.[75] Lombroso's algometrical studies found the "greatest deadness" on the hands of peasant women and in the clitorises of prostitutes. Twenty-eight percent of prostitutes were found to be completely insensitive to pain, although sensitivity increased if the prostitutes had borne children.[76] These results could be taken to mean either that maternity restored a more proper level of sensitivity or that prostitutes with children represented a category of "occasional" criminals who were not in fact degenerate and atavistic.

The project of (re)writing women into the criminologists' story of pain, civilization, and social dangerousness has all the appearances of a salvage operation. And yet it was precisely the challenge algometrical experiments appeared to offer to common sense that was put forward by Lombroso and his colleagues as the mark of science – the very counterintuitiveness of the claim that women are less sensitive than men was imagined to stand as a vindication of the will to quantify. And it is important to note that space for recording pain sensitivity would be routinely provided in the forms used by prison administrators, asylum doctors, and criminological expert witnesses at the beginning of the twentieth century.[77]

PRACTICING CRIMINOLOGY

I turn briefly now to 1905 and the publication of *La perizia*. Although Lombroso would soon be honored by his colleagues for his life's accomplishments, this could hardly be called a triumphant year for the Italian School, which had weathered attacks from abroad and had become internally fractured. Nor had criminology succeeded at establishing its authority in the courtroom in the way that its practitioners might have hoped: As

---

74 An exception seemed to be that prostitutes tested more sensitive on the hands than normal women, but the authors explained that prostitutes were diffident, egoistical, and irritable, and because the hand was the first part of the body tested, they were likely to react too quickly and overestimate their sensitivity. Gurrieri and Fornasari, *I sensi e le anomalie somatiche*, 17.

75 Ibid., 6. The breasts of women who had nursed were found to be less sensitive than those of childless women (10).

76 Lombroso and Ferrero, *La donna delinquente*, 138–9.

77 Of course, as Guarnieri notes for psychiatric records, these were not always completed by admitting physicians.

Patrizia Guarnieri has shown, when expert scientific witnesses were pitted against one another, quantification alone could not be expected to settle matters, and criminological theories, for all their reliance on folk wisdom, had run up against the common sense of juries when they suggested criminals should not be held responsible for their crimes.[78]

La perizia was, in some sense, a response to this crisis in the authority of the Lombrosian program, which aimed at consolidation rather than further elaboration. There is none of the brashness and excitement that mark the tone of Lombroso's early scientific reports, nor does the text have the scope and pastiche qualities of the various editions of *L'uomo delinquente*. Rather, the text reflects in its organization and content a renewed tension between the scientific and the commonsensical. Designed for the educated layman, it sought at the same time to shore up the wall dividing science from popular cultural practices. It attempted this by constructing forensic expertise as a form of *practice* or *discipline* – with its own tools, procedures, conventions, and specialized vocabulary.

The first part of the volume consists of a series of summarized case studies provided by various criminologists and alienists, many of which conclude in a perfunctory but triumphant declaration: "a clear case of irresponsibility" or "a true cretin." These examples of "classic expert testimony" were marshaled both to "confirm with secure documents the theories advanced in *L'uomo delinquente*" and "to guide the hand of the forensic neophyte."[79] The second part, devoted to expert-witness methodology, was intended to "meet the needs of those who complain they cannot follow these [earlier] studies because they lack ... a familiarity with specialized techniques." Lombroso proposed to teach readers "the few maneuvers necessary for anthropometric and psycho-physical measurements and research, and show how to apply these to expert testimony and to scientific investigations."[80] Finally, the text included a glossary of the most important terms in scientific criminology – terms whose meanings might otherwise remain elusive.

In his discussion of expert practices (Part II), Lombroso distinguished between "common" or "ordinary" kinds of forensic investigations, and cases of a particular or historic importance that demanded more detailed study. In either kind of case, Lombroso advised, the work of the forensic expert ought properly to resemble scientific research: "Both aim at the accumulation of objective proofs" and should therefore confine themselves to a somatic and

---

78 Guarnieri, "Misurare le diversità," 129. See also Guarnieri, *A Case of Child Murder*.
79 Lombroso, *La perizia*, viii.   80 Ibid., ix.

psychological study of the accused.[81] However, cautioned the author, the authority of science in the courtroom was far from assured: "Because judges and, even more so, members of the jury are not scientists and are instead for the most part averse to science, they would become fed up by an excess of subtle scientific analyses and would not be able to follow the witness; they might indeed arrive at a contrary verdict out of spite or boredom."[82] Thus, in the case of ordinary expert reports, Lombroso recommended that witnesses restrict their research and testimony. After a brief exposition of the case, he advised, experts should report the weight and height of the accused, then move quickly to the general anthropological characteristics, including thresholds of sensitivity. He further suggested that witnesses have before them one of the forms developed by Tamburini and Benelli, or by Carrara and Strassmann, "which in a few lines group together the most necessary investigations and determine the order in which one should proceed." The expert's final tasks were to link the anthropological characteristics to the acts in question and to provide a synthesis that would "illuminate" the judge.[83]

If the lists Lombroso recommended strike us as fairly exhaustive (including, for example, assessments of nine different sensory abilities) and therefore likely to try the patience of any judge or jury, Lombroso insisted upon a much more detailed investigation in criminal cases of special import. Here, as in scientific research, there were "never enough data."[84]

In both kinds of cases experts were advised to conduct measurements of pain sensitivity. And here there no longer was any question whether the Lombroso algometer was an appropriate device, whether it measured anything real, or whether the pain threshold was significant. Instead, the question with which the expert had to contend was whether a diminished sensitivity to pain was one of the facts that might productively be presented to a wary and disrespectful jury. When the expert took up his pen to complete the Tamburini-Benelli form and came to the line for pain threshold, the competition among instruments makers, the contests between anthropologists and physiologists, the debates about electricity and excitability, and the other ambiguities that attend the elaboration of a new science disappeared.

This is not to say criminology had, by 1905, put an end to such contingencies. Indeed, it would not have taken much for things to unravel: The expert might skip over the line in question or a jury might scoff at the

---

81 Ibid., 486. 82 Ibid., 487.
83 Ibid.
84 Ibid. "No naturalist," argues Lombroso by way of comparison, "would refuse to analyze, tissue by tissue, insofar as this were possible, an unknown animal before fixing its taxonomic position."

evidence when it was presented. And what was implicit in *La perizia* – that anyone with the right stuff (tools, techniques, rhetoric) might become a forensic expert – might actually have worked to undermine the authority of the scientist. Yet it is clear that by 1905 both criminological debates and trials were unfolding on a modified terrain, where a certain kind of attending to bodies could be taken for granted and where quantification proceeded silently, inexorably.

I suggest in conclusion that an unobtrusive circulation of tools and techniques, across both national and disciplinary boundaries, played a crucial role in reworking this terrain. More detailed – and comparative – research may enable us to understand the ways in which shared practices cut across discursive and theoretical debates (and not only between the Italians and the French), and helped to diffuse the scientific project of knowing the deviant body.

15

"One of the Strangest Relics of a Former State"

Tattoos and the Discourses of Criminality in Europe, 1880–1920

JANE CAPLAN

There is no law that is not inscribed on bodies. . . . It engraves itself on parchments made from the skin of its subjects. It articulates them in a juridical corpus. It makes its book out of them . . . through them, living beings are "packed into a text," . . . transformed into signifiers of rules (a sort of "intextuation"), and, on the other hand, the reason or *Logos* of a society "becomes flesh" (an incarnation).[1]

The tattooed man is thus the one who is excluded, the one who has no meaning, who does not belong to the system of written signifiers. From then on he is the target of literate societies that want to destroy him in order to give themselves the illusion that there is nothing that exists outside their system.[2]

I

In 1863 Cesare Lombroso (1836–1909), then a military physician stationed with an artillery regiment in Calabria, made an observation that, many years afterward, he claimed as the first dawning of his theory of criminality.[3] "As an army doctor, I beguiled my ample leisure with a series of studies on the Italian soldier. From the very beginning I was struck by a characteristic that distinguished the honest soldier from his vicious comrade: the extent to which the latter was tattooed and the indecency of the designs that covered his body."[4] Lombroso described this as the source of the first of his two "fundamental ideas," vis-à-vis that the point of criminology was to study

---

1 Michel de Certeau, *The Practice of Everyday Life* (Berkeley, Calif., 1988), 139–40.
2 Jean-Thierry Maertens, *Le dessein sur la peau* (Paris, 1978), 72.
3 This chapter draws partially on material published in my essay "'National Tattooing': Traditions of Tattooing in Nineteenth-Century Europe," in Jane Caplan, ed., *Written on the Body: The Tattoo in European and American History* (London, 2000). The quotation in the title comes from Gina Lombroso-Ferrero, *Criminal Man According to the Classification of Cesare Lombroso* (Montclair, N.J., 1972 [1911]), 45.
4 Cesare Lombroso, "Introduction," in Lombroso-Ferrero, *Criminal Man*, xxii.

not "crime in the abstract [but] the criminal himself"; however, in 1863 he had merely recorded his observations without quite knowing what to make of them. The more celebrated experience that completed his criminological epiphany occurred a little later, during his autopsy of the brigand Giuseppe Villela's anomalous skull, when he "seemed to see all of a sudden, lighted up as a vast plain under a flaming sky, the problem of the nature of the criminal – an atavistic being who reproduces in his person the ferocious instincts of primitive humanity and the inferior animals."[5] With this the tattoo fell into its privileged place as the most obtrusive and literal sign of criminal atavism.

Lombroso's retrospective gesture invested his own research with a reve-latory authority that certainly owed much of its conviction to his flair for the dramatic. Nevertheless, that twin reading of the body's surfaces and its depths, of optative inscription and involuntary anatomical anomaly, yielded the basic tools for his distinctive contribution to the late-nineteenth-century project of "creating born criminals," in Nicole Rafter's deft phrase.[6] By the time the tattoo was fully incorporated into Lombroso's theory of crimi-nal atavism in the 1870s, a modest corpus of research into tattooed Italians had accumulated. Virtually all of it was devoted to the study of convicts and prostitutes, thus annexing the tattoo's acknowledged association with lower-class men to a more inflexible union with criminality and deviance.

Although Lombroso's observations have come to dominate the field of memory, this was not the first time that academic attention had been attracted to the subject. The Italian account of tattoos as a characteristic of criminal identity infringed on an older French tradition of exploring their significance in the narrower medico-legal science of identification. This opposition between an existing police science of identification and a new criminological science of identities overdetermined the more celebrated col-lision between the ostensibly "biologistic-determinist" Italian criminologists and their "environmentalist–free will" counterparts in France.[7] It was there-fore not accidental that the tattoo launched the edgy encounter between Italian and French criminology when, in 1880, the Lyon criminologist

---

5 Ibid., xxv.
6 Nicole Hahn Rafter, *Creating Born Criminals* (Urbana, Ill., 1997).
7 For interpretations of the relationship between French and Italian criminology in the late nineteenth century, see Robert Nye, *Crime, Madness, and Politics in Modern France: The Medical Concept of National Decline* (Princeton, N.J., 1984), chap. 4; Ruth Harris, *Murders and Madness: Medicine, Law, and Society in the fin-de-siècle* (Oxford, 1989), 80–98; Marc Renneville, "La reception de Lombroso en France (1880–1909)," in Laurent Mucchielli, ed., *Histoire de la criminologie française* (Paris, 1994), 107–35; Laurent Mucchielli, "Hérédité et 'milieu social': le faux antagonisme franco-italien," in ibid., 190–211; Daniel Pick, *Faces of Degeneration: A European Disorder c. 1848–c. 1918* (Cambridge, 1989), 132–6; and Marie-Christine Leps, *Apprehending the Criminal: The Production of Deviance in Nineteenth-Century Discourse* (Durham, N.C., 1992), chap. 2.

Alexandre Lacassagne (1843–1924) published the results of his own research into the significance of tattooing. The Lombroso-Lacassagne dispute about the significance of "criminal" tattoos was widely known in European medico-legal and criminological circles by the 1890s, and it prompted a sudden flurry of publications on the subject in several European countries in the years before the outbreak of World War I. After the war, interest in the subject almost as suddenly subsided – what had previously been a steady stream of publications in the major criminological periodicals simply dried up.[8]

Although most of the surviving evidence of European tattooing in the nineteenth century was delivered by criminological controversy, it also was only through this controversy that the tattoo was vested with its association with criminality. Visibility and pathology arrived more or less simultaneously, engulfing a practice that had previously been defined by latency and marginality. Yet, as the research continued, it also generated information about tattoos that exceeded the existing medico-legal and criminological frameworks of interpretation. We can read the debate about this as a struggle not only to determine the limits of this association but also to manage the more diffuse uneasiness that was provoked by this curiously disturbing sign. Its ambivalent modality – was it an expression or an inscription? a voluntary or an involuntary sign? an indigenous or imported practice? – seems to have struck a cultural nerve among those who did not themselves bear it; the intensity of their reactions calls for explanation.

The tattoo also secured an imaginative grip on police science that seems to have been artificially enhanced by its lingering associations with criminal identity, its promise of an eloquence greater than that of individual identification alone.[9] Writers on the subject were fond of quoting Lacassagne's pithy characterization of tattoos as "speaking scars,"[10] but the language they spoke was, paradoxically, often mute: not exactly undecipherable or impenetrable, for the images were more likely to figure an excess of possible meanings, but incapable of communicating information that was any more valuable than

---

8 The role of tattoos in the debate between Lacassagne and Lombroso has been pointed out by Régine Plas, "Tatouages et criminalité," in *Histoire de la criminalité française*, 156–67; and see Peter Becker, "Physiognomie des Bösen: Cesare Lombrosos Bemühungen um eine präventive Entzifferung des Kriminellen," in Claudia Schmölders, ed., *Der exzentrische Blick: Gespräch über Physiognomik* (Berlin, 1996), 163–86.

9 See for example the discussion in Hans Gross's classic *Handbuch für Untersuchungsrichter*, first published in 1893 (English translation *Criminal Investigation: A Practical Textbook* [London, 1924], 112–14); and note the extended discussion in the 8th edition, revised by Ernst Seelig, *Handbuch der Kriminalistik* (Berlin, 1942), 404–16.

10 Alexandre Lacassagne, "Les cicatrices parlants" in *Les tatouages: Étude anthropologique et médico-légale* (Paris, 1881), 99.

that provided by a scar or a limp. That is to say, in certain finite circumstances this kind of feature might mark an individual as different from others in a set, but it did no more than this. As police techniques moved from observation to measurement, so the tattoo was left marooned, the ironic "relic of a former state" of surveillance and detection.

My focus in this chapter is how this interpretive deficit was produced and managed in the late-nineteenth-century project of "practical criminology," that is, the field research undertaken in the prisons, jails, and asylums of continental Europe. I begin by summarizing the contexts in which French and Italian research emerged and the encounter between these two approaches, and I then discuss the investigative projects that were stimulated by this public debate.

II

In France a combination of medico-legal and colonial interests sustained a research interest in tattoos at least from the 1830s. By the mid-nineteenth century these projects had accumulated a body of empirical evidence on the practice of tattooing in France. The usual inference was that it had spread since the 1770s from Pacific islanders to European sailors and then to soldiers and male manual laborers. Tattoos were generally seen as a foolish and uncivilized form of ornamentation – in the words of one early observer, "a bizarre decoration" borrowed by sailors from "savages" and propagated by "idleness and caprice."[11] This interpretation (which remains familiar) was in fact historically dubious in that it ignored, perhaps wilfully, an older history of tattooing within Europe itself, as well as evidence that the habit of tattooing among European and American sailors had been picked up much earlier, possibly from the pilgrim tattoos known in Mediterranean Europe from the seventeenth century.[12] But it established a durable association of tattoos with exoticism and primitivity, so that when European tattooing was

---

11 R. P. Lesson, "Du tatouage chez les différens peuples de la terre," *Annales maritimes et coloniales*, 1820, pt. 2, 289.

12 For the "discovery" of tattooing in Cook's voyages, see, e.g., Sydney Parkinson, *A Journal of a Voyage to the South Seas* (London, 1773), 25; John C. Beaglehole, ed., *The Journals of Captain Cook on His Voyages of Discovery* (Cambridge, 1955), 125; and Joseph Banks's descriptions in [James Cook], *The Three Famous Voyages of Captain Cook Round the World* (London, 1888–9), 80–81, 189–90. For American sailors, see Ira Dye, "The Tattoos of Early American Seafarers, 1796–1818," *Proceedings of the American Philosophical Society* 133 (1989), 520–54; and Simon P. Newman, "Reading the Bodies of Early American Seafarers," *William and Mary Quarterly*, 55 (1998), 61–82; for the history of tattooing in Europe, see Caplan, *Written on the Body*.

fully "rediscovered" later in the century, it was easily read as a survival or irruption of primitive practices.[13]

France's colonial projects created contacts with the societies of the South Pacific in which tattooing was culturally embedded, notably the Marquesas. One of the earliest French discussions of tattooing, published in 1820, was the work of a naval surgeon, R. P. Lesson, and it was another naval physician, Ernest Berchon, who was responsible for a series of influential publications on the subject beginning in the 1860s.[14] Berchon's firm though erroneous belief that tattooing was a serious health danger prompted the French admiralty to officially discourage tattooing among naval personnel and also led to more strictly medical studies of the anatomy of the tattoo in the context of early dermatological research (and because venereology was originally a subspecialty in dermatology, this led to investigations of the connection between tattooing and venereal disease).[15] Medical and forensic interest in the anatomy of tattooing overlapped in the question of the tattoo's permanence. Early French medico-legal specialists such as Mathurin Félix Hutin and Ambroise Tardieu had their interest piqued in the 1850s by two well-publicized criminal cases involving tattoos and disputed identities, a homicide victim in Prussia and an accused burglar in France.[16] They began carrying out empirical investigations into the tattoo, exploring its value as an aid to the identification of individuals by testing the crucial question of the indelibility of various colorants and observing the distribution of

---

13 For a profound interpretation of this relationship, see Alfred Gell, *Wrapping in Images: Tattooing in Polynesia* (Cambridge, 1993), chap. 1; and for the place of tattooing in the broader argument that "European modernism invents itself by inventing primitivism," see Mark Taylor, *Hiding* (Chicago, 1997), 95ff.

14 Lesson, "Du tatouage chez les différens peuples de la terre," 280–92; Ernest Berchon, "Le tatouage aux isles Marquises," *Bulletins de la société d'anthropologie de Paris*, I (1860), 99–117; Ernest Berchon, "Recherches sur le tatouage," *Comptes-rendus des séances et mémoires de la Société de Biologie*, 3rd. ser., III (1861), 13–37; and Ernest Berchon, *Histoire médicale du tatouage* (Paris, 1869).

15 See, e.g., Pierre Rayer, *Traité théorique et pratique des maladies de la peau*, 2d ed. (Paris, 1835), 3:602, 610–12; and "Lettre de M. Follin sur le transport des matières solides à travers l'économie" (1849), reprinted in Émile Littré and Charles Robin, eds., *Dictionnaire de médecine* (Paris, 1858). For venereal disease, see principally Jules Converset, *Syphilis et tatouage* (Lyon, 1888).

16 For the Ebermann/Schall case in Berlin, see Johann Ludwig Casper, "Über Tätowierungen: Eine neue gerichtlich-medizinische Frage. (Der Prozess Schall, eine cause célèbre)," *Vierteljahrsschrift für gerichtliche und öffentliche Medicin* 1 (1852): 274–92; for Tardieu's investigation of the case of the burglar Aubert, see Ambroise Tardieu, "Étude médico-légale sur le tatouage, considéré comme signe d'identité," *Annales d'hygiène publique et de médecine légale*, 2d ser., II (1855), 201–4; for Hutin, see his *Recherches sur les tatouages* (Paris, 1853). For fuller references on this and other aspects of the history of tattooing in Europe, see Jane Caplan, "'Speaking Scars': The Tattoo in Popular Practice and Medico-Legal Debate in Nineteenth-Century Europe," *History Workshop Journal* 44 (1997), 107–42.

tattoo images among the population. The first principle was, in Tardieu's words,

to fix [the tattoo's] value as a sign of identity.... Tattoos... can give positive or negative signs of identity, according to whether they are still apparent or whether they seem to have been effaced or have disappeared.... The confirmation of identity, whether its object is a mutilated or unknown corpse, or to overcome the silence or simulation of an accused person, demands... the most minute attention and the scrupulous examination of all parts of the body or the least remains of a cadaver. The tattoos that are discovered by this means should be described in every detail with the greatest care, and even on occasion depicted.[17]

Tattoos thus found a logical place in France among the developing techniques of specialist police science. Like any distinctive physical mark, they were a potential aid to identification, and the question of their indelibility carried serious consequences: As Bertillon later remarked, "The worst mistake an observer can make is to note down as indelible an identifying mark which may disappear or be effaced."[18] Tardieu's experiments and observations determined that tattoos in colors other than black had a tendency to fade (dyes such as vermilion and cinnabar were less stable), and that they could also be deliberately effaced, though with difficulty and at the cost of leaving a characteristic scar. He was especially intrigued by the idea that specific images could be clues to social class and occupational identity, just as many occupations left distinctive physical traces on the bodies (especially the hands) of their practitioners. He noted the case of a murder victim, the carpenter Chauvin, whose body had been identified by tattoos of his tools and of journeyman symbols, and concluded that "according to the location in which [the tattoo] is placed and the object it represents, it is a particular and sometimes decisive indicator of social condition and profession."[19]

---

17 Tardieu, "Étude médico-légale," 188.
18 Alphonse Bertillon, *Instructions for Taking Descriptions for the Identification of Criminals and Others by Means of Anthropometric Indications* (Chicago, 1889), 73.
19 Ibid., 192, 206; see also Achille Chereau, "Du tatouage: Nouvelle question médico-légale," *L'Union médicale* 6, no. 137 (16 Nov. 1852), 545–6, and Hutin, *Recherches sur le tatouage.* On physical traces left by the exercise of specific occupations, see, e.g., Alphonse Devergie, *Médecine légale, théorique et pratique* (Paris, 1840), vol. 2, 528–44; Ambroise Tardieu, "Mémoire sur les modifications physiques et chimiques que détermine dans certaines parties du corps l'exercice des diverses professions, pour servir à la recherche médico-légale de l'identité," *Annales d'hygiène publique et de médecine légale*, 1st ser., 42 (1849), 388–423, and 43 (1850), 131–44; Maxime Vernois, "De la main des ouvriers et des artisans au point de vue de l'hygiène et de médecine légale," *Annales d'hygiène publique et de médecine légale*, 2d. ser., 17 (1862), 104–90; and Ernest Morillon, *Identité en générale et signes professionnels en particulier* (Paris, 1865).

This pioneering work by Hutin and Tardieu received some further attention as French forensic science developed.[20] By the time of Lacassagne and
Lombroso, the tattoo had already secured itself a place among the repertoire
of identificatory techniques or *signalement* (descriptive particulars) pioneered
by the French police, a development that I can only briefly summarize here.
Policemen needed descriptive techniques that could support two different
identificatory tasks: not only techniques suitable for the identification of a
previously recorded criminal after his detention, but also those that could
be used for locating, shadowing, or arresting a suspect. Technically speaking the second type of identification was a considerably harder task because
the subject of the investigation was often not observable at close quarters,
let alone measurable for the purposes of comparison. Equally important
was that the data had to be easily classifiable and readily retrievable: This
set strict limits on the practical value of photographs, for example, despite
their promise of fidelity. These needs were addressed most imaginatively
by Alphonse Bertillon, founder and director of the Department of Judicial
Identity in the Paris district in the 1880s. Identification through "bertillonage," or the anthropometrical measurement of a series of physical dimensions (length and breadth of head, bizygomatic diameter, height of right
ear, etc.), created an exhaustive description that could be compared point
by point with a subject in custody. The *portrait parlé* and the standardized
description – aptly characterized in 1906 as "a photograph that can be
telegraphed"[21] – equipped the trained beat policeman or arresting officer with a practical summary of his quarry that could be committed to
memory.

The identification of known criminals was what came to link police
science (or criminalistics) to the core criminological pursuit of "the
recidivist" – an overlap that was important for both. But although tattoos on
convicts were certainly noticed, they were not necessarily the primary focus
of the earliest French investigations, which were as likely to be conducted in
the barracks or hospital as the prison. Of course, these were also types of confined male community at one time removed from "normal" conditions of
life, a fact that no doubt prepared the ground for the later conversion of tattoos to stigmata of deviance. Thus, Hutin, for example, claimed in his 1853
study of army veterans at the Paris Invalides that he had observed "remarkable

---

20 See Paul Hourteloup, "Du tatouage," *Annales d'hygiène publique et de médecine légale*, 2d ser., 34 (1870),
    440–72.
21 Edmond Locard, "Les services actuels d'identification et la fiche internationale," *Comptes-rendus du
    VIe congrès internationale d'anthropologie criminelle (1906)* (Turin, 1908), 399.

combinations of lubricious and religious symbols that one might associate carelessly at a certain age, but which almost all these old men now view with a sense of shame."[22] As the number of studies multiplied, increasing attention was paid to the easily studied prison populations.

However, as it matured, French police science was to discount the far-reaching significance attached to tattoos by criminal anthropology, concentrating instead on their purely forensic value as a mark of identification on criminals or on unidentified corpses. In the words of Edmond Locard, the preeminent French expert in police science in the generation after Bertillon, the tattoo was "so to speak privileged by virtue of its identificatory power . . . [it was] the model and archetype of the distinguishing mark."[23] Yet, as Locard was to concede after some two hundred pages of discussion in his mammoth *Traité de Criminalistique* (1932), the practical value of tattoos was limited to that of any other "distinguishing mark." Here he was repeating exactly the caveat that Tardieu had uttered seventy-five years earlier. Tattoos might be indelible, but the images could be substantially altered or their number augmented; also, because they were usually concealed they did not visibly identify a suspect or quarry during the chase. Moreover, experience had shown that tattoo images were not readily assimilable to the serialized systems of measurement and classification that had meanwhile been devised for the body's other physical signs and therefore had virtually no role to play in one of the central achievements of nineteenth-century French police science, the criminal *fiche*.

III

The new discourse of criminology of the 1880s launched a shift in the interpretation of the tattoo from a sign of individual identity to the stigma of a collectively pathological criminal class. It is tempting to see this semiotic move as a bid to vest the tattoo with the more special significance that its striking character appeared to deserve – surely these vivid images *had* to mean something more than a scar or a limp did? This was the status claimed for the tattoo in Lombroso's hypothesis of criminal atavism. His work first became widely known after the publication in 1878 of the second edition of *L'uomo delinquente*. The first edition (1876) had already included a chapter on tattoos that reproduced and expanded his 1860s investigations and that

22 Hutin, *Recherches sur les tatouages*, 8.
23 Edmond Locard, *Traité de criminalistique*, vol. 3: *Les preuves d'identité* (Lyon, 1932), 249, 418.

was embodied, with modifications, in all subsequent editions during his lifetime.[24]

With a certain impressive logic, the placement of the tattoo chapter constructed a bridge between the antecedent chapters on criminals' physical characteristics (craniometry and anthropometry) and the subsequent discussions of their moral and intellectual qualities. From his research in the military Lombroso had assembled a characteristically fragmented account of the custom of tattooing among specific Italian communities – principally peasants and rural workers in Lombardy, Piedmont, and the Marches, and pilgrims to the shrine of Loreto. Although these formed Lombroso's category of "the normal," they were hardly a control group in his eyes because they were the Italians among whom primitive Celtic influences still survived. He characterized them collectively as "those classes who, like the ocean floor, maintain the same temperature, repeat the customs, the superstitions, and even the songs of primitive peoples, and who share with them the same violent passions, the same dullness of sense, the same childish vanity, the long periods of idleness, and in the case of prostitutes the nakedness that among savages are the principal incentives to this strange usage." Savages, the lower classes, and criminals shared these and other generic motives for tattooing, but "the first and most primary cause of the diffusion of this custom among us is, in my view, atavism and that species of historical atavism that we call tradition, for tattooing is one of the special characteristics of primitive man and those in a state of savagery."[25]

Building on his own and others' subsequent observations of convicts (including military offenders) and prostitutes, Lombroso went on to make his familiar argument that "tattooing assumes a specific character, a strange tenacity and diffusion among the sad class of criminals...locked in combat with society," among whom "the tattoo can be considered, to use the medico-legal term, as a professional characteristic."[26] Criminals, tattooed in proportions varying from six to fifteen percent of the populations studied by Lombroso and his later collaborators, allegedly bore these marks "seven times more frequently" than soldiers, who themselves were "incalculably" more

---

24 Lombroso's original research on tattoos he found on 1,147 artillery soldiers was first published as "Sul tatuaggio degli Italiani," *Giornale di medicina militare*, 5/50 (1864), 36–43. This was extended between 1863 and 1874, and published as "Sul tatuaggio in Italia, in ispecie fra i delinquenti," *Archivio per l'antropologia e la etnologia*, vol. 4 (1874), 389–403. This text was reproduced verbatim as chapter 3 in the first edition of *L'uomo delinquente* (Milan, 1876), 43–56, from which the following citations are taken.
25 Lombroso, *L'uomo delinquente*, 54–5.
26 Ibid., 47, 56. For the question of tattooing among European female prostitutes – the only category of women regularly described as tattooed – see Caplan, "Educating the Eye."

likely to be tattooed than were civilians. Their tattoos were also, according to Lombroso, more violent or obscene in character, and more likely to be positioned on or near the genitals: this was succinctly demonstrated by the accompanying illustration (the only such image in the first edition of *L'uomo delinquente*) of a convict displaying numerous tattoos, including several serpents, an image of crossed daggers surrounded by the motto "Giuro di vendicarmi" (I swear to revenge myself), and a tattooed penis.[27] The alleged propensity of criminals to get multiple tattoos and tattoos on such delicate parts of the body also supported Lombroso's argument that they shared with "savages" a lesser sensitivity to pain. And despite mounting evidence to the contrary, he continued to argue that it was the worst, most "savage" criminals who bore the most numerous and indecent images.

These basic arguments survived the criticisms that led Lombroso to substantially modify his hypotheses about the proportion of criminality that could actually be attributed to atavism. In later editions of *L'uomo delinquente* the chapter on tattoos was expanded to include the data on tattooing that had meanwhile accumulated from ongoing ethnographic and criminological research.[28] These additions tended to reinforce the analysis, displacing the tattoo from contemporary popular culture and anchoring it more firmly in a terrain of primitiveness, deviance, and exoticism. Thus, Lombroso continued to insist on the "atavistic compulsion that drove criminals to undergo this strange operation" and made the highly charged claim that "if criminal tattoos are not atavistic, then there is no such scientific fact as atavism."[29] Apart from a brief chapter on the subject in his 1890 manual of forensic medicine, criminal anthropology remained the context in which he elected to discuss it.[30] In this way Lombroso unmistakably staked his general theory of criminal atavism on the wager of the tattoo, the wager that Lacassagne picked up.

That Lacassagne enjoyed an ambivalent intellectual relationship with Lombroso is well known, and this is manifest in his earliest publications on tattoos.[31] His first essay on the subject in 1880 was actually published in the inaugural volume of the *Archivio di psichiatria*, the house journal of Italian criminology. Here his guarded conclusion was that "the large number

---

27 Lombroso, *L'uomo delinquente*, 48–50.
28 See, e.g., the Italian editions of 1889 and 1896–7, and the French translation, *L'homme criminel* (Paris, 1895).
29 Cesare Lombroso, *L'anthropologie et ses récents progrès* (Paris, 1891), 85, 91.
30 Cesare Lombroso, *Sulla medicina legale del cadavare secondo gli ultimi studi di germania ed italia* (Pinerolo, 1890), 70–82.
31 This relationship of attraction and repudiation has been most closely examined by Mucchielli, "Hérédité et 'milieu social,'" and Renneville, "La reception de Lombroso en France."

of tattoos are the measure of the tattooed man's criminality, or at least the number of his convictions,"[32] and he continued to voice some equivocation initially. "Men have themselves tattooed as a way of passing the time," he wrote, but the number and location of their tattoos "are a manifestation of that instinctive vanity and need for display that are some of the characteristics of primitive men or criminal natures."[33] Thereafter, however, his critique of Lombroso became stronger as he expounded his own research at greater length.[34] The intellectual character of this disagreement – between theories of atavism and of degeneration – is familiar: "Where the Turin professor sees an interruption, then a backward regression, I demonstrate an uninterrupted series, a succession of transformations of an instinct.... Where Lombroso sees ancient types suddenly re-presenting themselves, we see only retardation."[35] This interpretive contrast between rupture and continuity, condensing the difference between theories of atavism and degeneration, also reflected differences in the two men's research strategy and presentation, which displayed a kind of inverse relationship between evidence and inference. In Lombroso's case, fragmented and disorderly data led rapidly to firmly tabulated conclusions; in Lacassagne's research, painstakingly assembled and catalogued data were built into a sequential exposition on the basis of which (at least in terms of presentation) a systematic interpretation was eventually proposed.

Lacassagne argued that the significance of tattoos could not be interpreted with confidence unless a very large number of examples had been collected and analyzed. Thus, in 1881 he explained at length precisely how he took copies of the 1600 tattoos in his "unique" (and growing) collection of images, how he catalogued them according to seven categories of image, ten specifications of location on the body, and so on. It was only later, under pressure of mounting data, that Lombroso adopted a similar taxonomic

---

32 Alexandre Lacassaigne [sic], "Ricerche su 1333 tatuaggi di delinquenti," *Archivio di pschiatria, scienze penali ed antropologia criminale* (hereafter *Archivio di psichiatria*), 1 (1880), 438–43. He also noted that Lombroso had anticipated this conclusion (439).

33 Alexandre Lacassagne, "Recherches sur les tatouages et principalement du tatouage chez les criminels," *Annales d'hygiène publique et de médecine légale*, 3rd. ser., 5 (1881), 291–2. This journal, published since 1829, was representative of earlier nineteenth-century French legal medicine, just as the *Archives de l'anthropologie criminelle et des sciences pénales* (hereafter *Archives de l'anthropologie*), founded by Lacassagne in 1885, was the flagship of French criminology (indicatively, it was renamed *Annales de médecine légale et de police scientifique* under Lacassagne's successor-editor in 1921).

34 Alexandre Lacassagne, *Les tatouages: Étude anthropologique et médico-légale* (Paris, 1881), and Alexandre Lacassagne and E. Magitot, "Tatouage," in Amédée Dechambre and Auguste Lereboullet, eds., *Dictionnaire encyclopédique des sciences médicales*, 3d ed. (Paris 1886), vol. 16, 95–160, which partially repeats the former work.

35 Lacassagne, *Les tatouages*, 115, repeated in Lacassagne and Magitot, "Tatouage," 158–9.

strategy for his own collection. As I have already suggested, Lacassagne also embedded his evidence in the historical context provided by the existing research tradition in the French science of identification. The literature on forensic identification drew Lacassagne's attention to the tattoo as a sign, which his own acute eye enrolled in a long historical series of similarly iconic but morally neutral means of representation and identification: "hieroglyphs, graffiti, professional emblems found on guild banners and seals, artisans' signatures, and even heraldic imagery."[36] It was this long sequence of signs that underwrote his proposition of "an uninterrupted series" in place of Lombroso's "backward regression." As the historical spread of literacy had provided new forms of expression for the educated, the need to exploit "a materialized expression of metaphor and a language of emblems" had drifted downward socially, ending up among those "poorly educated natures" who remained dependent on "material" means for "the objective or symbolic representation of an idea."[37] The tattoo was a creative way of meeting this need: It expressed simplicity and no doubt priority on a developmental scale, but not necessarily disreputability or savagery. Lacassagne thus was especially struck by the frequency with which he encountered the tattooed image of the pansy – a flower whose name in French, *pensée*, lent itself to touching invocations of distance bridged by memory. This is not to deny that Lombroso too was drawn to the symbolic value of the tattoo nor that Lacassagne acknowledged the power of heritage, but the emphasis was perceptibly different in each case. In the study of the criminal, Lombroso emphasized the anatomic and instinctual where Lacassagne privileged the extrinsic and semiotic.

IV

These differences in the sources of interest and the contexts of interpretation persisted as discussion of the significance of tattooing was taken up on a European scale between the 1890s and 1914. This discussion was not, of course, the only academic response to Lombroso's panoramic research into the anatomy of criminal identity, nor did it necessarily become the most significant, contentious, or creative site of debate – there was, after all, no corner of the body, however *recherché*, that was invisible to the criminal anthropologist's probing eyes and instruments.[38] But the tattoo's particular interest was its location in a field of cultural indeterminacy that rendered it a

---

36 Lacassagne, *Les tatouages*, 115.   37 Ibid., 61.
38 See the chapter by David Horn in this volume.

peculiarly slippery but at the same time oddly compelling sign. The tattoo – as Lombroso's chapter structure recognized – stood midway betwen the physical and moral indications of criminality. Even if it somehow expressed an involuntary instinct (which most authors in fact doubted), it did so by means of circuitous mediations that demanded explanation. It generated numerous publications in the major European journals of legal medicine and criminology, as well as some substantial monographs – as if to the surprise of the contributors themselves, who sometimes seemed almost to apologize for their curiosity about this peculiar subject. Still, it is not difficult to suggest some reasons for this.

First, there was the sheer visibility of the tattoo. Not only was it intensely provocative – once these images and inscriptions had been noticed, who could resist the temptation to classify and interpret them? – it also did not require any special techniques or measuring equipment, far less a pathologist's slab. Apart from the doctoral dissertations sponsored by the masters at Turin and Lyon, and a number of other quite substantial academic studies, numerous slighter publications were the work of ordinary prison and army medical officers, and sometimes judicial officials or asylum physicians, who came into regular contact with the tattooed bodies of their charges. For many of them this may have been their sole venture into print: They were practitioners, not academics, and the goals they set themselves were modest. Anyone could describe a tattoo verbally, and it was not much more difficult to make copies of the images and reproduce them for publication.[39] Once the images had been collected, their description and classification required only a reasonably tidy mind and a certain amount of spare time to prepare a piece of written work. The tattoo offered a readily available means of entering the field of criminology as it established itself in the late nineteenth century.

A typical report would consist of a brief contextualization in the existing literature, a summary of the author's research protocol, and descriptions of the tattoos he had seen, usually catalogued according to Lacassagne's categories. Some information about the bearer of the tattoo was normally included; this varied from a list of basic data (age, education, occupation,

---

39 The major collections of tattoos (both Lombroso and Lacassagne assembled libraries of several thousand images) were tracings or drawings. For descriptions of tracing and drawing techniques, see, e.g., Lacassagne, *Les tatouages*, 20; Battut, "Du tatouage," 90; and Karl Gotthold, "Vergleichende Untersuchungen über die Tätowierung bei Normalen, Geisteskranken und Kriminellen," *Klinik für psychische und nervose Krankheiten* 9 (1914), 196–7. For the Lacassagne collection, see Dominique Denis, "Les 7000 tatouages de la collection Locard: Emblèmes du crime ou ornamentation du corps?" *Cahiers d'histoire* 30 (1985), 107–37. (I am grateful to Peter Becker for this reference.)

date of tattoo(s), motives, and, where relevant, criminal record), to more
or less extensive biographies, sometimes in what was purported to be the
bearer's own words. The location, imagery, and number of tattoos were
always carefully noted, and if the scale of the evidence warranted it, reports
might include a statistical breakdown of the main findings. Yet very few
authors offered anything original in the way of interpretation, and some
contented themselves with simply listing the tattoos they had found, ostensibly as raw material for others to work on.[40] Others might submit a detailed
description of a single tattoo that seemed especially noteworthy, while journal editors sometimes unabashedly reprinted descriptions of unusual or sensational images taken directly from press reports.[41] Many accounts were
amply illustrated with tracings or sketches that recorded a rich iconography
of the tattoo images in circulation. However, these were often depicted in a
rough and reductive style that exaggerated the crudity of images that, as we
know from other sources, could be delicate and precise in composition and
execution. An especially noteworthy example was the publication of more
than fifty images, carefully drawn from photographs taken from the pattern
or "flash" book of an itinerant tattooist arrested in the Mainz/Mannheim
area in 1905.[42]

One can well imagine that, like Lombroso in the 1860s, these medical
and legal officials were happy to "beguile their leisure" by engaging in these
modest projects of research. Indeed, like so much else in the police and
prison world, their activities often formed an ironic parallel universe to that
of the prisoners who were their subjects of study, who had employed their
own "ample leisure" to inscribe the tattoos on their bodies in the first place.
The "idleness" and "boredom" of men confined for long periods without
adequate occupation were persistently identified as the principal motivations
for being tattooed, such that the tattoo became a virtual emblem of unfilled,
vitiated time. Understandably, the professional men who occupied their own
spare time studying them did not belabor this parallel (any more than that

40 See, e.g., J. Jaeger, "Tätowierungen von 150 Verbrechern mit Personalangaben," *Archiv für Kriminalanthropologie* 18 (1904), 141–68, and ibid., 21 (1905), 116–67. Plas, "Tatouages et criminalité,"
   160, notes this as the typical pattern in the French *Archives de l'anthropologie criminelle*.
41 See, e.g., Wolfgang Hauschild, "Zur Tätowierungsfrage: Ein Fall von Tätowierung des Hin-
   terkopfes," *Archiv für Kriminalanthropologie* 45 (1912), 60–80; Raffaele Gurrieri and G. B. Moraglia,
   "Note sul tatuaggio osceno ne delinquenti," *Archivio di pschiatria* 13 (1892), 145–51; F. Santangelo,
   "Tatuaggi e pazzia morale," ibid., 14 (1893), 115–23; Silvio Armando Neri, "Tatuaggi osceno in
   fratelli criminale," ibid., 23 (1902), 252–3 – a series of Prussian military images on two French
   brothers ("sodomites and onanists"); *Archiv für Kriminalanthropologie* 35 (1909), 375–6 – press report
   of a worker from Halle with a tattoo of his hero, Friedrich Nietzsche, on his lower arm; the *Archives
   de l'anthropologie criminelle* also carried intermittent brief reports of press stories.
42 Fritz Eller, "Ein Vorlagebuch für Tätowierungen," *Archiv für Kriminalanthropologie* 19 (1905): 60–67.

suggested by the tattooed man's susceptibility to "imitation" as a motive for his behavior). Still, one author did point out an ironic consequence of all the attention he was devoting to tattooed convicts: "My interest was one more reason for them to cultivate tattooing, even though I was always at pains to stigmatize this bad habit [*Unsitte*]. The fact that I spent time talking to the tattooed prisoners and stuck some of them in front of photographic apparatus seems to have been enough reason for some to get themselves tattooed."[43]

A second reason for paying attention to tattoos was that even the most dedicated criminal anthropologist had to recognize that these marks had a cultural as well as anatomical character. Unlike purely anatomical features, the tattoo as a physical image was not an involuntary or hereditary mark, but was a cultural product acquired in determinate social situations. It therefore positively incited national studies that could compare the history, the social diffusion, and the popularity of the practice in different countries, and the extent to which images were shared across national and linguistic boundaries. France and Italy generated the most numerous studies, and Germany (with Austria) was not far behind, but there also were scattered and sometimes individually voluminous contributions from observers in countries as varied as Belgium, Denmark, Portugal, Romania, and Spain, as well as outside Europe (for example, America, Japan, and Mexico). Occasional reports appeared in the proceedings of the International Congress of Criminal Anthropology, though less frequently than might be expected.[44] Most authors claimed to know at least some of the foreign literature, and many aimed to compare their local findings with those of their foreign colleagues. As the available literature expanded, a longer article might include a more or less compendious review of existing publications on the subject, although from the number of incomplete references, misspelled names, and so on it seems likely that much of this literature was known only by report and that the same basic information was repeatedly recycled. Nevertheless, an internationally cross-referenced discussion emerged in the pages of the new professional journals of criminology and forensic science, spurring subscribers to further efforts of investigation.

---

43 W. Maschka (military physician in Olmütz, Czecheslovakia), "Zur Tätowirungsfrage," *Archiv für Kriminalanthropologie* 1 (1899): 330.
44 I have found only two: Orazio de Albertis, "Cas de tatouage chez une femme," *Actes du premier Congrès internationale d'anthropologie criminelle, biologie et sociologie* (Turin, 1886–7), 456–8; and Edgar Berillon, "De la nécessité de pratiquer le détatouage chez les jeunes détenus dans les prisons et les maisons d'éducation correctionnelles," *Congrès internationale d'anthropologie criminelle, Compte-rendu des travaux de la 4. session* (Geneva, 1897), 228–31.

A final reason for the volume of publication was that the argument about the character of contemporary tattooing was not in itself so complicated or contentious that contributors ran any great intellectual risk by entering it. As suggested above, it was perfectly possible to avoid any deep engagement with the issues and yet have the satisfaction of making a modest contribution to the project of criminology. If most writers did line up against Lombroso, this was partly because degeneration was a more plastic concept than atavism, with a greater metaphorical reach. The original terms of the argument were in any case readily reformulated as the difference between internal and external motivations for prison tattooing, which also furthered the distinction between the motivation to get tattooed on the one hand and the specific choice of image on the other. The prison was, so to speak, a site of exchange or overlap between internal and external explanations, offering scope for the discussion of both. And as the Belgian criminologist Louis Vervaeck urged in 1906, the concepts of atavism and degeneration were "very close to identical": the distinction was less important than the fact that "the two theories make the tattooed individual into an abnormal being, whether this is because he has remained or has become a savage."[45]

This was indeed the crux of the matter: Was the tattoo to be seen as a normal or an abnormal preference in modern Europe? Important though this question was, Lombroso had immediately evaded it by simply equating tattooing and primitivity, thus guaranteeing the abnormality of the tattoo in a civilized society. Thereafter, virtually all the Italian research worked with the Lombrosian categories and was confined to the milieux of prison, military jail, or licensed brothel, where it was easy enough to find the original hypothesis confirmed.[46] It may therefore appear paradoxical that Italy seems to have been the one European country where tattooing could still demonstrate a deep cultural history by the nineteenth century. Lombroso's own evidence showed this, and it is supported by the well-documented practice of pilgrim tattooing in Loreto, as well as by other, more fragmentary evidence.[47] But, as is so often the case, the paradox here was resolved by the truth it embodied. Late-nineteenth-century Italy was still a country

---

45 Louis Vervaeck, "Le tatouage en Belgique," *Mémoires de la société d'Anthropologie de Bruxelles* 25 (1906): 16.

46 For a more extensive Italian study, see Abele de Blasio, *Il tatuaggio* (Naples, 1906); see also Antonio Marro, *I carratteri dei delinquenti* (Turin, 1887), chap. 8.

47 Lombroso, "Sul tatuaggio in Italia," 390–93; for religious and pilgrim tattooing see Catherina Pigorini-Beri, "Le tatouage religieux et amoureux au pélérinage de N.-D. de Lorette," *Archives de l'anthropologie criminelle*, 16 (1891), 5–16; de Blasio, *Il tatuaggio*, 148–54; and Italo Tanoni, "Il tatuaggio sacro a Loreto," *Ricerche di storia sociale e religiose* 12 (1977): 105–19. Tanoni suggests that the Loreto practice goes back at least to the sixteenth century.

of local cultures and languages, profoundly uneven in its cultural development, and facing specific and daunting challenges in the establishment of a national culture. It was precisely the widespread anxiety about this cultural imbalance between "civilization" and "savagery" *within* the newly unified country that generated Lombroso's project and hypotheses, and seemingly armed him and his collaborators to resist evidence that undermined their extreme interpretations.[48] They anticipated a continuing decline of this savage custom, which would further isolate criminal tattooing and highlight its atavistic character. In fact, in 1906 Abele de Blasio (the most intensive Italian researcher after Lombroso) expressed some frustration that tattooing had been on the verge of vanishing as a popular custom at the turn of the century when its unfortunate revival among the upper classes in Britain gave it a new lease on life.[49]

De Blasio apparently saw this fashionable revival as a perverse consequence of the amount of academic attention paid to tattooing, yet this seems an oddly inept judgment for the British case. Britain was distinctive among European countries in the almost total absence of any academic interest in tattooing, which was connected with the unusually wide distribution of tattooing across the male social spectrum. The reasons for this surely are deeply entangled in Britain's cultural and legal history, involving issues as varied as the persistence of exclusively male institutions from school to club to regiment, the rooted status of naval culture in an established maritime and colonial country, the strategic differences between the English common-law and continental Roman legal traditions, and the different trajectories of British and continental European criminology.[50] The upshot was that the tattoo seemed much more integrated into British masculine culture in the nineteenth century: Even before the turn-of-the-century craze tattoos could be found on public schoolboys and naval and military officers as well as on lower-class men and convicts. But to complicate the picture, the British army also used tattooing to identify two classes of offenders. The branding of criminals had been a common punishment throughout medieval and early modern Europe, but it appears that outside Britain (and possibly America) tattooing was not introduced as a more humane substitute when this stigmatizing penalty was abandoned in the course of penal reform.

---

48 For this political-cultural milieu, see Pick, *Faces of Degeneration*, Part II, and Silvana Patriarca, *Numbers and Nationhood: Writing Statistics in Nineteenth-Century Italy* (Cambridge, 1996), Epilogue.
49 De Blasio, *Il tatuaggio*, 119.
50 I discuss these issues more fully in "Speaking Scars" and "Educating the Eye"; see also James Bradley, "Body Commodification? Class and Tattoos in Victorian Britain," in Caplan, *Written on the Body*, 136–55.

In nineteenth-century Britain, however, army deserters were "marked on the left side . . . with the letter (D.) such letter not to be less than half an inch long, and to be marked upon the skin with some ink or gunpowder or other preparation so as to be visible, and conspicuous, and not liable to be obliterated," so that they could be easily identified on apprehension. Ignominiously discharged "bad characters" were marked on the right breast with the letters "BC" so as to prevent their fraudulent re-enlistment.[51] Yet official discussion of the practice in the late 1860s seemed pragmatic rather than prescriptive, and the character of tattoos and the tattooed was virtually ignored in the public discussion of criminality. One of the few English writers to refer to the subject while the European debate was at its height in the 1890s observed only that "We cannot think that tattooing has any special significance as regards criminals generally, for it is mainly found on those men who have either been soldiers or sailors."[52]

If Italian criminologists were fixated on the pathology of tattoos and the British simply ignored them, in France, Germany, and Austria (where most of the other nineteenth-century research was carried out), the conveniently confined and available convict populations were also the main object of study, but interest did not always stop short at the prison gate. Although researchers were usually defeated by the challenge of carrying out systematic research in the noncriminal population, they tried to incorporate comparative evidence of tattooing among nonoffenders and reached a somewhat better understanding of the scope of the practice in the working-class community at large.[53] The French naturally tended to follow the lead of Lacassagne, not only in the matter of interpretation but also in the scope and precision of their research. Lacassagne's pupil Mayrac noted ironically in 1900 that given the volume of interest in tattoos among criminal anthropologists, "the time is surely not far off when different crimes will have different tattoos as their equivalents, in a grand synoptic table — doubtless

---

51 The quotation is from the Mutiny Act of 1811 (51 Geo. III. c. 8), which is the first of these annual acts to make explicit reference to the punishment and its technique, but it was allegedly of earlier origin: see Ronald Scutt and Christopher Gotch, *Art, Sex and Symbol: The Mystery of Tattooing* (London, 1986), 162. See also Peter Burroughs, "Crime and Punishment in the British Army, 1815–1870," *English Historical Review* 100 (1985), 570f. The marking of bad characters began in the early 1860s; see "Report on the Discipline and Management of Military Prisons, 1859 and 1860," *Parliamentary Papers* 1861 (2900), vol. 30, 25, and the "Report" for 1864, *Parliamentary Papers* 1865 (3567), vol. 25, 23–4.

52 John Baker, "Some Points Connected with Criminals," *Journal of Mental Science* 38 (July 1892), 369.

53 See for example the studies published by the Austrian army officer Maschka, "Zur Tätowirungsfrage" (1899), the Frankfurt physician Karl Gotthold, "Vergleichende Untersuchungen" (1914), and the French naval officer J. Gouzer, "Tatoueurs et tatoués maritimes," *Archives de l'anthropologie criminelle* 9 (1894), 33–64, who compared shipboard tattooing to smoking as equally innocuous ways of passing time.

Italian – distinguished by number, location, character, and even age of acquisition."[54] However, although the Italians were certainly fond of tables, it was Mayrac's own countrymen who produced the most minute and well-organized research – notably an intricately detailed and richly illustrated analysis of over two thousand tattoos on inmates of the Nîmes central prison by its medical officer, Charles Perrier.[55] In Germany, too, where the issue of a national "school" was immaterial, there was a generally skeptical attitude toward Lombroso's arguments and a tendency among the leading researchers to look to environmental rather than constitutional explanations of tattooing. The prison physician Abraham Baer criticized not only Lombroso's account of "criminals' affinity with primitive peoples" but also Lacassagne's fainter echo of this; his colleague F. Leppmann deployed his own observations in a comprehensive attack on the interpretations advanced both by Lombroso and by his outspoken German disciple Hans Kurella.[56]

It was also typical of both the French and German accounts that they often included careful descriptions of the techniques and practitioners of tattooing. This conveyed a sense of tattooing as a normal practice in popular culture – fostered by fairground and circus entertainers, popular reportage, and in some countries by the tattooing craze that developed around the turn of the century – that was too often absent from the more focused Italian research. Leppmann, for example, attributed the growing penchant for tattooing among urban working-class youth to "the wars and the spirit of adventure encouraged by our colonial enterprises," also to the cultivation of the body fostered by the popularity of circuses and athletic clubs.[57] Within the German tradition of folklore studies (*Volkskunde*), an ultimately more serious interest emerged in mapping the popular history of the custom in Europe. Arguably, this kind of research was stimulated and supported by the availability of the forensic and criminological data: The folklorist Otto Lauffer, for example, had access to the Hamburg police archive of photographs and tattoo pattern books.[58]

---

54 Albert Mayrac, *Du tatouage* (Lyon, 1900), 39.

55 Charles Perrier, "Du tatouage chez les criminels," *Archives de l'anthropologie criminelle* 12 (1897), 485–552.

56 Abraham Baer, *Der Verbrecher in anthropologischer Beziehung* (Leipzig, 1893), 225–41, translated as "Tatouage des criminels," *Archives de l'anthropologie criminelle* 10 (1895), 153–74 (quotation is from 164); F. Leppmann, "Die criminalpsychologische und criminalpraktische Bedeutung des Tätowirens bei Verbrechern," *Vierteljahrsschrift für gerichtliche Medizin* 8 (1894): 193–218. For Kurella's extreme arguments, which directly echoed Lombroso, see his *Naturgeschichte des Verbrechers: Grundzüge der criminellen Anthropologie und Criminalpsychologie* (Stuttgart, 1893), 105–12.

57 Leppmann, "Die criminalpsychologische und criminalpraktische Bedeutung des Tätowirens," 197.

58 Otto Lauffer, "Über die Geschichte und den heutigen volkstümlichen Gebrauch der Tätowierung in Deutschland," *Wörter und Sachen: Kulturhistorische Zeitschrift für Sprache und Sachforschung* 6 (1914/5),

Nevertheless, despite the recognition of the cultural embeddedness of European tattooing, there evidently were strong inhibitions against accepting it as fully normal. Perhaps this is unsurprising: A social commentary conducted by the upper classes on the lower was likely to identify many practices as morally or socially reprehensible even if they did not rise to the level of the criminal. But this reluctance is worth looking at more closely. There was a widespread inference that modern tattooing was not indigenous to the country under discussion but had been imported from another European country. This desire to externalize tattooing even across Europe's own internal boundaries echoed the older argument that modern European tattooing was an exotic import from distant and less evolved cultures in the Pacific. The unease conveyed by Lombroso, de Blasio, Marro, and the Italian school at the evidence of a surviving culture of religious tattooing in Italy was paralleled by the reluctance of their northern European colleagues to see tattooing become fully domesticated into their own societies as a form of bodily pleasure. Thus, even those who rejected the implications of atavism or degeneration were inclined to insinuate deeply critical judgments of tattooing by the back door, in an attempt to bar it against further incursions.

The externalization of national tattooing is aptly illustrated by some less familiar studies published in Romania, Spain, and Belgium between 1899 and 1908. A study of tattooing in Romania by Nicolas Minovici, the head of the country's anthropometric service, found it to be so infrequent among convicts and nonconvicts alike (less than one percent of his 15,000 subjects were tattooed) that he concluded not only that tattooing in his country had "no connection whatsoever with atavism and even less with criminals" but that it had few indigenous roots and was a Greek import.[59] Minovici reported indigenous tattooing only among Romanians in Macedonia, who tattooed their children with a cross and their name, allegedly so that they could be identified if killed by Turks.[60] A similar argument was advanced for Spain, where Rafael Sallilas's data, collected from prison and police records,

---

1–14; see also Erhard Riecke, *Das Tatuierungswesen im heutigen Europa* (Jena, 1925). The precursor of this German research was the important study by Wilhelm Joest, *Tätowiren, Narbenzeichen und Körperbemalen: Ein Beitrag zur vergleichenden Ethnologie* (Berlin, 1887), especially 99–109. The outstanding German study was a later doctoral dissertation: Adolf Spämer, *Die Tätowierung in den deutschen Hafenstädten: Ein Versuch zur Erfassung ihrer Formen und ihres Bildgutes* (Bremen, 1934; reprinted Munich, 1993).

59 Nicolas Minovici, "Les tatouages en Roumanie," *Archives des sciences médicales* 4 (1899), 93.

60 For similar evidence of tattooing among Balkan Christians under Ottoman rule, see Leopold Glück, "Die Tätowirung der Haut bei den Katholiken Bosniens und der Hercegovina," *Wissenschaftliche Mittheilungen aus Bosnien und der Hercegovina* 2 (1894), 455–62, and Ciro Truhelka, "Die Tätowirung bei den Katholiken Bosniens und der Hercegovina," ibid., 4 (1896), 493–508.

led him to conclude that there was no indigenous tradition of popular or "normal" tattooing in Spain. (The fragmentary early evidence indicated that if it existed at all, it was socially exclusive.) He attributed this lack to the absence of Celtic influences in Spain (in contrast to France and Northern Italy), and to the Spanish predilection for brilliant clothing and ostentatious adornment, a cultural preference that ruled out the more isolated signals represented by tattoos, medals, and honorifics.[61] Tattooing in contemporary Spain was confined almost exclusively to sailors and prisoners: sailors because they were exposed to foreign influences, prisoners because confinement and idleness propagated the practice. Even so, Sallilas found tattooing to be less common than in France or Italy; moreover, the tattooists were more likely than not to be foreigners, and tattooed inscriptions were often in French or were obvious translations. Only in Barcelona was professional tattooing established, precisely because of the city's unusual openness to foreign influence. (The peculiarity of Barcelonan tattooing was also underlined by its inhabitants' uncharacteristic preference for political over religious and patriotic symbols.)[62] In Belgium, finally, a large-scale investigation of over 14,000 subjects carried out by Louis Vervaeck, the chief physician at the Brussels Minîmes jail, also attributed the spread of tattooing to foreign influences.[63] Vervaeck juggled with evidence both that tattooing was a recent import into Belgium from France (it was more common among Walloons than Flemings), and that it was becoming domesticated into characteristic national forms whose sentiments seemed almost to charm him:

Our national tattooing is essentially different from that of Germany and France.... Belgian tattooing is more modest, more ugly one must admit, less spiritual, but more naive and sincere. When we find on some depraved vagabond a Christ or a Virgin in veneration, or a scene of the Passion, how can we not think of the profound religious sentiments that are rooted in our rural populations? When we see on a daily basis tattoos of military emblems and inscriptions, how can we not recall the national virtues of this little country – attachment to the family hearth and to the motherland, sincere affections, a simple life?[64]

This sentimentalized evidence of popular tattooing led Vervaeck to criticize Lombroso and Lacassagne alike; he judged their theories of degeneration

---

61 Rafael Sallilas, *El tatauge en su evolución histórica, en sus differentes caracterizaciones antiguas y actuale y en los delincuentes franceses, italianos y espanoles* (Madrid, 1908), 146–9.
62 Ibid., 192–3.
63 Louis Vervaeck, "Le tatouage en Belgique," *Mémoires de la société d'Anthropologie de Bruxelles* 25 (1906), 1–239, summarized in "Le tatouage en Belgique," *Archives de l'anthropologie criminelle* 22 (1909), 333–62. All citations below are from the longer version in the *Mémoires*. I discuss this study in more detail in "National Tattooing."
64 Vervaeck, "Le tatouage," 232, 237.

(as we have seen) to be essentially indistinguishable and denied that "the tattooed man is an abnormal being who is developmentally arrested or degenerate."[65] But Vervaeck went on to draw a sharp distinction between tattooing as such, "which has no constant relation whatsoever with degeneration or criminality," and "the special tattooing that characterizes criminals and the depraved, a kind that bears the obvious imprint of vice and crime." With this he reinsinuated the degenerationist model by the back door:

> Once this distinction is made, we would be entirely in agreement with the Italian and French criminologists in saying that among this minority of the delinquent and the depraved tattooing presents *special* characteristics which suffice to classify the inmate who bears them. Tattooing is extremely common among the truly criminal and develops among them with great facility as a consequence of the degenerative taints, the sexual inversions and the subversive tendencies that are the lot of this sad class of prisoners.

Whereas Vervaeck conceded that it would be impracticable to ban tattooing outright, he argued that it should be generally discouraged, prohibited for young people, and proscribed in the army by severe penalties including "cauterization by fire" – an extraordinarily harsh suggestion that also contained disturbing implications of branding. Yet this was perhaps only consistent with the stated aim of these strategies: to remake tattooing into that which Lombroso claimed it already was, an irrevocable stigma of criminality. "Confining itself to those milieux that in essence tend to glorify it, it will become the true characteristic of the criminal, the depraved, and the degenerate."[66]

Vervaeck's paradoxical conclusion can be understood as a proposal that the incorrigible offender should stigmatize himself by inscribing a permanent physical mark that announced his criminal identity on his body's surface. He only articulated with unusual clarity a view that suffused the tattooing debate more nebulously and that represented a return of the repressed practice of penal branding and mutilation. Now that the state had abandoned the official marking of the body in the name of progress, humanity, and reform, the criminal was being asked to literally brand himself. This could be compared to expecting Kafka's convict to set in motion the "harrow" that carved his crime into the surface of his body and to survive this punishment as a marked man.[67] What is significant here is not merely the external sign, but the fact of its self-imposition by the delinquent: This voluntary act

---

65 This and the following quotations are from ibid., 234–6.
66 Ibid., 238.
67 Franz Kafka, "In der Strafkolonie," idem, *Erzählungen* (Berlin, 1963), 199–236.

would not only advertise a status but would express something inherent in the criminal himself. What was at stake was a permanent sign of the self, added to the external juridical categories of judgment and sentence, that dissolved confession in identity. This condition depended on a culture in which official branding had been abolished and body-marking stigmatized. To propose official tattooing as a more humane alternative to penal branding therefore missed the point.[68]

CONCLUSION

The desire to legislate the meaning of the tattoo by a regime of dissuasion, marginalization, and pathologization, rather than banning it outright, supports Marie-Christine Leps's proposition that "criminology's first function was to generate a discourse capable of widening the definition of deviance and of authorizing tighter control procedures"[69] – here, over the permitted functions of bodily expression. The tattoo thus became a kind of semiotic battleground on which criminologists skirmished with the tattooed over the significance of their marks, though they seemed uncertain whether the trophy was the meaning of specific images or of the sign as such. The hope that the tattoo was a species of language explains the iterative character of the treatments I have discussed, which piled up immense quantities of data without seeking to advance the interpretive agenda. This linguistic element was conveyed both by Lombroso's characteristic naked male figure inscribed with numerous tattoos, and even more by the much more frequently presented visual logs of single images isolated from the body that bore them – a body which itself had usually been yanked from its habitual cultural ambience in order to be isolated as a specimen.

Lombroso's presentation displayed the criminal's body as if it were an unmediated text narrating the story of his self, and this theme was taken up in the scattered attempts to read multiple tattoos as a kind of visual autobiography, as intimate clues to the bearer's personality or psychology.[70]

---

68 Dr. Liersch, "Zwangstätowierung zur Wiedererkennung von Verbrechern," *Vierteljahrsschrift für gerichtliche Medizin* 3rd ser., 21 (1901), 73–5; and see also Séverin Icard, "Procédé pour marquer d'un signe indélébile et non infamant les professionnels du crime," *Archives de l'anthropologie criminelle* 26 (1911), 30–34, which recommended something equivalent to a permanent symbolic prison number (but "legible" only to experts) marked on the body of released convicts.

69 Leps, *Apprehending the Criminal*, 43.

70 This was especially the focus of research into tattoos on the insane, discussed by Plas, "Tatouages et criminalité"; see, e.g., Dr. Christian, "Tatouage chez un aliéné," *Annales d'hygiène publique et de médecine légale*, 3rd ser., 25 (1891), 515–20; E. Marandon de Montyel, "Contribution à l'étude clinique des tatouages chez les aliénés," *Archives de l'anthropologie criminelle* 8 (1893), 373–413;

The second method of presentation imputed an almost pictographic character to tattoos, as if they were entries in a lexicon of images, a hidden compendium of subcultural meanings that could be translated into the dominant tongue in the same way as those graffiti, verbal argots, and *Gaunerzinken* (signs in tramps' code) that had long been intriguing to nineteenth-century police science. On occasion the resemblance and resistance to interpretation were blatant. Lacassagne described finding "on one man's left arm . . . a sort of mysterious alphabet composed of characters reminiscent of those employed by stenographers. The man in question did not want to reveal their meaning to us, and yet we know with certainty that in some penitentiaries . . . some inmates had adopted a special alphabet in which to write a secret journal."[71] If criminology monopolized language *about* tattoos, the tattooed had the language itself.

By the interwar period, at the latest, tattoo imagery appears to have established exactly this kind of proto-linguistic role in the *milieu*, the French underworld. In the words of an inspector in the forensic department of the French police in 1951, "Tattoos have become an almost exclusive appanage of the underworld [a fact which has] restored the utilitarian character of tattoo and [made] its bearer recognizable to his colleagues through the medium of a clandestine language, a sort of graphic argot."[72] If we can believe this claim, French criminal culture had endowed tattoo images with coded meanings that could in fact be deciphered as a system of speech, or rather as a primitive substitute for it. The lingering influence of Lacassagne is easily detectable here, establishing via Locard an unbroken line of French forensic semiotics, and suggesting a parallelism in national patterns of both police and criminal cultures: "For many frustrated beings, intellectually not far removed from primitive man, this art at once conventional and brutal remains the only means of expression for the confused and violent feelings that surge inside them. Its finality, its bizarre appearance, the blood and pain

---

L. Daguillon, "Contribution à l'étude des tatouages chez les aliénés," ibid., 10 (1895), 175–99; Gotthold, "Vergleichende Untersuchungen."

71 Lacassagne, *Les tatouages*, 90. The comparison of tattoos with graffiti was an obvious one: see, e.g., Louis Battut, "Du tatouage exotique et du tatouage en Europe," *Archives de l'anthropologie criminelle* 8 (1893), 84–5.

72 Jacques Delarue, "Florescence and Decadence of the Tattooist's Art," *Graphis* 7 (1951): 191. See also Jacques Delarue and Robert Giraud, *Les tatouages du "milieu"* (Paris, 1950). For the similar case of Russia, see A. Sudomir and P. Zeranskaja, "Die Psychologie der Tätowierung bei Verbrechern," *Archiv für Kriminologie* 85 (1929), 14–22 (a study of tattooed convicts in Kiev), and M. W. Solowjewa, "Die Tatauierung der jugendlichen Verbrecher," ibid., 87 (1930), 214–19 (a study of tattooed juvenile detainees in Saratow); for a full interpretation of Russian criminal tattooing, see Abby Schrader, "Branding the Other/Tattoing the Self: Bodily Inscription among Convicts in Russia and the Soviet Union," in Caplan, *Written on the Body*, 174–92.

that accompany its execution are well qualified to attract men who have remained as simple and cruel as children."[73]

This association of tattooing and primitivity invoked the values of a culture that had largely displaced decoration from the human body to its clothing, and fixed graphic speech in scriptorial rather than pictorial signs.[74] As a graphic language, the tattoo defied the ruling regime of literacy in modern Europe and resisted subjection to its laws. If we follow the anthropologist Alfred Gell's interpretation of tattooing as a "double skin," a kind of armor, that is, paradoxically, open to the multiplication of meanings, we can sense both its attractions for the bearer and the insult it conveyed to the literate interpreter.[75] Criminal speech seems to have escaped this opprobrium: tattooing and argot, it has been argued, actually followed inverse paths after the nineteenth century: while the once widespread custom of tattooing came to be disdained as a vicious and offensive practice suitable only for criminals and prostitutes, argot was able to make its way from criminal circles into general social speech.[76] How much criminology contributed to that transvaluation, or whether it merely recorded it, is debatable. It is hazardous to isolate any cultural practice from its broader social and aesthetic milieu and to concentrate on one context of criticism, though in this case there was not much to rival the criminological commentary on tattoos. But the quotations from Michel de Certeau and Thierry Maertens that preface this chapter suggest that the claims of the law converged on the tattooed body in a double sense, insisting on its own prerogative both to inscribe and to exclude. If the man who marked his own body thus presented a special challenge to the criminologists' project of calibrating the criminal body with the criminal law, the preemptive designation of the tattoo as already criminal seemed an almost inevitable response – even if it was not in fact the last word.

73 Delarue, "Florescence and Decadence," 191.
74 See Roy Harris, *The Origin of Writing* (London, 1986), 55–6.
75 Gell, *Wrapping in Images*, 38–9.
76 See Jean Graven, *L'argot et le tatouage des criminels* (Neuchatel, 1962).

16

What Criminals Think about Criminology

French Criminals and Criminological Knowledge at the End of the Nineteenth Century

PHILIPPE ARTIÈRES

For the past thirty years, historians of criminology have extensively studied the birth and development of criminology – from phrenology to criminal anthropology – and have reviewed the different debates about the criminal's personality that engaged the scientific community in the late nineteenth century.[1] More recently, these historians have taken an interest in the impact of criminology outside the scientific community. As a consequence, there have been studies to determine how the judicial system assessed and used this new knowledge.[2] Other historians have studied contemporary literature to find evidence of the spread of this specific knowledge, especially among naturalistic writers.[3] The press also has been the subject of some research, and it appears that tabloids tended to popularize criminology when reporting on famous criminal trials.[4]

But what about those most intimately involved, namely, the criminals themselves?[5] No one has tried to find out how they reacted to this scientific knowledge. Perhaps it has been assumed that they could not understand what was said about them, as if criminology was a science similar to botany or as if the discourse was irrelevant. Yet, just as a history of medicine is not complete if it does not include the point of view of those who benefit from it, so too the history of criminology and psychiatry must reckon with the way

Thanks to Michelle Perrot, Philippe Lejeune, and Dominique Kalifa for their help during the research on these criminals' autobiographies. This chapter was translated from French by Nicole Cesbron.

1 See Laurent Mucchielli (editor), *Histoire de la criminologie française* (Paris, 1994); Marc Renneville, *La Médecine du crime* (Thesis, Université de Paris 7, 1997).
2 Frédéric Chauvaud, *De pierre Rivière à Landru: La violence apprivoisée au XIXe siècle* (Bruxelles, 1991); Michel Porret and Vincent Barras, "Homo criminalis," *Revue Equinoxe* 22 (Fall 1999).
3 See Frédéric Chauvaud, *Les Experts du crime* (Paris, 2000); Jean-Marie Berlière, *L'Institution policière sous la IIIe République* (Thesis, Université de Bourgogne, 1991).
4 See, for example: Anne-Emmanuelle Demartini, *L'Affaire Lacenaire* (Paris, 2001).
5 See Dominique Kalifa, *L'Encre et le sang* (Paris, 1995); Philippe Artières and Dominique Kalifa, *Vidal: Le Tueur de femmes* (Paris, 2001).

criminals and insane people have reacted to this discourse, have used it, and have lived with it. I am convinced that we must attempt to write their story. Therefore, I plead for research that does not regard criminology exclusively as an activity of the scientific community but studies it in interaction with its subjects, the criminals.[6]

Two types of documents can primarily be used to conduct such a survey: (1) judicial documents, particularly the interrogations of prisoners; and (2) autobiographical papers written by criminals. Some were published by doctors in contemporary medico-legal journals and collections, such as those published by Alexandre Lacassagne in the *Archives d'anthropologie criminelle* and by Cesare Lombroso in his *Palimpsestes*.[7] However, texts published by criminologists mostly corroborated and validated their own theses. Consequently, a different corpus of documents may be more useful: the unpublished manuscripts of criminals. Although quite rare, they undoubtedly give a better reading of the responses of criminals to the novel approach of criminology.

I have been conducting research on the Lacassagne papers in Lyon and, more precisely, on autobiographies written by criminals in the late nineteenth century; here, I will advance some arguments resulting from my studies.[8] To identify the limits of such a survey, I will start by briefly recalling the circumstances in which the texts originated. In most cases, the criminals began to write because they wanted to produce scientific work and to have an influence in explaining the criminal phenomenon. I then give some examples that show what use these criminals made of criminological theories, either by adopting or repudiating them.

"DEAR PROFESSOR LACASSAGNE":
WHEN CRIMINALS WRITE TO CRIMINOLOGISTS

In the late nineteenth century, Lacassagne carried out an unprecedented experiment with some of the prisoners in St. Paul in Lyon.[9] His method was to select prisoners keen on writing or drawing and then to visit these "authors" in order to examine their notebooks. He suggested that they write

---

6 See the chapters by David Horn and Jane Caplan in this book.
7 Cesare Lombroso, *Les palimpsestes des prisons* (Lyon, 1894).
8 Fonds Lacassagne, Bibliothéque municipale de Lyon, fonds ancien; see *Catalogue du Fonds Lacassagne*, rédigé par Claudius Roux (Lyon: Imprimerie Lyonnaise, 1922).
9 On the importance of Lacassagne in the history of French criminology, see the chapters by Laurent Mucchielli and Martine Kaluszynski in this book.

their life stories, and he provided them with the necessary paper, ink, and pens. He came to see them every week to check on their progress. When a criminal's manuscript was finished and approved by Lacassagne, he gave the author another blank notebook with new instructions and occasionally some money. When a notebook was judged unsatisfactory, he made the prisoner rewrite it.

Thus, the first criminals that emerged from the silence were ordinary people, the "infamous" people about whom Michel Foucault has written, and the "common" people about whom Dubuffet has written – ordinary, faceless individuals who unexpectedly came into contact with a scientist.[10] Their names are Luigi Richetto, Charles Double, Henri Vidal, Camille Honoré Petitjean, Claude Carron, Pierre Tavernier, Louise Chardon, and Émile Nouguier. All were born between 1850 and 1875. Their lives were anchored in the Rhone-Alps region, but all traveled a great deal, in France or even in foreign countries. All remained single and some of the men never even had a relationship with a woman. Their family histories are full of violence, disease, and death, with much conflict and tension. The history of their education was also quite chaotic. Although some, like Louise Chardon, left school at the age of eleven to learn a trade as an apprentice, others attended secondary school. Their professional lives give more evidence of their marginality: Earning their living was a precarious matter, they were constantly changing jobs, and they generally lived in poverty. Charles Double, for example, lived on the money his mother sent him after he had repeatedly been dismissed by his employers. Banished by society, these figures came to engage in illegal activities. They therefore accumulated a sometimes serious criminal record and started serving time in prison as youths.

Such ordinary marginal people made up the "silent world" to be found in French prisons at the end of the nineteenth century. But their status as anonymous prisoners suddenly changed when they encountered the curious criminologist. Within a few months, sometimes within days, they broke their silence and turned into real autobiographical writers, simply by obeying Lacassagne's injunction to write.

It was very difficult for most to become writers because few had had any literary ambition and most knew nothing or only very little about writing, which is quite obvious in the texts Lacassagne collected. "A Loose Woman's

---

10 See Michel Foucault, "La vie des hommes infâmes," in *Dits et écrits* (Paris, 1995), v. III, 237; Jean Dubuffet, *Les Hommes du commun* (Paris, 1973).

Life" by Louise Chardon, for example, was written in complete ignorance of orthography and grammar, and the same is true of Tavernier's "My Life," which has all the characteristics of colloquial, spoken language.

There is a whole series of such texts, all produced under the same circumstances, that is, to gratify the criminologist's desires. The manuscripts Lacassagne collected consist of sixty-six small school notebooks of twenty-four or thirty-two pages each. The contribution of every prisoner to this corpus varied: Émile Nouguier undoubtedly was the most prolific, whereas most other prisoners were much more succinct. However, all the manuscripts were addressed to Lacassagne in one way or another. Charles Double, for instance, wrote Lacassagne's name on the cover of his notebook and added the words: "To be read by medical doctors only." Henri Vidal pointed out that his memoir was "offered to Monsieur Lacassagne who may use it as he wishes." The authors lavished great care and attention on their manuscripts: no words are crossed out and the handwriting is painstaking and regular. The prisoners adopted editorial standards akin to those of a printed book: They numbered the pages, underlined main points, dated their manuscript, respected the margins, inscribed annotations from poets, used paragraphing, and sometimes even included footnotes. They invented their own titles: "The Psychological and Mental State of a Homosexual Parricide" by Double; "A Loose Woman's Life" by Chardon; "This Is My Life" by Petitjean; and "A Sketch of the Life of Parricide" by Carron. They all divided their works into chapters with subtitles. Vidal, for example, deals successively with "The Origins of the Hatred of Women," "My Regrets," "Falling off the Bicycle," and "My Mother's Temperament."

These manuscripts are unique: Not only do they relate uncommon lives, but they also represent one of the first and rare examples in the nineteenth century of what might be called "constrained literature," which is different from commissioned literature (such as speech writing for someone else that is commissioned by contract). The prisoners are not in a position to refuse; they have to obey and write a text without profiting from it. Moreover, Lacassagne's injunction must be regarded as an act of coercion because writing is unfamiliar to most of the authors, because writing implies introspection (Nouguier, Double, and others complained about this difficulty on several occasions), and, above all, because achieving an autobiography requires coherence. Writing one's life story in the nineteenth century meant organizing all the events in a chronological order; it meant following an imposed pattern. As Pierre Bourdieu has explained, "Producing a life story, treating life as a coherent account of a meaningful sequence of events may mean sacrificing to a rhetorical illusion, a common representation of life that a long literary tradition has unceasingly imposed."[11] This tradition was either unknown to Lacassagne's prisoners or they had only recently discovered it (Nouguier, for example) by reading books in the prison library.

The authors Lacassagne chose were therefore in the same situation as Native Americans in the late nineteenth century, when anthropologists asked them to write the stories of their lives, although their own imagination and their own ideas of an autobiography were completely different.

Thus, in the case of White Bull's life story, minutely analyzed by David Brumble, the Sioux Chief chooses to leave out the events connected with his childhood.[12] The first episode that White Bull writes about is a bison hunt because, for him, the story of his life is the story of his actions, of his deeds as an adult. Brumble insists that if incidents belonging to childhood are to be found in the stories about warriors it is either because they serve as signs of future accomplishments or because the researcher insisted on obtaining some information about their childhood. It is precisely under this influence that autobiographies by Native Americans increasingly give more space to childhood stories, although writing about childhood is contrary to their idea of autobiography. This quotation from Yellow Wolf illustrates this same opinion: "It is not good to talk about the years when I grew up. It does not belong to history. It would mar the story I am writing. I do not want to spoil it, to blemish what I did during the war."[13]

Most anthropologists, partisans of autobiographies written according to the pattern prevailing in Western countries, refused any objection raised. This often resulted in violent confrontations, and the Indians offered strong resistance. Such was the case with a Papago Indian named Maria Chona and the anthropologist Ruth Underhill: "She [R. U.] did not let go until she got what she wanted, a word, a piece of information or anything else . . . Chona sometimes started shouting at Ruth, when asked the same question again and again. She was exasperated and would say, You milgahn [American] you are so stupid, you don't know anything."[14]

The autobiographies "initiated" by Lacassagne offer examples of similar confrontations: Carron reacted strongly when the criminologist asked him to rewrite his text; Vidal took great pleasure in making fun of the professor's obstinacy and would interrupt his confessions now and then to address him and remind him that, by asking Vidal to focus on some point or

---

11 See Pierre Bourdieu, "L'illusion biographique," *Actes en sciences sociales* nos. 62–3 (1986): 70.
12 See David Brumble, *Les Autobiographies d'indiens d'Amérique* (Paris, 1993).
13 Quoted by D. Brumble in *Les Autobiographies d'indiens d'Amérique*.
14 Maria Chona and Ruth Underhill, *The Autobiography of a Papago Woman*, Memoirs of the American Anthropological Association, no. 64 (1936).

another, the professor was completely neglecting other important matters. The notes written by Lacassagne in the margins of Vidal's manuscript also illustrate the tension between the two. There was less tension in the case of Nouguier, who seemed to be fascinated by Lacassagne; but his compliance was, of course, largely determined by his unequal position vis-à-vis the criminologist.

These autobiographies form part of the long history of confessions in Western countries. Émile Nouguier's *Memoirs of a Sparrow or the Confessions of a Prisoner*, which I published in 1998, was the first text produced in accordance with Lacassagne's method.[15] It exemplifies what is known as institutionalized confessions and undoubtedly gives evidence of the radicalization of this institutionalization in the second half of the nineteenth century. All these autobiographical writings originated under constraint, and yet they clearly reveal noticeable differences in the authors' responses to criminological views. Despite this constraint, some freedom becomes evident in the style and the ideas.

Before exploring this any further, it should be made clear that this corpus of autobiographies is not homogeneous. Some authors – like Louise Chardon, a prostitute who was an accomplice in the murder of her uncle – knew nothing at all about criminology and wrote brief accounts of their lives. But others adopted particular positions vis-à-vis Lacassagne's criminological theories. Moreover, the link between the criminologist and his authors could become strong. As the weeks passed, some prisoners no longer regarded Lacassagne as an ordinary visitor but rather as a confidant, father, or friend.

"I AM THE ONE YOU THINK I AM": WHEN CRIMINALS IDENTIFY THEMSELVES WITH THE CRIMINOLOGIST'S DISCOURSE

In our corpus of texts, the appropriation of criminological theories by the criminal writers is the most common scenario. Such cases were often advanced by criminologists themselves in order to validate their work. Such is the case with "Memories and Impressions of a Condemned Man," an autobiography that Lacassagne received from a prisoner in the early 1890s and then published in the *Archives d'Anthropologie criminelle* in 1893 "without altering a line." In this account the prisoner portrays in rapid sequence

15 See *Drôle d'oiseau: Autobiographie d'un voyou à la Belle Epoque*, texte présenté et etabli par Philippe Artières (Paris, 1998).

various criminals he came across while he was in jail: the Italian Mariani, a bloodthirsty born criminal who had no moral sense and enjoyed killing; the Austrian Umstasch, an insane criminal; and Cournon, a cold-blooded killer who carefully planned each murder. Although typological categories of criminals clearly inform the author's discourse, they remain implicit.[16]

The same applies to Jeanne Weiss, who poisoned her husband with the help of her lover. Before killing herself, she wrote "My Impressions in Prison," which Lacassagne quickly published in his journal in 1891 under the title "The Notebooks of Mrs. Weiss." In them the beautiful young poisoner drew a self-portrait that conformed to the picture of a hysterical female poisoner as described in contemporary academic publications.[17] But here, too, the scientific discourse is only alluded to and remains implicit. In contrast, it was much more explicit in the autobiography of Émile Nouguier, who was charged with the murder of a bar owner in Lyon in 1898.[18]

During the year he spent in St. Paul's prison, while awaiting trial and then execution, Émile Nouguier spent most of his time writing. On February 3, 1899, he obtained a small notebook and decided to keep a diary, which he did until he was executed in February 1900. Within a few days of getting the notebook, Nouguier wrote a first autobiographical text, which he called "The First Chapter of My Life: My Existence in General." At the end of this first text, he announced that he planned to write a second chapter about his faults. In early April, he was visited by Lacassagne, who asked him for permission to read his diary on a regular basis. In May, over the course of two days, Nouguier wrote the second chapter, titled "My Mistakes and My Faults." On July 2, Lacassagne came to see him again and suggested that he record his life story from a moral point of view. On the same day, Nouguier wrote an autobiographical text according to this new perspective. At month's end, Lacassagne visited again, approved of the work done, and urged Nouguier to develop the draft of July 2. On July 27, Nouguier started writing a fourth autobiography according to Lacassagne's advice. It was to fill six notebooks and was titled: "Memoirs of a Sparrow, or the Confessions of a Prisoner."[19]

In this document, Nouguier reorganizes all the important events of his life. He now constructs a fate designed to demonstrate the perfect coherence

---

16 Anonymous, "Souvenirs et impressions d'un condamné," *Archives d'Anthropologie criminelle* (1893): 326–33.
17 "Les Petits cahiers de Mme Weiss," *Archives d'Anthropologie criminelle* (1891): 420–30.
18 Affaire Nouguier, Ms 5279, Fonds Lacassagne, Bibliothèque municipale de Lyon.
19 See *Drôle d'oiseau*, 138.

of the episodes in his life. Whereas in "My Life in General" he had, as far as his memory permitted, adopted a chronological order, in "Memoirs" he completely rearranged the chronology. Consequently, Nouguier's first confession is not a narrative of his childhood but a self-portrait. It is as if Nouguier wanted to inscribe his story in a set shape, that of a child's unflattering portrait, in order to make the reader understand from the first pages that the murder he committed was mainly the consequence of his innate tendency toward evil. The following episodes appear to be nothing but the repetition of his early years. As a young boy he was greedy, self-indulgent, and a victim of his father's sadistic punishments; as an adult he became lazy, a thief, a gambler, and a lady's man, who broke the law and served the sentences imposed on him. At the end of his eighth confession he writes: "What was written is, what must be will be."

Nouguier does not stop with this self-portrait. In the following confessions, he tells us how, after his mother's death, he lived with his father. It was his father who incited him to steal. He also described how he encountered God when he was sent to the country in order to keep him away from bad friends. Back in Lyon, he found out his father had had an incestuous relationship with his older sister. He committed various offenses and, unable to put up with his father's scolding and remarriage, he ran away to his grandmother's. After robbing and beating her, he went back to Lyon, where he again committed minor offenses. While his father was temporarily away, he had an affair with his stepmother. He then increasingly stayed away from home, roaming Lyon in the company of other children. He was twelve when he left for Paris. On his way, he worked as a farmhand and fell in love with the farmer's daughter. Convinced that he could not declare his feelings publicly, because of his social status and because of his resentment of the rich, he went on to Paris, where he made a living as a thief. Through chance acquaintances he learned about anarchism and, when he returned to Lyon, he pursued his career as a thief and established contact with the local anarchist groups. In 1893 he was arrested for robbery and sentenced to prison for the first time. After his release, he was miserable and managed to survive by committing crimes at night, first on his own, and then with the help of a mate. They went together to Annecy and Paris, where Nouguier parted with his accomplice and converted to socialist ideas. He returned to Lyon, where he was arrested again for robbery and sent to prison, where he tried to commit suicide. After his release, he stayed with a gang of burglars for a while and then joined a circus with which he traveled all over France. He fell in love with the equestrienne, eloped with her, and eventually abandoned her.

He reappeared in Lyon where he made a living as a pimp and the leader of a gang of thieves. He was arrested and imprisoned once more. After being released, he went back to the family home and reconciled with his father, whose wife had left him and whose daughter had died. Because they often quarreled, Nouguier finally decided to leave his father and went to work as a construction worker. From that time forward, until his arrest at the end of 1898 for the murder of La Villette, he organized gangs that stole in the Lyon area; he was sentenced for multiple robberies and for being part of a criminal association.

This new autobiographical account in the form of a "destiny" is also punctuated with the recurrent figure of the father; the "Memoirs" focus on the father-and-son relationship. Whereas in his initial autobiographical text, written in February, the person of the father had been of secondary importance, here the father cannot be dissociated from the young man's misconduct: It is the father who mistreated him, who obliged him to steal, who had sex with his own daughter, and thus caused the family to disintegrate. These acts of the father drove the son into extreme poverty and made him become a thief.

In the "Memoirs," Nouguier not only organized events differently, but also increased the number of offenses he committed. In order to give his story more vividness, he blackens his own character: He claims to be not only a thief, but also a pimp, a forger, a hooligan, an anarchist, and so forth. This blackening of his own character sheds light on his writing strategy. Because Nouguier wants Lacassagne to take an interest in him, he deliberately exaggerates his own criminality by cleverly assembling a montage of episodes, by creating suspense through omissions, and by rewriting some events in order to more closely approximate Lacassagne's preoccupations, such as the innate tendency for some individuals to do evil and the influence of the social milieu on the individual. In this respect, the omission of the account of his birth and the emphasis on bucolic episodes are significant.

By contrast, the first autobiographical text, "My Life in General," began with details about his birth. In the "Memoirs," this episode was replaced by a tale about the birth of a sparrow. After the preface, Nouguier opened his confessions with a description of himself, not as an innocent baby but as a bad boy, as if he wanted to obliterate his early years. Thus he began his autobiography by describing a personal flaw – his desire, as a child, to touch everything, often breaking things – and his gluttony, which led to punishment by his parents. Hence his real birth did not occur on February 11,

1878, but on the day when he first began to steal. Nouguier tried to write a life story that was adapted to the viewpoint of his reader, Lacassagne, and, more generally, of society. He therefore adopted not only the contemporary views about criminals, but also the contemporary system of values: work, education, and religion.[20]

"GENTLEMEN, YOU ARE WRONG": WHEN CRIMINALS DISAGREE WITH CRIMINOLOGISTS

It sometimes happened that criminals began to write because they wanted to correct the views of criminologists and medical experts. In most cases, they did so not only with regard to their own case but also with regard to more general ideas about criminal behavior. Their wish often was to enlighten scientists: Henry Vidal wanted to generalize from his own case; Charles Double desired to set straight some contemporary ideas about homosexuality; and Émile Nouguier hoped to correct some errors with regard to the use of slang.

Henry Vidal: "Doctors, You Are Mistaking My Case"

Charged with several attempted murders and the killing of four women on the French Riviera between November 24 and December 11, 1901, Henry Vidal was tried by a court in the Alpes–Maritimes department. Several experts were heard during the trial. Dr. Boyer gave this description of the defendant's personality:

Vidal does not show any sign of madness or epilepsy; his crimes are not incoherent, impulsive actions. His parents were not epileptic. He may have been debilitated by typhoid fever. Vidal himself has given a careful description of his own mental condition. He has told us about his escapes, which always were motivated and not impulsive. He has spoken about his phobias – thanatophobia, the fear of death, and hemophobia, the fear of blood. He has never suffered from expressed anguish. Zoophilia may lead to aberrations, but it is not the case with Vidal. His thefts cannot be imputed to kleptomania. The stories he made up are very interesting. Vidal is not affected by delirium or by amnesia. Vidal was unsuccessful in business. He badly needed money. He decided to get some by any means.

Boyer gave a quick account of Vidal's crimes and the precautions he took and concluded: "No epilepsy, no hallucinations, only a slight trembling of his fingers. There are some signs of degeneration. He is debilitated. His

---

20 See Philippe Artières, "Ecriture contrainte," in *Genèses du "je,"* ed. Philippe Lejeune and Catherine Viollet (Paris, 2000); Philippe Artières, *Le livre des vies coupables* (Paris, 2000).

crimes reveal nothing delirious or impulsive. He must be held responsible for them."[21]

While in prison, Vidal wrote at great length and produced several memoirs. His purpose was to correct the opinion of medical experts who regarded him not as a sick person but as a murderer motivated by greed. "Listening to your discourse, I simply realize that you, gentlemen, haven't understood my case as it really is: No, you do not understand because you read me too quickly. You do not pay attention to many details you think unimportant but which are precisely the ones that make my case very different from those you have come across so far."

He thus pointed out his childhood diseases (and the accidents he had, for example, when he fell off his bicycle), his consumption of alcohol (he makes an extensive list of the times he drank heavily), and his fear of blood since birth. When he described his crimes, he underlined the impulsiveness of his actions: "As I walked into the room, the scent of perfume and the darkness suddenly flushed me with scorn and hatred. My eyesight was blurred, I was stammering, and at that moment I grabbed the knife and stabbed."[22]

Vidal's case is a good example because he made use of arguments often put forward by scientists, but he never worked out an original interpretation of his acts. In this respect, the case of Charles Double is more interesting.

Charles Double: "Homosexuality Is Not Really What You Think"

Double killed his mother in 1904 in Belley (Ain) in order to steal her savings, and took off with his young lover, Courgibet. In his memoir "The Mental and Psychological Condition of a Homosexual Who Killed His Mother," which Charles Double gave to Lacassagne in order to inform scientists about homosexuality, Double developed his own theory about his personality. He began by discussing the various contemporary theories on homosexuality, including the theory of the monster female and the theory of moral hermaphrodism. He then developed quite personal analyses, holding himself up as a fascinating example of this particular "perversion." In discussing the theory of mental hermaphrodism, Double did not deny the scientists' ideas but simply wished to complete them. Using his own life as a reference point, he depicted the life of homosexuals in the late nineteenth century.[23]

21 Alexandre Lacassagne, Jean Boyer, and F. Rebatel, *Vidal: Le Tueur de femmes* (Lyon, 1902).
22 Affaire Vidal, Ms 5268, Fonds Lacassagne, Bibliothèque municipale de Lyon.
23 Affaire Double, Ms 5366, Fonds Lacassagne, Bibliothèque municipale de Lyon.

Double's case is not unique; indeed, many other imprisoned criminals wrote to contribute toward better knowledge of criminality, probably in order to attract people's attention. This wish to add something to criminological knowledge also motivated Émile Nouguier.

Emile Nouguier: "You Don't Know the Criminal's Slang"

The dictionary of slang that Emile Nouguier compiled in prison is another example of the contribution of criminals to the discourse about them. Here it was not, strictly speaking, criminological theories that were at issue, but knowledge about the criminal underworld.

Nouguier commented on Delessale's dictionary of slang at some length. "In the preface, Richepoin says that to know the exact meaning of slang words it would be necessary to have a collaborator living amidst strange and closed circles and that such a man doesn't exist. . . . When you start reading the dictionary, you realize how justified Richepoin's remark was. When you see the dictionary, you are impressed by its size. But when you consult it, you have a totally different reaction. On one hand, there are words in it that are now part of the French language and are to be found in the standard dictionaries (Larousse, Bêcherel, etc.). . . . On the other hand, most of the words in it are not used by speakers of slang and have a different meaning or no meaning at all."[24]

Nouguier found that, out of ten thousand words in Delessale's dictionary, at most a thousand were spelled and explained correctly. Moreover, he explained that this dictionary was in fact merely an incomplete collection of words used in colloquial French, but not a dictionary of the slang used by criminals.

While he was in prison, Nouguier tried to compile his own dictionary of slang and gave a copy to Lacassagne. His aim was quite clear: He wanted not only to correct mistakes, but to play the part of the specialist himself and to become an expert on the world to which he belonged.[25]

The study of how criminals reacted to the scientific discourse about crimes could undoubtedly be more thorough and exhaustive if other corpuses and sources were analyzed. One could, for instance, write a monograph on

---

24 G. Delesalle, *Dictionnaire Argot-français et Français-argot*, avec préface par J. Richepin, Ms 5296, Fonds Lacassagne, Bibliothèque municipale de Lyon.

25 Emile Nouguier, "Notes sur l'argot," 50 pp., Ms 5301, Fonds Lacassagne, Bibliothèque municipale de Lyon.

parricide by comparing the criminological literature on the subject[26] and the statements made by contemporary criminals who committed this crime.

Having expressed these reservations, I would like to emphasize two conclusions: First, in the late nineteenth century, criminals were not ignorant of the scientific theories being postulated about them. On the contrary, they knew the criminological discourse, sometimes quite well. Second, this knowledge enabled criminals to develop more or less complex strategies of resistance, including conforming to them, exemplifying them, or critiquing them.

26 See, for example, Raoult, *Le Parricide au point de vue medico-legal* (Ph.D. diss., University of Lyon, 1901).

17

Talk of the Town

The Murder of Lucie Berlin and the Production of Local Knowledge

PETER FRITZSCHE

The newspaperman from the *Berliner Tageblatt* had taken the streetcar to the northern precincts of the city, to the corner of Franseckistrasse and Oderbergerstrasse, where the young girl, Margarete Koschorreck, had been murdered a few days earlier. The reporter walked along Franseckistrasse: In a bar across from the Schultheiss brewery he overheard conversations among patrons discussing a newspaper article about the crime, walked past the "blood-red" reward notices still pasted on the *Litfasssäulen*, or advertising pillars, and, finally, at the murder scene at Franseckistrasse Number 39, stumbled across two little girls on little chairs in front of a junk store absorbed by an account of the murder, slowly reading every word out loud. This story is revealing because it points to the increasingly textual nature of knowledge about the city. At every step, in streetcars, in bars, and in shops, Berliners debated and pored over newspaper articles; along Franseckistrasse they confronted advertisements and police notices. These illustrate not only that reading had become commonplace in even the most proletarian districts of Berlin but that reading about the city had become a habitual way of apprehending the city. The newspaperman's encounter on Franseckistrasse is also revealing because it re-enacted what was still a novelty among big-city newspapers, namely, sending observers to far-flung outskirts to report on working-class lives in feuilletonistic detail. This man from the *Berliner Tageblatt* quite self-consciously charted unknown territory "way out there," admitted his disorientation as he stepped from the streetcar after a "long, often circuitous journey," and took time to describe the urban characters and storefront horizons he saw around him.[1] In this case, a child's murder provided the opportunity for a "west-end" paper to cover a north Berlin

---

1 "Ecke Weissenburger- und Franseckistrasse," *Berliner Tageblatt*, no. 448, Sept. 3, 1904.

district, for a cosmopolitan daily to reflect on metropolitan circumstances. The long trip up from the prosperous "west" thereby established distance from conventional preconceptions and prejudices regarding the working-class north, which was usually represented in the prevailing naturalistic style with grey, monochromatic brush strokes but which this reporter sought to evoke with detail in precise, sharply drawn sketches.

The report from Franseckistrasse in September 1904 was one item in an increasingly voluble and open-ended conversation about the city that had been prompted by the molestation and murder earlier that summer of nine-year-old Lucie Berlin, which also had occurred in a typical proletarian neighborhood, on Wedding's Ackerstrasse. Lucie Berlin's death prompted a broad discussion concerning what elements constituted the metropolis, the social milieu of crime, the consequences of prostitution, and the efficacy of social reform. After the 1904 murders newspaper columns overflowed with feuilletonistic journeys to places of danger, poverty, and social intermixing; city readers, in turn, increasingly approached the metropolis as a social organism that was at once dreadful and delightful.[2] "Talk of the town" became much more garrulous. It admitted more tolerant and less dismissive attitudes regarding poverty, crime, and difference. Clearly defined zones of healthfulness and degeneration faded from view as literary encounters with the city imaginatively reconstructed the contours of metropolitan ecology. Once clear social-scientific divisions of metropolitan geography into territories and metropolitan sociology into types, which criminologists such as Cesare Lombroso had pioneered, no longer applied, whereas literary approaches that privileged case studies and firsthand documentation and investigation thrived. Sensationally detailed literature about crime increasingly informed professional analyses of crime and put stress on culture and circumstance, where before it had rested on race and heredity, and revalorized the juxtapositions, surprises, and hidden aspects of social formations, thus preparing the city as a terrain of sociological uncertainty and literary modernism.

Of course, the murder of Lucie Berlin was not the primary cause for more anthropological, less biological accounts of metropolitan space. The rise of an economically stable urban citizenry that crisscrossed the entire city to work, shop, and play and, at the same time, the development of mass-circulation newspapers that allowed readers to watch themselves using

---

2 Judith Walkowitz, *City of Dreadful Delight: Narratives of Sexual Danger in Late-Victorian London* (Chicago, 1992).

the city set the stage for more empathetic and investigative explorations of the metropolis. More readers wanted to know more about themselves: This was the formula of mass-circulation newspapers at the turn of the twentieth century.[3] The central role of the press in representing city lives corresponded to the rise of social realism and the practical and concrete particulars it favored. This enabled a more generous apprehension of society insofar as it challenged the application of gross scientific typologies even as it rejected overly sentimentalized renditions.[4] Although realism was superseded by modernism, both embellished an aesthetic of disorder.

Intellectual trends at the turn of the century were inclined to take more careful note of victims such as Lucie Berlin, and the horror of her murder, in turn, served to sanction more inductive, ethnographic, and socially conscientious apprehensions of the city. Indeed, no crime generated as much firsthand reporting and secondhand discussion of proletarian Berlin. The investigation of the murder sustained daily articles in all the big Berlin papers, and the trial of the murderer landed on front pages throughout Germany for ten days before Christmas 1904.[5] News of the trial was replenished by morning and evening editions, which provided nearly "live" reports. This complete coverage was all the more distinctive given the ordinary social background and hitherto anonymous lives of the main protagonists. Along Ackerstrasse, where Lucie Berlin had lived and died, the murder was still remembered a generation later, after war and revolution had completely reframed working-class life.[6] The murder also prompted the writer Hans Ostwald to pull together journalists, lawyers, social reformers, and sociologists to publish the fifty-volume *Grossstadt-Dokumente*, at the time among the

---

3 For details, see Peter Fritzsche, *Reading Berlin 1900* (Cambridge, 1996), chap. 2.

4 See, e.g., David E. Shi, *Facing Facts: Realism in American Thought and Culture, 1850–1920* (New York, 1995); Matthew Schneirov, *The Dream of a New Social Order: Popular Magazines in America, 1893–1914* (New York, 1994); and Carla Cappetti, *Writing Chicago: Modernism, Ethnography, and the Novel* (New York, 1993).

5 Berlin newspapers published the same nearly verbatim version of the trial. I relied on the reports in the *Berliner Tageblatt*, which appeared most complete. Individual newspapers also supplemented the transcripts with particular commentary.

6 *Berliner Morgenpost*, Oct. 31, 1929, quoted in Johann Friedrich Geist and Klaus Kürvers, *Das Berliner Mietshaus 1862–1945* (Munich, 1984), 408. The article misstates the date of the murder, which occurred in 1904, not 1891. Lucie Berlin still slips in and out of scholarship. See Fritzsche, *Reading Berlin 1900*, vi, 59, 193; inaccurately, in Eric Johnson, *Urbanization and Crime* (Cambridge, 1995), 78; Margitta-Sybille Fahr, *Pitaval Scheunenviertel* (Berlin, 1995), 5–89; and Margitta-Sybille Fahr, "Vom polizeilichen Leichenschauhaus zum Universitätsinstitute für Gerichtliche Medizin: 110 Jahre Gerichtsmedizin in Berlin-Mitte," *Humboldt*, no. 5 (1995–6), located at www.hu-berlin.de/presse/humboldt/num_596/8-gerich.html.

most comprehensive and innovative sociologies of a European metropolis, an effort that directly influenced the method of the Chicago School of Sociology. These documents, which were bestsellers in the years before 1914, are fascinating precisely because they crossed the professional analysis of crime with sensational literature about crime. Thus "talk of the town" refers to the various layers of the city as sites of crime and of criminological discourse.

It is not surprising that the murder story quickly found a large readership. Murders were not common in turn-of-the-century Berlin, a fast-growing city of nearly two million inhabitants (another two million lived in adjacent suburbs). A total of thirty-eight murders were reported in 1904, down from a prewar high of forty-six three years earlier; of these about half were infanticides.[7] Because Lucie was both female and a child she appeared to readers doubly innocent and doubly fragile, circumstances that only sustained the lurid coverage of the case. Her death was also plainly horrible.[8] Nine-year-old Lucie disappeared on the afternoon of June 9 from the tenement courtyard of Ackerstrasse Number 130, where she had apparently gone down to dance to the tunes of an itinerant organ-grinder. Two days later, her torso, which showed signs of sexual molestation, was found in the Spree River, by the Reichstagsufer, and put the story on the front pages. A few days later a white laundry basket was fished out of the river; it was later associated with the crime and examined for traces of blood and clothing. It was not until six days after Lucie's murder that three boys found the missing head and two arms wrapped in newspaper (the popular *Berliner Morgenpost*, no. 130, from June 9, the day of the murder) floating in the Charlottenburger Verbindungskanal.[9] Two days later, more than a week after Lucie had first disappeared, a worker on the Berlin-Spandauer Schiffahrtskanal found the right leg. Later that same day, her left leg was found in the Spree, near the Schiffbauerdamm. This slow, gruesome pace of discovery paralleled the prolonged police investigation. Seventy-two hours after the case had first been reported, an "army of policemen" worked "day and night" but were unable to locate crucial witnesses, the organ-grinder himself, or the missing body parts.[10] More and more readers were drawn to the unresolved story, which was picked up by papers outside Berlin as well. The initial missteps of the police generated further installments. Curbside informants at first led

---

7 Johnson, *Urbanization and Crime*, 132.
8 *Frankfurter Zeitung*, no. 344, Dec. 11, 1904, provides a thumbnail summary of the case and the charges.
9 On the *Morgenpost*, see Fahr, *Pitaval Scheunenviertel*, 29.
10 *Berliner Tageblatt*, no. 295, June 13, 1904.

the police to hold for questioning a petty underworld figure and sometime insurance clerk, Otto Lenz, who was later released for lack of evidence; they then arrested Theodor Berger, a pimp for Johanna Liebetruth, a prostitute who was the Berlin family's hallway neighbor. It was almost two weeks before the police were confident that they had the right man and had found all of Lucie Berlin's remains.

Over the course of the drawn-out investigation the police appeared repeatedly at the tenement building to inspect hallways and cellars, search and re-search Liebetruth's two-room apartment, and collect more forensic evidence. During these inconclusive visits, hundreds of neighbors gathered, hoping to learn of new developments in the case and eager to vent their anger on the suspects. Occasionally, overcrowded Ackerstrasse had to be closed to traffic.[11] At the same time the press continued to play the story, introducing readers into the lives of Lenz, Berger, and then Liebetruth, taking them along on explorations of the tenement at Ackerstrasse Number 130 and into Liebetruth's apartment, and passing along rumors heard on the street. In twice-daily installments for almost two weeks, newspaper coverage offered exceptional glimpses into proletarian lives. An indicator of just how large and absorbed the citywide readership had become, street corner crowds spontaneously assembled on several occasions to chase and nearly lynch luckless men after they had asked a little girl for directions or otherwise raised suspicions of passersby.[12] It is clear that Lucie Berlin's murder had set the city on edge.

Six months later the trial of Theodor Berger reassembled the citywide republic of readers. The trial was quite elaborate; more than one hundred witnesses were called over ten days and a half-dozen experts presented new methods in criminal forensics that allowed more positive identification of blood drops and woolen threads to link Berger to the crime.[13] Berger and his now estranged lover, Liebetruth, as well as the parents and brothers of Lucie Berlin, provided dramatic testimony. Underworld loyalties among prostitutes and pimps were exposed, and on the fourth day these even prompted a fistfight between two pimps outside the courtroom door. This procession of colorful characters speaking mouthfuls of Berlin dialect insured that the courtroom gallery was packed everyday: Lines began to form in the predawn

---

11 *Berliner Tageblatt*, no. 295, June 13, 1904; *Berliner Volks-Zeitung*, no. 279, June 17, 1904; no. 285, June 21, 1904; no. 583, Dec. 13, 1904.
12 *Berliner Volks-Zeitung*, no. 274, June 14, 1904; no. 287, June 22, 1904; *Berliner Tageblatt*, no. 295, June 13, 1904.
13 Fahr, "Vom polizeilichen Leichenschauhaus zum Universitätsinstitute."

winter darkness.[14] Newspapers around the nation provided ample coverage and added their own sidebar commentaries right up until the last day of the trial, on Christmas Eve.[15] Editors received stacks of letters regarding the case, the small selection that was published revealing just how carefully readers had pored over the transcripts to pick out the most shameful or prurient quotations. The unrehearsed testimony of ordinary Berliners in court became well-remembered items of illuminating knowledge about the city. "The most decisive thing from the proceedings was what the superintendent of the building on Ackerstrasse Number 130 said," commented Professor Friedrich Zimmer, director of the Evangelical Diakonieverein: "'I can't say how many prostitutes there are among the 160 renters in this building; the police refuse to tell me.'" "I simply want to draw attention to one point in this murder trial," rejoindered Dr. [first name] Dosquet-Manasse of the Berliner Frauen-Rettungs-Verein: "Liebetruth said the following: 'I got to know Berger as a 15-year-old. I was with a girlfriend. Berger saw us and greeted me with the words: "Good evening, Fräulein Hännchen!" That flattered me, a man calling me Fräulein. We spent the night together and met every day thereafter.'" Other letters raised familiar criticism: The salacious and unrelenting interest of the press in the case had disquieted the public and contributed to the decline in morals that had imperiled Lucie Berlin in the first place, further evidence of how thoroughly sensational crime stories underpinned metropolitan spectacles. In the wake of the trial, Berlin's underworld provided the stuff for all sorts of literary "exposures" and "revelations," which continued to frustrate legislative efforts such as the so-called Lex Heinze to censor pornographic texts and thereby protect public morals.[16] Lucie Berlin had loudly amplified the "talk of the town."

The trial provided fascinating glimpses into proletarian Berlin. The trial shone light into the narrow corridors, small rooms, and cellar taverns of Ackerstrasse. Called to testify, a procession of workers, coachmen, organ-grinders, grandmothers, laundrywomen, apprentices, as well as sometime pimps (Lenz, Rühr, Sander, and "Mulatten-Albert") and prostitutes (Seiler, Piatkowski, Koperski, and Fuhrmann), gave life and vibrancy to

14 *Berliner Tageblatt*, no. 634, Dec. 13, 1904.
15 In addition to the transcripts, see, e.g., Theodor Schäfer, "Die Welt der Lucie Berlin," *Berliner Tageblatt*, no. 644, Dec. 19, 1904; "Grossstadtjammer," ibid., no. 655, Dec. 24, 1904; "Die Erörterungen über den Prozess Berger," *Vossische Zeitung*, no. 601, Dec. 23, 1904; and *Frankfurter Zeitung*, no. 360, Dec. 28, 1904.
16 "Was lehrt der Mordprozess Berger?" *Berliner Lokal-Anzeiger*, no. 606, Dec. 27, 1904; and letters to the editor, ibid., no. 1, Jan. 1, 1905; no. 13, Jan. 8, 1905. See also *Frankfurter Zeitung*, no. 357, Dec. 24, 1904; and no. 360, Dec. 28, 1904.

a milieu that heretofore had remained largely unrepresented in popular chronicles. The trial transcript supplements a few documentary texts, and all remain key sources for historians.[17] Readers hardly resisted this voyeurism of the ordinary, which offered recognizable images of their own familiar surroundings. The trial allowed Berlin's primarily working-class population to watch themselves, a central pleasure provided by the modern mass media. Readers followed the *Berliner Volks-Zeitung* into the courtyard at Acker-strasse Number 130 and up the stairs: "A badly scuffed wooden stairway in the low-ceilinged entrance of the side building leads up to the second-floor apartments of Liebetruth and the Berlin family. Five doors open onto a nar-row hallway, on the left is the one to Liebetruth's rooms. From here it is just a couple of steps to the Berlin's apartment." "Next to the front door, before going into the kitchen," as the newspaper described Liebetruth's modest rooms, "is a bed draped with a little blanket embroidered with the words 'sleep well.' Behind the bed, right up against the wall, is where the omi-nous basket used to stand, before it was fished out of the river."[18] Other readers shared lunch with the Berlin family. At noon on the day of the murder, Lucie's mother testified, she had directed Lucie to meet her father as he walked home for lunch. Just then, though, Friedrich Berlin entered the apartment and Lucie and her parents sat down to eat: "Lucie ate a meat chop and potatoes – but not the cucumber salad," Anna Berlin remembered precisely. Because Lucie's father was in a bad mood, her mother asked her to make sure that he was in fact walking along Gerichtsstrasse when he headed off back to work and did not veer off to a bar or to visit friends. Shortly after Lucie returned, she needed to go to the toilet and reached for the key to the one in the hall: "She had to jump up to get it because she couldn't reach the bolt. She hopped two times and, as I later saw, she also took along the hall key." After awhile "I went to the stairs and saw that the key was not in the door." Anna Berlin never saw her daughter again, and readers did not soon forget the severe conditions of daily life in working-class tenements.[19] Around the same time the organ-grinder appeared in "the courtyard, which is partially paved with cobblestones, and partially with asphalt. As soon as he began playing, numerous kids from the building gathered on the asphalt and danced to his melodies. Lucie also went down and danced." A proces-sion of strangers followed the musician into the courtyard; "that's always the

---

17 See, e.g., Otto von Leixner, *Soziale Briefe aus Berlin 1888 bis 1891* (Berlin, 1891), and Gesine Asmus, ed., *Hinterhof, Keller und Mansarde: Einblicke in Berliner Wohnungselend 1901–1920* (Reinbek, 1982).
18 *Berliner Volks-Zeitung*, no. 583, Dec. 13, 1904.   19 *Berliner Tageblatt*, no. 642, Dec. 17, 1904.

case in Berlin when the organ-grinder plays," explained the well-informed *Volks-Zeitung*. "It's usually people from the neighborhood, but also idle young men who like to follow the organ-grinders for a couple of blocks or more."[20] "Sleep well," the uneaten cucumber salad, the key to the toilet just out of reach, the asphalt courtyard – details such as these conscripted readers into the drama of Lucie Berlin.

The murder had a long literary afterlife. Ackerstrasse, where Lucie Berlin had lived, was a quintessentially proletarian thoroughfare; at Number 132/133 could be found Berlin's largest tenement, Meyer's Hof, which was built in 1875 and until World War II housed 250 families in a complex encompassing six courtyards.[21] Meyer's Hof provided the scene for Max Kretzer's classic naturalist novel of degeneration and crime in the city, *Die Verkommenen* (1882).[22] Lucie Berlin's murder right next door, at Number 130, an older house dating from the 1850s, enhanced the street's status as a metonym for working-class Berlin. If a deadly crime took place in literary Berlin, as often as not it happened on Ackerstrasse: "Where? Ackerstrasse 210."[23] The crime also made popular the genre of urban case studies. Thus Margarete Koschorreck's murder later that same summer drew journalists all the way north to Franseckistrasse. Emblematic of the fresh focus on crime stories and other city matters was the speedy success of the *Berliner Morgenpost*, founded in 1898 and by the turn of the century Berlin's largest and genuinely hometown newspaper, and the publisher Ullstein's launch of the classic boulevard paper *BZ am Mittag* in 1904, just a few months before Lucie Berlin's murder, which suited *BZ*'s belligerent style and streetcorner focus. Newspapers *in* the city increasingly became newspapers *of* the city; they provided readers information on how to use the newfangled urban place and offered them places to advertise and purchase goods and services. Sensationalized front-page stories about corruption, murder, and suicide told inhabitants about the myriad ways to survive and succeed in the metropolis, and also revealed the many paths to misfortune. By introducing them to novel arenas and unlikely characters the press helped readers move about the labyrinthine city with greater certainty. The curbside feuilletons that could be found in the *Morgenpost*, in *BZ*, and in the *Berliner Tageblatt* were eventually turned into popular literary commodities by writers such as Hans Ostwald and, in the 1920s, Joseph Roth, Bernhard von Brentano, and Siegfried

---

20 *Berliner Volks-Zeitung*, no. 270, June 11, 1904.
21 Geist and Kürvers, *Das Berliner Mietshaus 1862–1945*.
22 Max Kretzer, *Die Verkommenen* (Berlin, 1882). The *Berliner Tageblatt*, no. 644, Dec. 19. 1904, identifies Meyer's Hof as the scene for Kretzer's novel.
23 Anonymous, *Berliner Polizei*, Grossstadt-Dokumente, no. 34 (Berlin, n.d.), 48.

Kracauer. Before World War I, Ostwald had fashioned metropolitan Berlin into a minor publishing industry, expanding the small magazine pieces he wrote immediately after the murder about Lucie Berlin and Berlin Nord into a series of *Grossstadt-Dokumente* (big-city documents) that modeled lurid and detailed explorations of crime, play, and sex in the big city on revelations and testimony, some of which had come directly from the investigation of Lucie Berlin's murder. Ostwald's popular explorations eventually filled fifty best-selling volumes easily identified by their tell-tale brown covers.[24] He understood his audience well, for as soon as fellow writers and journalists turned to the metropolis they found a mass readership that Berlin's newspapers had lacked just a few decades earlier. The busy circulation of feuilletons, exposés, and Ostwald's documentations had the effect of setting the big city as an encompassing stage for its own spectatorial pleasure. City matters fascinated city people, who were increasingly pulled together by distinctively metropolitan media, boulevard newspapers variety shows, and cinemas that styled their formats on Berlin's frenetic pace, visual delights, and tactile contrasts.[25] Reading and writing about Lucie Berlin or about Ackerstrasse characterized the new byways of popular culture at the turn of the century.

There is no doubt that melodrama sold, and a great many popular urban texts simply recycled tried-and-true melodramatic formulas.[26] Stories about murdered women or evil killers or tragic mother-and-child suicides that ended in the Spree appeared again and again in the metropolitan press; Weimar-era films such as *Berlin: Symphonie einer Grossstadt* and *M: eine Stadt sucht einen Mörder* simply continued feulletonistic traditions established in the prewar years.[27] At first glance, the murder of Lucie Berlin fit a melodramatic pattern: a young girl molested, murdered, butchered; a shadowy pimp who gained access to the girl through an unsuspecting prostitute; distraught, hardworking parents. On closer examination, however, the investigation and trial left questions unanswered and revealed the city to be a more complex, less

---

24 Hans Ostwald, *Dunkle Winkel in Berlin*, Grossstadt-Dokumente, no. 1 (Berlin, 1905), i. See also Hans Ostwald, "Aus Berlin N.," *Freistatt* 6 (1904): 1057–9; and Hans Ostwald, "Lucie Berlin," *Das neue Magasin* 73 (July 2, 1904), which provided the foundation for the much more ample investigations, Hans Ostwald, *Das Berliner Dirnentum*, 2 vols. (Leipzig, 1905); and Hans Ostwald, *Zuhältertum in Berlin*, Grossstadt-Dokumente, no. 5. On the distinctiveness of the documentary pamphlets, see Franz Diederich, "Aus den Tiefen des Lebens," *Das literarische Echo* 8 (Nov. 1905). See also Peter Fritzsche, "Vagabond in the Fugitive City: Hans Ostwald, Industrial Berlin, and the *Grossstadt-Dokumente*," *Journal of Contemporary History* 29 (1994): 385–402.
25 Peter Jelavich, *Berlin Cabaret* (Cambridge, Mass., 1993).
26 Peter Brooks, *The Melodramatic Imagination: Balzac, Henry James, Melodrama, and the Mode of Excess* (New Haven, Conn., 1976).
27 On disproportionate coverage for female victims, see Johnson, *Urbanization and Crime*, 212.

legible place. In the first place, the evidence that convicted Theodor Berger
to fifteen years imprisonment for sexual molestation and manslaughter was
circumstantial. The scene of the crime was never conclusively identified,
and neither Lucie Berlin nor Berger could be placed there with certainty.
Liebetruth's apartment appeared astonishingly clean to (male, class-bound)
police detectives, but no blood was found. None of Berger's personal effects
had traces of blood on them, and no one had seen him transport body
parts out of Ackerstrasse or throw them into the Spree. Although Berger
was drunk on the morning of the murder, and experts testified as to the
links between "Lustmord" and drunkenness, Berger had never displayed
the sexual interest in children reportedly cultivated by Otto Lenz, the initial suspect in the murder who had been released once his alibi proved
solid.[28] Moreover, neighbors repeatedly testified to seeing Lucie Berlin in
the tenement courtyard dancing with other children to the tunes of the
organ-grinder and, later, on the street with a bag of candy, whereas the
prosecutor constructed a scenario in which Lucie never left the third-floor
hallway from which Berger allegedly lured her into Liebetruth's rooms.
Indeed, some of the witnesses who placed Lucie outside in the courtyard
described her in the company of a man who sooner fit the description of
Lenz than Berger. Finally, other leads pointed to other men who on the day
of the murder had made improper overtures to young girls along Wedding's
busy streets, including an exhibitionist who allegedly offered children playing in the courtyard at Ackerstrasse 123 a handful of pennies if they would
touch him; these leads were not followed up.[29] The evidence against Berger
was not conclusive beyond a reasonable doubt.[30]

More importantly, the strict and transparent division between good and
evil on which melodrama relies was blurred by the very detail with which
the murder case was reported. Assumptions that the lives people lived were
clearly legible and conformed to physiognomical types were thoroughly
tested. Commentators did describe Johanna Liebetruth, the thirty-two year-
old prostitute who lived a few steps down the hall from the Berlins, in
knowing fashion. "There is no more humanity in her hard, rigid look
that reveals the typical traces of an elderly streetwalker's life of hardship
and depravity," certified the reporter from the *Berliner Tageblatt*: "Her voice

---

28 See the expert testimony of Medizinalrat Dr. Leppmann, *Berliner Tageblatt*, no. 649, Dec. 21, 1904.
     On the sexual interests of Berger and Lenz, *Berliner Tageblatt*, no. 641, Dec. 17, 1904; and *Berliner
     Volks-Zeitung*, no. 584, Dec. 13, 1904.
29 Fahr, *Pitaval Scheunenviertel*, 61.
30 *Frankfurter Zeitung*, no. 357, Dec. 24, 1904, admitted as much. Fahr, *Pitaval Scheunenviertel*, 6–7,
     comes to the same conclusion.

is dry, brassy, without heart. She resembles a lifeless, covetous Salome."[31] Berger's physiognomy was plainly readable to investigating detectives as well. As Berger's attorney ruefully pointed out: "If he blushes, he betrays his great anxiety and thus his guilty conscience; if he stays totally calm, he shows himself to be a totally hardened criminal who doesn't flinch at the charges."[32] In the end, in the opinion of the court, these physiognomies implicated Berger, but among the wider circle of readers the testimony of one hundred witnesses disassembled stereotyped images, made it difficult to sort out honest proletarians from rapacious criminals, and thus raised probing questions about the nature of crime in the city.

Berger was not what many people took to be the typical pimp, "that is to say, a man with a checked cap and neckerchief, a bulldog face, and a blackjack in his hand."[33] According to testimony by Liebetruth's father, Berger was seventeen and Liebetruth not yet fifteen when the two met and she moved in with him and began to prostitute herself to pay the bills. Although the father had Berger locked up for a time, he was unable to stop Liebetruth from seeing her lover. At first glance, Berger appeared to be a predator whose molestation of Lucie Berlin recapitulated his attraction to Liebetruth almost twenty years earlier. And yet Liebetruth testified to Berger's charm. He flattered the fourteen-year-old Liebetruth by calling out to her: "Good Evening, Fräulein Hännchen." They came to meet daily "at an advertising pillar," and she eventually moved in with him. Again and again, Liebetruth returned to Berger despite other affairs, his jealousy, and his drunken rages (he once threw an alarm clock out the window) because she "had a thing for him." Hans Ostwald would later pick up this theme, claiming that most prostitutes associated with pimps out of emotional need, out of love: "Even the prostitute does not want to be alone."[34] ("He never had to protect me. I liked the guy," recounted one prostitute to Ostwald, "and 'cause I didn't want him straying, that's why I gave him money.")[35] Himself once "down and out," Ostwald insisted that prostitutes, and pimps for that matter, led full lives in Berlin's diverse human ecology and could not be dismissed as

31 *Berliner Tageblatt*, no. 640, Dec. 16, 1904.
32 Walter Bahn, *Meine Klienten: Beiträge zur modernen Inquisition*, Grossstadt-Dokumente, no. 42, 13, commenting on testimony by Kriminalkommissar Wannowski in which he described Berger turning "deathly pale and almost unconscious" when confronted with a witness who purportedly had seen him with Lucie Berlin and later becoming "very weak" during interrogation. See *Berliner Tageblatt*, no. 645, Dec. 19, 1904; and no. 646, Dec. 20, 1904.
33 Bahn, *Meine Klienten*, 37.
34 Ostwald, "Aus Berlin N.," *Freistatt* 6 (1904), 1059; *Zuhältertum*, 3; *Dirnentum*, 5 of the introductory section.
35 Ostwald, *Zühaltertum*, 17.

disabled or pathological. This is the conclusion that Liebetruth's father, a seventy-five-year-old furniture maker who had lived in Berlin since 1866, reached as well. He ended up befriending Berger, trying without luck to offer him a job as a polisher in his furniture business, and even calling him "Theodor" and being called "Father" in return, although keeping some distance: "I always said '*Sie*' to him."[36] What these well-known measures of reserve and familiarity revealed were regular bonds of sociability that connected the extended family. Berger also was close to his sister, who on the day of the murder came by to cook a lunch of potatoes and herring for her brother. Klara Walter reported that her brother expressed his intention to marry "Hännchen."[37] In any case, Liebetruth and Berger socialized with their respective families and cannot be regarded as outcasts.

Arriving everyday at the trial on the arm of her new lover – a certain Schadow – Liebetruth did not appeal to the sympathies of the court or the public. Nonetheless, she could be engaged as a victim. The *Berliner Tageblatt* admitted that one reason she moved in with Berger as a fourteen-year-old was because she feared physical assaults from her father. In a rather remarkable letter for its time another reader found the meeting between Berger and Liebetruth typical of the city's predatory gender relations: "What a charming child! Where's today taking you, my pretty Fräulein?" "How often can one hear this sort of thing?" Obviously "it is one of the prerogatives of men to size up the girls they see."[38] The trial raised questions about how and why young girls became prostitutes and amidst the welter of circumstantial detail offered little support for arguments that explained crime in terms of biological predisposition or individual disability. Rather, observers insisted on the relevance of broader contexts: abusive families, overcrowded apartments, economic hardships, and the desire for independence. As a result, newspaper commentaries after the trial dismissed righteous indignation about immorality and extramarital sex and called for municipal housing and other practical reforms.[39]

Easy determinations about good and bad became more and more difficult as the trial revealed the remarkable ease with which Liebetruth moved back and forth between life as a prostitute and the world of friends and neighbors. Intimate details broke down physiognomical types; family scenes trumped

---

36 *Berliner Tageblatt*, no. 640, Dec. 16, 1904.   37 *Berliner Tageblatt*, no. 642, Dec. 17, 1904.
38 Frau Dr. A. Dosquet-Manasse in *Berliner Lokal-Anzeiger*, no. 13, Jan. 8, 1905.
39 Schäfer, "Die Welt der Lucie Berlin"; "Grossstadtjammer," *Berliner Tageblatt*, no. 655, Dec. 24, 1904; "Die Erörterungen über den Prozess Berger," *Vossische Zeitung*, no. 601, Dec. 23. 1904; *Frankfurter Zeitung*, no. 360, Dec. 28, 1904. More generally, see Richard J. Evans, *Tales from the German Underworld* (New Haven, Conn., 1998).

class differences. This certainly was the effect of descriptions of Liebetruth's return to her apartment after serving a three-day sentence at the women's prison on Barnimstrasse; it was during these crucial seventy-two hours that Berger had exclusive access to the apartment and the killing occurred. As she entered her rooms on the Saturday morning after the murder her pet poodle ran up to her, and Berger, who had been lying on her bed, got up to give her a kiss. After awhile, Berger and Liebetruth discussed marriage, a regular topic of conversation between them. "I always wanted to marry Berger," Liebetruth admitted in court, which had been afforded a glimpse into the sentimental nature of this woman whose blanket was embroidered with the words "sleep well" and whose bag wished "sweet dreams." She continued: "We agreed that we would go to city hall on Monday. Saturday night I was away, you know, working; Sunday night too." Late Sunday, Berger picked her up as planned at Cafe Heidelberg and revealed to Liebetruth that he had been summoned by the police to appear for questioning the next day; Berger found himself placed under arrest soon thereafter and the wedding never took place.[40]

The almost seamless transition between Berger's homecoming kiss and Liebetruth's work paralleled the easygoing sociability among residents at Ackerstrasse Number 130. Lucie Berlin, who was known as an extremely friendly child, often played with Liebetruth's dog and did the same shopping chores for her as she did for her mother and other neighbors, most of whom were employed as home workers, stitching clothes in their apartments or manufacturing small items, such as the cigar wrappers that occupied Anna Berlin. On the day of the murder, for example, Lucie was sent out to get "eggs and hot buns"; when she returned, she went out again to pick up "meat chops" for Frau Höhler, who paid her two pfennigs for a visit to the candy counter in return and arranged for Lucie to accompany her to Leipzigerstrasse later that afternoon.[41] With her mother's permission, Lucie undertook similar chores for Liebetruth, who lived right down the hall, and another neighbor (and prostitute), Emma Seiler. Indeed, Anna Berlin admitted that her daughter often played in Liebetruth's apartment and had said of Berger: "Uncle is very nice!" Lucie's father also knew about these contacts with "uncle" and Liebetruth.[42]

Uncle Berger notwithstanding, Lucie was apparently even closer to Seiler and the pimp she supported, the one-time murder suspect Lenz. On the occasion of Seiler's birthday, an organ-grinder had been hired to play some

40 *Berliner Tageblatt*, no. 641, Dec. 17, 1904.   41 *Berliner Tageblatt*, no. 642, Dec. 17, 1904.
42 *Berliner Tageblatt*, no. 642, Dec. 17, 1904; no. 643, Dec. 17, 1904.

dance tunes. Lucie, who again and again was described as well developed
for her age (a further departure from melodrama's projection of the innocent
victim), was among the guests and danced with "Herr Lenz," who not only
took pride in his talents as a "smooth" dancer but felt expert enough to
confide in the Berlins that "Lucie has it in her to become a *Balleteuse*."
The gossip on the courtyard was that Lenz had flattered Lucie's parents
into thinking that their daughter had a future as an artist.[43] Another time
Lucie had even bought schnapps for Lenz. When questioned about these
contacts with prostitutes, Lucie's nineteen-year-old brother Karl admitted
they had existed and claimed he had warned his parents.[44] Casual contacts
between the Berlin family and Ackerstrasse prostitutes continued even after
it had become clear that Lucie had been murdered; Lucie's mother had
a long enough discussion about the case with Liebetruth and Berger for
Berger to raise his suspicions concerning Lenz and to pass along a story
he had picked up on the street about Lucie being killed in a tunnel under
the nearby Stettiner Bahnhof.[45] That her parents had warned Lucie about
talking to strangers generally underscored how untroubled they were about
her friendships down the hall and across the courtyard. After notices had
gone up throughout the city revealing that the butchered parts of a woman
had been found in Charlottenburg, Lucie replied to her mother's concerns:
"Mutti, I'm not that dumb. I know they'll cut my head off and throw me
into the river."[46] Lucie disappeared eight days later.

The seemingly insouciant attitude of Friedrich and Anna Berlin and the
intertwined nature of tenants' lives shocked some observers. Yet, what was
troublesome about the case was not so much that Lucie's mother or father
had acted irresponsibly but that good and bad were not easily distinguishable.
The building superintendent, Rudolf Möbius, for example, admitted that
he had no idea how many among Ackerstrasse's 160 tenants were prostitutes;
the police refused to provide him with any figures, and these would have
included only registered prostitutes. With so many people, he added, the
front gate to the tenement was often left open at night. Unknown people
walked in and out of the building, following the organ-grinder's tune by
day or taking up a one-night stand by night. It was entirely possible for
someone to sneak out a basket filled with body parts without being seen,
Möbius replied under questioning; he himself had recently lost a wardrobe

---

43 *Berliner Volks-Zeitung*, no. 275, June 15, 1904; no. 586, Dec. 14, 1904.
44 *Berliner Volks-Zeitung*, no. 584, Dec. 13, 1904.
45 *Berliner Volks-Zeitung*, no. 583, Dec. 13, 1904; *Berliner Tageblatt*, no. 642, Dec. 17, 1904.
46 *Berliner Tageblatt*, no. 642, Dec. 17, 1904.

that someone had lugged across the courtyard and out the front gate under cover of night. The fact was, as the *Frankfurter Zeitung* commented, "it is not possible to clearly distinguish honest proletarians from prostitutes and their pimps." These busy comings and goings facilitated friendships as much as they jeopardized neighbors. Tenants lived "door to door," participating in corridor gossip (*Flurgespräche* and *Treppengespräche*) that took place between Liebetruth and the Berlins or extending a helping hand as had Lucie Berlin for her mother's workmates or "Uncle" Berger. "Of course one knows," the *Frankfurter Zeitung* argued, rehearsing the reasoning of Ackerstrasse residents, "that prostitutes lead a life that one cannot condone, but on the whole they come from the same background as the rest of the building, and besides, they are as poor as everyone else."[47] The newspaper could have added that both Liebetruth and Berger saw their families regularly. Neither stood outside the bounds of working-class sociability. Theirs was not what Lombroso and his followers postulated as a self-enclosed criminal world marked out by tattoos, slang, hieroglyphics, and other purportedly primitive practices. Residents of Ackerstrasse Number 130 approached each other with a mixture of reserve and intimacy that allowed a diverse but supportive "brightly colored, kaleidoscopic" group to prosper.[48] What made the trial so compelling was that it put forward a more complicated picture of Berlin's proletariat, one in which prostitutes and pimps mingled regularly with tenement-house society and in which they could not be mistaken as strangers or monsters but rather appeared as emotionally robust individuals.

If "the world of Lucie Berlin" indicated just how indistinguishable the criminal world was from the "busyness" of the "crowded lives" in the Ackerstrasse tenement, the adventures of Berger and his mate, Albert Klein, the night before the murder revealed how proximate that world was with other, more respectable precincts of the city.[49] Klein was the first witness to testify on the fifth day. Known to associates in the underworld as "Mulatten-Albert," he had already provided great entertainment a day earlier when he got into a fight with Liebetruth's new lover, whom he claimed was securing false testimony against Berger. Hauled in front of the judge, Klein explained his actions in Berlin's unmistakable dialect: "Look, when I see a guy like that, I have to punch him in the face." The obviously charmed judge asked an overexcited Klein if he wanted to postpone his testimony until the following day. "Better tomorrow, but then first thing in the morning!" he

---

47 *Frankfurter Zeitung*, no. 360, Dec. 28, 1904.
48 Theodor Schäfer, "Die Welt der Lucie Berlin," *Berliner Tageblatt*, no. 644, Dec. 19, 1904.
49 Ibid.

replied to the amusement of the court. The judge played along: "Right, you will appear as the first witness; by then your excitement will have subsided."[50] Klein's testimony was worth the wait. "On this day," reflected the *Berliner Tageblatt*, "the witnesses who were called to testify came from the lowest orders of society." "Mulatten-Albert," a pimp who could be found in dives such as "Lokomotive" and the "Zur Goldenen Kugel," a bar that won lasting notoriety thanks to the trial, told a captivating story about two unsavory men about town. "You could not have asked for more vulgar features or common gestures," commented one paper.[51] On June 8, the day before Lucie Berlin's disappearance, Klein met Berger in the afternoon, when they started drinking in various bars "in the Linden." In the evening, they wandered over to the "Passagen," the famous arcade that connected Friedrichstrasse and Unter den Linden. "Look over there, that's a pretty girl," Klein remembered exclaiming. Klein, Berger, and the woman Berger described as "an artist, officially registered with the police as a prostitute," then had drinks together at the Linden Café. Because Berger's "old lady" was not at home, Berger agreed to lend Klein the key to Liebetruth's apartment. The threesome took a streetcar to Ackerstrasse and, while Berger waited in a bar outside, Klein and the woman went upstairs. Little more than a half-hour later Klein started downstairs but then turned around to find the woman rummaging in Liebetruth's clothes: "Her underwear was dirty, and she apparently wanted to find something clean." Klein warned her to leave Liebetruth's stuff alone, left the apartment, and tossed Berger the key, telling him to get upstairs before the woman caused trouble. Berger rushed back to Liebetruth's apartment and accompanied the "artist" out the door before he rejoined Klein in the "Kugel" on Elsässer Strasse. Later that night Berger got into a brawl, reportedly poked his fingers into the eyes of a rival, and did not return to Liebetruth's until the next morning, by which time his sister had arrived to prepare him his lunch of herring and potatoes.[52]

The testimony of "Mulatten-Albert" fascinated readers because it introduced them to the daily life of a pimp in sensational detail. It surveyed a rich ecology, indicating the ties and loyalties that bound together petty criminals and describing dangerous places like "Zum Goldenen Kugel" on Elsässer Strasse and immoral women in the "Passagen." At the same time there was something completely ordinary about Berger and Klein: the dirty

---

50 *Berliner Tageblatt*, no. 639, Dec. 16, 1904.   51 Ostwald, *Zuhältertum in Berlin*, 76.
52 This is drawn from Klein's and Berger's testimony, *Berliner Tageblatt*, no. 640, Dec. 16, 1904; and
   Frankfurter Zeitung, no. 346, Dec. 13, 1904.

clothes, the drunken fight, the herring at lunch. It was possible for readers to imagine themselves bumping into the two pimps on the streetcar, trolling the Kaiserpassagen, or drinking at the Linden Café. Mulatten-Albert belonged to the Linden as much as anyone, reminding even Berlin's most well-born readers that they could not expect to orient themselves in the city according to sharply drawn lines between sin, depravity, and respectability.

Ostwald elaborated these insights in the *Grossstadt-Dokumente*. He revealed a city that constantly mixed types and mixed up typologies: Points of circulation, such as Friedrichstrasse, Unter den Linden, and Potsdamer Platz, and also streetcars and the most ordinary tenement courtyards and dance halls, were the focus of Ostwald's investigations. In many respects he simply followed the geography laid out in the trial testimony. Moreover, Ostwald credited the trial for exposing not only the lifestyles of pimps and prostitutes but also the ease with which honest and well-meaning Berliners had turned to pimping or prostitution. As he recounted the life stories of pimps, including "der grobe Eugen" from the "Zur Goldenen Kugel," but also "the student," "the doctor," "the confectioner," "the young worker," "the soldier," and "the schoolteacher," he indicated just how fluid the boundaries were between respectability and crime.[53] Only few pimps worked full-time. As a result, it was wrong to think of Mulatten-Albert or Berger as hardened criminals or to imagine their haunts on Friedrichstrasse or Elsässer Strasse as "dens of thieves." "In the dives," he wrote, "things are not much different from what they are in other bars. No louder, no rougher, no more vulgar."[54] The "Kugel," for example, "consists of two big rooms that are decorated in a friendly, even modern style; yellow drapes hang across the high picture windows." Indeed, many pimps were indistinguishable from other small-time entrepreneurs, shopkeepers, and agents, and they belonged to ordinary athletic associations and busied themselves in glee clubs around Alexanderplatz, just as they circulated among the social circles of their own families.

The fugitive nature of city appearances and the promiscuous admixtures of city places became one of the characteristics of an urban modernism that emerged after 1900. Sociologists such as Georg Simmel, painters Heinrich Zille, Ludwig Meidner, and Ernst Ludwig Kirchner, and poets gathered around Jakob van Hoddis and Georg Heym explored Berlin as a brand new place, terrain shaped and reshaped by the accidental surprises, unsettled flux, and weird juxtapositions of city life. To talk about the city at

---

53 Ostwald, "Aus Berlin N.," *Freistatt* 6 (1904), 1059; Ostwald, *Zuhältertum in Berlin*, 20–36.
54 Ostwald, *Zuhältertum*, quoted in Evans, *Tales*, 190.

the turn of the century was to confront its indeterminacies and illegibilities and as a consequence to challenge epistemological confidences. Naturalism, which had painted the poverty of the city in deep and fateful colors, yielded to a more curious and playful approach that inquired about the particulars of metropolitan life and refrained from making broad generalizations or adhering to melodramatic formulas.[55] The recognition that "various existences are thrown together pell-mell," as the *Frankfurter Zeitung* put it, had the effect of overturning conventional notions regarding the malignant constitution of the metropolis, which had been circulated by Lombroso, by Emile Zola, and by Berlin's own Max Kretzer, and in turn of encouraging more anthropological or ecological readings.[56]

Among academics, Ostwald acquired authority as an interpreter of the city and its crimes. He was best known for his writings on tramps, who fascinated observers because they were mobile, hard to track, and moved in and out of respectable trades. Thanks to widely read novels by Jack London, Maxim Gorky, and Ostwald himself, the tramp stood as a powerful transgressive figure: not quite a criminal, not yet a respectable citizen, and therefore not completely knowable. Indeed, scientists avidly took up studies of tramps precisely because they eluded hard and fast criminological categorization. But they resisted Ostwald's larger thesis that prostitutes, hucksters, and city people in general had to be understood as a collection of so many tramps who, only with difficulty, made their way in conditions of economic uncertainty but did so as fully developed individuals and moral agents. And, at least in Germany, there was no professional recognition of the novelty of Ostwald's method, which rejected academic surveys to gather knowledge by tramping around.[57] It was journalists who pioneered the case study, which, while not necessarily "real," illuminated the city in a new way.

55 On naturalism, degeneration, and views on the city, see Klaus-Michael Bogdal, *Schaurige Bilder: Der Arbeiter im Blick des Bürgers am Beispiel des Naturalismus* (Frankfurt am Main, 1978); and Andrew Lees, *Cities Perceived: Urban Society in European and American Thought, 1820–1940* (New York, 1985).

56 *Frankfurter Zeitung*, no. 360, Dec. 28, 1904. See also Fritzsche, "Vagabond in the Fugitive City."

57 Ostwald wrote about tramps for the *Archiv für Kriminalanthropologie*: see "Das Leben der Wanderarmen," *Archiv für Kriminal-Anthropologie* 13 (1903): 297–315. This article was discussed further in the *Zeitschrift für die gesamte Strafrechtswissenschaft* 24 (1904): 788–90. Interest in tramps as former criminals is underscored by the translation and publication of Josiah Flynt, "Tramping with Tramps," *Zeitschrift für die gesamte Strafrechtswissenschaft* 24 (1904): 129–47. Ostwald's work was reviewed regularly in the *Archiv für Kriminalanthropologie*. See volumes 23 (1906): 379, and 27 (1907): 376–7. See also Hans Landsberg, "Die Grundlagen der Kriminalpolitik und die Bekämpfung des Zuhältertums," *Monatsschrift für Kriminalpsychologie und Strafrechtsreform* 7 (1910–11): 673; and a review in *Monatsschrift für Kriminalpsychologie und Strafrechtsreform* 2 (1905–6): 528. Concerns about the legibility of the city are discussed in Hans Landsberg, "Die Grossstadt in unserem Rechtsgange," *Monatsschrift für Kriminalpsychologie und Strafrechtsreform*, 4 (1907–8): 209–28. Hans Ostwald discussed his method in *Dunkle Winkel in Berlin*, Grossstadt-Dokumente, no. 1, i.

Eschewing physiognomic methods and smudging danger zones, Ostwald argued in vain against the prevailing assumptions of criminologists discussed in this volume by David Horn. But the knowledge he offered about the city was taken up by an eclectic group that included American sociologists, newspaper reporters, and secessionist artists. A few weeks after Lucie Berlin's murder, Ostwald urged judgmental Berliners to visit the scene of the crime, the tenement building at Ackerstrasse Number 130: "Just go there," he wrote. "See what a real tenement and courtyard look like. Don't just examine some sort of reproduction," a circulated image made up of old clichés and faulty assumptions.[58] The point was to leave the newspaper offices downtown and to travel to neighborhoods uptown, to quit Unter den Linden and Friedrichstrasse and to inspect Ackerstrasse, to go into inner courtyards and up tenement staircases, and to dismiss the cast of types and physiognomies choreographed by scientists and to meet the inhabitants and listen to their stories. This was the case-study method that the intensive reportage of Lucie Berlin's murder in fact came to embrace: It increasingly became the credo of metropolitan journalists, such as the one from the *Berliner Tageblatt* who covered the September 1904 murder of Margarete Koschorreck and remained quite self-reflective about this specific journey all the way up to Berlin N., and it served as the organizing principle for Ostwald's *Grosstadt-Dokumente*. Ostwald claimed that new types of textual productions were necessary to understand the new terrain of the city. Statistics and academic handbooks were inadequate to comprehend the dark corners, the labyrinthine angles, and the fast-changing contents of the big city. To make sense of metropolitan variety, Ostwald recommended feuilletonistic forms, letters, sketches, case studies, and *Augenblicksbilder* that would resist authoritative conclusions. Moreover, Ostwald proposed to document what the eye saw, without making sentimental or scandal-mongering commentaries about the episode. As aids to documentation he selected for readers firsthand texts: verbatim dialog, lyrics, slang, transcripts, letters, pamphlets, inventories, and the like. The *Grosstadt-Dokumente* were unique in gathering so many metropolitan documents and interspersing them, collage-like, in the published texts. Ostwald took up where Charles Dickens and Charles Booth had left off, making the digressive documentary method central to his investigations and laying the disordered streets that resulted down the middle of the fast-changing industrial city.[59] "Just go there": This was the approach

---

58 Ostwald, "Lucie Berlin," *Das neue Magasin* 73 (July 2, 1904), 12.
59 Albert Fried and Richard M. Elman, eds., *Charles Booth's London: A Portrait of the Poor at the Turn of the Century, Drawn from His "Life and Labor of the People in London"* (New York, 1968), xvi, xix;

that Robert Parks, founder of the Chicago School of Sociology and himself deeply influenced by Ostwald's project, called "nosying around." The result in the case of both Berlin and Chicago was a view of the city that stressed the singular, the protean, and the different. This challenged the premises of criminologists, who sought typological keys to render the city and its inhabitants legible.[60]

"Just go there" to Ackerstrasse Number 130 appealed to an increasingly citywide readership that not only lived in the city but clamored for stories about the city. It was in the ten years on either side of Lucie Berlin's murder that metropolitan newspapers transformed themselves into mass-circulation newspapers by assiduously reporting on city life. For the majority of Berlin's largely working-class population, modest discretionary incomes allowed new modes of consumption. More and more families not only could afford a local newspaper – either the *Morgenpost*, to which Liebetruth subscribed, or, among more conservative circles, the *Lokal-Anzeiger* – but read newspapers in order to use the city in distinctly metropolitan ways: to keep up with new streetcar routes, to buy goods and services, to learn about department-store sales, to schedule theater visits, and to plan excursions into the countryside. These same newspapers also reported back on the carnivals, Sunday outings, train wrecks, and the murders like the one on Ackerstrasse that constituted the fabric of ordinary life in the city. To read about the city was to watch oneself using the city. Once newspapers and illustrated magazines adhered to this formula they found a mass readership. In this sense, the extensive coverage of the investigation and trial of Lucie Berlin's murder signaled new modes of reading in the city and new kinds of readers in the city. It pulled together a citywide audience of spectators.

"Just go there" to Ackerstrasse Number 130 also produced new kinds of knowledge about the city. Ostwald took walking to and around places seriously. Born in 1873, the son of an impoverished blacksmith, Ostwald was forced to tramp around Germany at a young age in order to find itinerant work as an artisan.[61] He came to befriend a highly mobile population of seasonal laborers, part-time criminals, and prostitutes that lived along the

---

Charles Booth, *Life and Labor of the People of London* (London, 1889). See also Fritzsche, "Vagabond in the Fugitive City," 395–7.

60 On the links between Ostwald and the Chicago School of Sociology, see Dietmar Jazbinsek and Ralf Thies, "Berlin/Chicago 1914: Die Berliner Grossstadt-Dokumente und ihre Rezeption durch die Gründergeneration der Chicago School of Sociology," *Papers*, Wissenschaftszentrum für Sozialforschung (Berlin, 1998). See also Rolf Lindner, *Die Entdeckung der Stadtkultur: Soziologie aus der Erfahrung der Reportage* (Frankfurt am Main, 1990); Fred H. Matthews, *Quest for an American Sociology: Robert E. Park and the Chicago School* (Montreal, 1977); and Cappetti, *Writing Chicago*.

61 Hans Ostwald, *Vagabunden*, ed. Klaus Bergmann (Frankfurt am Main, 1980).

margins of settled society, and he quickly abjured the dismissive judgments he might have held had he remained well employed in the city. Only the margins provided a complete picture of society and the economic and social forces that were at work. Indeed, the vagabond or *Landstreicher* served as the model for his *Stadtstreichereien*, eclectic literary tours of the city that he would later write up in feuilletons and in the *Grossstadt-Dokumente*. Moreover, Ostwald recognized his itinerant past in the prostitutes and pimps, whom he repeatedly compared to vagabonds. They too were forced out of their homes by poverty or misunderstanding, and they too moved in and out of relationships trying to find emotional anchorage or personal independence. In this sense, the testimony of Liebetruth and particularly her recollection of meeting Berger perfectly illustrated Ostwald's arguments that prostitutes were complete personalities whose work on the streets occurred for complicated reasons. Repeatedly, Ostwald hoped to erase the line between depravity and virtue by introducing readers to particular individuals, to the specific social interactions that continually connected the most diverse city people, and to the difficult, changing circumstances of the city that had unexpectedly uprooted even Ostwald himself.[62] The documentary method – "Just go there" – facilitated the accumulation of this knowledge, which was at odds with standard criminological or sociological practice. Of course, Ostwald's method obscured the work of larger social processes, even as it enabled a new metropolitan aesthetic.

The murder of Lucie Berlin in June 1904 elicited a horrified fascination in this city of readers, but it also served to represent that city in a fundamentally differrent way. As the investigative reportorial style more interested in case studies than melodrama made increasingly clear, the city was not easily divided into zones of depravity and civilization and its inhabitants into criminals and citizens. Neither Liebetruth nor Berger – nor Anna and Friedrich Berlin, for that matter – could be set apart as distinct racial or physiognomic types, even in the layman's imagination. Whether on Unter den Linden or on Ackerstrasse, they belonged to wider social circles that frustrated what Walter Benjamin once referred to as "botanizing on the asphalt."[63] Far from leading viewers to see general characteristics, a necessary task if the city was to become familiar and safe, the urban tours to Ackerstrasse and other improbable Berlin destinations became more and more digressive

---

62 The emphasis on contingency is apparent in Ostwald's foray into criminology: Ostwald, "Das Leben der Wanderarmen."

63 Walter Benjamin, "The Paris of the Second Empire in Baudelaire," in Walter Benjamin, *Charles Baudelaire: A Lyric Poet in the Era of High Capitalism*, trans. Harry Zohn (London, 1973), 36.

and took note of precise details, singular occasions, and chance encounters. They did not construct an authoritative map to the city but rather fashioned an impressionistic surface to reveal juxtapostions, transitions, and surprises. "Talk of the town" did not nail down city matters, it alerted readers to detail and fluctuation. As a result, the city became more unknowable and more astonishing for readers. Berlin appeared as a fantastic, dreadful garden of possibility.

FOUR

Criminology in the First Half of the Twentieth Century

The Case of Weimar and Nazi Germany

18

Criminology in Weimar and Nazi Germany

RICHARD F. WETZELL

THE EMERGENCE OF GERMAN CRIMINOLOGY AS A RECOGNIZED SCIENTIFIC FIELD IN THE LATE NINETEENTH CENTURY

Modern German criminology originated from a conjunction of two developments: the formation, in the 1880s, of the so-called modern school of criminal law under the leadership of Franz von Liszt, and the influence of Cesare Lombroso's famous work on the "born criminal."[1]

Liszt and his fellow legal reformers argued that the purpose of punishment did not lie in retribution or general deterrence but in preventing each individual criminal from offending again in the future. To achieve this purpose, they proposed that an offender's punishment should no longer depend on the offense committed, but on the individual's future dangerousness. Having decided that punishments ought to be individualized in form and preventive in function, the penal reformers became interested in the person of the criminal and in the causes of criminal behavior, that is, in criminological research, which they hoped would provide answers to two questions. First, how could one assess an offender's dangerousness and corrigibility? And second, which kind of treatment would be most effective in preventing a particular criminal from offending again? Although the practical questions that motivated the reformers' interest in criminology revolved around the personality of the criminal, the reformers did not assume that the criminal's personality was a more important cause of crime than the social environment. On the contrary, Liszt himself always insisted that both sets of factors

---

1 For a fuller version of the argument presented here, see Richard Wetzell, *Inventing the Criminal: A History of German Criminology, 1880–1945* (Chapel Hill, N.C., 2000).

had to be investigated and at times even suggested that social factors were more important than individual ones.[2]

Although the legal reformers called for criminological research, most did not consider themselves qualified for this task and looked to social scientists and medical experts to undertake such research. Since German sociologists did not show much interest in crime, the study of its social causes was left largely to statisticians and jurists. Their most important finding was that the rate of property crime was closely correlated to economic indicators such as the price of grain.[3] However, the statistical literature on crime was quickly overshadowed by the medical literature. For unlike German sociologists, German doctors – mainly prison doctors and psychiatrists – began to take a keen interest in crime, which was largely due to the impact of Cesare Lombroso's notion of the "born criminal."

In his study *L'uomo delinquente* (Criminal Man), first published in 1876, Lombroso had argued that criminals were characterized by certain physical characteristics (including a receding forehead and handle-shaped ears) that marked them as a distinct anthropological type, which Lombroso interpreted as an atavistic throwback to primitive man. In later editions of his work Lombroso modified his teaching by allowing that born criminals accounted for only about a third of all criminals and by explaining the born criminal in terms of mental illness rather than atavism, but his conviction that the born criminal was an anthropological type with distinct physical characteristics remained unchanged.[4]

Like their French and British colleagues, in the 1890s a number of German prison doctors responded to and refuted Lombroso by conducting their own examinations of prisoners.[5] They found that many prisoners did

2 Franz von Liszt, "Der Zweckgedanke im Strafrecht" [1882], in Liszt, *Strafrechtliche Aufsätze und Vorträge*, 2 vols. (Berlin, 1905), 1:126–79; Liszt, "Über den Einfluß der soziologischen und anthropologischen Forschungen auf die Grundbegriffe des Strafrechts" [1893], *Strafrechtliche Aufsätze*, 2:83; Liszt, "Das Verbrechen als sozialpathologische Erscheinung" [1898], ibid., 2:234–6; Liszt, "Die Aufgabe und die Methode der Strafrechtswissenschaft" [1899], ibid., 295. On Liszt and his reform movement see Richard Wetzell, "Criminal Law Reform in Imperial Germany" (Ph.D. diss., Stanford University, 1991).

3 Georg von Mayr, *Statistik der gerichtlichen Polizei im Königreiche Bayern und in einigen anderen Ländern* (Munich, 1867); Mayr, *Statistik und Gesellschaftslehre*, vol. 3, *Moralstatistik mit Einschluß der Kriminalstatistik* (Tübingen, 1917).

4 Cesare Lombroso, *L'uomo delinquente* (Milan, 1876); I have used the German translation: *Der Verbrecher (homo delinquens) in anthropologischer, ärztlicher und juristischer Beziehung*, trans. M. Fränkel, 2 vols. (Hamburg, 1887–90).

5 My analysis of the birth of German criminology in the years 1880–1914 is developed at greater length in Wetzell, "Criminal Law Reform in Imperial Germany" and Wetzell, "The Medicalization of Criminal Law Reform in Imperial Germany," in *Institutions of Confinement: Hospitals, Asylums and Prisons in Western Europe and North America, 1500–1950*, ed. Norbert Finzsch and Robert Jütte (Cambridge, 1996), 275–84. See also Mariacarla Gadebusch Bondio, *Die Rezeption der kriminalanthropologischen*

indeed display some of the physical abnormalities that Lombroso had described, but argued that these abnormalities were also found among the general population, especially the poorer classes, and therefore interpreted them as signs of degeneration.[6] Although these studies established a medical consensus that born criminals with distinct physical characteristics did not exist, some German psychiatrists redefined the notion of the born criminal in psychological terms, as a person whose criminal behavior resulted from an innate defect of the moral sense.[7]

The dominant figures in the emerging field of "criminal psychology," however, did not believe in the existence of an isolated moral defect and concentrated on the finding that many criminals displayed signs of degeneration. This approach was best exemplified by Gustav Aschaffenburg's *Das Verbrechen und seine Bekämpfung* [Crime and its Repression] (1903), Germany's first survey of criminology, which remained the standard work for the next thirty years. Aschaffenburg, a psychiatrist who had worked as a prison doctor, stressed that the physical and mental abnormalities commonly found among criminals were also widespread among the general population, especially its poorer stratum, and therefore not distinctive of criminals. He showed little interest in criminals' physical defects and focused on their mental deficiencies, primarily *Schwachsinn* (imbecility or feeblemindedness) and *Haltlosigkeit* (unsteadiness or lack of resilience). He referred to these mental conditions as *geistige Minderwertigkeiten*, that is, mental abnormalities or personality disorders situated in the borderland between mental health and full-fledged mental illness.

Estimating that about half of all criminals were *geistig minderwertig*, Aschaffenburg faced two main questions: What caused these mental deficiencies? And how were they connected to criminal behavior? What was remarkable about Aschaffenburg and the dominant strand of prewar criminal psychology was that he explained both problems in environmental rather than hereditarian terms. First, drawing on degeneration theory, he argued that the causes of these physical and mental deficiencies lay mainly in noxious environmental factors such as lack of prenatal care, malnutrition, and parental neglect. Second, he argued that the resulting mental deficiencies, such as

Theorien von Cesare Lombroso in Deutschland von 1880–1914 (Husum, 1995) and her chapter in this volume.

6 Abraham Baer, *Der Verbrecher in anthropologischer Beziehung* (Leipzig, 1893); Paul Näcke, *Verbrechen und Wahnsinn beim Weibe. Mit Ausblicken auf die Criminal-Anthropologie überhaupt* (Vienna/Leipzig, 1894).

7 Robert Sommer, "Die Criminalpsychologie," *Allgemeine Zeitschrift für Psychiatrie* 51 (1895), 782–803; Julius Koch, *Die Frage nach dem geborenen Verbrecher* (Ravensburg, 1894); Eugen Bleuler, *Der geborene Verbrecher* (Munich, 1896).

feeblemindedness and unsteadiness, often led to crime, not because their bearers had a moral defect or were otherwise biologically predisposed toward crime, but because they were handicapped in economic life and turned to crime as a last resort.

When it came to the implications of his findings for penal policy, however, Aschaffenburg was ambivalent. On the one hand, he thought that the large role of social factors offered hope for preventing crime by changing social circumstances. On the other hand, he was deeply pessimistic about the prospects for social change and feared that in the absence of such change most mentally deficient criminals would have to be considered incorrigible.[8]

CRIMINAL BIOLOGY IN THE WEIMAR YEARS (1918–1933): AN OVERVIEW

The tremendous increase in crime during the First World War renewed interest in the social causes of crime. Two major studies of wartime and post-war crime, written by jurists, treated the war as a "gigantic experiment" on the question of social versus individual-biological causes of crime. Since the war could not have changed the biological characteristics of the population, these studies concluded that the wartime increase in crime (mainly property crime) demonstrated the overwhelming importance of social causes of crime. Moreover, since the same surge in property crime had occurred in neutral countries, the wartime increase in crime was clearly due to the economic hardships of the war rather than the effects of military combat.[9] Although these two studies of wartime crime were influential, they remained virtually the only works of criminal sociology during the Weimar years, because German sociologists took little interest in the subject of crime.

Weimar psychiatrists, by contrast, produced a large body of work on what was coming to be called "criminal biology." Their research received an important institutional boost when the Bavarian Justice Ministry established a Criminal-Biological Service (Kriminalbiologischer Dienst) to administer criminal-biological examinations of Bavarian prisoners. Introduced gradually between 1923 and 1925, this agency gathered criminal-biological reports from all Bavarian prisons in a central Sammelstelle (Record Office). Later associated with the prestigious Deutsche Forschungsanstalt für Psychiatrie in Munich, the Sammelstelle gathered a unique collection of

8 Gustav Aschaffenburg, *Das Verbrechen und seine Bekämpfung* (Heidelberg, 1903); English translation: *Crime and Its Repression* (1913, reprint Montclair, N.J., 1968).
9 Franz Exner, *Krieg und Kriminalität in Oesterreich* (Vienna, 1927); Moritz Liepmann, *Krieg und Kriminalität in Deutschland* (Stuttgart, 1930).

criminal-biological data, which was used by many of the studies discussed below.[10]

Most criminal-biological research of the Weimar period can be divided into five strands:

1. Psychoanalytic works, which explained criminal behavior as a manifestation of acquired psychological maladjustments. Since the field of criminal biology was dominated by the psychiatric profession, which was generally hostile to psychoanalysis, psychoanalytic research was marginalized by mainstream criminal biology throughout the interwar period.[11]

2. Somatotyping (*Konstitutionslehre*): efforts to establish correlations between criminal behavior and certain physique types, on the basis of Ernst Kretschmer's typology of physique and character types as set forth in his influential work *Physique and Character* (*Körperbau und Charakter*), first published in 1921. This type of research, too, remained highly controversial among criminal biologists.[12]

While psychoanalysis and somatotyping represented the two extremes on the criminal-biological spectrum, three other strands of research dominated criminal-biological research during the Weimar years:

3. Research on the connections between criminal behavior and "mental abnormalities" (that is, borderline personality disorders) based on the new typology of "psychopathic" or "abnormal personalities" developed by Kurt Schneider in the early 1920s (*Psychopathenforschung*).[13]

4. Research on the role of genetic factors in criminal behavior, which entered a new stage when the psychiatrist Johannes Lange conducted the first twin study on criminal behavior (1929).[14]

5. Research on "criminal psychology," which was closely tied to the emerging field of *Persönlichkeitslehre* (study of personality and character) and sought to redirect the focus of research from the biology of the criminal to the criminal's psychology, and from the study of abnormal criminals to the study of all criminals, whether normal or abnormal.[15]

---

10 *Der Stufenstrafvollzug und die kriminalbiologische Untersuchung der Gefangenen in den bayerischen Strafanstalten*, 3 vols. (Munich, 1926–9). On the Kriminalbiologischer Dienst see also Oliver Liang's chapter in this volume.

11 Major psychoanalytic works on crime include Theodor Reik, *Gedächtniszwang und Strafbedürfnis* (Wien, 1925); Franz Alexander and Hugo Staub, *Der Verbrecher und seine Richter* (Wien, 1929); Hans Coenen, *Strafrecht und Psychoanalyse* (Breslau, 1929). Major *individualpsychologisch* publications on crime: Alfred Adler, "Neurose und Verbrechen," *Internationale Zeitschrift für Individualpsychologie* [hereafter: *IZI*] 3 (1924): 1–11; Sonderheft "Menschen vor dem Richter" *IZI* 9 (1931), Heft 5 (321–407); Eugen Schmidt, "Verbrechen und Strafe," *Handbuch der Individualpsychologie*, ed. Erwin Wexberg, v. 2 (Munich, 1926), 150–79. See also Gabriel Finder's chapter in this volume.

12 Ernst Kretschmer, *Körperbau und Charakter* (Berlin, 1921); idem, "Biologische Persönlichkeitsdiagnose in der Strafrechtspflege," *Deutsche Juristen-Zeitung* 31 (1926): 782–7.

13 Kurt Schneider, *Die psychopathischen Persönlichkeiten*, 1st ed. (1923), 2d ed. (Leipzig, 1928); Karl Birnbaum, *Die psychopathischen Verbrecher*, 2d ed. (Leipzig, 1926).

14 Johannes Lange, *Verbrechen als Schicksal* (Leipzig, 1929).

15 Here the major figures were Birnbaum and Hans Gruhle. See, for instance: Birnbaum, *Kriminalpsychopathologie und psychobiologische Verbrecherkunde*, 2d ed. (Berlin, 1931); Hans Gruhle,

Overall, criminal biology in the Weimar years reflected two opposing tendencies. On the one hand, much criminal-biological work pathologized the criminal and explained criminal behavior primarily as the result of biological abnormality. This approach, however, was challenged by an equally powerful trend toward regarding the criminal as biologically normal and explaining crime as the result of a complex interaction between biological and social factors.

Reflecting the first tendency, many criminologists not only treated a criminal's personality as the decisive criminogenic factor, but often insisted that this personality was "pathological" or "abnormal."[16] Although estimates varied, most researchers agreed that a large percentage of habitual, recidivist criminals were abnormal personalities. Criminal biologists' sophistication in defining normality and abnormality varied greatly. Whereas some used highly subjective and value-laden notions of normality, the psychiatrist Kurt Schneider insisted on a quantitative definition of the norm as the statistical average, and defined "abnormal personalities" as deviations from a statistical average. But since the notion of an "average personality" was subject to interpretation, Schneider's norm, too, was ultimately subjective. Schneider's definition of "psychopathic" personalities as a subset of "abnormal" personalities – those abnormal personalities who "suffered from their abnormality or whose abnormality made society suffer" – also had contradictory implications. On the one hand, this distinction was meant to emphasize that mental abnormalities as such were infinite in number (and hence, to some extent, "normal") and in most cases unconnected with antisocial behavior. On the other hand, Schneider's focus on the "psychopathic" subset ended up reinforcing the connection between abnormality and antisocial behavior.

Furthermore, despite Schneider's efforts to construct his psychopathic types on the basis of "objective" psychological criteria, categories like his *gemütlose* (compassionless) or *willenlose* (weak-willed) psychopaths were subjective and value-laden. For if, in the case of *gemütlose*, Schneider regarded a lack of "compassion, shame, sense of honor, remorse, conscience" as a biological abnormality, this was because he defined biological normality to

"Kriminalbiologie und Kriminalpraxis," *Kriminalistische Monatshefte* 2:242; idem, "Wesen und Systematik des biologischen Typus," *Mitteilungen der Kriminalbiologischen Gesellschaft* 2 (1928): 15–21; idem, "Aufgaben der Kriminalpsychologie," *Zeitschrift für die gesamte Strafrechtswissenschaft* 51 (1930/1931): 469–80; idem, "Vererbungsgesetze und Verbrechensbekämpfung," *Monatschrift für Kriminalpsychologie und Strafrechtsreform* 23 (1932): 559–68.
16 For our present purposes, these terms will be treated as synonyms.

reflect contemporary morality and social conventions.[17] Likewise, the psychiatrist Karl Birnbaum thought that psychopathic *Haltlosigkeit* (unsteadiness) manifested itself, among other things, in the "inability to properly emphasize important values such as honor and morality, duty and responsibility."[18] Although criminal biologists insisted that criminal behavior itself could never be regarded as evidence of a criminal's abnormality, they were clearly inclined to interpret deviations from social norms as deviations from biological norms. In short, social deviance became evidence of biological abnormality.

The focus on biological abnormality was reinforced by an increasing emphasis on the role of heredity over that of the environment in explaining the etiology of these abnormalities. In the prewar era most psychiatrists had subscribed to the theory of degeneration, which had attributed such abnormalities to a combination of hereditary and environmental factors. In the Weimar years, most researchers abandoned degeneration theory, thus paving the way for Kurt Schneider's hereditarian position that "abnormal personalities" were always congenital (and therefore in most cases hereditary) and never the result of external influences. But while Schneider and Birnbaum believed that *abnormal (psychopathic) personalities* were always congenital, they did not claim that *criminal behavior* was determined by heredity: whether a psychopathic personality committed a crime always depended on environmental factors. Regarding criminal behavior itself, the question of the relative weight of heredity and environment remained open. This was the question that Johannes Lange's twin research sought to address. And there can be no doubt that his results – the high concordance rate for criminal behavior among identical twins – were widely regarded as proof that heredity played a preponderant role in criminal behavior. In short, Lange's research held out the promise of explaining crime not just biologically, but genetically.

Finally, the tendency to pathologize the criminal manifested itself in the persistence of the notion of the "born criminal." Most remarkable was the fact that the concept survived German psychiatry's virtually unanimous rejection of Lombroso's theories. In the prewar years, this rejection had resulted in a split between those who rejected the notion entirely and those who rejected only Lombroso's claim that the "born criminal" was a physical type, while continuing to believe in the "born criminal" as a manifestation

---

17 Kurt Schneider, *Die psychopathischen Persönlichkeiten*, 2d ed. (Leipzig, 1928), 1–5, 69–70, 73–5.
18 Karl Birnbaum, *Die psychopathischen Verbrecher*, 2d ed. (Leipzig, 1926), 46.

of a mental disorder called "moral insanity" or merely "moral defect." In the Weimar years, this psychiatric version of the born criminal was transformed into one of the "psychopathic types," namely Schneider's *gemütloser* (compassionless) and Birnbaum's "amoral" psychopath, both characterized by a lack of altruistic or moral feelings. Both Schneider and Birnbaum insisted that compassionless psychopaths did not necessarily commit antisocial acts. If born into a wealthy family, their lack of scruples might result in worldly success. If born into the working class, however, they were quite likely to become criminal. But despite this insistence on the importance of the social milieu, Schneider and Birnbaum admitted that the compassionless psychopath came closest to the "born criminal."[19] As a result, the two were often treated as synonyms and the notion of the "born criminal" lived on. Contemporary critics of Lombroso might point out that Lombroso, in his later years, claimed that born criminals accounted for about a third of all criminals, whereas Schneider and Birnbaum regarded the compassionless psychopath as an extremely rare phenomenon. But the mere survival of the concept of the "born criminal" allowed others to insist that Lombroso's theories contained an important kernel of truth: that, in the most severe cases, crime was indeed the result of biological abnormality.[20]

The tendency to pathologize criminals, however, competed with another, equally powerful trend to treat criminals as biologically normal and to explain crime as a complex interaction between environment and heredity. Above all else, this trend manifested itself in the gradual disintegration of the notion of "the criminal" or "the criminal character" as a distinct biological phenomenon. In every area of research, criminal biologists arrived at the conclusion that there was no such thing as "the criminal." To be sure, this trend had begun with the first German studies refuting the existence of Lombroso's born criminal. But in the prewar period Aschaffenburg had still described about half of all criminals as *geistig minderwertig* (mentally abnormal), that is, as a unified group with certain characteristics. By the Weimar period, however, not only the notion of "the criminal" but more restricted concepts such as the "psychopathic criminal" or "habitual criminal" disintegrated into a myriad of different "psychopathic personalities" or "types."

---

19 Schneider, *Die psychopathischen Persönlichkeiten*, 69–73; Birnbaum, *Die psychopathischen Verbrecher*, 53–5, 62, 154–5.
20 See, for example: Friedrich von Rohden, "Lombrosos Bedeutung für die moderne Kriminalbiologie," *Archiv für Psychiatrie und Nervenkrankheiten* 92 (1930): 140–54.

The pluralistic, typological approach transformed both the study of mental abnormalities (psychopathies) and the study of general criminal psychology. The notion of a "criminal character" or "criminal disposition" had become untenable, because criminal biologists had become convinced that: (1) criminal behavior could result from a great variety of motivations and character traits; (2) criminal behavior arose from complex combinations of character traits which were in no way "criminal" in themselves; and (3) since hereditary traits (*Anlagen*) were only potentials, criminal behavior was always the result of genetic and environmental factors.[21] In short, the causes of criminal behavior were seen to be as diverse and complex as the causes of all other human behavior. As a result, the criminal began to look more and more like any other normal human being, and criminal biology became inextricably bound up with the general study of human behavior, human psychology, and human genetics. But since, by general consensus, all these fields were still in very early stages of development, the goal of understanding criminal behavior, let alone prognosticating an offender's dangerousness or corrigibility, became more elusive than ever. Ironically, the increasing sophistication of criminal biologists had made their goal harder to reach.

The disintegration of the notion of a "criminal disposition" also complicated research into the role of heredity in crime and made the implications of Johannes Lange's twin research appear much less clear cut. At first glance, Lange's finding that identical twins had a high (77%) concordance rate, whereas nonidentical twins had a low one (12%) seemed to suggest that heredity played an overwhelming role in criminal behavior. But if there was no such thing as a "criminal disposition," what exactly was being "passed on" through heredity? Lange himself admitted that his research shed no light on the nature of the "hereditary disposition" (*Anlage*) that predisposed its bearers to antisocial behavior. Recognizing that hereditary character traits were only potentials, he also conceded that the criminal behavior of his concordant identical twins was not determined by heredity alone, but by external influences as well. The same point was driven home by the very existence of discordant identical twins (23%), which could only be explained by environmental factors.[22]

---

21 These points were made especially clear by Hans Gruhle (see his publications cited in note 15) and by Hans Luxenburger, "Anlage und Umwelt beim Verbrecher," *Allgemeine Zeitschrift für Psychiatrie* 92 (1930): 411–38.
22 Lange, *Verbrechen als Schicksal*, 82–3, 90–92, 96.

In summary, we find that the widespread inclination to explain criminal behavior as the result of hereditary abnormalities was counterbalanced by an equally widespread recognition that criminal behavior was as diverse and complex as all human behavior and always subject to environmental influences. As a result, Weimar criminal biologists perceived the futility of approaching heredity and milieu as alternative explanations and concluded that both factors played a role in criminal behavior.

Nevertheless, the recognition of both factors allowed for differences in emphasis. Some criminal biologists, like Karl Birnbaum and Hans Gruhle, never tired of pointing out that even persons with potentially highly criminogenic "psychopathic personalities" did not usually become criminal unless, as Gruhle put it, "fate put them in this world as members of the proletariat."[23] Others, like Gustav Aschaffenburg, presented heredity as the "decisive" factor. Dire need, he acknowledged, could be a cause of crime. But in a situation of need "one person will endure hunger, another person might commit suicide, but a third person will steal – a highly personal reaction." By presenting the situation in this manner, Aschaffenburg was able to conclude that, although the environment played a role, the "ultimately decisive" factor was the criminal's personality, which he considered "overwhelmingly" a matter of heredity.[24]

Although Aschaffenburg felt confident in stressing the importance of personality and heredity, he also admitted that criminal-biological research was still in its early stages. The increasing sophistication of criminal-biological research and the resulting disintegration of the notion of a "criminal disposition" had so immensely complicated the questions under investigation that progress became ever more elusive. Summarizing the state of the field in 1932, Aschaffenburg therefore concluded that criminal biology was "far from possessing reliable methods for examining and evaluating the personality of the criminal"; that research on human heredity met with "almost insurmountable difficulties" and would therefore be slow to produce reliable results; and that it was "currently impossible to separate corrigibles from incorrigibles with criminal-psychological methods."[25] In short, Aschaffenburg had to acknowledge that after forty years of research criminal biology had produced virtually no results and was indeed still a science in its infancy.

---

23 Hans Gruhle, "Wesen und Systematik des biologischen Typus," *Mitteilungen der Kriminalbiologischen Gesellschaft* 2 (1928): 21.
24 Gustav Aschaffenburg, "Kriminalanthropologie und Kriminalbiologie (Überblick)," *Handwörterbuch der Kriminologie*, v. 1 (Berlin/Leipzig, 1933), 830–32.
25 Aschaffenburg, "Kriminalanthropologie und Kriminalbiologie," 825, 828, 840.

CRIMINAL BIOLOGY UNDER THE NAZI REGIME (1933–1945):
AN OVERVIEW

The Nazis' attitude toward criminology was conflicted. On the one hand, Nazi leaders themselves subscribed to a biological approach to crime; on the other hand, a number of Nazi jurists were hostile to criminology, because they blamed it for the "emasculation" of Weimar criminal justice. Quick to grasp the dangers and opportunities inherent in this situation, leading criminologists made a strong effort to dissociate criminology from the supposed failures of Weimar criminal justice, while capitalizing on Nazi racial-eugenic ideology by linking criminology with the broader eugenic agenda of the Nazi state. By 1935, the expansion of criminal-biological examinations in the prisons to the national level demonstrated the success of this strategy for winning Nazi support. At the same time, the anti-Semitic component of the Nazi racial ideology ended the careers of Jewish criminologists Gustav Aschaffenburg and Karl Birnbaum, both of whom emigrated to the United States.[26]

A variety of historical studies have shown that many people in Nazi Germany endorsed genetically determinist or racist explanations of criminal behavior. In their study of the Nazi racial state Michael Burleigh and Wolfgang Wippermann argued that "[i]n the Nazis' view of the world, 'asocial' and criminal behavior was not determined by either individual choice or the social environment, but rather was innate and hence heritable." In the case of the police, Patrick Wagner has shown that by the late 1930s, the police leadership in the Reichskriminalpolizeiamt had come to regard "professional and recidivist crime as a genetically produced phenomenon." Likewise, a number of studies have demonstrated that doctors and others involved in the persecution and eventual murder of the handicapped, Jews, and gypsies claimed that these groups were characterized by "criminality" as a racial characteristic. Thus Robert Proctor has argued that Nazi medical leaders believed that "Jews were racially disposed to commit crime." Henry Friedlander has shown that "race hygiene had always linked the handicapped to criminal and antisocial behavior," that researchers on gypsies claimed that "gypsies as a group were degenerate, criminal and asocial and that this condition was hereditary"; and that as a result, "the Nazi killers used the language of Lombroso to target . . . gypsies and the handicapped."[27] In short, there

---

26 For a detailed account see Wetzell, *Inventing the Criminal*, 179–90.
27 Michael Burleigh and Wolfgang Wippermann, *The Racial State: Germany 1933–1945* (Cambridge, 1991), 167; Patrick Wagner, *Volksgemeinschaft ohne Verbrecher: Konzeptionen und Praxis der Kriminalpolizei in der Zeit der Weimarer Republik und des Nationalsozialismus* (Hamburg, 1996), 265; Robert

is considerable evidence that the police and other Nazi officials subscribed
to genetic explanations of crime; and that a substantial number of medical
doctors, especially those involved in the persecution and killing of Jews,
gypsies, and the handicapped, regarded those groups as racially predisposed
toward crime.

The researcher whose views on crime are most frequently cited in
the existing historical literature is the psychiatrist Robert Ritter, who headed
the Rassenhygienische und bevölkerungsbiologische Forschungsstelle
(Research Institute for Eugenics and Population Policy) of the Reichsge-
sundheitsamt (Reich Health Office) since 1936, where he conducted
research on gypsies. Starting in 1940, Ritter took over the direction of two
institutes concerned with criminal-biological matters. That year Ritter's
Research Institute for Eugenics was merged with the Reichsgesundheits-
amt's Kriminalbiologische Forschungsstelle (Criminal-Biological Institute),
which collected the reports generated by the criminal-biological examinations conducted in German prisons. And in late 1941, Ritter's connections
with the German police led to his appointment as director of the newly created Kriminalbiologisches Institut of the Sicherheitspolizei (Security Police),
which also collected criminal-biological reports and conducted criminal-
biological screenings of juvenile delinquents interned in reeducation camps
(Jugendschutzlager).[28] Ritter figures prominently in the existing historical
literature because he played a key role in three important areas that have
been the focus of recent research: the persecution and eventual murder of
the Sinti and Roma (gypsies);[29] juvenile justice and the treatment of juvenile delinquents;[30] and the expansion of the power of the police in the Nazi
state.[31] While his activities in these three areas of Nazi policy make him an
important figure in the history of the Nazi "racial state," it would be wrong
to assume that Ritter's deterministic and racist approach to the etiology of

---

Proctor, *Racial Hygiene: Medicine under the Nazis* (Cambridge, Mass., 1988), 204–5; Henry Friedlander, *The Origins of Nazi Genocide: From Euthanasia to the Final Solution* (Chapel Hill, N.C., 1995), 3,
23, 252.

28 On Ritter see Joachim Hohmann, *Robert Ritter und die Erben der Kriminalbiologie* (Frankfurt, 1991);
    Patrick Wagner, *Volksgemeinschaft ohne Verbrecher* (Hamburg, 1996), esp. 274–9, 378–84; Michael
    Zimmermann, *Verfolgt, vertrieben, vernichtet: Die nationalsozialistische Vernichtungspolitik gegen Sinti und
    Roma* (Essen, 1989), esp. 25–39; idem, *Rassenutopie und Genozid: Die nationalsozialistische 'Lösung der
    Zigeunerfrage'* (Hamburg, 1996).

29 See Zimmermann, *Verfolgt;* idem, *Rassenutopie;* Friedlander, *The Origins,* esp. 246–62; Burleigh and
    Wippermann, *The Racial State,* 113–35.

30 See Jörg Wolff, *Jugendliche vor Gericht im Dritten Reich* (Munich, 1992); Detlev Peukert, "Arbeits-
    lager und Jugend-KZ," in *Die Reihen fast geschlossen,* ed. Peukert and Jürgen Reulecke (Wuppertal,
    1981).

31 See Wagner, *Volksgemeinschaft ohne Verbrecher.*

criminal behavior was representative of German criminology as a field of research under the Nazi regime.

The largest and most influential research project in criminal biology during the prewar years of the Nazi regime was the work of Friedrich Stumpfl, who had joined the Deutsche Forschungsanstalt für Psychiatrie in Munich in 1930 to continue the criminal-biological research program initiated by Johannes Lange. Stumpfl's large-scale "family study," which compared the extended families of a group of multiple recidivists with those of a group of one-time offenders (*Heredity and Crime*, 1935), and his twin study (*The Origins of Crime*, 1936) impacted criminal-biological research in a number of ways. Stumpfl's finding that the families of recidivists showed no increased incidence of *mental illness* refuted the longstanding theory of a genetic connection between mental illness and a disposition toward criminal behavior. At the same time, his findings of widespread mental abnormalities ("psychopathy") among recidivists and their families reinforced the view, popularized by Schneider and Birnbaum, that many habitual criminals were "psychopathic."

Concerning the key question of genetic versus environmental causes of crime, Stumpfl's work sent contradictory messages. On the one hand, Stumpfl's first book claimed that the clusters of psychopathic traits found among recidivist criminals were "genuine causes of crime" that were genetically transmitted, and therefore characterized the recidivist criminal as a "genetically determined criminal personality."[32] And his twin study claimed to have confirmed this finding. On the other hand, Stumpfl also demonstrated unprecedented methodological sophistication, which obliged him to qualify his hereditarian claims. This was especially evident in his twin study, in which he conceded, first, that recidivists could become criminal as a result of milieu-induced "psychological deformations" rather than genetic psychopathic traits; and second, that because of the greater similarity of the environments of identical as compared to fraternal twins, differences in concordance rates could not be regarded as proof of the influence of genetic factors, as had previously been assumed by Lange.[33]

---

32 *anlagemässig bedingte Täterpersönlichkeit.*

33 Friedrich Stumpfl, *Erbanlage und Verbrechen: Charakterologische und psychiatrische Sippenuntersuchungen* (Berlin, 1935); idem, *Die Ursprünge des Verbrechens: dargestellt am Lebenslauf von Zwillingen* (Leipzig, 1936). Stumpfl also disseminated the results of these two studies in numerous articles, including "Kriminelle Psychopathen," *Der Erbarzt* (1936): 134; "Kriminalbiologische Forschung und der Vollzug von Strafen und sichernden Massnahmen," *Gerichtssaal* 108 (1936): 338–61; "Untersuchungen an kriminellen und psychopathischen Zwillingen," *Öffentlicher Gesundheitsdienst* 2 (1936); "Die Persönlichkeit im Lichte der Erblehre," *Die Vererbung des Charakters* (Leipzig, 1936); "Erbanlage und Verbrechen," *Monatsschrift für Kriminalpsychologie und Strafrechtsreform* (1937): 92–8; "Vortrag auf der

Perhaps even more important than Stumpfl's methodological sophistication is the fact that his hereditarian conclusions met with a remarkably critical reception among major criminologists. Indeed, it would be fair to say that most of the criticisms that could be leveled at research on the genetic causes of crime were in fact articulated by contemporary critics like Hans Gruhle, Hellmuth Mayer, and Franz Exner during the Nazi period.[34]

The two major surveys of criminology written by Edmund Mezger (1934, 2d ed. 1942) and Franz Exner (1939) generally reflected the increasing sophistication of criminological research since the time of Aschaffenburg's 1903 survey. It must be noted, however, that both Mezger and Exner asserted that race played a role in criminal behavior and made explicitly anti-Semitic comments, although neither of them described Jews or gypsies as inherently criminal. Generally, Exner concluded that statistical family studies and twin studies had demonstrated that genetic factors played a "prominent role among the causes of crime," so that purely environmental explanations, whether of a materialist or psychoanalytic variety, were clearly refuted. At the same time, however, he insisted that purely genetic explanations were refuted as well, since the existence of discordant identical twins (amounting to about a third of all cases) clearly demonstrated that genetic factors did not always play a decisive role. The importance of genetic factors, he suggested, was most likely different for different groups of criminals. Although past research studies showed that genetic factors played a more frequent role among recidivists than among occasional offenders, recidivist criminality was not always attributable to genetic factors. Hence the problem of "identifying those groups of criminals in which genetic factors play a practically decisive role" remained an "unresolved task" for future research.[35]

In conclusion, we find that the development of criminal biology and criminology in the Nazi period presents a picture that differs from what

Jahresversammlung der Vereinigung für gerichtliche Psychologie und Psychiatrie am 17.4.1937," *Deutsches Recht* (1937): 336; "Psychopathenforschung und Kriminalbiologie: Erbbiologische Ergebnisse 1933–1937," *Fortschritte der Neurologie, Psychiatrie und ihrer Grenzgebiete* 9 (1937): 167–76; "Über Erbforschung an Rechtsbrechern," *Mitteilungen der Kriminalbiologischen Gesellschaft* 5 (1937): 111–15; "Über kriminalbiologische Erbforschung," *Allgemeine Zeitschrift für Psychiatrie* 107 (1938): 38–63; "Verbrechen und Vererbung," *Monatsschrift für Kriminalpsychologie und Strafrechtsreform* 29 (1938): 1–21; "Psychopathenforschung unter dem Gesichtspunkt der Erbbiologie, 1937–1939," *Fortschritte der Neurologie, Psychiatrie und ihrer Grenzgebiete* 11 (1939): 409–16; "Gutachten zum Thema: Studium der Persönlichkeit des Verbrechers," in *Römischer Kongress für Kriminologie* (Berlin, 1939), 217–27; "Kriminalität und Vererbung," in *Handbuch der Erbbiologie des Menschen*, v. 5, part 2 (Berlin, 1939): 1223–74.

34 On Stumpfl's reception, see Wetzell, *Inventing the Criminal*, 202–9.

35 Edmund Mezger, *Kriminalpolitik auf kriminologischer Grundlage* (Stuttgart, 1934), 2d ed. (1942), 3d ed. (1944); Franz Exner, *Kriminalbiologie in ihren Grundzügen* (Hamburg, 1939), 2d ed. (1944).

one might have expected in the Nazi racial state. To be sure, prominent Nazi leaders, high-ranking police officials, doctors involved in the euthanasia program, and researchers like Robert Ritter believed in genetically deterministic and often racist explanations of crime. On the other hand, however, we have seen that such genetically deterministic and racist explanations of crime did not predominate in mainstream criminal biology and criminology as a field of scientific research. Instead, we found that Nazi-era criminology was characterized by a continuing tension between hereditarian biases and an ongoing process of increasing methodological sophistication. In sum, these findings support the argument that a certain amount of "normal science" continued under the Nazi regime, as has been suggested by some recent work in the history of German science.[36]

This said, it must be acknowledged that what mattered most for practical purposes was not criminological research as such, but its reception and application, especially regarding the eugenics question. Weimar sterilization debates reveal that criminal-biological research did indeed foster a widespread belief that genetic factors played a major role in criminal behavior. But they also demonstrate that the sophistication of criminal-biological research was not lost on most nonspecialists, who clearly understood that the role of genetic factors in crime remained obscure and as yet unproven. Given the tension between hereditarian beliefs and the lack of evidence, different groups disagreed on the policy implications. Most psychiatrists decided to support the sterilization of at least some criminals despite the lack of evidence, whereas government officials and most members of the Reichstag penal reform committee concluded that current research could not justify the sterilization of criminals.[37]

What is most remarkable is that such differences of opinion continued to persist even during the Third Reich. Even after the Nazis made quick passage of a sterilization law a priority and placed a eugenic hardliner (Arthur Gütt) in charge of its preparation, the Ministry of Justice succeeded in blocking his plans for the inclusion of criminals in the 1933 sterilization law. Determined to prevail, Gütt and the prominent eugenicist Ernst Rüdin used their official commentary on the law to encourage the sterilization of criminals through an expanded definition of "feeblemindedness," which violated both the intent of the law and well-established medical definitions.

---

36 See Arleen Tuchmann, "Institutions and Disciplines: Recent Work in the History of German Science," *Journal of Modern History* 69 (1997): 300, 316, 317; Kristie Macrakis, *Surviving the Swastika: Scientific Research in Nazi Germany* (New York, 1993), 3–4, 199, passim.
37 On Weimar debates concerning the sterilization of criminals, see Wetzell, *Inventing the Criminal,* 233–54.

As a result, some Hereditary Health Courts did order sterilizations of criminals for supposed "feeblemindedness," diagnosed solely on the basis of their criminal behavior. But many of these decisions were struck down on appeal. The appeals court rulings resulted in a compromise that allowed sterilization courts to use criminal behavior as a criterion in "borderline" cases of feeblemindedness. Statistics show that, because of this loophole, criminals were indeed more likely to be sterilized than nondelinquent citizens. But since this loophole was a small one, proponents of the sterilization of criminals continued to demand the expansion of the sterilization law to include criminals. Even in the late 1930s, however, these demands were met with opposition from a number of criminologists, who succeeded in blocking the inclusion of criminals in the sterilization law. In sum, the examination of Nazi sterilization policy with regard to criminals shows that before Nazi biological politics took its turn to mass murder with the killing of the handicapped in 1939 there was some room for debate and dissent in the Nazi "racial state," even in the crucial area of eugenic policy.[38]

THE PREDOMINANCE OF CRIMINAL-BIOLOGICAL RESEARCH: CRIMINOLOGY AND PSYCHIATRY

Reviewing the development of German criminology from the late nineteenth century to 1945, the most noticeable feature is the predominance of research on the biological causes of crime over research on its social causes. This prevalence of the criminal-biological approach was in large part due to the fact that most criminological research was conducted by psychiatrists. As we have seen, the field of criminology developed from a conjunction of interests among criminal jurists and psychiatrists. The penal reformers around Franz von Liszt looked to criminological research to provide a scientific foundation for penal policy. Although the reformers were inclined to attribute greater importance to social rather than biological causes of crime, in practice criminal-sociological investigations soon lagged behind criminal-biological research, both because German sociologists showed little interest in crime and because the penal reformers proved reluctant to undertake criminal-sociological research themselves. This situation changed only after the First World War, when a number of jurists, most notably Franz Exner and Moritz Liepmann, did begin to conduct criminal-sociological research.

---

38 For a detailed analysis of Nazi sterilization policy with regard to criminals see Wetzell, *Inventing the Criminal*, 254–80; on sterilization under the Nazi regime in general see Gisela Bock, *Zwangssterilisation im Nationalsozialismus* (Opladen, 1986).

But the resurgence of criminal sociology under Exner's aegis was never enough to overcome the continuing predominance of criminal biology.

Hence, most criminological research during our period was conducted by German doctors, primarily psychiatrists. Why did they take such an interest in criminological questions? To a considerable extent, the late-nineteenth-century surge in the medical profession's interest in crime was due to the fact that Lombroso's theory of the born criminal advanced a biological explanation of crime to which the German medical profession, like their colleagues in other countries, felt compelled to respond. Moreover, as Lombroso came to equate his "born criminal" with the psychiatric diagnosis of "moral insanity," not just prison doctors but psychiatrists in general felt called upon to react to Lombroso's theories.

Besides the impact of Lombroso's theories, there were a number of other reasons why the psychiatric profession took a sustained interest in criminological research. First, the reception of Lombroso's theories occurred at a time when German psychiatry was expanding its expertise from the area of full-fledged mental illnesses into the borderland of mental "abnormalities" (now termed "personality disorders") that the late-nineteenth-century psychiatrist Julius Koch called "geistige Minderwertigkeiten," and which Kraepelin and Schneider referred to as "psychopathic personalities." Since these conditions were associated with deviant behavior, including crime, psychiatrists' interest in colonizing this vast new borderland of "abnormalities" also fueled their interest in criminological research.

Second, the psychiatric profession's interest in criminological research was closely tied to its ambition to expand psychiatry's role in the criminal justice system. This ambition found its earliest and most radical expression in Emil Kraepelin's *Die Abschaffung des Strafmasses* (1880), in which Kraepelin called for the abolition of fixed "punishments" in favor of indefinite, individualized treatment and the reorganization of the penal system along the lines of psychiatric clinics. Since Kraepelin's scheme did not distinguish between punishment and medical treatment, the question of legal responsibility became moot, so that psychiatrists would no longer have to serve as expert witnesses in cases of the insanity plea. As a result, the traditionally adversarial relationship between criminal justice and psychiatry, in which jurists frequently resented psychiatrists for "getting criminals off," would be transformed into a symbiotic one, in which psychiatrists played a key role in determining the proper individualized treatment for every offender. Although most psychiatrists stopped well short of Kraepelin's demands, and accepted the distinction between legally responsible and irresponsible offenders (calling only for the introduction of "diminished responsibility"), they all shared the ambition of expanding the role of psychiatry in the criminal justice system. After all, the whole idea behind criminal-biological examinations was that psychiatric evaluations ought to play a role in determining an offender's individualized penal treatment.

Finally, the psychiatric profession's eagerness to play a major role in the criminal justice system reflected another characteristic of late-nineteenth and twentieth-century German psychiatry: its willingness to place the interests of society above the welfare of the individual patient.[39] This attitude emerged quite clearly in pre-1914 discussions on the introduction of "diminished responsibility," in which psychiatrists seized on the "abnormality" of *Minderwertige* to justify their indefinite detention for the sake of protecting society without, however, insisting that this same "abnormality" ought to qualify Minderwertige for purely medical treatment and thus exempt them from the rigors and stigma of imprisonment.[40] The same attitude received its most explicit formulation when Aschaffenburg defended psychiatrists against the accusation that their "excessive humanitarianism" had undermined criminal justice. Psychiatrists, he insisted, routinely "deprive[d] patients of their freedom in order to protect the public" and were therefore well aware that "the interests of the patient must come second to the general welfare."[41]

TWO PARADIGMS

From the outset, the biological explanations of criminal behavior offered by German psychiatrists took the form of two different paradigms. Although the turn-of-the-century pioneers of German "criminal psychology" were unanimous in rejecting Lombroso's claim that the "born criminal" represented a distinct anthropological type, the explanations of criminal behavior that they offered split them into two camps. The proponents of what we might call the "Kraepelin paradigm" stripped the notion of the "born criminal" of Lombroso's anthropological characteristics and redefined it in purely psychiatric terms as someone with a criminogenic "moral defect." After the

---

39 See Heinz-Peter Schmiedebach, "The Mentally Ill Patient Caught between the State's Demands and the Professional Interests of Psychiatrists," in *Medicine and Modernity: Public Health and Medical Care in Nineteenth- and Twentieth-Century Germany*, Manfred Berg and Geoffrey Cocks, eds. (Cambridge, 1997), 99–119.

40 On these debates see Wetzell, "Criminal Law Reform."

41 Aschaffenburg, "Neue Horizonte?" *Monatsschrift für Kriminalpsychologie und Strafrechtsreform* 24 (1933): 159. While the date might lead one to wonder whether Aschaffenburg's comment was simply designed to ward off Nazi attacks, the historical record shows that this had indeed been the prevalent attitude among German psychiatrists at least since the turn of the century.

First World War, this paradigm took the form of Birnbaum's and Schneider's *gemütlos* (compassionless) or "amoral" psychopaths. The most interesting feature of the "Kraepelin paradigm" was its blatant conflation of moral and medical norms, for which Kraepelin's definition of "moral insanity" as "the lack or weakness of those sentiments which counter the ruthless satisfaction of egotism" provides perhaps the most egregious example. Remarkably, even Kurt Schneider, who criticized the conflation of medical and moral criteria in Kraepelin's definitions and made a special effort to establish objective psychological criteria for his "psychopathic personalities," committed the same error when he defined the *gemütlos* or amoral psychopathic type as lacking "compassion, shame, honor, remorse, conscience." The inclusion of moral criteria in psychiatric diagnoses greatly increased the risk of tautological reasoning in which a person's deviant or criminal behavior became a medical symptom of psychopathy simply because it violated conventional moral and social norms.

Since Schneider and Birnbaum regarded the *gemütlos* or amoral psychopathic types as a tiny minority among criminals, the scope of the Kraepelin paradigm was severely restricted from the Weimar period onward, allowing the competing paradigm to gain ascendancy. Already at the turn of the century, a second group of psychiatrists, including Gustav Aschaffenburg and Paul Näcke, had denied the existence of a "moral defect" and taken a more complex view of the interaction of heredity and environment. They established what we might call the "Aschaffenburg paradigm," which argued that many criminals suffered from general mental abnormalities (described in terms of degeneration, *Minderwertigkeit*, or psychopathy) that made them more likely to succumb to a life of crime under certain external circumstances — not because these abnormalities were directly criminogenic, but because they handicapped their carriers in social and economic life. By the Weimar period this paradigm had become the predominant one. Virtually every criminal biologist of the interwar period, including those most committed to the search for genetic factors, like Johannes Lange and Friedrich Stumpfl, agreed that, except for the rare cases of *gemütlos* psychopaths, the congenital or genetic factors that played a role in criminal behavior did not consist of some kind of criminogenic "moral defect" but of various psychopathic traits that were not inherently criminogenic, but that could develop a criminogenic potential in certain combinations and under certain environmental circumstances. In short, the Aschaffenburg paradigm acknowledged that criminal behavior was always the result of a complex interaction between genetic and environmental factors.

THE TENSION BETWEEN INCREASING METHODOLOGICAL
SOPHISTICATION AND HEREDITARIANISM

The most important effect of the Aschaffenburg paradigm was that its complex view of the interaction of heredity and environment promoted methodological and conceptual sophistication in criminal-biological research. If we compare Weimar-era to pre-1914 research, there can be no doubt that the work of Karl Birnbaum, Kurt Schneider, Hans Gruhle, and Johannes Lange was considerably more sophisticated in its approach to the interaction of heredity and environment than the prewar theories of Emil Kraepelin, Eugen Bleuler, Gustav Aschaffenburg, or Paul Näcke. Remarkably, this long-term trend toward increasing methodological sophistication in mainstream criminal biology continued even under the Nazi regime. Friedrich Stumpfl had a much better grasp of the methodological problems of twin studies than Lange, just as Franz Exner's 1939 survey of criminology represented a considerable advance over Aschaffenburg's standard work. Perhaps the most important result of this increasing sophistication was that it immensely complicated criminal-biologists' task. For as their understanding of the interaction of heredity and environment became more complex, criminologists' goal to identify criminogenic genetic factors and distinguish between corrigibles and incorrigibles became ever more elusive.

Having established the increasing sophistication of criminal-biological research, we are faced with a paradox. For even though most criminal biologists appreciated the complexity of the interaction of heredity and milieu, most (though not all) consistently privileged the search for genetic factors, arguing that genetic factors were somehow of "primary" importance. Such an assertion would have been warranted only if it had been shown that genetic factors often led to crime without any significant environmental co-factors or that the criminogenic force of such genetic factors was not usually amenable to rehabilitative measures. In fact, however, there was no evidence for either proposition. On the contrary, Lange admitted that environmental factors played a role in the cases of all his criminal twins, and Stumpfl estimated that at most 20 percent of criminals could be considered incorrigible.

Why, then, did most criminal biologists nevertheless claim "primacy" for genetic factors? The answer, I would argue, has to do with a number of fundamental biases and assumptions that were characteristic of German psychiatry during the period under investigation. First, German psychiatry during our period was characterized by a strong hereditarian bias; that is, by the assumption that individual differences, including mental illness, were primarily due to genetic factors. This hereditarianism, which was by no means unique to German psychiatry, derived at least in part from psychiatry's failure to make progress in the treatment of mental illnesses. Unable to cure most of their patients, it was tempting for psychiatrists to explain their therapeutic failures with a theory that attributed the cause of mental illness to immutable genetic factors. Furthermore, although human genetics remained in a primitive state throughout our period, hereditarianism also received a boost from the rediscovery of Mendel's laws around the turn of the century.

Second, by the mid-1920s at the latest, the vast majority of German physicians and psychiatrists were enthusiastic supporters of eugenics, at least in principle. That qualification is important, because the details of practical implementation, including the question of who exactly should be sterilized, gave rise to significant disagreements. Nevertheless, the almost universal enthusiasm for eugenics among German psychiatrists clearly helps to explain why they privileged the search for genetic factors over environmental research.[42]

Finally, although most criminal biologists acknowledged the role of social factors in crime, they were generally pessimistic about being able to change the social conditions that pushed so many people into a life of crime. Gustav Aschaffenburg, Theodor Viernstein, Ernst Rüdin, and others, explicitly admitted that in many cases changes in the social milieu of a recidivist could, in principle, prevent that person from offending again. But such acknowledgments were always followed by the qualification that this environment could not, in practice, be changed, so that the criminal in question would have to be considered "incorrigible." In other words – and this is crucial – the prognosis of incorrigibility was not based on the conviction that the individual's criminal behavior was rooted in unalterable genetic factors, but on the judgment that it was simply too difficult to change the social factors involved. The reasons for this pessimism about the possibility of changing the social environment, or more accurately, the lack of interest in trying to effect such social change, were deeply rooted in the traditions of the medical profession but also reflected a basic political conservatism. A similar point holds for the penal reformers. For although Liszt and his fellow reformers frequently stressed the role of social factors, their reform

---

42 On German eugenics see Peter Weingart, Jürgen Kroll, and Kurt Bayertz, *Rasse, Blut und Gene: Geschichte der Eugenik und Rassenhygiene in Deutschland* (Frankfurt, 1988); Paul Weindling, *Health, Race and German Politics between National Unification and Nazism, 1870–1945* (Cambridge, 1989); Hans-Walter Schmuhl, *Rassenhygiene, Nationalsozialismus, Euthanasie*, 2d ed. (Göttingen, 1992). The connection between eugenics and criminology is examined at greater length in Wetzell, *Inventing the Criminal*.

proposals focused on the individualization of punishment, that is, on the transformation of the offender rather than social change. From this perspective, criminal biology was welcome because it promised the knowledge about individual criminals that was crucial for an offender-oriented reform effort.

After examining why so many criminal biologists and criminologists continued to privilege biological and genetic explanations of criminal behavior over sociological ones, we must also note that the sophistication of criminal-biological research did impose some checks on hereditarian beliefs and led a number of psychiatrists and jurists to stress the importance of environmental factors. Among the psychiatrists pursuing criminal-biological research, Hans Gruhle remained highly critical of genetic explanations of crime and emphasized the role of social factors, including social class. Moreover, jurists conducting criminological research, especially Franz Exner and Moritz Liepmann, but even Edmund Mezger, tended to be much more even-handed in their treatment of biological and social factors in the etiology of crime. Finally, it must be remembered that because criminal-biological research successfully conveyed the complexity of the interaction of genetics and environment in the etiology of crime, many psychiatrists and most jurists opposed the targeting of criminals as such for sterilization during the Weimar and Nazi years.

CRIMINOLOGY AND NAZISM

The relationship between criminology and Nazism was a complex one. On the one hand, the longstanding predominance of criminal-biological over criminal-sociological research undoubtedly helped to popularize the notion that it might be possible to provide medical solutions to the crime problem. Criminal biology thus contributed to the rise of the eugenics movement and a climate of opinion that facilitated the implementation of Nazi eugenic policy. The disproportionate targeting of criminals for eugenic sterilization under the Nazi sterilization law that was promoted by Ernst Rüdin and Arthur Gütt would have been inconceivable without decades of hereditarian criminal-biological rhetoric. Moreover, leading criminal biologists, including Theodor Viernstein, appealed for the Nazi regime's support by arguing that criminal-biological examinations could serve a useful function in Nazi eugenic policy, and this appeal resulted in the expansion of the Criminal-Biological Service to the national level. In all these respects, our findings reinforce the thrust of recent research on the Nazi "racial state," which has argued that Nazi anti-Semitism and the murder of the European

Jews were part of a larger vision of "biological politics" that targeted a wide variety of groups perceived as biologically inferior.[43]

On the other hand, however, careful study of mainstream criminological research and of Nazi sterilization policy with regard to criminals shows that the triumph of genetic determinism under the Nazi regime was not as complete as has sometimes been assumed. While crude genetic determinism and racism did indeed pervade not just the Nazi elite but many sectors of society, including the leadership of the police and significant portions of the medical profession, we have seen that they did not supplant a more nuanced and complex discourse among mainstream criminal biologists and criminologists. As we have noted, this finding supports the argument that a certain amount of "normal science" did indeed continue under the Nazi regime.

Furthermore, the history of the genesis and implementation of the Nazi sterilization law demonstrates that the sophistication of criminal biological research, which acknowledged its inability to identify criminogenic genetic traits, made the sterilization of criminals controversial and contentious not only during the Weimar Republic but even under the Nazi regime. The opponents of the sterilization of criminals succeeded in having criminals excluded from the sterilization law of 1933 and subsequently in preventing the law from being amended to include criminals. And even as Gütt and Rüdin used their influence to target criminals through an expanded definition of feeblemindedness, a significant number of Superior Hereditary Health Courts ruled against the sterilization of criminals as such. When the regime took the step from forced sterilization to mass murder with the "euthanasia" killings of the mentally ill and handicapped in 1939, these disagreements over sterilization policy became sadly irrelevant. The victims of the "euthanasia" program were selected by doctors sworn to secrecy; no court reviewed their fate; "euthanasia" could not be publicly discussed, because the program was secret. Nevertheless, the story of continued academic, official, and judicial disagreements over the sterilization of criminals during the Nazi regime suggests that Nazi biological politics left more room for contention and disagreement than has often been assumed.

43 See especially Burleigh and Wippermann, *The Racial State.*

19

The Biology of Morality

Criminal Biology in Bavaria, 1924–1933

OLIVER LIANG

Faced with growing crime and recidivism rates after World War I, Bavarian penal officials in 1920 introduced a "progressive system" (*Stufensystem*) in prisons, whereby inmates were classified according to "corrigibility" and placed into appropriate "steps" or "levels" (*Stufen*), each with corresponding rights and privileges. The idea behind the system was to separate hardened criminals and recidivists from occasional criminals, many of whom were driven to crime by the hardships of the war. By 1923 the progressive system was in trouble, foundering on an ill-defined classification method and an inmate population clever enough to exploit its weaknesses. At this point the prison doctor at the penitentiary in Straubing, Dr. Theodor Viernstein, suggested that "biological" criteria be used to evaluate and classify prisoners in the progressive system. Drawing on a rich legacy of criminal-anthropological and criminal-psychological theories, Viernstein argued that a thorough medical and psychological evaluation of an inmate would provide the precise "scientific" classification of prisoners that the progressive system required. As a result, in 1924 a Criminal-Biological Service (Kriminalbiologischer Dienst) was established in Bavaria, which eventually collected over 20,000 "criminal-biological evaluations" (*kriminalbiologische Gutachten*) of prison inmates that contained information about more than 100,000 family members and associates throughout Germany. These evaluations were used in criminal and civil cases, and even by local authorities in such matters as issuing driver's licenses.[1]

Viernstein's notion of criminal biology marked a significant departure from contemporaneous criminological theories. Like many so-called "criminal psychologists," Viernstein believed that a large number of criminals

---

[1] Bayerisches Hauptstaatsarchiv (BHStA), MJu 22507: Bericht des fünften Arbeitsjahres, Oct. 31, 1930.

Oliver Liang

were mentally ill, in some cases due to hereditary factors, and that this inclined them toward criminal behavior. Viernstein, however, emphasized the idea that hereditary mental deficiencies were apparent through physiological characteristics of "degeneration" – tuberculosis, alcoholism, the size and shape of the ears, nose, head, and other parts of the body – as well as somatic "character types." Criminal-biological evaluations therefore assembled a wide range of data, including full medical and psychiatric evaluations, physiometric measurements, and "subjective" impressions gained by the evaluator from interviews with the inmate. Reports from schools, parishes, and local police precincts – often filled with local hearsay and rumors – rounded out the background information in the evaluations. From this information Viernstein and other evaluators sought to determine whether a prisoner was "corrigible," "incorrigible," or "questionable," so as to place him or her in the appropriate level of the progressive system.[2] These classifications were important because they could be used as evidence in future penal procedures or be invoked to have inmates placed in insane asylums or in preventive detention.

At first glance the Bavarian criminal-biological project might appear simply as another European eugenic project that arose from the crisis of the welfare state in the 1920s. Certainly Bavaria had the highest recorded crime rate in Germany, and Munich had become a center for psychological and neurological research, creating an unusually high concentration of medically oriented social policy experts. Nevertheless, it would be too simple to explain the Bavarian criminal-biological service as a response to a high crime rate or as a means to bring about economic efficiency in public administration, a motive ascribed to German eugenics by much of the scholarly literature on the topic.[3] In fact, many types of crime declined in Bavaria during the Weimar years, as did the overall prison population, thus diffusing

2 Theodor Viernstein, "Entwickelung und Aufbau eines kriminalbiologischen Dienstes im bayerischen Strafvollzug," in *Stufenstrafvollzug und die kriminalbiologische Untersuchung der Gefangenen in den bayerischen Strafanstalten*, 3 vols. (Munich, 1926–9), 1:86–110.

3 Broadly speaking, most of the recent literature on German eugenics has stressed its "rational," "modern," and economic aspects. Detlev J. K. Peukert, "The Genesis of the 'Final Solution' from the Spirit of Science," in Thomas Childers and Jane Caplan, eds., *Reevaluating the Third Reich* (New York, 1993); Elizabeth Harvey, *Youth and the Welfare State in Weimar Germany* (Oxford, 1993); Sheila Faith Weiss, *Race Hygiene and the Rational Management of National Efficiency: Wilhelm Schallmeyer and the Origins of German Eugenics, 1890–1920* (Baltimore, 1983); Paul Weindling, *Health, Race, and German Politics Between National Unification and Nazism* (Cambridge, 1989); Peter Weingart, Jürgen Kroll, and Kurt Bayertz, *Rasse, Blut und Gene* (Frankfurt am Main, 1988); Hans-Walter Schmuhl, *Rassenhygiene, Nationalsozialismus, Euthanasie: Von der Verhütung zur Vernichtung "lebensunwerten Lebens"* (Göttingen, 1987); Detlev J. K. Peukert, *Grenzen der Sozialdisziplinierung: Aufstieg und Krise der deutschen Jugendfürsorge* (Cologne, 1986).

the argument that criminal biology was a reaction to high crime rates.[4] The Catholic Church, always a powerful force in Bavaria, initially had difficulty reconciling the idea of hereditary criminality with the idea of sin, redemption, and freedom of will.[5] The Criminal-Biological Service was expensive, requiring equipment, training, additional staff, and a photographic service to take pictures of unclothed criminal "specimens" (a practice against which the Catholic Church protested vehemently); it was therefore not an ideal means to reduce the cost of running prisons. The German criminological community was keenly aware that the notion of "crime" was a social construct that was difficult to link with physiology and heredity. Finally, it was unclear why a more "scientific" selection of prisoners could not have been attained through academically accepted criminal-psychological theories without resorting to the radical theories of an obscure prison doctor.

Nevertheless, by 1933 much of the Bavarian penal establishment had been won over by criminal-biological thought. The interest in linking theories of crime to hereditary biology was only in part a response to the perception of rising crime rates and the search for administrative efficiency. The most compelling reason that motivated Bavarian supporters of criminal biology was an interest in recasting a bourgeois vision of morality through a religious interpretation of biology. The notion of "biology" allowed elite groups to buttress their crumbling social positions, reinforce their moral values and taboos against certain forms of behavior, and in general recast a bourgeois moral discourse against what was perceived as cosmopolitanism, moral relativism, cultural decadence, urbanism, and socialism – in short, modernity.

BAVARIAN PRISON OFFICIALS

The Bavarian criminal-biological project was supported by a prison establishment composed of civil servants, medical doctors, and members of the Catholic and Protestant clergy. These groups did not share an identical agenda; instead, they appear to have stressed particular strands of criminal-biological theory to suit their professional interests. Nonetheless, these groups shared a number of common characteristics. They all belonged to what could be loosely called the German bourgeoisie and petit-bourgeoisie

---

4 Bavaria, like the rest of Germany, experienced a sharp rise in crime after World War I that peaked in 1924. Thereafter, crime rates fell, often to levels lower than the period between 1890 and 1913. Although Bavaria had the highest crime rate in Germany, most Bavarian cities had lower crime rates than cities in the Ruhr or in Prussia. On Bavarian criminal statistics, see *Verbrechen und Verbrechertum in Bayern*, Bayerisches Statistisches Landesamt (Munich, 1944).

5 BHStA, MJu 22516: Bishopric Speyer to the MJu, June 4, 1925.

(*Bürgertum* and *Kleinbürgertum*). Jurists and doctors were part of the educated bourgeoisie, whereas clerics and minor penal officials constituted part of the German lower middle-class. These strata of society faced increasing professional hardships during the Weimar period and generally believed that their social status and well-being were being threatened by revolution and mass politics.

As a result, many Bavarian jurists, medical doctors, and clergy gravitated toward conservative and nationalist politics. For example, the Bavarian justice minister (and later Reich justice minister) Franz Gürtner, whose support was crucial for the Criminal-Biological Service, participated in the trials of left-wing political radicals after the failed Bavarian socialist republics. He joined the conservative German National People's Party (DNVP) but reserved sympathies for Hitler after his failed 1923 Munich putsch.[6] Hans Frank, the National Socialist justice minister of Bavaria, praised Gürtner in 1933 for having staffed the Justice Ministry with acceptable national-conservative men throughout his tenure.[7] Bavarian doctors who supported the criminal-biological project also came from similar backgrounds. Hans Otto Luxenburger, a researcher at the German Psychiatric Research Institute in Munich and a member of the board of the Criminal-Biological Service, served as an officer in a military hospital after the war, where he examined a number of leading figures of the Bavarian revolution.[8] Politically, Luxenburger was conservative and anti-Semitic.[9] The eugenicist Ernst Rüdin, who also served on the board of the Criminal-Biological Service, prepared psychiatric evaluations of indicted revolutionaries such as Ernst Toller for the Munich criminal courts.[10] Viernstein, the father of Bavarian criminal biology, also evaluated Munich revolutionaries and was a staunch monarchist and supporter of the conservative Bavarian People's Party. Not only did these conservative doctors have to worry about left-wing radicalism in the initial years of Weimar; they also faced deteriorating professional conditions.[11] The clergy, too, faced unprecedented challenges to their status and place in Bavarian society. In prisons the clergy confronted hostile prisoners, in many cases anticlerics who used mass and other religious rites as opportunities to break up the monotony of prison life.[12] Attendance at religious services declined, reflecting a general trend of secularization in

---

6 Lothar Gruchmann, *Justiz im Dritten Reich 1933–1940: Anpassung und Unterwerfung in der Ära Gürtner* (Munich, 1988), 10–26.

7 Ibid., 231–2.

8 Luxenburger quoted in Matthias Weber, *Ernst Rüdin: Eine politische Biographie* (Berlin, 1993), 142.

9 Ibid., 179.   10 Ibid., 1–92.

11 Michael Kater, *Doctors Under Hitler* (Chapel Hill, N.C., 1989), 12–53.

12 BHStA, MJu 22508: Bericht des Evang. Luth. Anstaltsgeistlichen, June 11, 1931.

Bavaria, especially in the larger cities.[13] Many clerics found it difficult to deal with socialist inmates, who were perceived to be corroding the faith of their fellow prisoners.

These convergent social and political backgrounds prompted Bavarian jurists, doctors, and clergy to support the criminal-biological project with particular fervor. This is not to say that humanitarian or administrative motives were entirely absent: Richard Degen, a senior official in the Bavarian justice ministry who was a fervent supporter of the progressive system, hoped that better prison conditions and humane treatment by prison officials would ignite a spark of kindness and humanity in convicted criminals and lead them toward redemption. Degen strengthened the position of teachers and clergy in prisons and provided cinemas and music halls, lectures on cultural and political issues, concerts, and theater and music groups in an effort to develop the educational aspects of incarceration.[14]

Despite lectures and concerts, however, problems of recidivism and prison discipline remained. Although statistics are not available on discipline matters, reports from prison staff indicated a high level of uneasiness about prisoners who screamed a lot ("Schreier") and other uncooperative inmates who defied prison authority.[15] After 1929, prison officials became increasingly aware of discipline problems, especially in politicized inmates. Even at the juvenile prison in Niederschönfeld, the prison doctor complained that he feared physical assault by his patients.[16] Increasingly aware of the high costs of penal reform and frustrated by a core of inmates who, for one reason or another, would not or could not be rehabilitated through prison pedagogy, penal officials in Bavaria experienced what Detlev Peukert aptly described as the "limits of social discipline."[17] By 1930 Degen consequently conceded that it was only possible to treat prisoners to sports and concerts at state expense if he could convince the public that the "strictest selection" (*strengste Auslese*) of prisoners had been made.[18] As a result, a different notion of redemption came to the fore. Instead of "uplifting" the entire prison population, those capable of "redemption" had to be selected from those who were "incorrigible."

---

13 Werner K. Blessing, *Staat und Kirche in der Gesellschaft: Institutionelle Autorität und mentaler Wandel in Bayern während des 19. Jahrhunderts* (Göttingen, 1982), 245ff.

14 BHStA, MJu 22504: Degen an die Verwaltungen der Strafanstalten, July 16, 1920.

15 BHStA, MJu 22508: Bericht des katholischen Anstaltsgeistlichen Niederschönfeld, July 14, 1931, Halbjahresbericht 1931; BHStA, MJu 22509: Bericht des Anstaltslehrers Gensberger an die Direktion Niederschönfeld, June 15, 1933.

16 BHStA, MJu 22509: Bericht des Strafanstaltsarztes Niederschönfeld, Jan. 11, 1932.

17 Peukert, *Grenzen der Sozialdisziplinierung*, 249–50.

18 BHStA, MJu 22507: Besprechung der Strafvollzugsreferenten, June 18, 1930.

The discourse on criminal biology thus shifted toward a second theme, that of economic efficiency. The state's attorney Emil Lersch in Munich saw criminal biology as a needed corrective against "the cult of the socially inferior" and the "feminism" he perceived to be running rampant in the legal system.[19] Degen envisioned expanding the Criminal-Biological Service to include schoolchildren and the chronically poor in an effort to compose a racial-hygienic portrait of Bavaria for a more efficient allocation of welfare resources.[20] Medical doctors such as Viernstein believed that the Criminal-Biological Service would allow corrigible criminals to be identified quickly and released on probation, thus saving the cost of their incarceration.

Criminal-biological discourse thus reflected both the humanitarian tradition of penal reform and the increasing anxieties about national economic efficiency that arose in Germany after World War I. Yet beyond these themes existed a far more powerful discourse which suggested that biological selection would recast a bourgeois vision of morality and society based on the science of biology. There was, of course, no fixed canon of moral values that constituted "bourgeoisness" (*Bürgerlichkeit*). Values associated in scholarly literature with the German bourgeoisie – prudence, religion, sexual restraint, hard work, education – are in many ways the universal values of the economically dynamic classes in Western societies. Nonetheless, within the discourse of criminal biology, a consistent set of moral values was repeatedly identified as traits of bourgeois respectability: industriousness, sexual decorum, veneration for rural life and order, rejection of "proletarian" and modern culture, political conservatism, and a social order based on defined gender, class, and professional roles. These values were perceived to be embodied by upstanding members of the middle class. Significantly, these ideals of moral behavior were defined in opposition to depictions of lower-class immorality and socialism, and as a result, they gained a certain identity-creating function, especially because they were perceived as threatened by mass politics, revolution, and crime. Criminal-biological theory allowed penal officials to construct a distinctly bourgeois "Self" in opposition to a dangerous, lower-class "Other." This Self was not simply based on political conservatism, nationalism, racism, or *völkisch* ideology: instead, criminal-biological discourse defined the identity of a middle-class German who eschewed both modernism and cosmopolitanism, as well as the idealistic zealotry of political revolutionaries. Thus defined as a moral and social identity, *Bürgerlichkeit* was

---

19 Emil Lersch, "Die Strafrechtliche Verwertung der kriminalbiologischen Gutachten," *Mitteilungen der Kriminalbiologischen Gesellschaft* (hereafter *MKG*) 3 (1930): 47–53.

20 *Stufenstrafvollzug* 1:6–7.

no longer linked directly with a particular class or social-political milieu; as Charles Maier has observed, the notion of the German "bourgeois" in the interwar period came to signify a "common denomination of social anxiety and political defense."[21]

In order to preserve this sense of bourgeois moral identity, prison officials hoped that the progressive system and criminal-biological selection would lead prisoners to adopt a religious and socially conservative moral outlook. The director of the penitentiary in Straubing, Franz Koch, for example, believed that prison pedagogy should go beyond just instructing prisoners: It was to lead to a fundamental change in their personalities. Koch concluded that "more important than formal church and confessional activities is . . . the guidance toward and eventual bonding of the personality to the moral/ethical content of religion."[22] Koch warned against what he perceived as sham religiosity; instead, he envisioned a more robust, "manly" religious feeling that would result in redemption: "Especially with men, an unequivocal parting with superficial piousness is necessary; a new, robust piousness has to be presented as the ideal."[23] From the outset the criminal-biological project was gendered, represented as a "manly" alternative to the penal "feminism" that pedagogical approaches implied.

A similar attitude was voiced by Otto Kahl, the director of the Nuremberg prison. For Kahl, criminal biology was to assist in making a prisoner "morally, spiritually, mentally, and physically stronger and more resistant for the battle of life."[24] Beyond this, Kahl envisioned a widening of the criminal-biological project to include schoolchildren. His objective was not only to conduct a racial hygienic survey of the population, but to make the population aware of the biological roots of social cohesion. Quoting Degen, Kahl believed that "a loving immersion into the history of one's ancestors . . . would revive the sense of family that has been buried in part by the material woes of our *Volk* and in part by the superficiality of

---

21 Charles S. Maier, *Recasting Bourgeois Europe: Stabilization in France, Germany, and Italy in the Decade after World War I* (Princeton, N.J., 1975; reprint, 1988), 6–7, 36–7. For a discussion of the notion of *Bürgertum*, see Jürgen Kocka, "Bürgertum und Bürgerlichkeit als Probleme der deutschen Geschichte vom späten 18. zum frühen 20. Jahrhundert," in Jürgen Kocka, ed., *Bürger und Bürgerlichkeit im 19. Jahrhundert* (Göttingen, 1987), 21–63; Hans Mommsen, "The Decline of the Bürgertum in Late Nineteenth- and Early Twentieth-Century Germany," in Hans Mommsen, ed., *From Weimar to Auschwitz*, trans. Philip O'Connor (Cambridge, 1991), 11–27; David Blackbourn, "The German Bourgeoisie: An Introduction," in David Blackbourn and Richard J. Evans, eds., *The German Bourgeoisie* (London, 1991), 1–45; Doris Kaufmann, *Aufklärung, bürgerliche Selbsterfahrung, und die "Erfindung" der Psychiatrie in Deutschland 1770–1850* (Göttingen, 1995).
22 Robert Koch, "Kriminalpönologie," *Stufenstrafvollzug* 3 (1929): 173.
23 Koch, quoting J. Schneider, in "Kriminalpönologie," 174.
24 Otto Kahl, "Die Kriminalbiologische Untersuchung der Strafgefangenen in Bayern," *MKG* 3 (1930): 17.

modern life."[25] For Kahl and Koch, criminal biology went beyond a means for achieving greater efficiency and pedagogical success: It was a means of describing the essence of ethics, morality, and decency that they perceived to be crumbling beneath their feet. The concept of criminal biology imparted to the prison regime a robust, religious, and "manly" sense of ethics that was based on the seemingly unshakable foundation of "biology." For Viernstein the religious and moral aspects of criminal biology were evident as well. In 1923 Viernstein noted that:

For us Germans today, the flourishing of the race must be an object of utmost concern, after the negative selection of the war has removed colossal masses of valuable racial elements. Research that reveals the physical and mental structure of the population is crucial to identify the direction in which the population is heading. This is especially relevant for a knowledge of those parts of the population whose calling it is to supply the new generation of leaders. So it has, for example, been rightly claimed that the civil-servant class [*Beamtenstand*], which has always represented a certain selection in the population, should in the future consist only of personalities whose psychological, especially characterological, familial, and civic qualities guarantee their suitability for public office.[26]

The key idea in this passage was that of "characterology," a field developed by the German psychiatrist Ernst Kretschmer, among others, which linked certain personality traits with particular body types.[27] Because body types were inherited, the theories of characterology closely linked character with heredity. Thus, for Viernstein the characterological qualities of the future civil-servant class (*Stand*) were inextricably linked with their hereditary qualities. Those who represented the characterologically and biologically select were already endowed, in essence, with superior bourgeois moral traits. Moral traits were not learned or acquired from one's milieu but were an inherent part of a given *Stand*. Having gone this far, Viernstein then postulated that not only personal morality but ethics on the whole were in essence biological: "Criminal law is, in the end, applied ethics. And ethics measures its postulates according to the standard of the biologically best, the most valuable of the race."[28]

Viernstein's self-perceived function as the arbiter of morality shifted the role of the doctor into the jurisdiction of the clergyman. Like Koch,

---

25 Ibid., 29.
26 BHStA, MJu 22504: Viernstein to Degen, Feb. 28, 1923.
27 Ernst Kretschmer, *Körperbau und Charakter: Untersuchungen zum Konstitutionsproblem und zur Lehre von den Temperamenten* (Berlin, 1922).
28 BHStA, MJu 22511: Viernstein, "Denkschrift über die wissenschaftlichen Grundlagen für den Betrieb einer kriminalbiologischen Sammelstelle," n.d.

Viernstein believed that the science of biology could offer a clearer basis for moral values than religious institutions. Nevertheless, Viernstein conceded that the functions of religion and biology were similar, as were the roles of the clergyman and the medical doctor:

> It is . . . sheer nonsense when one repeatedly sees a doctor and a theologian feuding in some village [*Bierdorf*] because the doctor does not attend church (which has nothing to do with his religion) and the pastor understands nothing about biology. Both are talking "past each other," yet have the same earthly goal . . . the elevation of the race, each after his own fashion.[29]

Viernstein hoped that his rapprochement with religion would lead to the building of an "intellectual bridge" between theology and medicine.[30] Although he believed that morality was based on biology, it was nonetheless important for him that morality also coincide with religious principles. Writing in the Catholic publication *Hochland* in 1926, Viernstein affirmed that criminal-biological investigations into a prisoner's psyche did not entail "for the biologist a weakening, a watering-down of the irrevocable demands of law, religion and custom."[31] For Viernstein, biology in essence reaffirmed in a modern, scientific language what religion had rightly suspected all along. A doctor who did not attend church or squabbled with the village priest was not irreligious: He simply had found a language with which to describe religious notions of morality that was more credible and more effective than concepts offered by declining religious institutions.

Despite being the antagonists of doctors, members of the clergy entertained an equally flexible and ambiguous concept of "biology" with which they bolstered religious conceptions of morality. The Bavarian clergy were, of course, pledged to help all prisoners find redemption, yet in the face of the challenges mentioned above, many harbored less than charitable views of their charges and were eager to remove "big-city Bolshevists" and other troublemakers from the ordinary prison population.[32] This sentiment eventually led to the stigmatization in eugenic terms of all nonreligious inmates. One priest suggested the removal from the normal prison population of all "asocials, communists, severe psychopaths, incorrigible complainers, sexual delinquents, homosexuals, and so forth."[33] Another Catholic priest declared that: "All historical experiences and biological facts indicate that the real

29 Viernstein to Wallner, Feb. 16, 1926, Viernstein papers, currently in author's possession.
30 Ibid.
31 Viernstein, "Biologische Probleme im Strafvollzug," offprint from *Hochland* (June 1926): 10.
32 BHStA, MJu 22508: Bericht des katholischen Anstaltsgeistlichen bei Zweibrücken, June 27, 1931.
33 BHStA, MJu 22509: Bericht des katholischen Anstaltsgeistlichen bei Niederschönfeld, June 15, 1932.

subhuman race (*Untermenschentum*), spiritually and morally inferior persons, severe psychopaths, asocials, atavistic persons, whose attitude corresponds to an outdated and inferior level of cultural developement, are, with few exceptions, impossible to educate and reform, and cannot be lifted up."[34] Members of the Protestant clergy voiced a similar opinion.[35]

The particularly warm endorsement the clergy gave to criminal biology is interesting in view of the clergy's traditional interest in championing redemption through religion. This problem was addressed by Ignaz Klug, a professor of moral theology in Passau and a member of the academic board of the Criminal-Biological Service, who attempted to reconcile the Catholic notion of free will and salvation with the hereditary determinism of criminal biology. Klug argued that criminal biology did not signify "predestination" but allowed for the possibility of freedom of choice. Criminals, even if they were biologically disposed toward crime, could choose whether or not to follow their biological inclinations. Thus, the first step in redeeming a prisoner was a criminal-biological evaluation that would help the prisoner "recognize his heredity."[36] If the inmate recognized his or her hereditary inclination toward crime, Klug argued, inner moral salvation might be achieved. Much like Kahl, Klug saw the essence of morality in biology. Klug thus argued that the criminal-biological evaluation should not simply take account of the medical facts but attempt to grasp the essence of the inmate's inner biological morality.[37] Once an inmate's "inner morality" – for Klug a part of a prisoner's hereditary character – had been determined, it was up to the clergyman to guide him toward behavior that would prevent this born criminality from emerging. In terms of therapy this meant that the prisoner should establish an "affective relationship" with a religious counselor. Because this counselor – be it a cleric, prison warden, or pedagogue – would embody the "Christ ideal," this cathexis could result in redemption.[38] Judges were equally empowered through their religious qualities because Klug believed that "the judge is the conscience, the divine, the incorruptible righteousness in mankind."[39]

Concurring with Viernstein, Klug thus saw the role of the clergyman as equal to that of the medical doctor: "Body and soul stand in close

34 BHStA, MJu 22509: Bericht des katholischen Anstaltsgeistlichen bei Niederschönfeld, Dec. 7, 1932.
35 BHStA, MJu 22509: Bericht des protestantischen Anstaltsgeistlichen bei Zweibrücken, June 30, 1932.
36 Notes on a lecture by Ignaz Klug, n.d., Viernstein papers.
37 Ignaz Klug, "Kriminalpädagogik," in *Stufenstrafvollzug*, 3:104.
38 Ibid., 153.
39 Ibid., 68.

connection; therefore, priest and doctor are – if not by the same means or in the same areas – equal helpers of humanity."[40] Nonetheless, Klug's interpretation of criminal biology was tailored to the needs of the clergy. It permitted the clergyman to play the role both of the merciful warden of souls and of the scientific fighter of crime. Klug allowed for the redemption even of "incorrigible" criminals, as long as they recognized their sinful heredity, and he pleaded for a more forgiving classification system, suggesting that the category incorrigible be replaced with "unsuitable for freedom."[41] At the same time, Klug supported calls for the compulsory sterilization of prisoners and other "inferiors," believing it was an ethical question that religion had to face.[42] This combination of Catholic charity and eugenic firmness secured the place of the clergy in the modern prison order, and permitted Klug to declare in 1932, a period of intense social turmoil, that "there is no relative morality."[43]

The actual evaluations of prisoners also indicate that clergymen were the strictest evaluators in the Bavarian penal system. Already in 1923 the clergy at Straubing were condemning prisoners to "Level 1" (incorrigible) in the progressive system at a higher rate than their medical and juridical colleagues. Of approximately 950 prisoners, the Protestant pastor placed 506 at Level 1, and his Catholic counterpart placed 577 at that level. One teacher placed a similar number, relegating 502 inmates to the lowest level. By contrast, a second teacher placed only 271 inmates at Level 1; the director of Straubing prison, a jurist, classified only 94 prisoners as incorrigible.[44] Overall in Bavaria, jurists classified 29.3 percent of inmates as incorrigible; doctors believed the rate to be 36.1 percent, whereas the clergy (both Catholic and Protestant) judged 38.5 percent of all prisoners to be beyond any hope of redemption.[45]

CRIMINAL–BIOLOGICAL EVALUATIONS

It is clear that criminal biology represented more than just a "hardline" application of eugenic theory. For doctors, jurists, and clerics alike, criminal

---

40 Ignaz Klug, "Willensfreiheit – Willenshemmungen – Willenserziehung," in *Stufenstrafvollzug*, 2:107.
41 Ibid., 124.   42 Ibid., 137.
43 Ignaz Klug, *Willensfreiheit und Persönlichkeit: Moralpsychologische Vorträge* (Paderborn, 1932), 3. The Bavarian Catholic establishment largely shared Klug's attitude toward criminal biology. See BHStA, MK 11779: *Amtsblatt für die Erzdiözese Bamberg*, no. 22, July 9, 1925; *Würzburger Diözesen-Blatt*, no. 17, May 20, 1925.
44 BHStA, MJu 22504: Report of the Directorate at Straubing, Mar. 5, 1923.
45 Staatsarchiv Amberg, Strafgefangenenanstalt Amberg, no. 139: Statistische Unterlagen des Gutachten, Feb. 4, 1930.

biology was vested with deep implications concerning their professional status, the importance of religion and morals in society, and, ultimately, fundamental questions concerning human nature. The actual criminal-biological evaluations of prisoners duly reflected this level of meaning. Criminal-biological evaluations were drawn up by prison doctors and were rounded out by clerics, teachers, and other prison officials. True to their criminal-anthropological origin, criminal-biological evaluation forms called for precise data concerning the subject's ancestry, health, physiology, and psyche. A much more extensive part of the evaluation was the "subjective" report, where the evaluator freely recorded his personal impressions of the prisoner's character and criminal deeds. These often long and convoluted reports projected the particular bourgeois social vision – based on concepts of class, gender, and religion – that criminal-biologists sought to anchor through biology.

For the most part, classification as "incorrigible" was tightly linked with behavior that was demarcated as the "clever" but nevertheless "dangerous" comportment of members of the working class or peasantry. To get an idea of how a prisoner was evaluated, it is worth examining two cases in detail. Josef V. was convicted of grand larceny and evaluated on April 5, 1928, in Straubing. Drawing on parish and police reports, the evaluation illustrates the inmate's family life. We are informed that the subject was an illegitimate child. The father was an "amiable person, but quick to anger"; other reports indicate that he was a tyrant and often beat the mother, who was "thrifty, kept the house well, and was religious and friendly." Although both parents had no criminal record, they performed the "theater of concubinage" during the inmate's youth. In all, the report notes that this was the "typical proletarian milieu of the lower classes."

School reports indicate Josef V. was a truant; during World War I he spent three years at the front, where he was wounded and consequently suffered from "the shakes." He was married in 1927 to a woman whom V.'s clergyman – in a parish report furnished for the criminal-biological evaluation – referred to as an "unlucky star," a woman who supposedly demanded a luxurious lifestyle and drove the subject into a life of crime. The inmate admitted to keeping "bad company." The evaluator concluded that Josef V. was too accustomed "to living off others," and because it would be impossible for him to break off his uxorious relationship with his wife, he should be classified as "incorrigible."[46]

46 BHStA, MJu 22512: Gutachten Josef V., Apr. 5, 1928.

A second representative case involved Alois D., convicted of arson and evaluated in Straubing in 1928 by Viernstein himself. D.'s father was "not a drinker, hard-working, domestic, amiable"; the mother also was "friendly, good, and pious." These descriptions did not come from local reports but from the inmate himself, whom Viernstein believed, because fabrication would be beyond an "uncomplicated and primitive person, such as Alois D." Alois D.'s wife was "overpious" and "would prefer to abstain from her marital duties." Because Alois D. claimed he was innocent, Viernstein came to the conclusion that he was either a hysteric who was convinced of his innocence or an innocent man who had become hysterical because he was being convicted of a crime he did not commit. In Viernstein's view, there was sufficient exculpatory evidence to leave open the possibility that Alois D. was corrigible.[47]

Both Josef V.'s and Alois D.'s evaluations are unique in many ways because evaluators delved deep into the personal history of their subjects. No doubt many of the factors cited in evaluations were an accurate reflection of a particular person's character; nevertheless, the evaluations contain three elements that appeared repeatedly, raising them to the status of being specific indicators that were invoked to justify a classification of either corrigible or incorrigible.

1. *Sexuality and gender relations.* The nature of an inmate's sexuality and his relationship with women and men were characteristics on which evaluators could inscribe a host of social and moral concerns. The "incorrigible criminal" was depicted as having a strong sex drive that was mostly "misdirected" – either toward no one (onanism), inappropriate partners (homosexuality, incest), or toward women who were not their spouse. One inmate was described thus: "sex-life awakened early, first intercourse at seventeen, strong drive, copulated frequently, no perversions, no autoeroticism."[48] Nearly all evaluations of "incorrigible" prisoners sampled listed "dangerous" sexuality as a reason for their criminality.[49] In the cases of Josef V. and Alois D. the significant sexual themes evoked were the sexual natures of their respective spouses. Josef V.'s wife was overly demanding, Alois D.'s spouse was sexually inactive; each behavior was cited in the context of explaining the inmate's character. Josef V. was condemned for indulging his "dissolute" wife, whereas Alois D. was exculpated for having been "betrayed"

47 BHStA, MJu 22512: Gutachten Alois D., Mar. 7, 1928.
48 Staatsarchiv Augsburg: Gefangenenakten, no. 359.
49 Staatsarchiv Landshut (StaLands), Rep. 176: JVA Straubing, Krankenakten, Box 7. Bericht und Befundbogen (BuB) Otto A., 1925.

by his. Overall, the character of the mother or wife of a male inmate played an important role in the explanation of an evaluation. Characteristics of a "good" woman were exemplified by this positive evaluation of a "good" wife: "no criminal record, not a drinker, a respectable woman, lively, friendly, amiable, warm–hearted, willing to make sacrifices, not anxious, not quarrelsome, beloved in the neighborhood, goes to church, no children before marriage, always healthy, never mentally ill."[50] The "good" wife or mother was rarely used to exculpate a prisoner; instead, they often acted as foils to a criminal who "deceived" or "betrayed" a "good" woman with a warm heart. Criminal-biological evaluations thus acted to define desirable and undesirable behavior not only in male inmates but in their female acquaintances as well.

Although the appearance of "good" women had little effect on a prisoner's evaluation, "bad" women were often a sign of undesirable heredity or a bad influence on the prisoner. A "bad" woman might exhibit the characteristics attributed to the mother of a minor Nazi party official, who in 1921 allegedly had a spat with Hitler and left the National Socialist Party: "The mother has a good education. . . . She is very irritable, but has a good personality; today like this, the next day like that, one can't rely on her; sometimes mean; mood swings; no [hysterical] attacks; gives away gifts given to her; no feelings of gratitude."[51] Instances of venereal disease, illicit love affairs, and extramarital children also weighed heavily in the description of what one evaluator called "dissolute women."[52] The spouses of prisoners were especially penalized for such misbehavior and were often depicted as being the inmate's "curse."[53]

2. *Milieu.* The evaluation of Josef V. described his parental home as "the typical proletarian milieu of the lower classes, even if both parents worked and were not criminal. . . . This type of inferiority is very possible in the case of both the mother and father of J. V."[54] Criminal biologists acknowledged that the milieu played a role in shaping an inmate's behavior, but the extent of that role remained powerfully ambiguous. In V.'s case, the evaluator acknowledged the difficult circumstances of V.'s home but then inverted the

50 StaLands, Rep. 176: JVA Straubing, Box 7, BuB Adolf A., Jan. 16, 1925; Viernstein papers: Gutachten Johann A., 1924.
51 BHStA, MJu 22512: BuB, Ernst E., Oct. 14, 1925; ibid.: BuB Christian J. S., May 5, 1928; Viernstein papers: Gutachten Franz K., May 11, 1928; ibid.: Gutachten Urban D., Aug. 29, 1928.
52 Viernstein papers: Gutachten Oskar B., Jan. 26, 1928; BHStA, MJu 22512: Gutachten Alois H., May 30, 1928; BHStA, MJu 22512: Gutachten Wilhelm P., May 30, 1928.
53 BHStA, MJu 22512: Gutachten Josef V., Apr. 5, 1928; Viernstein papers: Gutachten Franz K., May 11, 1928; ibid.: Gutachten Aug. S., 1924.
54 BHStA, MJu 22512: Gutachten Josef V.

causality to indicate that these conditions were a sign of the already present inferiority of the parents. The notion that a bad social environment was simply an indication of the inferiority of its inhabitants became a key concept in establishing a connection between specific "dangerous milieus" and natural-born criminality. Indeed, the evaluator revealed his preconception of the working class, registering surprise at the fact that both parents were employed and had no criminal record.

Dangerous milieus consisted of previously mentioned "dissolute women," communists, political agitators, other criminals, and drinking establishments of the lower classes. Thus evaluators noted the political associations of prisoners, their associations with known criminals in the community, and often recorded the alcohol-tolerance level of individual inmates.[55] All these observations expressed disapproval of an urban milieu, or as one evaluator described it, "environmental conditions, as they exist in the deepest proletariat and particularly during the immediate postwar period, with its depravation of customs and the unleashing of inconsiderate, self-centered attitudes."[56] "Dangerous women," bad company, and communists were all signifiers of the cosmopolitan city and its concomitant immorality.

This mistrust of cities is especially apparent in contrast to the evaluation of Alois D., who was described as part of the "country folk of the low, primitive strata."[57] Although criminal-biological evaluators looked on rural inhabitants with a certain contempt, the rural milieu also was considered naïve, good-hearted, and less insidiously criminal. Alois D.'s statements were taken at face value because he was from the country and was seen as too naive to lie; other evaluations spoke, with respect, of a certain "farmer cleverness."[58] Echoing Bavarian critics of big cities like Wilhelm Heinrich Riehl, criminal biologists used evaluations to express their support for the steady, conservative, and pious peasant in contrast to the urban proletariat.[59]

3. *Religion and politics.* Linked to the milieu were two other factors regularly noted by evaluators: religion and politics. Although evaluators were not supposed to inquire directly about a prisoner's political affiliation, politics were regularly mentioned in the psychological part of the evaluation,

55 StaLands, Rep. 176 JVA, Box 3: BuB Oswald S., Feb. 1920; ibid.: BuB Ferdinand R., July 7, 1920; ibid.: Gutachten Oskar B., Jan. 26, 1928; Viernstein papers: Gutachten Wilhelm P., May 30, 1929.
56 StaLands, Rep. 176 JVA, Box 3: BuB Anton S., June 6, 1920.
57 BHStA, MJu 22512: Gutachten Alois D., Mar. 7, 1928.
58 BHStA, MJu 22512: Gutachten Josef M., Jan. 14, 1928.
59 On German anti-urbanism, see Andrew Lees, *Cities Perceived: Urban Society in European and American Thought* (New York, 1985), 82–5.

presumably as they arose in police or parish reports. A few cases before 1933 mentioned links to the extreme right, such as the member of the Nazi Party mentioned above. For the most part, conservative politics were mentioned in a favorable light, as in the case of one prisoner, in which the evaluator noted: "attitude toward state: positive. 'Military belongs in power again...because the parties have not achieved anything.'"[60] By contrast, inmates who were socialists or who sympathized with the left were often described as "psychopaths" or "hysterics."[61]

Equally as important as political sympathies was the piousness of the inmate. In general, religiosity and piousness served as indicators of reformability. Thus, in the case of one inmate who was classified as corrigible, the evaluator noted that the subject was "not deeply religious, ambivalent, but does go to church."[62] Another prisoner had several redeeming features – "no political interests, beloved in his social circles and amiable" – but failed at religion: "religion Catholic, does not attend church; despite his good Catholic upbringing, his stepfather nearly was not buried due to lack of money; he is simply not convinced [of religion]."[63] Consequently, he was labeled "incorrigible." Similarly condemned was a prisoner convicted of larceny who "showed himself as an indomitable and undisciplined person, who caused trouble, slandered religion, and spouted off spiteful communist views... [his family] obviously constituted a typical proletarian milieu."[64]

What is striking about these evaluations is that, despite their reference to criminal biology, there was very little biology in them. The required anthropometric data were perfunctory compared to the rich discussions of sex, gender, social class, politics, and religion that were evoked in rendering judgment on a prisoner. These factors were not cited as a direct cause of the inmate's behavior; rather, they were cited in the context of the explanation of the prisoner's classification. Criminal biologists never bluntly stated that nonreligiosity or sexual promiscuity were direct causes of criminality; instead, such factors were evoked as a trope within the evaluation. The causality was inferred yet nevertheless explicit. Criminal biology drew its power precisely from this extreme flexibility and ambiguity, allowing it to glibly suggest that working-class males were mostly hereditary criminals without actually having to serve up any definitive proof.

60 StaLands, Rep. 176 JVA, Box 13: Psychologischer und Soziologischer Befundbogen, Karl A., 1929.
61 BHStA, Stufenstrafvollzug 1919–1930: Direktion Lichtenau an das MJu, Oct. 22, 1919; BHStA, MJu 22507: Direktion Ebrach an das MJu, Oct. 17, 1919.
62 Staatsarchiv Augsburg (StaAugs): BuB Wilhelm M., Jan. 10, 1927; BHStA, MJu 22512: KBuB Johann M.
63 StaAugs: Gefangenenakten, no. 363.
64 BHStA, MJu 22512: Gutachten Ludwig G., 2 May 1928; ibid.: Gutachten Karl R., Apr. 26, 1928.

Criminal-biological evaluations were effective in defining a range of undesirable behaviors, yet their implicit purpose was to present these as a backdrop to a canon of desirable moral, bourgeois behaviors. Thus, evaluations that deemed an inmate corrigible cited a catalogue of bourgeois behavioral traits to justify their conclusion: industriousness, religiosity, honesty, decency, political conservatism, and respect for rural traditionalism. These traits were listed as the desired characteristics in inmates who were to be advanced through the ranks of the progressive system, corresponding to the characteristics of what Viernstein called the "ideal type of person": "diligence," "steadiness of character," "practice of his respective faith," and "a certain honest and believable thankfulness to the administrative organs."[65] Inevitably, "good" character traits were linked to certain social positions. Thus, one corrigible prisoner, a bank director convicted of fraud, was described as "politically inactive . . . was in the Stahlhelm, always nationally-patriotically engaged."[66] Apparently, membership in the Stahlhelm, a right-wing paramilitary group, was not considered political activity but merely a sign of decent character. Rural persons could be portrayed as errant but stalwart farmers, as in the case of a wealthy farmer convicted of performing abortions. Although abortion was almost unanimously considered an "incorrigible" crime among women, certain factors redeemed the farmer in the eyes of the evaluators. He came from a good family, yet was betrayed by a wife who had an affair and spent all his money while he served in the military during World War I. Psychologically, he was described as "of average talents, earnest and quiet, independent, natural, docile and seeking company, trusting, hard-working, loving, friendly and has community-spirit, more oriented toward the exterior in religious matters, but a believer, without particular desire for education."[67] The narrative of a misguided country person who was betrayed by an "evil" woman, but who was otherwise amiable, clever but not intellectual, and pious but not zealous, fit well into the bourgeois ideal of a country bumpkin and thus justified a favorable classification.

Broadly speaking, criminal-biological evaluations had more to do with upholding a particular ideal of social order than with rooting out the psychological and physiological causes of criminality. In fact, criminal-biological evaluations concentrated more on describing the social circumstances of

---

65 BHStA, MJu 22507: Gutachten, signed Viernstein and Trunk, Feb. 4, 1930.
66 StaAugs, Gefangenenakten aus dem Zuchthause Kaisheim: Criminal-biological evaluations from Kaisheim, nos. 363, 455.
67 BHStA, MJu 22512: Gutachten Josef M., Jan. 14, 1928.

a prisoner, yet suggested that these very circumstances were indications of inferior heredity. Moreover, milieu, behaviors, and comportment were evoked in the context of "incorrigible" prisoners less to sentence the prisoner than to demonstrate that particular behaviors were signs of a degenerate biology and thus could not be defended by morally relativist arguments. The statistics on particular crimes compiled by criminal biologists bear out this trend as well. Of all criminals, those convicted of property crimes, such as theft and robbery, were perceived to have the highest rate of "incorrigibility." In 1925, 33.6 percent of criminals convicted of property crimes were considered "incorrigible," followed by 20 percent of those convicted of sex offenses and 16 percent of those convicted of violent crimes.[68] By 1930, 45 percent of perpetrators convicted of property crimes were classified as "incorrigible," followed by 29 percent for sex offenders, and 23 percent for inmates convicted of violent crimes.[69]

A reading of the evaluations provides an explanation for these somewhat surprising conclusions. Theft and robbery were crimes often associated with social conflict, of lower classes disrupting the social order.[70] Thieves and robbers were described as "do-nothings," "vagabonds," or "complainers." They were associated with "proletarian milieus" and were labeled as work-shy, lazy, and indolent – going to the heart of what evaluators perceived to be the decline of moral society. One thief was described as "what one calls the 'professional poor': ethically defective, unsteady in will . . . unwilling to work, socially ill-kempt, and inclined to criminal behavior, a psychopath who through his egotistical deeds and mischief harms society without remorse."[71] Viernstein believed that the majority of burglars and robbers suffered from "moral insanity."[72]

By contrast, sex crimes such as incest and sexual assault were treated as lapses of male restraint. Despite admissions from inmates that they actually committed these crimes, the evaluations took into mitigating account such protestations from inmates as "the mother [the wife of the subject] precipitated the offense" by her own reluctance for sexual relations.[73] More commonly, evaluators gave credence to protestations that "the girl was worse then he [the inmate] was himself," and that the victim was to blame for

68 BHStA, Stufenstrafvollzug: Table III, Kriminalbiologische Sammelstelle.
69 Staatsarchiv Amberg, Strafgefangenenanstalt Amberg, no. 139: Statistische Unterlagen des Gutachten, Apr. 2, 1930.
70 Dirk Blasius, *Kriminalität und Alltag* (Göttingen, 1978), 46–64.
71 BHStA, MJu 22512: BuB Gregor G., Jan. 27, 1928.
72 Theodor Viernstein,"Über Typen des verbesserlichen und unverbesserlichen Verbrechers," offprint from *MKG*, Viernstein papers, 39.
73 StaAugs: Gefangenenakten, no. 362, May 25, 1927.

arousing a man's natural sex drive.[74] In many evaluations of sex offenders, the male sexual prerogative in the home was preserved. This led Viernstein to later conclude, in a study on incest, that in certain cases the crime could be followed back to "a weak and timid male" faced with a dominant woman.[75] In the case of incest or sexual assault, the focus of criminal-biological investigation often shifted from perpetrators to victims and bystanders. Similarly, violent crimes such as assault and murder were often viewed in the context of another male prerogative: drunken brawls and altercations.[76] Evaluations often fashioned narratives to diminish the seriousness of violent crimes, as in the case of one inmate who attempted to poison his rival for a woman's affection. The evaluator found the inmate corrigible because the woman "betrayed" him.[77] A poacher convicted of shooting a game warden was deemed "corrigible" on the grounds that he knew his victim, reflecting the prevalent view that poaching was a rural man's sport, a violent but essentially private game.[78] Nonpolitical violence did not interfere with the evaluators' vision of a social order; instead it was frequently treated as honorable, manly dispute settlement or lusty inebriation gone out of control. Only when it directly challenged the prevailing social order, as in the case of left-wing political and politicized prisoners, was violence condemned with full criminal-biological force.

CONSTRUCTING A BOURGEOIS MORAL ORDER

The concerns expressed by prison administrators, clergymen, and doctors indicate that their support for the criminal-biological project went far beyond an interest in rationalizing the penal aspects of the welfare state. Dominating criminal-biological discourse was a concern for outlining and maintaining an imagined bourgeois social order based on traditional class and gender roles. By linking the term "biology" with "crime," diverse elite groups were able to anchor their social visions in a tangible "science" and overcome the moral relativism that many saw as the root of social decay.

---

74 StaAugs: Gefangenenakten Kaisheim, no. 4166, Mar. 20, 1927; StaLands, Rep. 176 JVA, Box 19: BuB Franz X., June 13, 1932.
75 Hans von Hentig and Theodor Viernstein, *Untersuchungen über den Inzest* (Heidelberg, 1925), 12.
76 BHStA, MJu 22512: Gutachten Michael S., Nov. 9, 1927; StaLands, Rep. 176 JVA, Box 7: BuB Thomas B., Feb. 12, 1925; Viernstein papers: Gutachten Urban D., Aug. 29, 1928.
77 Viernstein papers: Gutachten Franz E., May 22, 1928.
78 Viernstein papers: Gutachten Jakob E., 1924. On poaching as a tolerated rite of manhood, see Regina Schulte, *Das Dorf im Verhör* (Reinbeck bei Hamburg, 1989), 192ff.

This quest for a moral anchor undoubtedly stemmed from the overall unease felt by members of the Bavarian bourgeoisie throughout the Weimar Republic. The perception of a crumbling society in which morals and ethics fall by the wayside fits in many ways Richard Bessel's description of a general "moral panic" after World War I.[79] Not only were the instances of crime, venereal disease, abortion, and divorce perceived to be rising, but many Bavarians believed they were battling urbanism, cosmopolitanism, and socialism – the many-headed monster of modernity. Attempts at introducing secular public schools were labeled "socialist evils," and modernist theater and art were stifled by the Bavarian government in an effort to combat "cultural Bolshevism."[80] It is not surprising that prison reform reflected the same level of cultural conflict.

Consequently, concerns about national efficiency, sparked by the lack of cell space and dwindling resources in prisons, if anything sharpened this perception of failing law and order. In 1923 the administration of Zweibrücken complained that the lack of cell space was "felt severely in this present and revolutionary time, when discipline and order, as well as respect for the law and for other people are almost lost."[81] Degen believed that he lived in a time "when the general morality is shaken at its foundation, respect for authority, justice and law has declined,"[82] and shortly before Hitler's ascension to power, the Protestant pastor at the prison in Zweibrücken gave the following impression of the political situation at hand:

Dark storm clouds hover over Germany. Thunder rumbles eerily. A storm sweeps over mountains and valleys, over cities and towns, and shakes palaces and huts. . . . In the western sky it flares up still, again and again: Versailles! And in the eastern sky it still flares, again and again, ever more eerily: Moscow! And like a screaming gale the words fly about: World revolution! "Stir up the fire that consumes worlds, that destroys churches and prisons for ever!"[83]

The fear of revolution that would destroy the pillars of bourgeois moral order – the church and, more recently, the prison – sealed the support of Bavarian clergy, pedagogues, and prison administrators for criminal-biological theory.

---

79 Richard Bessel, *Germany after the First World War* (Oxford, 1993), 252ff.
80 Friederike Euler, "Theater zwischen Anpassung und Widerstand: Die Münchner Kammerspiele im Dritten Reich," in Martin Broszat and Elke Fröhlich, eds., *Bayern in der NS-Zeit*, 6 vols. (Munich, 1977), 2:91–169.
81 BHStA, MJu 22504: Direktion Zweibrücken an das MJu, Dec. 27, 1923.
82 Richard Degen, "Die Einführung eines Stufensystems in den bayerischen Strafanstalten," *Monatsschrift für Kriminalpsychologie und Strafrechtsreform* 14 (1923): 7.
83 BHStA, MJu 22509: Protestantischer Anstaltsgeistlicher an die Direktion Zweibrücken, Jan. 6, 1933.

As the religious underpinnings of the bourgeois moral order crumbled, doctors, prison administrators, and the very guardians of the moral order, the clergy, turned to the powerfully multifarious concept of "biology" to recast their world. Outwardly, these groups had successfully shed the traditional trappings of premodernity by rejecting formal religion and embracing rational science and positivist law. Inwardly, however, they longed for a clearly marked moral order that would ensure both the social and moral superiority of their class in a society rapidly modernizing, industrializing, and moving toward mass politics. As the traditional means of maintaining bourgeois identity – three-class voting, formal religion, and rigidly defined class culture – became archaic, criminal biology offered a viable language in which bourgeois notions of morality could be preserved.

This cultural dimension of criminal biology offers an explanation as to why, as Gabriel Finder indicates in his contribution to the present volume, criminal psychology did not significantly shape German penal law after 1918; it might further explain why, as Richard Wetzell discusses in his chapter, German criminologists embraced hereditarian views on crime despite overwhelming evidence that such views were untenable. Criminal psychology, with its promise of reform and its implicit focus on the individual – and for some, its inherent Jewishness – could not fulfill criminal biology's role as a cultural means of value creation. Only criminal biology could endow a bourgeois elite with biological superiority and set forth an entire strategy to discursively refound and reshape the moral universe of mass society. Those who did not fit this vision of a social order – socialists, non-churchgoers, nontraditional women, unruly peasants and workers – were deemed biologically inferior and punished accordingly. There was nothing to fear from a mass society that, as unwieldy as it threatened to become, could be tamed by the seemingly immutable laws of heredity. These laws provided important guiding moral values in a society confronted with cosmopolitan culture, cinema, avant-garde art, feminism, cultural and moral relativism, even temporal-spatial relativity. Biology corresponded to the emotive and religious needs of a social elite that felt betrayed by positivist law and social science, by offering them a re-enchanted vision of a bourgeois moral order.[84] This cultural significance of the notion of biology ensured criminal biology's growing success during Weimar Germany and

---

84 Woodruff D. Smith, *Politics and the Sciences of Culture in Germany, 1840–1920* (Oxford, 1991). On the concept of enchantment in politics, see Philippe Burrin, "Political Religion: The Relevance of a Concept," in Michael Ley and Julius H. Schoeps, eds., *Der Nationalsozialismus als politische Religion* (Bodenheim b. Mainz, 1997), 168–85.

later a dominant and nefarious role in criminological discourse and penal practice under the National Socialists.[85]

85 In 1923 the medical doctor Rainer Fetscher set up a "hereditary biological registry" of prison inmates in Saxony. In 1929 Prussia established criminal-biological research facilities in conjunction with its progressive system. Baden and Hamburg followed with similar measures. Under Hitler a Criminal-Biological Research Station was created under the Health Ministry in 1936, and the Criminal- Biological Institute was attached to the security police in 1941. See Oliver Liang, "Criminal-Biological Discourse, Theory, and Practice in Germany, 1918–1945," (Ph.D. diss., Johns Hopkins University, 1999).

20

Criminals and Their Analysts

Psychoanalytic Criminology in Weimar Germany and the First Austrian Republic

GABRIEL N. FINDER

A MODERN FORM OF SOCIAL DEFENSE

The time in the Weimar Republic (1918–33) and the First Austrian Republic (1918–34) was ripe for rethinking the tenets of criminal justice. Many Germans and Austrians, feeling increasingly vulnerable and insecure, blamed the apparent unraveling of the social fabric in the aftermath of World War I in large measure on an irrepressible rise in criminality of all kinds, from the petty to the psychopathic. This perception naturally intensified calls for law and order. However, the authoritative prescriptions of criminal justice in the imperial era appeared not only moribund but also sterile. Many contemporary observers questioned the efficacy and legitimacy of traditional straightforward punishment, in part because they no longer felt angry enough to need to stigmatize all offenders. Friedrich Nietzsche (1844–1900) had already articulated this sentiment in 1887 in *Zur Genealogie der Moral* (*On the Genealogy of Morality*). There he traced the origins of punishment to the debtor–creditor relationship. The lawbreaker was simply someone who owed a debt to society, and punishment was tantamount to repayment of this unpaid obligation. Thus, justice originated not in *ressentiment* – that is, reactive sentiments of revenge – but rather in the containment of fratricidal hatred. Only much later did society transform an objective "feeling of guilt" or "feeling of indebtedness" (*Gefühl der Schuld*; the German word *Schuld* yields this twofold meaning) into a "bad conscience" (*schlechtes Gewissen* or *Gewissensbiss*) in the offender. In this climate the legitimacy of capital punishment and the desirability of prison reform became topics of intense debate. Thus, demands for law and order in Germany and Austria coexisted with appeals for

447

a more rational – and, in some quarters, even humane – treatment of criminals.[1]

Psychiatry sought to fill the void created by this state of uneasy equipoise by expanding and diversifying its criminological arsenal. But this attempt was hindered by tension between the judicial and psychiatric realms. In the first place, psychiatry always threatened, in principle, to frustrate the requirements of the state by declaring insane those whom the state wanted to punish. This potential opposition explains the indifference, if not hostility, of many criminal justice officials to forensic medicine. When the presiding judge in the 1925 trial of serial killer Fritz Haarmann rejected a request by the defense to introduce the expert testimony of psychiatrists and psycho-analysts on the defendant's behalf, he ruled that "Psychology has no place in the courtroom."[2] The sentiment of the prosecutor Andergast in Jakob Wassermann's popular novel *Der Fall Maurizius* (*The Maurizius Trial*, 1928) probably reflected the prevailing attitude of the majority of contemporary prosecutors: "I place no value on the soul."[3]

Furthermore, the psychiatric grid increasingly appeared too rigid and crude to be of much use. Psychiatry's postwar preoccupation with the bio-logical basis of mental illness, which found expression in the construction of the "psychopathic personality," seemed inadequate to unravel the secrets of criminal motivation in the minds of many contemporary observers. In the opinion of one judge, the diagnostic tendency of forensic psychiatry to reduce so many criminals to a psychopathic personality, "[did] not offer a key to the complexities of the inner life."[4] Indeed, in his interwar magnum opus *Berlin Alexanderplatz* (1929), the German novelist Alfred Döblin (1878–1957), who was in a position to know because he was not only a writer but also an asylum psychiatrist, sheds light on the mentality of contemporary psychiatry. In his ruminations on the challenge of Freudianism to biological psychiatry the medical director of the asylum where the protagonist, Franz Biberkopf, is under observation thinks to himself: "The soul, the soul – it's

---

1 On the impact of post–World War I criminality on Germans' (and, I would argue, Austrians') attitudes, see the editors' observations in Anton Kaes, Martin Jay, and Edward Dimendberg, eds., *The Weimar Republic Sourcebook* (Berkeley, Calif., 1994), 718–20, and therein the 1931 piece by cultural critic Siegfried Kracauer, "Murder Trials and Society," 740–41. On Nietzsche, see Friedrich Nietzsche, "Zur Genealogie der Moral," in *Sämtliche Werke: Kritische Studienausgabe*, ed. Giorgio Colli and Mazzino Montinari, 15 vols. (Munich, 1980), 5:291–337.

2 Theodor Lessing, *Haarmann: Die Geschichte eines Werwolfs* (Frankfurt am Main, 1989), 211; see also Erich Frey, *Ich beantrage Freispruch* (Hamburg, 1959), 82; and Maria Tatar, *Lustmord: Sexual Murder in Weimar Germany* (Princeton, N.J., 1995), 49.

3 Jakob Wassermann, *Der Fall Maurizius* (Munich, 1988), 425.

4 Quoted in Rainer Marwedel, "Vom Schlachthöfen und Schlachtfeldern," introduction to Lessing, *Haarmann*, 18–19.

simply sentimental modern gush. Medicine soaring on the wings of a song."[5]

Frustration with the limits of forensic psychiatry in an atmosphere of social reconstruction helped create curiosity in, if not responsiveness to, novel ideas in criminology. The 1920s and early 1930s in Germany and Austria were conducive to the dismantlement of jaded authoritative criminological blueprints in favor of bold experiments in the spirit of what Peter Fritzsche aptly calls Weimar – and, I would add, interwar Austrian – "eclectic experimentalism."[6] Among these experiments criminal biology would ultimately dominate the investigation of criminal behavior from the middle of the 1920s until 1945.[7] But dissatisfaction with the sterility of biological psychiatry to explain, predict, and – from the perspective of an engaged minority – treat criminal behavior generated efforts in the spirit of contemporary psychoanalysis to grasp the "total personality" (*Gesamtpersönlichkeit*) of the criminal.[8] Whereas criminal biology embarked on a biomedical conceptualization of the criminal personality, a new trend or – to be more precise – new trends in criminology predicated on Freudian psychoanalysis and Adlerian individual psychology strove to evaluate and modify the dynamic processes of criminal motivation.[9] The initiative in Germany and Austria to establish psychoanalytic criminology traces its origins to the initial investigations in the mid-1920s of the Berlin psychoanalyst Franz Alexander (1891–1964) and the (psychoanalyzed) jurist Hugo Staub. Together with a version of criminology founded on individual psychology, psychoanalytic criminology gestated in a dissatisfaction (also shared by practitioners of other forms of criminal psychology) with the determinism of hereditarian criminology, which largely cloaked authoritarian moral values in the vernacular of science. Psychoanalytic criminology offered a potentially more sophisticated and open-ended alternative to – so Alexander and Staub – "crude psychiatric diagnoses of a 'psychopathic personality'" in criminal biology.[10]

5 Alfred Döblin, *Berlin Alexanderplatz*, trans. Eugene Jolas (New York, 1997), 593.
6 Peter Fritzsche, "Did Weimar Fail?" *Journal of Modern History* 68 (1996): 629–56, quotation on 631.
7 See the chapters by Oliver Liang and Richard F. Wetzell in this volume.
8 See Franz Alexander, *Psychoanalyse der Gesamtpersönlichkeit: Neun Vorträge über die Anwendung von Freuds Ichtheorie auf die Neurosenlehre* (Leipzig, 1927).
9 For a useful synopsis and comparison of Freudian psychoanalysis and Adlerian individual psychology, see Henri F. Ellenberger, *The Discovery of the Unconscious: The History and Evolution of Dynamic Psychiatry* (New York, 1970), chaps. 7–8.
10 Franz Alexander and Hugo Staub, *Der Verbrecher und seine Richter: Ein Psychoanalytischer Einblick in die Welt der Paragraphen* (Vienna, 1929), 24; translated by Gregory Zilboorg as *The Criminal, the Judge, and the Public: A Psychological Analysis* (New York, 1931). The quotations from this work here and throughout this chapter are my translations from the German edition.

Psychoanalytic criminology was heir to the late-nineteenth-century mutation of criminal law. In the spirit of the legacy bequeathed by Paul Johann Anselm Feuerbach (1775–1833), until approximately 1880 guilt was in theory predicated exclusively on the commission of a criminal act, and the criminal's internal motivation for the crime was irrelevant to a determination of his culpability and punishment. After 1880 the initiative of Franz von Liszt (1851–1919) to "rationalize" punishment redirected criminal law from the promotion of individual responsibility through legal intimidation to the suppression of socially harmful and antisocial acts in the name of "social defense." This redirection of penal policy entailed consideration not only of the offense but also of the personality of the offender. Although Liszt stressed the "incapacitation" (*Unschädlichmachung*) of incorrigible criminals, interest in the resocialization of offenders who were deemed corrigible was almost an inevitable outcome of his reconceptualization of punishment. Incapacitation through repressive discipline and the threat of physical force coexisted tentatively with a constructive disciplinary trend to abandon the old concept of breaking the vicious will of criminals in favor of encouraging promising candidates to adopt certain standards of conduct. In other words, social defense was promoted under the proper circumstances not only through incapacitation but also through rehabilitation. Before World War I rehabilitation more or less entailed an offender's mechanistic reproduction of his compulsory submission to the internal standards of his institutional confinement. But after the war the rhetoric of rehabilitation gradually and partially metamorphosed into a concept of personal regeneration, though still in the service of social defense.

Alexander and Staub, the authors of *Der Verbrecher und seine Richter* (*The Criminal and his Judges*, 1929), the preeminent text in psychoanalytic criminology, traced its lineage to Liszt, liberally invoking the nomenclature of social defense from "criminal danger to society" to "incapacitation." Indeed, Liszt's demand to individualize punishment, they contended, was ultimately unattainable before the advent and maturation of psychoanalysis: "The introduction of psychoanalysis into the courtroom will signify the first step in the realization of [Liszt's] demand."[11] What distinguished their approach to social defense from Liszt's was their conceptualization of justice. Liszt had invoked the principle of justice when he argued for individualized punishment, but his notion of justice was exceedingly instrumental. For Liszt, individualized punishment was solely a means to the end of protecting

---

11 Alexander and Staub, *Der Verbrecher und seine Richter*, 25.

society.[12] For their part, Alexander and Staub justified their enterprise through an appeal to the emotional sources and meaning of justice. Justice is a form of social contract between the individual and society (and earlier in life between children and their parents), whereby the individual refrains from gratifying some of his desires, to which society objects, in order to keep its love. This contract loses its power over the antisocial impulses of the average individual whenever justice miscarries.[13] In other words, a correct judgment is essential to human organization because a miscarriage of justice can subvert the functioning of societal institutions that are responsible for preventing crime and combating criminals. Psychoanalytic criminology was vital to social defense, they argued, because it assured that a person would be sentenced for the real – that is, unconscious – motivation for his crime.[14] For this reason the psychoanalytic concept of justice demands acute knowledge of a criminal's motivation, which, they contended, only psychoanalysis could render. Unlike psychiatry, psychoanalytic criminology – and its cousin based on individual psychology – promised to compel criminals to confront the essential question of who they were and why they had committed the crime.

THEORETICAL FOUNDATIONS

The theories of Sigmund Freud (1856–1939) indelibly shaped criminology in the spirit of psychoanalysis (whereas defensive reactions to it shaped the Adlerian strand of criminology). Freud's most influential, direct contribution to psychoanalytic criminology was his 1915 essay titled "Einige Charaktertypen aus der psychoanalytischen Arbeit" ("Some Character Types Encountered in Psychoanalytic Work"). In the essay's final section Freud discussed his discovery of "criminals out of a sense of guilt" (*"Verbrecher aus Schuldbewusstsein"*). Most people are deterred from committing crime because of a latent sense of guilt that comes to the fore only after its commission, in the form of remorse. However, on the basis of his examinations of patients who from all appearances were law-abiding but during psychoanalysis admitted to the commission of criminal acts, Freud described the discovery of the

---

12 Franz von Liszt, "Der Zweckgedanke im Strafrecht," in *Strafrechtliche Vorträge und Aufsätze*, 2 vols. (Berlin, 1905), 1:161.

13 Hugo Staub, "Psychoanalyse und Strafrecht," *Imago* 17 (1931): 205; see also the untitled paper of Thomas M. French, in Institute for Psychoanalysis, *Franz Alexander, M.D., 1891–1964* (Chicago, 1964), 42.

14 Alexander and Staub, *Der Verbrecher und seine Richter*, 7–8.

following criminal type: A man who commits a criminal act precisely "because it was forbidden and because its implementation was connected with emotional relief for the offender." This person did not lack a conscience; to the contrary, he suffered from an unconscious "oppressive sense of guilt." But after he committed the offense, the pressure was relieved. An intrigued Freud added: "As paradoxical as it may sound, I must maintain that the sense of guilt was present before the offense, that it did not arise from it, but rather, to the contrary, the offense arose from the sense of guilt." Without much ado, Freud attributed the psychological basis for this sense of guilt to an unresolved Oedipus complex, leaving it to others to work out the details.[15] On this basis, however tentative Freud's exploration of criminal motivation may have been, conflict theory underlay the conceptualization of criminal behavior in psychoanalytic criminology.[16]

The paramount work of Freudian psychoanalytic criminology was the aforementioned *Criminal and His Judges* by Alexander and Staub. The authors acknowledged the socioeconomic etiology of a large percentage of criminality, but they were intrigued by chronic criminals, those who seemed capable of committing crime under any circumstances. Furthermore, a significant proportion of these criminals seemed to resemble neurotics because they appeared to act out of unconscious motives. In this spirit, Alexander and Staub "discovered" the "neurotic criminal" with his unresolved Oedipus complex.

Every criminal act, they argued, was determined by a variety of motives, the majority of which remain buried in the unconscious of the criminal. Furthermore, they universalized the criminal predisposition: All human beings are potential criminals when they are born with antisocial impulses demanding satisfaction, and they become socially adjusted only when the Oedipus complex is ultimately overcome. Normal individuals succeed in repressing their illicit instinctual drives, which originate in the dual infantile desire to kill the father and possess the mother, transforming them into socially acceptable behavior. But criminals suffering from neuroses are characterized by their incapacity for the psychological management of conflicts in family relations. Unconscious motives are primarily responsible for the impulsive conduct of the neurotic criminal. These unconscious motives arise from

---

15 Sigmund Freud, "Einige Charaktertypen aus der psychoanalytischen Arbeit," in *Gesammelte Werke*, 18 vols. (London, 1946), 10:389–91.

16 Freud himself was rather wary of the applicability of psychoanalysis to criminology, counseling caution in attributing an unresolved Oedipus complex to a son's murder of his father in the absence of incontrovertible evidence to this effect. Sigmund Freud, "Das Fakultätsgutachten im Prozess Halsmann," in *Gesammelte Werke*, 14:541–2.

strong infantile desires to redress his unresolved relationship with his father and mother. Thus the neurotic criminal's offense has a strong symbolic character, whereas the actual utility of the act remains peripheral. The neurotic criminal perpetrates an offense primarily to relieve his unconscious feelings of guilt. Through the often relatively harmless transgression of the law for which he is punished, the neurotic criminal displaces his feelings of guilt for his patricidal tendencies to a lesser offense.[17]

Central to Alexander's and Staub's investigation were the degree and form of the "participation of the ego" (*Beteiligung des Ich*) in the criminal act, which they considered integral not only to psychoanalytic understanding but also to a determination of criminal responsibility under the law. In neurotic criminal behavior, the ego is insufficiently supported by an independent superego, which in Freudian terms is the watchful, judging, and punishing agency in the psychic structure. Thus the ego is able to isolate the superego within the psychic organization and circumvent or deceive it, and the superego loses its inhibitory power over the ego. But the ego itself is too weak to control the regressive and aggressive demands of the id, the amoral agency in the psychic structure, and succumbs to it, allowing the repressed impulses of the id to assert themselves. In this manner, the ego is granted a free hand in satisfying its antisocial tendencies, through which the unadjusted prohibited drives of the id derive substitute gratification in spite of the prohibitory demands of the superego. If criminal responsibility is determined by the degree of the participation of "the conscious ego" (*das bewusste Ich*) in the act, then the criminal liability of the neurotic criminal, who acts under the strong pressures of unconscious motives, should be minimal, if not nonexistent.[18]

From the perspective of individual psychology, which was pioneered by Freud's antagonist Alfred Adler (1870–1937), criminal traits are acquired reactive aggressive formations. These traits arise from instinctive aspirations to prove one's superiority or from overcompensation for one's feelings of inferiority. The criminal pursues his objective largely on the basis of

---

17 A few years earlier (*Psychoanalyse der Gesamtpersönlichkeit*, 134, 136) Alexander had equated the neurotic psyche with a "primitive criminal code," locating "the social and biological roots of the neurotic punishment mechanism . . . in a primitive level of human social organization founded on punishment."

18 Alexander and Staub, *Der Verbrecher und seine Richter*, 25–52, 84–5. The other most influential treatise in psychoanalytic criminology was Theodor Reik, *Geständniszwang und Strafbedürfnis: Probleme der Psychoanalyse und der Kriminologie* (Vienna, 1925). Reik, a disciple of Freud, emphasized the dynamic processes of guilt feelings in criminal behavior. Other major works in psychoanalytic criminology included Franz Wittels, *Die Welt ohne Zuchthaus* (Stuttgart, 1928); and Hans Coenen, *Strafrecht und Psychoanalyse* (Breslau, 1929). See also the special issue of *Imago* (vol. 17, 1931), the authoritative organ of Freudian psychoanalysis, devoted to criminology.

unconscious motives; these objectives arise under the pressure of "errors" (*Irrtümer*), whose origins lie in his childhood. His confrontation with society is undesired and symbolic. Alienated from society in his youth and driven to an antisocial attitude by emotionally detrimental circumstances (for example, being pampered), he becomes cowardly, losing faith in the possibility of succeeding through socially acceptable means. From an unadjusted youth emerges the error of the criminal who must assert himself through false, antisocial means because he knows of no other way. Criminal behavior is therefore overcompensation for an extreme sense of inferiority, or − in the parlance of individual psychology − an error provoked by "discouragement" (*Entmutigung*).[19]

Although sexuality became the hallmark of psychoanalytic criminology in the Freudian tradition on the one hand and psychosocial causation in Adlerian criminology on the other, they shared important features. Both strands attributed criminal behavior to acquired psychological maladjustment in childhood (unlike criminal biology, which explained criminal behavior on the basis of inherited traits). In neither perspective is criminal behavior entirely the result of conscious processes. And in the view of both Freudian and Adlerian criminology, legal punishment (of neurotic criminals in Freudian criminology, of all criminals in the Adlerian version because all criminals are socially maladjusted) is meaningless and even harmful to society's interests.

These Freudian and Adlerian classifications of the criminal personality had drastic implications for the rationale of punishment. According to Alexander and Staub, the neurotic criminal is "sick," his psychoneurotic illness characterized by an imbalance between the instinctive powers of his drives and the inhibitory function of his ego. His antisocial acts are the result of unconscious drives to which his ego has no access whatsoever. In this light, to punish him would be not only senseless but also counterproductive. In the first place, he would be punished for actions over which he has no control. Moreover, he is not inhibited by punishment because his unconscious need for punishment actually welcomes the expectation of it. The neurotic criminal whose acts are driven by an unconscious sense of guilt actively seeks punishment because it constitutes the main motive for his transgression. Punishment becomes not a disincentive but rather an incentive to

---

19 The approach of individual psychology to criminal behavior is articulated in Alfred Adler, "Neurose und Verbrechen," *Internationale Zeitschrift für Individualpsychologie* 3 (1924): 1–11; and Eugen Schmidt, "Verbrecher und Strafe," in Erwin Wexberg, ed., *Handbuch der Individualpsychologie*, 2 vols. (Munich, 1926), 2:150–79.

commit a criminal act. "Punishment," Alexander and Staub argued, "cannot make these people better because . . . their conscious willpower cannot overcome the forces operating in the unconscious. Their punishment *is psychologically meaningless and sociologically harmful.*" They are curable, but what they require is psychoanalytic therapy.[20] From the perspective of individual psychology, legal punishment was counterproductive because it was tantamount to another form of discouragement; the criminal sees in punishment only an affirmation of the rectitude of his antisocial orientation.[21]

Thus, inherent in both the Freudian and Adlerian strands of criminology was a reproach of the provision in the German and Austrian penal codes that governed legal insanity (*Unzurechnungsfähigkeit*). Paragraph 51 of the German penal code and Paragraph 2 of the Austrian penal code were predicated on the traditional psychiatric notion that restricted the plea of insanity to defendants whose inability to distinguish between right and wrong amounted to complete psychological disorganization and ensued from either a mental illness or a state of unconsciousness. In reality, the applicability of the law was limited to comparatively few cases. But the findings of Freudian and Adlerian criminology questioned whether the punishment provisions in the codes even had a rational basis because a large group of criminals could not be assessed on the basis of conventional psychiatric wisdom, since their criminal acts were committed under the pressure of unconscious motives. Indeed, if instead of prevention and rehabilitation legal punishment only led to the commission of crime in the first place, then the law was inherently flawed. "Legal punishment," Staub wrote in another context, "in this case is probably the most irrational form of social reaction."[22] On these grounds Alexander and Staub urged the modification of the German provision, arguing for a new legal interpretation of mental incapacitation based on the interplay of the conscious ego and unconscious impulses in the commission of the criminal act. If a neurotic criminal was a sick person whose delinquency was the outcome of his mental disturbances, his criminal liability would perforce be limited, if not nonexistent.[23] Clearly, the implementation of this provision would have required diagnostic evaluation by psychiatric experts trained in psychoanalysis, thus opening

---

20 Alexander and Staub, *Der Verbrecher und seine Richter*, 67–71, 76–7, quotation on 76 (original emphasis).
21 Heinrich Zeller, "Das Strafrecht in seinen Beziehungen zur Individualpsychologie," *Zeitschrift für Individualpsychologie* 1 (1916): 145–56; and Emil Hauser, "Individualpsychologie und Kriminalpolitik," *Zeitschrift für Individualpsychologie* 1 (1916): 174–85.
22 Hugo Staub, "Psychoanalyse und Strafrecht," in Paul Federn and Heinrich Meng, eds., *Das psychoanalytische Volksbuch*, 2 vols., 2d ed. (Stuttgart, 1928), 2:187.
23 Alexander and Staub, *Der Verbrecher und seine Richter*, 44–51.

the portals of the courthouse to psychoanalysis. (Criminologists in the Adlerian tradition doubtless would have stressed training in individual psychology.) Needless to say, a penal provision of this kind would have acquired great symbolic significance because it would have represented official acknowledgment of unconscious motivations in criminal if not all human behavior and thus, by implication, acknowledgment of the social value of psychoanalysis.

CRIMINOLOGICAL PRACTICES

The practitioners of psychoanalytic criminology actively sought practical applications of their expertise. In *Berlin Alexanderplatz*, Döblin, himself a psychiatrist whose literary oeuvre displays a lively interest in criminal psychology, renders an ironic, plastic, and in all likelihood autobiographical account of young psychiatrists employing psychoanalytic techniques to diagnose their criminal patient, the protagonist Franz Biberkopf:

The doctors put on their white blouses in the consultation room . . . [and] they all say it's a case of stupor. The younger gentlemen have opinions of their own about the case: they are inclined to consider Franz Biberkopf's trouble as psychogenic, that is, his rigidity comes from the soul, it is a pathological condition of inhibitions and constraint which could be cleared up by an analysis (perhaps it emanates from early psychic levels) if – the big If, a most regrettable If, it's too bad, a most irritating If – if only Franz Biberkopf would talk and sit down with them at the conference table to liquidate the conflict with them. . . . These younger gentlemen . . . go, one by one, to the little ward, after the morning inspection and again in the afternoon, and visit Franz; each of them tries to start a conversation with him as best he can. They experiment, for instance, with the device of pretending nothing's wrong, and talk to him as if he were listening to everything, and that's all right, and as if they could coax him out of his isolation and break down his blockade.

But it doesn't work so well. . . .

"Well, what's to be done about this Biberkopf case, what's the Chief's opinion?" "Make the right diagnosis. Which, according to my naturally old-fashioned diagnostics, is called in this case: Catatonic stupor. . . ." "Catatonic stupor? . . . And what's to be done for a man with such a diagnosis, Doctor, that alone won't help him a great deal." . . . The chief laughs heartily and gets up. He steps to the window and slaps the assistant's shoulder: "Well, in the first place, he'll get out of both your clutches, my dear fellow. Don't you think that in the end he gets a bit bored with all the prayers you and your colleague recite over him? As a matter of fact, do you know what I'm going to base my iron diagnosis on? You see, I've got it. Why, man alive, he would have made a grab for it long ago, if his trouble had been your so-called soul. When a confirmed jail-bird such as he is sees for himself two young gentlemen who, of course, know a lot of rubbish about him . . . and they want to do some prayer-healing with him, well, take it from me, a chap like that has been looking for you all his life." . . . "But he's inhibited, Chief, in our view it is a repression, conditioned by a psychic crisis, a loss of contact with reality, due to disappointments, failures, then infantile and instinctive demands on reality and a fruitless attempt to re-establish contact." "Psychic crisis be damned! In that case he would have other psychic moments. He's handing it to you as a Christmas present. In a week he'll be up and about with your assistance, good Lord, you really are a master-healer, bravo for the new therapy, you can send a telegram of congratulations to Freud in Vienna."[24]

In the end, the younger generation triumphs over obscurantism; the diagnosis of catatonic stupor is displaced by one of psychic trauma. In any case, Franz survives and, after a discourse with death, a new ego emerges in a form of rebirth – but no thanks to the physicians. His survival cannot be explained by science, and his psychoanalytically inclined doctors cannot take credit for it because in this ironic text they do not understand it.

In principle, the role in court of the psychoanalytic expert witness was to illuminate all of the defendant's motivations, conscious and unconscious alike, and thereby allow the judge to reach the correct verdict. Part of the expert witness's function was to make the judge himself aware, even if only subliminally, of his own biases against criminal defendants that were caused by his own repressed aggressive impulses.[25] In his examination of the defendant the expert witness would seek to identify certain typical characteristics of the neurotic criminal: the lack of any sufficient rationale for the offense; a stereotypical offense; and an inner psychic conflict, deriving particularly from guilt feelings or the need for self-punishment.[26]

Alexander actually testified several times to the mental state of criminal defendants. (Staub and the Berlin psychoanalyst Ernst Simmel [1882–1947] were also summoned on occasion to be expert witnesses.) This was no minor achievement because in Germany no expert witness but a conventional psychiatrist had testified to the mental state of a defendant before 1925. The defendants whom he examined and testified for included a female kleptomaniac, a young man who would take long rides in taxicabs only to refuse to pay upon completion of the journey and then vanish, and a juvenile double murderer. In all of these defendants he identified characteristic traits of neurotic criminals acting out of unconscious motives. His testimony led to the acquittal of the accused kleptomaniac, but the uncovering of the truth revealed the aggravated circumstances of the juvenile murderer's offense, for

24 Döblin, *Berlin Alexanderplatz*, 492–6; quoted partially in Edward Shorter, *A History of Psychiatry: From the Era of the Asylum to the Age of Prozac* (New York, 1997), 158–9.
25 Staub, "Psychoanalyse und Strafrecht," in Federn and Meng, eds., *Das psychoanalytische Volksbuch*, 185–6.
26 Franz Alexander, "Psychische Hygiene und Kriminalität," *Imago* 17 (1931): 161–4.

which the defendant was sentenced to prison. Alexander's recommendation to acquit the delinquent taxicab passenger and commit him to an asylum for therapy was approved by the court, only to be thwarted by the defendant's later theft of a large sum of money, for which he was sentenced to prison. All in all, Alexander found judges and prosecutors receptive to his psychoanalytic approach.[27]

Nevertheless, Alexander conceded that methodological obstacles stood in the way of expert testimony. Most important, the threat of punishment could distort the psychoanalytic assessment of the defendant. First, it would most probably diminish his openness during examination; unlike the private client who was inclined to be forthcoming because he expected the therapist to want to help him, in the eyes of the criminal defendant the psychoanalyst represented the authorities. Furthermore, the psychological tension of a person who expects to be imprisoned would in all likelihood impede the therapist from engaging in techniques vital to the success of the psychoanalytic method.[28]

The therapeutic goal of the Freudian and Adlerian approaches to criminal behavior was the resocialization of the offender. Because psychoanalytic criminology was founded on conflict theory, the aim of therapy was, through extensive and intensive analysis, to make the offender's repressed desires accessible to his conscious thinking and thus unmask the unconscious motivation for seemingly incoherent and uncontrolled criminal actions. Once these unconscious motives rose to the surface, the objective was to help him channel his antisocial impulses, be they caused by an inadequate repression mechanism in the process of adjustment to social life or by a sense of guilt, into socially acceptable behavior. For its part, the objective of therapy in the criminological version of individual psychology was to "encourage" (*ermutigen*) the criminal to overcome his feeling of inferiority. In effect, this meant awakening in the offender a "social interest" (*soziales Interesse*), which he lacked by virtue of his extreme inferiority complex and which curbed antisocial behavior, by stressing the benefits of social altruism, cooperation, and accountability.[29]

In practice, the impact of psychoanalytic techniques on contemporary penal therapy appears to have been relatively modest and largely untested.

27 Franz Alexander, "Psychoanalytisches Gutachen vor Gericht," *Internationale Zeitschrift für Psychoanalyse* 11 (1925): 128–9; Franz Alexander, "Ein besessener Autofahrer: Ein psychoanalytisches Gutachten," *Imago* 17 (1931): 174–93; Alexander, "Psychische Hygiene," 165; and Franz Alexander, "Der Doppelmord eines 19jährigen," *Die psychoanalytische Bewegung* 2 (1930): 80–93.

28 Alexander and Staub, *Der Verbrecher und seine Richter*, 88–90.

29 For the approaches of psychoanalytic criminology and criminological individual psychology to therapy respectively, see Alexander, "Psychische Hygiene," 166–7; and Alfred Adler, "Die kriminelle Persönlichkeit und ihre Heilung," *Internationale Zeitschrift für Individualpsychologie* 9 (1931): 321–9.

Clearly, this was so in large measure because observation and treatment, which required both proper facilities and personnel, were financially prohibitive in an era of severe financial constraints. In addition, many inmates were deemed insufficiently motivated to undergo, or intelligent enough to grasp, the principles essential to a fruitful analysis.[30] Moreover, prison officials wanted to test their own ideas for reform, one of which was the systematic introduction of the so-called progressive system (*Stufensystem*), which was then in vogue, into the prison system.[31] For these reasons, carceral therapy seems to have been practiced only sporadically. When it was attempted, analytic techniques included free association, the reclamation of childhood memories, the interpretation of dreams, and transference and countertransference – all in an effort to decipher the symptoms of criminal motivation until they were to all appearances successfully overcome.[32] The pressure of the sense of guilt was expected to make the criminal patient more susceptible to psychoanalytic influence. Through psychoanalysis this sense of guilt was to be converted into a confession, which would mark the beginning of the emergence of the repressed material to consciousness and hence recovery.[33] In addition, psychoanalytic therapy was extended to traditional private consultations of middle-class offenders who, cognizant of their emotional disposition to commit an offense and fearful of detection by the law in the future, themselves sought treatment from the practitioners of psychoanalytic criminology.[34] In general, they were more receptive to therapy than working-class offenders, the majority of criminals for whom criminality compensated for their daily frustrations. In any case, to the deep chagrin of its practitioners, even when it was employed psychoanalytic therapy more often than not did not result in a cure regardless of the origins of the patient.[35]

30 See Hans Lungwitz, "Nochmals: Psychoanalyse und Kriminalität," *Archiv für Kriminologie* 77 (1925): 309–11.

31 For a psychoanalyst's criticism of the progressive system and a plea for the introduction of psychotherapy in every prison, see Erich Fromm, "Psychologie des Verbrechers und Strafvollzugsreform," *Soziale Praxis* 39 (1930): 489–94, 513–18.

32 See Werner Lippmann, "Analyse eines Kriminellen," *Fortschritte der Sexualwissenschaft und Psychoanalyse* 2 (1926): 288–316; and Hugo Sonnenschein, "Analyse eines Kriminellen," *Fortschritte der Sexualwissenschaft und Psychoanalyse* 3 (1928): 116–30.

33 See Coenen, *Strafrecht und Psychoanalyse*, 76–82; and Staub, "Psychoanalyse und Strafrecht," in Federn and Meng, eds., *Das psychoanalytische Volksbuch*, 187.

34 See, e.g., Ernst Simmel, "Neurotische Kriminalität und Lustmord," in Ludger M. Hermanns and Ulrich Schultz-Venrath, eds., *Psychoanalyse und ihre Anwendung: Ausgewählte Schriften* (Frankfurt am Main, 1993), 176–94. Freud also seems to have provided private consultations to patients with criminal urges, from which he drew his theory of the "criminal out of a sense of guilt" (see "Einige Charaktertypen aus der psychoanalytischen Arbeit," 389).

35 Hugo Staub, "Einige praktische Schwierigkeiten der psychoanalytischen Kriminalistik," *Imago* 17 (1931): 220–21.

Individual psychology appears to have penetrated prison walls with more success than psychoanalysis. Treatment was offered both on an individual basis and in group sessions, but its availability was sporadic and depended on the predilections of prison personnel. Fritz Kleist, for a time the director of a prison in Celle, near Hannover, was in the vanguard of the movement to provide therapy in prison. In his prison and others in Prussia a new inmate submitted to an examination inspired by research in criminal biology. If the diagnosis ruled out congenital defects as an explanation for his criminal behavior, the inmate would be treated on the basis of individual psychology techniques, from earliest childhood recollections and childhood behavior disorders to dreams and exogenous pathogenic factors, with the goals of explaining the criminal patient to himself, encouraging him, and awakening his social interest. Group therapy was endorsed both because it was economical and because it exposed an individual's problems to a group, where they could be detached from his private interpretation of them and become objectified through group discussion.[36] Kleist and his colleagues reported several successes, though there doubtless were just as many, if not more, failures.[37]

Because the Freudian and Adlerian theories of criminality ascribed delinquent behavior to the effects of psychological trauma in the earliest stages of childhood and claimed to be able to reeducate the emotions of chronic juvenile offenders through psychotherapy, they were both incorporated into intervention strategies in juvenile justice, which in both Germany and Austria was finally codified in the 1920s. Many activists in the juvenile justice movement, from juvenile court judges to administrators of juvenile prisons and reformatories, believed in the potential of psychoanalysis to contribute to the regeneration of juvenile offenders.[38] Their faith was buoyed by the contemporary Austrian example of August Aichhorn (1878–1949). This psychoanalytically trained director of a reformatory on the outskirts of Vienna spearheaded the application of psychoanalytic techniques

---

36 Fritz Kleist, "Erfahrungen eines Individualpsychologen im Strafvollzug," *Internationale Zeitschrift für Individualpsychologie* 9 (1931): 381–8; and Heinz Jacoby, "Wie ich zum Verbrecher wurde," *Internationale Zeitschrift für Individualpsychologie* 9 (1931): 389–95.

37 For a general endorsement of carceral psychotherapy, see Schaefer, "Psychotherapie und Strafvollzug," *Zeitschrift für die gesamte Strafrechtswissenschaft* 49 (1929): 98–107. Schaefer, a traditional prison psychiatrist, was open to psychoanalysis and individual psychology as well as criminal biology as long as they could help prison officials understand inmates better.

38 See the comments of Hamburg juvenile court judge Bruno Müller, "Die praktischen Aufgaben des Jugendrichters und der Jugendgerichtshilfe in der Gegenwart," in Max Grünhut and Bruno Müller, *Zwei Vorträge über Jugendgerichtsbarkeit* (n.p., n.d. [1927]), 40; and those of one of the directors of the progressive juvenile prison in Hahnöfersand near Hamburg and a leading figure in prison reform, Curt Bondy, *Pädagogische Probleme im Jugend-Strafvollzug* (Mannheim, 1925), 26–9, 67–70.

to the management of carceral institutions with the goal of promoting the self-understanding of inmates. In his own institution for delinquent youth Aichhorn fostered an environment of almost unrestricted freedom. Even chronically aggressive youths were left undisciplined (to the sheer amazement and utter disapproval of many outside observers). According to Aichhorn, they eventually became aware of their own self-destructiveness and turned to adult counselors for protection and then management of their own impulsive behavior.[39] Aichhorn also was a leading figure in the establishment of "educational counseling stations" (*Erziehungsberatungsstellen*) in Vienna, whose clientele largely comprised delinquent juveniles. In these facilities Aichhorn fostered the use of transference to achieve therapeutic results.[40]

One juvenile court judge, Otto Nägele of Munich, was trained in individual psychology and kept its principles in mind when he decided the fates of the juvenile defendants in his courtroom. In court he would try to ascertain their motivation, often through confessions, and he would do his utmost within the confines of the law to avoid imprisonment and impose pedagogically designed remedies.[41]

The tenets of individual psychology were also tested in various juvenile prisons and reformatories. After his transfer to the juvenile wing of the prison in Breslau, Fritz Kleist became the leader of this endeavor. The primary goal of individual psychology in juvenile institutions was to create a "therapeutic pedagogical atmosphere" (*heilpädagogische Atmosphäre*), from the dismantlement of the typical physical geography of the prison to the creation of civics, vocational, and sex education classes.[42] The ultimate goal of the pedagogical atmosphere was to instill a "sense of responsibility" (*Verantwortungsbewusstsein*) in the juvenile inmates.[43]

---

39 August Aichhorn, *Verwahrloste Jugend: Die Psychoanalyse in der Fürsorgeerziehung*, 10th ed. (Bern, 1987), 144–56; see also Wiener Psychoanalytische Vereinigung, ed., *Wer war August Aichhorn?* (Vienna, 1976).
40 Aichhorn, *Verwahrloste Jugend*, chap. 6; and August Aichhorn, "Zur Technik der Erziehungsberatung: Die Übertragung," *Zeitschrift für psychoanalytische Pädagogik* 10 (1936): 5–74.
41 See Otto Nägele, "Jugendlicher und Justiz," in Erwin Wexberg, ed., *Handbuch der Individualpsychologie*, 2 vols. (Munich, 1926), 1:382–418; Otto Nägele, "Richter und Jugendlicher," *Zeitschrift für die gesamte Strafrechtswissenschaft* 44 (1924): 420–39; and Otto Nägele, "Kriminalität und Justiz," *Internationale Zeitschrift für Individualpsychologie* 9 (1931): 350–57.
42 Fritz Kleist, "Jugendstrafvollzug und Heilpädagogik," *Die Justiz* 3 (1927–8): 368–74; Fritz Kleist, "Jugendstrafvollzug und Heilpädagogik," *Zeitschrift für Kinderforschung* 34 (1928): 213–17; and Fritz Kleist, *Jugend hinter Gittern: Im Jugendgefängnis*, 2d ed. (Jena, 1931), 131–43. See also Oskar Beck, "Jugendliche nach der Straftat," *Internationale Zeitschrift für Individualpsychologie* 6 (1928): 100–107; and Oskar Beck, "Ursache und Therapie bei verwahrlosten Jugendlichen," *Internationale Zeitschrift für Individualpsychologie* 9 (1931): 396–402.
43 Fritz Kleist, "Der Lehrer in der Strafanstalt," *Die Justiz* 4 (1928–9): 181–91.

In spite of these valiant efforts, proponents of psychoanalysis and individual psychology were stymied in their attempts to make deep inroads into the juvenile justice system. The employment of psychotherapy to cure both the symptoms and underlying causes of juvenile maladjustment encountered practical hindrances. Therapy was prohibitively expensive because it was so labor intensive. Moreover, directors of juvenile institutions who were novices in the psychological sciences were uncertain which therapy was the correct one to utilize. Even progressive juvenile prison administrators, such as Curt Bondy and Walter Hermann in the model institution of Hahnöfersand near Hamburg, were too preoccupied with the daily management of their own educational programs to be able to integrate therapy into their institution's routines.[44] In any case, such facilities could not handle all the youngsters in need of therapy. The ambulatory educational counseling station under Aichhorn's direction handled 336 youngsters in 1932, 459 in 1933, and 517 in 1934. Because it functioned only 35 days a year, on working days it treated nearly seven youngsters on average in 1932 and almost twelve in 1934. The ability to offer sufficient therapy to all these young people must have been limited.[45] Moreover, members of the Christian charity leadership, who ran many of the correctional education facilities, were suspicious of proposals by practitioners of psychoanalysis and individual psychology to replace religious values like original sin and traditional disciplinary practices like corporal punishment. The educators in Christian, and especially Catholic, correctional education institutions considered such initiatives immoral and impractical, and were oblivious to the realities of life in the reformatories.[46] In a similar vein, Herman Nohl, a leading educator in the Weimar Republic, was wary of the initiative of psychoanalysis and individual psychology in juvenile institutions to dismantle punishment, which in his view was designed precisely to persuade juvenile offenders to accept responsibility through atonement for their unlawful actions.[47]

The potential of psychoanalytic criminology to aid in the detection of crime was explored by Freud himself as early as 1906. This cooperation made sense because, Freud argued, the tasks of psychoanalysis and criminal

---

44 Walter Hermann, *Das Hamburgische Jugendgefängnis Hahnöfersand: Ein Bericht über Erziehungsarbeit im Strafvollzug*, 2d ed. (Mannheim, 1926), 23.
45 See Wolfgang Huber, "Psychoanalytische Pädagogik in der Zeit des Ständestaates," *Zeitgeschichte* 6 (1979): 394.
46 See Edward Ross Dickinson, *The Politics of German Child Welfare from the Empire to the Federal Republic* (Cambridge, Mass., 1996), 184, 202.
47 Herman Nohl, "Gedanken für die Erziehungstätigkeit des Einzelnen," in Herman Nohl, *Jugendwohlfahrt: Sozialpädagogische Vorträge* (Leipzig, 1927), 71–83.

detection resembled each other: to uncover unrevealed psychic material. Doubtful of the trustworthiness of confessions in large part because neurotics, even if innocent, might confess to satisfy their sense of guilt, Freud advocated the use of psychoanalytic techniques to compel the accused to establish their guilt or innocence by manifestations of resistance to verbal suggestions.[48]

Theodor Reik (1888–1969), a disciple of Freud who was an important figure in the development of psychoanalytic criminology, went to great lengths to refine the application of psychoanalytic techniques to the detection of crime, especially through the return of repressed knowledge to consciousness in confessions. According to Reik, because criminal behavior is the expression of a preexisting sense of guilt and legal punishment serves to gratify a "need for self-punishment" (*Strafbedürfnis*), which itself constitutes the unconscious motive for the criminal act, a substitute formation and gratification of the inner desire for punishment finds expression in the form of a "compulsion to confess" (*Geständniszwang*). The unconscious confession (characterized by parapraxes) of a neurotic criminal represents the attempt of the superego to reconcile the tension between the ego and the id, offering psychic relief to the ego from the feeling of guilt through reproduction of the act in narrative form.[49]

Notwithstanding this criminalistic potential of psychoanalysis, Freud counseled caution because of one fundamental difference between psychoanalysis and criminal detection: Whereas the patient assists the analyst in overcoming his psychic resistance because his goal is recovery, the criminal would resist the overtures of judicial officials because revelation of the truth in his case is frequently to his own detriment.[50] Moreover, the use of psychoanalytic technique in crime detection underlined the fundamental dilemma of psychoanalytic criminology: Whom did it seek to benefit, the troubled individual or society? Reik doubtless intended to use the evidence adduced from confessions to protect the innocent from mistaken accusations as well as to identify the guilty, but when he placed the expertise of psychoanalytic criminology in the service of judicial officials, did he not risk reducing it to an appendage of state police powers? At any rate, there is no evidence that psychoanalytic techniques were actually applied to criminal detection.

---

48 Sigmund Freud, "Tatbestandsdiagnostik und Pyschoanalyse," in *Gesammelte Werke*, 7:1–15.
49 Theodor Reik, *Geständniszwang und Strafbedürfnis: Probleme der Psychoanalyse und der Kriminologie* (Vienna, 1925), 20–159. See also his *Der unbekannte Mörder* (1925; reprint, Frankfurt am Main, 1983). For another endorsement of the use of psychoanalysis in crime detection, see Coenen, *Strafrecht und Psychoanalyse*, 37–55.
50 Freud, "Tatbestandsdiagnostik und Psychoanalyse," 12–13.

Interest generated by the appearance of Alexander and Staub's book persuaded the Berlin Psychoanalytic Institute to sponsor a workshop in 1930 for members of the legal profession under the guidance of the two authors.[51] Erich Fromm led similar workshops in 1930 and 1931 under the auspices of the Frankfurt Psychoanalytic Institute.[52] In addition, these men and many others, especially Reik and Aichhorn, lectured frequently and not only to the converted. But they all operated in the metropolis; psychoanalytic criminology, let alone psychoanalysis, rarely infiltrated the provinces.[53]

LUKEWARM RECEPTION

Many judicial officials, including several judges, attended the institutes' workshops. Among them was the rather well-known judge Albert Hellwig of the Potsdam district court. Hellwig's ambivalent view of the role of psychoanalysis in the courtroom represented the opinion of many more-or-less open-minded metropolitan judges regarding the benefits and drawbacks of psychoanalysis. He was willing to invite psychoanalytic expert witnesses to his courtroom but only on a restricted basis. Their testimony would have to afford unique insight into the personality of the defendant, which he believed it could in exceptional cases, and thereby yield practical results, especially in sentencing. He was clearly discouraged by the practical burden of psychoanalytic testimony on criminal procedure from the length of time required to analyze a defendant to the cost of analysis. Hellwig was loath to permit psychoanalysts to testify to a defendant's mental capacity because the law did not recognize an exemption from criminal responsibility for neurotic behavior. He was, moreover, suspicious of what he considered psychoanalytic criminology's dogmatic approach to the etiology of criminal behavior.[54] This dogmatism clearly deterred many judges from inviting psychoanalysts to testify. In the words of a judge sympathetic to the introduction of psychoanalysis into the criminal justice system, "If psychoanalysis frees

---

51 See the calendar of the Berlin Psychoanalytic Institute in Anna Freud, "Korrespondenzblatt der Internationalen Psychoanalytischen Vereinigung," *Internationale Zeitschrift für Psychoanalyse* 16 (1930): 525–6.

52 Michael Laier, *Das Frankfurter Psychoanalytische Institut (1929–1933): Anfänge der Psychoanalyse in Frankfurt am Main* (Frankfurt am Main, 1989), 42, 64, 66.

53 Marwedel, "Vom Schlachthöfen und Schachtfeldern," 19. In an ironic twist, in Fritz Lang's classic film from 1922, "Dr. Mabuse, der Spieler" ("Dr. Mabuse, the Gambler"), the main character, a criminal mastermind who possesses ominous psychic powers, lectures to a distinguished audience on the benefits of psychoanalysis while impersonating a psychiatrist.

54 Albert Hellwig, "Psychoanalyse und Strafrechtspflege," *Juristische Rundschau* 6 (1930): 133–7, 146–50, 160–63, 173–6.

itself from this self-limitation, even courtrooms, whose doors were until now almost completely closed to it, will open to it."[55] Thus, even the relatively open-minded judges who attended the seminars gradually left the auditorium when the discussion turned to matters like the roles of the Oedipus complex and incest in criminal behavior.[56]

The majority of judges, who had recently made their peace with forensic psychiatry in part because they were able in large measure to co-opt it, were even less inclined to welcome a controversial and unverified science into their courtrooms. In their view they had nothing to gain from bringing psychoanalysis into their courtrooms. Astute and honest proponents of psychoanalytic criminology like Staub understood this.[57]

In light of this prevailing attitude it should come as no surprise that psychoanalytic criminology was marginalized, if not simply ignored, in the courtroom. Alexander and Staub contended that "psychoanalysis belongs to the most important weapons in the arsenal of the judge."[58] But, unlike Hellwig, very few judges felt compelled to invest in either psychoanalytic experts or their own psychoanalytic training.[59] Perhaps most important, judicial suspicions of the inclination of psychoanalytic criminology to exonerate criminals on the basis of an abstract emotional disturbance made it anathema to the courts. Society simply felt compelled to eliminate the perpetrators of particularly depraved crimes, such as the highly publicized sexual murders of the 1920s. Advocates of the notorious sexual murderers Haarmann and Kürten requested psychoanalytic examinations of their clients, but the judges in these cases denied their pleas doubtless because even the most remote possibility of finding them innocent by reason of mental incapacity was unthinkable.[60] A practical outcome of this judicial attitude was that psychoanalytic criminology suffered from a lack of case material in large part because judges preferred to refer suitable cases to forensic psychiatrists.[61]

For its part, the psychiatric profession's reception of psychoanalytic criminology was generally lukewarm, but it could turn hostile. Only the rare psychiatrist wholeheartedly endorsed the introduction of psychoanalysis and individual psychology into the criminal justice system. Several psychiatrists

---

55 Sachs, "Strafrichter und Psychoanalyse," *Juristische Rundschau* 6 (1930): 85–9, quotation on 88.
56 Staub, "Einige praktische Schwierigkeiten der psychoanalytischen Kriminalistik," 217.
57 Ibid., 218–21.
58 Alexander and Staub, *Der Verbrecher und seine Richter*, 49.
59 See Lindenau's review of *Der Verbrecher und seine Richter* in *Archiv für Kriminologie* 86 (1930): 77–9.
60 Staub, "Psychoanalyse und Strafrecht," *Imago* 17 (1931): 203; see also Richard J. Evans, *Ritual of Retribution: Capital Punishment in Germany, 1600–1987* (Oxford, 1996), 600.
61 Staub, "Einige praktische Schwierigkeiten der psychoanalytischen Kriminalistik," 221.

active in criminological research acknowledged the need, stimulated by the investigations of psychoanalytic criminology, to explore unconscious motivations for criminal behavior. A few even conceded the usefulness of the Freudian or Adlerian paradigm for explaining the causes of criminal behavior in isolated individual cases. But for the most part forensic psychiatrists dismissed the general validity of theories like the Oedipus complex as simplifications of complex criminogenic factors.[62] Ultimately, though, forensic psychiatry cast Freudian and Adlerian criminology into the role of apologist for criminal behavior. In the opinion of forensic psychiatrists, the practitioners of Freudian and Adlerian criminology failed to comprehend the true, adversarial nature of criminal law. In the words of the eminent forensic psychiatrist Edmund Mezger, "in the final analysis, legally organized society finds itself in a state of war with the criminal in which the decisive question is who in the end remains the victor." Armed merely with notions like the neurotic criminal or discouragement, "society's battle cannot be successfully conducted if it does not simultaneously function ... 'to intimidate' further criminal tendencies and further criminal acts."[63]

CONCLUSION

As Richard F. Wetzell has shown, criminal law and forensic psychiatry eventually developed a symbiotic relationship because they came to share a vision in which confinement in prison and confinement in an asylum became functionally equivalent.[64] This vision would not have been drastically threatened by judicial cooperation with psychoanalytic criminology. Alexander and Staub unblinkingly endorsed not only imprisonment of the "normal" criminal but also indefinite confinement of emotionally troubled lawbreakers. "It is self-evident," they asserted, "that independent from treatment all chronically harmful criminals will have to be interned or otherwise confined

62 See Gustav Aschaffenburg, "Psychoanalyse und Strafrecht," *Süddeutsche Monatshefte* 28 (1931): 793–6; and Müller-Hess and Ferdinand Wiethold, "Psychoanalyse und Strafrecht," *Jahreskurse für ärztliche Fortbildung* 21 (1930): 32–48.
63 Edmund Mezger, "Psychoanalyse und Individualpsychologie in der Strafrechtspflege," *Gerichtssaal* 102 (1933): 1–29, quotation on 26. Although he rejected the utility of Freudian and Adlerian criminology in determining criminal liability, Mezger was relatively open to their potential therapeutic role in prison. Edmund Mezger, "Die Bedeutung der Psychoanalyse für die Rechtspflege," in Hans Prinzhorn, ed., *Krise der Psychoanalyse*, vol. 1: *Auswirkungen der Psychoanalyse in Wissenschaft und strafrechtliche Schuld* (Leipzig, 1928), 361–71; and Edmund Mezger, "Psychoanalyse und strafrechtliche Schuld," *Schweizerische Zeitschrift für Strafrecht* 44 (1930): 185–93.
64 Richard F. Wetzell, "The Medicalization of Criminal Law Reform in Imperial Germany," in Norbert Finzsch and Robert Jütte, eds., *Institutions of Confinement: Hospitals, Asylums, and Prisons in Western Europe and North America, 1500–1950* (New York, 1996), 283.

throughout the course of their harmfulness to society."[65] Thus, for emotionally disturbed neurotic criminals Alexander and Staub may have recommended "*the abolition of all forms of punishment* and leading them to *reeducation* or *treatment* on the basis of a psychoanalytic foundation," but their recommendation "signifies no *fundamental* reconstruction of criminal law" because "we remove from [the jurisdiction of] criminal law only ... a portion of its objects in order to transfer them into the competent hands of the educator or doctor."[66]

Notwithstanding their efforts to be integrated into the criminal justice system, Freudian and Adlerian criminology were bedeviled by an inherent contradiction. How could they even recognize the concept of criminal liability, which is a "social construction," an interpretation of social behavior by means of artificially conceived, value-laden norms? Their practitioners seem never to have confronted their complicity, to borrow from Heinz-Peter Schmiedebach, in the "transformation of social abnormality into pathological normalcy." "Defining 'mental illness,'" he writes, "inevitably involves making value judgments about individual behavior with regard to social rules of society and applying medical concepts to social phenomena."[67] Practitioners of Freudian and Adlerian criminology hardly bothered to reconcile the claim of psychoanalysis and individual psychology to value-neutral healing with their active promotion of condemnatory official social policies. Indeed, in their defense of psychoanalytic criminology, Alexander and Staub took pains to disabuse readers of even the slightest intimation of its disloyalty to the state.

This striving to be part of a rationalized system of criminal justice casts into sharp relief the ambiguity of criminology founded on psychoanalysis or individual psychology. It both palliated and succumbed to the darker aspects of contemporary practices in the administration of criminal justice. In large part it posed a challenge and occasionally offered an alternative to state-sponsored violence in the form of criminal law. Recall the practice of Kleist in the Celle penitentiary, where individual psychology enjoyed a robust application in the shadow of the limited applicability of criminal biology. Indeed, if it had been allowed to operate within the margins of criminal

---

65 Alexander and Staub, *Der Verbrecher und seine Richter*, 87.
66 Ibid., 115–16 (original emphasis). Reik (*Geständniszwang und Strafbedürfnis*, 157–9) was able to imagine a future in which confession would supplant legal punishment, but he conceded that his dream was more likely than not utopian.
67 Heinz-Peter Schmiedebach, "The Mentally Ill Patient Caught Between the State's Demands and the Professional Interests of Psychiatrists," in Manfred Berg and Geoffrey Cocks, eds., *Medicine and Modernity: Public Health and Medical Care in Nineteenth- and Twentieth-Century Germany* (New York, 1997), 99–119, quotations on 99–100.

justice, psychoanalytic criminology may just have been able to compel German and Austrian society to honestly confront the imposition of the death penalty on offenders with diminished mental capacity. Perhaps the unnerving quality of such an acknowledgment could have unbound this repressed open secret from the collective unconscious into public debate over the merits of Germany's Paragraph 51 and Austria's Paragraph 2, although in the climate of the terminal years of both republics the champions of the modification of this provision would have stood virtually no chance of success.[68] Moreover, to its credit and unlike so many other criminological alternatives in the 1920s and 1930s, psychoanalytic criminology removed the categories of race and heredity from the analysis of crime, rendering criminal behavior universal.[69] Perhaps most important in its favor, if allowed to function, psychoanalytic criminology might have been conducive to the personal freedom of the condemned. If society can demand that people govern themselves and obey the law or face penal consequences, it is important that they know themselves – including their dark sides – because only when they comprehend their irrational proclivities for aggression can they make informed behavioral choices.[70] In this spirit a contemporary psychoanalyst wrote in his examination of psychoanalytic criminology that "a psychoanalyzed person has made peace with his environment and its organization, and as a member of society shares its common destiny as well."[71] To be sure, Alexander and Staub went so far as to claim that "the psychological understanding of the criminal does not primarily help the criminal but, on the contrary, serves the interests of society."[72] But even if the practitioners of psychoanalytic criminology saw their primary task as promoting official social goals, they did not abandon the promise of healing.[73] To their credit,

68 See Evans, *Rituals of Retribution*, 599–602.

69 See Michel Foucault, *The History of Sexuality*, vol. 1: *An Introduction*, trans. Robert Hurley (New York, 1980), 109, 150, for commendation of this particular aspect of psychoanalysis by one of its otherwise staunchest critics. See also John E. Toews, "Foucault and the Freudian Subject: Archaeology, Genealogy, and the Historicization of Psychoanalysis," in Jan Goldstein, ed., *Foucault and the Writing of History* (Oxford, 1994), 117–34; and Sander L. Gilman, *The Case of Sigmund Freud: Medicine and Identity at the Fin de Siècle* (Baltimore, 1993), 175.

70 See Jonathan Lear, *Open Minded: Working Out the Logic of the Soul* (Cambridge, Mass., 1998), 174–8.

71 Hans Lungwitz, "Psychoanalyse und Kriminalität," *Archiv für Kriminologie* 77 (1925): 304–6, quotation on 306.

72 Alexander and Staub, *Der Verbrecher und seine Richter*, 7.

73 Cf. Peter Strasser, *Verbrechermenschen: Zur kriminalwissenschaftlichen Erzeugung des Bösen* (Frankfurt am Main, 1984), 193–4, who regards the psychoanalytic criminology of Alexander and Staub, first and foremost, as a vehicle for state control over deviants in the population. See also the essays on German psychiatry by Schmiedebach, "Mentally Ill Patient," and Paul Lerner, "Rationalizing the Therapeutic Arsenal: German Neuropsychiatry in World War I," both in Berg and Cocks,

the majority of the practitioners of Freudian and Adlerian criminology seem genuinely to have wanted to help troubled individuals.

But even if psychoanalytic criminology and its cousin individual psychology were not merely an alibi to redescribe punitive sanctions in the vocabulary of Freud or Adler, they were not without potentially dangerous ramifications, either. Psychoanalytic criminology depersonalized criminal responsibility because in its insistence on the universality of criminal neurosis, a pathological condition, it rendered criminals typical rather than individual and, in turn, invalidated the principle of retributive justice. But if criminal responsibility is depersonalized and retribution no longer viable, then rights are arguably no longer fundamental, including the right to a fixed punishment. Jacques Donzelot has argued that the essential function of psychoanalysis in the welfare state was to create a new system of "flotation." Psychoanalysis operated to displace public norms by private principles and detached them from fixed standards – that is to say, social norms and private desires "floated" in relation to one another, reducing the risk of conflict between them while combining their functions. In the legal system "flotation" functioned to loosen the rigidity of the law by significantly widening the margins of its flexibility – and by implication, its arbitrariness.[74] By subordinating the right to a fixed punishment to the uncertain diagnosis of criminal motivation or the uncertain success of posttrial therapy, Freudian and Adlerian criminology, in a deep sense, reaffirmed the violent character of criminal law by enhancing its potential for arbitrariness. Freudian psychoanalytic criminology and its Adlerian variant – characterized, not unlike myriad other reform movements of the era, by vexing ambiguities – were thus ultimately caught in a contradiction of their own making between the promise to liberate criminals from the unconscious compulsion to punish themselves and the punitive character of criminal justice.

eds., *Medicine and Modernity*, 121–48, which argue that German and Austrian psychiatrists were traditionally more concerned with endorsing official policies than helping patients.

74 Jacques Donzelot, *The Policing of Families*, trans. Robert Hurley (New York, 1979), 211, 216–17; see also Gilles Deleuze's foreword to *Policing of Families*, xv–xvii.

21

Drinking and Crime in Modern Germany

GEOFFREY J. GILES

Prior to the foundation of the German Empire in 1871, drunkenness as such was not prosecuted under the law, but the consequences of it were, inasmuch as they were criminal offenses. By the middle of the century, however, German physicians, well aware of the worldwide respect that German science enjoyed, became increasingly active in public policymaking on health questions. In the 1860s, their investigations into the workings of the human brain convinced them that a person delirious with fever, drugged with sleep (drunk with sleep, *schlaftrunken*, in German phraseology), or drunk from alcohol might not be responsible for his or her actions. Under Prussian law only mental illness (*Geisteskrankheit*) could exonerate a criminal from legal responsibility; if he were declared *non compos mentis*, of unsound mind, there were grounds for acquittal from any crime. The Prussian doctors successfully pressed for the inclusion of the new categories in the criminal code of the North German Confederation, which was then carried over into the new Empire. The amendment was effected in broad rather than specific terms. The term *mental illness* was replaced with the imprecise phrase, "a pathological disturbance of mental activity" (*krankhafte Störung der Geistesthätigkeit*), which left open the question of precisely how drunk a person had to be in order to have himself declared not responsible for his actions.[1] Subsequent legal practice demonstrated the welcome flexibility this provided to exonerate the upper classes while allowing punishment of the lower classes for

Research for this chapter was generously supported by a fellowship from the Alexander von Humboldt Foundation, and the hospitable institutional support of Professor Hugo Ott and the University of Freiburg.

1 See comments by Staatssekretär des Reichsjustizamtes Dr. Ludwig von Schelling in the Reichstag debate on the law to punish drunkenness, April 5, 1881, Bundesarchiv Lichterfelde (hereafter BAL) 30.01 RJM 6065. In his chapter in this volume, Gabriel Finder notes that forensic psychiatrists were still struggling to achieve professional legitimacy in the 1920s. See also Richard Wetzell's comments, in his chapter, on the attempts of psychiatrists to "colonize" this borderland of abnormalities.

similar offenses. Initially, however, even the latter benefited from the new legislation.

On the night of October 15, 1879, Karl Berger, a worker, was involved in a drunken brawl in the Lützowstrasse in Berlin, where he was apprehended by a policeman. Already convicted seven times for resisting arrest, he was determined not to be run in on this occasion, too, and bit off the end of the policeman's finger. This was not only foolish but, to the police, was also a sign of positive madness, and Berger was carted off to the lunatic ward of Berlin's famous Charité Hospital. The doctors soon released him, however, asserting that their tests had revealed not a trace of mental illness. In court the prosecution was therefore confident that it would succeed in winning a prison conviction. The judge dashed these hopes by bowing to science, in the form of Professor Carl Liman, the medical expert called by the defense. The doctor argued that the defendant's father's alcoholism had induced a condition in which Berger himself was not responsible for his actions after taking even moderate amounts of alcohol. The injured policeman watched helplessly as Berger was acquitted of the charges.[2]

Otto von Bismarck was livid when he read of this in the newspaper and immediately scribbled a note to Ludwig von Schelling, his minister of justice, ordering him to draft legislation to ensure that this kind of outrage would not go unpunished in the future.[3] He was especially appalled at the thought that someone who knowingly got drunk might escape the consequences. Socialists, his current archenemies, might get deliberately drunk in order to commit mischief with impunity.

The justice minister's response was slightly, but significantly, different from what Bismarck had suggested. Schelling proposed a law that placed "publicly manifested alcoholism" under the jurisdiction of the criminal code if other crimes had been committed. The parallel he saw was with the certification of the insane; thus, drunkards no longer would be set free on technicalities but would be automatically locked up. Bismarck, himself a friend of the bottle, thought the equation of "drunkard" with "lunatic" went too far but urged his minister to close the current loopholes in the law.[4]

2 *Norddeutsche Allgemeine Zeitung*, July 16, 1880.
3 Bismarck knew his Reichstag and opined in his note that "the first attempt in this direction will have little chance of success in the Reichstag, although I have no doubt that in time we shall win over the level-headed elements who are loyal to the state to cooperation for a reform in this direction." In fact it took almost fifty years before the drunkenness bill was finally pushed through the Reichstag. Bismarck's brief note set in motion one of the most voluminous sets of files among the Reich Ministry of Justice records. Bismarck to Schelling, July 20, 1880, BAL 30.01 RJM 6064.
4 Schelling to Bismarck, Aug. 3, 1880; Bismarck to Schelling, Aug. 6, 1880, ibid. The Kaiser's formal charge to Bismarck (doubtless drafted by the latter) was to prepare legislation "against the vice of

The unsuccessful Reichstag debate on the bill in April 1881, a hurried affair with the deputies eager to travel home for the Easter recess, betrayed the shift from the specific desire to provide protection against acts of violence to the general wish to punish drunkenness. Schelling reported in regretful tones that of the 7,377 people arrested for drunkenness in Berlin in 1879, more than 80 percent were released without charges being pressed, as soon as they had sobered up. Most of the deputies found in this no reason to pass new laws, however. Deputy Albert Traeger, for example, felt that drunkenness in public had actually declined over recent decades; most of the cases he encountered were in fact older gentlemen in white tie and tails, returning home from a banquet. He found them amusing rather than threatening. A rash of finger biting would indeed have been alarming, but Traeger undertook a little research into the incidence of drunken violence against the police on which the government was basing its case. Unfortunately, the ministry had not done its homework very carefully in preparing this bill. There were merely three other cases recorded, two of them committed by men suffering from delirium tremens who, as incontrovertibly sick people, would not be punishable even under the proposed law. The third case, the only one comparable to the finger-biting rage of Karl Berger, involved a man who had reached too often for the brandy bottle in order to dull the pain from his hemorrhoids. On a particularly bad day he had committed a minor assault. It became especially clear that the government was straining desperately to find evidence when it emerged that this last incident had not even taken place in Germany but involved a Spanish tailor in Madrid. The bill failed.[5]

After this unsuccessful attempt to pass a law against drunkenness, the government initiated more systematic attempts at gathering information on criminal acquittals on grounds of inebriation. The Ministry of Justice of the largest state, Prussia, compiled detailed statistics from all its judicial districts for 1880–81. But the results were less than striking: A mere thirty-five cases showed up for the period, with the largest group of seven involving cases of theft and a further six cases concerned with lèse-majesté (a charge typically brought against Socialists). Of the remainder, five cases involved acquittals in cases of resisting arrest, and a further four involved physical assault. In the latter category, one of the cases is illuminating, in that it demonstrates the class-based partiality of the judges.

---

drunkenness, and against the exemption from punishment of criminal offenses committed in a state of drunkenness." Wilhelm I to Bismarck, Sept. 13, 1880, ibid.

5 Erste Berathung des Gesetzentwurfs, betr. die Bestrafung der Trunkenheit, *Stenographische Berichte des Deutschen Reichstages*, 4. Legislaturperiode, 4. Session, 31. Sitzung, 5. April 1881, pp. 781–6. Albert Traeger was a member of the Progressive Party.

In July 1880, Anton Ellebrecht, a twenty-five-year-old Bonn University student, was returning home drunk from a doctoral graduation party when he set upon a passerby and knocked him out with his walking stick. The victim was so badly injured that he was unable to return to work for seventeen days. Incredibly, the case never even reached the courts. Ellebrecht was able to find a doctor who made a deposition that he (Ellebrecht) "had been, as a result of acute alcohol poisoning, in a state of temporary insanity that precluded the exercise of his free will." The state prosecutor thereupon unhesitatingly dropped the charges. There are no examples of such leniency when the perpetrator was a member of the lower classes and the victim from the bourgeoisie.[6]

An especially fond focus for the temperance movement, too, was the connection between alcohol and criminality. The supporting justification of the draft bill for Bismarck's desired legislation to punish drunkenness, prepared by the Ministry of Justice, already noted this as an accepted fact and embraced the issue of heredity: "It is sufficient to point out that . . . a large proportion of suicides (8–16 percent in Germany) and a still greater proportion of mental illnesses derive from excessive alcohol abuse, that the latter also represents the most common source of pauperism, encourages prostitution, undermines the sense of public order and respect for law, and that its effects on physical and mental being are inherited by future generations, leading to degeneration." Eugenic issues did not, then, suddenly take hold in the 1930s or just before, but already formed part of the government's narrative here in 1880. The deputies were told categorically that the number of crimes rose when drunkenness increased, and fell when there was less drunkenness.[7]

If civil servants were putting forward this official view, the temperance movement could be even more insistent with its dire warnings. Among full-color pictures of diseased kidneys, livers, hearts, and brains, one book by two prominent temperance advocates, directed specifically at elementary school students, hammered home the already clichéd case of Ida Tuke, a drunkard whose descendants had been followed down through the nineteenth century. Out of 709 of them, the children were told, 550 had descended into drunkenness, poverty, and misery, and many had become outright criminals. The offspring of this one woman had allegedly cost the state a total of more than

---

6 Zusammenstellung: Fälle von Freispruch wegen Trunkenheit, November 1881, Geheimes Staatsarchiv Dahlem (GStA) I HA Rep 84a 5233.
7 Entwurf: Gesetz Bestrafung der Trunkenheit, October 1880, Zentrales Staatsarchiv Potsdam 30.01 RJM 6064.

five million Marks in prison expenses and other support over a seventy-five-year period. Ida Tuke was held up again and again as a terrible example of the "heritability of alcoholism."[8] Temperance pamphlets were flooded with tables showing the high proportion of crimes committed by drinkers. Studies that provided conveniently alarming results were utilized for decades afterward, with no attempt at follow-up investigations. Often they were based on data from other countries altogether. A set of wall charts widely distributed before World War I by the German Association Against the Abuse of Spirits (*Deutscher Verein gegen den Missbrauch geistiger Getränke* or DVMGG) included a ubiquitous table on alcohol and crime, showing how many convicted criminals had been found to be habitual or occasional drinkers. Although the table was lifted from a 1907 publication, the figures were far more dated and derived from a review carried out in 1876.[9] A similar publication in 1931 was still using data from the 1870s because it happened to suit the argument that the organization wished to project.[10] But who precisely was a "drinker"? And did drinkers mean drunks? Did drunks mean alcoholics? The definition was blurred all the more so because the German word *Trinker* can signify all of these. In a 1907 speech, the temperance activist Immanuel Gonser called for a standardization of terminology, but nothing was done because greater precision in this area would have made the statistics look less alarming, and this was hardly the intention of the anti-alcohol movement.[11]

Only one German state, Bavaria, prepared detailed statistics over an extended period of time on what it termed "alcohol criminality," which were published annually between 1910 and 1930, except during World War I. The Bavarian government ultimately halted the scheme, admitting the inaccuracy and unreliability of much of the data, despite the pleas of the anti-alcohol movement to continue publication of these lurid figures.[12] The

---

8 Geh. Sanitätsrat Dr. [Ewald] Dicke and Knappschaftsarzt Dr. [Emil] Kohlmetz, *Die Schädlichkeit des Missbrauchs geistiger Getränke: Ein Lehr- und Lesebuch für Schüler der Volkschulen, Fortbildungsschulen und der höheren Lehranstalten*, 3d ed. (Leipzig, n.d. [1912]), 36.

9 Obermedizinalrat Hofrat Professor Dr. [Max] von Gruber and Hofrat Professor Dr. [Emil] Kraepelin, eds., *Verkleinerte Abdrücke der 10 Wandtafeln zur Alkoholfrage* (Munich, n.d.), plate IX, "Alkohol und Verbrechen." Note the attempt to lend greater scientific authority to the publication by the concatenation of titles for the authors.

10 See especially plate 10, "Anteil der Gewohnheitstrinker und der Gelegenheitstrinker an einigen Hauptarten von Vergehen und Verbrechen," in [Willibald] Ulbricht, *Abriss der Alkoholfrage in 14 Tafeln: Zugleich Erläuterungsheft für das Wandtafelwerk zur Alkoholfrage*, 3d ed. (Berlin-Dahlem, 1931), 13.

11 Immanuel Gonser, *Alkohol und Verbrechen: Vortrag auf der 23. Jahresversammlung der Gefängnisgesellschaft für die Provinz Sachsen und das Herzogtum Anhalt* (Berlin, 1907).

12 Bayerischer Landesverband des Deutschen Vereins gegen den Alkoholismus to Bayerisches Staatsministerium der Justiz, Jan. 7, 1931; and reply, Jan. 31, 1931, Bayerisches Hauptstaatsarchiv (hereafter BHStA) MJu 12578.

problem arose from a relaxation of the stringent police reporting procedures after the war. Whereas the number of alcohol-related crimes in the years 1910–13 was reported to be around eight thousand per annum in Bavaria, from 1920 onward, when the Ministry of Justice resumed collection of data, it could find only a few hundred cases each year.[13]

Broadly, the results were the same, however. In prewar figures, cases of physical assault constituted around 50 percent of total crimes. About half the perpetrators came from the working class, among whom casual and unskilled laborers received a disproportionately high ranking. The low proportion from the self-employed classes involved in drink-related crime and the noticeably high share of foreigners in the figures probably reflect the class and ethnic prejudices of the police and judicial system. The fact that only one student is to be found among 830 convicted people in 1926 (and the proportion of students in the figures never rose much above 1 percent) clearly is not representative of the reality of student rowdiness.[14] Similarly, the fact that women represented less than half of 1 percent of the "alcohol delinquents" (as the Bavarians called them) should not be taken as a sign that women were immune from problems of alcohol abuse but rather that they were viewed by the police as less threatening and as inappropriate inmates of the prisons.

A claim that strained credulity still further was the connection between occasional drinking and crime. Here the statistics used were invariably those that had first appeared in Abraham Baer's early study of alcoholism, published in 1878. Baer conducted a survey of a number of German prisons and drew up tables on the drinking habits of 7,392 prisoners. He concluded that 3,324 of them, or 45 percent, were "drinkers." The rates varied for the different categories of crime. The most alcoholic group of prisoners were those convicted of morals offenses (77 percent), closely followed by those imprisoned for obstructing a police officer (76 percent); 63 percent of those charged with physical assault were drinkers. But just what did this mean in terms of the *amount* consumed by typical criminals? Baer further distinguished between "habitual drinkers" and "occasional drinkers." In fact, the numbers of habitual drinkers was rather small, a total of 859 or 12 percent. All that the figures really showed, then, was that 33 percent of the prisoners were people who sometimes used but did not necessarily abuse alcohol. Yet, it was this group that the anti-alcohol movement seized upon, in order to

13 Alkoholstatistik, Zahl der Verurteilungen, 1910–29, table in ibid. On the Bavarian Criminal-Biological Service, see Oliver Liang's chapter in this volume.

14 Ergebnisse der Alkoholstatistik, drafts for 1926 and other years, BHStA MJu 12578.

produce the greatest shock effect. The proportion of habitual drinkers was lowest among the crimes of violence (assault, obstructing an officer, morals offenses), representing only 230 prisoners (6 percent); whereas 1,139 of these convicts (29 percent) sometimes drank. The lesson drawn from this was that it was even more dangerous to drink occasionally than to drink regularly, for it was the occasional drinker who was much more likely to lose control of himself and commit rape or punch a policeman in the nose. The moral was that only total abstention could save one from prison![15] In actuality the inquiry, which did not investigate the amount drunk or the frequency of drinking, is of little value. The historical question of how many prisoners were drinkers or alcoholics is not a significant one because those who were sent to jail were not a representative cross-section of offenders but often rather narrowly selected, I would suggest, along class lines.

There was little agreement on the necessary measures to cure drinking problems. The main temperance group, the German Association Against the Abuse of Spirits (DVMGG), thought that all drinks were fine in moderation. Their main rival, the Good Templars, believed that everybody should abstain completely from alcohol. The often vicious battles between these two organizations periodically threatened to cripple all work for the relief of drink-related illness. Was there at least agreement, by the turn of the century, that chronic alcoholism was a disease that could be cured only by serious medical attention? Not at all, for some church-related groups stressed the central importance of prayer in any cure. As late as 1927, the Protestant Blue Cross organization was still issuing pamphlets that talked of alcoholism as a sin that could never be healed by medicine alone.[16] The fact was that this complicated disease was not fully understood.

The possibility created by the new Civil Code of 1900 for the involuntary committal of an alcoholic to an asylum gave rise to expectations of an increased demand for institutional spaces. In May 1900, the Prussian ministry of the interior instituted an enquiry into the adequacy of facilities for the care of alcoholics in Prussia. No fewer than 10,237 men and 746 women were treated in Prussian institutions for alcohol-related illnesses in 1895. The practice differed from state to state in the treatment of the most severely sick patients, those with delirium tremens or "drinker's madness"

---

15 Table from Abraham Baer, *Der Alkoholismus, seine Verbreitung und seine Wirkung auf den individuellen und socialen Organismus* (Berlin, 1878), quoted in J. Stump and Robert Willenegger, *Zur Alkoholfrage* (Zurich, 1907), table A3. A similar but more detailed table utilizing the same source is part of a set of lantern slides on alcoholism, dating from about 1920, which are preserved in the Westphalian School Museum in Dortmund.

16 Walther to Preussisches Justizministerium, Sept. 10, 1927, GStA I HA Rep. 84a 5238.

(*Säuferwahnsinn*), as it was also called. Saxony and Alsace-Lorraine sent most of them directly to the lunatic asylum, whereas elsewhere, such as in Hamburg, they were treated in ordinary hospitals.

The state, then, was already treating large numbers of people who had fallen ill as a result of excessive drinking. They had developed a variety of physical or mental diseases that doctors were trained to cure. Yet those patients who did not exhibit ancillary symptoms beyond either acute alcoholism (intoxication and inebriation) or chronic alcoholism (including delirium tremens) did not receive such clear-cut care in hospitals and asylums. Doctors had no definite cure for alcoholism as such, and these patients were largely "unwelcome guests," as a study in 1901 discovered. "Acute" alcoholics were discharged on average in one to four days, and "chronic" alcoholics, although needing care for at least six to twelve months, were being discharged as "cured" within two to four weeks. In overcrowded Prussian hospitals alcoholics were regarded as troublemakers occupying beds that were needed by more docile patients with "real" illnesses.[17]

The expense of treatment for alcoholism was the subject of some controversy. As late as 1912, the Berlin Ladies' Society against Alcoholism had noted the common view that ran: "Let the boozers drink themselves to death, it's no loss to the nation."[18] That, of course, ran counter to the belief of all the abstinence and temperance organizations. In Hamburg no person was left alone to drink himself into the grave but was pursued as part of a comprehensive project to encompass all the city's thousands of alcoholics in a central file of the municipal welfare authority. The purpose was primarily benevolent, although this data-gathering zeal was bound up with broader plans to chart and study all aspects of the poor, diseased, and criminal parts of the population. This database was co-opted by the police in the Nazi state after 1933, but in the 1920s elaborate maps were drawn up, shaded to show the density of the alcoholic population in certain districts. The "Old Town" area in the center came off worst, with about five times as many taverns per capita as the average (namely, one tavern for every twenty-nine men over the age of eighteen); and the Sankt Pauli district near the docks was not far behind.[19] In an enormous city like Hamburg, the sheer numbers of those who needed alcohol counseling made it impossible for the public authorities to cope, and so the procedure was initially to refer each case to

17 J. Waldschmidt, "Die Trinkerfürsorge in Preussen," *Zeitschrift des Königlich Preussischen Statistischen Bureaus*, 41 (1901):193–208.

18 Berliner Frauenverein gegen den Alkoholismus, *Bericht über das 5. Geschäftsjahr* (Berlin, 1913), 10.

19 Map "Trinkerfürsorge der Wohlfahrtsbehörde Hamburg," Ausgabe 1928, Staatsarchiiv Hamburg (StAHH) 351–10 I Sozialbehörde I GF41.19.

one of the private organizations. The organization was then requested to submit a report on the alleged alcoholic within fourteen days to the central welfare authority. If necessary, the police could be brought in to take the person into custody.

The city of Hamburg had three institutions to which its residents with drinking problems were sent. Its main facility was at Farmsen, to which curable alcoholics were transferred; incurable cases went to an institution where the regime was much stricter and more Spartan; and finally, in certain cases alcoholics were assigned to the lunatic asylum.[20] Even in Farmsen the atmosphere was scarcely one of human warmth and trust. An exposé in the Hamburg press in 1929 drew parallels with life in a penitentiary, protesting that prospective inmates were frequently picked up without warning at their home or workplace by the police and driven off in a paddy wagon for all to see. An air of resignation descended upon most inmates, none of whom were said to have any hopes of recovery, and they merely counted the days until their "punishment" was ended. Liquor was regularly smuggled in, and "schnapps orgies" were not uncommon.[21] Those who tried to escape were locked in the cellar with a hard wooden bed and put on a bread-and-water diet with no reading materials permitted, just like prisoners. The wardens were criticized for their lack of any training in medical or welfare matters: One of them (barely twenty years old) was said to strut around in his jackboots "like a cock on a dung heap." In short, the unfortunates who were consigned to the mildest of Hamburg's three levels of institutionalization were in fact stamped as second-class human beings, and very little was done for them, least of all in helping them to find work after their release.[22]

It was the statistics on expense that struck home with the average newspaper reader, especially in a time of economic hardship. They prepared the ground all too smoothly for the more drastic measures of the National Socialist regime that were shortly to be introduced. Even one of Hamburg's liberal newspapers asserted in the spring of 1933 in a matter-of-fact manner that, in order to save money, incurable alcoholics should be placed

---

20 Richtlinien für die Zusammenarbeit der Wohlfahrtsbehörde Hamburg mit den Vereinen der freien Trinkerfürsorge, November 1928, StAHH 361–2 V Oberschulbehörde V 674c/II.
21 This seems to be a universal problem with institutionalized alcoholics. See, for example, Cheryl Krashnick Warsh, *Moments of Unreason: The Practice of Canadian Psychiatry and the Homewood Retreat, 1883–1923* (Montreal, 1989). A similar complaint from 1923 is mentioned by Hauschildt, who also notes that seven inmates were carried out drunk from the 1924 Christmas party at the Hamburg institution. Hauschildt, "Die erste . . . .," 5, 8–9.
22 "In den Klauen der Trinkerfürsorge," *Hamburger Volkszeitung*, Mar. 20, 1929; "Die brutale Wirklichkeit der Trinkerfürsorge," ibid., Mar. 25, 1929.

in a detention center, not a treatment center.[23] But which alcoholics were incurable? Where did the threshold lie between treatable and hopeless cases? This is a question that the experts failed to resolve throughout the Third Reich. The degradation of their aims from healing to permanent supervision did not signal resignation and defeat, but a shift in values. A semiofficial 1936 pamphlet from the Reich Committee for Public Health (*Reichsausschuß für Volksgesundheit*) made clear the intrusive nature of the state. Healthcare professionals even today would be wary of alcoholics who discharged themselves as cured and requiring no further treatment or counseling. In a benevolent climate the promise to "never again let the client out of sight, in defiance of every resistance and excuse of the person himself and of his family," might merely sound like creditable thoroughness, until one understands the real meaning of this in a police state. What the Nazi government had in mind for those carefully watched alcoholics was "preventive detention in the workhouse for an extended period, or even for life in the case of work-shy, incorrigible, degenerate drinkers."[24]

Public acceptance of the slide in the perception of alcoholics as willful criminals toward their categorization as irremediable degenerates was boosted by the widely read pronouncements of some well-known university professors. Ernst Rüdin, a psychiatrist and an enthusiastic protagonist of compulsory sterilization for psychopaths and the "whole, great army" of incorrigible criminals in Nazi Germany, called early on for the sterilization of incurable alcoholics as well.[25] His mentor, Emil Kraepelin, was among the many scholars who published colored charts purporting to offer dramatic proof of the inevitability of racial degeneration from alcoholism, which then became part of the rationale for sterilization.[26]

Adolf Hitler himself warmed to such plans. In the spring of 1933, in an article about alcohol, the new chancellor claimed that the numbers of those "valuable human beings" who had been destroyed or made "useless for the nation" by drink was far higher than all German losses on battlefields over the last century. This comment in itself is significant in its reflection

23 "Aus der Trinkerfürsorge Hamburg," *Hamburger Anzeiger*, Mar. 7, 1933.

24 Max Fischer, *Organisierte Abwehr der Alkoholschäden*. Schriftenreihe des Reichsausschusses für Volksgesundheit (Berlin, 1936), 11.

25 Rüdin described the former groups as "ballast existences" at a meeting of the Commission on Population and Racial Policies. Benno Müller-Hill, *Tödliche Wissenschaft: Die Aussonderung von Juden, Zigeuner und Geisteskranken 1933–1945* (Reinbek, 1984), 35. His remarks in 1903 were made at the Ninth International Congress for the Prevention of Alcoholism in Bremen. Manfred Hüllemann, "50 Jahre 'Gesetz zur Verhütung erbkranken Nachwuchses,'" *Suchtgefahren*, 29, no. 4 (1983):387.

26 A chart on "Alcohol and Degeneracy," for example, compares the incidence of stillborn children, early childhood death, deformities, and disease in families of moderate drinkers and alcoholics. Von Gruber and Kraepelin, *Verkleinerte Abdrücke der 10 Wandtafeln zur Alkoholfrage*.

of Hitler's central motive in the alcohol question, as in population policies overall: to boost the size of the cohort of men fit for military service to its utmost limit. Beyond this, Hitler was a staunch believer in hereditary defects and illnesses, and warned in the article of the "terrible certainty that the effects of this poison do not, alas, remain restricted to the individual drinker, but are transmitted to his children and his children's children. In alcohol we have to recognize one of the most dreadful causes of the degeneration of mankind."[27]

The initial legal basis for sterilization during the Third Reich was the Law for the Prevention of Hereditary Illness (*Gesetz zur Verhütung erbkranken Nachwuchses*) of July 14, 1933. As the standard commentary on the sterilization law pointed out, "According to the sense and purpose of the law, chronic alcoholism is to be understood as a *symptom of a sick personality structure*, in other words an alcoholism that is based on a predominantly sick, hereditary disposition" [author's emphasis].[28] Alcoholism does, of course, have an effect on the personality of the sufferer. A few days before the Nazi seizure of power the Prussian Interior Ministry issued guidelines for the identification of alcoholics who needed to be institutionalized, which included rather vague phraseology on conditions certainly not peculiar to alcoholics. The characteristics of alcoholism were said to include a "heightening of egoism to a degree where the drinker acts without consideration or love for his family . . . a marked decline of community feeling that makes the drinker asocial or anti-social, and the loss, or at least the morbid decline, of feelings of honor, morality, and decency."[29] What was dangerous about such imprecise guidelines, which were intended primarily for police and municipal officials (and not for addiction specialists), was that they could be used against almost anyone, regardless of the medical seriousness of the disease. Indeed, the standard commentary on the law spoke strongly in favor of sterilization *before* incontrovertible symptoms of alcoholism had shown themselves. It ought to be possible, the authors claimed, to tell from the overall personality of the patient whether severe alcoholism was "to be expected with great probability." An "inclination to criminal and asocial activity" might be a good enough indication of a likely future chronic

---

27 Hitler's article in the *Linksrheinische Rundschau*, 94 (Apr. 22, 1933), quoted in Herbert Thiess, "25 Jahre Auskunfts- und Fürsorgestelle für Alkoholismus in Halle/Saale," Archiv des Diakonischen Werkes, Berlin (hereafter ADW) CA 1853/37.
28 Gütt/Rüdin/Ruttke, *Zur Verhütung erbkranken Nachwuchses* (1936), quoted in Ferdinand Goebel, *Tatsachen zur Alkoholfrage* (Berlin, 1939), 32.
29 Runderlass Preuss. MdI, "Anstaltsunterbringung gemeingefährlicher Trinker," Jan. 27, 1933, ADW BP I 191/3,4.

alcoholic and one should waste no time in sterilizing him right away. Documenting how much a person drank, or how often, was a matter of little importance:

> It would be a complete mistake to be so pedantic as to demand the presence of all or even most of the criteria [for alcoholism]. For example, it is perfectly sufficient to have solid proof of just one attack of alcoholic hallucination, because only a person whom one would characterize as a severe alcoholic would have an alcoholic hallucination in the first place. . . . Objective signs of chronic alcoholism (such as polyneuritis, abnormalities of the tendon reflexes, slight trembling of the fingers, etc.) are occasionally desirable for the diagnosis but should never be demanded as a sine qua non, for these signs often develop very late.[30]

This last point is a valid one about alcoholism, but the commentary to the law taken as a whole underlines the indecent haste with which eugenicists in the Third Reich tried to select the "racially unfit." The tendency was to base the decision to sterilize less on the medical aspects of the disease than on the social results. In his chapter, Richard Wetzell makes the important point that the acceptance of hereditarianism can be explained in some measure by the failure of psychiatry to make progress in the treatment of mental illnesses. The same is certainly true in the more specific case of physicians and alcoholism.

The notes of examining doctors in individual cases are revealing. One Hamburg physician admitted that his patient responded adequately to intelligence tests, yet still characterized her as "dull (and) primitive" on the grounds of her poor housekeeping ability and inadequacies in educating her children. Her "occasional" alcohol abuse merely confirmed her in his eyes as a "weak, inferior woman," and the nicotine stains on her teeth and fingers clinched the matter for him: She was to be treated as "a feeble-minded, inferior woman of weak character whose reproduction (was) not desirable for the national community," and therefore to be sterilized.[31] The Hereditary Health High Court (*Erbgesundheitsobergericht*) in Nuremberg (a body issuing rulings about sterilization policy) repeated in 1935 the official line that it was not the excessive amount consumed by the alcoholic that was crucial. After all, there were many people who drank very large quantities in the course of their occupation without being regarded as "boozers" – the court was doubtless thinking of brewery and tavern workers here. Rather,

---

30 Gütt/Rüdin/Ruttke, 170ff., mimeographed extract, June 10, 1938, in Archiv des Deutschen Caritasverbandes, Freiburg im Breisgau 259.3 Fasz 2.
31 Andrea Brücks, "Zwangssterilisation gegen 'Ballastexistenzen,'" in Projektgruppe für die vergessenen Opfer des NS-Regimes in Hamburg e.V., ed., *Verachtet-verfolgt-vernichtet–zu den "vergessenen" Opfern des NS-Regimes* (Hamburg, 1988), 105.

it was the manifestation of asocial behavior, which became apparent "above all in the commission of criminal offenses," that would identify the people who needed to be sterilized.[32]

The Marienwerder high court passed down an important decision in 1935, in which it expressed the opinion that "it is not necessary for the sterilization subject's passion for drinking to have manifested itself in physical or mental illness, or in reduced capability. Rather, it must be regarded as sufficient if frequent alcohol abuse leads him *repeatedly to molest or harm his neighbors and break the laws of the state*" [emphasis added].[33] A more elastic guideline for state intrusion is hard to imagine.

On top of this came the encouragement of the Nazi movement to characterize alcoholism as a crime rather than as an illness. The SS newspaper *Das Schwarze Korps* carried an article on the "Concentration Camp and its Inmates" in February 1936, in which a photograph of a supposedly handsome SS guard was juxtaposed with an allegedly degenerate-looking prisoner. The latter caption read: "A typical representative of the camp: habitual drunkard and lecher."[34] Some doctors were positively eager to send alcoholic patients for a stay at a concentration camp. A doctor in Regensburg found it a splendid educational tool. His patients developed such a "fear of being sent back again" that they kept away from the bottle. He continued to recommend this treatment for a string of patients at least through 1940.[35]

Even the anti-alcohol organizations spoke with such strong language that their acceptance of the worst kind of Nazi racial thinking was unmistakable. A 1936 booklet for helpers in alcohol treatment centers, co-authored by one of the leading officials of the DVMGG, was strident in its tone. It offered lavish praise for the twin Nazi concepts of selection of the racially fit and eradication of the hereditarily tainted. What was to be done with the latter? "Even if one cannot kill them," one could at least make sure that they produced no offspring by sterilizing them. The introduction of such a thought into the argument carries the implication that killing such unfortunates would really be the most practical solution, particularly when

---

32 "Der schwere Alkoholiker," *Hofer Anzeiger*, July 13, 1935.

33 Short reports in *Juristische Wochenschrift*, 26 (1935):1874; 30 (1935):2149; 39 (1935):2747. The hope that sterilization would reduce overall criminality by as much as 6 percent follows this preventive, rather than simply corrective, rationale.

34 "K. Z. und seine Insassen," *Das Schwarze Korps*, Feb. 13, 1936.

35 From 1934 straightforward alcoholism (without the commission of a crime) no longer was sufficient grounds to commit someone to a concentration camp. Hans Simon-Pelanda, "Medizin und Trinkerfürsorge: Ein Amtsarzt bekämpft den Alkoholismus mit KZ-Haft," *Dachauer Hefte* 4 (November 1988):215–24, here 218–22. The article does not name the doctor in question, identifying him only as Bezirksarzt Dr. S.

the authors then bemoaned the expense of treatment for the afflicted. For asocial drunkards, they felt the proper answer was the workhouse and congratulated the city of Berlin for creating one for drinkers without waiting for the necessary legal provisions that should have been used to commit a person to such an institution. Sterilization was not a violation of, but a good turn for, the individual. Finally, they quoted with approval the commentary to the heredity law regarding chronic alcoholism, which stressed that "proof of the hereditary basis [of alcoholism] is *not required* because such alcoholism arises almost without exception on hereditary, psychopathic grounds, and therefore offspring are not desirable" [emphasis added]. In other words, only a hereditarily inferior person could become a chronic alcoholic in the first place.[36]

Heinrich Himmler built special quarters at Buchenwald for alcoholic SS officers in 1941. The buildings were just outside the camp proper, but the inmates were nevertheless in solitary confinement, which was broken only by communal early morning and afternoon sport; even the strictly vegetarian meals were not taken as a group.[37] This is an extreme outcome rather than the logical conclusion of the German attitude toward excessive drinking in the century leading up to World War II. Treatment was often harsh and unsympathetic in other countries, too. What is special about the German case is that it provides an example of how ideas of degeneracy among criminals, fostered by eugenics advocates in several countries, took hold in Germany with an unusual tenacity and merged with that country's virulent racism to devastating effect.

The voices that suggested that there were social causes for excessive drinking – and there were a few, including a Nazi district police chief – were lonely ones and generally went unheeded.[38] Drinking was a central part of German culture, and in order to preserve that, for economic as

---

36 Dr. Ottokar Brunzlow and Ferdinand Goebel, *Erbgesundheitspflege im Dritten Reich: Was muss der Helfer in der Trinkerfürsorge von der Vererbungslehre und Gesetzgebung wissen?* (Berlin, 1936), esp. 3, 5, 8, 12, 18.

37 Franz W. Seidler, "Alkoholismus und Vollrauschdelikte in der deutschen Wehrmacht und bei der SS während des Zweiten Weltkrieges," *Wehrwissenschaftliche Rundschau* 6 (1979):185.

38 It is significant that the heightened social concerns of the Weimar Republic brought a greater awareness of such problems. A 1928 report on alcohol problems in industrial areas reported agreement on the absence of adequate and congenial housing (accompanied by stimulating cultural amenities) as the principal contributory factor. Generaloberarzt a.D. Dr. Ottokar Brunzlow, *Die Bekämpfung des Alkoholismus in den Industriegebieten* (Berlin, n.d. [1928]), 5. A report by the police president of Gleiwitz in industrial Silesia, Dr. Palten, concluded that sending individual alcoholics to concentration camps was not the answer to the problem, which was altogether more extensive: "A really lasting and crucial change for the better [will come] only with a decisive improvement in the social conditions of the industrial work force." Bericht Palten, "Bekämpfung des Alkoholmissbrauchs," Jan. 31, 1939, BA 36/1356.

much as for nostalgic reasons, it was infinitely easier to punish the victims of alcohol than to address the causes of their excess, or even to trust in the ability of medical science. Most people were not alcoholics, but thousands of Germans drank to excess. Were they alcoholics? Were they criminals? They certainly did not think so. Only degenerates had these authentic failings, they were persuaded. It was reassuring to be able to look down on these and other "outsiders" who were the real cause of Germany's problems. By locking them up, and by making sure they could not have children, the "alcohol problem" would apparently be solved without most Germans having to adjust their own behavior. When their statistics had revealed in the nineteenth century that most criminals were drinkers, temperance leaders sought to show conversely that drinkers were likely criminals. The increasing medicalization of the question had the effect of relieving the majority of drinkers from such odium. They might not drink with impunity, because excessive consumption could cause degeneracy, but no one had a handy definition of "excessive" in this context. The ordinary drinker, then, might be forgiven for believing that things had been worse under the Kaiser than in Hitler's Third Reich. Back then, the government had tried repeatedly to pass laws, criminalizing simple, public drunkenness. Now, the rowdy binges of Stormtroopers and other Nazi Party officials, the very officers of the state, were as evident as they were legion. Despite schoolmasterly rhetoric, the regime seemed more tolerant in practice to the man in the street in this regard. Was not the Party itself founded in a beer hall? For the vast majority of Germans who felt themselves to be "insiders" within the racial community, empirical policy on the alcohol question seemed to be building consensus, rather than rejecting large sectors of society. The price of that comforting belief was the acceptance of Nazi eugenic policy, and the turning of a blind eye to the fate of the rejected. The dynamics of the Nazi state demanded the numbers of such "outsiders" to grow and grow.

Index

Lightning Source UK Ltd.
Milton Keynes UK
03 August 2010

157803UK00001B/17/P